W9-BAA-384

MAR CARIBE

OCÉANO ATLÁNTICO

Barranquilla
Maracaibo
Caracas
PANAMÁ
GUYANA
VENEZUELA
Georgetown
Medellín
Paramaribo
Panamá
Río Orinoco
Cayena
Bogotá
SURINAME
GUYANA FRANCESA
Cali
COLOMBIA
Quito
Ecuador
ECUADOR
Río Amazonas
Belém
Guayaquil
Manaus
PERÚ
BRASIL
CORDILLERA DE LOS ANDES
Recife
Cuzco
Lima
La Paz
Brasília
Arequipa
BOLIVIA
Sucre
PARAGUAY
Río de Janeiro
Antofagasta
Trópico de Capricornio
CHILE
Asunción
San Miguel
São Paulo
de Tucumán
OCÉANO
PACÍFICO
La Serena
OCÉANO
ATLÁNTICO
Córdoba
Rosario
URUGUAY
Valparaíso
ARGENTINA
Santiago
Montevideo
Buenos Aires
Concepción
Río de la Plata
Bahía Blanca
Puerto Montt
Bariloche
Chiloé

N

Islas Malvinas

AMÉRICA DEL SUR

0	1500 kilómetros

Estrecho de Magallanes

0	1000 millas

Punta Arenas
Tierra del Fuego

Cabo de Hornos

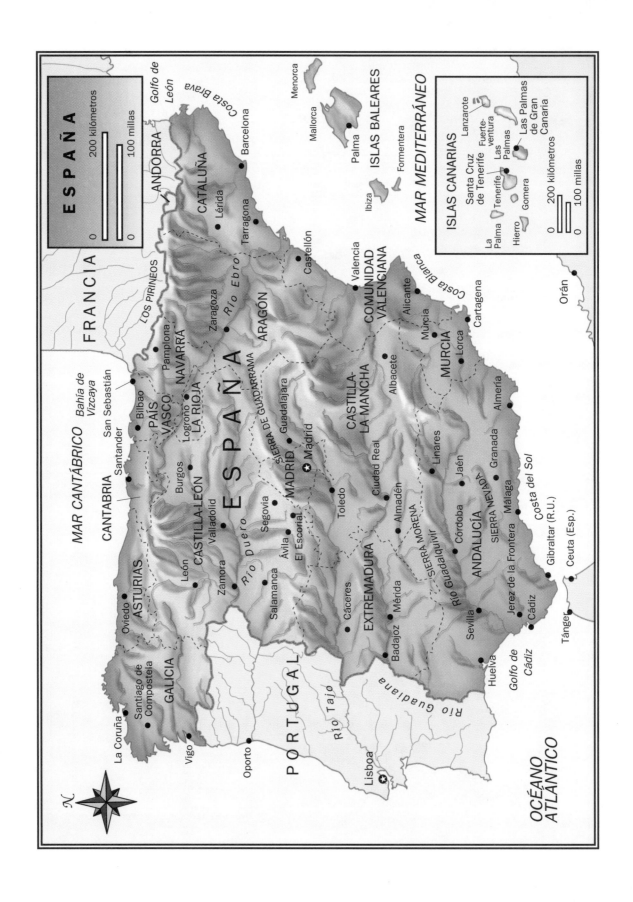

¿Qué tal?

¿Qué tal?

AN INTRODUCTORY COURSE
Fourth Edition

Thalia Dorwick

Ana María Pérez-Gironés
Wesleyan University

Marty Knorre

William R. Glass
Pennsylvania State University

Hildebrando Villarreal
California State University, Los Angeles

McGraw-Hill, Inc.
New York • St. Louis • San Francisco • Auckland • Bogotá • Caracas •
Lisbon • London • Madrid • Mexico City • Milan • Montreal • New Delhi •
San Juan • Singapore • Sydney • Tokyo • Toronto

This is an  book.

¿Qué tal?
An Introductory Course

Portions of this book reprinted by permission from *Puntos de partida: An Invitation to Spanish*, Fourth Edition, by Marty Knorre et al., published by McGraw-Hill, Inc. Copyright © 1993 by McGraw-Hill, Inc.

3 4 5 6 7 8 9 0 VNH VNH 9 0 9 8 7

ISBN 0-07-017956-5 (Student Edition)
ISBN 0-07-017957-3 (Instructor's Edition)

This book was set in Berkeley Book by GTS Graphics, Inc.
The editors were Sharla Volkersz and Marie Deer.
The design manager was Francis Owens.
Cover and text design was by Vargas/Williams Design.
Cover illustration was by Iikka Valli, Paloma Design and Production.
Cover photos: (*top left*) © Peter Menzel, (*top*) © Beryl Goldberg, (*top right*) © Stuart Cohen, (*middle right*) © Bob Daemmrich/Stock Boston, (*bottom left*) © Beryl Goldberg, (*bottom middle*) © Peter Arnold, Inc.
The production supervisor was Diane Renda.
The photo researcher was Darcy Wilding.
Production and editorial assistance was provided by Edie Williams, Ralph Kite, Scott Tinetti, and Michelle Lyon.
Von Hoffman Press was printer and binder.

Library of Congress Cataloging-in-Publication Data
¿Qué tal? : an introductory course / Thalia Dorwick . . . [et al.]. — 4th ed.
    p. cm.
    Includes index.
    ISBN 0-07-017956-5 (student ed.). — ISBN 0-07-017957-3 (teacher ed.)
    1. Spanish language—Textbooks for foreign speakers—English.
  I. Dorwick, Thalia, 1944–   .
  PC4129.E5Q4   1995
  468.2'421—dc20   94-39641
                                       CIP

Grateful acknowledgment is made for use of the following:

Photographs: *Page 1* © Peter Menzel/Stock Boston; *3* © Robert Frerck/Odyssey/Chicago; *7* (*left*) © Yoram Kahana/Shooting Star; (*right*) © Steve Allen/Gamma Liaison; *21* (*top and center*) © Robert Frerck/Odyssey/Chicago; (*bottom*) © John Phelan/D. Donne Bryant Stock Photo; *27* © Crandall/The

(*Continued on p. 418*)

Contents

THEME/VOCABULARIO	GRAMMAR AND FUNCTIONAL USES

Preface

The coauthors of *¿Qué tal?* have approached this new edition, its fourth, with excitement and energy. The importance of knowing Spanish has become more evident not only in this country but in the global community as well, making this an exciting time to be involved in Spanish instruction. And we are delighted that so many instructors have found and continue to find *¿Qué tal?* to be an appropriate vehicle for implementing a communicative approach with a brief, manageable textbook.

Based on the highly successful *Puntos de partida*, this fourth edition continues to emphasize essential vocabulary and grammar. We believe that the text continues to provide a flexible framework adaptable to individual teaching situations and goals—among them, a proficiency orientation and teaching for communicative competence.

Why Look at *¿Qué tal?* Again?

The overall goals of this edition of *¿Qué tal?* are identical to those of the first: "to help students develop proficiency in the four language skills essential to truly communicative language teaching." The text's teachability, its abundance of lively communicative activities, and its emphasis on meaningful use of Spanish by students have been enhanced in this edition. Chapters continue to be organized around contemporary cultural or everyday themes, and grammar is introduced and practiced within that real-world context. Thus, grammar, vocabulary, and culture work together as interactive elements. The text was prepared and revised with today's students in mind—to help them learn *how* to learn Spanish and to give them the opportunity to use it to express their own meaning.

The following is a brief list of the major features of the fourth edition.

- A reduction of the number of chapters, to make the text even more manageable than previous editions

- A consistent chapter structure, to make course planning easier
- New **Voces del mundo hispánico** sections that include non-edited literary and journalistic readings as well as geographic, historic, and political information about the different regions of the Hispanic world, including the main groups of Spanish-speaking people in the United States
- An annotated *Instructor's Edition,* with extensive on-page support for all sections
- New communicative activities throughout
- Enhancement of the doability of new and existing communicative activities via an easily implemented step-by-step approach
- New input-based activities at the beginning of many **Práctica** sequences that model new grammar and engage students in using new material before having to generate it in speaking
- New **Vocabulary Library** boxes that offer students vocabulary needed for communication without increasing the overall vocabulary load of the text
- Incorporation of authentic readings in the **Lectura cultural** sections
- Spiraled presentation of the uses of **por** and **para** throughout the text (highlighted in **¿Por o para?** boxes)
- Earlier introduction of the preterite (**Capítulo 8**) and of reflexive pronouns (**Capítulo 7**)
- A completely new **Capítulo 24,** with an engaging end-of-year activity
- New, more accessible realia throughout (with more in-text support), as well as new and improved drawings for vocabulary presentation and communicative activities
- Computer exercises in a revised software program for IBM and Macintosh equipment, new video materials, and other exciting new supplements

Instructors will find a more detailed discussion of these features in the *Instructor's Manual* for the fourth edition.

▼ ▼

Organization of the Fourth Edition

The chapter organization has been slightly altered in this edition of *¿Qué tal?* The text begins with a preliminary chapter of three mini-lessons, **Primeros pasos,** which provide a functional introduction to Spanish language and culture that enables students to express themselves on a wide variety of topics before the formal presentation of grammar begins.

The preliminary chapter is also set apart from the other chapters because its structure is different. After the **Primeros pasos, Capítulos 1–23** follow a consistent format:

    Primer paso
        Vocabulario
        Pronunciación (first seven chapters)
        Estructuras
    Segundo paso
        Vocabulario
        Estructuras
    Un paso más
        Un poco de todo
        Situación
        Para escribir
        Vocabulario (end-of-chapter list)
    Lectura cultural (after odd-numbered chapters) or
    Voces del mundo hispánico (after even-numbered
        chapters)

The following discussion of each repeating section of the chapters highlights their function as well as some features of the fourth edition.

• **Primer paso: Vocabulario** This section presents and practices thematic vocabulary and other simple structures that students will need for self-expression as they progress through the chapter.
• **Segundo paso: Vocabulario** This section either expands the theme vocabulary of the chapter or introduces a paradigm that fits in the theme, for example, **estar** with names of places; **estar** with adjectives; place prepositions; demonstratives; and so on. Although some of these items are typically found in the grammar sections of language textbooks, *¿Qué tal?* approaches them as vocabulary sets.
• **Pronunciación** This section focuses on individual sounds that are particularly difficult for native speakers of English.
• **Estructuras** This heading presents grammar topics, each introduced by a minidialogue, cartoon, or brief narrative, and followed by a series of contextualized exercises and activities that progress from more controlled to open-ended. Practice materials, carefully sequenced to lead students from

guided to free responses, include story sequences, paraphrase, interview, role-playing, and self-expression activities.

Throughout the text, you will note the attempt to introduce major grammar topics as background elements (in direction lines, dialogues, readings, lexical items) before the text formally presents the grammar for full student production and control.

• **Un poco de todo** These optional exercises and activities combine and review grammar presented in the chapter with that of previous chapters. Major topics consistently recycled in **Un poco de todo** include **ser** and **estar,** preterite and imperfect, gender, indicative and subjunctive, and so on.
• **Situación** These optional dialogues illustrate functional language and practical situations related to the chapter theme. In each chapter, students are given a task to perform as they read the dialogue. In most chapters, the dialogue is followed by **Notas comunicativas sobre el diálogo,** which highlight aspects of the language or culture that are of particular interest in the dialogue. Related role-plays are presented in **Comunicación.**
• **Para escribir** These brief optional composition topics guide students toward self-expression in writing.

The text concludes with **Capítulo 24 (Planeando un viaje al mundo hispánico),** which leads students through an end-of-text activity, the organization of a trip, step by step.

Additional features of importance include:

• **Notas (comunicativas, lingüísticas, culturales)** These boxes highlight functional material or cultural information at logical points throughout all sections of the text.
• **De aquí y de allá** Occuring once in each **Primer paso: Vocabulario** section, these boxes highlight up-to-date vocabulary and expressions from all parts of the Hispanic world, with special emphasis in the diversity of Spanish worldwide.
• **Reciclado** These brief review boxes provide a link between previous grammar points and new material that builds on those grammar points.
• **Study Hints** These boxes give students specific advice about how to acquire language skills: how to learn vocabulary, how to study verbs, and so on. They occur at logical points throughout the text.
• **Vocabulary Library** These boxes offer students vocabulary needed for communication without increasing the overall vocabulary load of the text. They occur at logical points throughout the text.

▼ ▼

Using *¿Qué tal?* in the Classroom: Statement of Purpose

The authors believe that students' *class time* is best spent in *using* Spanish: listening to and speaking with the instructor and each other, listening to and viewing audiovisual materials of many kinds and reading in-text and supplementary materials. It is recommended that instructors spot-check text exercises in class but devote more time to the marginal-note extensions and their variations in the *Instructor's Edition,* as well as to the many optional exercises and activities found there. Consequently, class time can be focused on new material and on novel language experiences that will maintain student interest and provide more exposure to spoken and written Spanish. Students make few gains in language learning when all their class time is spent correcting exercises. Answers for most exercises are provided in the *Instructor's Manual* and may be copied and distributed to students, for self-checking.

All exercises and activities in the *¿Qué tal?* program have been designed to help students develop proficiency in Spanish rather than simply display their grammatical knowledge. The authors believe that the process of attempting to use language provides an optimal language learning situation—one that will prepare students to function in Spanish in the situations that they are most likely to encounter outside the classroom.

¿Qué tal? and Developing Language Proficiency

The conceptualization of all editions of *¿Qué tal?* makes it an appropriate text to use for developing language proficiency.

• An insistence on the acquisition of vocabulary during the early stages of language learning (**Primeros pasos**) and then in each chapter throughout the text
• An emphasis on personalized and creative use of language to perform various functions or achieve various goals
• Careful attention to skills development rather than grammatical knowledge alone
• A cyclical organization in which vocabulary, grammar, and language functions are consistently reviewed and reentered
• An integrated cultural component that embeds practice in a wide variety of culturally significant contexts
• Content that aims to raise student awareness of the interaction of language, culture, and society

Within each chapter, text materials are sequenced to facilitate and maximize progress in communication skills: from vocabulary acquisition activities, to grammar practice, to divergent activities that stimulate student creativity. The overall text organization progresses from a focus on formulaic expressions, to vocabulary and structures relevant to the "here and now" (descriptions, student life, family life), to survival situations (ordering a meal, travel-related activities), and to topics of broader conceptual interest (current events, the environment). Some material is introduced functionally in small chunks before the entire paradigm is presented. Major grammar topics such as the past tenses and the subjunctive are introduced and then reentered later in the text; most grammar topics and language functions are continually reviewed and reentered throughout the text and its ancillaries.

Supplementary Materials for the Fourth Edition

A variety of additional components have been developed to support *¿Qué tal?* Many are free to adopting institutions. Please contact your local McGraw-Hill representative for details on policies, prices, and availability.

Components that are new to this edition or significantly changed are marked with violet bullets.

• The **Workbook,** by Alice Arana (Fullerton College) and Oswaldo Arana (formerly of California State University, Fullerton), continues the successful format of previous editions by providing additional practice with vocabulary and structures through a variety of controlled and open-ended exercises, review sections, and guided compositions. More realia- and drawing-based activities have been included in the fourth edition. In addition, personalized input-based activities help to make practice with the forms of Spanish more meaningful to students. A new journal-writing section, **Mi diario,** encourages students to express themselves about aspects of the chapters' cultural themes, as does the new **En primera persona** feature.
• The **Laboratory Manual** and **Tape Program,** by María Sabló-Yates (Delta College), continue to emphasize listening comprehension activities. New listening activities in this edition include a **Los hispanos hablan** feature as well as completely new cultural listening passages with listening strategies. Most major sections begin with personalized activities that allow students to think about aspects of the chapter theme in their own lives as they listen to focused input with grammar. One section of each chapter, **Un paso más,** is now designed to be turned in to the instructor; no answers are

▼ ▼

given for it on the tape or in the laboratory manual. Chapters continue to offer mechanical speaking practice as well as interview and dialogue-based activities. Many activities are realia- or drawing-based. One tape in the set includes all of the words in the end-of-chapter **Vocabulario** lists. You may wish to have copies of this tape made for student use. A **Tapescript** is also available. Cassette tapes are free to adopting institutions and are also available for student purchase upon request.

- The **Student Tapes** (new to the fourth edition) offer a self-test to help students review each chapter's structures and vocabulary. Designed for listening practice only, the *Student Tapes* do not depend on any written material.
- The **Instructor's Edition** of the student text (new to the fourth edition), contains on-page suggestions, many supplementary exercises for developing listening and speaking skills, and abundant variations and follow-ups on student text materials. Most annotations for the **Vocabulario** sections are bound into the back of the *Instructor's Edition* rather than appearing directly on the page.
- The **Instructor's Manual/Testbank** offers an extensive introduction to teaching techniques, general guidelines for instructors, suggestions for lesson planning and for semester/quarter schedules, a testing program, models for vocabulary introduction, supplementary exercises, and suggestions for the **Lectura cultural** and **Voces del mundo hispánico** sections of the student text. Answers to the text's mechanical exercises are also provided; you may wish to have them copied and distributed to students. The **Instructor's Manual** also now offers a wide variety of interactive and communicative games for practicing vocabulary and grammar, created by Linda H. Colville and Deana Alonso (Citrus College). Also included are two sets of structured role-plays, **Situaciones,** coordinated with each chapter's vocabulary and grammar. Supplementary exercises and activities are also included for these **Situaciones.**
- The **Destinos Video Modules** (vocabulary, functional language, situational language, and culture, taken from the popular *Destinos* television series as well as original footage shot on location), is also available for use with *¿Qué tal?*, along with a videodisc version of the situational language module.
- Additional video supplements include the **McGraw-Hill Video Library of Authentic Spanish Materials.**
- The **McGraw-Hill Electronic Language Tutor (MHELT 2.0)** offers many of the more controlled exercises from the student text and workbook. The *MHELT* program is available in both IBM and Macintosh formats. It has been thoroughly revised for this edition, in response to the compliments and suggestions from users of the original *MHELT* program.

- Also available is the innovative **Juegos comunicativos,** an interactive program by John Underwood (Western Washington University) and Richard Bassein (Mills College), which stresses communication skills in Spanish—ordering a meal, giving directions, and so on. (Available only in Apple II format.)
- Also available (and new to this edition) is a new software program for purchase by students, **Spanish Partner.** Developed at Vanderbilt University by Monica Morley and Karl Fisher, *Spanish Partner* is a user-friendly program that helps students master vocabulary and grammar topics that all beginning Spanish students need to know. *Spanish Partner* offers clear, user-oriented feedback that helps students learn from their mistakes.
- **Overhead Transparencies** offer all new visuals in four color, appropriate for vocabulary or grammar presentations.
- A set of **slides** from various parts of the Spanish-speaking world, with activities for classroom use, is also available to adopting institutions.
- A training/orientation **manual** for use with teaching assistants, by James F. Lee (University of Illinois, Urbana-Champaign), offers practical advice for beginning language instructors and language coordinators.
- **A Practical Guide to Language Learning,** by H. Douglas Brown (San Francisco State University), provides beginning foreign language students with a general introduction to the language learning process. This guide is free to adopting institutions, and it can also be made available for student purchase.

Acknowledgments

The suggestions, advice, and work of the following friends and colleagues is gratefully acknowledged by the authors of the fourth edition.

- Dr. Bill VanPatten (University of Illinois, Urbana-Champaign), whose creativity has been an inspiration to us for a number of editions and from whom we have learned so very much about language teaching and about how students learn.
- The friends, students, and colleagues who contributed materials on which many exercises and some reading selections are based.

In addition, the publishers wish to acknowledge the suggestions received from the following instructors and professional friends across the country. The appearance of their names in this list does not necessarily constitute their endorsement of the text or its methodology.

▼ ▼

Jonathan Arries
  Old Dominion University
Margaret A. Ballantyne
  York University/CUNY
Priscilla Byerly
  University of Vermont
Jaime Calvillo
  Anoka-Ramsey Community College
Richard K. Curry
  Texas A & M University
Alice Edwards
  Mercyhurst College
James Fonseca
  California Lutheran University
Virginia Ramos Foster
  Phoenix College
Juan Carlos Galeano
  Utica College of Syracuse University
Bruce A. Gamble
  Owens Technical College
Jorge García-Gómez
  Long Island University
Sharon M. Gormley
  Austin Community College
Anita Gowin
  Mississippi College
Pilar F. Cañadas Greenwood
  Wells College
Linda Gresham
  Minot State University

Lisa Huempfner
  University of Vermont
Ellen C. Lavroff
  Front Range Community College
Guadalupe López-Cox
  Austin Community College
Mary Loud
  Youngstown State University
Domenico Maceri
  Allan Hancock College
Lisa A. Martin
  South Mountain Community College
Thomas M. McTigue
  Indiana University Southeast
Sister Michael Raymond Moore
  Immaculata College
John D. Nesbitt
  Eastern Wyoming College
Ted Olsen
  Lee College
Amanda Plumlee
  Davis & Elkins College
Harriet N. Poole
  Lake City Community College
Marcie J. Pyper
  Reformed Bible College
David Quinn
  Western Illinois University
Shelley Quinn
  Memorial University of Newfoundland

M. Mercedes Rahilly
  Lansing Community College
Monroe Harland Rall
  Abilene Christian University
MaryAnne Rangel
  Western Washington University
Susan M. Riddell
  University of New Hampshire
Claire H. Rogers
  Arapahoe Community College
M. Salama
  Memorial University of Newfoundland
Delia E. Sánchez
  Phoenix College
George R. Shivers
  Washington College
Eileen Smith
  Shasta College
Marina Valenzuela Smith
  Antelope Valley College
Augustina López Snideman
  Santa Fe Community College
Daniela Stewart
  Everett Community College
Elizabeth Willingham
  The College of William and Mary

Many other individuals deserve our thanks and appreciation for their help and support. Among them are the people who, in addition to the authors, read the fourth edition at various stages of development to ensure its linguistic and cultural authenticity and pedagogical accuracy: Alice Arana (United States), Oswaldo Arana (Perú), Laura Chastain (El Salvador), and María Sabló-Yates (Panamá).

Within the McGraw-Hill family, the "cast of characters" from the development and production staff has become too large to acknowledge individually. You can find many of their names on the copyright page. We would be remiss, however, if we did not recognize the special contributions of Scott Tinetti, Sharla Volkersz, and Francis Owens, who really helped to make this text and its ancillaries "happen"; these materials would not be here without them. Special thanks are due

Eirik Børve, who originally brought some of us together; to the McGraw-Hill sales staff, for their constant support and efforts; and to Margaret Metz, whose suggestions and input from a marketing perspective are always insightful.

The only reasons for publishing a new textbook or to revise an existing one are to help the profession evolve in meaningful ways and to make the task of daily classroom instruction easier and more enjoyable for experienced instructors and teaching assistants alike. Foreign language teaching has changed in important ways in the decade since the publication of the first edition of ¿Qué tal?. We are delighted to have been—and to continue to be—one of the agents of that evolution. And we are grateful to McGraw-Hill for its continuing creative support for our ideas.

Primeros pasos

Salamanca, España.

¿Qué tal? means *"Hi, how are you doing?"* in Spanish. This textbook, called *¿Qué tal?,* will help you to begin learning Spanish and to become more familiar with the many people here and abroad who use it.

Language is the means by which humans communicate with one another. To learn a new language is to acquire a new way of exchanging information and of sharing your thoughts and opinions with others. *¿Qué tal?* will help you use Spanish to communicate in various ways and function in many kinds of real-life situations: to understand Spanish when others speak it, to speak it yourself, and to read and write it. This text will also help you to communicate with Spanish speakers in nonverbal ways through an awareness of cultural differences.

Learning about a new culture is an inseparable part of learning a language. "Culture" can mean many things: everything from great writers and painters to what time people usually eat lunch. Throughout *¿Qué tal?* you will have the opportunity to find out about the daily lives of Spanish-speaking people and the kinds of things that are important to them. Knowing about all these things will be important to you, too, when you visit a Spanish-speaking country, and it may even be useful to you here. If you look around, you will see that Spanish is not really a foreign language, but rather a widely used language in this country today.

Primeros pasos (*First steps*), a three-part chapter, will introduce you to the Spanish language and to the format of *¿Qué tal?*

1

Primer paso

SALUDOS[a] Y EXPRESIONES DE CORTESÍA

[a]*Greetings*

Here are some words, phrases, and expressions that will enable you to meet and greet others appropriately in Spanish.

▼ 1. ANA: Hola, José.
▼   JOSÉ: ¿Qué tal, Ana? (¿Cómo estás?)
▼   ANA: Regular. ¿Y tú?
▼   JOSÉ: ¡Muy bien! Hasta mañana, ¿eh?
▼   ANA: Adiós.
▼
▼ 2.
▼
▼   2. SEÑOR ALONSO: Buenas tardes, señorita López.
▼   SEÑORITA LÓPEZ: Muy buenas, señor Alonso.
▼   ¿Cómo está?
▼   SEÑOR ALONSO: Bien, gracias. ¿Y usted?
▼   SEÑORITA LÓPEZ: Muy bien, gracias. Adiós.
▼   SEÑOR ALONSO: Hasta luego.

¿Qué tal?, **¿Cómo estás?**, and **¿Y tú?** are expressions used in informal situations with people you know well, on a first-name basis.

¿Cómo está? and **¿Y usted?** are used to address someone with whom you have a formal relationship.

▼ 3. MARÍA: Buenos días, profesora.
▼   PROFESORA: Buenos días. ¿Cómo se llama usted?
▼   MARÍA: (Me llamo) María Sánchez.
▼   PROFESORA: Mucho gusto.
▼   MARÍA: Igualmente. (Encantada.)

---

[1]ANA: Hi, José. JOSÉ: How are you doing, Ana? (How are you?) ANA: OK. And you? JOSÉ: Fine! (Very well!) See you tomorrow, right? ANA: Bye.
[2]MR. ALONSO: Good afternoon, Miss López. MISS LÓPEZ: 'Afternoon, Mr. Alonso. How are you? MR. ALONSO: Fine, thanks. And you? MISS LÓPEZ: Very well, thanks. Good-bye. MR. ALONSO: See you later.
[3]MARÍA: Good morning, professor. PROFESSOR: Good morning. What's your name? MARÍA: (My name is) María Sánchez. PROFESSOR: Pleased to meet you. MARÍA: Likewise. (Delighted.)

¿**Cómo se llama usted?** is used in formal situations. ¿**Cómo te llamas?** is used in informal situations—for example, with other students. The phrases **mucho gusto** and **igualmente** are used by both men and women when meeting for the first time. In response to **mucho gusto**, a woman can also say **encantada**; a man can say **encantado**.

OTROS SALUDOS Y EXPRESIONES DE CORTESÍA

buenos días	good morning (*used until the midday meal*)
buenas tardes	good afternoon (*used until the evening meal*)
buenas noches	good evening; good night (*used after the evening meal*)
señor (Sr.)	Mr., sir
señora (Sra.)	Mrs., ma'am
señorita (Srta.)	Miss

Note that there is no standard Spanish equivalent for *Ms.* Use **Sra.** or **Srta.**, as appropriate.

Práctica

A **Minidiálogos.** Practice the three dialogues on the preceding page several times with another student, using your own names.

B **Saludos.** How many different ways can you respond to the following greetings and phrases?

1. Buenas tardes.
2. Adiós.
3. ¿Qué tal?
4. Hola.
5. ¿Cómo está?
6. Buenas noches.
7. Hasta mañana.
8. ¿Cómo se llama usted?
9. Mucho gusto.

C **Entrevista** (*Interview*). Turn to the person sitting next to you and do the following.

- Greet him or her appropriately, that is, with formal or informal forms.
- Find out his or her name.
- Ask how he or she is.
- Conclude the exchange.

Now have a similar conversation with your instructor, using the appropriate formal forms.

México, D.F. (Distrito Federal).

NOTA CULTURAL: Greetings in the Hispanic World

Hispanics tend to greet more physically than English speakers. For instance, Hispanic women regularly kiss on the cheek while greeting, even if they are meeting for the first time. A kiss is also common between men and women, especially adolescents and young adults. Men often hug while greeting one another, and it is common to see two male friends strolling arm in arm.

NOTA COMUNICATIVA: Speaking Politely

The material in this recurring section of **¿Qué tal?** will help you deal with everyday situations in Spanish, such as how to accept or decline an invitation and how to order in a restaurant. Here are some words and phrases that will help you speak politely.

gracias	thanks, thank you
muchas gracias	thank you very much
de nada, no hay de qué	you're welcome
por favor	please; excuse me (*to get someone's attention*)
perdón	pardon me; excuse me (*to apologize or to get someone's attention*)
con permiso	pardon me, excuse me (*to request permission to pass by or through a group of people, or to leave a group*)

D **Descripciones.** Are the numbered people in the drawing saying **por favor, con permiso,** or **perdón?**

EL ALFABETO ESPAÑOL

▼ ▼

There are thirty letters in the Spanish alphabet (**el alfabeto**)—four more than in the English alphabet. The **ch,*** **ll,*** and **rr** are considered single letters even though they are two-letter groups; the **ñ** is the fourth extra letter. The letters **k** and **w** appear only in words borrowed from other languages.

---

*Several Hispanic language academics have recently decided that **ch** and **ll** should no longer be considered separate letters of the Spanish alphabet. It is difficult to predict what effect this decision may have on Spanish usage throughout the world.

Listen carefully as your instructor pronounces the names listed with the letters of the alphabet.

LETTERS	NAMES OF LETTERS	EXAMPLES		
a	a	**A**ntonio	**A**na	(l**a**) **A**rgentin**a**
b	be	**B**enito	**B**lanca	**B**olivia
c	ce	**C**arlos	**C**ecilia	**C**áceres
ch	che	Pan**ch**o	Con**ch**a	**Ch**ile
d	de	**D**omingo	**D**olores	**D**urango
e	e	**E**duardo	**E**lena	(**e**l) **E**cuador
f	efe	**F**elipe	**F**rancisca	(la) **F**lorida
g	ge	**G**erardo	**G**loria	**G**uatemala
h	hache	**H**éctor	**H**ortensia	**H**onduras
i	i	**I**gnacio	**I**nés	**I**biza
j	jota	**J**osé	**J**uana	**J**alisco
k	ca (ka)	(**K**arl)	(**K**ati)	(*Kansas*)
l	ele	**L**uis	**L**ola	**L**ima
ll	elle	Gui**ll**ermo	Gui**ll**ermina	Sevi**ll**a
m	eme	**M**anuel	**M**aría	**M**éxico
n	ene	**N**icolás	**N**ati	**N**icaragua
ñ	eñe	Í**ñ**igo	Bego**ñ**a	Espa**ñ**a
o	o	**O**ctavio	**O**livia	**O**vied**o**
p	pe	**P**ablo	**P**ilar	**P**anamá
q	cu	Enri**q**ue	Ra**q**uel	**Q**uito
r	ere	Álva**r**o	Cla**r**a	(el) Pe**r**ú
rr	erre *or* ere doble	**R**afael	**R**osa	Monte**rr**ey
s	ese	**S**alvador	**S**ara	**S**an Juan
t	te	**T**omás	**T**eresa	**T**oledo
u	u	Ag**u**stín	L**u**cía	(el) **U**r**u**guay
v	ve *or* uve	**V**íctor	**V**ictoria	**V**enezuela
w	doble ve, ve doble, *or* uve doble	Os**w**aldo	(**W**ilma)	(*Washington*)
x	equis	**X**avier	**X**imena	E**x**tremadura
y	i griega	Pela**y**o	**Y**olanda	(el) Paragua**y**
z	ceta (zeta)	**G**on**z**alo	Esperan**z**a	**Z**aragoza

Práctica

A **Letras.** The letters on the next page represent the Spanish letters and sounds that are the most different from their English counterparts. You will practice the pronunciation of some of these letters in upcoming sections of *¿Qué tal?* For the moment, pay particular attention to their pronunciation when you see them. Can you match the Spanish spelling with its equivalent pronunciation?

SPELLING	PRONUNCIATION
1. ch	**a.** like the *g* in English *garden*
2. g before **e** or **i**; also **j**	**b.** similar to *tt* of *butter* when pronounced very quickly
3. h	
4. g before **a, o,** or **u**	**c.** like *ch* in English *cheese*
5. ll	**d.** like Spanish **b**
6. ñ	**e.** similar to a "strong" English *h*
7. r	**f.** like *y* in English *yes* or like the *li* sound in *million*
8. r at the beginning of a word or **rr** in the middle of a word	
	g. a trilled sound, several Spanish r's in a row
9. v	**h.** similar to the *ny* sound in *canyon*
	i. never pronounced

B **Nombres.** Spell your own name in Spanish, and listen as your classmates spell their names. Try to remember as many of their names as you can.

MODELO: Me llamo María: **M** (eme) **a** (a) **r** (ere) **í** (i acentuada) **a** (a).

LOS COGNADOS

▼ ▼

Many Spanish and English words are similar or identical in form and meaning. These related words are called *cognates* (**los cognados**). Spanish and English share so many cognates because a number of words in both languages are derived from the same Latin root words—and also because Spanish and English are "language neighbors," especially in the southwestern United States. Each language has borrowed words from the other and adapted them to its own sound system. Thus, the English word *leader* has become Spanish **líder**, and Spanish **el lagarto** (*the lizard*) has become English *alligator*. The existence of so many cognates will make learning some Spanish words easier for you and increase the number of words that you can recognize immediately. Many cognates are used in **Primeros pasos**. Don't try to memorize all of them—just get used to the sound of them in Spanish.

Here are some Spanish adjectives (words used to describe people, places, and things) that are cognates of English words. Practice pronouncing them, imitating your instructor. These adjectives can be used to describe either a man or a woman.

arrogante	importante	pesimista
cruel	independiente	realista
eficiente	inteligente	rebelde
egoísta	interesante	responsable
elegante	liberal	sentimental
emocional	materialista	terrible
flexible	optimista	valiente
idealista	paciente	

The following adjectives change form. Use the **-o** ending when describing a man, the **-a** ending when describing a woman.

extrovertido/a	religioso/a	serio/a
generoso/a	reservado/a	sincero/a
impulsivo/a	romántico/a	tímido/a

Práctica

Personalidades. Think of a well-known person—real or imaginary—and describe him or her using **es** (*is*) or **no es** (*isn't*). Try to describe as many qualities of the person as you can. For example:

Andy García es / no es...   Gloria Estefan es / no es...

Servicios De Información En Español

1310	Noticias Locales
1315	Temperatura Locales
1320	Deportes Locales
1325	Informacion Sobre La Salud
1330	Información Legal
1335	Asuntos Locales

If you were in Miami, you could tune in to this radio station to get information in Spanish. Can you find the Spanish equivalent of the following English phrases?

- Community Events
- The "Top Ten" Songs
- What's Happening in Miami
- Local Temperature
- Legal Information

1075	Las 10 Canciones Principales
1140	Eventos Comunitarios
1881	Línea Abierta
1882	¿Qué Pasa En Miami?

¿CÓMO ES USTED?[a]

▼ ▼

[a]*¿Cómo... What are you like?*

You can use these forms of the verb **ser** (*to be*) to describe yourself and others.

(yo)	**soy**	*I am*
(tú)	**eres**	*you* (familiar) *are*
(usted)	**es**	*you* (formal) *are*
(él, ella)	**es**	*he/she is*

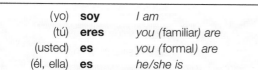

Práctica

A ¿**Cómo es usted?** Describe yourself, using adjectives from **Los cognados**. Begin with **Yo soy...** or **Yo no soy...**

B Reacciones.

Paso 1. Use the following adjectives, or any others you know, to create one sentence about a classmate.

> MODELO: USTED: Alicia, **eres** generosa
>   ALICIA: Sí, **soy** generosa. (Sí, **soy** muy generosa.) (No, no **soy** generosa.)

    Adjetivos: sincero/a, eficiente, emocional, inteligente, impulsivo/a, liberal

Paso 2. Now find out what kind of person your instructor is, using the same adjectives. Use the appropriate formal forms.

> MODELO: ¿Es usted optimista (generoso/a)?

NOTA CULTURAL: Spanish as a World Language

There are more than 350 million native speakers of Spanish, making it one of the five most spoken languages in the world.* It is the language spoken in Spain, in all of South America (except Brazil and the Guyanas), in most of Central America, in Cuba, in Puerto Rico, and in the Dominican Republic. Spanish is also heard in Andorra, Belize, and the United States.

Like all languages spoken by large numbers of people, Spanish varies from country to country and region to region. The Spanish of Madrid is different from that spoken in Mexico City or Buenos Aires, just as the English of London differs from that of Sydney or Chicago. Although these differences are most noticeable in pronunciation ("accent"), they are also evident in varying vocabulary and in special expressions used in different geographical areas. In Great Britain the word *lift* is used to describe the apparatus known in other English-speaking areas as an *elevator*. What is called an **autobús** in Spain is called a **guagua** in the Caribbean and a **bus** in Uruguay. Although such differences are noticeable, they rarely result in misunderstandings among native speakers, since the majority of structures and vocabulary are common to all varieties of each language.

---

*Top 5 languages (source: *World Almanac 1994*): Chinese (Mandarin), 930 million; English, 463 million; Hindi, 400 million; Spanish, 371 million; and Russian, 291 million.

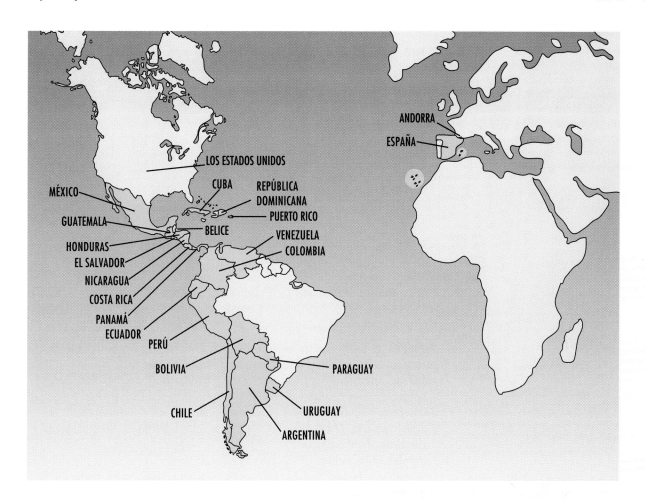

MÁS COGNADOS

▼ ▼

Although some English and Spanish cognates are spelled identically (*idea, general, gas, animal, motor*), most will differ slightly in spelling: *position*/**posición**, *secret*/**secreto**, *student*/**estudiante**, *rose*/**rosa**, *lottery*/**lotería**, *opportunity*/**oportunidad**, *exam*/**examen.**

   The following exercises will give you more practice in recognizing and pronouncing cognates. Remember: don't try to learn all of these words. Just get used to the way they sound.

Many of the Spanish words used to talk about technology and recent inventions, including the latest in electronic equipment, are cognates of English words. What piece of equipment is this ad for? Can you find the Spanish word for it? How many other cognates are there in the text of the ad?

Monolith 70-490 NIC

Técnica fascinante y línea clara con perfiles estrechos: esto es un televisor al más alto nivel. 2 × 50 W Hifi stéreo a través de dos cajas acústicas exponenciales. Doble reproducción del sonido stéreo/dual (Nicam 728 y sistema alemán).

Práctica

A **Categorías.** Pronounce each of the following cognates and give its English equivalent. You will also recognize the meaning of most of the categories (**Naciones, Personas,** . . .). Based on the words listed in the group, can you guess the meaning of the categories indicated with a gloss symbol (°)?

Naciones: el Japón, Italia, Francia, España, el Brasil, China, el Canadá, Rusia
Personas: líder, profesor, actriz, pintor, político, estudiante
Lugares:° restaurante, café, museo, garaje, bar, banco, hotel, oficina, océano, parque
Conceptos: libertad, dignidad, declaración, cooperación, comunismo
Cosas:° teléfono, fotografía, sofá, televisión, radio, bomba, novela, diccionario, dólar, lámpara, yate
Animales: león, cebra, chimpancé, tigre, hipopótamo
Comidas y bebidas:° hamburguesa, cóctel, patata, café, limón, banana
Deportes:° béisbol, tenis, vólibol, fútbol americano
Instrumentos musicales: guitarra, piano, flauta, clarinete, trompeta, violín

B **¿Qué es esto?** (*What is this?*)

Paso 1. Being able to tell what something is or to identify the group to which it belongs is a useful strategy in conversation. Begin to practice this strategy by pronouncing these cognates and identifying the category from **Práctica A** to which they belong. Use the following sentences as a guide.

Es **un** lugar (concepto, animal, deporte, instrumento musical).
Es **una** nación (persona, cosa, comida, bebida).

MODELO: béisbol → Es un deporte.

1. calculadora	**6.** actor	**11.** universidad
2. burro	**7.** clase	**12.** fama
3. sándwich	**8.** limonada	**13.** terrorista
4. golf	**9.** elefante	**14.** acordeón
5. México	**10.** refrigerador	**15.** democracia

Paso 2. With a classmate, practice identifying words, using the categories given in **Paso 1.** In the question, **¿qué?** means *what?*

MODELO: ESTUDIANTE 1: ¿Qué es un hospital?
              ESTUDIANTE 2: Es un lugar.

The English equivalent of these sentences is *It is a place (concept,* . . .); *It is a country (person,* . . .). Note that Spanish has two different ways to express *a (an):* **un** and **una.** All nouns are either masculine (*m.*) or feminine (*f.*) in Spanish. **Un** is used with masculine nouns, **una** with feminine nouns. You will learn more about this aspect of Spanish in **Capítulo 1.** Don't try to learn the gender of nouns now. You do not have to know the gender of nouns to do this activity.

1. un saxofón
2. un autobús
3. un rancho
4. un doctor
5. Bolivia
6. una Coca-Cola
7. una enchilada
8. una jirafa
9. una turista

PRONUNCIACIÓN

▼ ▼

You have probably already noted that there is a very close relationship between the way Spanish is written and the way it is pronounced. This makes it relatively easy to learn the basics of Spanish spelling and pronunciation.

Many Spanish sounds, however, do not have an exact equivalent in English, so you should not trust English to be your guide to Spanish pronunciation. Even words that are spelled the same in both languages are usually pronounced quite differently. It is important to become so familiar with Spanish sounds that you can pronounce them automatically, right from the beginning of your study of the language.

Las vocales (*Vowels*): *a, e, i, o, u*

Unlike English vowels, which can have many different pronunciations or may be silent, Spanish vowels are always pronounced, and they are almost always pronounced in the same way. Spanish vowels are always short and tense. They are never drawn out with a *u* or *i* glide as in English: **lo** ≠ *low*; **de** ≠ *day*.

¡OJO!   The *uh* sound or schwa (which is how most unstressed vowels are pronounced in English: *canal, waited, atom*) does not exist in Spanish.

a: pronounced like the *a* in *father,* but short and tense
e: pronounced like the *e* in *they,* but without the *i* glide
i: pronounced like the *i* in *machine,* but short and tense*
o: pronounced like the *o* in *home,* but without the *u* glide
u: pronounced like the *u* in *rule,* but short and tense

A Pronounce the following Spanish syllables, being careful to pronounce each vowel with a short, tense sound.

1. ma fa la ta pa
2. me fe le te pe
3. mi fi li ti pi
4. mo fo lo to po
5. mu fu lu tu pu
6. mi fe la tu do
7. su mi te so la
8. se tu no ya li

B Pronounce the following words, paying special attention to the vowel sounds.

1.	hasta	tal	nada	mañana	natural	normal	fascinante
2.	me	qué	Pérez	Elena	rebelde	excelente	elegante
3.	sí	señorita	permiso	terrible	imposible	tímido	Ibiza
4.	yo	con	cómo	noches	profesor	señor	generoso
5.	uno	usted	tú	mucho	Perú	Lupe	Úrsula

---

*The word **y** (*and*) is also pronounced like the letter **i**.

Here is part of a rental car ad in Spanish. The names of the countries should be familiar to you. Can you find the following information in the ad?

- How many cars does the agency have available?
- How many offices does the agency have?
- What Spanish word expresses the English word *immediately*?
- If not confirmed immediately, when are reservations confirmed by the agency?

LOS NÚMEROS 0-30; HAY

▼ **Canción infantil**

Dos y dos son cuatro,
cuatro y dos son seis,
seis y dos son ocho,
y ocho dieciséis.

0	cero				
1	uno	11	once	21	veintiuno
2	dos	12	doce	22	veintidós
3	tres	13	trece	23	veintitrés
4	cuatro	14	catorce	24	veinticuatro
5	cinco	15	quince	25	veinticinco
6	seis	16	dieciséis*	26	veintiséis
7	siete	17	diecisiete	27	veintisiete
8	ocho	18	dieciocho	28	veintiocho
9	nueve	19	diecinueve	29	veintinueve
10	diez	20	veinte	30	treinta

A children's song: Two and two are four, four and two are six, six and two are eight, and eight (makes) sixteen.

*The number 16 to 19 and 21 to 29 can each be written as one word (**dieciséis... veintiuno...**), as shown in the chart, or as three words (**diez y seis... veinte y uno...**).

The number *one* has several forms in Spanish.

* **Uno** is the form used in counting.
* **Un** is used before masculine singular nouns: **un señor.**
* **Una** is used before feminine singular nouns: **una señora.**
* The number **veintiuno** becomes **veintiún** before masculine nouns and **veintiuna** before feminine nouns: **veintiún señores, veintiuna señoras.**

Use the word **hay** to express both *there is* and *there are* in Spanish. **No hay** means *there is not* or *there are not.* **¿Hay... ?** asks *Is there . . . ?* or *Are there . . . ?*

¿Cuántos estudiantes **hay** en la clase? —**(Hay)** Treinta.
¿**Hay** chicos en la clase? —**Hay** veinte chicas, pero **no hay** chicos.

How many students are there in the class? —*(There are) Thirty.*
Are there any young men in the class? —*There are twenty young women, but there aren't any young men.*

> Notice how plural nouns in Spanish, like most plurals in English, end in **-s** or **-es: una clase → dos clases, un señor → dos señores.** You will learn how to form plurals in **Capítulo 1.** You don't have to form them to do the activities in this section.

Práctica

A **¡Practique los números!** Empiece (*Begin*) con **Hay...**

1. 4 señoras
2. 12 estudiantes
3. 1 café (*m.*)
4. 21 cafés (*m.*)
5. 14 días
6. 1 clase (*f.*)
7. 21 ideas (*f.*)
8. 11 personas
9. 15 estudiantes
10. 13 teléfonos
11. 28 naciones
12. 5 guitarras
13. 1 león (*m.*)
14. 30 señores
15. 20 oficinas

B **Problemas de matemáticas.** Note: + (**y**), − (**menos**), = (**son**).

MODELOS: $2 + 2 = 4$ → Dos y dos son cuatro.
$4 - 2 = 2$ → Cuatro menos dos son dos.

1. $2 + 4 = ?$
2. $8 + 17 = ?$
3. $11 + 1 = ?$
4. $3 + 18 = ?$
5. $9 + 6 = ?$
6. $5 + 4 = ?$
7. $1 + 13 = ?$
8. $15 - 2 = ?$
9. $9 - 9 = ?$
10. $13 - 8 = ?$
11. $14 + 12 = ?$
12. $23 - 13 = ?$

GUSTOS[a] Y PREFERENCIAS

[a]*Likes*

▼ ▼

▼ —¿Te gusta jugar al béisbol?

▼ —Sí, me gusta, pero me gusta más el vólibol.

To indicate that you like something in Spanish, say **Me gusta** _____. To indicate that you don't like something, use **No me gusta** _____. Use the question **¿Te gusta** _____**?** to ask a classmate if he or she likes something. Use **¿Le gusta** _____**?** to ask your instructor the same question.

In the following conversations, you will use the word **el** to mean *the* with masculine nouns and the word **la** with feminine nouns. Don't try to memorize which nouns are masculine and which are feminine. Just get used to using the words **el** and **la** before nouns.

You will also be using a number of Spanish verbs in the infinitive form, which always ends in **-r.** Here are some examples: **estudiar** = *to study;* **comer** = *to eat.* Try to guess the meanings of the infinitives used in these activities from context. If someone asks you, for instance, **¿Te gusta *beber* Coca-Cola?,** it is a safe guess that **beber** means *to drink.*

Práctica

Los gustos.

Paso 1. Indicate whether you like the following things, people, or activities.

MODELOS: ¿la clase de español? → (No) Me gusta la clase de español.
¿estudiar? → (No) Me gusta estudiar.

1. ¿la música moderna? ¿la música clásica? ¿la música rap?
2. ¿la universidad? ¿la cafetería de la universidad?
3. ¿la actriz María Conchita Alonso? ¿el actor Edward James Olmos? ¿la tenista Mary Jo Fernández? ¿el cantante Julio Iglesias? ¿el conjunto (*group*) Los Lobos?
4. ¿estudiar español? ¿estudiar en la cafetería? ¿estudiar en la residencia (*dorm*)? ¿estudiar en la biblioteca (*library*)?
5. ¿esquiar (*to ski*)? ¿jugar al tenis? ¿jugar al fútbol americano? ¿jugar al golf? ¿jugar a la lotería?
6. ¿beber vino? ¿beber café? ¿beber té? ¿beber limonada? ¿beber chocolate?

Paso 2. Now use the preceding cues to interview your instructor about his or her likes and dislikes.

MODELO: **¿Le** gusta la música moderna?

—Do you like to play baseball? —Yes, but I like volleyball more.

¿QUÉ HORA ES?ᵃ

ᵃ¿Qué... *What time is it?*

Dé (*Give*) el nombre de...

- un melodrama
- un programa cómico
- un programa de deportes (*sports*)
- un programa de los Estados Unidos (*U.S.*)
- un programa infantil

¿Qué significa en inglés... ?

- dibujos animados (dibujo = *drawing*)
- telediario (diario = *newspaper*)
- territorial
- nacional

TVE-1	
7,45	**Carta de ajuste.**
7,59	**Apertura.**
8,00	**Buenos días.**
10,00	**El día por delante.** Incluye las series: «Webster» y «Santa Bárbara».
13,05	**Dibujos animados.** «El pájaro loco».
14,00	**Informativos territoriales.**
14,55	**Conexión con la programación nacional.**
15,00	**Telediario 1.**
15,30	**A mi manera.** Incluye la serie: «Cheers».
17,50	**Avance telediario.**
17,55	**Los mundos de Yupi.**
18,20	**Erase una vez... la vida.** «Las vacunas».
18,50	**Sopa de gansos.**
19,20	**Con las manos en la masa.**
19,50	**Murphy Brown.** «Firmado, sellado y marcado».
20,20	**Informativos territoriales.**
20,29	**Conexión con la programación nacional.**
20,30	**Telediario 2.**
21,00	**El tiempo.**
21,10	**Treinta y tantos.** «¿De quién es este bosque?»
22,10	**Punto y aparte.**
23,50	**Enredo.**
0,15	**Telediario 3 y Teledeporte.**
1,00	**Producción española.** «A los cuatro vientos», 1987, 93 minutos. Dirección: José A. Zorrilla. Intérpretes: Xabier Elorriaga, Anne Louis Lampert, Peter Leeper, Jean Claude Bouillaud. En la primavera de 1937 los ejércitos de Franco, paralizados ante Madrid, abren un segundo frente: Bilbao. El general Mola asedia con un cerco que llega hasta el mar. Entre aquellos vascos de los caseríos está un poeta y periodista, Esteban Urkeaga, llamado Lauaxeta.
2,35	**Despedida y cierre.**

Es la una.

Son las dos.

Son las cinco.

¿Qué hora es? is used to ask *What time is it?* In telling time, one says *Es* **la una** but *Son* **las dos** (**las tres, las cuatro,** and so on).

Es la una y { cuarto. / quince.

Son las dos y { media. / treinta.

Son las cinco **y diez.**

Son las ocho **y veinticinco.**

Note that from the hour to the half-hour, Spanish, like English, expresses time by adding minutes or a portion of an hour to the hour.

Son las dos { cuarto. / quince. } menos   Son las ocho **menos diez**.   Son las once **menos veinte**.

From the half-hour to the hour, Spanish usually expresses time by subtracting minutes or a part of an hour from the *next* hour.

OTRAS EXPRESIONES ÚTILES

de la mañana	A.M., in the morning	**en punto**	exactly, on the dot, sharp
de la tarde	P.M., in the afternoon (and early evening)	**¿a qué hora?**	(at) what time?
de la noche	P.M., in the evening	**a la una (las dos, ...)**	at 1:00 (2:00, ...)

Son las cuatro de la tarde **en punto**.   *It's exactly 4:00 P.M.*

¿A qué hora es la clase de español?   *(At) What time is Spanish class?*

Hay una recepción **a las once** de la mañana.   *There is a reception at 11:00 A.M.*

¡OJO!   Don't confuse **Es/Son la(s)...** with **A la(s)...** The first is used for telling what time it is currently, the second for telling at what time something happens (at what time class starts, at what time one arrives, and so on).

Práctica

A **¿Qué hora es?** Listen as your instructor says a time of day; then say in Spanish the number of the clock or watch face that corresponds to the time you heard.

1.   **2.**   **3.**   **4.**   **5.**   **6.**   **7.**   **8.**

B **¿Qué hora es?**

1. 1:00	**4.** 1:30	**7.** 4:15	**10.** 9:50 sharp
2. 6:00	**5.** 3:15	**8.** 11:45 exactly	
3. 11:00	**6.** 6:45	**9.** 9:10 on the dot	

C **Entrevista.** Ask a classmate at what time the following events or activities take place. He or she will answer according to the cue.

MODELO: la clase de español (10:00 A.M.) →
ESTUDIANTE 1: ¿A qué hora es la clase de español?
ESTUDIANTE 2: A las diez de la mañana... ¡en punto!

1. la clase de francés (1:45 P.M.)
2. la sesión de laboratorio (3:10 P.M.)
3. la excursión (8:45 A.M.)
4. el concierto (7:30 P.M.)

D **Situaciones.** How might the following people greet each other if they met at the indicated time? With a classmate, create a brief dialogue for each situation.

1. el profesor Martínez y Gloria, a las diez de la mañana
2. la Sra. López y la Srta. Luna, a las cuatro y media de la tarde
3. usted y su (*your*) profesor(a) de español, en la clase de español
4. Jorge y María, a las once de la noche

El mundo^a hispánico (Parte 1)   ^a*world*

This first brief reading in *¿Qué tal?* will give you a lot of information about the Spanish-speaking world outside of this country: the names of the countries and their capitals, as well as the approximate number of people who live in each country. Look at the maps before you begin the reading to get a general idea of the reading's content. And, in the reading, watch for the use of a Spanish phrase whose meaning you will probably recognize: **se habla español** (*Spanish is spoken*).

  Many readings in *¿Qué tal?* are preceded by **Antes de leer** (*Before Reading*) sections. Be sure to work through them before beginning the reading. The suggestions in them will help you become a better reader in Spanish.

Antes de leer: Recognizing Interrogatives and *estar*

In the following reading, note that the word **está** means *is located;* **está** and other forms of the verb **estar** (*to be*) are used to tell where things and people are. You will learn more about the uses of **estar** in later chapters.

  The reading also contains a series of quotations with interrogative words. You are already familiar with **¿cómo?** and **¿qué?** The word **¿cuántos?**, which you have seen only once, means *how many;* you should be able to guess the meaning of

¿**cuántas?** easily. The meaning of other interrogatives may not be immediately obvious to you, but the sentences in which the words appear may offer some clues to meaning. You probably do not know the meaning of ¿**dónde?** and ¿**cuál?**, but you should be able to guess what they mean in the following sentences.

> Cuba está en el Mar Caribe. ¿**Dónde** está la República Dominicana?
> Managua es la capital de Nicaragua. ¿**Cuál** es la capital de México?

Use the statements in the reading as models to answer the questions contained in the reading. The information you need about geography and population is in the maps.

Las naciones del mundo hispánico

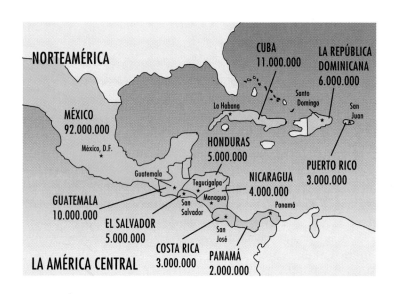

H ay noventa y dos millones de habitantes en México. ¿Cuántos habitantes hay en Guatemala? ¿en El Salvador? ¿en las demás[b] naciones de la América Central? ¿En cuántas naciones de la América Central se habla español? México es parte de Norteamérica. ¿En cuántas naciones de Norteamérica se habla español? ¿Cuál es la capital de México? ¿de Costa Rica?

Cuba está en el Mar Caribe. ¿Dónde está la República Dominicana? ¿Qué parte de los Estados Unidos está también[c] en el Mar Caribe? ¿Dónde está el Canal de Panamá?

[a]*noventa . . . ninety-two*   [b]*other*   [c]*also*

¿En cuántas naciones de Sudamérica se habla español? ¿Se habla español o[d] portugués en el Brasil? ¿Cuántos millones de habitantes hay en Venezuela? ¿en Chile? ¿en las demás naciones? ¿Cuál es la capital de cada[e] nación?

España está en la Península Ibérica. ¿Qué otra nación está también en esa[f] península? ¿Cuántos millones de habitantes hay en España? No se habla español en Portugal. ¿Qué lengua se habla allí[g]? ¿Cuál es la capital de España? ¿Está en el centro de la península?

[d]*or*   [e]*each*

[f]*that*   [g]*there*

PALABRAS INTERROGATIVAS • Un resumen
▼ ▼

You have already used a number of interrogative words and phrases to get information. (You will learn more in subsequent chapters of *¿Qué tal?*) Note the accent over the vowel you emphasize when you say the word, and the use of the inverted question mark.

¿a qué hora?	¿A qué hora es la clase?
¿cómo?	¿Cómo estás? ¿Cómo es Gloria Estefan? ¿Cómo te llamas?
¿cuál?*	¿Cuál es la capital de Colombia?
¿cuántos?, ¿cuántas?	¿Cuántos estudiantes hay en la clase? ¿Cuántas naciones hay en Sudamérica?
¿dónde?	¿Dónde está España?
¿qué?*	¿Qué es un hospital? ¿Qué es esto? ¿Qué hora es?

Note that in Spanish the voice falls at the end of questions that begin with interrogative words.

¿Qué es un tren?   ¿Cómo estás?

Práctica

A **Preguntas** (*Questions*).

Paso 1. What interrogative words do you associate with the following information?

1. Son las once.
2. En el Mar Caribe.
3. Muy bien, gracias.
4. ¡Es muy arrogante!
5. Hay 5 millones (de habitantes).
6. (La fiesta) Es a las ocho.
7. (La capital) Es Caracas.
8. Es un instrumento musical.

Paso 2. Now ask the questions that would result in the answers given in **Paso 1**.

---

*Use **¿qué?** to mean *what?* when you are asking for a definition or an explanation. Use **¿cuál?** to mean *what?* in all other circumstances. See also **Capítulo 16**.

B **Más preguntas.** What questions are being asked by the numbered people in this picture? More than one answer is possible for some items. Select questions from the following list or create your own questions.

PREGUNTAS

¿A qué hora es el programa sobre (*about*) México?
Hola. ¿Cómo estás?
¿Cuál es la capital de Colombia?
¿Cuántas personas hay en la fiesta?
¿Dónde está Buenos Aires?
¿Dónde está el diccionario?
¿Qué es esto?
¿Qué hay en la televisión hoy?

LECTURA

cultural

El mundo hispánico [Parte 2]

Antes de leer: Guessing Meaning from Context

You will recognize the meaning of a number of cognates in the following reading about the geography of the Hispanic world. In addition, you should be able to guess the meaning of the underlined words from the context (the words that surround them); they are the names of geographical features. The photo captions below will also be helpful. You have learned to recognize the meaning of the word **¿qué?** in questions; in this reading, **que** (with no accent mark) means *that* or *which*.

La geografía del mundo hispánico

La geografía del mundo hispánico es impresionante. En algunas[a] regiones hay de todo.[b] Por ejemplo, en la Argentina hay pampas extensas en el sur[c] y la cordillera de los Andes en el oeste. En partes de Venezuela, Colombia y el Ecuador, hay regiones tropicales de densa selva. En el Brasil está el famoso río Amazonas. En el centro de México y también en El Salvador, Nicaragua y Colombia, hay volcanes activos. El Perú y Bolivia comparten[d] el enorme lago Titicaca, situado en una meseta entre los dos países.[e]

Cuba, Puerto Rico y la República Dominicana son tres islas situadas en el Mar Caribe. Las bellas[f] playas[g] del Mar Caribe y de la península de Yucatán son populares entre[h] los turistas de todo el mundo.

España y Portugal forman la Península Ibérica. España, como Latinoamérica, tiene[i] una geografía variada. En el norte están los Pirineos, la cordillera que separa a España del[j] resto de Europa. Madrid, la capital del país, está situada en la meseta central. En las costas del sur y del este hay playas tan bonitas como las de[k] Latinoamérica y el Caribe.

Es importante mencionar también la gran diversidad de las ciudades del mundo hispánico. En la Argentina está la gran[l] ciudad de Buenos Aires. Muchos consideran a Buenos Aires «el París» o «la Nueva York» de Sudamérica. En Venezuela está Caracas, y en el Perú está Lima, la capital, y Cuzco, una ciudad antigua de origen indio.

En fin,[m] el mundo hispánico es diverso respecto a la geografía. ¿Y Norteamérica?

Una meseta de la Mancha, España.

La ciudad de Valparaíso, Chile.

La cordillera de los Andes, Perú.

[a]*some*   [b]*de... a bit of everything*   [c]*south*   [d]*share*   [e]*naciones*
[f]*beautiful*   [g]*beaches*   [h]*among*   [i]*has*   [j]*from the*   [k]*tan... as pretty as those of*   [l]*great*   [m]*En... In short*

Comprensión

Demonstrate your understanding of the words underlined in the reading and other words from the reading by giving an example of geographical features from the Spanish-speaking world. Then give an example of a similar feature found in the United States or Canada or close to them.

MODELOS: el río... → el río Orinoco, *the Mississippi*
la isla de... → la isla de Cuba, *Newfoundland*

1. el lago...
2. la cordillera de...
3. el río...
4. la isla de...

5. la playa (las playas) de...
6. la costa (las costas) de...
7. el mar...
8. la península (de)...

▼▼▼▼▼▼▼▼▼▼▼▼▼▼ **VOCABULARIO** ▼▼▼▼▼▼▼▼▼▼▼▼▼▼

Although you have used and heard many words in this preliminary chapter of *¿Qué tal?*, the following words are the ones considered to be active vocabulary. Be sure that you know all of them before beginning **Capítulo 1**.

Saludos y expresiones de cortesía

Buenos días. Buenas tardes. Buenas noches.
Hola. ¿Qué tal? ¿Cómo está(s)?
Regular. (Muy) Bien.
¿Y tú? ¿Y usted?
Adiós. Hasta mañana. Hasta luego.
¿Cómo te llamas? ¿Cómo se llama usted? Me llamo... .
señor (Sr.), señora (Sra.), señorita (Srta.)
(Muchas) Gracias. De nada. No hay de qué.

Self-Test

Use the tape that accompanies this text to test yourself briefly on the important points of the **Primeros pasos**.

Por favor. Perdón. Con permiso.
Mucho gusto. Igualmente. Encantado/a.

¿Cómo es usted?

soy, eres, es

Los números

cero, uno, dos, tres, cuatro, cinco, seis, siete, ocho, nueve, diez, once, doce, trece, catorce, quince, dieciséis, diecisiete, dieciocho, diecinueve, veinte, treinta

Gustos y preferencias

¿Te gusta... ? ¿Le gusta... ? Sí, me gusta... . No, no me gusta... .

Palabras interrogativas

¿cómo?, ¿cuál?, ¿cuántos/as?, ¿dónde?, ¿qué?

¿Qué hora es?

Es la... , Son las... y/menos cuarto, y media, en punto, de la mañana (tarde, noche)
¿A qué hora... ? A la(s)...

Palabras adicionales

sí yes
no no

hay there is/are
no hay there is not / are not
está is (located)

y and
o or

a to; at (*with time*)
de of; from
en in; at

que that; which
también also

INTRODUCTION TO *¿QUÉ TAL?*

▼ ▼

¿Qué tal? is divided into twenty-four chapters, each with its own theme —themes such as university life here and abroad, travel and food. Each chapter is divided into three parts, called **Primer paso** (*First Step*), **Segundo paso** (*Second Step*), and **Un paso más** (*One More Step*). **Primer paso** and **Segundo paso** each have a theme vocabulary section (**Vocabulario**) and one grammar section (**Estructuras**). In the first seven chapters, sections called **Pronunciación** will introduce you to more aspects of the Spanish sound system.

Estructuras sections are introduced with brief dialogues, drawings, realia, or readings. The grammar explanations are followed by exercises and activities (**Práctica**) that will help you function in realistic situations in Spanish, and express yourself creatively (by answering questions, describing pictures and cartoons, completing sentences, and so on). You have already seen materials such as these in the **Primeros pasos.** You will often be asked to work with another student or in small groups.

Throughout the text, the word **¡OJO!** (*Watch out!*) will call your attention to areas where you should be especially careful when using Spanish. Brief sections called **Reciclado** (*Recycling*) will help you review structures you have already studied before you learn new structures based on these points.

¿Qué tal? presents several types of dialogues that serve as models for conversation throughout the text. 1. Minidialogues introduce many of the grammar topics by showing how a structure can be used in an everyday situation. 2. Functional minidialogues called **Situación** (in the **Un paso más** sections) demonstrate brief conversational exchanges in specific situations. They are particularly useful for handling situations you might encounter in a Spanish-speaking country or area of the United States.

Throughout the text you will find real materials from Spanish-speaking countries—ads, tickets, forms, clippings from newspapers and magazines, and the like. (You have already seen authentic materials of this kind in the **Primeros pasos,** and you may have been surprised by how much in them you could understand!)

The **Un paso más** sections at the end of each chapter offer various kinds of material. 1. Exercises and activities in **Un poco de todo** (*A little bit of everything*) sections combine and review all grammar presented in the chapter, along with important grammar from previous chapters. 2. The **Situación** dialogues are described above. 3. **Para escribir** (*For writing*) sections offer guidance for writing about the chapter's theme. Each chapter ends with **Vocabulario,** a list of all important words and expressions actively used in the chapter. Remember to use the tape that accompanies this text to test yourself on the chapter.

In between chapters, you will find special sections that deal with culture. Odd-numbered chapters are followed by a **Lectura cultural** section, which offers readings about the chapter theme or realia from Spanish-speaking areas of the world. In the **Voces del mundo hispánico** sections that follow even-numbered chapters, you will have the opportunity to learn about specific countries and groups of Spanish speakers, and the tape will let you hear what a typical accent from that area sounds like.

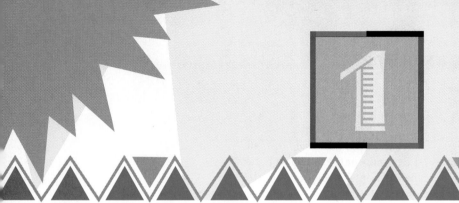

Primer paso

Escenas universitarias

la pizarra

la profesora

la puerta

la ventana

la estudiante

el estudiante

la silla

el diccionario

la mesa

la calculadora

el libro
de texto

el cuaderno

el papel

el libro
el bolígrafo

la mochila

el escritorio

el lápiz

En la UNIVERSIDAD

¿Quién?ª Personas

ªWho?

el compañero de clase	classmate	**la estudiante**	(female) student
la compañera de clase	classmate	**el profesor**	(male) professor
el estudiante	(male) student	**la profesora**	(female) professor

Práctica

A ¿Dónde está... ?

Paso 1. Look at the drawing and tell where the persons and items are.

MODELO: el libro → El libro está en el escritorio.

1. el cuaderno → El cuaderno está en...
2. la mochila
3. la estudiante
4. el diccionario
5. el lápiz
6. la profesora
7. la puerta
8. el libro de texto
9. el papel
10. el bolígrafo

25

B **Identificaciones.** ¿Es hombre o mujer (*man or woman*)?

MODELO: ¿la profesora? → Es mujer.

1. ¿el profesor?   **3.** ¿el compañero?
2. ¿la estudiante?   **4.** ¿el estudiante?

C **¿Qué es esto** (*this*)**?** Working with a classmate, identify the following items with the categories you used in **Primeros pasos: una cosa, un lugar, una persona.**

MODELO: un libro → ESTUDIANTE 1: ¿Qué es un libro?
                      ESTUDIANTE 2: Un libro es una cosa.

1. una profesora
2. un diccionario
3. una clase
4. una puerta
5. un estudiante
6. un compañero
7. una mochila
8. un lápiz
9. una calculadora

STUDY HINT: Learning New Vocabulary

Vocabulary is one of the most important tools for successful communication in a foreign language. What does it mean to "know vocabulary"? And how can you best learn vocabulary?

1. Memorization is only part of the learning process. Using new vocabulary to communicate requires practicing that vocabulary in context. What do you associate with this word? When might you want to use it? Create a context—a place, a situation, a person, or a group of people—for the vocabulary that you want to learn or use a context from the text. The more associations you make with the word, the easier it will be to remember. Practice useful words and phrases over and over—thinking about their meaning—until you can produce them automatically. You may find it useful to "talk to yourself," actually saying aloud the words you want to learn.

2. Carefully study the words in vocabulary lists and drawings. If a word is a cognate or shares a root with an English word, be especially aware of differences in spelling and pronunciation. For example, note that **clase** is spelled with only

one **s;** that there is no *th* in **matemáticas;** and that **ciencias** does not begin with an **s.** Keep in mind that an "almost but not quite perfect" spelling may lead to a miscommunication: **el libro** (*the book*) versus **la libra** (*the pound*); **la mesa** (*the table*) versus **el mes** (*the month*); **el profesor** (*male professor*) versus **la profesora** (*female professor*). You also need to remember which words require **el** and which require **la** to express *the,* as well as which words require a written accent—**el lápiz, el bolígrafo,** for example—and where the accent occurs.

3. After studying the list or drawing, cover the English and give the English equivalent of each Spanish word.

4. When you are able to give the English without hesitation and without error, reverse the procedure; cover the Spanish and give the Spanish equivalent of each English word. Write out the Spanish words (using **el** or **la** where appropriate) once or several times and say them aloud.

5. Vocabulary lists and flash cards can also be useful as a review or as a self-test.

DE AQUÍ Y DE ALLÁ[a]

[a]*De... From here and there*

The words **compañero** and **compañera** are frequently used in Spanish but they don't have just one English equivalent. You already know one meaning of **compañero/a:** *mate,* as in **compañero/a de clase** (*classmate*). Here are some other ways in which **compañero/a** is used.

el compañero (la compañera) de trabajo   co-worker
el compañero (la compañera) de cuarto   roommate

Compañero/a is also the word used by many people to refer to a "significant other," especially a person with whom they are living without being married.

Varadero, Cuba.

PRONUNCIACIÓN

Diphthongs and Linking

Two successive weak vowels (**i, u**) or a combination of a strong vowel (**a, e,** or **o**) and a weak vowel (**i** or **u**) are pronounced in the same syllable, forming a *diphthong* (**un diptongo**): **Luis, siete, cuaderno.**

When words are combined to form phrases, clauses, and sentences, they are linked together in pronunciation. In spoken Spanish, it is usually impossible to hear the word boundaries—that is, where one word ends and another begins.

A Más práctica con las vocales.

1. hablar	regular	reservar	conservar
2. trece	clase	papel	general
3. mochila	silla	bolígrafo	libro
4. hombre	profesor	escritorio	los
5. calculadora	gusto	lugar	mujer

B Practique las siguientes (*following*) palabras.

1. media	Colombia	gracias	estudiante	materia
2. bien	Oviedo	siete	también	diez
3. escritorio	expresión	adiós	diccionario	Antonio
4. cuaderno	Eduardo	el Ecuador	Guatemala	Managua
5. bueno	nueve	luego	pueblo	Venezuela

C Practice saying each phrase as if it were one long word, pronounced without a pause.

1. el papel y el lápiz
2. la profesora y la estudiante
3. la puerta y la ventana
4. el libro en la mochila

ESTRUCTURAS ▼▼▼▼▼▼▼▼▼▼▼▼▼▼▼▼▼▼▼▼▼

1. Identifying People, Places, and Things

Singular Nouns: Gender and Articles*

▼ **En *la clase* de composición: *El primer día***

▼ PROFESORA: ...y para mañana, es necesario traer *el libro* de texto, *papel, un cua-*
▼ *derno* y *un diccionario.*
▼ ANA: Perdón, *profesora,* pero... ¿hay *libros* para esta *clase* en *la librería?*
▼ PROFESORA: Creo que sí.
▼ ANA: ¿Y *diccionarios?*
▼ PROFESORA: ¿No hay en *la librería?*
▼ PEDRO: Sí hay. *El problema* es que no son *diccionarios* bilingües...

▲ ▲ ▲

▼ ¿Cierto o falso? Corrija (*Correct*) las oraciones falsas.

▼ 1. Para mañana no es necesario traer el libro de texto.
▼ 2. Hay libros de texto en la librería.
▼ 3. No hay diccionarios en la librería.
▼ 4. El problema con los diccionarios es el precio (*price*).

To name persons, places, things, or ideas, you need to be able to use nouns. In Spanish, all *nouns* (**los sustantivos**) have either masculine or feminine *gender* (**el género**). This is a purely grammatical feature of nouns; it does not mean that Spanish speakers perceive things or ideas as having male or female attributes.

	MASCULINE NOUNS		FEMININE NOUNS	
Definite articles	**el** hombre	*the man*	**la** mujer	*the woman*
	el libr**o**	*the book*	**la** mes**a**	*the table*
Indefinite articles	**un** hombre	*a (one) man*	**una** mujer	*a (one) woman*
	un libr**o**	*a (one) book*	**una** mes**a**	*a (one) table*

A. Nouns that refer to male beings and most nouns that end in **-o** are *masculine* (**masculino**) in gender: **hombre, libro.**

Nouns that refer to female beings and most nouns that end in **-a, -ción, -tad,** and **-dad** are *feminine* (**femenino**): **mujer, mesa, nación** (*nation*), **libertad** (*liberty*), **universidad** (*university*).

---

*The grammar sections of *¿Qué tal?* are numbered consecutively throughout the book. If you need to review a particular grammar point, the index will refer you to its page number.

In composition class: The first day PROFESSOR: . . . and for tomorrow, it's necessary to bring the textbook, paper, a notebook, and a dictionary. ANA: Pardon me, ma'am [professor], but . . . are there books for this class in the bookstore? PROFESSOR: I think so. ANA: And (what about) dictionaries? PROFESSOR: Aren't there any in the bookstore? PEDRO: Yes, there are. The problem is that they aren't bilingual dictionaries . . .

¡OJO!   A common exception is the word **día**, which ends in -**a** but is masculine in gender: **el día**. Many words ending in -**ma** are also masculine: **el problema, el programa,** and so on.

Nouns that have other endings and that do not refer to either males or females may be masculine or feminine. Their gender must be memorized: **el lápiz, la clase, la tarde, la noche,** and so on.

B.   In English, *the* is the *definite article* (**el artículo definido**). In Spanish, the definite article for masculine singular nouns is **el**; for feminine singular nouns it is **la**.

C.   In English, the singular *indefinite article* (**el artículo indefinido**) is *a* or *an*. In Spanish, the indefinite article, like the definite article, must agree with the gender of the noun: **un** for masculine nouns, **una** for feminine nouns. **Un** and **una** can also mean *one* as well as *a* or *an*. Context determines the meaning.

[Práctica A–B]*

D.   Some nouns that refer to persons indicate gender according to the following patterns.

If the masculine ends in -**o,** the feminine ends in -**a:**

> **el** compañer**o**   *the (male) classmate* → **la** compañer**a**   *the (female) classmate*
> **el** consejer**o**   *the (male) advisor* → **la** consejer**a**   *the (female) advisor*
> **el** amig**o**   *the (male) friend* → **la** amig**a**   *the (female) friend*
> **el** secretari**o**   *the (male) secretary* → **la** secretari**a**   *the (female) secretary*

If the masculine ends in a consonant, the feminine has a final -**a:**

> **un** profeso**r**   *a (male) professor* → **una** profeso**ra**   *a (female) professor*

Many other nouns that refer to people have a single form. Gender is indicated by the article: **el estudiante, la estudiante; el cliente** (*the male client*), **la cliente** (*the female client*). A few nouns that end in -**e** have a feminine form that ends in -**a:** **el dependiente** (*the male clerk*), **la dependienta** (*the female clerk*).

E.   Since the gender of all nouns must be memorized, it is best to learn the definite article along with the noun; that is, learn **el lápiz** rather than just **lápiz**. The definite article will be given with nouns in vocabulary lists in this book.

[Práctica C–D]†

Práctica

A   **Artículos.** Dé el artículo definido (**el, la**).

1. escritorio	**5.** hombre	**9.** mujer
2. mesa	**6.** diccionario	**10.** nación
3. bolígrafo	**7.** universidad	**11.** escritorio
4. mochila	**8.** libro	**12.** calculadora

---

*This type of reference is a regular feature of some grammar sections of *¿Qué tal?* This reference means that you are now prepared to do Exercises A and B in the **Práctica** section.

†You are now prepared to do the rest of the activities in the **Práctica** section.

Dé el artículo indefinido (**un, una**).

13. día	**16.** lápiz	**19.** papel
14. mañana	**17.** clase	**20.** condición
15. problema	**18.** noche	**21.** programa

B **Escenas de la universidad.** Haga una oración con las palabras indicadas.

MODELO: estudiante/clase → Hay un **estudiante** en la **clase.**

1. pizarra/clase	**5.** cuaderno/escritorio
2. profesora/universidad	**6.** libro/mochila
3. lápiz/mesa	**7.** papel/silla
4. compañero/cuarto	**8.** palabra/pizarra

C **¿Quién es?**

Paso 1. Give the male or female counterpart of each of the following persons.

MODELO: Pablo Ortiz es consejero. (Paula Delibes) →
Paula Delibes es consejera también.

1. Camilo es estudiante. (Conchita)
2. Carmen Leal es profesora. (Carlos Ortega)
3. Juan Luis es dependiente. (Juanita)
4. Josefina es mi (*my*) amiga. (José)
5. El Sr. Romero es mi consejero. (la Srta. Green)

Paso 2. Now identify as many people as you can in your class and on campus.

NOTA COMUNICATIVA: Working with a Partner

As you have already seen, many of the exercises and activities in *¿Qué tal?* work well with a classmate. It is likely that you did some of the preceding partner activities with the person sitting next to you. This time, when your instructor says **"Busque un compañero,"** find a different partner. Here are some phrases to use.

¿Tienes compañero?		Do you have a partner?
Todavía no.		Not yet.
¿Deseas } **trabajar**		Do you want } to work
¿Te gustaría } **conmigo?**		Would you like } with me?
Sí, cómo no.		Yes, of course.

D **Entrevista. ¿Te gusta... ?** Find out whether a classmate likes the following things. Remember to use the definite article.

MODELO: comida (*food*) en McDonald's →
ESTUDIANTE 1: ¿Te gusta la comida en McDonald's?
ESTUDIANTE 2: Sí, me gusta. (No, no me gusta.)

1. comida en McDonald's (en la cafetería, en...)
2. música rock (clásica,...)
3. programa *General Hospital* (*All My Children, . . .*)
4. drama *Northern Exposure* (*NYPD Blue, . . .*)

▼   **VOCABULARIO**

¿Dónde está? Lugares y el verbo *estar*

Otros lugares de la universidad

la cafetería	cafeteria
el edificio	building
la oficina	office

As you know, **estar** means *to be,* and you have already used forms of it to ask how others are feeling or to tell where things are located.

¿Dónde está Alicia?

A las diez de la mañana, está en una clase.

A la una, está en **la biblioteca.** Le gusta estudiar allí.

A las tres, está en **la librería.** Es dependienta.

A las once de la noche, está en **la residencia,** en su **cuarto.**

(yo)	estoy	*I am*
(tú)	estás	*you (familiar) are*
(usted)	está	*you (formal) are*
(él, ella)	está	*he/she is*

You will learn all of the uses of the verb **estar,** along with those of **ser** (the other Spanish verb that means *to be*), gradually, over the next several chapters. For now, just review what you already know about **estar** by answering the following questions. Then do the activities that follow.

1. ¿Cómo está usted en este momento (*right now*)? Y su (*your*) profesor(a) de español, ¿cómo está?
2. ¿Dónde está usted en este momento?

Práctica

A **Es lógico.** With a classmate, tell where the following people probably are. React to your partner's reaction, as indicated.

MODELOS: la consejera →

ESTUDIANTE 1: ¿Dónde está la consejera?
ESTUDIANTE 2: Está en la oficina.
ESTUDIANTE 1: Es lógico.

el profesor →

ESTUDIANTE 2: ¿Dónde está el profesor?
ESTUDIANTE 1: Está en la residencia.
ESTUDIANTE 2: No es lógico.

1. el cliente
2. el estudiante
3. el compañero de cuarto
4. el bibliotecario (*librarian*)
5. la dependienta
6. la secretaria
7. la profesora
8. su (*your*) compañero/a para esta (*this*) actividad (**¡OJO!** ¿Dónde estás?)

B **Preguntas.** ¿Dónde están los siguientes países (*countries*)?

Sugerencias: Norteamérica, la América Central, el Caribe, Sudamérica, Europa

1. México
2. la Argentina
3. España
4. Chile
5. Nicaragua
6. el Canadá
7. Cuba
8. Costa Rica
9. Puerto Rico

ESTRUCTURAS ▼

What part of the newspaper do you think this clipping is from? How many nouns can you recognize in it? You have already seen some of these nouns, and many others are cognates.

2. Identifying People, Places, and Things

Nouns and Articles: Plural Forms

	SINGULAR	PLURAL	
Nouns ending in a vowel	**el** libro **la** mesa **un** libro **una** mesa	**los** libro**s** **las** mesa**s** **unos** libro**s** **unas** mesa**s**	*the books* *the tables* *some books* *some tables*
Nouns ending in a consonant	**la** universidad **un** papel	**las** universidad**es** **unos** papel**es**	*the universities* *some papers*

A. Spanish nouns that end in a vowel form plurals by adding **-s**. Nouns that end in a consonant add **-es**. Nouns that end in the consonant **-z** change the **-z** to **-c** before adding **-es**: **lápiz** → **lápices.**

B. The definite and indefinite articles also have plural forms: **el** → **los, la** → **las, un** → **unos, una** → **unas. Unos** and **unas** mean *some, several,* or *a few.*

C. In Spanish, the masculine plural form of a noun is used to refer to a group that includes both males and females.

los amig**os**	*the friends* (both male and female)
unos profesor**es**	*some professors* (both male and female)

Práctica

A **Singular y plural.** Dé la forma plural.

1. la mesa
2. el libro
3. el amigo
4. la oficina
5. un cuaderno
6. un lápiz
7. una librería
8. un bolígrafo
9. un edificio

Dé la forma singular.

10. los profesores
11. las calculadoras
12. las residencias
13. los lápices
14. unos papeles
15. unas tardes
16. unas bibliotecas
17. unas sillas
18. unos escritorios

B **Identificaciones.** Which of the words listed to the right might be used to refer to the person(s) named on the left?

1. Ana María: consejero   mujer   dependiente   estudiante
2. Tomás: compañero   consejera profesor   secretaria
3. Margarita y Juan: clientes   amigos   hombres   estudiantes

C **Más identificaciones.** Identifique a las personas, las cosas y los lugares.

MODELO: Hay _____ en _____. → Hay unos estudiantes en la clase.

Palabras útiles: la computadora, la planta, el teléfono

Un paso más

UN POCO DE TODO

A **Asociaciones.**

Paso 1. Write the names of five things or people and five places in two separate lists: **Cosas o personas, Lugares**

Paso 2. Working with a classmate, name the first person or thing you wrote down. Your classmate will respond with the first place he or she wrote. Then you react to the random pairing by saying whether that thing or person is likely to be in the place mentioned.

MODELOS: exámenes / cafetería →
             ESTUDIANTE 1: ¡Imposible! No hay exámenes en la cafetería.

             libros / biblioteca →
             ESTUDIANTE 2: ¡Claro que sí! (*Of course!*) Hay libros en la biblioteca.

Taking turns, continue to pair vocabulary items in the order in which you wrote them.

B **Semejanzas** (*Similarities*) **y diferencias.**

Paso 1. ¿Cuáles son las semejanzas y las diferencias entre los dos cuartos? Hay por lo menos (*at least*) seis diferencias.

Ⓐ Ⓑ

MODELOS: En el dibujo A, hay _____ .
           En el dibujo B, hay sólo (*only*) _____ .
           En el escritorio del dibujo A, hay _____ .
           En el escritorio del dibujo B, hay _____ .

Palabras útiles: la cama (*bed*), la computadora, la lámpara, la planta

Paso 2. Ahora indique qué hay en su propio (*your own*) cuarto. Use palabras del Paso 1.

MODELO: En mi (*my*) cuarto hay _____ . En mi escritorio hay _____ .

SITUACIÓN   Hablando de[a] las clases

Useful words and phrases from the **Situación** dialogues will often be highlighted in boxes called **Notas comunicativas sobre el diálogo**, which follow the dialogue. It is a good idea to scan the information in the box before reading the dialogue.

—¿Cuántos estudiantes hay en tu[b] clase de español?
—Creo[c] que hay quince o dieciséis.
—¿Y quién es el profesor?
—Es profesora. Se llama Lidia Ortega y es de[d] Panamá.
—¡Ah, sí! Ella es muy simpática. ¿A qué hora es la clase?
—A las 9 de la mañana.

[a]Hablando... *Talking about*   [b]*your*   [c]*I think*   [d]es... *she's from*

NOTAS COMUNICATIVAS SOBRE EL DIÁLOGO

To ask where someone is from: **¿De dónde es usted?**
                                ¿De dónde eres (tú)?
To tell where you are from: **Soy de...**

Conversación

Practice the dialogue with a classmate. When you are familiar with it, vary some of the details.

Universidad Iberoamericana, México, D.F.

PARA ESCRIBIR

Complete the following paragraph about your Spanish class. All you have to do is to fill in the blanks and select the appropriate information when two choices are given.

En mi clase de español hay _____ personas, _____ hombres y _____ mujeres.

La clase es a la/las _____ (hora) de la _____. Mi profesor(a) se llama _____. Es

de _____. La clase está en el edificio _____. Hay / No hay un laboratorio de

lenguas. Me gusta mucho / No me gusta mi clase de español.

▼ ▼ ▼ ▼ ▼ ▼ ▼ ▼ ▼ ▼ ▼ ▼ ▼ ▼ **VOCABULARIO** ▼ ▼ ▼ ▼ ▼ ▼ ▼ ▼ ▼ ▼ ▼ ▼ ▼

Verbos

estar (*irreg.*) to be
  estoy I am
  estás you (*fam.*) are
  está you (*form.*) are; he/she is

Lugares

la biblioteca library
la cafetería cafeteria
la clase class
el cuarto room
el edificio building
la librería bookstore
la oficina office
la residencia dormitory
la universidad university

Personas

el/la amigo/a friend
el/la cliente client

el/la compañero/a
  de clase classmate
  de cuarto roommate
el/la consejero/a advisor
el/la dependiente/a clerk
el/la estudiante student
el hombre man
la mujer woman
el/la profesor(a) professor
el/la secretario/a secretary

Cosas

el bolígrafo (ballpoint) pen
la calculadora calculator
el cuaderno notebook
el diccionario dictionary
el escritorio desk
el lápiz (*pl.* **lápices**) pencil
el libro (de texto) (text)book
la mesa table
la mochila backpack

el papel (piece of) paper
la pizarra chalkboard
la puerta door
la silla chair
la ventana window

Otros sustantivos

el día day
la noche night
el problema problem
la tarde afternoon; evening

Palabras adicionales

¡claro que sí! of course!
¿quién? who?

Self-Test

Use the tape that accompanies this text to test yourself briefly on the important points of this chapter.

LECTURA
cultural

As you learned in **El mundo hispánico (Primeros pasos)**, you can often guess the meaning of unfamiliar words from the context (the words that surround them) and by using your knowledge about the topic in general. Making "educated guesses" about words in this way should be an important part of your reading skills in Spanish.

Can you guess the meaning of the underlined words in these phrases?

Información <u>para</u> turistas
Información <u>sobre</u> cursos

If you guessed that **para** means *for* and **sobre** means *about,* you are right. The context around each word helped you to make a logical guess.

The text in this section comes from a university brochure. Look at it now. Can you guess what part of the brochure it is? If you said the *table of contents,* you are right. It is called an **índice** in Spanish. Does **índice** have an English cognate?

As you scan the brochure and do the **Comprensión** items that follow it, keep in mind the information that you would expect to find in a university or college brochure in this country.

NOTA CULTURAL: The Hispanic Educational System

The educational system in Hispanic countries differs considerably from that of the United States. The **escuela primaria**—sometimes called the **colegio**—corresponds to our elementary school and consists of from five to eight years of instruction. The **escuela secundaria** (also called **liceo, instituto,** or **colegio**) provides secondary education. Students who complete their secondary education receive the **bachillerato.** In some countries, students attend an additional year or two of **preparatoria** before entering the university.

At the university, students immediately begin specialized programs leading to a professional degree (**título** or **licenciatura**) in areas such as law, medicine, engineering, or the humanities. These university-level programs of study are established by ministries of education, and there are almost no electives. Students are required to take as many as eight different subjects in a single academic term.

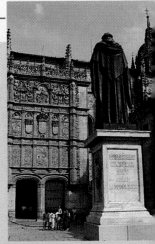

Esta estatua de Fray Luis de León está en la Universidad de Salamanca. La Universidad data del año 1220 (mil doscientos veinte).

Un folleto universitario

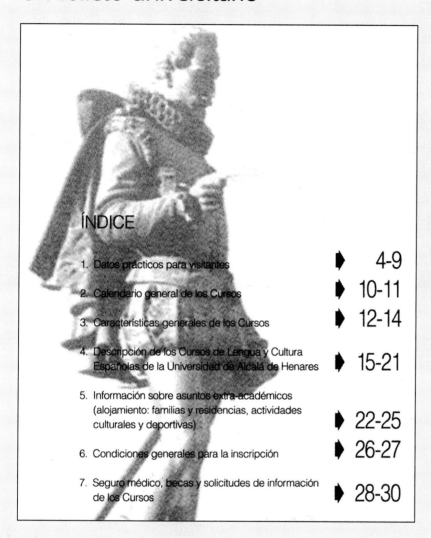

Comprensión

A Give the number of the section in the brochure that probably deals with the following topics. Then explain your choice by giving the Spanish words that you associate with each topic.

1. information for visitors to the university
2. lodging
3. medical coverage
4. holidays and duration of the program
5. course offerings
6. information about tuition (**inscribirse** = *to register*)

B What is the name of the university that the brochure is about? Once you find it, you will also find the name of the specific program that is advertised in the brochure.

Primer paso

Las materias

la física

la química

la sicología

las matemáticas

la administración de empresas

la computación

¿Qué ESTUDIA USTED?

Otras materias

el arte
las ciencias naturales
las ciencias políticas
las ciencias sociales
las comunicaciones
la economía
la filosofía
la historia
la literatura

Las lenguas extranjeras

el alemán   (German)
el chino
el español
el francés
el inglés
el italiano
el japonés
el ruso

The names of most of these academic subjects are easily recognizable cognates. Can you guess what they mean in English? If you cannot guess the meaning of a word, look it up in the vocabulary at the end of this book, or ask your instructor or a classmate for help. An expression used to ask for a translation is: **Perdón, ¿qué significa _____ en inglés?**

Práctica

A **Asociaciones.** ¿Con qué materia(s) asocia usted a... ?

1. Louis Pasteur, Marie Curie
2. la doctora Joyce Brothers, B. F. Skinner
3. Dan Rather, Peter Jennings
4. Aristóteles, Confucio
5. Mark Twain, Alice Walker
6. Frida Kahlo, Pablo Picasso
7. Donald Trump, Lee Iacocca
8. Microsoft, IBM

B **¿Qué estudias?** (*What are you studying?*) The right-hand column lists a number of university subjects. Tell about your academic interests by creating sentences using one word or phrase from each column. You can tell what you *are* studying, *want* to study, *need* to study, and *like* to study.

(No) Estudio _____.
(No) Deseo estudiar _____.
(No) Necesito estudiar _____.
(No) Me gusta estudiar _____.

español, francés, inglés
arte, filosofía, literatura, música
ciencias políticas, historia
antropología, sicología, sociología
biología, física, química
matemáticas, computación
¿ ?

DE AQUÍ Y DE ALLÁ

Some Spanish words useful for discussing university life are false cognates; that is, they do not mean what their nearest English equivalent means.

- **La facultad** does not mean *faculty* but rather *department* or *school* of a university: **La Facultad de Filosofía y Letras** (*the School of Liberal Arts*), for example. To express *faculty* in Spanish, use **el profesorado**, that is, **los profesores**.
- Each **facultad** often has its own **cafetería**, also called **un bar**. In most Spanish-speaking cultures, the word **bar** does not have the connotations that it has in English. While alcoholic beverages are served, **un bar** is just a place where people get together to chat and have a snack.

PRONUNCIACIÓN ▼▼▼▼▼▼▼▼▼▼▼▼▼▼▼▼▼▼▼▼▼

Stress and Written Accent Marks (Part 1)

By now you will have noticed that some Spanish words have *written accent marks* over one of the vowels. That mark is called **el acento** (**ortográfico**). It means that the syllable containing the accented vowel is stressed when the word is pronounced, as in the word **bolígrafo** (**bo-LI-gra-fo**), for example.

Although all Spanish words of more than one syllable have a stressed vowel, most words do not have a written accent mark. Most words have the spoken stress exactly where native speakers of Spanish would predict it. These two simple rules tell you which syllable is accented when a word does not have a written accent.

In this chapter you will learn those predictable patterns. In the next chapter, you will learn when the written accent mark is needed.

- Words that end in a vowel, **-n**, or **-s** are stressed on the next-to-last syllable.

ru-so	**co**-sa	e-**xa**-men	i-ta-**lia**-no
gra-cias	**e**-res	**len**-guas	

- Words that end in any other consonant are stressed on the last syllable.

us-**ted**	es-pa-**ñol**	doc-**tor**	pa-**pel**
na-tu-**ral**	pro-fe-**sor**	es-**tar**	

A The following words have been separated into syllables for you. Read them aloud, paying careful attention to where the spoken stress should fall.

1. Stress on the next-to-last syllable

chi-no	me-sa	li-bro	cien-cias
ru-so	si-lla	con-se-je-ra	o-ri-gen
cla-se	Car-men	li-te-ra-tu-ra	com-pu-ta-do-ra

2. Stress on the last syllable

se-ñor	ac-tor	li-ber-tad	lu-gar
mu-jer	co-lor	ge-ne-ral	u-ni-ver-si-dad
fa-vor	po-pu-lar	sen-ti-men-tal	con-trol

B Indicate the stressed vowel in each of the following words.
1. mo-chi-la   3. re-gu-lar   5. E-cua-dor   7. li-be-ral
2. me-nos   4. i-gual-men-te   6. e-le-gan-te   8. hu-ma-ni-dad

▼ **ESTRUCTURAS**

STUDY HINT: Learning Grammar

Learning a language is similar to learning any other skill; knowing *about* it is only part of what is involved. Consider how you would acquire another skill—swimming, for example. If you read all the available books on swimming, you would probably become an expert in talking *about* swimming and you would know what you *should* do in a pool. Until you actually got into a pool and practiced swimming, however, you would probably not swim very well. In much the same way, if you memorize all the grammar rules but spend little time *practicing* them, you will not be able to communicate very well in Spanish.

As you study each grammar point in **¿Qué tal?**, you will learn how the structure works; then you need to put your knowledge into practice. First, read the grammar discussion, study and analyze the examples, and pay special attention to any **¡OJO!** sections, which will call your attention to problem areas. Then begin the **Práctica** section. Do the exercises. When you are certain that your

answers are correct, practice doing each exercise several times until the answers sound and "feel" right to you. As you do each item, think about what you are conveying and the context in which you could use each sentence, as well as about spelling and pronunciation. Then you will be well prepared to conclude the **Práctica** section with the more open-ended situations in which, in general, there are no "right" or "wrong" answers.

Always remember that language learning is cumulative. This means that you are not finished with a grammar point when you go on to the next chapter. Even though you are now studying the material in **Capítulo 2,** you must still remember how to form plurals and how to conjugate the verb **estar,** because **Capítulo 2** builds on what you have learned in the previous chapters—just as all subsequent chapters will build on the material leading up to them. A few minutes spent each day reviewing "old" topics will increase your confidence—and success—in communicating in Spanish.

3. Expressing Actions

Subject Pronouns; Present Tense of *-ar* Verbs; Negation

▼ **Una fiesta con unos amigos extranjeros**
▼
▼   CARLOS: ¿No *desean* Uds. *bailar*?
▼   ALFONSO: ¡Cómo no! Yo *bailo* con Mary. Ella *habla* español. ¿Dónde *está*?
▼   TERESA: Yo *hablo* francés y *bailo* con Jacques.
▼   CARLOS: Y yo *bailo* con Gretchen.
▼ GRETCHEN: Sólo si *pagas* las cervezas. ¡*Bailas* muy mal!

 ▲ ▲ ▲

A party with some foreign friends CARLOS: Don't you want to dance? ALFONSO: Of course! I'll dance with Mary. She speaks Spanish. Where is she? TERESA: I speak French and I'll dance with Jacques. CARLOS: And I'll dance with Gretchen. GRETCHEN: Only if you buy (pay for) the beers. You dance very badly!

▼ Who made—or might have made—each of the following statements?

▼ 1. Yo bailo con Jacques.
▼ 2. Yo hablo español.
▼ 3. Yo hablo alemán.

4. Nosotros (*We*) hablamos francés.
5. Yo bailo con Alfonso.
6. ¡Yo no bailo mal!

In **Primeros pasos** and **Capítulo 1**, you have already used a number of Spanish verbs—and some subject pronouns—to talk about actions and states of being. In this section you will learn more words for expressing actions. The following chart contains most of the important information you will learn in this section.

hablar (*to speak*): **habl-**					
SINGULAR			PLURAL		
(*I*)	yo	habl**o**	(*we*)	nosotros / nosotras	habl**amos**
(*you*)	tú	habl**as**	(*you*)	vosotros / vosotras	habl**áis**
(*you*)	usted (Ud.)*	habl**a**	(*you*)	ustedes (Uds.)*	habl**an**
(*he*) / (*she*)	él / ella	habl**a**	(*they*)	ellos / ellas	habl**an**

Subject Pronouns

The preceding chart shows a number of Spanish subject pronouns you have already seen (**yo, tú, usted, él, ella**), with the corresponding forms of **hablar.** Here are some additional comments about these *pronouns* (**los pronombres**).

- Several subject pronouns have masculine and feminine forms: **él, ella; nosotros, nosotras** (*we*); **vosotros, vosotras** (*you*); **ellos, ellas** (*they*). The masculine plural form is used to refer to a group of males as well as to a group of males and females.
- Spanish has two different words for *you* (singular): **tú** and **usted. Usted** is generally used to address persons with whom the speaker has a formal relationship. Use **usted** with people whom you call by their title and last name (**Sr. Gutiérrez, profesora Hernández**), or with people you don't know very well. Students generally address their instructors with **usted.** In some parts of the Spanish-speaking world, children use **usted** with their parents.

  Tú implies a familiar relationship. Use **tú** when you would address a person by his or her first name, with close friends or relatives, and with children and pets. Students usually address each other as **tú.** The native speaker can always suggest that you use **tú** if that form is more appropriate.
- The plural of **usted** is **ustedes.** In Latin America, as well as in the United States, **ustedes** also serves as the plural of **tú.** In Spain (and other parts of the Spanish-speaking world), however, there are two different plural forms for *you:* **ustedes** and **vosotros/vosotras. Ustedes** is used when speaking with two or

Latin America

tú ⟶
      ⟶ ustedes
usted ⟶

Spain

tú ⟶ vosotros/as

usted ⟶ ustedes

---

*Usted and **ustedes** are frequently abbreviated in writing **Ud.** or **Vd.,** and **Uds.** or **Vds.,** respectively. **Ud.** and **Uds.** will be used in *¿Qué tal?*

Cuarenta y cinco **45**

more persons whom you address individually as **usted. Vosotros/vosotras** is used when speaking with two or more persons whom you address individually as **tú.**

Subject pronouns are not used as frequently in Spanish as they are in English. You will learn more about the uses of Spanish subject pronouns in **Capítulo 4.**

[a] ¿Qué... *What the devil is that?*
[b] tú en la Argentina y el Uruguay
[c] *Do you understand?*

Infinitives and Personal Endings

A. The *infinitive* (**el infinitivo**) of a verb indicates the action or state of being, with no reference to who or what performs the action or when it is done (present, past, or future). In English the infinitive is indicated by *to: **to run, to be.*** In Spanish all infinitives end in **-ar, -er,** or **-ir.**

B. To *conjugate* (**conjugar**) a verb means to give the various forms of the verb with their corresponding subjects: *I speak, you speak, he (she, it) speaks,* and so on. All regular Spanish verbs are conjugated by adding *personal endings* (**las terminaciones personales**) that reflect the subject doing the action. These are added to the *stem* (**la raíz** or **el radical**), which is the infinitive minus the infinitive ending: **hablar** → **habl-.**

C. The following personal endings are added to the stem of all regular **-ar** verbs: **-o, -as, -a, -amos, -áis, -an.**
  Some important **-ar** verbs in this chapter include the following.

bailar	to dance	**hablar**	to speak; to talk
buscar	to look for	**necesitar**	to need
cantar	to sing	**pagar**	to pay (for)
comprar	to buy	**practicar**	to practice
desear	to want	**regresar**	to return (*to a place*)
enseñar	to teach	**tocar**	to play (*a musical instrument*)
escuchar	to listen (to)	**tomar**	to take; to drink
estudiar	to study	**trabajar**	to work

¡OJO! In Spanish the meaning of the English word *for* is included in the verbs **pagar** (*to pay for*) and **buscar** (*to look for*); *to* is included in **escuchar** (*to listen to*).

D. As in English, when two Spanish verbs are used in sequence and there is no change of subject, the second verb is usually in the infinitive form.

Necesito **trabajar.**	*I need to work.*
También desean **bailar.**	*They want to dance, too.*

You have already learned the singular forms of **estar** (*to be*), another **-ar** verb. Note that the **yo** form of **estar** is irregular: **estoy.** The other forms take regular **-ar** endings, but some have a shift in the stress pattern (indicated by the accented **á**):

estoy	estamos
estás	estáis
está	están
está	están

English Equivalents for the Present Tense

In both English and Spanish, conjugated verb forms also indicate the *time* or *tense* (**el tiempo**) of the action: *I speak* (present), *I spoke* (past).

The present tense forms of Spanish verbs correspond to three English equivalents.

▼
▼ **hablo** ⎰ *I speak*   Simple present tense
▼   ⎱ *I am speaking* Present progressive to indicate an action in progress
             I will speak   Near future action

Note that another word or phrase may indicate future time when the present is used to describe near future actions.

Hablo con Juan **mañana**.	*I'll speak with John tomorrow.*
¿Estudiamos **por la noche**?	*Shall we study at night?*

Negation

A Spanish sentence is made negative by placing the word **no** before the conjugated verb. There is no Spanish equivalent for the English words *do* or *does* in negative sentences.

El señor **no** habla inglés.	*The man doesn't speak English.*
No, **no** necesitamos dinero.	*No, we don't need money.*

Práctica

A Mis compañeros y yo.

Paso 1. Read the following statements and tell whether they are true for you and your classmates and for your classroom environment. If any statement is not true for you or your class, make it negative or change it in another way to make it correct.

MODELO: Toco el piano. → Sí, toco el piano.
                     (No, no toco el piano. Toco la guitarra.)

1. Necesito dinero.
2. Trabajo en la biblioteca.
3. Tomo ocho clases este semestre/trimestre (*this term*).
4. En clase, cantamos en francés.
5. Deseamos practicar el español.
6. Tomamos cerveza en clase.
7. El profesor / La profesora enseña español.
8. El profesor / La profesora habla muy bien el alemán.

Paso 2. Now turn to the person next to you and rephrase each sentence as a question, using **tú** forms of the verbs in all cases. Your partner will answer the question.

MODELO: ¿Tocas el piano? → Sí, toco el piano. (No, no toco el piano.)

B **En una fiesta.** The following paragraphs describe a party that might happen on your campus. Scan the paragraphs first, to get a general sense of their meaning. Then complete the paragraphs with the correct form of the infinitives.

Esta noche[a] hay una fiesta en el apartamento de Marcos y Julio. Todos[b] los estudiantes (cantar[1]) y (bailar[2]). Una persona (tocar[3]) la guitarra y otras personas (escuchar[4]) la música.

Jaime (buscar[5]) un café. Marta (hablar[6]) con un amigo. María José (desear[7]) enseñarles a todos[c] un baile[d] de Colombia. Todas las estudiantes desean (bailar[8]) con el estudiante mexicano—¡él (bailar[9]) muy bien!

La fiesta es estupenda, pero todos (necesitar[10]) regresar a casa[e] o a su[f] cuarto temprano.[g] ¡Hay clases mañana!

[a]Esta... *Tonight*   [b]*All*   [c]enseñarles... *to teach everyone*   [d]*dance*   [e]a... *home*   [f]*their*   [g]*early*

Tell whether these statements are true (**cierto**) or false (**falso**), based on information in the paragraph.

1. Marcos es un profesor de español.   **3.** María José es de Colombia.
2. A Jaime le gusta la cerveza.   **4.** Los estudiantes desean bailar.

C **Oraciones lógicas.** Form complete logical sentences by using one word or phrase from each column. The words and phrases may be used more than once, in many combinations. Be sure to use the correct form of the verbs. Make any of the sentences negative, if necessary.

MODELO: Yo no estudio francés.

yo	comprar	la guitarra, el piano, el violín
(estudiante) , tú	regresar	el edificio de ciencias
nosotros (los miembros de esta clase)	buscar	en la cafetería, en la universidad
los estudiantes de aquí (*here*)	trabajar	en una oficina, en una librería
el extranjero	hablar	a casa por la noche, a la biblioteca a las dos
	tocar	cerveza, café, Coca-Cola
un secretario (no)	enseñar	francés, alemán
una profesora de español	pagar	bien el español
un dependiente	tomar	los libros de texto con un cheque
una cliente	estudiar	libros y cuadernos en la librería
	desear	tomar una clase de computación
	necesitar	hablar bien el español
		estudiar más (*more*)
		comprar una calculadora, una mochila
		pagar la matrícula (*tuition*) en septiembre

D **¿Dónde están?** Tell where these people are (using **estar**) and what they are doing. Note that the definite article is used with titles when you are talking about a person: **el señor, la señora, la señorita, el profesor, la profesora.**

MODELO: La Sra. Martínez _____ . →
          La Sra. Martínez está en la oficina. Busca un libro, trabaja...

Frases útiles: hablar por teléfono, preparar la lección, pronunciar las palabras, usar una computadora

1. Estas (*These*) personas _____.
La profesora Gil _____.
Casi (*Almost*) todos los estudiantes _____.
Unos estudiantes _____.

2. Estas personas _____.
El Sr. Miranda _____.
La bibliotecaria _____.
El secretario _____.

2.

3. Estas personas _____.
El cliente _____.
La dependienta _____.

3.

Segundo paso

VOCABULARIO ▼▼▼▼▼▼▼▼▼▼▼▼▼▼▼▼▼▼▼▼▼▼▼▼▼▼▼▼▼

¿Qué día es hoy?

lunes	Monday
martes	Tuesday
miércoles	Wednesday
jueves	Thursday
viernes	Friday
sábado	Saturday
domingo	Sunday

el lunes, el martes...	on Monday, on Tuesday . . .
los lunes, los martes...	on Mondays, on Tuesdays . . .
Hoy (Mañana) es viernes.	Today (Tomorrow) is Friday.
el fin de semana	(on) the weekend
pasado mañana	the day after tomorrow

Except for **el sábado / los sábados** and **el domingo / los domingos,** all the days of the week use the same form for the plural as they do for the singular. The definite articles are used to express *on* with the days of the week. The days are not capitalized in Spanish, and the week begins with Monday (not with Sunday).

Práctica

A Preguntas

1. ¿Qué día es hoy? ¿Qué día es mañana? ¿pasado mañana?
2. Si hoy es sábado, ¿qué día es mañana? ¿pasado mañana? Si hoy es jueves, ¿qué día es mañana? ¿pasado mañana?
3. ¿Qué días de la semana hay clases de español? ¿Qué días no hay clases de español? ¿Qué día estudia Ud. en el laboratorio de lenguas? ¿Qué días de la semana trabaja Ud.?

Adivinanza[a]

¿Qué fiesta será[b] que entre[c] sábado y lunes está?

[a]*Riddle* [b]*can it be* [c]*between*

¿POR O PARA?

Just as there are two Spanish verbs that mean *to be* (**ser** and **estar**), there are two Spanish words that often express English *for:* **por** and **para.** These prepositions (words that express the relationship between other words) have other English equivalents as well. You will learn about the uses of **por** and **para** gradually, throughout the chapters of *¿Qué tal?* Boxes like this one will call your attention to their uses.

In the following questions, you will use **por** in one of its most important meanings: *in, during.*

Estudio **por** la mañana y trabajo **por** la tarde. **Por** la noche, estoy en casa con la familia.	*I study in the morning and I work in the afternoon. During the evening (At night), I'm at home with my family.*

Remember that the phrases **de la mañana (tarde, noche)** are used when a specific hour of the day is mentioned.

B **¿Cuándo... ?** (*When . . . ?*) When do you do the following activities, **por la mañana, por la tarde,** or **por la noche**? Add a day of the week when appropriate.

MODELO: Practico un deporte (*sport*) ... →
              Practico un deporte (los sábados) por la tarde.

1. Hablo por teléfono con mis amigos...
2. Practico un deporte...
3. Miro (*I watch*) la televisión...

4. Escucho música...
5. Bailo en una fiesta...
6. Estudio en (casa, la biblioteca,...)...
7. Trabajo en (la librería...)...
8. Tomo (café, cerveza, Coca-Cola)...

ESTRUCTURAS ▼

4. Getting Information

Asking Yes / No Questions

▼ **En una universidad: La oficina de matrícula**
▼
▼ ESTUDIANTE: Necesito una clase más por la mañana. *¿Hay sitio* en la clase
▼   de sicología 2?
▼ CONSEJERO: Imposible, señorita. No hay.
▼ ESTUDIANTE: *¿Hay un curso* de historia o de matemáticas?
▼ CONSEJERO: Sólo por la noche. *¿Desea Ud. tomar* una clase por la noche?
▼ ESTUDIANTE: Trabajo por la noche. Por eso necesito una clase por la mañana.
▼ CONSEJERO: Pues... ¿qué tal el francés 10? Hay una clase a las diez de la mañana.
▼ ESTUDIANTE: *¿El francés 10?* Perfecto. Pero, *¿no necesito tomar* primero el
▼   francés 1?
▼
▼   ▲ ▲ ▲
▼
▼ 1. ¿Necesita la señorita dos clases más?
▼ 2. ¿Hay sitio en sicología 2?
▼ 3. ¿Hay cursos de historia o de matemáticas por la mañana?
▼ 4. ¿A qué hora es la clase de francés 10?
▼ 5. ¿Cuál es el problema con la clase de francés 10?

There are two kinds of questions: information questions and yes/no questions.
Questions that ask for new information or facts that the speaker does not know
often begin with *interrogative words* such as *who* and *what*. You learned many interrogative words in **Primeros pasos.** *Yes/no questions* are those that permit a simple
yes or *no* answer.

Do you speak French? → No, I don't (speak French).

Rising Intonation

A common way to form yes/no questions in Spanish is simply to make your voice
rise at the end of the question.

At a university: The registration office STUDENT: I need one more class in the morning. Is there space in
Psychology 2? ADVISOR: Impossible, Miss. There's no room. STUDENT: Is there a history or math class? AD-
VISOR: Only at night. Do you want to take a night course? STUDENT: I work at night. That's why I need a
class in the morning. ADVISOR: Well . . . what about French 10? There's a class at ten in the morning.
STUDENT: French 10? Perfect. But don't I need to take French 1 first?

STATEMENT:	Ud. trabaja aquí todos los días. *You work here every day.*	Arturo regresa a casa hoy. *Arturo is returning home today.*
QUESTION:	¿Ud. trabaja aquí todos los días? *Do you work here every day?*	¿Arturo regresa a casa hoy? *Is Arturo returning home today?*

There is no Spanish equivalent to English *do* or *does* in questions. Note also the use of an inverted question mark (¿) at the beginning of a question.

Inversion

Another way to form yes/no questions is to invert the order of the subject and verb, in addition to making your voice rise at the end of the question.

STATEMENT:	**Ud.** trabaja aquí todos los días.	**Arturo** regresa a casa hoy.
QUESTION:	¿Trabaja **Ud.** aquí todos los días?	¿Regresa **Arturo** a casa hoy?

Práctica

A **En la librería.** With a classmate, look carefully at the following drawing. Then, as your classmate looks away from the drawing, ask him or her questions about it based on the following statements. Your classmate should try to answer without looking at the drawing.

MODELO: El dependiente toma café: →
ESTUDIANTE 1: ¿El dependiente toma café? (¿Toma café el dependiente?)
ESTUDIANTE 2: No. Ramón toma café.

Alicia   Hildebrando   Ramón   Miguel   Irma

1. Miguel habla con el dependiente.
2. Irma desea pagar una mochila.
3. Hildebrando busca un libro de historia.

4. Irma busca un libro de historia.
5. Alicia estudia historia.
6. Ramón es una persona impaciente.
7. Hay tres dependientes en la librería hoy.

B **En la cafetería.** Imagine that you have just overheard the following answers. Ask the questions that led to them. Follow the model.

MODELO: «Sí, estudio con él (*him*).» → ¿Estudia Ud. con Guillermo?
¿Estudias (tú) con Guillermo?

1. «No, no trabajo aquí todos los días.»
2. «Sí, ella baila muy bien.»
3. «No, no regreso a casa hoy.»
4. «Sí, estudiamos mucho para esa (*for that*) clase.»
5. «Sí, él busca una clase por la noche.»
6. «No, no necesitamos hablar con el profesor.»

C **¡Firma aquí, por favor!** (*Sign here, please!*)

Paso 1. Use the following cues as a guide to form questions to ask classmates. Write the questions on a sheet of paper first, if you like.

1. estudiar en la biblioteca por la noche   _____
2. practicar español con un amigo / una amiga   _____
3. tomar café por la mañana   _____
4. bailar mucho (*a lot*) en las fiestas   _____
5. tocar un instrumento musical   _____
6. regresar a casa muy tarde a veces (*sometimes*)   _____
7. estudiar los domingos por la noche   _____
8. practicar español en el laboratorio de lenguas   _____

Paso 2. Now use the questions to get information from your classmates. When a person answers a question affirmatively, ask him or her to sign his or her name (**¡Firma aquí, por favor!**) next to the question, if you have written it out, or next to the appropriate item above.

Un paso más

UN POCO DE TODO

A Conversaciones en la cafetería.

Paso 1. Form complete questions and answers based on the words given, in the order given. Conjugate the verbs and add other words if necessary. Do not use the subject pronouns in parentheses.

PREGUNTAS

1. ¿buscar (*tú*) / libro de español?
2. ¿no trabajar / Paco / aquí / en / cafetería?
3. ¿qué más / necesitar / Uds. / en / clase de matemáticas?
4. ¿dónde / estar / Juanita?
5. ¿no desear (*tú*) / estudiar / más?

RESPUESTAS

1. no, / (*yo*) necesitar / regresar / a casa
2. no, / (*yo*) buscar / mochila
3. (*nosotros*) necesitar / calculadora / y / cuaderno
4. no, / él / trabajar / en / biblioteca
5. ella / trabajar / en / librería / por / tarde

Paso 2. Now match the answers with the questions to form short conversational exchanges.

B **¿Qué pasa** (*What's up*) **y dónde?** Scan the vocabulary in the following Vocabulary Library before you begin this activity.

Vocabulary Library

descansar	to rest
escuchar (**música, discos, cintas**)	to listen to (music, records, tapes)
fumar	to smoke
mirar (**películas, la televisión**)	to watch (movies, TV)
tocar (**la batería, la trompeta**)	to play (drums, the trumpet)

Boxes like this will appear throughout **¿Qué tal?** whenever a bit of extra vocabulary might be useful to you. This vocabulary is not considered to be "active" vocabulary that you should learn (although you know some of the verbs already). But you may wish to learn those words and phrases that are especially useful for talking about your life and activities.

Paso 1. Tell what you and your friends do in each of the following places. Use the verbs you have already learned plus some listed in the Vocabulary Library.

MODELO: en el laboratorio de lenguas →
          Cuando estamos en el laboratorio de lenguas, escuchamos cintas, hablamos español,...

1. en la biblioteca, por la noche
2. en casa, por la noche
3. en un bar estudiantil
4. en el pasillo (*hallway*) antes de (*before*) clase

Paso 2. Now tell what is happening in the following scene. Use complete sentences and describe as many details as possible so that a person who has not seen it can visualize it.

SITUACIÓN   En la biblioteca, antes de[a] clase

ALICIA: Oye, ¿cuándo es tu clase de cálculo?
TOMÁS: A las once. ¿Qué hora es?
ALICIA: Son las diez y veinte.
TOMÁS: Entonces,[b] ¿estudiamos diez minutos más?
ALICIA: Está bien. ¿Qué tal si tomamos un café antes de tu clase?
TOMÁS: ¡De acuerdo!

[a]antes... before   [b]Well, then

NOTAS COMUNICATIVAS SOBRE EL DIÁLOGO

To get a friend's attention: **Oye...**
To suggest activities to a friend: **¿Qué tal si + nosotros** verb form**?**
To express agreement or to accept an **invitation: Está bien.   De acuerdo.**

Conversación

Practice the dialogue with a classmate. Then vary some of the details.

- Mention a class you are taking this term.
- Give the time the class meets.
- Invite your friend to have a soft drink (**un refresco**) or an ice cream (**un helado**).

Cafetería estudiantil de la Universidad Iberoamericana, México, D.F.

NOTA CULTURAL: Las universidades hispanas

¡OJO!   Can you guess the meaning of the underlined verbs in the following brief note about Hispanic universities? Note also: **muchos/muchas** = many.

En el mundo hispánico, el concepto de vida[a] universitaria es diferente. La universidad no es un centro de actividad social. No hay muchas residencias estudiantiles. La mayoría[b] de los estudiantes habitan con sus familias en la ciudad[c] donde está la universidad.

Si en la universidad hay un campus similar al de[d] las universidades norteamericanas, se llama la «ciudad universitaria». Muchas universidades ocupan un solo[e] edificio grande[f] o varios edificios en el centro de la ciudad. No tienen[g] zonas verdes.[h]

Otra diferencia es que los deportes no son muy importantes en las universidades hispanas. Muchos estudiantes practican deportes, pero[i] no en la universidad sino[j] en clubes deportivos.

[a]life [b]majority [c]city [d]al... to those of [e]un... one single [f]large [g]No... They don't have [h]zonas... landscaped areas [i]but [j]but rather

PARA ESCRIBIR

Complete the following paragraph about your university. All you have to do is fill in the blanks. Then, if you wish, add additional information, modeling your sentences after those in **Nota cultural: Las universidades hispanas.**

Mi universidad se llama _____. Está en _____, en el estado de _____. En mis clases generalmente hay _____ estudiantes. En cuanto a (*As for*) los estudiantes, _____. El estudio de lenguas _____.

VOCABULARIO

Verbos

bailar to dance
buscar to look for
cantar to sing
comprar to buy
desear to want
enseñar to teach
escuchar to listen (to)
estar (*irreg.*) to be
estudiar to study
hablar to speak; to talk
mirar to look (at); to watch
necesitar to need
pagar to pay (for)
practicar to practice
regresar to return
      (*to a place*)
   regresar a casa to go home
tocar to play (*a musical
      instrument*)
tomar to take; to drink
trabajar to work

Materias y cursos

**la administración de
      empresas** business
la computación computer science
Otras materias: el arte (*but f.*),
      las ciencias (naturales, políticas, sociales), las comunicaciones, la economía, la filosofía, la física, la historia,
la literatura, las matemáticas,
la química, la sicología

Lenguas (extranjeras)

**el alemán, el chino, el español,
      el francés, el inglés, el italiano, el japonés, el ruso**

Cosas

el café coffee
la cerveza beer
el deporte sport
el dinero money
la fiesta party
la matrícula tuition; registration

¿Cuándo?

el fin de semana (on) the
      weekend
hoy today
mañana tomorrow
pasado mañana the day after
      tomorrow
por in, during (*with time*)
por la mañana (tarde, noche) in
      the morning (afternoon,
      evening)
todos los días every day

Los días de la semana

**lunes, martes, miércoles, jueves,
      viernes, sábado, domingo**

Palabras adicionales

aquí here
bien well
con with
en casa at home
mal badly
más more
muy very
por teléfono by telephone
si if
sólo only

Self-Test

Use the tape that accompanies this text to test yourself briefly on the important points of this chapter.

VOCES

There is material for this section on the tape that accompanies this text.

del mundo hispánico 1
Hispanics in the United States

You don't need to go abroad to find evidence of the importance of Spanish. The Spanish language and people of Hispanic descent have been an integral part of life in what is today the United States for centuries. Hispanic colonizers arrived in what is now Florida, Texas, and California in the early sixteenth century. A quick glance at the map of the United States—from Puerto Valdez in Alaska to Colorado (meaning *red* in Spanish) to Florida (meaning *flowered* or *flowering*)—shows how extensive the influence of Spanish in this country has been.

Bailadoras mexicanoamericanas en San Antonio, Texas.

Today there are more than twenty-four million people of Hispanic descent in the United States, and Hispanics are currently one of the fastest growing cultural groups. In fact, the United States is now the fifth largest Spanish-speaking country in the world.

Who are the twenty-four million Hispanics living in the United States today? If we are tempted to think of all U.S. Hispanics as similar, we soon discover how untrue that is! Hispanics in this country are characterized by great diversity, reflecting the natural diversity of the Spanish-speaking world. Ethnically and racially, Hispanics can be Indian (descendants of the many native indigenous groups that populated the Americas before the arrival of the Europeans), European, African, Asian, and all possible combinations of these groups. And, of course, there is national, regional, dialectal, socioeconomic, and professional diversity as well.

The U.S. Hispanic population is also diverse in terms of its arrival in this country. Some Hispanic families, including many Mexican American families, have lived on what is now U.S. soil for centuries. Other groups—like the Cubans and Central Americans—have arrived in recent years as the result of political and social changes in their countries of origin.

Most U.S. Hispanics strive to maintain aspects of their unique heritage while at the same time entering the mainstream of American culture. Although not all people of Hispanic origin speak Spanish, many are in fact bilingual and bicultural, able to move back and forth between their own and the mainstream culture with ease. This dual cultural identity is being increasingly recognized by the media and by the business community.

Comparing origins of U.S. Hispanic population

Total population as of 1990:
22 million

Percentages:

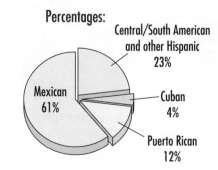

Central/South American and other Hispanic 23%

Mexican 61%

Cuban 4%

Puerto Rican 12%

Who are the U.S. Hispanics?

Mexicans: This is the oldest and largest group of U.S. Hispanics. There is a constant migration from Mexico to the United States due to the long border that the two countries share along the Rio Grande (called the **Río Bravo** in Mexico). Although there are Mexican Americans in all states, this group is particularly concentrated in the Southwest (mostly Texas, New Mexico, Arizona, and California) as well as in large Midwestern cities like Chicago.

Puerto Ricans: All Puerto Ricans are U.S. citizens by birth, since Puerto Rico is a Commonwealth of the United States. There are many Puerto Ricans in the large cities of the Northeast.

Cubans: A large part of this group arrived in the United States as the result of the political situation in Cuba in the late 1950s. Cuban-Americans live mainly in Florida.

Central Americans: This group of recent arrivals—which includes many Nicaraguans, Salvadorans, and Guatemalans—tends to settle in large urban areas like Washington, D.C., San Francisco, and Los Angeles.

South Americans: Mainly Colombians, Argentines, and Ecuadorans, this group tends to settle in large cities as well.

Basques: This small group, originally from Spain, has lived in the Southwest for centuries, especially in Nevada and Colorado.

Bailadores colombianos, en San Mateo, California.

Una tienda de la Pequeña Habana, el barrio cubano de Miami, Florida.

Un desfile (*parade*) puertorriqueño en Nueva York.

¡Qué interesante!

▼ **1.** What information in this reading surprised you the most?
▼ **2.** Working in a group, make a list of the names of places in the United States or Canada that you know to be of Spanish origin. Then share your list with the whole class.
▼ **3.** Is there a large group of Hispanics in your home town or in the city where your college or university is located? What country or countries are they from? What do you know about them?

Primer paso

Adjetivos

casado

soltero

alto

grande

pequeño

joven

vieja

bajo

corto

largo

morena

rubia

trabajador

perezoso

To describe a masculine singular noun, use **alto, bajo,** and so on;
use **alta, baja,** and so on for feminine singular nouns.

¿Cómo eres?

Más adjetivos

guapo	handsome, good-looking	**listo**	smart, clever	**rico**	rich
bonito	pretty	**tonto**	silly, foolish	**pobre**	poor
feo	ugly				
		simpático	nice, likeable	**delgado**	thin, slender
bueno	good	**antipático**	unpleasant	**gordo**	fat
malo	bad				

Práctica

A **Preguntas.** Conteste según los dibujos.

1. Einstein es listo. ¿Y el chimpancé?

2. Roberto es trabajador. ¿Y José?

3. El libro es viejo y corto. ¿Y el lápiz?

4. El ángel es bueno y simpático. También es guapo. ¿Y el demonio?

5. Ramón Ramírez es casado. También es viejo. ¿Y Paco Pereda?

6. Pepe es bajo. ¿Y Pablo?

7. Elena es gorda y morena. ¿Y Marta? **(¡OJO!)**

8. La familia Pérez es grande y rica. ¿Y la familia Gómez? **(¡OJO!)**

B **¿Cómo son?** Your elderly uncle Guillermo is not familiar with these famous personalities. Describe them to him, using as many adjectives as possible. Don't forget to use cognate adjectives you have already seen.

1. Spike Lee   **2.** Joe Montana   **3.** la princesa Diana   **4.** Roseanne

DE AQUÍ Y DE ALLÁ

Here are some adjectives to use in informal situations to compliment someone or to describe things that you feel positive about.

chulo	nice; pretty	**genial**	witty; great
mono *(Spain, Cuba)*	cute	**bárbaro**	great, impressive

Descriptive adjectives are frequently used by Spanish speakers with **¡Qué _____!,** to express English *how* + adjective.

¿El bebé? ¡Qué mono!
¿Michael Jordan? ¡Qué alto! ¡Y qué bárbaro!

PRONUNCIACIÓN ▼▼▼▼▼▼▼▼▼▼▼▼▼▼▼▼▼▼▼▼▼▼▼

Stress and Written Accent Marks (Part 2)

The written accent mark is used in the following situations.

As you know, most Spanish words do not need a written accent mark because their pronunciation is completely predictable by native speakers. Here are the two basic rules.

- A word that ends in a vowel, **-n,** or **-s** is stressed on the next-to-last syllable.
- A word that ends in any other consonant is stressed on the last syllable.

1. A written accent mark is needed when a word does not follow the two basic rules.
   Look at the words in this group.

   ta-bú   a-le-mán   na-ción   in-glés   es-tás

   Since these words end in a vowel, **-n,** or **-s,** one would predict that they would be stressed on the next-to-last syllable. But the written accent mark shows that they are in fact accented on the last syllable.

   Now look at the words in this group.

   lá-piz   dó-lar   ál-bum   á-gil   dó-cil

   Since these words end in a consonant (other than **-n** or **-s**), one would predict that they would be stressed on the last syllable. But the written accent mark shows that they are in fact accented on the next-to-last syllable.

2. All words that are stressed on the third-to-last syllable must have a written accent mark.

   bo-lí-gra-fo   ma-trí-cu-la   ma-te-má-ti-cas

3. When two consecutive vowels do not form a diphthong, the vowel that receives the spoken stress will have a written accent mark. This pattern is very frequent in words that end in **-ía.**

   Ma-rí-a   dí-a   po-li-cí-a   bio-lo-gí-a   as-tro-no-mí-a

   Contrast the pronunciation of those words with the following words in which the vowels **i** and **a** *do* form a diphthong: **Patricia, Clemencia, Francia, infancia.**

4. Some one-syllable words have accents to distinguish them from other words that sound like them. For example:

   él (*he*) / el (*the*)   tú (*you*) / tu (*your*)
   sí (*yes*) / si (*if*)   mí (*me*) / mi (*my*)

5. Interrogative and exclamatory words have a written accent on the stressed vowel. For example:

   ¿quién? (*who?*)   ¿dónde? (*where?*)   ¡Qué bárbaro!

A The following words have been separated into syllables for you. Read them aloud, paying careful attention to where the spoken stress should fall. The lists include some words that you have never heard before in Spanish. That does not matter, since the rules you have learned will help you pronounce them correctly.

1. a-quí   pa-pá   a-diós   bus-qué
2. prác-ti-co   mur-cié-la-go   te-lé-fo-no   ar-chi-pié-la-go
3. Ji-mé-nez   Ro-drí-guez   Pé-rez   Gó-mez
4. si-co-lo-gí-a   so-cio-lo-gí-a   sa-bi-du-rí-a   bu-jí-as
5. his-to-ria   te-ra-pia   Pre-to-ria   me-mo-ria

B Indicate the stressed vowel of each word in the list that follows. Give the rule that determines the stress of each word.

1. exámenes   **5.** actitud   **9.** están   **13.** plástico
2. lápiz   **6.** acciones   **10.** hombre   **14.** María
3. necesitar   **7.** dólares   **11.** peso   **15.** Rodríguez
4. perezoso   **8.** francés   **12.** mujer   **16.** Patricia

▼▼▼▼▼▼▼▼▼▼▼▼▼▼▼▼▼▼▼▼▼▼▼▼▼ **ESTRUCTURAS**

RECICLADO

Before beginning Grammar Section 5, review the forms and uses of **ser** that you have already learned by answering these questions.

1. ¿Eres estudiante o profesor(a)?
2. ¿De dónde eres?
3. ¿Cómo eres? ¿Eres una persona sentimental? ¿inteligente? ¿paciente? ¿elegante?
4. ¿Qué hora es? ¿A qué hora es la clase de español?
5. ¿Qué es un hospital? ¿Es una persona? ¿una cosa? ¿una institución?

5.   Expressing *to be*

Present Tense of *ser;* Summary of Uses

▼ **En la oficina de la profesora Castro**

▼
▼ PROFESORA: *¿Es* este su examen, Sr. Bermúdez?
▼   RAÚL: *Es* posible. *¿Es* el examen de Raúl Bermúdez o de Jaime Bermúdez?
▼   *Somos* hermanos.
▼ PROFESORA: *Es* de Jaime Bermúdez, y *es* un suspenso.
▼   RAÚL: Pues el suspenso *es* de Jaime. ¡Yo *soy* Raúl!
▼
▼   ▲ ▲ ▲
▼
▼ 1. ¿Con quién habla Raúl?
▼ 2. ¿Raúl y Jaime son amigos?
▼ 3. ¿Es Jaime profesor o estudiante?
▼ 4. ¿Es el examen de Raúl o de Jaime?

As you know, there are two Spanish verbs that mean *to be:* **ser** and **estar.** They are not interchangeable; the meaning that the speaker wishes to convey determines their use. In this chapter, you will review the uses of **ser** that you already know and learn some new ones. Remember to use **estar** to express location and to ask how someone is feeling. You will learn more about the uses of **estar** in **Capítulos 4** and **5.**

ser *(to be)*			
yo	**soy**	nosotros/as	**somos**
tú	**eres**	vosotros/as	**sois**
Ud.	**es**	Uds.	**son**
él / ella	**es**	ellos / ellas	**son**

Here are some basic language functions of **ser.** You have used or seen all of them already in this and previous chapters.

• To *identify* people and things

  Yo soy **estudiante.**   **Alicia y yo** somos **amigas.**
  La doctora Ramos es **profesora.**   **Esto** es **un libro.**

In Professor Castro's office   PROFESSOR: Is this your exam, Mr. Bermúdez? RAÚL: It's possible. Is it Raúl Bermúdez's exam or Jaime Bermúdez's? We're brothers. PROFESSOR: It's Jaime Bermúdez's, and it's an "F." RAÚL: Well, the "F" is Jaime's. I'm Raúl!

- To *describe* people and things*

Soy **sentimental.**	*I'm sentimental (a sentimental person).*
El coche es **muy viejo.**	*The car is very old.*

- With **de,** to express *origin*

Somos **de los Estados Unidos.**	*We're from the United States. Where*
¿**De dónde** es Ud.?	*are you from?*

[Práctica A]

- To express *generalizations* (only **es**)

Es **importante** estudiar, pero no es	*It's important to study, but it's not*
necesario estudiar todos los días.	*necessary to study every day.*

[Práctica B]

Here are two basic language functions of **ser** that you have not yet practiced.

- **Ser** is used with the preposition **de** to express *possession.*

Es el perro **de** Carla.	*It's Carla's dog.*
Son las gatas **de** Jorge.	*They're Jorge's cats.*
—¿**De** quién es el examen?	*Whose exam is it?*
—Es (el examen) **de** Raúl.	*It's Raúl's (exam).*

Note that there is no *'s* in Spanish.

¡**OJO!** The masculine singular article **el** contracts with the preposition **de** to form **del.** No other article contracts with **de.**

Es la casa **del** niño.	*It's the boy's house.*
Es la casa **de las** niñas.	*It's the girls' house.*

[Práctica C]

- **Ser** is used with **para** to tell for whom or what something is *intended.*

¿POR O PARA?

In **Capítulo 2** you learned one of the most important uses of the preposition **por.** Here is the first important use of the preposition **para. Para** introduces the recipient of an object or tells what something will be used for.

¿*Romeo y Julieta?* Es **para** la clase de inglés.	Romeo and Juliet? *It's for English class.*
¿**Para** quién son todos los regalos? —**Para** mis amigos.	*Who are all the presents for? —For my friends.*

[Práctica D]

---

*You will practice this language function of **ser** in Grammar Section 6 in this chapter and in subsequent chapters.

Práctica

A **Identificaciones.** ¿Quiénes son, de dónde son y dónde trabajan ahora?

MODELO: Teresa: profesora / de Madrid / en Cleveland →
Teresa es profesora. Es de Madrid. Ahora trabaja en Cleveland.

1. Carlos Miguel: profesor / de Cuba / en Milwaukee
2. Maripili: consejera / de Bogotá / en Miami
3. Mariela: dependienta / de Buenos Aires / en Nueva York
4. Sara y Juan: estudiantes / de San Juan / en Boston
5. Julio y Raúl: atletas / de Caracas / en Chicago
6. yo: estudiante / de ¿ ? / en ¿ ?

Now use the same pattern to tell about a friend of yours.

B **¿Qué opinas?** (*What do you think?*) Exprese opiniones originales, afirmativas o negativas, con una frase de cada (*each*) columna.

(No) Es importante / Es muy práctico / Es necesario / Es tonto (*foolish*) / Es fascinante / Es una lata (*pain, drag*) / Es (im)posible

mirar la televisión todos los días
hablar español en clase
tener (*to have*) muchos hermanos / muchos gatos y perros
tomar cerveza en clase
hablar con los animales / las plantas
tomar mucho café y fumar muchos cigarrillos
trabajar dieciocho horas al día
pasar (*to spend*) el fin de semana con la familia
estudiar para un examen el sábado por la noche
regresar a casa a las tres de la mañana
¿ ?

C **¡Seamos** (*Let's be*) **lógicos!** ¿De quién son estas (*these*) cosas? Con un compañero / una compañera, haga y conteste preguntas según los modelos.

MODELOS: E1: ¿De quién es el perro?
E2: Es de...

E2: ¿De quién son las mochilas?
E1: Son de...

Personas: los estudiantes, la actriz, el niño, el estudiante extranjero, los señores Schmidt, la familia con diez niños

1. la casa en Beverly Hills
2. la casa en Viena
3. la camioneta (*station wagon*)
4. el perro
5. las fotos de la Argentina
6. las mochilas con todos los libros

D **¿Para quién son los regalos?** The first column lists gifts, the second, friends and other individuals. Decide who receives which gift, then explain why.

MODELO: _____ es para _____. →
El dinero es para mi amiga Anita. Ella es estudiante. Necesita dinero.

el dinero (para comprar una mochila, para
    pagar la matrícula, para ¿ ?)
la camioneta
el coche, un Mercedes
la cerveza
la silla mecedora (*rocking chair*)
las cintas (*tapes*) de U2 y Jon Secada
el televisor (*TV set*)
¿ ?

Ernesto y Lupita: pasan todos los días en casa; son viejos
Juan: mira el fútbol en la tele
mi amigo Raúl y su esposa (*his wife*): ¡tienen ocho niños!
mi amiga Anita: estudia en la universidad
Marcos: escucha la música moderna
Armando: es actor

Segundo paso

▼ **VOCABULARIO**

Los números 31–100

Para dormirse (*To get to sleep*), ¿quién cuenta cintas y discos compactos?
¿Quién cuenta gatos? ¿Quién cuenta atletas?

Continúe la secuencia:

    treinta y uno, treinta y dos...
    ochenta y cuatro, ochenta y cinco...
    cincuenta y seis, cincuenta y siete...

treinta y uno,
  treinta y dos...

cincuenta y seis,
  cincuenta y siete...

ochenta y cuatro,
  ochenta y cinco...

31	treinta y uno*	35	treinta y cinco	39	treinta y nueve	70	setenta
32	treinta y dos	36	treinta y seis	40	cuarenta	80	ochenta
33	treinta y tres	37	treinta y siete	50	cincuenta	90	noventa
34	treinta y cuatro	38	treinta y ocho	60	sesenta	100	cien, ciento

Cien is used before nouns and in counting.

cien casas	a/one hundred houses
noventa y nueve, **cien**	ninety-nine, one hundred

Práctica

A Más problemas de matemáticas.

1. $30 + 50 = ?$ **4.** $77 + 23 = ?$ **7.** $84 - 34 = ?$

2. $45 + 45 = ?$ **5.** $100 - 40 = ?$ **8.** $78 - 36 = ?$

3. $32 + 58 = ?$ **6.** $99 - 39 = ?$ **9.** $88 - 28 = ?$

B Los números de teléfono.

LAZARO AGUIRRE, A. –Schez Pacheco, 17	415 0046
LAZCANO DEL MORAL, A. –E. Larreta, 14	215 8194
LAZCANO DEL MORAL, A. –Ibiza, 8	274 6868
LEAL ANTON, J. –Pozo, 8	222 3894
LIEBANA RODRIGUEZ, A.	
Guadarrama, 10	463 2593
LOPEZ BARTOLOME, J. –Palma, 69	232 2027
LOPEZ CABRA, J. –E. Solana, 118	407 5086
LOPEZ CABRA, J. –L. Van, 5	776 4602
LOPEZ GONZALEZ, J. A. –Ibiza, 27	409 2552
LOPEZ GUTIERREZ, G. –S. Cameros, 7	478 8494
LOPEZ LOPEZ, J. –Alamedilla, 21	227 3570
LOPEZ MARIN, V. –Illescas, 53	218 6630
LOPEZ MARIN, V. –N. Rey, 7	463 6873
LOPEZ MARIN, V. –Valmojado, 289	717 2823
LOPEZ NUÑEZ, J. –Pl. Pinazo, s/n	796 0035
LOPEZ NUÑEZ, J. –Rocafort, Bl. 321	796 5387
LOPEZ RODRIGUEZ, C. –Pl. Jesus, 7	429 3278
LOPEZ RODRIGUEZ, J. –Pl. Angel, 15	239 4323
LOPEZ RODRIGUEZ, M. E.	
B. Murillo, 104	233 4239
LOPEZ TRAPERO, A. –Cam. Ingenieros, 1	462 5392
LOPEZ VAZQUEZ, J. –A. Torrejón, 17	433 4646
LOPEZ VEGA, J. –M. Santa Ana, 5	231 2131
LORENTE VILLARREAL, G. –Gandia, 7	252 2758
LORENZO MARTINEZ, J. –Moscareta, 5	479 6282
LORENZO MARTINEZ, A. –P. Laborde, 21	778 2800
LORENZO MARTINEZ, A.	
Av. S. Diego, 116	477 1040
LOSADA MIRON, M. –Padilla, 31	276 9373
LOSADA MIRON, M. –Padilla, 31	431 7461
LOZANO GUILLEN, E.	
Juan H. Mendoza, 5	250 3884
LOZANO PIERA, F. J. –Pinguino, 8	466 3205
LUDEÑA FLORES, G. –Lope Rueda, 56	273 3735
LUENGO CHAMORRO, J.	
Gral Ricardos, 99	471 4906
LUQUE CASTILLO, J. –Pto Arlaban, 121	478 5253
LUQUE CASTILLO, L. –Cardeñosa, 15	477 6644
LLANES FERNANDEZ CAPALLEJA, R.	
Galileo, 93	234 7204
LLOMBART GALIANO, J. –Cavanilles, 37	433 6711
LLOVEZ FERNANDEZ, R.	
Av. N. Sra Fátima, 17	461 7935

Paso 1. Here are parts of several pages from Hispanic telephone books. Do you notice anything different about the names? (The next **Nota cultural** feature will give you information about them.)

Note also that telephone numbers in many Hispanic countries are written and said slightly differently than in the United States. Here is one model for asking for and giving phone numbers.

MODELO: 4-33-28-21 →

E1: ¿Cuál es tu (número de) teléfono?

E2: Es el cuatro, treinta y tres, veintiocho, veintiuno.

Use the preceding model to say the following telephone numbers aloud.

LA GUÍA TELEFÓNICA

Fierro Aguilar	Amalia	Avenida Juárez 86	7-65-03-91
Fierro Navarro	Teresa	Calle Misterios 45	5-86-58-16
Fierro Reyes	Gilberto	Avenida Miraflores 3	5-61-12-78
Figueroa López	Alberto	Calle Zaragoza 33	5-32-97-77
Figueroa Pérez	Julio	Avenida Iglesias 15	5-74-55-34
Gómez Pérez	Ana María	Calle Madero 7	7-94-43-88
Gómez Valencia	Javier	Avenida Córdoba 22	3-99-45-52
Guzmán Ávila	José Luis	Avenida Montevideo 4	6-57-29-40
Guzmán Martínez	Josefina	Avenida Independencia 25	2-77-22-70

Paso 2. Now use the model in **Paso 1** to find out the phone numbers of several classmates. Write down the numbers as you hear them, then say them back. Your classmates will verify the accuracy of the numbers.

---

*Beginning with 31, Spanish numbers are *not* written in a combined form: **treinta y uno, cuarenta y dos, sesenta y tres,** and so on must be three separate words.
Remember that when **uno** is part of a compound number (**treinta y uno,** and so on), it becomes **un** before a masculine noun and **una** before a feminine noun: **cincuenta y una** mesas; **setenta y un** coches.

NOTA CULTURAL: Hispanic Last Names

As you probably noted in the preceding excerpts from Hispanic telephone books, two last names **(apellidos)** were given for each entry: **Amalia Fierro Aguilar.** The first last name **(Fierro)** is that of Amalia's father; the second **(Aguilar)** is her mother's. This system for assigning last names is characteristic of all parts of the Spanish-speaking world, although it is not widely used by Hispanics living in the United States.

▼▼▼▼▼▼▼▼▼▼▼▼▼▼▼▼▼▼▼▼▼▼▼▼▼▼▼▼▼   **ESTRUCTURAS**

6. Describing

Adjectives: Gender, Number, and Position

Adjectives (**los adjetivos**) are words used to talk about nouns or pronouns. Adjectives may describe (*large desk*, **tall** *woman*) or tell how many there are (*a few desks*, **several** *women*).

You have been using adjectives to describe people since **Primeros pasos.** In this section, you will learn more about describing the people and things around you.

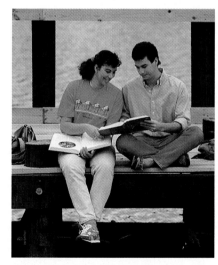

Un poema sencillo

Amiga	Amigo
Fiel	Fiel
Amable	Amable
Simpática	Simpático
¡La admiro!	¡Lo admiro!

▲ ▲ ▲

According to their form, which of the adjectives below can be used to describe each person? Which can refer to you?

Marta:
Mario: { fiel   amable   simpática   simpático

A simple poem Friend Loyal Kind Nice I admire him/her!

Adjectives with *ser*

In Spanish, forms of **ser** are used with adjectives that describe basic, inherent qualities or characteristics of the nouns or pronouns they modify.

Antonio **es interesante.**	*Antonio is interesting. (He's an interesting person.)*
Tú **eres amable.**	*You're nice. (You're a nice person.)*
El diccionario **es largo.**	*The dictionary is long.*

Forms of Adjectives

Spanish adjectives agree in gender and number with the noun or pronoun they modify. Each adjective has more than one form.

- Adjectives that end in **-e** (**inteligente**) and most adjectives that end in a consonant (**fiel**) have only two forms, a singular form and a plural form. The plural of adjectives is formed in the same way as that of nouns.

	MASCULINE	FEMININE
Singular	amigo inteligent**e** amigo fie**l**	amiga inteligent**e** amiga fie**l**
Plural	amigos inteligente**s** amigos fiel**es**	amigas inteligente**s** amigas fiel**es**

- Adjectives that end in **-o** (**alto**) have four forms, showing gender and number.*

	MASCULINE	FEMININE
Singular	amigo alt**o**	amiga alt**a**
Plural	amigos alt**os**	amigas alt**as**

[Práctica A–B]

- Most adjectives of nationality have four forms.

  Note: The names of many languages—which are masculine in gender—are the same as the masculine singular form of the corresponding adjective of nationality: **el español, el inglés, el alemán, el francés,** and so on. Note that in Spanish the names of languages and adjectives of nationality are not capitalized, but the names of countries are: **español, española,** but **España.**

---

*Adjectives that end in **-dor, -ón, -án,** and **-ín** also have four forms: **trabajador, trabajadora, trabajadores, trabajadoras.**

	MASCULINE	FEMININE
Singular	el doctor mexican**o** español alemán inglés	la doctor**a** mexican**a** español**a** aleman**a** ingles**a**
Plural	los doctor**es** mexican**os** español**es** aleman**es** ingles**es**	las doctor**as** mexican**as** español**as** aleman**as** ingles**as**

NOTE: This adjective of nationality has only two forms, singular and plural: **canadiense, canadienses.**

[Práctica C]

Placement of Adjectives

As you have probably noticed, adjectives do not always precede the noun in Spanish as they do in English. Note the following rules for adjective placement.

- Adjectives of quantity, like numbers, *precede* the noun, as do the interrogatives **¿cuánto/a?** and **¿cuántos/as?**.

Hay **muchas** sillas y **dos** escritorios.	*There are many chairs and two desks.*
Busco **otro*** coche.	*I'm looking for another car.*
¿Cuánto dinero necesitas?	*How much money do you need?*

- Adjectives that describe the qualities of a noun and distinguish it from others generally *follow* the noun. Adjectives of nationality are included in this category.

un perro **bueno**	un dependiente **trabajador**
una joven **delgada** y **morena**	un joven **español**

- The adjectives **bueno** and **malo** may precede or follow the noun they modify. When they precede a masculine singular noun, they shorten to **buen** and **mal** respectively.

un **buen** perro / un perro **bueno**	una **buena** perra / una perra **buena**
un **mal** día / un día **malo**	una **mala** noche / una noche **mala**

- The adjective **grande** may also precede or follow the noun. When it precedes a singular noun—masculine or feminine—it shortens to **gran** and means *great* or *impressive*. When it follows the noun, it means *large* or *big*.

Nueva York es una ciudad **grande.**	*New York is a large city.*
Nueva York es una **gran** ciudad.	*New York is a great (impressive) city.*

[Práctica D–F]

*****Otro** by itself means *another* or *other.* The indefinite article is not used with **otro.**

Forms of *this/these*

The demonstrative adjective *this/these* has four forms in Spanish. Learn to recognize them when you see them.

est**e** coche	*this car*	est**a** casa	*this house*
est**os** coches	*these cars*	est**as** casas	*these houses*

You have already seen the neuter demonstrative **esto.** It refers to something that is as yet unidentified: **¿Qué es esto?**

Práctica

A **Hablando de la universidad.** Tell what you think about aspects of your university by telling whether you agree (**Estoy de acuerdo.**) or disagree (**No estoy de acuerdo.**) with the statements. If you don't have an opinion, say **No tengo opinión.**

1. En esta universidad, hay suficientes actividades sociales.
2. Los profesores son excelentes, por lo general (*in general*).
3. Las residencias son buenas, por lo general.
4. Hay suficientes gimnasios y facilidades para practicar muchos deportes.
5. Es fácil aparcar el coche.
6. Los restaurantes, cafeterías y cafés son buenos.

B **¿Cómo son?** Complete each sentence with all the adjectives that are appropriate according to form and meaning.

1. Anita es _____. (morena / casado / jóvenes / lista / bonito / trabajadora)
2. Ernesto es _____. (viejo / alto / nueva / grande / fea / interesante)
3. Los clientes son _____. (rubio / antipático / inteligentes / viejos / ricos / práctica)
4. Las niñas son _____. (malo / cortas / sentimental / buenas / casadas / joven)

C **Nacionalidades.** Tell what nationality the following persons could be and where they might live: **Portugal, Alemania, la China, Inglaterra, España, Francia, Italia**

1. Monique habla francés; es _____ y vive (*she lives*) en _____.
2. José habla español; es _____ y vive en _____.
3. Greta y Hans hablan alemán; son _____ y viven en _____.
4. Gilberto habla portugués; es _____ y vive en _____.
5. Gina y Sofía hablan italiano; son _____ y viven en _____.
6. Winston habla inglés; es _____ y vive en _____.
7. Hai (*m.*) y Han (*m.*) hablan chino; son _____ y viven en _____.

D **¡María es igual!** Cambie: Miguel → María.

Miguel es un buen estudiante. Es listo y trabajador y estudia mucho. Es argentino, de la gran ciudad de Buenos Aires. Por eso[a] habla español. Desea ser

[a]Por... *That's why*

profesor de español.

Miguel es alto y guapo; también es muy delgado, pues hace[b] mucho ejercicio. Le gustan las fiestas grandes de la universidad. Es un buen amigo para todos porque[c] es comprensivo y tolerante.

[b]*pues... since he gets* [c]*because*

E **Asociaciones.** Working with several classmates, how many names can you associate with the following phrases? Everyone in the group must agree with the names you decide on. To introduce your suggestions, you can say **Creo** (*I think*) **que (____ es un gran hombre).** To express agreement or disagreement, use **(No) Estoy de acuerdo.**

1. un mal restaurante
2. un buen programa de televisión
3. una gran mujer, un gran hombre
4. un buen libro (¿una novela?), un libro horrible
5. una gran ciudad

F **Descripciones.** Describa a* su (*your*) familia, a* sus amigos y su universidad. Haga oraciones completas con palabras de cada (*each*) columna.

mi familia	(no) ser	interesante, importante, amable,
mis padres (*parents, m.*)		(im)paciente, grande, ¿ ?
mi profesor(a) de ____		intelectual, fiel, ¿ ?
mi amigo/a [nombre]		nuevo, viejo, pequeño, bueno, malo,
mi perro/gato		famoso, ¿ ?
mi universidad		

Un paso más

UN POCO DE TODO

A **La familia hispánica típica: ¿Existe?** Complete the following paragraphs about families. Give the correct form of the words in parentheses, as suggested by the context. When two possibilities are given in parentheses, select the correct word.

Muchas personas creen[a] que (todo[1]) las familias (hispánico[2]) son (grande[3]), pero no es así[b]. Como en todas las partes (de/del[4]) mundo[c], el concepto (del / de la[5]) familia ha cambiado[d] mucho, especialmente en las ciudades (grande[6]).

[a]*believe* [b]*pero... but that isn't so* [c]*world* [d]*ha... has changed*

---

*Note the use of the word **a** here (**a su familia, a sus amigos**). In this context, the word **a** has no equivalent in English. It is used in Spanish before a direct object that is a specific person. You will learn more about this use of **a** in **Capítulo 9.** Until then, the exercises and activities in *¿Qué tal?* will indicate when to use it.

Es verdad[e] que la familia campesina[f] (típico[7]) es grande, pero es así en casi[g] (todo[8]) las sociedades[h] rurales del mundo. Cuando los hijos[i] (trabajar[9]) la tierra con sus[j] padres, es bueno y (necesario[10]) tener[k] muchos niños. Pero en los grandes centros (urbano[11]) las familias con sólo[l] dos o tres hijos (ser[12]) más comunes. Es caro mantener[m] a (mucho[13]) hijos en una sociedad (industrializado[14]).

Es realmente difícil (hablar[15]) de una sola[n] familia (hispánico[16]) típica. ¿Hay una familia (norteamericano[17]) típica?

[e]*true* [f]*country, rural* [g]*almost* [h]*societies* [i]*children* [j]*their* [k]*to have* [l]*only* [m]Es... *It's expensive to support* [n]*single*

¿Cierto o falso? Corrija las oraciones falsas.

1. Todas las familias hispánicas son iguales (*the same*).
2. Las familias rurales son grandes en casi todas partes del mundo.
3. Las familias rurales necesitan muchos niños.
4. Por lo general, las familias urbanas son más pequeñas.

B **¿De dónde eres tú?** With a classmate, ask and answer questions according to the model.

MODELO: Atlanta → E1: ¿De dónde eres tú?
E2: Soy de *Atlanta.*
E1: Ah, eres *norteamericano/a.*
E2: Sí, por eso hablo *inglés.*

1. Guadalajara	**3.** Roma	**5.** Madrid	**7.** Lima	**8.** Berlín
2. París	**4.** Houston	**6.** Londres	(peruano)	**9.** Lisboa

SITUACIÓN Hablando[a] de otras personas

—¿Conoces[b] al joven moreno de la foto?
—No. ¿Quién es?
—Es mi compañero de cuarto. Es de Guatemala.
—¡Qué guapo es!, ¿verdad? ¿Cómo se llama?
—Se llama Fernando y es muy simpático. ¿Te gustaría conocerlo?
—¡Sí, claro[c]!

[a]*Talking* [b]*Do you know* [c]*of course*

NOTAS COMUNICATIVAS SOBRE EL DIÁLOGO

¿Te gustaría conocer**lo**?	*Would you like to meet him?*
¿Te gustaría conocer**la**?	*Would you like to meet her?*

Conversación

Practice the dialogue with a classmate. When you are comfortable with it, vary it to talk about other people you know or know about: an instructor, a good friend, a singer (**un/una cantante**), an actor or actress (**un actor / una actriz**) you like a lot, and so on.

PARA ESCRIBIR

Write a poem about what a friend means to you, like the one on page 67. Use adjectives different from those in the model poem. If you prefer, use the same structure but write a simple poem about a different topic, following this model.

MODELO: La familia   [*noun*]
         Cariñosa   [*adjective*]
         Comprensiva   [*adjective*]
         Tolerante   [*adjective*]
         ¡Es importante!   [Es + *adjective*]

Temas: el amor (*love*), la familia, la universidad, la vida (*life*)

▼▼▼▼▼▼▼▼▼▼▼▼▼ VOCABULARIO ▼▼▼▼▼▼▼▼▼▼▼▼▼

Verbos

pasar to spend (*time*)
ser (*irreg.*) to be

Adjetivos

alto/a tall
amable kind, nice
antipático/a unpleasant
bajo/a short (*in height*)
bonito/a pretty
buen, bueno/a good
casado/a married
corto/a short (*in length*)
delgado/a thin, slender
este/a this
   estos/as these
feo/a ugly
gordo/a fat
gran(de) large, big; great
guapo/a handsome, good-looking
joven young
largo/a long
listo/a smart, clever
mal, malo/a bad
moreno/a brunette
muchos/as many
norteamericano/a North American

nuevo/a new
otro/a other, another
pequeño/a small
perezoso/a lazy
pobre poor
rico/a rich
rubio/a blond(e)
simpático/a nice, likeable
soltero/a single (*not married*)
todo/a all, every
tonto/a silly; foolish
trabajador(a) hardworking
viejo/a old

Sustantivos

la camioneta station wagon
la casa house
la cinta tape
la ciudad city
el coche car
los Estados Unidos United States
el examen test
la familia family
el gato cat
el hermano brother
el/la niño/a boy/girl
los padres parents

el perro dog
el regalo gift

Los números

treinta, cuarenta, cincuenta, sesenta, setenta, ochenta, noventa, cien(to)

Palabras adicionales

estar de acuerdo to agree
para (intended) for
por eso that's why
por lo general in general
porque because

Self-Test

Use the tape that accompanies this text to test yourself briefly on the important points of this chapter.

LECTURA
cultural

Antes de leer: Recognizing Cognate Patterns

You already know that cognates are words that are similar in form and meaning from one language to another: for example, English *poet* and Spanish **poeta**. The endings of many Spanish words correspond to English word endings according to fixed patterns. Learning to recognize these patterns will increase the number of close and not-so-close cognates that you can recognize.

-dad → -ty	**-ción** → -tion	**-ico** → -ic, -cal
-mente → -ly	**-sión** → -sion	**-oso** → -ous

What are the English equivalents of these words?

1. unidad
2. reducción
3. explosión
4. idéntico
5. dramático
6. estudioso
7. famoso
8. reacción
9. recientemente
10. frecuentemente
11. religioso
12. religiosidad

Try to spot cognates in the following reading, and remember that you should be able to guess the meaning of underlined words from context.

Note: The reading is about the concept of family in this country and in Hispanic cultures. It contains some verb forms with endings different from those you have learned about. You will recognize the meaning of most of those verbs easily, however. A verb whose meaning may not be immediately obvious to you is **vivir.** Associate it with *vivisection* and *vivid.* Then read it in this context and guess its meaning: **Mi amigo Julio** *vive* **en la Argentina, en Buenos Aires.**

Another verb whose meaning is not easy to guess is **tener** (with its irregular forms: **tengo, tienes, tiene,** etc.), which means *to have.* Be aware of the meaning of **tener** in the phrase **tener... años** (*to be . . . years old*): **Tengo/Tiene veinte años** (*I'm / He / She is 20*).

Una familia hispánica, de Austin, Texas.

La unidad familiar

Cuando una persona hispana observa la estructura de la familia norteamericana, puede llegar[a] a esta conclusión: la familia ya no[b] existe en los Estados Unidos. ¿Por qué cree esto?[c]

El hispano observa que, cuando los hijos[d] tienen 18 años, aproximadamente, comienzan a vivir en otro lugar independientes de sus padres. Con frecuencia, los hijos trabajan y estudian en otras ciudades y, a veces,[e] abandonan el hogar familiar sólo porque sí.[f]

Los padres viejos viven solos porque, cuando los hijos tienen su propia[g] familia, los padres son para ellos una gran molestia. Los muy viejos están en residencias especiales para viejos y no con su familia. Por estas razones,[h] el hispano puede concluir que entre[i] los padres y los hijos norteamericanos, no hay unión; son muy indiferentes.

Por otra parte,[j] un norteamericano que mira la estructura de la familia hispánica puede creer que la influencia de la familia es demasiado fuerte.[k] ¿Por qué cree esto?

En muchas familias hispanas, hay hijos de 30 años y más que todavía[l] viven con sus padres. Muchas veces estos hijos tienen buenos trabajos y suficiente dinero para no depender de sus padres. Pero obviamente los padres no educan a los hijos para ser independientes. Por eso, el norteamericano puede concluir que los padres hispanos no tienen confianza en sus hijos y que no los[m] preparan para la vida.[n]

¿Son válidas estas conclusiones? El concepto de la unidad familiar existe en las dos culturas. En los Estados Unidos, la independencia personal tiene gran importancia social. Es una gran responsabilidad de los padres educar a sus hijos para ser independientes desde que[o] son jóvenes. La integridad de la familia depende menos de la cercanía[p] física y geográfica.

En cambio,[q] en la cultura hispánica, es muy importante preservar intacto el núcleo familiar. En muchos casos, los hijos sólo dejan[r] la casa familiar cuando se casan[s] y no cuando terminan sus estudios o comienzan a trabajar. Las dos sociedades tienen perspectivas diferentes; es imposible evaluar una cultura según[t] las normas de la otra.

[a]puede... *he can arrive* [b]ya... *no longer* [c]¿Por... *Why does he believe this?* [d]*children*
[e]a... *sometimes* [f]sólo... *just because they want to* [g]*own* [h]Por... *For these reasons* [i]*between*
[j]Por... *On the other hand* [k]demasiado... *too strong* [l]*still* [m]*them* [n]*life* [o]desde... *from the time that* [p]*closeness* [q]En... *In contrast* [r]*leave* [s]se... *they marry* [t]*according to*

Comprensión

A ¿Opinión o hecho (*fact*)? Indique si las siguientes oraciones representan una opinión o un hecho.

	HECHO	OPINIÓN
1. A veces los hijos norteamericanos trabajan en otras ciudades porque sus padres no los quieren (*don't love them*).	☐	☐
2. En muchos casos, los hijos hispanos viven con su familia aun (*even*) cuando tienen buenos trabajos.	☐	☐
3. La proximidad de los parientes es muy importante para la familia hispana.	☐	☐
4. Los padres ancianos representan una molestia para los hijos norteamericanos.	☐	☐

B Indique quién habla en las siguientes oraciones. ¡OJO! Hay diferentes normas culturales.

	UN HISPANO	UN NORTE-AMERICANO
1. «Tengo 38 años. Soy soltero y vivo con mis padres.»	☐	☐
2. «Necesito visitar a mi madre. Tiene 79 años y vive en el Meadowbrook Home.»	☐	☐
3. «La independencia es muy importante para mí. No deseo depender de mis padres el resto de mi vida.»	☐	☐
4. «Mi hija (*daughter*) tiene un buen trabajo en la IBM. Vive con una amiga en Los Ángeles y yo vivo aquí, en Nueva York.»	☐	☐

4

Primer paso

La familia y los parientes[a]

[a] *relatives*

los abuelos — Joaquín · Josefina

los padres — Mercedes · Luis · Elena · Juan

los hijos — Carmencita · Manolito · Elenita · Juanito

Michín · Sultán

Las relaciones FAMILIARES

Los parientes

el padre (papá)	father (dad)	**el nieto**	grandson
la madre (mamá)	mother (mom)	**la nieta**	granddaughter
el esposo/marido	husband	**el tío**	uncle
la esposa/mujer	wife	**la tía**	aunt
el hijo	son	**el primo**	(male) cousin
la hija	daughter	**la prima**	(female) cousin
el hermano	brother	**el sobrino**	nephew
la hermana	sister	**la sobrina**	niece
el abuelo	grandfather		
la abuela	grandmother		

To refer to a group of relatives who all bear the same relation to one person, use the masculine plural form. The group may be all male, or it may include males and females.

los padres	parents
los abuelos	grandparents
los hermanos	brothers and sisters

The feminine plural is used when there are no males in the group.

las hermanas	sisters (*no brothers*)
las tías	aunts (*no uncles*)

Las mascotas

el gato	cat	**el perro**	dog
el pájaro	bird	**el pez**	fish

Vocabulary Library

Remember that the words in these sections are for you to use if you want to, for what you personally need to express.

el padrastro / la madrastra	stepfather / stepmother
el hijastro / la hijastra	stepson / stepdaughter
el medio hermano / la media hermana	half-brother / half-sister

See also the words in **De aquí y de allá** (page 78).

Adivinanza

Dos hermanas,
mentira[a] no es,
la una es mi tía,
la otra no lo es.

[a]*lie*

Práctica

A **¿Cierto o falso?** Corrija las oraciones falsas.

1. Juan es el hermano de Elena.
2. Josefina es la abuela de Elenita.
3. Carmencita es la sobrina de Joaquín.
4. Carmencita y Juanito son primos.
5. Luis es el tío de Elenita.
6. Juanito es el sobrino de Juan.
7. Elena es la esposa de Luis.

B **¿Quién es?** Complete las oraciones lógicamente.

1. La madre de mi* padre es mi _____.
2. El hijo de mi tío es mi _____.
3. La hermana de mi padre es mi _____.
4. El esposo de mi abuela es mi _____.
5. Soy el/la _____ de mis abuelos.

Ahora (*Now*) defina estas personas, según el mismo (*same*) modelo.

6. prima   **7.** sobrino   **8.** tío   **9.** abuelo

C **¿Recuerdas a mi familia?** (*Do you remember my family?*)

Paso 1. Following the model on page 76, draw your own family tree (**el árbol genealógico**). Make it as complete as possible.

Paso 2. Exchange trees with a classmate. Study each other's tree for two minutes and then return them.

Paso 3. Taking turns, ask each other questions about your respective families: **¿Cómo se llama la hermana de mi madre?** The loser is the first person who can't remember two names. **¡Buena suerte (***luck***)!**

DE AQUÍ Y DE ALLÁ

To refer to your in-laws in Spanish, you can use the adjective **político/a** with the term describing the family member.

el padre político	father-in-law
la hermana política	sister-in-law

But there are also specific names for in-laws, and they are more commonly used.

el suegro / la suegra	father-in-law/mother-in-law
el yerno / la nuera	son-in-law/daughter-in-law
el cuñado / la cuñada	brother-in-law/sister-in-law

*Use **mi** to mean *my* with singular nouns and **mis** with plural ones. You will learn more about using words of this type in Grammar Section 8.

PRONUNCIACIÓN

r and rr

Spanish has two **r** sounds, one of which is called a *flap*, the other a *trill*. The rapid pronunciation of *tt* and *dd* in the English words *Betty* and *ladder* produces a sound similar to the Spanish flap **r**: the tongue touches the alveolar ridge (behind the upper teeth) once. Although English has no trill, when people imitate a motor, they often produce the Spanish trill **r**, which is a rapid series of flaps.

The trilled **r** is written **rr** between vowels (**carro, correcto**), and **r** at the beginning of a word (**rico, rosa**). Any other **r** is pronounced as a flap. Be careful to distinguish between the flap **r** and the trilled **r**. A mispronunciation will often change the meaning of a word—for example, **pero** (*but*) / **perro** (*dog*).

A inglés: *potter   ladder   cotter   meter   total   motor*
español: para   Lara   cara   mire   toro   moro

B
1. rico
2. ruso
3. rubio
4. Roberto
5. Ramírez
6. rebelde
7. reportero
8. real
9. corro
10. carro
11. corral
12. error

C
1. coro/corro
2. coral/corral
3. pero/perro
4. vara/barra
5. ahora/ahorra
6. caro/carro
7. cero/cerro

D
1. el nombre correcto
2. un corral grande
3. una norteamericana
4. Puerto Rico
5. rosas grandes
6. un libro corto
7. una mujer refinada
8. Carlos y Rosita
9. El perro está en el corral.
10. Los errores son raros.

ESTRUCTURAS

STUDY HINT: Studying and Learning Verbs

Knowing how to use verb forms quickly and accurately is one of the most important parts of learning how to communicate in a foreign language. These suggestions will help you recognize and use verb forms.

1. Study carefully any new grammar section that deals with verbs. Are the verbs regular? What is the stem? What are the personal endings?

Don't just memorize the endings (**-o, -as, -a,** and so on). Practice the complete forms of each verb (**hablo, hablas, habla,** and so on) until they are "second nature" to you. Be sure that you are using the appropriate endings: **-ar** endings with **-ar** verbs, for example. Be especially careful when you write and pronounce verb endings, since a misspelling or mispronunciation can convey inaccurate information. Even though there is only a one-letter difference between **hablo** and **habla** or between **habla** and **hablan,** that single letter makes a big difference in the information communicated.

2. Are you studying irregular verbs? If so, what are the irregularities? Practice the irregular forms many times so that you "overlearn" them and will not forget them: **soy, eres, es, son.**

3. Once you are familiar with the forms, practice asking short conversational questions using **tú/**

Ud. and **vosotros/Uds.** Answer each question, using the appropriate **yo** or **nosotros** form.

¿Hablas español? ⎫
¿Habla español? ⎭ Sí, hablo español.

¿Comen Uds. en clase? ⎫ No, no comemos
¿Coméis en clase? ⎭ en clase.

4. Be sure that you always know both the spelling *and* the meaning of all verb forms, just as you must for any new vocabulary word. Practice new verb forms in original sentences.

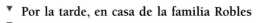

RECICLADO

The personal endings used with **-ar** verbs (**Capítulo 2**) share some characteristics of those used with **-er** and **-ir** verbs, which you will learn in the next section. Review the endings of **-ar** verbs by telling which subject pronoun(s) you associate with each of these endings.

1. **-amos**   2. **-as**   3. **-áis**   4. **-an**   5. **-o**   6. **-a**

7.   Expressing Actions

Present Tense of *-er* and *-ir* Verbs; More About Subject Pronouns

▼ **Por la tarde, en casa de la familia Robles**

SR. ROBLES: Paquita, *debes* estudiar ahora.

PAQUITA: Pero, papá, *asisto* a todas mis clases y saco buenas notas. Además, todos mis amigos están en el centro comercial esta tarde.

SR. ROBLES: Tus amigos no son mis hijos. Nunca *abres* los libros en casa. Nunca *lees* el periódico. Nunca *lees* una novela. Nunca...

PAQUITA: ¡Ay, papá! ¡No me *comprendes*! ¡Eres terrible a veces!

▲ ▲ ▲

¿Quién... ?

1. debe estudiar más
2. está en el centro comercial esta tarde
3. asiste a todas las clases
4. nunca abre los libros en casa
5. no comprende la situación

Afternoon at the Robles' house   MR. ROBLES: Paquita, you should study now. PAQUITA: But, Dad, I go to all of my classes and I get good grades. Besides, all my friends are at the mall this afternoon. MR. ROBLES: Your friends aren't my children. You never open your books at home. You never read the newspaper. You never read a novel. You never . . . PAQUITA: Oh, Dad! You don't understand me! You're terrible sometimes!

▼ En su opinión, ¿es Paquita una estudiante universitaria o de secundaria? ¿Por
▼ qué? ¿Es Ud. más como (*like*) Paquita o más como su (*her*) padre? Si Ud. tiene
▼ hijos, ¿son como Paquita? ¿Por qué (*Why*) sí o por qué no?

Verbs That End in *-er* and *-ir*

comer *(to eat)*		vivir *(to live)*	
como	comemos	vivo	vivimos
comes	coméis	vives	vivís
come	comen	vive	viven

The present tense of **-er** and **-ir** verbs is formed by adding personal endings to the
stem of the verb (the infinitive minus its **-er/-ir** ending). The personal endings are
the same for both **-er** and **-ir** verbs except for the first and second person plural.

Remember that the Spanish present tense has a number of present tense equivalents in English and can also be used to express future meaning:

como = *I eat, I am eating, I will eat*

Some important **-er** and **-ir** verbs in this chapter include the following.

aprender	to learn	**abrir**	to open
beber	to drink	**asistir (a)**	to attend, go to (*a class, function*)
comer	to eat	**escribir**	to write
comprender	to understand	**recibir**	to receive
creer (en)	to think, believe (in)	**vivir**	to live
deber (+ *inf.*)	should, must, ought to (*do something*)		
leer	to read		
vender	to sell		

Use and Omission of Subject Pronouns

In English, a verb must have an expressed subject (a noun or pronoun): *he/she
says, **the train** arrives*. In Spanish, however, as you have probably noticed, an expressed subject is not required. Verbs are accompanied by a subject pronoun only
for clarification, emphasis, or contrast.

* *Clarification:* When the context does not make the subject clear, the subject pronoun is expressed: ***Ud. / él / ella* vende; *Uds. / ellos / ellas* venden**. This happens most frequently with third person singular and plural verb forms.
* *Emphasis:* Subject pronouns are used in Spanish to emphasize the subject when
in English you would stress it with your voice.

  ¿Quién debe pagar? —¡**Tú** debes   *Who should pay? —**You** should pay!*
  pagar!

* *Contrast:* Contrast is a special case of emphasis. Subject pronouns are used to
contrast the actions of two individuals or groups.

  Ellos leen mucho; **nosotros** lee-   *They read a lot; we read little.*
  mos poco.

Práctica

A En la clase de español

Paso 1. Read the following statements and tell whether they are true for you and your classmates and for your classroom environment. If any statement is not true for you or your class, make it negative or change it in another way to make it correct.

> MODELO: Bebo café en clase. → Sí, bebo café en clase.
>   (No, no bebo café en clase. Bebo café en casa.)

1. Debo estudiar más para esta clase.
2. Leo todas las partes de las lecciones.
3. Comprendo bien cuando el profesor / la profesora habla.
4. Asisto al laboratorio con frecuencia.
5. Abrimos los libros en clase.
6. Escribimos mucho en clase.
7. Aprendemos a hablar español en esta clase.*
8. Vendemos los libros al final del año (*year*).

Paso 2. Now turn to the person next to you and rephrase each sentence, using **tú** forms of the verbs and **¿verdad?** (*right?*). Your partner will indicate whether the sentences are true for him or her.

> MODELO: E1: Debes estudiar más para esta clase, ¿verdad? →
>   E2: Sí, debo estudiar más. (No, no debo estudiar más.) (No. Debo estudiar más para la clase de matemáticas.)

B Unas diferencias familiares: Habla Paquita. The following paragraphs tell Paquita's side of the disagreement you read about in the minidialogue. Complete them with the correct form of the infinitives.

Según mi padre, los jóvenes (deber[1]) asistir a clase todos los días. Papá también (creer[2]) que nosotros (deber[3]) estudiar con frecuencia. Papá (creer[4]) que no es necesario mirar la televisión. Según él, es más interesante (leer[5]) el periódico o una novela. Él sólo trabaja, (comer[6]) y (leer[7]).

Yo no soy como papá. Me gusta mirar la televisión todas las noches. (*Yo:* abrir[8]) los libros a veces y (leer[9]) cuando es necesario, pero... tengo[a] muchos amigos y (*yo:* creer[10]) que es más interesante estar con ellos.

[a]*I have*

C En casa, con la familia

Paso 1. Form complete sentences about a Saturday morning spent at home with the family, based on the cues given and adding words when needed. When the subject pronoun is given in parentheses, do not use it in the sentence. Before you start,

---

*Note: **aprender** + **a** + *infinitive* = to learn how to (*do something*).

scan through the sentences to get their gist, and make sure you know the meaning of all of the words.

1. (*yo*) leer / periódico / como siempre (*as always*)
2. niños / leer / y / mirar / televisión
3. Paquita / escribir / ejercicios / para / clase de español
4. hoy por la tarde / (*ella*) asistir / a / fiesta
5. por eso / (*ella*) deber / estudiar / por / mañana
6. (*yo*) creer / que / Paquita / aprender / a / ser / más responsable
7. mi esposa / abrir / carta (*letter*) / de / abuelo
8. él / vivir / en / otro / ciudad
9. (*nosotros*) creer / que / (*él*) deber / pasar / las vacaciones / con nosotros
10. a las doce y media / todos / (*nosotros*) comer / juntos (*together*)

Paso 2. From whose point of view is the story told? If you said Paquita's father, you are right. Now retell the story as if you were Paquita, using the same cues as a guide and making the necessary adjustments: **1. Mi padre lee...**

NOTA COMUNICATIVA: Telling How Frequently You Do Things

Use the following words and phrases to tell how often you perform an activity.

todos los días,	every day, always	**a veces**	at times
siempre		**casi nunca**	almost never
con frecuencia	frequently	**nunca**	never

Hablo con mis amigos **todos los días.** Hablo con mis padres **una vez a la semana. Casi nunca** hablo con mis abuelos. Y **nunca** hablo con mis tíos que viven en Italia.

For now, use the expressions **casi nunca** and **nunca** only at the beginning of a sentence. You will learn more about how to use them in Grammar Section 17.

D **¿Con qué frecuencia?**

Paso 1. How frequently do you do the following things?

	CON FRECUENCIA	A VECES	CASI NUNCA	NUNCA
1. Asisto al laboratorio de lenguas (o uso las cintas).	☐	☐	☐	☐
2. Recibo paquetes (*packages*).	☐	☐	☐	☐
3. Escribo poemas.	☐	☐	☐	☐
4. Leo novelas románticas.	☐	☐	☐	☐
5. Como en una pizzería.	☐	☐	☐	☐
6. Hablo con mis abuelos/hijos.	☐	☐	☐	☐
7. Aprendo palabras nuevas en español.	☐	☐	☐	☐
8. Escucho música mientras (*while*) estudio.	☐	☐	☐	☐
9. Compro regalos para los amigos.	☐	☐	☐	☐
10. Vendo los libros al final del semestre/trimestre.	☐	☐	☐	☐

Paso 2. Now compare your answers with those of another student in the class. Then answer the following questions with that student. *Note:* **ninguno/a** = *neither of us.*

	YO	MI COMPAÑERO/A	LOS/LAS DOS	NINGUNO/A
1. ¿Quién estudia mucho el español?	☐	☐	☐	☐
2. ¿Quién come más (*the most*) pizza?	☐	☐	☐	☐
3. ¿Quién es muy generoso/a?	☐	☐	☐	☐
4. ¿Quién es muy romántico/a?	☐	☐	☐	☐
5. ¿Quién recibe más paquetes?	☐	☐	☐	☐

Segundo paso

VOCABULARIO ▼▼▼▼▼▼▼▼▼▼▼▼▼▼▼▼▼▼▼▼▼▼▼

Estar with adjectives

¿Cómo te sientes hoy? (*How do you feel today?*)
This is another way of asking **¿Cómo estás?**

Estar is used with adjectives to express temporary conditions or observations that are true at a given moment but that do not describe inherent qualities of the noun. The following adjectives are generally used with **estar.** Some of them are cognates. Can you guess their meaning?

abierto/a	open	**limpio/a**	clean
aburrido/a	bored	**nervioso/a**	¿ ?
cansado/a	tired	**ocupado/a**	¿ ?
cerrado/a	closed	**ordenado/a**	¿ ?
contento/a	¿ ?	**preocupado/a**	¿ ?
desordenado/a	¿ ?	**solo/a**	alone
enfermo/a	sick, ill	**sucio/a**	dirty
furioso/a	¿ ?	**triste**	sad

Práctica

A **¡Un día desastroso para los Rodríguez!** This Sunday, the Rodríguez family cannot go to the park with their children and have lunch with the grandparents, as they usually do. Complete the description of their day with appropriate adjectives. More than one answer is possible in some cases.

1. El Sr. Rodríguez necesita trabajar hoy porque esta semana está muy _____ en la oficina.
2. Martita, la hija pequeña, no está bien hoy. Está _____. Desgraciadamente (*Unfortunately*), la oficina del médico está _____. Por eso la Sra. Rodríguez está _____.
3. Pepito está muy _____ hoy porque no está en el parque con sus abuelos. Está muy _____ en casa.
4. Los abuelos están _____, en casa. Hoy no comen con la familia.
5. Hoy la casa de los Rodríguez es un desastre. Está muy _____ y muy desordenada, con cosas por todas partes.

B **Reacciones.** ¿Cómo está Ud. en las siguientes (*following*) situaciones?

1. Cuando saco (*I get*) A en un examen, estoy _____.
2. Cuando trabajo mucho, estoy _____.
3. Cuando bebo mucho café, estoy _____.
4. Cuando no estoy con mis amigos, estoy _____.
5. Por lo general, cuando estoy en clase, estoy _____.
6. Los lunes por la mañana, estoy _____.
7. Los viernes por la tarde, estoy _____.

▼    **ESTRUCTURAS**

RECICLADO

Before beginning Grammar Section 8, review what you already know about expressing possession. Tell which of your friends or relatives has something that you like. Use **de** + noun as well as the possessive adjective **mi** or **mis.**

MODELO: Me gusta mucho el coche **de mi tío Harry.** Me gusta la casa **de mis abuelos.**

Sugerencias: coche, casa (apartamento, cuarto), computadora, mascota

8. Expressing Possession

Possessive Adjectives (Unstressed)*

▼ **En el periódico**

▼ Querida Antonia,
▼ Tengo un problema muy grave con *mis* padres. *Mi* hermana y yo siempre
▼ compramos cintas y discos compactos en el centro comercial los fines de semana.
▼ *Nuestros* padres no creen que debemos gastar *su* dinero en cosas tontas. *Nuestra*
▼ situación es desesperada. ¿Cuál es *tu* consejo?
▼ Sin Música... y sin dinero

▼ Querida Sin Música,
▼ *Tu* situación es difícil, pero no es imposible de solucionar. Tú y *tu* hermana
▼ deben hablar con *sus* padres. Deben explicarles que *su* interés por la música es
▼ serio. Por otro lado, deben recordar que gastan el dinero de *sus* padres. Ellos
▼ tienen el derecho de imponer límites. ¡Buena suerte!
▼ Antonia

▲ ▲ ▲

▼ ¿Qué usa Sin Música, **mi** o **mis**?

▼ 1. _____ padres tienen dinero.
▼ 2. _____ hermana desea comprar más cintas.
▼ 3. _____ situación es terrible.

¿Qué usa Antonia, **tu** o **tus**?

4. _____ padres están preocupados.
5. _____ problema es difícil.
6. _____ hermana debe hablar con _____ padres.

You have already used **mi(s)**, one of the possessive adjectives in Spanish. Here is the complete set.

POSSESSIVE ADJECTIVES			
my	**mi** libro/mesa **mis** libros/mesas	*our*	nuestr**o** libro nuestr**a** mesa nuestr**os** libros nuestr**as** mesas
your	**tu** libro/mesa **tus** libros/mesas	*your*	vuestr**o** libro vuestr**a** mesa vuestr**os** libros vuestr**as** mesas
your, his, *her, its* }	**su** libro/mesa **sus** libros/mesas	*your,* *their* }	**su** libro/mesa **sus** libros/mesas

---

*There is another set of possessives called the *stressed possessive adjectives,* which can be used as nouns. For information on them, See Appendix 1, *Using Adjectives as Nouns.*

In the newspaper Dear Antonia, I have a very serious problem with my parents. My sister and I always buy tapes and CDs at the mall on the weekends. Our parents don't think that we should spend their money on foolish things. Our situation is desperate. What is your advice? Without Music . . . and without money   Dear Without Music, Your situation is difficult, but it isn't impossible to solve. You and your sister should talk to your parents. You should explain to them that your interest in music is serious. On the other hand, you should remember that you're spending your parents' money. They have the right to impose limits. Good luck! Antonia

In Spanish, the ending of a possessive adjective agrees in form with the person or thing possessed, not with the owner or possessor. Note that these possessive adjectives are placed before the noun.

$$\text{Son} \left\{ \begin{array}{l} \text{mis} \\ \text{tus} \\ \text{sus} \end{array} \right\} \text{libros.} \qquad \text{Es} \left\{ \begin{array}{l} \text{nuestra} \\ \text{vuestra} \\ \text{su} \end{array} \right\} \text{casa.}$$

The possessive adjectives **mi(s)**, **tu(s)**, and **su(s)** show agreement in number only with the nouns they modify. **Nuestro/a/os/as** and **vuestro/a/os/as**, like all adjectives that end in **-o**, show agreement in both number and gender.

¡OJO!   Su(s) can have several different equivalents in English: *your* (*sing.* or *pl.*), *his, her,* and *their.* Usually its meaning will be clear in context. For example, if you are admiring the new car of someone you address as **Ud.** and ask **¿Es nuevo su coche?**, it is clear from the context that you mean *Is your car new?* But when context is not enough, **de** and a noun or pronoun are used instead of **su(s)** to indicate the possessor.

$$\left. \begin{array}{l} \text{el coche} \\ \text{la casa} \\ \text{los parientes} \\ \text{las primas} \end{array} \right\} \begin{array}{l} \textbf{de} \text{ él / ella / Ud. / ellos / ellas / Uds. /...} \\ \textbf{de} \text{ Raúl / los niños / Marcos y Patricia} \end{array}$$

Note how the meaning of **su** is clarified in this brief exchange.

—¿Son jóvenes sus hijos?
—¿Los hijos de quién?
—Los hijos de Roberto (de él).
—Ah, sí. Sus hijos son muy pequeños.

Práctica

A **Descripciones.** Which nouns can these possessive adjectives modify without changing form?

1. **su:** padre / casas / madre / abuelos / foto / esposas
2. **tus:** discos / amigas / primo / compañera de cuarto / clases / cursos
3. **mi:** abuelos / dinero / música / mesas / librerías / compañera / hija
4. **sus:** estudiantes / esposos / hija / nación / lugar / ciudades
5. **nuestras:** primos / abuelas / madres / padres / clases / noches
6. **nuestro:** escritorio / consejera / profesor / tío / esposos / libro
7. **vuestros:** padres / amigas / prima / dinero / abuelos

B **¿Cómo está la familia de Pepe García?** Conteste según el modelo.
¡OJO!   Use **estar** para describir su condición o estado.

MODELO: familia / contenta → Su familia está contenta.

1. abuelos / cansados
2. hermanos / furiosos
3. mamá / enferma
4. papá / preocupado por el dinero
5. primas / nerviosas
6. tíos / ocupados

C **El día de nuestros padres.** Miguel and Maripepa are talking about their parents. Form complete sentences based on these words and phrases, making any necessary changes.

1. nuestro / padres / estar / ocupado / hoy
2. papá / estar / en / su / oficina

3. su / papeles / estar / muy / desordenado...
4. y / su / clientes / estar / muy / preocupado
5. mamá / estar / con / su / hermanas
6. (*ellas*) estar / en / casa / de / su / padres
7. su / padres / ¡nuestro / abuelos! / estar / enfermo / hoy
8. por eso / nuestro / tías / estar / muy / preocupado

D **Entrevista.** You have already learned a great deal about the families of your classmates and instructor. This interview will help you gather more information. Use the questions as a guide to interview your instructor or a classmate and take notes on what he or she says. (Use **tu[s]** when interviewing a classmate.) Then report the information to the class. *Note:* To indicate that you do not have a particular family member, say **No tengo** (**padre, hermanos, ...**).

1. ¿Cómo es su familia? ¿grande? ¿pequeña? ¿Cuántas personas viven en su casa? ¿en la casa de sus padres?
2. ¿Son norteamericanos sus padres? ¿hispanos? ¿De dónde son?
3. ¿Son simpáticos sus padres? ¿generosos? ¿cariñosos?
4. ¿Trabaja su padre/madre? ¿Dónde?
5. ¿Cuántos hijos tienen sus padres?
6. ¿Cómo son sus hermanos? ¿listos? ¿traviesos (*mischievous*)? ¿trabajadores?
7. ¿Viven sus padres en una casa o en un apartamento? ¿Cómo es su casa/apartamento?
8. ¿Sus abuelos viven también en la casa / el apartamento?
9. ¿De dónde son sus abuelos? ¿Cuántos hijos tienen?
10. ¿Tiene Ud. esposo/a (compañero/a de cuarto)? ¿Quién es? ¿Cómo es? ¿Trabaja o estudia?

A **La familia del nuevo nieto.** The following sentences will form a description of a family in which there is a new grandchild. The name of the person described is given in parentheses after each description (if necessary). Form complete sentences based on the words given, in the order given. Conjugate the verbs and add other words if necessary.

As you create the sentences, complete the family tree given on page 89 with the names of the family members. *Hint:* Hispanic families pass on first names just like families in the United States.

1. yo / ser / abuela / panameño (Anita)
2. nuevo / nieto / ser / de / Estados
   Unidos (Juan José)
3. Juan José / ser / padre / nieto
4. Juan José / también / ser / abuelo /
   panameño
5. uno / de / tías / de / nieto / ser / médico (Pilar)
6. otro / tía / ser / profesor / famoso (Julia)
7. madre / niño / ser / norteamericano (Paula)
8. hermana / niño / se llama / Concepción

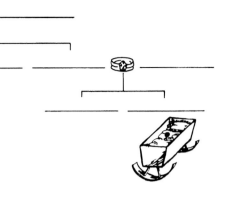

Ahora conteste estas preguntas según la descripción de la familia.

1. ¿De dónde son los abuelos y tías?
2. ¿De dónde es la madre del niño?

NOTA CULTURAL: Saints' Days

Hispanics traditionally celebrate their saint's day (**el día del santo**). Each day of the year on the Catholic calendar has the name of a different saint. If your name is Ana, you celebrate the day of Saint Anne, July 26, as your saint's day. If your name is Juan, you celebrate Saint John's day on June 24.

Since the Hispanic world is primarily Catholic, the saint's day celebration is a widespread tradition. Birthdays are celebrated as well. Sometimes one's birthday is the same as one's saint's day.

> Te felicito el Día
> de tu Santo
> Deseando que la dicha
> y alegría
> De este venturoso día
> Llenen tu vida de ilusión
> y encanto.

B **El Día de San José.** Complete the following paragraphs about a saint's day celebration. Give the correct form of the words in parentheses, as suggested by the context. When two possibilities are given in parentheses, select the correct word.

Hoy (*nosotros:* celebrar[1]) el día de San José* en (nuestro[2]) casa. Hay (veintiún/veintiuna[3]) personas para comer y mi madre (preparar[4]) una (gran/grande[5]) comida.[a] El día de San José (ser[6]) una fiesta muy importante para (nuestro[7]) familia porque hay (mucho[8]) cosas que celebrar. Primero,[b] es (el/la[9]) día del santo de mi padre y de mi abuelo. Por eso ellos (recibir[10]) muchos regalos. También es el santo de mi tío Pepe y de (su[11]) hijo Pepito.[†] Finalmente, es el cumpleaños[c] de mi (hermano[12]) Luisa.

[a]*meal*   [b]*First*   [c]*birthday*

---

*The day of Saint Joseph is celebrated on March 19 (**el 19 de marzo**).
[†]**Pepe** and **Pepito** are nicknames for **José**.

Felicidades
en el Día
de tu Santo

(Mi[13]) abuelos están (contento[14]) porque todos (su[15]) hijos y nietos están (junto[16]). Nosotros (estar[17]) contentos porque ellos no (estar[18]) enfermos. (El/La[19]) problema es que mi madre (necesitar[20]) trabajar mucho y está muy (cansado[21]). ¡Mi familia (comer[22]) mucho los días de fiesta!

¿Cierto o falso? Corrija las oraciones falsas.

1. Muchas personas comen en casa hoy.
2. El padre prepara la comida.
3. Cinco personas celebran algo (*something*).
4. Todos están muy contentos.

SITUACIÓN   Hablando de la familia y de la edad[a]

—¿Cuántos hermanos tienes?
—Tengo cuatro hermanas y dos hermanos.
—¡Madre mía![b] ¿Y tienes muchos parientes?
—¡Uf! Tengo un montón.[c] Mis padres tienen muchos hermanos también. Tengo más de[d] veinte primos.
—¿Cuántos años tiene tu hermana pequeña?
—Once. ¡No, perdón, doce! Hoy es su cumpleaños.[e]

[a]*age*   [b]Madre... *Wow!*   [c]un... *a lot*   [d]más... *more than*   [e]*birthday*

NOTAS COMUNICATIVAS SOBRE EL DIÁLOGO

In Spanish, age is expressed with the verb **tener** + **... años** (literally, *to have . . . years*). In the dialogue, you have seen many of the forms of **tener.** Use them in the following sentences to ask and tell about age.

¿Cuántos años tiene(s)?
Tengo... años.

Conversación

Practice the dialogue with a classmate. When you are comfortable with it, vary it to talk about members of your family.

PARA ESCRIBIR

Write two brief paragraphs that describe your family. Use the questions in **Entrevista** (page 88) as a guide for the first paragraph, which should contain details about who is in your family. For the second paragraph, think about the following questions.

1. ¿Es muy unida (*close-knit*) su familia?
2. ¿Con quién habla Ud. cuando tiene problemas?
3. ¿Cree Ud. que es una familia típica? ¿Por qué sí o por qué no?

▼ ▼ ▼ ▼ ▼ ▼ ▼ ▼ ▼ ▼ ▼ ▼ ▼ ▼ ▼ ▼ **VOCABULARIO** ▼ ▼ ▼ ▼ ▼ ▼ ▼ ▼ ▼ ▼ ▼ ▼ ▼ ▼ ▼

Verbos

abrir to open
aprender to learn
asistir (a) to attend, go (to) (*a class, function*)
beber to drink
comer to eat
comprender to understand
creer (en) to think, believe (in)
deber (+ *inf.*) should, must, ought to (*do something*)
escribir to write
leer to read
recibir to receive
vender to sell
vivir to live

Los parientes

el/la abuelo/a grandfather/ grandmother
los abuelos grandparents
la esposa/mujer wife
el esposo/marido husband
la hermana sister
el/la hijo/a son/daughter
los hijos children
la madre (mamá) mother (mom)
el/la nieto/a grandson/ granddaughter
el padre (papá) father (dad)
el/la primo/a cousin
el/la sobrino/a nephew/niece
el/la tío/a uncle/aunt

Repaso: la familia, el hermano, los padres

Las mascotas

el pájaro bird
el pez (*pl.* **peces**) fish

Repaso: el gato, el perro

¿Con qué frecuencia?

a veces at times
casi nunca almost never
con frecuencia frequently
nunca never
siempre always

Repaso: todos los días

Otros sustantivos

la carta letter
el centro comercial mall
la novela novel
el periódico newspaper

Adjetivos

cariñoso/a affectionate
familiar family-related, of the family
junto/a together

Adjetivos posesivos

mi(s), tu(s), su(s), nuestro/a(s), vuestro/a(s)

Adjetivos con *estar*

abierto/a open
aburrido/a bored

cansado/a tired
cerrado/a closed
contento/a happy
desordenado/a messy
enfermo/a sick, ill
furioso/a angry
limpio/a clean
nervioso/a nervous
ocupado/a busy
ordenado/a neat, orderly
preocupado/a worried
solo/a alone
sucio/a dirty
triste sad

Palabras adicionales

ahora now
pero but
¿por qué? why
según according to
sin without
tener... años to be . . . years old
tengo I have
tiene(s) you have

Self-Test

Use the tape that accompanies this text to test yourself briefly on the important points of this chapter.

del mundo hispánico 2
La comunidad mexicanoamericana

Los mexicanoamericanos forman el grupo más grande[a] de hispanos en los Estados Unidos, el 60% (por ciento) aproximadamente. La gran mayoría[b] vive en el sudoeste[c] de los Estados Unidos: en Texas, Nuevo México, California, etcétera. También hay importantes comunidades mexicanas en otras grandes ciudades del medio oeste,[d] como Chicago.

Los mexicanoamericanos son también el grupo hispano más antiguo[e] en los Estados Unidos. De hecho,[f] todo el actual sudoeste de los Estados Unidos perteneció[g] primero[h] a México hasta 1848 (mil ochocientos cuarenta y ocho). Aztlán, la legendaria «tierra blanca[i]» de origen de los aztecas, hoy está al norte de la frontera[j] de México y forma parte de los Estados Unidos.

[a]más... *biggest* [b]La... *The vast majority* [c]*southwest* [d]medio... *midwest* [e]más... *oldest* [f]De... *In fact,* [g]*belonged* [h]*originally* [i]tierra... *white land* [j]*border, frontier*

Para la gente (*people*) que vive en la frontera, esta (*it*) es sólo una línea artificial, una realidad política que no divide dos pueblos.

La frontera de 1.952 (mil novecientos cincuenta y dos) millas que separa a EE UU[a] de México es el único límite internacional en el mundo[b] donde un país pobre y en desarrollo[c] bordea una nación poderosa[d] y desarrollada. En el siglo pasado,[e] esta atmósfera originó[f] un estilo de vida y unas reglas[g] diferentes para los millones de habitantes de las ciudades gemelas[h] de El Paso–Ciudad Juárez, Laredo–Nuevo Laredo, Brownsville–Matamoros y otras.»

Extraído de «La frontera: ¿une o separa?», *Más.*

[a]*abbreviation for* Estados Unidos [b]*world* [c]un... *a poor developing country* [d]*powerful* [e]siglo... *last century* [f]*gave rise to* [g]*rules* [h]*twin*

Un niño juega a romper (*is trying to break*) una piñata. ¿Sabía Ud. (*Did you know*) que la piñata es una tradición mexicana? La piñata es una figura de papel (un animal, un objeto) que contiene regalos y dulces (*candy*). En las fiestas para niños, se suspende del techo (*ceiling*) para que los niños jueguen a romperla (*try to break it*) con un palo (*stick*).

«Cake-Walk», de Carmen Lomas Garza, pintora mexicanoamericana de Kingsville, Texas, que ahora vive en San Francisco. Este cuadro (*painting*) representa la vida y el ambiente (*atmosphere*) de un barrio mexicanoamericano. ¿Le gusta?

Una niña mexicanoamericana de Chicago, Illinois.

Yo soy hijo de la tierra,[a]
y heredero[b] de la raza[c];
tengo rasgos[d] de españoles
y de aztecas en mi alma.[e]

Mario Benítez, poeta chicano, de «Yo soy hijo de la tierra»

[a]*land*   [b]*heir*   [c]*Spanish-speaking peoples*
[d]*tengo... I have traces*   [e]*soul*

Henry Cisneros, Ministro de Vivienda y Desarrollo Urbano (*Secretary of Housing and Urban Development*). Anteriormente fue (*he was*) alcalde (*mayor*) de San Antonio, Texas.

¡Qué interesante!

▼ En todos los casos, compare sus respuestas (*your answers*) con las de otros
▼ compañeros.

▼
   1. En grupos, hagan una lista de personas importantes y famosas de origen
▼   mexicano que Uds. conocen (*you know*).
▼
   2. ¿Qué cosas o ideas relaciona Ud. con los mexicanoamericanos?
▼
   3. ¿Qué lugares de los Estados Unidos relaciona Ud. con los hispanos de
▼   origen mexicanoamericano?

Primer paso

La ropa

¿Qué LLEVAS HOY?

Más vocabulario

un par de (zapatos, medias...)	a pair of (shoes, stockings, . . .)	llevar	to wear; to carry; to take
es de (lana, algodón, seda)	it is made of (wool, cotton, silk)	usar	to wear; to use
Está de moda.	It's in style.		

Note another use of **ser** + **de:** to tell what material something is made of.

Práctica

A **Descripciones.** ¿Qué ropa llevan estas personas?

1. El Sr. Rivera lleva _____.
2. La Srta. Alonso lleva _____. El perro lleva _____.
3. Sara lleva _____.
4. Alfredo lleva _____. Necesita comprar _____.

De estas personas, ¿quién está de vacaciones? ¿Quién trabaja hoy? ¿Quién se prepara (is getting ready) para una fiesta? ¿Quién no trabaja en este momento (right now)?

¿POR O PARA?

Another important use of the preposition **para** is to express *in order to,* followed by an infinitive.

Para llegar al centro, tomo el auto-   *(In order) To get downtown, I take*
bús número 16.   *the number 16 bus.*

B **Ud. y la ropa.** Complete estas oraciones lógicamente.

1. Para ir (*go*) a la universidad, me gusta usar _____.
2. Para ir a las fiestas con los amigos, me gusta usar _____.
3. Para pasar un día en la playa (*beach*), me gusta llevar _____.
4. Cuando estoy en casa todo el día, llevo _____.
5. Nunca uso _____.
6. _____ es/son un artículo de ropa absolutamente necesario para mí.
7. Muchos ejecutivos (Muchas ejecutivas) llevan _____.
8. Para practicar deportes la gente lleva _____.
9. La ropa de _____ [*material*] es muy elegante.
10. La ropa de _____ [*material*] es muy práctica.

DE AQUÍ Y DE ALLÁ

There are a number of synonyms for **bonito/a** that you can use to talk about clothing (or people as well). **Lindo/a** and **mono/a** both mean *cute*. **Hermoso/a** and **bello/a** are the equivalents of *beautiful* or *handsome*. The word **precioso/a** is also frequently used, without the "cutesy" connotations of its English cognate *precious*. And Puerto Ricans frequently use **chévere** to describe anything that they like a lot. Here are some additional phrases to use to talk about what's "in" . . . and what's not.

WHAT'S "IN"?

Está(n) en onda (*the latest*).
Es el último grito (*last word, latest*) de la moda (española, norteamericana, francesa...)
Se llevan (*People are wearing*) los *bluejeans,* las faldas cortas...

WHAT'S "OUT"?

Está muy visto/a. (Están muy vistos/as.) (*You see it/them everywhere.*)
Está pasado/a (Están pasados/as) de moda.
No se llevan (las camisetas, las faldas largas)...

C Comentando sobre (*about*) la moda.

Paso 1. Diga si Ud. cree que las siguientes oraciones
son ciertas o falsas. Corrija las oraciones falsas.

1. Los *bluejeans* siempre están de moda.
2. Actualmente (*Currently*) no se llevan las faldas cortas.
3. Los pantalones de campana (*bell-bottom*) son el último
   grito en los Estados Unidos.
4. ¡La ropa de Madonna es horrible!
5. La ropa de Eddie Vedder es muy bonita.
6. Me gusta mucho la ropa estilo *rap*.

Paso 2. Ahora invente tres oraciones que expresan sus
ideas sobre la moda. Luego compárelas con las de sus
compañeros. ¿Están todos de acuerdo sobre la moda?

Sugerencias: los abrigos largos, los *bluejeans,* las chaquetas
de cuero (*leather*), las gorras de béisbol, la moda francesa

PALOMA PICASSO nació en
Francia, pero pasó parte de
sus años juveniles en España
y se considera una diseñadora hispana. Se especializa en joyería y diseña

para la famosa casa Tiffany.
Los pendientes con el diseño
"XX" se han convertido en
su marca de fábrica. También diseña porcelana fina,
cristalería y azulejos para
Villeroy & Boch, y perfumes
y cosméticos para Cosmair.
En 1988 Paloma Picasso recibió el premio MODA.

*"Los accesorios
son la clave
del buen vestir"*

▼ **PRONUNCIACIÓN**

b/v

In Spanish, the pronunciation of the letters **b** and **v** is identical. At the beginning of
a phrase or sentence—that is, after a pause—or after **m** or **n,** the letters **b** and **v**
are pronounced just like the English stop [b]. Everywhere else they are pronounced
like the fricative [ƀ], produced by creating friction when pushing the air through
the lips. This sound has no equivalent in English.

A. [b] bueno viejo veinte Vicente bota también hombre sombrero
  bienvenido vocabulario

B. [ƀ] llevar libro pobre abrir abrigo universidad abuelo palabras
  sobrino chévere

C. [b / ƀ] bueno / es bueno busca / Ud. busca bien / muy bien
  en Venezuela / de Venezuela visita / él visita en Bolivia / de Bolivia
  baño / traje de baño

D. [b / ƀ] beber bebida vivir biblioteca Babel vívido

ESTRUCTURAS ▼▼▼▼▼▼▼▼▼▼▼▼▼▼▼▼▼▼▼▼▼

9. Expressing Actions and States

Tener and *venir*; *preferir*, *querer*, and *poder*; Some Idioms with *tener*

▼ **Decisiones instantáneas**

▼ Conteste rápidamente.

▼ —¿Qué **prefieres**?
▼ —**Prefiero**...

▼ 1. los zapatos o los zapatos de tenis
▼ 2. un traje o unos *bluejeans*
▼ 3. leer una novela o mirar la televisión
▼ 4. los gatos o los perros
▼ 5. los coches japoneses o los
▼   norteamericanos

tener (to have)	**venir** (to come)	**preferir** (to prefer)	**querer** (to want)	**poder** (to be able, can)
tengo	vengo	prefiero	quiero	puedo
tienes	vienes	prefieres	quieres	puedes
tiene	viene	prefiere	quiere	puede
tenemos	venimos	preferimos	queremos	podemos
tenéis	venís	preferís	queréis	podéis
tienen	vienen	prefieren	quieren	pueden

The **yo** forms of **tener** and **venir** are irregular: **tengo, vengo.** In other forms of **tener, venir, preferir,** and **querer,** when the stem vowel **e** is stressed, it becomes **ie: tienes, vienes, prefieres, quieres,** and so on. Similarly, the stem vowel **o** in **poder** becomes **ue** when stressed. In vocabulary lists these changes are shown in parentheses after the infinitive: **poder (ue).** You will learn more verbs of this type in Grammar Section 12.

Some Idioms with *tener*

An *idiom* (**un modismo**) is a group of words that has meaning to the speakers of a language but that does not necessarily appear to make sense when examined word by word. Idiomatic expressions are often different from one language to another. For example, in English, *to pull Mary's leg* usually means *to tease her,* not *to grab her leg and pull it.* In Spanish, *to pull Mary's leg* is **tomarle el pelo a María** (literally, *to take Mary's hair*).

Adivinanza

You can find the answer to this **adivinanza** in the explanation of what an idiom is.

Soy sublime en la mujer, pero cortito en el hombre y sin pudor a mi nombre[a] me toman sin yo querer.[b]

[a]sin... *with no regard for my (good) name* [b]me... *they pull me against my will*

Many ideas expressed in English with the verb *to be* are expressed in Spanish with idioms using **tener**. You have already used one **tener** idiom: **tener... años.** Here are some additional ones. Note that they describe a condition or state that a person can experience.

tener miedo (de)	to be afraid (of)	**tener razón**	to be right
tener prisa	to be in a hurry	**no tener razón**	to be wrong

Other **tener** idioms include **tener ganas de** (*to feel like*) and **tener que** (*to have to*). The infinitive is always used after these two idiomatic expressions.

Tengo ganas de comer.	*I feel like eating.*
¿No **tienes ganas de descansar**?	*Don't you feel like resting?*
Tienen que ser prácticos.	*They have to be practical.*
¿No **tiene Ud. que leer** este capítulo?	*Don't you have to read this chapter?*

Práctica

A **Sara tiene mucha tarea.**

Paso 1. Haga oraciones con las palabras indicadas.

1. Sara / tener / muchos exámenes
2. (*ella*) venir / a / universidad / todos los días
3. hoy / trabajar / hasta / nueve / de / noche
4. preferir / estudiar / en / biblioteca
5. querer / leer / más / pero / no poder
6. por eso / regresar / a / casa
7. tener / ganas de / leer / más / pero / es / imposible
8. unos amigos / venir a mirar / televisión
9. Sara / decidir / mirar / televisión / con ellos

Paso 2. Now retell the same sequence of events, first as if they had happened to you, using **yo** as the subject of all but sentence number 8, then as if they had happened to you and your roommate, using **nosotros/as**.

B **Situaciones.** Expand the situations described in these sentences by using an appropriate idiom with **tener.** There is more than one possible answer.

MODELO: Tengo un examen mañana. Por eso... → Por eso **tengo que estudiar.**

1. ¿Cuántos años? ¿Cuarenta? No, yo...
2. Un perro feroz vive en esta casa. Por eso yo...
3. Sí, la capital de la Argentina es Buenos Aires. Tú...
4. No, dos y dos no son cinco. Son cuatro. Tú...
5. Tengo que estar en el laboratorio a las tres. Ya son las tres menos cuarto. Yo...
6. Cuando hay un terremoto (*earthquake*), todos...
7. ¿Los exámenes de la clase de español? ¡Son siempre muy fáciles! Yo no...
8. Esta noche hay una fiesta en el apartamento de un amigo. Yo...

C **Estereotipos.** Draw some conclusions about Lourdes based on this scene. Think about things that she has, needs to or has to do or buy, likes, and so on. When you have finished, compare your assumptions with those of others in the class. Did you all reach the same conclusions?

Palabras útiles: los aretes (*earrings*), el juguete (*toy*), llamar por teléfono, los muebles (*furniture*), el sofá, tener alergia a (*to be allergic to*)

NOTA COMUNICATIVA: More About Getting Information

Tag phrases can change statements into questions.

Venden de todo aquí,	¿**no?**	*They sell everything here, right?*
	¿**verdad?**	*(don't they?)*
No necesito impermeable hoy,		*I don't need a raincoat today,*
	¿**verdad?**	*do I?*

¿**Verdad?** is found after affirmative or negative statements; ¿**no?** is usually found after affirmative statements only. The inverted question mark comes immediately before the tag question, not at the beginning of the statement.

D **Entrevista: Preferencias.** Try to predict the choices your instructor will make in each of the following cases. Then, using tag questions, find out if you are correct.

MODELO: El profesor / La profesora tiene...
(muchos libros)/ pocos libros →
Ud. tiene muchos libros, ¿verdad?

1. El profesor / La profesora tiene...
   mucha ropa / poca ropa
   sólo un coche / varios coches
2. Prefiere...
   los gatos / los perros
   la ropa elegante / la ropa informal
3. Quiere comprar...
   un coche deportivo, por ejemplo, un Porsche / una camioneta
   un abrigo / un impermeable
4. Viene a la universidad...
   todos los días / sólo tres veces a la semana
   en coche / en autobús / en bicicleta / a pie (*on foot*)
5. Esta noche tiene ganas de...
   mirar la tele / leer
   comer en un restaurante / comer en casa

Segundo paso

VOCABULARIO

¿De qué color es?

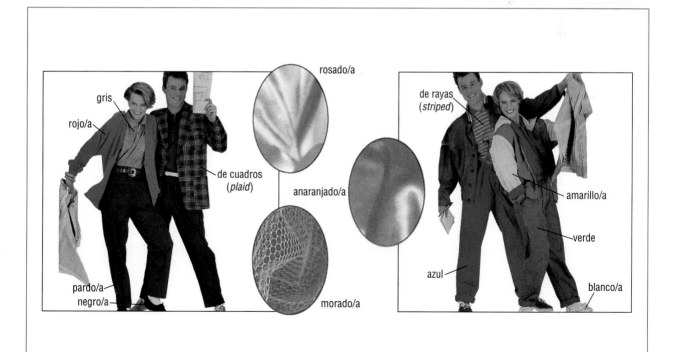

gris
rojo/a
de cuadros (*plaid*)
pardo/a
negro/a
rosado/a
anaranjado/a
morado/a
de rayas (*striped*)
amarillo/a
verde
azul
blanco/a

Práctica

A **Asociaciones.** ¿Qué colores asocia Ud. con... ?

¿el dinero? ¿la una de la mañana? ¿una mañana bonita? ¿una mañana fea? ¿el demonio? ¿los Estados Unidos? ¿una jirafa? ¿un pingüino? ¿un limón? ¿una naranja? ¿un elefante? ¿las flores (*flowers*)?

B **¿De qué color es?** Tell the color of things in your classroom, especially the clothing your classmates are wearing.

MODELOS: El bolígrafo de Anita es amarillo.

            Los calcetines de Roberto son azules. Los de Jaime* son pardos. Los de Julio...

Now describe what someone is wearing, without revealing his or her name. Using your clues, can your classmates guess whom you are describing?

Puerto Rico.

NOTA CULTURAL: Las guayaberas

In the warm parts of Latin America, many men wear a typical article of masculine clothing called **la guayabera.** It's an elegant short-sleeved shirt—often lightly embroidered or with pleats—that is worn outside the pants. It can take the place of the shirt/tie/jacket combination and is much more comfortable in a warm, humid climate. It can be worn in formal or informal situations, to go to the office or to class.

    By the way, the famous Colombian writer Gabriel García Márquez wore a **guayabera** when he accepted his Nobel Prize for Literature.

ESTRUCTURAS ▼

10. ¿Ser o estar?

Summary of the Uses of *ser* and *estar*

▼ Aquí hay un lado (*side*) de la conversación entre una esposa que **está** en un viaje
▼ de negocios (*business trip*) y su esposo, que **está** en casa. Habla el esposo.

---

*You can avoid repeating the noun **calcetines** just by dropping it and retaining the definite article. Here are some other examples of the same construction: **la camisa de Janet y la camisa de Paula** → **la camisa de Janet y *la de* Paula**; **el sombrero del niño y el sombrero de Pablo** → **el sombrero del niño y *el de* Pablo.** For more information on this topic, see Appendix 1, Using Adjectives as Nouns.

▼ Aló. [... [1]] ¿Cómo **estás**, mi amor? [... [2]] ¿Dónde **estás** ahora? [... [3]] ¿Qué hora **es**
▼ allí? [... [4]] ¡Huy!, **es** muy tarde. Y el hotel, ¿cómo **es**? [... [5]] ¿Cuánto cuesta por
▼ noche? [... [6]] **Es** barato para Nueva York, ¿no? Oye, ¿qué haces ahora? [... [7]] Ay,
▼ pobre, lo siento. **Estás** muy ocupada. ¿Con quién **estás** citada mañana? [... [8]]
▼ ¿Quién **es** el dueño de la compañía? [... [9]] Ah, él **es** de Cuba, ¿verdad? [... [10]]
▼ Bueno, ¿adónde vas mañana? [... [11]] ¿Y cuándo regresas? [... [12]] **Está** bien, mi vida.
▼ Hasta luego, ¿eh? [... [13]] Adiós.
▼

▼
▼   ▲ ▲ ▲
▼
▼ Aquí está el otro lado de la conversación... pero las respuestas no están en orden.
▼ Ponga las respuestas en el orden apropiado.
▼
▼ a. _____ Es muy moderno. Me gusta mucho.
▼ b. _____ Sí, pero vive en Nueva York ahora.
▼ c. _____ Son las once y media.
▼ d. _____ Hola, querido. ¿Qué tal?
▼ e. _____ Es el Sr. Cortina.
▼ f. _____ Pues, todavía (*still*) tengo que trabajar.
▼ g. _____ Sí, hasta pronto.
▼ h. _____ Estoy en Nueva York.
▼ i. _____ Mañana todavía estoy en Nueva York. Luego me voy (*I'm going*) a
▼   Boston.
▼ j. _____ Un poco cansada, pero estoy bien.
▼ k. _____ Creo que noventa y cinco dólares.
▼ l. _____ Con un señor de Computec, una nueva compañía de computadoras.
▼ m. _____ Creo que regreso el domingo, pero no estoy segura todavía.

SUMMARY OF THE USES OF *SER*

• To *identify* people and things	Ella **es doctora.**
• To express *nationality;* with **de** to express *origin*	**Son cubanos. Son de** la Habana.
• With **de** to tell of what *material* something is made	El suéter **es de lana.**
• With **para** to tell *for whom something is intended*	El regalo **es para Sara.**
• To tell *time*	**Son las once. Es la una y media.**
• With **de** to express *possession*	**Es el libro de Carlota.**
• With *adjectives* that describe *basic, inherent characteristics*	Ramona **es inteligente.**
• To form many *generalizations*	**Es necesario** llegar temprano. **Es importante** estudiar.

Hello . . . How are you, dear? . . . Where are you now? . . . What time is it there? . . . Boy, it's very late.
And how's the hotel? . . . How much is it per night? . . . That's cheap for New York, isn't it? Hey, what
are you doing now? . . . You poor thing, I'm sorry. You're very busy. Who are you meeting with tomorrow? . . . Who's the owner of the company? . . . Ah, he's from Cuba, isn't he? . . . Well, where are you
going tomorrow? . . . And when are you coming back? . . . OK, sweetheart. See you later, OK? . . .
Goodbye.

SUMMARY OF THE USES OF *ESTAR*

- To tell *location*
- To describe *health*
- With *adjectives* that describe *conditions*
- In a number of *fixed expressions*

El libro **está en la mesa.**
Estoy muy **bien,** gracias.
Estoy muy **ocupada.**

(No) Estoy de acuerdo. Está bien.

Ser and *estar* with Adjectives

Remember: **Ser** is used with adjectives that describe the fundamental qualities of a person, place, or thing. Many adjectives used with **ser** are found in **Capítulo 3.**

Esa mujer es muy **baja.**	*That woman is very short.*
Sus calcetines son **morados.**	*His socks are purple.*
Sus padres son **cariñosos.**	*Their parents are affectionate people.*

Remember: **Estar** is used with adjectives to express conditions or observations that are true at a given moment but that do not describe inherent qualities of the noun. Many adjectives used with **estar** are found in **Capítulo 4.**

Many adjectives can be used with either **ser** or **estar**, depending on what the speaker intends to communicate. In general, when *to be* implies to *look, feel,* or *appear,* **estar** is used. Compare the following pairs of sentences.

Daniel **es** guapo.	*Daniel is handsome. (He is a handsome person.)*
Daniel **está** muy guapo esta noche.	*Daniel looks very nice (handsome) tonight.*
¿Cómo **es** Amalia? —**Es** simpática.	*What is Amalia like (as a person)? —She's nice.*
¿Cómo **está** Amalia? —**Está** enferma todavía.	*How is Amalia (feeling)? —She's still feeling sick.*

Práctica

A **Un regalo especial.** Hay algo nuevo en el cuarto. Es una camisa. ¿Qué puede Ud. decir de ella (*say about it*)? Haga oraciones completas con **es** o **está.**

La camisa es/está...

1. en el escritorio de mi compañero.
2. un regalo de cumpleaños.
3. para mi compañero de cuarto.
4. de la tienda Gap.
5. en una caja (*box*) verde.

6. del padre de mi compañero
7. muy bonita
8. de algodón de cuadros
9. nueva
10. limpia

B **¿Quiénes son?** Ahora identifique a los jóvenes que aparecen en esta foto.

Los jóvenes son/están...

1. mis primos argentinos
2. de Buenos Aires
3. aquí este mes para visitar a la familia
4. al lado de (*alongside*) los abuelos en la foto
5. muy simpáticos
6. muy contentos con el viaje (*trip*) en general
7. un poco cansados hoy

C **Actividades sociales.** Complete the following description with the correct form of **ser** or **estar,** as suggested by the context.

LAS FIESTAS: Las fiestas (ser/estar[1]) populares entre los jóvenes de todas partes del mundo. Ofrecen una buena oportunidad para (ser/estar[2]) con los amigos y conocer[a] a nuevas personas. Imagine que Ud. (ser/estar[3]) en una fiesta con unos amigos hispanos en este momento: todos (ser/estar[4]) alegres, comiendo,[b] hablando y bailando... ¡Y (ser/estar[5]) las dos de la mañana!

LA PANDILLA:[c] Ahora en el mundo hispánico no (ser/estar[6]) necesario tener chaperona. Muchas de las actividades sociales se dan[d] en grupos. Si Ud. (ser/estar[7]) miembro de una pandilla, sus amigos (ser/estar[8]) el centro de su vida social y Ud. y su novio[e] o novia salen[f] frecuentemente con otras parejas[g] o personas del grupo.

[a]*to meet*   [b]*eating*   [c]*group of friends*   [d]*se... occur*   [e]*boyfriend*   [f]*go out*   [h]*couples*

¿Sí o no? ¿Son estas las opiniones de un joven hispano?

1. Me gustan mucho las fiestas.
2. Nunca bailamos en las fiestas.
3. Es necesario salir con chaperona.
4. La pandilla tiene poca importancia para mí.

D **Dos compañeras de cuarto.** Describa este dibujo de un cuarto típico de la residencia. Invente los detalles necesarios. ¿Quiénes son las dos compañeras de cuarto? ¿De dónde son? ¿Cómo son? ¿Dónde están en este momento? ¿Qué hay en el cuarto? ¿En qué condición está el cuarto? ¿Son ordenadas o desordenadas las dos?

Palabras útiles: el cartel (*poster*), la foto

Ana   Estela

Un paso más

Un POCO DE TODO

A **¿Somos tan diferentes?** Answer the following questions. Then ask the same questions of other students in the class to try to find at least one person who answered a given question the way you did.

1. De la siguiente lista, ¿qué cosa tienes ganas de tener? ¿Por qué? **¡OJO!** También es posible contestar: **No quiero tener ninguna** (*any*).
   _____ un abrigo de pieles (*fur*)
   _____ unas botas de cuero (*leather*)
   _____ aretes de oro (*gold*)
   _____ un reloj de diamantes

2. ¿Cuál de las siguientes cosas que dicta la moda es la más tonta, en tu opinión?
   _____ llevar aretes en la nariz (*nose*)
   _____ las gorras puestas (*worn*) al revés
   _____ los *bluejeans* de los grandes diseñadores como Ann Klein o Ralph Lauren
   _____ la ropa de estilo *rap*

3. ¿Cierto o falso?
   _____ Las personas mayores (*older*) deben llevar siempre ropa de colores oscuros, como negro, gris, etcétera.
   _____ Una mujer que tiene más de 30 años nunca debe llevar minifalda.
   _____ Sólo las mujeres deben usar arete(s).
   _____ Cuando la moda cambia (*changes*), es necesario comprar mucha ropa nueva.

NOTA LINGÜÍSTICA: Using *mucho* and *poco*

In the first chapters of **¿Qué tal?**, you have seen and used the words **mucho** and **poco** as both adjectives and adverbs. *Adverbs* (**Los adverbios**) are words that modify verbs, adjectives, or other adverbs: ***quickly, very** smart, **very** quickly*. In Spanish and in English, adverbs are invariable in form.

ADVERB
Rosario estudia **mucho** hoy.   *Rosario is studying a lot today.*

> ADJECTIVE
>
> Rosario tiene **mucha** ropa.   *Rosario has a lot of clothes. She*
> Sobre todo tiene **muchos**   *especially has a lot of shoes.*
> zapatos.

B **Las obligaciones y preferencias universitarias.** Describe the things you have to do as students. Follow the model, giving as many examples as you can for each item.

MODELO: escribir: Como estudiantes, tenemos que... →
          Como estudiantes, tenemos que escribir mucho. Escribimos muchos ejercicios, muchas...

Palabras útiles: oraciones, palabras, composiciones, ejercicios, cartas, novelas, periódicos, poemas, diálogos, personas, estudiantes, compañeros, amigos

1. escribir: Como estudiantes, tenemos que...
2. leer: Debemos...
3. estudiar: También es necesario...
4. Este fin de semana, ¡tenemos ganas de... !

SITUACIÓN   Presentaciones

As you read the following brief dialogues, which offer different ways to introduce people to one another, try to think about the circumstances in which each would be used. Are the situations and language formal or informal?

En casa...

EDUARDO: Abuelo, quiero presentarte[a] a un compañero de clase. Se llama Adolfo Domínguez.
ABUELO: Mucho gusto, Adolfo. ¿Qué tal?
ADOLFO: Muy bien. ¿Y Ud.?

En la universidad...

ADELAIDA: Profesora Benítez, quisiera[b] presentarle a Laura Sánchez, una amiga salvadoreña.[c] Laura, esta es la profesora Rosa María Benítez.
PROFESORA: Mucho gusto, Laura.
LAURA: El gusto es mío, profesora.

Con amigos...

LUIS: Escuchen.[d] Este es Pedro. Es un amigo español que estudia aquí.
PEDRO: ¡Hola a todos!
JULIO: Hola, Pedro. Bienvenido.[e]

[a]*to introduce you*   [b]*I would like*   [c]*de El Salvador*   [d]*Listen up.*   [e]*Welcome.*

NOTAS COMUNICATIVAS SOBRE EL DIÁLOGO

Here's a quick, informal way to introduce one person to another.

To introduce a man: Este es mi amigo (profesor, esposo).
To introduce a woman: Esta es mi amiga (profesora, esposa).

Conversación

With other students, practice making the following introductions, using formal or informal phrases, as appropriate. Tell something about the person you are introducing.

1. You are at home, and a good friend stops by for a few minutes. Introduce him or her to your family.
2. You are in the library and happen to run into two of your professors at the circulation desk. Introduce them to each other.
3. You are at a party. Introduce one good friend to another.
4. Introduce the student next to you to another student.

PARA ESCRIBIR

Tell about your clothing habits by completing the following paragraphs.

Por lo general, prefiero la ropa (elegante/informal). Para ir (*going*) a las clases, generalmente uso _____. Para ir al cine (*movies*) con los amigos, uso _____. Cuando estoy en casa los sábados y domingos, llevo _____. ¡No me gusta nada (*I hate*) llevar _____!

Mi prenda (*article*) favorita es _____. Me gusta porque es (viejo/a, cómodo/a [*comfortable*], de mi color favorito, ¿ ?).

VOCABULARIO

Verbos

llevar to wear; to carry; to take
poder (ue) to be able, can
preferir (ie) to prefer
querer (ie) to want
tener (*irreg.*) to have
usar to wear; to use
venir (*irreg.*) to come

La ropa

el abrigo coat
los aretes earrings
los *bluejeans* jeans
la blusa blouse
la bolsa purse
la bota boot
los calcetines socks
la camisa shirt
la camiseta T-shirt
la cartera wallet
el cinturón belt
la corbata tie
la chaqueta jacket
la falda skirt
la gorra cap
el impermeable raincoat
las medias stockings
los pantalones pants

el par pair
el reloj watch
la sandalia sandal
el sombrero hat
el suéter sweater
el traje suit
el traje de baño swimsuit
el vestido dress
el zapato (de tenis) (tennis) shoe

Los colores

amarillo/a yellow
anaranjado/a orange
azul blue
blanco/a white
gris gray
morado/a purple
negro/a black
pardo/a brown
rojo/a red
rosado/a pink
verde green

Materiales

es de... it is made of . . .
   algodón cotton
   lana wool
   seda silk

Otros sustantivos

el mundo world
la tienda shop, store

Palabras adicionales

de cuadros plaid
de rayas striped
en este momento right now, at
   this very moment
está de moda it's in style
mucho (*adv.*) a lot
mucho/a (*adj.*) a lot
para + *inf.* in order to (*do
   something*)
poco (*adv.*) not much, little
poco/a (*adj.*) not much, little
no tener razón to be wrong
tener...
   ganas de (+ *inf.*) to feel like
      (*doing something*)
   miedo (de) to be afraid (of)
   prisa to be in a hurry
   que (+ *inf.*) to have to (*do
      something*)
   razón to be right
todavía still, yet

¿no?   right?, isn't that so?,
¿verdad?   don't they (you, *etc.*)?

Self-Test

Use the tape that accompanies this text to test
yourself briefly on the important points of this chapter.

LECTURA
cultural

Antes de leer: Finding the Main Parts of a Sentence

When reading Spanish, it's easy to "get lost" in long sentences. Here is a way to get around that difficulty: first omit the words and information set off by commas and concentrate on the main verb and its subject. Try this strategy in this sentence.

> En muchos lugares del mundo hispánico, especialmente en las tierras templadas, los hombres casi siempre llevan camisa con corbata y una chaqueta.

Once you have located the subject and verb (**los hombres, llevan**), you can read the sentence again, adding more information to the framework provided by the phrase *men wear . . .* Men from what part of the world? What, specifically, do they wear? Try the strategy again in this sentence.

> Aunque mi mamá parece tímida, es una mujer independiente con ideas fijas que no tiene miedo de ofrecer su opinión.

The following reading was adapted from an article written for native speakers of Spanish. For this reason, the language in it may seem difficult to you, and there are a lot of words in it that you will not understand. Nevertheless, if you apply the strategy you have just learned to the reading, you will be able to get the gist of it, which is all you have to do. Scan through the reading quickly, resisting the temptation to look up words. The activities in the **Comprensión** section that follows the reading will help you understand more of it.

Jeans, la prenda[a] menos[b] elitista del mundo

Sus orígenes perdidos en el polvo de Texas, los *jeans* sobreviven en nuestra cultura consumista como la prenda más duradera del guardarropa[c] masculino, inscritos para siempre en los anales de la elegancia desde que James Dean y Marlon Brando los consagraron[d] como prenda preferida de los jóvenes rebeldes en la América de la posguerra. Diana Vreeland denomina los *jeans* como el elemento de moda más famoso del siglo,[e] que se lleva de todas las maneras posibles e imaginables. Hay quien los lleva el fin de semana, otros, para ir al trabajo o para salir por la noche. El pantalón vaquero es la única[f] prenda que se puede llevar a

[a]*article of clothing* [b]*least* [c]*wardrobe* [d]*los... anointed them* [e]*century* [f]*only*

cualquier hora del día y en casi todas las ocasiones. Ya sean universitarios o cantantes de rock, hay gente[g] que parece vivir siempre en vaqueros.

Esta prenda no discrimina, no clasifica. Muchos han intentado[h] hacer un vaquero de lujo[i] y ninguno ha rozado siquiera el éxito[j] de los *jeans* normales. Las grandes casas de moda internacionales producen sus propios vaqueros, basados en el famoso y duradero 501.

Los *jeans* son únicos.[k] No responden a las modas y tienen una imagen fuerte y bien definida dentro de la memoria colectiva. Son internacionales, ubicuos,[l] unisex. En definitiva, ningún guardarropa puede estar sin ellos y cada hombre los personaliza llevándolos cuando le parezca oportuno, con corbata o camiseta, a su modo.[m]

[g]personas   [h]han... *have tried*   [i]de... *luxury, high fashion*
[j]ninguno... *none has even touched the success*   [k]*unique*
[l]*found everywhere*   [m]a... *in his own way*

¿Le gusta la ropa que llevan estos jóvenes de México?

Comprensión

A As you were reading, did you apply the reading strategy recommended in **Antes de leer**? Here are some suggestions to help you do so.

- In the first sentence of the text, can you identify the subject and the verb? If you said **los *jeans*** and **sobreviven**, you're right.
- Did you notice the verb **viven** in the longer verb **sobreviven**? The infinitive is **sobrevivir**. Can you conjugate it? Can you deduce its meaning? It is very similar to its English equivalent, *to survive*. What other information can you now "get" about the subject of the sentence?
- What about the last sentence in the second paragraph? Can you find the subject and the verb? The subject is **las casas de moda** and the verb is **producen**. The adjectives **grandes** and **internacionales** modify the subject in this sentence.

B Find at least two other words and phrases in the reading that refer to jeans.

C ¿Cierto o falso?

1. La popularidad de los *jeans* oscila; es decir (*that is*), no es estable.
2. Los vaqueros son de origen norteamericano.
3. El uso de los *jeans* está muy limitado.
4. Los vaqueros son populares en los Estados Unidos pero no en otras partes del mundo.

Primer paso

¿Dónde venden... ?

el supermercado

el centro comercial

las tiendas

la joyería

la zapatería

la boutique

el mercado al aire libre

De Compras

Más vocabulario

comprar	to buy	el precio (fijo)	(fixed, set) price
regatear	to haggle, bargain	las rebajas	sales, reductions
vender	to sell		
¡Venden de todo!	They sell everything!	barato/a	inexpensive
		caro/a	expensive
el almacén	department store		
el centro	downtown; center		

Práctica

A **De compras.** Complete las oraciones lógicamente.

1. Un _____ es una tienda grande.
2. No es posible _____ cuando hay precios fijos.
3. En la librería, _____ de todo: textos y otros libros, cuadernos, lápices, cintas... y hay grandes _____ al final del semestre/trimestre, cuando todo es muy barato.
4. Siempre hay boutiques en los _____.
5. El _____ de una ciudad es la parte central.
6. La tienda donde venden libros se llama la librería. Venden cuadernos y artículos de papel en una papelería. Venden zapatos en _____ y joyas (*jewels*) en una _____.
7. Es posible regatear en _____.

B **Preguntas.** Using tag questions, ask a classmate questions based on the following statements. He or she will answer based on general information.

MODELO: E1: Venden libros en la biblioteca, ¿verdad?
E2: No. No venden libros allí.

1. En un almacén hay precios fijos.
2. Regateamos mucho en los Estados Unidos.
3. No hay muchos mercados al aire libre en esta ciudad.
4. Los *bluejeans* Guess son muy baratos.

113

5. No hay supermercados en el mundo hispano.
6. Hay muchos en el centro de esta ciudad.

DE AQUÍ Y DE ALLÁ

Here are some more ways to talk about prices.

barato:	¡Es/Fue...	It is/was . . .
	una ganga!	a bargain!
	regalado/a!	a gift (so cheap that it was given away)!
caro:	¡Cuesta/Costó...	It costs/cost . . .
	un dineral!	a fortune!
	un ojo de la cara!	an arm and a leg! (lit., an eye from my face!)

Here are more names of stores that end in **-ería.** Can you guess what they sell?

España.

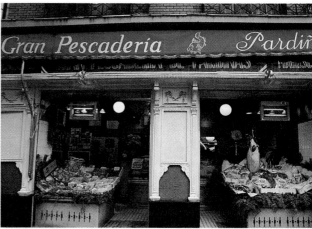

Madrid, España.

PRONUNCIACIÓN ▼

Some sounds, such as English [b], are called *stops* because, as you pronounce them, you briefly stop the flow of air and then release it. Other sounds, such as English [f] and [v], pronounced by pushing air out with a little friction, are called *fricatives*.

Spanish **d** has two basic sounds. At the beginning of a phrase or sentence or after **n** or **l**, it is pronounced as a stop [d] (similar to English *d* in *dog*). Like the Spanish [t], it is produced by putting the tongue against the back of the upper teeth. In all other cases, it is pronounced as a fricative [đ], that is, like the *th* sound in English *they* and *another.*

A [d] diez   dos   doscientos   doctor
            ¿dónde?   el doctor   el dinero   venden

B [đ] mucho dinero adiós   usted   seda
            ¿adónde?   la doctora   cuadros   todo

C 1. ¿Dónde está el dinero?   4. ¿Qué estudia Ud.?
       2. David Dávila es doctor.   5. Venden de todo, ¿verdad?
       3. Dos y diez son doce.   6. Hay de todo en el mercado.

▼▼▼▼▼▼▼▼▼▼▼▼▼▼▼▼▼▼▼▼▼▼▼▼▼▼

11. Expressing Destination and Future Actions

Ir; ir + *a* + Infinitive

▼ **Bueno... ¡pero barato, por supuesto!**
▼
▼   BETO: Esta tarde *voy a ir* de compras. ¿Quieres *ir* conmigo?
▼ MILTON: Es posible. ¿Adónde *vas* y qué *vas a comprar*?
▼   BETO: *Voy* a un centro comercial. Quiero comprar un regalo de cumpleaños
▼   para mi hermana Lourdes... algo bueno pero barato.
▼ MILTON: *Vamos a ver.* A Lourdes le gusta usar aretes, ¿verdad?
▼   BETO: Sí, pero los aretes son muy caros.
▼ MILTON: Normalmente, sí, pero en el centro hay unas tiendas donde venden
▼   cosas de artesanía. Allí estoy seguro que *vas a encontrar* unas gangas.
▼   BETO: ¡Qué buena idea! ¿Vamos?
▼
▼   ▲ ▲ ▲
▼
▼ ¿Quién... ?
▼
▼ 1. va a ir de compras con un amigo
▼ 2. va a comprar algo
▼ 3. va a recibir un regalo
▼ 4. va a ir al centro
▼ 5. va a vender algo

Good . . . but inexpensive, of course!   BETO: I'm going shopping this afternoon. Do you want to come with me? MILTON: Maybe. (It's possible.) Where are you going and what are you going to buy? BETO: I'm going to a shopping center. I want to buy a birthday present for my sister Lourdes . . . something nice but inexpensive. MILTON: Let's see. Lourdes likes to wear earrings, doesn't she? BETO: Yes, but earrings are very expensive. MILTON: Normally, yes, but downtown there are some stores where they sell crafts. I'm sure that you can find some bargains there. BETO: What a great idea! Shall we go?

ir *(to go)*	
voy	vamos
vas	vais
va	van

The first person plural of **ir, vamos** (*we go, are going, do go*), is also used to express *let's go.*

> **Vamos** a clase ahora mismo.   *Let's go to class right now.*

Ir + **a** + *infinitive* is used to describe actions or events in the near future.

> **Van a llegar** esta noche.   *They're going to arrive tonight.*
> **Voy a ir** de compras esta tarde.   *I'm going to go shopping this afternoon.*

The Contraction *al*

In **Capítulo 3** you learned about the contraction **del**, formed by combining **de** with the masculine singular article **el**. There is one other contraction in Spanish: **al** is formed by combining **a** with **el**. Both contractions are obligatory. No other articles contract with **de** or **a**.

> Voy **al** centro comercial.   *I'm going to the mall.*
> ¡Vamos **a la** tienda de la señora   *Let's go to Mrs. Hernandez's store!*
>   Hernández!

Práctica

A **¿Adónde van de compras?** Haga oraciones completas usando **ir.**
¡OJO! **a** + **el** = **al.**

1. Ud. / el centro
2. Francisco / el almacén Goya
3. Jorge y Carlos / el centro comercial
4. tú / un mercado
5. nosotros / una tienda pequeña
6. yo / ¿ ?

B **¡Vamos de compras!** Describa la tarde, usando **ir** + **a** + el infinitivo, según el modelo.

MODELO: Raúl compra un regalo para Estela. →
          Raúl **va a comprar** un regalo para Estela.

1. Llegamos al centro a las diez de la mañana.
2. Compro unos chocolates para Lupita.
3. Raúl busca una blusa de seda.
4. No compras esta blusa de rayas, ¿verdad?
5. Buscamos algo más barato.
6. ¿Vas de compras mañana también?

C Entrevista: El fin de semana.

Paso 1. Interview a classmate about his or her plans for the weekend. Try to "personalize" the interview by asking additional questions. If your partner is going to read a novel, ask questions like **¿Qué novela? ¿Quién es el autor?**

¿Vas a... ?	SÍ	NO
1. ir de compras	☐	☐
2. leer una novela	☐	☐
3. asistir a un concierto	☐	☐
4. estudiar para un examen	☐	☐
5. ir a una fiesta	☐	☐
6. escribir una carta	☐	☐
7. ir a una discoteca	☐	☐
8. escribir los ejercicios para la clase de español	☐	☐
9. practicar un deporte	☐	☐
10. mirar mucho la televisión	☐	☐

Paso 2. En general, ¿es muy activo/a su compañero/a? ¿O prefiere la tranquilidad? Los números pares (2, 4, 6, ...) son actividades más o menos pasivas o tranquilas. Los números impares (1, 3, 5, ...) representan actividades más activas. ¿Cómo es su compañero/a?

> # NOTA COMUNICATIVA: ¿Cuándo? Las preposiciones
>
> Prepositions express relationships in time and space.
>
> The book is **on** the table.   The homework is **for** tomorrow.
>
> Some common prepositions you have already used include **a, con, de, en, para,** and **por.**
>
> Here are some prepositions that express time relationships.
>
> | | | | |
> |---|---|---|---|
> | **antes de** | before | **durante** | during |
> | **después de** | after | **hasta** | until |
>
> The infinitive is the only verb form that can follow a preposition in Spanish.
>
> ¿Adónde vas **después de**   *Where are you going after study-*
> **estudiar**?   *ing (after you study)?*

D ¿Cuándo? Complete las oraciones lógicamente, con una preposición.

1. Voy a la clase de español _____ preparar la lección.
2. Esta noche voy a estudiar _____ mirar la televisión.
3. Prefiero comer _____ ir al cine.
4. Voy a estudiar mucho _____ tomar el próximo examen.
5. No voy a estudiar _____ las vacaciones.
6. Mañana, voy a leer _____ la hora de ir a la universidad.

What stores and services are available at the Arturo Soria Plaza? Make a list of as many as you can find, then compare your list with those of other classmates. *Note:* in this context, **servicios** is a false cognate. Can you guess what it means?

VOCABULARIO ▼▼▼▼▼▼▼▼▼▼▼▼▼▼▼▼▼▼▼▼▼▼

Los números 100 y más

¿tres mil doscientos? ¡imposible!

Palo

Continúe la secuencia: noventa y nueve, cien, ciento uno, ...
mil, dos mil, ...
un millón, dos millones, ...

100	cien, ciento		700	setecientos/as
101	ciento uno/una		800	ochocientos/as
200	doscientos/as		900	novecientos/as
300	trescientos/as		1.000*	mil
400	cuatrocientos/as		2.000	dos mil
500	quinientos/as		1.000.000	un millón
600	seiscientos/as		2.000.000	dos millones

- **Ciento** is used in combination with numbers from 1 to 99 to express the numbers 101 through 199: **ciento uno, ciento dos, ciento setenta y nueve,** and so on. **Cien** is used in counting and before numbers greater than 100: **cien mil, cien millones.**
- When the numbers 200 through 900 modify a noun, they must agree in gender: **cuatrocientas niñas, doscientas dos casas.**
- **Mil** means *one thousand* or *a thousand.* It does not have a plural form in counting, but **millón** does. When used with a noun, **millón (dos millones,** and so on) must be followed by **de.**

1.899	mil ochocientos noventa y nueve
3.000 habitantes	tres mil habitantes
14.000.000 de habitantes	catorce millones de habitantes

Práctica

A **¿Cuánto es?** Diga los precios.

     el dólar (los Estados Unidos, el Canadá)
     el peso (México)

---

*In many parts of the Spanish-speaking world, a period in numerals is used where English uses a comma, and a comma is used to indicate the decimal where English uses a period: **$10,45.**

el bolívar (Venezuela)
la peseta (España)
el quetzal (Guatemala)

1. 7.345 pesetas
2. $100
3. 5.710 quetzales
4. 670 bolívares
5. 2.486 pesetas
6. $1.000.000

7. 528 pesos
8. 836 bolívares
9. 101 pesetas
10. $4.000.000,00
11. 6.000.000,00 pesos
12. 25.000.000,00 pesetas

B ¿Cuánto es? ¿Cuánto son?

Paso 1. With a classmate, determine how much the following items probably cost, using the question that is the title of this activity or **¿Cuánto cuesta(n) ... ?** Keep track of the prices that you decide on.

1. una calculadora pequeña
2. un coche nuevo
3. un coche usado
4. un estéreo
5. una computadora Mac o IBM

6. un reloj Timex
7. un reloj de diamantes
8. unos zapatos de tenis Nike
9. unos *bluejeans* Levi's
10. una casa en esta ciudad

Paso 2. Now compare the prices you selected with those of others in the class. What is the most expensive thing on the list? (**¿Cuál es la cosa más cara?**) What is the least expensive? (**¿Cuál es la cosa más barata?**)

¿POR O PARA?

An important use of **por** is to express English *in exchange for.* **Por** is frequently used with the verb **pagar** in the context. Here are some additional examples, with the forms of **pagar** given in the past.

¿Cuánto **pagaste por** el coche?	*How much did you pay for the car?*
¿**Pagaste** mucho **por** el coche?	*Did you pay a lot for the car?*
Pagué cien dólares **por** el vestido.	*I paid one hundred dollars for the dress.*

Use these phrases to ask several classmates how much they paid for something that they have with them today or something that you think they own. (Use **pagó** to ask your instructor a similar question.) These are indiscreet questions, but for once it's OK to ask them, since you are practicing Spanish!

ESTRUCTURAS ▼▼▼▼▼▼▼▼▼▼▼▼▼▼▼▼▼▼▼▼▼▼▼▼▼

12. Expressing Actions

Present Tense of Stem-Changing Verbs

▼ **¡Nunca más!**

▼ ALICIA: ¡No *vuelvo* a comprar en la papelería Franco!

▼ MIGUEL: Yo también *empiezo* a cansarme de esa tienda. Nunca tienen los materiales que les *pido.*

▼ ALICIA: ¿Y no *piensas* que los precios son muy caros? Yo creo que siempre *perdemos* dinero cuando compramos allí.

▼ MIGUEL: Te *entiendo* perfectamente. Los precios son horribles. Como la papelería está tan cerca de la facultad, ¡*piensan* que *pueden* pedir mucho dinero por todo!

▲ ▲ ▲

▼ ¿Quién piensa que... ?

▼ 1. los precios de la papelería son muy caros
▼ 2. la papelería no tiene muchas cosas necesarias
▼ 3. pueden pedir mucho dinero porque la papelería está muy cerca de la facultad
▼ 4. los estudiantes pierden dinero cuando compran en la papelería Franco

e → ie	o (u) → ue	e → i
pensar (ie) *(to think)*	**volver (ue)** *(to return)*	**pedir (i)** *(to ask for; to order)*
p**ie**nso pensamos	v**ue**lvo volvemos	p**i**do pedimos
p**ie**nsas pensáis	v**ue**lves volvéis	p**i**des pedís
p**ie**nsa p**ie**nsan	v**ue**lve v**ue**lven	p**i**de p**i**den

You have already learned three *stem-changing verbs* (**los verbos que cambian el radical**): **querer, preferir,** and **poder.** In these verbs the stem vowels **e** and **o** become **ie** and **ue,** respectively, in stressed syllables. The stem vowels are stressed in all present tense forms except **nosotros** and **vosotros.** All three classes of stem-changing verbs follow this regular pattern in the present tense. In vocabulary lists, the stem change will always be shown in parentheses after the infinitive: **volver (ue).**

Some stem-changing verbs practiced in this chapter include the following.

Never again! ALICIA: I'm not going to shop at Franco's stationery store again! MIGUEL: I'm also beginning to get fed up with that store. They never have the things I ask them for. ALICIA: And don't you think that the prices are very expensive? I think that we always lose money when we buy there. MIGUEL: I understand you perfectly. The prices are awful. Since the stationery store is so close to the campus, they think that they can ask a lot of money for everything!

e → ie		o (u) → ue		e → i	
cerrar (ie)	*to close*	almorzar (ue)	*to have lunch*	pedir (i)	*to ask for; to order*
empezar (ie)	*to begin*	costar (ue)	*to cost*	servir (i)	*to serve*
entender (ie)	*to understand*	dormir (ue)	*to sleep*		
pensar (ie)	*to think*	jugar (ue)*	*to play* (a game,		
perder (ie)	*to lose; to miss*		sports)		
	(a function)	volver (ue)	*to return*		

- When used with an infinitive, **empezar** is followed by **a**.

  Uds. **empiezan a hablar** muy bien el español.   *You're beginning to speak Spanish very well.*

- When used with an infinitive, **volver** is also followed by **a**. The phrase then means *to do* (something) *again.*

  ¿Cuando **vuelves a jugar** al tenis?   *When are you going to play tennis again?*

- When followed directly by an infinitive, **pensar** means *to intend, plan to.*

  ¿Cuándo **piensas contestar** la carta?   *When do you intend to answer the letter?*

Práctica

A **¿Cuánta imaginación tiene Ud.?** Identifique a qué se refieren las siguientes definiciones. ¡Las respuestas posibles son muchas!

1. Una cosa que cierra una puerta.
2. Una cosa que los estudiantes pierden con frecuencia.
3. Una cosa que cuesta mucho dinero y no sirve para nada (*is useless*).
4. Un animal que vuelve cada año (*every year*) al mismo (*same*) lugar.
5. Un deporte que se juega (*is played*) con once personas o más.
6. Un juego que se juega en las iglesias (*churches*). Es el favorito de muchas personas viejas.
7. Una cosa que sirve para ser feliz (*happy*).
8. Una cosa que pedimos en un restaurante caro.
9. Cada (*Each*) cosa que pensamos.
10. Una cosa que no entienden los niños de cuatro años.

los pensamientos

la langosta

la tarea

el amor

las golondrinas

una llave

---

*Jugar is the only **u → ue** stem-changing verb in Spanish. **Jugar** is often followed by **al** when used with the name of a sport: **Juego *al* tenis.** Some Spanish speakers, however, omit the **al**.

B Hoy queremos comer paella.

Paso 1. Using the following cues as a guide, tell about the visit of Ismael's family to a restaurant that specializes in Hispanic cuisine. Use **ellos** as the subject except where otherwise indicated.

1. familia / de / Ismael / tener ganas / comer / paella
2. volver / a / su / restaurante / favorito
3. pensar / que / paella / de / restaurante / ser / estupendo
4. pedir / paella / para / 6 / persona
5. pero / hoy / sólo / servir / menú (*m.*) / mexicano
6. por eso / pedir / tacos / y / guacamole (*m.*)
7. almorzar / mucho / y / ahora / querer / dormir la siesta
8. pero / también / querer / estar / más tiempo / junto
9. por eso / jugar / al dominó / en / parque (*m.*)

Paso 2. Now retell the story as if it were your family, using **nosotros** as the subject, except in item 5, where you will use **ellos.**

C Un día normal. María es dependienta en una tienda de ropa para jóvenes en El Paso. ¿Cómo es un día normal de trabajo para ella? Complete la narración en la página 123 con los verbos apropiados, según los dibujos.

NOTA COMUNICATIVA: ¿Cuándo?

These adverbs (**los adverbios**) will help you express the sequence of events.

primero	first
entonces	then, next
luego	then, afterward
finalmente	finally

1.

2.

3.

4.   **5.**   **6.**

1. Llego a la tienda a las 9:50 de la mañana con mis compañeros de trabajo. Primero (*yo*) _____ a ordenar (*put in order*) la ropa. La ropa de la tienda _____ bonita y no _____ mucho dinero.

2. A las 10 abren la tienda y entonces los clientes _____ a llegar.

3. Mis compañeros no _____ español. Por eso yo siempre atiendo a los clientes hispanos.

4. (*Yo*) _____ a las 12:30 con mi amiga Susie, que trabaja en una zapatería. Normalmente (*nosotras*) _____ en la pizzería San Marcos y casi siempre _____ pizza.

5. Luego, (*yo*) _____ a la tienda y _____ a trabajar. Nunca _____ la siesta.

6. Finalmente, la supervisora _____ la tienda a las 6:00 en punto. Entonces yo _____ a casa.

D **¿Quién lo hace** (*does it*)**?** Haga oraciones completas con una palabra o frase de cada columna para expresar algunas (*some*) acciones típicas de las personas indicadas. Añada (*Add*) los detalles necesarios.

yo	(no) almorzar	descansar (*to rest*),
mi padre/madre	perder	dormir
mi hermano/a	jugar (al)	trabajar, estudiar
mi mejor amigo/a	pedir	español, inglés
mi perro/gato	dormir	golf, tenis,
mi compañero/a (de	entender	básquetbol
cuarto/clase)	volver (a)	la siesta, 8 horas
mi profesor(a) de	preferir	la ropa de los años
español	pensar	60, ropa vieja
_____ y yo	empezar (a)	regatear, pagar el
¿ ?	¿ ?	precio fijo
		los mercados, las
		boutiques
		¿ ?

Más frases útiles: siempre, nunca, con frecuencia, mucho, poco, por la mañana (tarde, noche)

Un paso más

UN POCO DE TODO

A **Pero, ¿no podemos regatear?** Complete the following paragraph with the correct form of the words in parentheses, as suggested by the context. When two possibilities are given in parentheses, select the correct word.

El mercardo de artes de Granada, España.

En (los/las[1]) ciudades hispánicas, hay una (grande[2]) variedad de tiendas para (ir[3]) de compras. Hay almacenes, centros comerciales y boutiques (elegante[4]), como en (los/las[5]) Estados Unidos, donde los precios son siempre (fijo[6]).

También hay tiendas (pequeño[7]) que venden un solo[a] producto. Por ejemplo,[b] en una zapatería sólo hay zapatos. En español el sufijo **-ería** se usa[c] para (formar[8]) el nombre de la tienda. ¿Dónde (creer[9]) Ud. que venden papel y (otro[10]) artículos de escritorio? ¿A qué tienda (ir[11]) a ir Ud. a comprar fruta?

Si Ud. (poder[12]) pagar el precio que piden, (deber[13]) comprar los recuerdos[d] en (los/las[14]) almacenes o boutiques. Pero si (tener[15]) ganas o necesidad de regatear, tiene (de/que[16]) ir a un mercado: un conjunto[e] de tiendas o locales[f] donde el ambiente[g] es más (informal[17]) que[h] en los (grande[18]) almacenes. Ud. no (deber[19]) pagar el primer[i] precio que mencione el vendedor. ¡Casi siempre va (a/de[20]) ser muy alto!

[a]*single* [b]*Por... For example* [c]*se... is used* [d]*souvenirs* [e]*group* [f]*stalls* [g]*atmosphere* [h]*than* [i]*first*

¿Cierto o falso? Corrija las oraciones falsas.

1. En el mundo hispánico, todas las tiendas son similares.
2. Uno puede regatear en un almacén hispánico.
3. Es posible comprar limones en una papelería.
4. En los mercados, el vendedor siempre pide un precio bajo al principio (*beginning*).

NOTA CULTURAL: Prices and Sizes

Here are two pieces of advice about shopping in the Spanish-speaking world.

- In Hispanic countries, shoe and clothing sizes are different from those in this country. It's a good idea to ask the clerk to help you with sizes. **La talla** means clothing size; **el número** is shoe size. If you are unsure of the equivalent of your size, simply ask the clerk: **¿Qué talla/número uso?**
- Although it is often possible to bargain over the price of an item in some shops or open-air markets, merchandise is generally sold at a fixed price in Hispanic stores, just as in this country.

NOTA COMUNICATIVA: What Do You Think About . . . ?

One way to ask for someone's opinion with the verb **pensar** is to use the phrase **¿Qué piensas de... ?** (*What do you think about . . . ?*) The answer can begin with **Pienso que...** (*I think that . . .*)

> —¿**Qué piensas de** la clase de química?
> —¡**Pienso que** es muy difícil!

B Entrevista: Por lo general,

Paso 1. With a classmate, explore your general preferences in at least two of the following areas by asking and answering questions based on the cues. Try to get as much information as you can about each question you choose. Keep track of the information you learn about your partner.

Form your questions with expressions like these: **¿Prefieres... o... ?**, **¿Te gusta más** (*infinitive*) **o** (*infinitive*)?, **¿Qué piensas de... ?**, **¿Piensas que... o... ?** If you have no opinion about a given question, say **No tengo preferencia/opinión.**

1. **¿Qué tipo de clases prefieres?** ¿las clases fáciles o las difíciles?* ¿las clases que empiezan a las ocho o las que empiezan a la una? ¿O prefieres tomar clases por la noche? ¿Prefieres clases con profesores que piden mucho o poco trabajo? ¿clases donde es necesario escribir muchas o pocas composiciones?
2. **¿Qué bebidas prefieres?** ¿el café o el té? ¿con o sin azúcar (*sugar*)? ¿los refrescos (*soft drinks*) con calorías o los dietéticos? ¿los refrescos con o sin cafeína? Por lo general, ¿pides refrescos, jugos (*juices*) naturales o cerveza? ¿Pides cerveza o vino?
3. **¿Qué piensas de nuestra universidad?** ¿Piensas que el *campus* es bonito? ¿Hay muchas zonas verdes o es un *campus* urbano? ¿Qué piensas de los edificios? ¿Son modernos o anticuados? ¿bonitos o feos? ¿Qué piensas de los estudiantes? ¿Estudian mucho o poco? ¿O prefieren ir a fiestas?

Paso 2. Now report some of your findings to the class. If you both agree, you will express this with phrases like **Pensamos que...** , (**Los/Las dos** [*Both of us*]) **Preferimos...** If you do not agree, give the preferences of both persons: **Yo prefiero/pienso que... Pero Gustavo prefiere/piensa que...**

SITUACIÓN   En una tienda de ropa

The following dialogue takes place in a clothing store. Try to guess the meaning of the phrases glossed with question marks. (You can find the meaning of most of them in **Notas comunicativas sobre el diálogo.**) Let the context guide you. What

---

*Note again the use of the definite article with an adjective to express English *ones: easy classes or difficult ones?* Something similar happens in the next question: *classes that start at eight or ones (those) that start at one?* You will see this use of the definite article throughout *¿Qué tal?* You can learn more about it in Appendix 1 if you like.

is the first thing a clerk might ask you? What place might you inquire about after you have found something that you like? And so on.

DEPENDIENTA: ¿En qué puedo servirle[a]?
CLIENTE: Busco un pantalón de algodón de color oscuro,[b] para mí.
DEPENDIENTA: ¿Qué talla usa?
CLIENTE: La trece, por lo general.
DEPENDIENTA: ¿Le gusta este pantalón negro?
CLIENTE: No está mal. Y ¿qué tal una blusa de seda también?
DEPENDIENTA: Cómo no. En su talla tenemos blusas de seda en color *beige,* rojo y gris perla. Son perfectas para este pantalón.
CLIENTE: ¿Dónde me los puedo probar[c]?
DEPENDIENTA: Allí están los probadores.[d]

[a]¿ ?   [b]*dark*   [c]¿ ?   [d]¿ ?

NOTAS COMUNICATIVAS SOBRE EL DIÁLOGO

Here are some other phrases that will be useful when you go shopping.

DEPENDIENTE

¿Qué desea (Ud.)?	
¿En qué puedo servirle?	*Can I help you?*
Allí están los probadores.	*There are the fitting rooms.*
¿De qué color?	*What color?*
No hay. No tenemos.	*We don't have any.*
Lo siento.	*I'm sorry.*
No nos quedan.	*We don't have any left.*

CLIENTE

¿Tienen Uds. ... ?	*Do you have . . . ?*
¿Cuánto es/son?	
¿Cuánto cuesta(n)?	*How much is it / are they?*
¿Qué precio tiene(n)?	
¿Me lo (la/los/las) puedo probar?	*May I try it (them) on?*
Necesito algo más barato.	*I need something cheaper.*
¿Se aceptan tarjetas de crédito?	*Do you take credit cards?*
Me lo/la llevo.	*I'll take it* (m. or f.).

Conversación

With another student, play the roles of customer and salesperson in the following situations. Use the phrases from **Notas comunicativas** as well as strategies you have learned from listening to the preceding dialogues.

1. En la librería de la universidad: Ud. desea comprar dos cuadernos pequeños.
2. En una tienda pequeña: Ud. desea comprar una blusa azul para su hermana (madre, amiga, tía).
3. En un almacén: Ud. quiere comprar un regalo barato para un amigo.
4. En una tienda de flores: Ud. necesita comprar seis rosas rojas.

PARA ESCRIBIR

Write a paragraph about your ideas on fashion. Here are some ideas to get you started.

- Personalmente, la moda (no) me interesa (mucho).
- Mis colores favoritos son...
- Las prendas (*clothing items*) que prefiero usar son...
- Mi tienda favorita para comprar ropa es... La tienda está...

▼ ▼ ▼ ▼ ▼ ▼ ▼ ▼ ▼ ▼ ▼ ▼ ▼ ▼ ▼ ▼ **VOCABULARIO** ▼ ▼ ▼ ▼ ▼ ▼ ▼ ▼ ▼ ▼ ▼ ▼ ▼ ▼

Verbos

almorzar (ue) to have lunch
cerrar (ie) to close
costar (ue) to cost
dormir (ue) to sleep
empezar (ie) to begin
  empezar a (+ *inf.*) to begin to (*do something*)
entender (ie) to understand
ir (*irreg.*) to go
  ir a (+ *inf.*) to be going to (*do something*)
  ir de compras to go shopping
jugar (ue) (al...) to play (*a sport*)
llegar to arrive
pedir (i) to ask for; to order
pensar (ie) to think
  pensar (+ *inf.*) to intend, plan to (*do something*)
perder (ie) to lose; to miss (*a function*)
regatear to haggle, bargain
servir (i) to serve
volver (ue) to return
  volver a (+ *inf.*) to do (*something*) again

Repaso: **comprar, vender**

¿Cuándo?

antes de before
después de after
durante during
entonces then, next
finalmente finally
luego then, afterward
primero first

Repaso: **hasta**

De compras

el precio (fijo) (fixed) price
las rebajas sales, reductions

Los lugares

el almacén department store
la boutique boutique
el centro downtown
la joyería jewelry store
el mercado (al aire libre) (outdoor) market(place)
el supermercado supermarket
la zapatería shoe store

Repaso: **el centro comercial, la tienda**

Otros sustantivos

la llave key
el/la vendedor(a) seller

Adjetivos

barato/a inexpensive
caro/a expensive

Los números

cien(to), doscientos/as, trescientos/as, cuatrocientos/as, quinientos/as, seiscientos/as, setecientos/as, ochocientos/as, novecientos/as, mil, un millón (de)

Palabras adicionales

algo something
de todo everything
por (in exchange) for

> **Self-Test**
>
> Use the tape that accompanies this text to test yourself briefly on the important points of this chapter.

VOCES

del mundo hispánico 3
La comunidad puertorriqueña

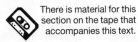
There is material for this section on the tape that accompanies this text.

L a isla de Puerto es un Estado Libre Asociado (ELA)[a] de los Estados Unidos. Por eso los puertorriqueños son ciudadanos[b] norteamericanos de nacimiento.[c]

Actualmente hay aproximadamente dos millones y medio (2,5) de puertorriqueños en los Estados Unidos. Las mayores concentraciones de puertorriqueños están en los grandes núcleos urbanos del nordeste: Nueva York, Nueva Jersey, Pensilvania y también en Chicago. Hay mucho movimiento entre esta zona y la Isla (como los puertorriqueños llaman[d] a Puerto Rico), porque muchas personas tienen familia y amigos en los dos lugares. La mayoría de los puertorriqueños que están en el continente vinieron[e] para encontrar mejores oportunidades económicas y educativas.

El estado Libre Asociado de Puerto Rico tiene los ingresos[f] anuales per cápita más altos de Latinoamérica. Pero a su vez[g] son menores[h] que los ingresos medios más pobres de los Estados Unidos. Los puertorriqueños mantienen un continuo debate sobre la situación de Puerto Rico con los Estados Unidos. En noviembre de 1993 se hizo[i] un referéndum en la Isla para votar sobre ello[j]. Los defensores del *status quo* de Puerto Rico ganaron[k] por un pequeño margen a los que quieren ver a Puerto Rico convertido en el Estado 51.

Nueva York.

[a]Estado... *Commonwealth State* [b]citizens [c]de... *by birth* [d]call [e]came
[f]income [g]a... *at the same time* [h]lower [i]se... *was held* [j]this issue [k]won

Cuando a sus playas[a] llegó[b] Colón
exclamó,[c] lleno[d] de admiración
¡Oh! ¡Oh! ¡Oh!
Esta es la linda tierra[e]
que busco yo,
es Borinquen,[f] la hija
del mar y el sol.[g]

[a]beaches [b]arrived [c]he exclaimed [d]full [e]linda... *beautiful land* [f]nombre indio de la isla de Puerto Rico [g]sun

De «La borinqueña», himno nacional de Puerto Rico.

El Viejo San Juan, Puerto Rico.

Puerto Rico, Isla del Encanto[a]

Puerto Rico es un centro turístico por excelencia. ¿Cuántos de estos atractivos turísticos reconoce Ud.?

- el Viejo San Juan, un barrio[b] colonial, con restaurantes, bares, galerías de arte, museos, monumentos históricos
- el Morro, una fortaleza que protegía[c] a la ciudad contra los ataques de los piratas
- el Festival de Música Casals, fundado[d] en 1957 por el violoncelista español Pablo Casals y su esposa Marta Istomín (exdirectora del *John F. Kennedy Center for the Performing Arts*)
- las playas[e] y los hoteles de El Condado, en San Juan
- el Yunque, un bosque[f] tropical

[a]*Enchantment* [b]*neighborhood* [c]*used to protect*
[d]*founded* [e]*beaches* [f]*forest*

Betsy Padín, «Vigilante de mis dominios».
Padín representa la otra dirección del intercambio humano entre los Estados Unidos y Puerto Rico. Esta norteamericana de nacimiento vive en Puerto Rico desde hace más de 30 años. Es fundadora del Museo de Arte Contemporáneo y del Grupo de Mujeres Artistas de Puerto Rico. Su pintura refleja su obsesión por los paisajes naturales.

¡Qué interesante!

▼ En todos los casos, compare sus respuestas
▼ (*answers*) con las de otros compañeros.
▼
▼
▼ **1.** En grupos, hagan una lista de personas importantes y famosas de origen puertorriqueño que Uds. conocen (*you know*).
▼
▼
▼ **2.** ¿Qué cosas o ideas relaciona Ud. con los puertorriqueños?
▼
▼ **3.** ¿Qué sentimientos evoca el poema de Julia de Burgos?
▼
▼ **4.** Para investigar (*research*): ¿Qué importancia tiene Ponce de León, el explorador español, para la isla de Puerto Rico? Y ¿qué es la Casa Blanca, que está en San Juan?

Desde adentro[a]

Es un lamento.
Es un grito[b] sin lágrimas.[c]
Desde adentro.
Desde el fondo[d] de todo lo inevitable.
Desde el sollozo[e] en espiral de espadas.[f]
Desde la rama[g] trágica
de un silencio perfecto.
Desde el azul caído[h]
en los pies[i] de la noche.
Desde la tempestad de
un sueño[j] solitario.
Desde ti
y desde mí
grita[k] un lamento
sin lágrimas
diciendo
¡Adiós!

Julia de Burgos (1914–1953), poeta puertorriqueña, de *El mar y tú.*

[a]*Desde... From within* [b]*cry* [c]*tears* [d]*depths* [e]*sob*
[f]*swords* [g]*branch* [h]*fallen* [i]*feet* [j]*dream* [k]*shouts*

Primer paso

¿Qué tiempo hace hoy?[a]

[a] ¿Qué... *What's the weather like today?*

Hace frío.

Hace calor.

Hace viento.

Hace sol.

Está (muy) nublado.

Llueve.

Nieva.

Hay mucha contaminación.

Las estaciones
Y EL TIEMPO

Más vocabulario

Hace (mucho) frío (calor, viento, sol).	It's (very) cold (hot, windy, sunny).
Hace fresco.	It's cool.
Hace (muy) buen/mal tiempo.	It's (very) good/bad weather.
	The weather is (very) good/bad.
la lluvia	rain
la nieve	snow

In Spanish, many weather conditions are expressed with **hace.** Note that the adjective **mucho** is used with the nouns **frío, calor, viento,** and **sol** to express *very.*

Pronunciation: In most parts of the Spanish-speaking world, **ll** is pronounced like **y: llueve, la lluvia.**

Práctica

A **El tiempo y la ropa.** Diga qué tiempo hace, según la ropa de cada persona.

1. San Diego: María lleva pantalones cortos y una camiseta.
2. Madison: Juan lleva suéter, pero no lleva chaqueta.
3. Toronto: Roberto lleva suéter y chaqueta.
4. San Miguel de Allende: Ramón lleva impermeable y botas y también tiene paraguas (*umbrella*).
5. Buenos Aires: Todos llevan abrigo, botas y sombrero.

B **El tiempo y las actividades.** Haga oraciones completas, indicando una actividad apropiada para cada situación.

cuando llueve	me quedo (*I stay*) en casa
cuando hace buen tiempo	juego al básquetbol/vólibol con
cuando hace calor	mis amigos
cuando hace frío	almuerzo afuera (*outside*) / en el
cuando nieva	parque
cuando hay mucha contaminación	estoy en el parque / en la playa
	(*beach*) con mis amigos
	vuelvo a casa y trabajo o estudio
	¿ ?

131

NOTA LINGÜÍSTICA: More *tener* Idioms

Several other conditions expressed in Spanish with **tener** idioms—not with *to be,* as in English—include the following.

tener (mucho) calor   to be (very) warm
tener (mucho) frío   to be (very) cold

These expressions are used to describe people or animals only. *To be comfortable*—neither hot nor cold—is expressed with **estar bien.**

C   **¿Tienen frío o calor? ¿Están bien?** Describe the following weather conditions and tell how the people pictured are feeling.

DE AQUÍ Y DE ALLÁ

Here are some colorful expressions for commenting on the weather.

Llueve a cántaros.	*It's raining cats and dogs* (lit., *raining jugfuls*).
Estoy calado/a hasta los huesos.	*I'm soaking wet* (lit., *soaked to the bones*).
Hace un frío/calor de morirse.	*It's extremely cold/hot* (lit., *so cold/ hot you could die*).
Hace un frío/calor espantoso.	*It's awfully (frightfully) cold/hot.*

LOS MESES Y LAS ESTACIONES[a] DEL AÑO

[a] *seasons*

se(p)tiembre		diciembre		marzo		junio	
octubre	el otoño	enero	el invierno	abril	la primavera	julio	el verano
noviembre		febrero		mayo		agosto	

La fecha[b]

^b*date*

¿Cuál es la fecha de hoy?	What is today's date?
(Hoy) Es el primero de abril.	(Today) It is the first of April.
(Hoy) Es el cinco de febrero.	(Today) It is the fifth of February.

- The ordinal number **primero** is used to express the first day of the month. Cardinal numbers (**dos, tres,** and so on) are used for other days.
- The definite article **el** is used before the date. However, when the day of the week is expressed, **el** is omitted: **Hoy es jueves, tres de octubre.**
- Use **mil** to express the year (**el año**) after 999.

1994   mil novecientos noventa y cuatro

En esta foto de Mar del Plata, Argentina, las personas toman el sol en una playa (*beach*) en el mes de diciembre. ¿Qué estación es en la foto?

Práctica

A Fechas.

Paso 1. ¿Qué día de la semana es el 12 (1, 20, 16, 11, 4, 29) de noviembre?

Paso 2. Ahora exprese estas fechas en español. ¿En qué estación caen (*do they fall*)?

1. March 7
2. August 24
3. December 1
4. June 5
5. September 19, 1993
6. May 30, 1842
7. January 31, 1660
8. July 4, 1776

B ¿Cuándo se celebran?*

1. el Día de la Raza (*Columbus Day*)
2. el Día del Año Nuevo
3. el Día de los Enamorados (de San Valentín)
4. el Día de la Independencia de los Estados Unidos
5. el Día de los Inocentes (*Fools*), en los Estados Unidos
6. la Navidad (*Christmas*)
7. su cumpleaños (*birthday*)

Adivinanzas

1. El sol tiene frío;
   no quiere salir;[a]
   metido entre nubes[b]
   se ha puesto[c] a dormir.

   ^a*to come out* ^b*clouds* ^c*se... it has gone*

2. Entre defectos y dones,[a]
   para hinchar[b] un almacén,
   yo tengo cuatro estaciones,
   por las que[c] no pasa el tren.

   ^a*gifts* ^b*para... enough to fill* ^c*por... through which*

---

*¡**OJO!** Note that the word **se** before a verb changes the verb's meaning slightly. **¿Cuándo se celebran?** = *When are they celebrated?* You will see this construction throughout *¿Qué tal?* Learn to recognize it, for it is frequently used in Spanish.

C **¿En qué año... ?** Lea los siguientes años en español. ¿A qué hecho (*event*) corresponden?

1.	1492	**a.**	el año de mi nacimiento (*birth*)
2.	1776	**b.**	la Declaración de la Independencia de los Estados Unidos
3.	1945	**c.**	el asesinato de John F. Kennedy
4.	2001	**d.**	la llegada (*arrival*) de Cristóbal Colón a América
5.	1963	**e.**	la bomba atómica
6.	1984	**f.**	una película famosa
7.	¿ ?	**g.**	la novela de George Orwell
		h.	este año

D **¿Cómo se siente Ud.** (*do you feel*) **cuando... ?** Complete las oraciones lógicamente.

1. En otoño generalmente estoy _____ porque _____.
2. Cuando hace frío (calor) estoy _____ porque _____.
3. En verano estoy _____ porque _____.
4. Cuando llueve (nieva) estoy _____ porque _____.

PRONUNCIACIÓN

▼ ▼

g, gu, j

In Spanish, the letter **g** followed by **e** or **i** has the same sound as the letter **j** followed by any vowel: [x]. It is similar to the English **h**, although in some dialects it is pronounced with a harder sound.

	jamón, jota, jugo
general	jersey
gigante	jirafa

As you know, the letter **g** has another pronunciation, similar to **g** in the English word *go:* [g]. The Spanish letter **g** is pronounced [g] when it is followed directly by **a, o,** or **u** or by the combinations **ue** and **ui.**

galante   gorila   gusto   guerrilla   siguiente

The Spanish **g** is also pronounced [g] at the beginning of a phrase (that is, after a pause) or after the letter **n.**

mango   tango   ángulo

In any other position, the Spanish **g** is a fricative: [g̶]. It sounds very soft.

el gato   el gorila   el gusto

A [x]

jamón	Juan	Jesús	joya	rojo
geranio	genio	gimnasio	gitano	germinal
Jijona	Jorge	jipijapa		

B [g]

gato	negro	gas	abrigo	algodón

C [g / g̶]

un gato / el gato   un grupo / el grupo ·
gracias / las gracias   guapos niños / niños guapos

D [x / g]

gigante   jugoso   jugar   jugamos   juguete

▼▼▼▼▼▼▼▼▼▼▼▼▼▼▼▼▼▼▼▼▼▼▼▼▼▼ **ESTRUCTURAS**

13.   Expressing Actions

Hacer, poner, salir

▼ **Unas preguntas para una persona desordenada**
▼
▼ «¿Por qué no *pones* las cosas en su lugar cuando
▼   *sales* de casa?»
▼ «¿Por qué siempre tengo que *hacer* yo tu trabajo?»
▼ «¿Cuándo vas a *hacer* tu parte? Yo estoy cansado/a
▼   de esta situación.»
▼ «Si tú no arreglas el cuarto inmediatamente... »
▼
▼   ▲ ▲ ▲
▼
▼ ¿Con quién habla esta persona? ¿con su esposo/a? ¿con su hijo/a? ¿con su
▼ compañero/a de cuarto/casa?
▼
▼ Complete la última (*last*) oración lógicamente para las siguientes personas.
▼
▼ 1. un padre o una madre que habla con un hijo pequeño
▼ 2. un esposo que habla con su esposa (o vice versa)
▼ 3. un compañero / una compañera de cuarto que habla con su compañero/a
▼
▼ ¿Ha querido Ud. (*Have you ever wanted*) hablar así con alguien? ¿Con quién?

hacer *(to do; to make)*		poner *(to put; to place)*		salir *(to leave; to go out)*	
ha**g**o	hacemos	pon**g**o	ponemos	sal**g**o	salimos
haces	hacéis	pones	ponéis	sales	salís
hace	hacen	pone	ponen	sale	salen

Here are some frequent uses of **hacer, poner,** and **salir.**

• **hacer**

   ¿Por qué no **haces** los ejercicios?   *Why aren't you doing the exercises?*

Three common idioms with **hacer** are **hacer un viaje** (*to take a trip*), **hacer una
pregunta** (*to ask a question*), and **hacer ejercicio** (*to exercise*).
   You have already learned to use the third person singular form of **hacer,
hace,** in many weather expressions. **Hace** + [a period of time] + **que** is also
used to tell how long something has been going on.

A few questions for a messy person   "Why don't you put things in their place when you leave the house?"
"Why do I always have to do your work?" "When are you going to do your part?" "I'm tired of this situation." "If you don't straighten up the room immediately . . ."

Hace tres horas **que** miran la tele.	*They've been watching TV for three hours.*
Hace dos meses **que** estudio español.	*I've been studying Spanish for two months.*

The exercises and activities in *¿Qué tal?* will not actively practice this structure, but you should learn to recognize it when you see it.

- **poner**

Siempre **pongo** leche y mucho azúcar en el café.	*I always put milk and a lot of sugar in my coffee.*

Many Spanish speakers use **poner** with appliances to express *to turn on.*

Voy a **poner** el televisor.	*I'm going to turn on the TV.*

- **salir**

Salen de clase ahora.	*They're getting out of (leaving) class now.*

Note that **salir** is always followed by **de** to express leaving a place. **Salir con** can mean *to go out with, to date.*

Salgo con Miguel.	*I'm going out with (dating) Miguel.*

¿POR O PARA?

Use **para,** along with **salir,** to indicate someone's destination.

Salimos para la sierra pasado mañana.	*We're leaving for the mountains the day after tomorrow.*
Salgo para la oficina a las siete de la mañana.	*I leave for the office at 7:00 A.M.*

Práctica

A ¿Cierto o falso?

Paso 1.

1. Hago ejercicio en el gimnasio con frecuencia.
2. Todas las noches pongo el televisor a las seis.
3. Nunca salgo con los amigos.
4. Siempre hago los ejercicios para la clase de español.
5. Salgo para la universidad a las ocho de la mañana.
6. Nunca pongo la ropa en la cómoda (*closet*).

Paso 2. Now turn to the person next to you and rephrase each sentence as a question, using **tú** forms of the verbs. Your partner will indicate whether the sentences are true (**sí**) or not (**no**) for him or her.

B **Consecuencias lógicas.** Indique una acción lógica para cada situación, usando (*using*) estas frases: **poner el televisor / el radio, salir con/de/para..., hacer un viaje a..., hacer una pregunta**

1. Me gusta esquiar. Por eso...
2. Quiero practicar el español. Por eso...
3. Mis compañeros hacen mucho ruido (*noise*).
4. Hay un programa interesante en la televisión.
5. Estoy en la biblioteca y... ¡no puedo estudiar más!
6. Queremos bailar y necesitamos música para hacerlo.
7. No comprendo la explicación del profesor.

C **Preguntas**

1. ¿Qué pone Ud. en el café? ¿en el té? ¿en una limonada? ¿Pone Ud. hielo (*ice*) en los refrescos (*soft drinks*)? ¿limón en la cerveza?
2. ¿Qué quiere Ud. hacer esta noche? ¿Qué necesita hacer? ¿Qué va a hacer? ¿Va a salir con sus amigos? ¿Adónde van? ¿Sale con alguien en particular?
3. ¿A qué hora sale Ud. de la clase de español? ¿de otras clases? ¿A veces sale tarde de clase? ¿Por qué? ¿Le gusta salir temprano? ¿Siempre sale Ud. temprano para la universidad? ¿Sale tarde a veces?

D **¿Qué tienes ganas de hacer?** We all have things we've wanted to do for some time but never get around to or never have the chance to do. Express at least three things you've wanted to do for some time, using the model provided.

MODELO: Hace tiempo que tengo ganas de...

Palabras útiles: leer, ver (*to see*), ir a..., comprar...

Segundo paso

VOCABULARIO

¿Dónde está? Más preposiciones

¿Dónde está España? Está **en** la Península Ibérica, **al lado de** Portugal. **Al norte** está Francia, y el continente de África está **al sur. Al oeste** está el Océano Atlántico y **al este** está el Mar Mediterráneo. La capital de España es

Madrid. **Cerca de** la Península Ibérica están las Islas Baleares, que son parte de España. Las Islas Canarias, también parte de España, están **al oeste de** África. Gibraltar está **entre** España y África. No es parte de España. Pertenece a Inglaterra.

cerca de	close to	**delante de**	in front of
lejos de	far from	**detrás de**	behind
debajo de	below	**a la derecha de**	to the right of
encima de	on top of	**a la izquierda de**	to the left of
al lado de	alongside of		
entre	between, among		

al este/oeste/norte/sur de   to the east/west/north/south of

In Spanish, the pronouns that serve as objects of prepositions are identical in form to the subject pronouns, except for **mí** and **ti**.

Julio está delante de **mí**.	*Julio is in front of me.*
María está detrás de **ti**.	*María is behind you.*
Estoy a la izquierda de **ella**.	*I'm on her left.*

Práctica

A **¿De qué país** (*country*) **se habla?**

Paso 1. Escuche la descripción que da su profesor(a) de un país de Sudamérica. ¿Puede Ud. identificar el país?

Paso 2. Ahora describa un país de Sudamérica. Sus compañeros de clase van a identificarlo. Siga el modelo, usando (*using*) todas las frases que sean apropiadas.

MODELO: Este país está al norte/sur/este/oeste de _____.
También está cerca de _____. Pero está lejos de _____. Está entre _____ y _____. ¿Cómo se llama?

Paso 3. Ahora trate de (*try to*) emparejar los nombres de estas capitales de Sudamérica con sus países.

MODELO: _____ es la capital de _____.

Capitales: Brasilia, Buenos Aires, Bogotá, Santiago, La Paz, Asunción, Quito, Caracas, Montevideo, Lima

B **¿Qué o quién es?** Describe the location of someone or something in your classroom as accurately as you can, but without naming the person or thing. Your classmates will try to guess what you are describing.

MODELOS: Esta persona está al lado de Sara. Está delante de Mario y está detrás de mí.

Esta cosa / Este objeto está encima de la mesa del profesor. Está a la izquierda de su libro de español.

C ¿**De dónde es Ud.?** Give as much information as you can about the location of
your hometown or state or the country you are from. You should also tell what
the weather is like there.

MODELO: Soy del pueblo (de la ciudad) de _____. Está cerca de la ciudad de
_____. En verano hace _____. En invierno _____. (No) Llueve
mucho en primavera.

▼▼▼▼▼▼▼▼▼▼▼▼▼▼▼▼▼▼▼▼▼▼▼▼▼▼▼ **ESTRUCTURAS**

14.   Expressing *-self/-selves*

Reflexive Pronouns

▼ **Un día típico**

1. *Me llamo* Alicia; mi esposo *se llama* Miguel.   2. *Me despierto* y *me levanto*
temprano, a las seis. Él también *se levanta* temprano.   3. *Nos bañamos* y *nos*
vestimos.   4. Luego yo pongo la mesa y él prepara el desayuno.   5. ¡Por fin!
Estamos listos para salir para la oficina.   6. Pero... un momentito. ¡Es un día
feriado! ¿Es demasiado tarde para *acostarnos* otra vez? No, pero...
desgraciadamente, ¡ya no tenemos sueño!

1.   **2.**   **3.**   **4.**   **5.**   **6.**

▲ ▲ ▲

Imagine que Ud. es Alicia y complete las oraciones.

1. _____ llamo Alicia y mi esposo _____ llama Miguel.
2. _____ levanto a las seis y Miguel _____ levanta a las seis y diez.
3. _____ baño; luego él _____ baña.
4. _____ visto y él _____ viste al mismo tiempo.

Ahora imagine que Ud. es Miguel y complete las oraciones describiendo las
acciones de los dos.
1. Alicia y yo _____ levantamos temprano.
2. _____ bañamos y _____ vestimos con prisa (*quickly*) por la mañana.
3. Casi siempre _____ acostamos temprano también.

A typical day   1. My name is Alicia; my husband's name is Miguel. 2. I wake up and get up early, at six.
He also gets up early. 3. We bathe and get dressed. 4. Then I set the table, and he makes breakfast.
5. Finally! We're ready to leave for the office. 6. But . . . just a minute. It's a holiday (day off)! Is it too
late to go back to bed? No, but . . . unfortunately, we're not sleepy anymore!

Many English verbs that describe parts of one's daily routine—*to get up, to take a bath,* and so on—are expressed in Spanish with a reflexive construction: *I take a bath* → **me baño** (literally, *I bathe myself*). In this section you will learn to use reflexive pronouns, as well as other verbs that are used reflexively, to talk about your daily routine.

Uses of Reflexive Pronouns

bañarse (*to take a bath*)		
(yo)	**me** baño	*I take a bath*
(tú)	**te** bañas	*you take a bath*
(Ud.) (él) (ella)	**se** baña	*you take a bath* / *he takes a bath* / *she takes a bath*
(nosotros)	**nos** bañamos	*we take baths*
(vosotros)	**os** bañáis	*you take baths*
(Uds.) (ellos) (ellas)	**se** bañan	*you take baths* / *they take baths*

In Spanish, whenever the subject does anything to or for him-/her-/itself, a *reflexive pronoun* (**un pronombre reflexivo**) is used. The Spanish reflexive pronouns are **me, te,** and **se** in the singular; **nos, os,** and **se** in the plural. English reflexives end in *-self/-selves: myself, yourself,* and so on.

The pronoun **-se** at the end of an infinitive indicates that the verb is used reflexively. When the verb is conjugated, the reflexive pronoun that corresponds to the subject must be used: (*yo*) *me* **baño,** (*tú*) *te* **bañas,** and so on.

The following Spanish verbs are used with reflexive pronouns. Many of them are also stem-changing.

Note also the verb **llamarse** (*to be called*), which you have been using since **Primeros pasos: Me llamo _____. ¿Cómo se llama Ud.?**

acostarse (ue)	to go to bed	**ducharse**	to take a shower
afeitarse	to shave	**levantarse**	to get up; to stand up
bañarse	to take a bath	**ponerse**	to put on (*clothing*)
despertarse (ie)	to wake up	**quedarse**	to stay; remain
divertirse (ie)	to have a good time, enjoy oneself	**quitarse**	to take off (*clothing*)
		sentarse (ie)	to sit down
		vestirse (i)	to get dressed
dormirse (ue)	to fall asleep		

¡OJO!   After **ponerse** and **quitarse,** the definite article (*not* the possessive, as in English) is used with articles of clothing.

Se pone **el** abrigo.   *He's putting on his coat.*
Se quitan **el** sombrero.   *They're taking off their hats.*

¡OJO!   All of these verbs used with reflexive pronouns can also be used nonreflexively, often with a different meaning. For example, you have used **dormir** to mean *to* *sleep;* note that **dormirse** means *to* ***fall*** *asleep.* **Poner** means *to put* or *to place;* when used reflexively it means *to put* **on.**

[Práctica A–B]

Placement of Reflexive Pronouns

Reflexive pronouns are placed before a conjugated verb but after the word **no** in a negative sentence: **No** *se* **bañan.** They may either precede the conjugated verb or be attached to an infinitive.

Me tengo que levantar temprano. ⎫
Tengo que levantar**me** temprano. ⎬ *I have to get up early.*
⎭

¡OJO!   Regardless of its position, the reflexive pronoun reflects the subject of the sentence.

[Práctica C–F]

NOTA LINGÜÍSTICA: Another *tener* Idiom

Here is another **tener** idiom useful for talking about one's daily routine.

tener sueño   to be sleepy

Práctica

A **Su rutina diaria.** ¿Hace Ud. lo mismo (*the same thing*) todos los días? Conteste sí o no.

	LOS LUNES		LOS SÁBADOS	
	SÍ	NO	SÍ	NO
1. Me levanto antes de las ocho.	☐	☐	☐	☐
2. Siempre me baño o me ducho.	☐	☐	☐	☐
3. Siempre me afeito.	☐	☐	☐	☐
4. Me pongo un traje / un vestido / una falda.	☐	☐	☐	☐
5. Me quito los zapatos después de llegar a casa.	☐	☐	☐	☐
6. Me quedo en casa por la noche.	☐	☐	☐	☐
7. Me acuesto antes de las once de la noche.	☐	☐	☐	☐

¿Tiene Ud. una rutina diferente los sábados? ¿Qué día prefiere? ¿Por qué?

B **La rutina diaria.** ¿Qué acostumbran hacer los miembros de la familia Hernández? Conteste, imaginando (*imagining*) que Ud. es el esposo / la esposa. Use el pronombre de sujeto cuando sea (*whenever it is*) necesario.

1. yo / levantarse / a las siete
2. mi esposo/a / levantarse / más tarde
3. nosotros / ducharse / por la mañana
4. por costumbre / niños / bañarse / por la noche
5. yo / vestirse / antes de / tomar / café
6. mi esposo/a / vestirse / después de / tomar / té (*m.*)
7. por la noche / niños / acostarse / muy temprano
8. yo / acostarse / más tarde, a las once
9. por lo general / mi esposo/a / acostarse / más tarde que (*than*) yo

En la familia Hernández, ¿quién... ?

1. se levanta primero
2. se acuesta primero
3. no se baña por la mañana
4. se viste antes de tomar el café

C **Conclusiones lógicas.** Complete las oraciones, usando la forma correcta de los verbos de la derecha (*right*). **¡OJO!** Después de una preposición, sólo puede usarse el infinitivo.

1. Los niños _____ en el suelo (*floor*) con frecuencia. Por lo general los adultos prefieren _____ en una silla.
2. Es hora de salir. Yo voy a _____ un abrigo. ¿No vas a _____ una chaqueta o un abrigo?
3. Yo voy a _____ por la noche hoy. Pero mi esposo/a va a _____ mañana por la mañana.
4. Nosotros _____ muy temprano, a las seis de la mañana. Y tú, ¿a qué hora te gusta _____?
5. Después de hacer ejercicios aeróbicos, es buena idea _____ (*infinitivo*) la ropa y los tenis inmediatamente y _____ (*infinitivo*).
6. Yo _____ cuando tengo sueño, no importa la hora. En cambio, mi compañero/a de cuarto siempre _____ a las once.
7. Yo siempre _____ en las fiestas, pero no tengo que estar en una fiesta para _____.

acostarse
bañarse
despertarse
divertirse
ducharse
ponerse
quitarse
sentarse

D **Un día típico.**

Paso 1. Complete las siguientes oraciones lógicamente para describir su rutina diaria. Use pronombres reflexivos cuando sea (*whenever it is*) necesario. **¡OJO!** Use el infinitivo después de las preposiciones.

1. Me levanto después de _____.
2. Primero (*yo*) _____ y luego _____.
3. Me visto antes de / después de _____.
4. Luego me siento a la mesa para _____.
5. Me gusta estudiar antes de _____ o después de _____.
6. Por la noche me divierto un poco y luego _____.
7. Me acuesto antes de / después de _____ y finalmente _____.

Paso 2. Con las oraciones del **Paso 1,** describa los hábitos de su esposo/a, su compañero/a de cuarto/casa o de sus padres.

E Preguntas

1. Por lo general, ¿se afeitan los hombres todos los días? ¿Se afeita Ud. todos los días? ¿Prefiere no afeitarse los fines de semana? ¿Cuántos años hace que se afeita? Por lo general, ¿cuándo empiezan a afeitarse los jóvenes?

2. Por lo general, ¿se viste Ud. elegante o informalmente? ¿Qué ropa se pone cuando quiere estar elegante? ¿cuando quiere estar muy cómodo/a (*comfortable*)? ¿Qué se pone para ir a las clases? ¿para jugar al tenis o hacer ejercicio?

3. ¿Cuál es la última (*last*) cosa que hace antes de acostarse? ¿Cuál es la última cosa o persona en que piensa antes de dormirse? ¿Se duerme Ud. fácilmente (*easily*) o con dificultad? ¿Qué hace cuando no puede dormirse? Cuando se despierta por la noche, ¿puede volver a dormirse fácilmente? ¿Se despierta fácilmente por la mañana o vuelve a dormirse con frecuencia?

F Una mañana magnífica hasta que...

[a] *cigarette with light tobacco*
[b] *deja... stops being the way it is in the ads*

Paso 1. Mafalda es una niña argentina de una tira cómica muy famosa, creada por el humorista argentino Quino. Aquí está en el tercer cuadro (*third frame*). Describa lo que (*what*) pasa en su casa por la mañana. Puede inventar detalles.

   Palabras útiles: la bata (*bathrobe*), besar a (*to kiss* [*a person*]), la calle (*street*), fumar (*to smoke*)

Paso 2. Para el padre de Mafalda, la mañana deja de ser (*stops being*) perfecta cuando sale a la calle. Y para Ud., ¿cuándo deja de ser perfecto su día, como en los avisos comerciales?

UN POCO DE TODO

A Un día en la vida de...

Paso 1. Domingo Meléndez es un estudiante graduado en la Universidad de Sevilla. Los siguientes verbos sirven para hacer una descripción de un día típico de su vida.

Hay toda clase de verbos en las lista. Use los adverbios de tiempo siempre que pueda (*whenever possible*).

despertarse a las ocho	divertirse con ellos	salir a las once a reunirse con
levantarse	ir a la biblioteca	unos amigos en un bar
bañarse	quedarse allí para estudiar	tomar unas copas (*drinks*) con ellos
vestirse	toda la tarde	bailar un poco con una amiga
desayunar	volver a casa a las ocho	volver a casa a la una
tomar sólo un café con leche	poner la mesa y comer	quitarse la ropa y acostarse
ir a la universidad	tener ganas de estudiar	leer un poco
asistir a clases toda la mañana	no poder (estudiar)	poner el despertador (*alarm clock*)
almorzar con unos amigos a las	mirar la televisión	dormirse pronto
tres en una cafetería		

Paso 2. Use los mismos verbos para hablar de su propia rutina.

Neliquén, Argentina.

B **Dos hemisferios.** Complete the following paragraphs with the correct forms of the words in parentheses, as suggested by the context. When two possibilities are given in parentheses, select the correct word.

Hay (mucho[1]) diferencias entre el clima del hemisferio norte y el del hemisferio sur. Cuando (ser/estar[2]) invierno en los Estados Unidos, por ejemplo, (ser/estar[3]) verano en la Argentina, en Bolivia, en Chile... Cuando yo (salir[4]) para la universidad en enero, con frecuencia tengo que (llevar[5]) abrigo y botas. En (los/las[6]) países del hemisferio sur, un estudiante (poder[7]) asistir (a/de[8]) clases en enero llevando[a] sólo pantalones (corto[9]), camiseta y sandalias. En muchas partes de los Estados Unidos, (antes de/durante[10]) las vacaciones en diciembre, casi siempre (hacer[11]) frío y a veces (nevar[12]). En (grande[13]) parte de Sudamérica, al otro lado del ecuador, hace calor y (muy/mucho[14]) sol durante (ese[15]) mes. A veces en enero hay fotos, en los periódicos, de personas que (tomar[16]) el sol y nadan[b] en las playas sudamericanas en enero.

Tengo un amigo que (ir[17]) a (hacer/tomar[18]) un viaje a Buenos Aires. Él me dice[c] que allí la Navidad (ser/estar[19]) una fiesta de verano y que todos (llevar[20]) ropa como la que[d] llevamos nosotros en julio. Parece increíble, ¿verdad?

[a]*wearing*   [b]*are swimming*   [c]*Él... He tells me*   [d]*la... that which*

SITUACIÓN   Haciendo planes para el fin de semana

—Hace un frío espantoso hoy, ¿verdad? Hace dos horas que nieva.
—Sí, y la radio dice[a] que va a nevar toda la noche.
—Oye, ¿qué piensas hacer este fin de semana? ¿Por qué no vamos a esquiar? Seguro que[b] hay mucha nieve en las montañas.
—¡Qué buena idea! ¿Qué día y a qué hora salimos?
—Mañana, después de clases. Mi última clase es a las 11.

[a]*says*   [b]*Seguro... There's sure to be*

Conversación

After practicing the dialogue, use it as a model to make plans with a classmate to do something together this week-end. Change the details, as necessary.

PARA ESCRIBIR

¿Cómo es el clima donde Ud. vive? Describa el tiempo en las cuatro estaciones del año y algunas (*some*) actividades que a Ud. le gusta hacer durante cada (*each*) estación. ¿Qué ropa le gusta llevar o tiene que llevar?

▼▼▼▼▼▼▼▼▼▼▼▼▼▼▼▼ VOCABULARIO ▼▼▼▼▼▼▼▼▼▼▼▼▼▼▼

Verbos

hacer (*irreg.*) to do; to make
poner (*irreg.*) to put; to place; to turn (*an appliance*) on
salir (*irreg.*) (**de**) to leave (*a place*)

La rutina diaria

acostarse (ue) to go to bed
afeitarse to shave
bañarse to bathe
despertarse (ie) to wake up
divertirse (ie) to have a good time, enjoy oneself
dormirse (ue) to fall asleep
ducharse to take a shower
levantarse to get up; to stand up
ponerse to put on (*clothing*)
quedarse to stay, remain
quitarse to take off (*clothing*)
sentarse (ie) to sit down
vestirse (i) to get dressed

Sustantivos

el azúcar sugar
el clima climate
el hielo ice
la leche milk
el país country
la playa beach
el refresco soft drink
el televisor television (*set*)
el tiempo weather; time

¿Qué tiempo hace?

está (muy) nublado it's (very) cloudy, overcast

hace...
  (muy) buen/mal tiempo it's (very) good/bad weather
  (mucho) calor it's (very) hot
  fresco it's cool
  (mucho) frío it's (very) cold
  (mucho) sol it's (very) sunny
  (mucho) viento it's (very) windy
hay (mucha/poca) contaminación there's (a lot of / little) pollution, smog
llover (ue) to rain
  la lluvia rain
nevar (ie) to snow
  la nieve snow

estar bien to be comfortable (*temperature*)
tener calor to be warm/hot
tener frío to be cold

¿Cuál es la fecha?

el cumpleaños birthday
el primero de... the first of . . .

Los meses del año

enero, febrero, marzo, abril, mayo, junio, julio, agosto, se(p)tiembre, octubre, noviembre, diciembre

Las estaciones del año

la primavera, el verano, el otoño, el invierno

Las preposiciones

a la derecha de to the right of
a la izquierda de to the left of
al este/oeste/norte/sur de to the east/west/north/south of
al lado de alongside of
cerca de close to
debajo de below
delante de in front of
detrás de behind
encima de on top of
entre between, among
lejos de far from

Palabras adicionales

afuera outside
hacer ejercicio to exercise
hacer un viaje to take a trip
hacer una pregunta to ask a question
mí me (*obj. of prep.*)
para for (*destination*)
salir con to go out with, date (*someone*)
tarde late
temprano early
tener sueño to be sleepy
ti you (*fam.*) (*obj. of prep.*)

Self-Test

Use the tape that accompanies this text to test yourself briefly on the important points of this chapter.

LECTURA
cultural

Antes de leer: Getting a General Idea About Content

Before starting a reading or looking at a piece of realia, it is a good idea to try to get a general sense of the content. The more you know about the reading before you begin to read, the easier it will seem to you. Here are some things you can do to prepare yourself for readings.

1. Make sure you understand the title. Think about what it suggests to you and what you already know about the topic. Do the same with any subtitles that the reading contains.
2. Look at the drawings, photos, or other visual cues that are included. What do they indicate about the content?
3. Read the comprehension questions before starting to read. They will tell you what kind of information you should be looking for.

NOTA CULTURAL: The Southern Hemisphere

Seasons are reversed in the Southern Hemisphere, where many Spanish-speaking countries lie. This means, of course, that when it is summer in this country, it is winter in Argentina, and vice versa. You may never have thought about the effect of this phenomenon on the celebration of many traditional holidays. Christmas and New Year's Eve, winter holidays for residents of this country, are generally associated with snow and ice, snow figures, winter sports, and so on. What does this ad for a Chilean hotel reveal about the kind of holiday New Year's Eve is in the Southern Hemisphere?

TIEMPO DE VERANO EN PUCON !!
tiempo de vacaciones, de pesca, de descanso y de placer....

¡MARAVILLOSA NOCHE DE AÑO NUEVO!

$ 5.976 c/IVA POR PERSONA

Incluye:
· 2 Noches - desayuno
· Cena Año Nuevo
· Cotillón
· Niños hasta 10 años: aloj. gratis

RESERVAS:
SANTIAGO: Alameda 949 Of.603 · Telfs: 86112 · 83711
64924
TEMUCO: Casilla 511 Telf. 36190
PUCON: Holzapfel 190 Telf. 1

CHILE
lo espera....

35912 - Tco

Gran Hotel Pucón

146

Informe meteorológico para el 24 de julio

Este informe sobre el tiempo es de un periódico español. Incluye información meteorológica para las ciudades españolas más importantes y también para las capitales de muchos países.

Use el mapa y las preguntas de **Comprensión** para aprender algunas palabras importantes relacionadas con el tiempo y a expresar las temperaturas en grados centígrados.

EL TIEMPO

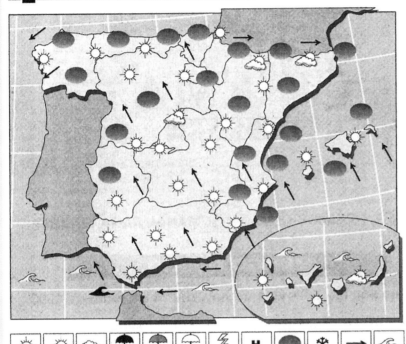

ESPAÑA		MÁX.	MÍN.
Albacete	D	34	15
Alicante	C	30	20
Almería	D	36	17
Ávila	C	28	11
Badajoz	D	35	15
Barcelona	c	27	20
Bilbao	Q	25	12
Burgos	c	25	10
Cáceres	D	35	18
Cádiz	D	32	19
Castellón	C	28	20
Ceuta	c	25	20
Ciudad Real	D	35	17
Córdoba	D	36	17
Coruña, La	P	21	16
Cuenca	D	32	14
Gerona	D	27	15
Gijón	Q	23	14
Granada	D	36	14
Guadalajara	D	34	12
Huelva	D	35	17
Huesca	D	27	15
Ibiza	D	28	18
Jaén	D	36	20
Lanzarote	D	26	19
León	Q	26	10
Lérida	C	29	18
Logroño	D	27	12
Lugo	D	20	12

		MÁX.	MÍN.
Madrid	D	35	17
Mahón	D	28	21
Málaga	D	27	17
Melilla	D	29	19
Murcia	D	35	18
Orense	c	26	12
Oviedo	Q	22	12
Palencia	c	26	12
Palma	D	29	20
Palmas, Las	D	24	19
Pamplona	c	24	9
Pontevedra	A	22	12
Salamanca	c	27	12
San Sebastián	Q	22	12
S. C. Tenerife	c	26	22
Santander	Q	25	14
Santiago de C.	D	19	12
Segovia	D	29	13
Sevilla	D	36	18
Soria	c	27	11
Tarragona	c	25	19
Teruel	C	29	11
Toledo	D	35	17
Valencia	C	30	23
Valladolid	c	28	12
Vigo	A	20	15
Vitoria	c	26	10
Zamora	c	28	14
Zaragoza	D	19	15

EXTRANJERO		MÁX.	MÍN.
Amsterdam	Q	19	12
Atenas	D	31	21
Berlín	S	19	12
Bruselas	Q	19	13
Buenos Aires *	D	16	6
Cairo, El	D	33	21
Estocolmo	P	14	13
Francfort	P	17	11
Ginebra	C	20	14
Lisboa	D	29	15
Londres	Q	18	10

		MÁX.	MÍN.
México *	P	21	12
Miami *	P	31	27
Moscú	A	19	9
Nueva York *	Q	31	19
Oslo	P	18	13
París	A	18	11
Rabat	D	38	22
R. de Janeiro *	D	25	13
Roma	D	30	17
Tokio *	D	29	24
Viena	Q	17	14

A, agradable / C, mucho calor / c, calor / D, despejado / F, mucho frío / f, frío /H, heladas / N, nevadas / P, lluvioso / Q, cubierto /S tormentas / T, templado / V, vientos fuertes.
* Datos del día anterior.

Despejado — Nubes y claros — Cubierto — Lluvia — Chubascos — Llovizna — Tormenta — Heladas — Niebla — Nieve — Viento — Marejada

Comprensión

A Busque en el informe del tiempo las palabras equivalentes en español a las siguientes expresiones.

1. *high tides*
2. *very light rain*
3. *partially cloudy skies*
4. *clear*
5. *icy* (**Recuerde:** el hielo)
6. *overcast* (cubrir = *to cover*)

B **Temperaturas centígradas.** El termómetro indica las equivalencias entre los grados Fahrenheit y los grados Celsius o centígrados. (En los países europeos y americanos, excepto en la Gran Bretaña, el Canadá y los Estados Unidos, usan la escala de grados Celsius para medir las temperaturas.) Mire la lista de las predicciones del tiempo para el 24 de julio en las siguientes ciudades e indique qué tiempo va a hacer y qué ropa van a llevar los habitantes de esa ciudad.

1. Madrid
2. París
3. El Cairo
4. Miami
5. Nueva York
6. Moscú

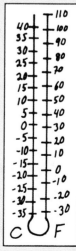

Primer paso

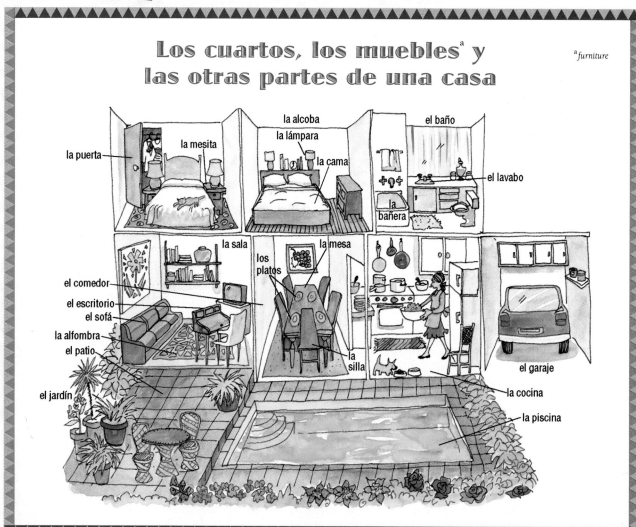

8

Los cuartos, los muebles[a] y las otras partes de una casa

[a]*furniture*

la alcoba
la lámpara
la cama
la mesita
la puerta
el baño
el lavabo
la bañera
la sala
la mesa
los platos
el comedor
el escritorio
el sofá
la alfombra
el patio
la silla
el jardín
el garaje
la cocina
la piscina

En CASA

Más vocabulario

el armario	closet	**la pared**	wall
la cama de agua	water bed	**el sillón**	armchair
la cómoda	bureau, dresser	**el televisor**	TV set
el estante	bookshelf		

Práctica

A **Las partes de una casa.** Identifique las partes de esta casa y diga lo que hay en cada cuarto. ¿Qué hay en el patio? ¿Hay una piscina? ¿O solamente hay plantas?

B **Asociaciones.** ¿Qué muebles o partes de la casa asocia Ud. con las siguientes actividades?

1. estudiar para un examen
2. dormir la siesta por la tarde
3. pasar una noche en casa con la familia
4. tener una comida (*meal*) especial para celebrar algo
5. tomar el sol
6. hablar de temas (*topics*) serios con los amigos (padres, hijos)
7. hacer ejercicio
8. leer novelas o revistas (*magazines*)
9. sentarse a almorzar
10. despertarse

C **Mi casa (apartamento, cuarto en la residencia).**

Paso 1. Dé tres adjetivos o frases que describan su casa (apartamento, cuarto).

Palabras útiles: cómodo (*comfortable*), con mucha luz (*light*), elegante, espacioso, modesto

Paso 2. ¿Cuáles son los cuartos de su casa (o de la casa de su familia)? Indique el número de cuartos también.

Paso 3. ¿Cuál es su cuarto favorito? ¿Por qué? ¿De qué color son las paredes? ¿Qué le gusta hacer en este cuarto?

DE AQUÍ Y DE ALLÁ

Spanish speakers in different areas express the names of rooms of a house in several ways. Here are some typical variations.

> *bedroom:* la alcoba, el dormitorio, la recámara, la habitación, el cuarto
> *living room:* la sala, la salita, el cuarto de estar, la sala de estar

Common to Spanish-speaking areas are these names for parts of a house. Can you match the definitions with the names?

la azotea	algo que abre la puerta de la calle desde el apartamento, sin necesidad de ir a abrir personalmente
la despensa	
el portero automático	terraza encima del techo (*roof*) del edificio
	lugar donde se almacenan (*are stored*) las provisiones, dentro o cerca de la cocina

ESTRUCTURAS ▼▼▼▼▼▼▼▼▼▼▼▼▼▼▼▼▼▼▼▼▼▼

15. Describing

Comparisons

▼ **Tipos y estereotipos**

▼ Adolfo es muy atlético y extrovertido, pero estudia poco.

▼ • Es una persona **más** atlética **que** Raúl y Esteban.
▼ • Es **menos** estudioso **que** Raúl.
▼ • Es **tan** extrovertido **como** Esteban.

▼ Y Raúl, ¿cómo es?

▼ • Es menos extrovertido que _____.
▼ • Es más estudioso que _____.
▼ • No es una persona tan atlética como _____.

▼ Esteban trabaja en la cafetería y también estudia—tiene cinco clases este
▼ semestre.

▼ • No estudia **tanto como** Raúl.
▼ • No tiene **tanto** tiempo libre **como** Adolfo.
▼ • Tiene **más** amigos **que** Raúl pero **menos** amigos **que** Adolfo.

▼ Y Adolfo, ¿cómo es?

▼ • No estudia tanto _____.

▼ • Tiene más tiempo libre _____.

▼ • Tiene más amigos _____.

As you have just seen while you were describing Adolfo, Raúl, and Esteban, comparative forms enable you to compare and contrast people, things, and characteristics or qualities. Similar—but not identical—forms are used with adjectives, nouns, verbs, and adverbs.

The following chart summarizes the patterns you will learn to use in this section. Compare these patterns with those you saw in **Tipos y estereotipos** and those you will see in the example sentences that follow. The _____ indicates where the adjective (noun, etc.) occurs in the pattern.

	UNEQUAL COMPARISONS	EQUAL COMPARISONS
with adjectives or adverbs	más/menos ___ que	tan _____ como
with nouns		tanto/a/os/as _____ como
with verbs	_____ más/menos que	_____ tanto como

Regular Comparisons of Adjectives

Alicia es **más** <u>perezosa</u> **que** Marta.   *Alicia is lazier than Marta.*
Julio es **menos** <u>listo</u> **que** Pablo.   *Julio is less bright than Pablo.*
Enrique es **tan** <u>trabajador</u> **como**   *Enrique is as hardworking as Alicia.*
  Alicia.

The *comparative* (**el comparativo**) of most English adjectives is formed by using the adverbs *more* or *less* (**more** *intelligent,* **less** *important*), or by adding **-er** (*taller, longer*).

In Spanish, unequal comparisons are usually expressed with **más** (*more*) + [adjective] + **que** (*than*) or **menos** (*less*) + [adjective] + **que** (*than*).

Equal comparisons are expressed with **tan** + [adjective] + **como**.

[Práctica A–B]

más _____ que
menos _____ que
tan _____ como

Irregular Comparative Forms

Spanish has the following irregular comparative forms:

mejor(es) better   **mayor(es)** older
peor(es)   worse   **menor(es)** younger

  Estos coches son **buenos,** pero   *These cars are good, but those are*
    esos son **mejores.**   *better.*

[Práctica C]

mejor
peor
mayor
menor

Comparison of Nouns

más _____ que
menos _____ que
tanto/a/os/as _____ que

Alicia tiene **más/menos** <u>bolsas</u> **que** Susana.

Nosotros tenemos **tantas** <u>revistas</u> **como** ellas.

Alicia has more/fewer purses than Susana (does).

We have as many magazines as they (do).

Nouns are compared with the expressions **más/menos** + [*noun*] + **que** and **tanto/a/os/as** + [*noun*] + **como**. **Más/menos** *de* is used when the comparison is followed by a number.

Tengo más **de un** hijo.

Tanto must agree in gender and number with the noun it modifies.

[Práctica D]

Comparison of Verbs and Adverbs

más _____ que, más que
menos _____ que, menos que
tan _____ que, tanto como

Me levanto **más** <u>tarde</u> **que** mi compañera. **No** me acuesto **tan** <u>temprano</u> **como** ella. Y no estudio **tanto como** ella.

No <u>llueve</u> **tanto** en junio **como** en abril.

I get up later than my roommate (does). I don't go to bed as early as she (does). And I don't study as much as she (does).

It doesn't rain as much as in June as (it does) in April.

Actions expressed by verbs are compared with **más/menos que** and **tanto como**. **Tanto** is invariable in this construction. Qualities expressed by adverbs are compared with **más/menos** _____ **que** and **tan** _____ **como**.

[Práctica E]

Práctica

A **¿Estereotipos?** Conteste según el dibujo.

1. Micaela, ¿es más alta o más baja que Sancho?
2. ¿Es tan tímida como Sancho? ¿Quién es más extrovertido?
3. Sancho, ¿es tan atlético como Micaela?
4. ¿Quién es más intelectual? ¿Por qué cree Ud. eso?
5. ¿Es Micaela tan estudiosa como Sancho? ¿Es tan trabajadora como él?
6. ¿Quién es más listo? ¿Por qué cree Ud. eso?

B **Mi universidad.** Cambie las siguientes descripciones de su universidad para expresar su opinión personal: **tan** _____ **como** → **más/menos** _____ **que**. Si está de acuerdo con la oración tal como es (*just as it is*), diga **Estoy de acuerdo**.

1. Aquí, la primavera es tan agradable como el invierno.
2. El béisbol es tan popular como el fútbol americano.
3. Los profesores son tan dedicados como los estudiantes.
4. Las artes son tan importantes como las ciencias.
5. Las pruebas (*quizzes*) son tan fáciles como los exámenes.
6. Los estudios son menos importantes que los deportes.
7. Los hombres son tan estudiosos como las mujeres.
8. Las clases son tan importantes como las telenovelas (*soap operas*) de la tarde.

C **La familia de Micaela y Sancho Jordán.** Mire la siguiente foto e (*and*) identifique a los miembros de esta familia. Luego compárelos (*compare them*) con otro
pariente. **¡OJO!**   Micaela tiene dos hermanos y un sobrino.

MODELO: Micaela es la hermana de Sancho. Ella es menor que Sancho, pero es
más alta que él.

D **Alfredo y Gloria.** Compare la casa y las posesiones que tienen Alfredo y Gloria,
haciendo oraciones con **más/menos _____ que** o **tanto/a/os/as _____ como.**

	ALFREDO	GLORIA
cuartos en total	8	6
baños	2	1
alcobas	3	3
camas	3	5
coches	3	1
dinero en el banco	$500.000	$5.000

E **La rutina diaria... en invierno y en verano.** ¿Es diferente nuestra rutina diaria
en diferentes estaciones?

Paso 1. Complete las siguientes oraciones sobre su rutina.

Palabras útiles: el gimnasio, el parque, la cafetería estudiantil, afuera

EN INVIERNO...

1. me levanto a _____ (hora)
2. almuerzo en _____ (lugar)
3. me divierto con mis amigos en _____ (lugar)
4. estudio _____ horas todos los días
5. estoy / me quedo en _____ (lugar) por la noche

EN VERANO...

me levanto a _____
almuerzo en _____
me divierto con mis amigos en _____
(no) estudio _____ horas todos los días
estoy / me quedo en _____ por la noche

Paso 2. Ahora compare sus actividades en invierno y en verano, según el modelo.

MODELO: En invierno me levanto más temprano/tarde que en verano.
(En invierno me levanto a la misma [*same*] hora que en verano.)
(En invierno me levanto tan temprano como en verano.)

Adivinanzas

¿Quién seré yo[a],
quién seré yo,
que cuanto más[b] lavo[c]
más sucia voy yo?

[a]seré... *can I be*   [b]cuanto... *the more*   [c]*I wash*

1. una madre   **2.** el agua
(*water*)   **3.** el aire

Segundo paso

VOCABULARIO ▼▼▼▼▼▼▼▼▼▼▼▼▼▼▼▼▼▼▼▼▼▼▼▼

RECICLADO

You have seen forms of **este** (*this*), one of the Spanish demonstrative adjectives, in activities throughout *¿Qué tal?,* especially since **Capítulo 3.** Can you give the four forms of the adjective?

Demonstrative Adjectives

«Hay muchos invitados... y no hay cama para todos, con tantas personas en casa. ¿Dónde quieres dormir? **Este** sillón grande es muy cómodo. **Ese** sofá es viejo pero cómodo. Y también tenemos **aquella** hamaca en el patio.»

	SINGULAR		PLURAL
this	este libro	*these*	estos libros
that {	ese libro	*those* {	esos libros
	aquel libro allí		aquellos libros allí

¡OJO! est**e** *but* est**os**, es**e** *but* es**os** (no **o** in the masculine singular forms).

Demonstrative adjectives (**los adjetivos demostrativos**) are used to point out or indicate a specific noun or nouns. In Spanish, demonstrative adjectives precede the nouns they modify. They also agree in number and gender with the nouns.

- There are two ways to say *that/those* in Spanish. Forms of **ese** refer to nouns that are not close to the speaker in space or in time. Forms of **aquel** are used to refer to nouns that are even farther away.

Este niño es mi hijo. **Ese** joven es mi hijo también. Y **aquel** señor allí es mi esposo.

This boy is my son. That young man is also my son. And that man over there is my husband.

- To express English *this one* (*that one*), just drop the noun.

  este coche y ese   aquella casa y esta*

- Use the neuter demonstratives **esto, eso,** and **aquello** to refer to as yet unidentified objects or to a whole idea, concept, or situation.

  ¿Qué es **esto**?   *What is this?*
  Eso es todo.   *That's it. That's all.*
  ¡**Aquello** es terrible!   *That's terrible!*

Práctica

A **Comparaciones.** Restate the sentences in the plural, following the model.

> MODELO: Este garaje es más grande que ese. →
>   **Estos** garajes son más grandes que **esos**.

1. Esta mesita es más baja que esa.
2. Este televisor es más nuevo que ese.
3. Esta lámpara es tan bonita como esa.
4. Este estante es menos alto que ese.

Now change the **ese/a** forms to **aquel(la)**. Then make the sentence plural.

> MODELO: Este garaje es más grande que ese. →
>   Este garaje es más grande que **aquel**. **Estos** garajes son más grandes que **aquellos**.

B **Situaciones.** Find an appropriate response for each situation: **¡Eso es un desastre!, ¿Qué es esto?, ¡Eso es magnífico!, ¡Eso es terrible!**

1. Aquí hay un regalo para Ud.
2. Hay un accidente en la cocina. Desgraciadamente, todos los platos...
3. No hay clases mañana.
4. El profesor de química cancela el examen.
5. Su gato destruye (*destroys*) su sillón favorito.

C **En casa de Soledad Santana**

Paso 1. Soledad Santana es la mujer que está en primer plano (1) a la izquierda en este dibujo. Es la dueña (*owner*) de esta bonita casa mexicana. Hoy tiene invitados: el hombre que también está en el primer plano (1) y las personas de los planos 2 y 3.

En este momento, como Ud. puede ver (*see*), Soledad habla con

---

*Some Spanish speakers prefer to use accents on these forms: **este coche y ése, aquella casa y ésta.** However, it is acceptable in modern Spanish, per the **Real Academia de la Lengua** in Madrid, to omit the accent on these forms when context makes the meaning clear and no ambiguity is possible. To learn more about these forms, consult Appendix 1, Using Adjectives as Nouns.

uno de sus invitados. Complete las siguientes oraciones de Soledad con formas de **este, ese** o **aquel**, según el dibujo.

1. _____ hombre cerca de la puerta es mi primo Ricardo. Está de visita este fin de semana.
2. No, _____ sofá no es mi favorito. Mi favorita es _____ sofá, donde está mi primo, sí. Es muy antiguo, estilo colonial.
3. No, _____ pájaro no es un loro (*parrot*); es una cacatúa (*cockatoo*). Las cacatúas tienen más colores.
4. _____ planta, aquí, es una palmera. Y _____ planta que está detrás de Ud. es un cacto.
5. No, la esposa de mi primo es _____ mujer que habla con él, junto a la puerta.

Paso 2. Ahora invente Ud. las preguntas de la persona con quien habla Soledad.

Paso 3. Finalmente, imagine que Ud. es la mujer que está junto a la silla. Describa el patio del dibujo, con todos los detalles posibles.

NOTA CULTURAL: Las casas del mundo hispánico

Balcón de una casa de San Juan, Puerto Rico.

Es imposible decir[a] qué estilo de casa es típico del mundo hispánico. El estilo depende del área geográfica. Por ejemplo, en las regiones cálidas,[b] muchas casas son planeadas alrededor de[c] un patio central interior. Estos patios se adornan con plantas y, a veces, con una fuente.[d] Pero, por lo general, la población de los países hispanos se concentra normalmente en las zonas urbanas. Por eso, en muchos lugares, la mayoría de la gente[e] que vive en una ciudad vive en apartamentos, como en las ciudades grandes de los Estados Unidos. Aquí hay algunos detalles más sobre las casas hispánicas.

- **Hogar** literalmente significa *home.* Pero normalmente se habla de **casa,** aunque[f] uno viva[g] en un apartamento.

  Voy a casa.   *I'm going home.*

- A los hispanos, por lo general, les preocupa más el interior de su casa que el exterior.
- Un balcón o terraza[h] es una cosa muy deseada[i] en un apartamento.
- En muchos hogares hay pájaros. Normalmente son pájaros pequeños que cantan muy bonito, como los canarios.

[a]*to say* [b]*hot* [c]*alrededor... around* [d]*fountain* [e]*people* [f]*although* [g]*uno... one may live* [h]*balcony* [i]*desirable*

ESTRUCTURAS

▼▼▼▼▼▼▼▼▼▼▼▼▼▼▼▼▼▼▼▼▼▼▼▼▼▼▼▼▼▼▼

¿POR O PARA?

The preposition **por** is used in a number of fixed expressions. So far you have used two of them frequently: **por lo general** (*generally, in general*) and **por eso** (*that's why*). Be alert to other expressions with **por.** You will find them listed in the **Vocabulario** sections as they occur throughout the text.

16. Talking About the Past (1)

Some Forms of the Preterite

▼ **¿Qué *hizo* Ricardo ayer?**[a]   [a]*¿Qué... What did Ricardo do yesterday?*

RICARDO MALDONADO: Ayer, *me desperté* muy temprano, a las seis. Pero no *me levanté* en seguida. *Me quedé* en cama una hora. *Escuché* la radio y *pensé* en mi horario para el día. Por fin *me levanté, me duché,* me *vestí* y *salí* para la universidad. No *tomé* el desayuno[a] porque no *tuve* tiempo.

Llegué tarde a mi primera clase. Después de otra clase, *almorcé* en la cafetería estudiantil y *hablé* con varios amigos. *Tuve* dos clases más por la tarde. Luego *fui* al gimnasio y *jugué* al básquetbol. *Me divertí* mucho.

Más tarde, *volví* a casa, *preparé* la cena[b] y *estudié* unas horas. *Miré* la televisión un rato y *hablé* con un buen amigo que *llamó* muy tarde. Por fin *me acosté* a las once y media. *Empecé* a pensar en el examen de mañana... Pero, ¿por qué preocuparme[c]? *Me dormí* en seguida.

[a]*breakfast* [b]*dinner* [c]*worry*

All of the verb forms in this monologue are in the past. Note also the meaning of these words and phrases: **en seguida** = *right away,* **un rato** = **un breve período de tiempo** (*time*); **por fin** = *finally.*

▲ ▲ ▲

Ponga en orden cronológico (de 1 a 5) las siguientes oraciones sobre lo que Ricardo hizo ayer.

_____ Se acostó y se durmió por fin.

_____ Llegó tarde a una clase.

_____ Se despertó temprano pero no se levantó en seguida.

_____ En casa, comió, estudió, miró la tele y habló con un amigo.

_____ Almorzó con unos amigos, asistió a dos clases y jugó al básquetbol.

In previous chapters of *¿Qué tal?*, you have talked about a number of your activities, but always in the present tense. In this section, you will begin to work with the forms of the preterite tense in Spanish, one of the tenses that will allow you to talk about the past. Here are the singular forms of the preterite for regular verbs. In this section you will use them to talk about your daily routine and other activities, as well as those of your classmates.

Note that the endings of **-er** and **-ir** verbs are identical in the singular forms of the preterite.

hablar: hablé (*I spoke*), hablaste (*you [fam.] spoke*), habló (*you [form.],
he/she spoke*)

comer: comí, comiste, comió

vivir: viví, viviste, vivió

You have already seen the irregular third person preterite form of **ser: Fue una ganga.** Here are some additional irregular preterite forms. Note that the forms of **ir** and **ser** are identical in the preterite:

hacer: hice (*I did*), hiciste, hizo

ser/ir: fui (*I was / I went*), fuiste, fue

tener: tuve (*I had*), tuviste, tuvo

In Ricardo's description of what happened to him yesterday, did you notice some minor spelling changes? For example: **llegué, almorcé.** You will learn about these and other simple changes in **Capítulos 10, 12,** and **13.** Until then, let yourself be guided by the forms you see in exercises and activities.

Práctica

A ¿Qué hizo Ud. anoche (*last night*)? Conteste sí o no.

Las actividades de los números impares (1, 3, 5...) son «externas» y las de los números pares (2, 4, 6...) son «internas». Piense en sus respuestas. ¿Qué tipo de persona es Ud.? ¿Prefiere salir o quedarse en casa?

		SÍ	NO
1.	Fui al cine.	☐	☐
2.	Miré la televisión.	☐	☐
3.	Estudié en la biblioteca o en casa de un amigo / una amiga (de mi novio/a [*boy / girlfriend*]).	☐	☐
4.	Estudié en mi alcoba.	☐	☐
5.	Comí en un restaurante.	☐	☐
6.	Preparé algo para comer en casa.	☐	☐
7.	Fui a casa de un amigo / una amiga (mi novio/a) para charlar (*to chat*).	☐	☐
8.	Hablé con un amigo / una amiga (un pariente, mi novio/a) por teléfono.	☐	☐
9.	Asistí a un concierto.	☐	☐
10.	Escuché la radio / el estéreo.	☐	☐

B ¿Y el horario de Uds.?

Paso 1. Look back at the description of what Ricardo did yesterday. Think about your last school day and, one by one, decide if each sentence is true for you. If it is, repeat it. If it is not, change it to make it correct or simply add **no.**

Paso 2. Now use the same sentences to interview a classmate about what he or she did. Change the **yo** forms to **tú.**

MODELO: E1: Ayer, ¿te levantaste muy temprano?
           E2: Sí, (me levanté) a las siete. Es muy temprano para mí.

C **¿Quién fue?** Ayer, en la clase de español, ¿quién hizo lo siguiente? Si una actividad no ocurrió, conteste **Nadie** (*No one*).

MODELOS: ¿Quién no entendió una pregunta? →
            Fue Bob Anderson. (Bob Anderson no entendió una pregunta.)
            Fui yo. (Yo no entendí una pregunta.)

¿Quién... ?

1. no entendió una pregunta
2. llegó tarde a clase
3. escribió en la pizarra

4. habló en inglés
5. hizo muchas preguntas
6. salió de clase temprano

Un POCO DE TODO

A **La casa ideal**

Paso 1. Lea estos anuncios de casas en venta (*sale*) en Puerto Rico. Preste (*Pay*) atención a la influencia del inglés. Algunas palabras aparecen en inglés directamente. Por ejemplo, la palabra *family* aparece en tres anuncios. ¿A qué tipo de cuarto se refiere? ¿Qué otras palabras en inglés puede Ud. encontrar?

❶ **Alto Apolo**	❷ **LOMAS DEL SOL**	❸ **Borinquen Gardens**	❹ **TORRIMAR I**	❺ **Sta. María**
Bonito «townhouse», área exclusiva. 3 dorms., 3 baños. Equipado. «Family», tres terrazas. Cerca centros comerciales, transportación. Bajos $80s. <u>Hipoteca</u> $57.250 al 8½%. Mens. $478. 790-6811, 789-9331.	Hermosa res. 3 dorms., 2 baños. Fabulosa <u>vista</u> con lago en el patio. Gallinero, árboles frutales, marq. doble. 2.179 mts. de solar. Hip. $64.000 al 8%. Mens. $489. Pronto $36.000. Información 725-0773.	Con un poquito de amor usted <u>arregla</u> esta amplia casa de 4 dorms., 2 baños. Su precio en los $60s.	Recién remodelada con buen gusto, casa de 5 dorms., 4 baños, en calle tranquila. Dueños bajan precio para <u>venta</u> rápida. Haga un cita exclusiva, hoy.	Preciosa residencia de ejecutivo con: • 4 dorms • 3 baños • cuarto de servicio • amplia terraza • barra • piscina • y mucho más. Haga su cita exclusiva, hoy.
	❻ **Santa Paula**	❼ **CAPARRA HILLS**	❾ **Villa Ávila.** Encantadora	
	Amplísima residencia 4 dorms., 4 baños. Moderna <u>fachada</u>, espaciosa cocina. Inmenso <u>cuarto de juego</u>. Estudio, «family». Piscina. Solar sobre 1.000 metros. Medios $100s. Financiamiento especial. 790-6811, 789-9331.	Atractiva res. de 2 años construida, moderna, sencilla. Perfecta para familia pequeña. Con doble garaje, patio interior, terraza cubierta, en más de 650 m.s. Con hipoteca alta. En los medios $100s. Llama ahora. UNIVERSAL HOMES (Selected Homes Specialista) 781-7605.	residencia totalmente redecorada. 3 dorms., 2 baños. Cocina y equipos nuevos. Toda empapelada y alfombrada. «Family». Preciosa piscina. Cable TV. Bajos $100s con términos. Conveniente mensualidad $509. 790-6811, 789-9331.	

Paso 2. Ahora vuelva a leer los anuncios rápidamente para indicar cuáles de estas casas pueden ser apropiadas para los Juárez, una familia que consiste en los padres, cuatro hijos y una abuela.

Torrimar I   Caparra Hills   Villa Ávila   Lomas del Sol

Paso 3. Ahora que Ud. tiene práctica en buscar casas para familias, busque la casa ideal para las siguientes personas.

1. Pedro Aquino, un carpintero a quien le gusta el trabajo manual.
2. Los Pino, un matrimonio mayor (*elderly couple*) que no tiene coche.
3. Óscar Sifuentes, un banquero que se divierte con la mecánica: Los fines de semana le gusta reparar su coche antiguo.
4. Los Pérez, un matrimonio con cuatro hijos muy activos. Necesitan una casa espaciosa donde los hijos puedan (*can*) jugar sin molestar a los adultos.

Paso 4. Ahora es el momento de elegir su propia (*own*) casa. ¿Cuál le gusta más? ¿Por qué?

B **¡Firma** (*Sign*) **aquí, por favor!** Complete these sentences with real information. Then, for each separate item, ask your classmates questions to find someone who answered the same way you did.

MODELO: El año pasado, leí *cinco* novelas. →
        E1: ¿Cuántas novelas leíste el año pasado?
        E2: No estoy seguro/a. Probablemente cinco.
        E1: Muy bien. Firma aquí, por favor.

NOMBRES

1. El año pasado leí _____ novelas.   _____
2. Anoche volví a casa a la(s) _____.   _____
3. Me gusta el invierno más que _____.   _____
4. Estoy triste cuando _____ (llueve, nieva, hace ¿ ?).   _____
5. Ayer me levanté a la(s) _____.   _____
6. Este verano, pienso hacer un viaje a _____.   _____
7. En mi casa (apartamento, residencia), hay _____ baños.   _____
8. Mi cuarto favorito es _____.   _____
9. Leo más revistas que _____.   _____

SITUACIÓN Hablando del nuevo apartamento

—¿Qué más necesitas para tu apartamento?
—Practicamente lo necesito todo.[a]
—Entonces, ¿por qué no vamos de compras esta tarde? Podemos ir a una tienda de decoración estupenda en el centro comercial.
—Porque no tengo un chavo.[b] El cheque de la ayuda financiera no llega hasta final de mes.
—Bueno, no importa. Podemos ir sólo a mirar. Además, yo quiero comprarte un regalo por tu santo.
—¡Eres un amor! Pero no tienes que comprarme nada.

[a]lo... *I need everything*   [b]no... *I'm broke*

Conversación

Después de leer y repetir el diálogo con un compañero / una compañera, cambie los detalles para hablar de su apartamento (casa, cuarto, ...) y de sus necesidades y posibilidades económicas.

PARA ESCRIBIR

Escriba dos párrafos describiendo el lugar donde Ud. vive con su familia. En el primer párrafo diga cuánto tiempo hace que su familia vive allí. Dé (*Give*) también todos los detalles posibles sobre su hogar (*home*). En el segundo párrafo exprese sus sentimientos sobre su hogar, si le gusta o no, y por qué.

VOCABULARIO

Los cuartos y las otras partes de una casa

la alcoba bedroom
el baño bathroom
la cocina kitchen
el comedor dining room
el garaje garage
el jardín garden
el patio patio; yard
la piscina pool
la sala living room

Los muebles y otras cosas en una casa

la alfombra rug
el armario closet
la bañera bathtub
la cama (de agua) (water) bed
la cómoda bureau, dresser
el estante bookshelf
la lámpara lamp
el lavabo (bathroom) sink
la mesita end table
la pared wall
el plato plate, dish
el sillón armchair
el sofá sofa

Repaso: el escritorio, la mesa, la puerta, la silla, el televisor

Otros sustantivos

el horario schedule
el/la invitado/a guest
el/la novio/a boyfriend/girlfriend
la prueba quiz
la revista magazine

Adjetivos

antiguo/a old, ancient; antique
cómodo/a comfortable
extrovertido/a outgoing, extroverted
primero/a first

Formas demostrativas

aquel, aquella, aquellos/as that, those (over there)
ese/a, esos/as that, those
esto, eso, aquello this, that, that thing, fact, idea (over there)

Repaso: este/a, estos/as

Las comparaciones

más que more than
menos que less than
tan... como as . . . as
tanto/a/os/as... como as much/many . . . as

mayor older
mejor better
menor younger
peor worse

¿Cuándo?

anoche last night
ayer yesterday
en seguida immediately
un rato a while

Palabras adicionales

por ejemplo for example
por fin finally

Self-Test

Use the tape that accompanies this text to test yourself briefly on the important points of this chapter.

VOCES

There is material for this section on the tape that accompanies this text.

del mundo hispánico 4
La comunidad cubanoamericana

Los cubanos son principalmente un grupo de inmigrantes. La primera ola[a] migratoria llegó al final del siglo[b] XIX a Florida para trabajar en las fábricas[c] de tabaco. El segundo movimiento migratorio, más importante en número que el primero, ocurrió en los años 60, debido[d] a la revolución de Fidel Castro. Estos cubanos también se establecieron[e] el sur de Florida.

Lo más importante de la segunda inmigración cubana es que los inmigrantes que llegaron en los años 60 eran[f] en su mayoría[g] profesionales de las clases media y alta. Llegaron a los Estados Unidos sin dinero, pero con su cultura y su educación.

En sólo una generación los inmigrantes cubanos han recuperado[h] gran parte de la situación económica que tuvieron que abandonar,[i] y ahora ejercen[j] una enorme influencia en la vida del sur de Florida, donde todavía se concentra la mayoría.

[a]*wave* [b]*century* [c]*factories* [d]*due* [e]*se... settled*
[f]*were* [g]*en... for the most part* [h]*han... have regained*
[i]*tuvieron... they had to leave behind* [j]*they exert*

I t's one thing to speak English, even to require it. It's quite another to *think and feel English,* and *that* you can't legislate.

"I am blessed, and I mean that sincerely, in that I can think and feel in both circles. But I cannot, and I shall not, forget that my father died in Cuba because he loved it so, and that I am part of that land that he loved so much."

María C. García, periodista cubanoamericana.

Festival en la famosa Calle Ocho, Miami.

Gloria Estefan está feliz con el próximo lanzamiento[a] de su disco en español (¡fabuloooooso!), donde encontrarás[b] boleros, cha-cha-chá, rumba y otros ritmos latinos "calientes".[c] Imagínate, en la grabación[d] de este LP participaron la Filarmónica de Londres y un conocido[e] trío de cantantes mexicanos. Sumado a esto, Gloria recibió el pasado mes de febrero su estrella[f] (la número 1974) en el famoso "Paseo de la fama" en Hollywood. ¡Este va a ser un año tremendo para ella!!!

[a]debut [b]you will find [c]hot [d]recording [e]well-known [f]star

Yo soy un hombre sincero
de donde crece[a] la palma;
y antes de morirme,[b] quiero
echar[c] mis versos del alma.[d]

Mi verso es de un verde claro[e]
y de un carmín encendido:[f]
mi verso es un ciervo herido[g]
que busca en el monte amparo.[h]

[a]grows [b]dying [c]to cast [d]soul [e]light [f]firey
[g]ciervo... wounded deer [h]refuge

José Martí (1853–1895), héroe nacional de Cuba y poeta, de *Versos sencillos*.

Miami esencialmente se ha profesionalizado[a] en general. Esto se refleja inclusive en la manera en la que visten las personas... Estamos llegando a nivel[b] de gran metrópolis internacional. Nosotros como arquitectos nos damos cuenta[c] de eso... La combinación de idiomas, la combinación de ideologías sociales y políticas... todo esto ha hecho que[d] muchos describan a Miami como la Suiza del Hemisferio.»

[a]se... has become more professional [b]Estamos... We are getting to the level
[c]nos... are aware [d]ha... has made

Hilario Candela, arquitecto cubano, en *Miami Mensual*.

Xavier Suárez, ex alcalde (*mayor*) de Miami. Llegó a los Estados Unidos a los 11 años. Obtuvo (*He earned*) el título de abogado (*lawyer*) en la Universidad de Harvard.

¡Qué interesante!

▼ En todos los casos, compare sus respuestas con las de otros compañeros.

▼ **1.** En grupos, hagan una lista de personas importantes y famosas de origen cubano que Uds. conocen (*you know*).

▼ **2.** ¿Qué cosas o ideas relaciona Ud. con los cubanos?

▼ **3.** ¿Por qué piensa Ud. que los cubanos que emigraron por razones políticas se establecieron (*settled*) en Florida? ¿Qué tiene en común Miami con Suiza, según el señor Candela?

9

Primer paso

La comida y las bebidas

¿estilo norteamericano o estilo hispano?

El desayuno →
desayunar

el jamón

el café

las galletas

los huevos el jugo de fruta el pan tostado

un bollo el café con leche

¿una comida grande o un almuerzo rápido?

la hamburguesa

El almuerzo →
almorzar (ue)

una papa
al horno

el flan

la
cerveza

el pan

el pavo los espárragos el refresco

el helado las papas fritas

¿una cena ligera o una cena elegante?

el vino blanco

La cena → cenar

la
manzana

el
pastel

el pan

el arroz el pollo las arvejas el agua mineral la langosta la sopa la ensalada de lechuga
y tomate

The noun **agua** (*water*) is feminine, but the masculine articles are used with it in the singular: **el agua.** This phenomenon occurs with all feminine nouns that begin with a stressed **a** sound: **el ama de casa** (*the homemaker*).

¿Qué VAMOS A PEDIR?

Las bebidas

la leche   milk
el té   tea
el vino blanco   white wine

La carne

el bistec   steak
la chuleta (de cerdo)   (pork) chop

Los mariscos

los camarones   shrimp

El pescado

el atún   tuna
el salmón   salmon

Las verduras

los frijoles   beans
la zanahoria   carrot

Otros platos y comidas

el queso   cheese
el sándwich   sandwich

La fruta

la banana   banana
la naranja   orange

Los postres

el flan   custard
la galleta   cookie; cracker

Práctica

A ¿Qué quiere tomar? Match the following descriptions of meals with these categories: **un menú ligero para una dieta, una comida rápida, una cena elegante, un desayuno estilo norteamericano.**

1. una sopa fría, langosta, espárragos, una ensalada de lechuga y tomate, todo con vino blanco y, para terminar, un pastel
2. jugo de fruta, huevos con jamón, pan tostado y café
3. pollo al horno, arroz, arvejas, agua mineral y, para terminar, una manzana
4. una hamburguesa con papas fritas, un refresco y un helado

B Definiciones. ¿Qué es?

1. un plato de lechuga y tomate
2. una bebida alcohólica blanca o roja
3. un líquido caliente (*hot*) que se toma con cuchara (*spoon*)
4. una verdura anaranjada
5. la carne típica para barbacoa en los Estados Unidos
6. una comida muy común en la China y en el Japón
7. la comida favorita de los ratones

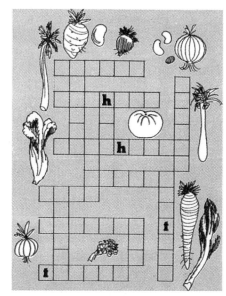

Cruciletras
En este cruciletras deberás encajar los siguientes nombres: ajo - apio - haba - brecol - tomate - rábano - judías - acelgas - puerro - lechuga - lenteja - cebolla - zanahoria.

165

8. una verdura frita que se come con las hamburguesas
9. una fruta roja o verde
10. una fruta amarilla de las zonas tropicales
11. un líquido de color blanco que se sirve especialmente a los niños
12. la bebida tradicional de los ingleses
13. se usa para preparar sándwiches
14. un postre muy frío
15. un postre que se sirve en las fiestas de cumpleaños
16. una comida que tiene el centro amarillo y el resto blanco

NOTA LINGÜÍSTICA: More *tener* Idioms

Here are two additional **tener** idioms related to foods and eating.

tener (mucha) hambre	to be (very) hungry
tener (mucha) sed	to be (very) thirsty

C **Consejos a la hora de comer.** ¿Qué debe Ud. comer o beber en las siguientes situaciones? (¿O qué comió o bebió una vez [*once*]?)

1. Ud. quiere comer algo ligero porque no tiene hambre.
2. Ud. quiere comer algo fuerte (*heavy*) porque tiene mucha hambre.
3. Ud. tiene un poco de sed y quiere tomar algo antes de la comida.
4. Ud. quiere comer algo antes del plato principal.
5. Ud. quiere comer algo después del plato principal.
6. Después de jugar al tenis, Ud. tiene mucha sed.
7. Ud. está a dieta.
8. Ud. es vegetariano/a. Come en un restaurante con unos amigos.
9. Ud. está de vacaciones en Maine (o Boston).
10. Ud. está enfermo/a.
11. Ud. no puede dormirse.
12. Después de levantarse, Ud. no está completamente despierto/a (*awake*).

DE AQUÍ Y DE ALLÁ

Here are some phrases to use at mealtimes.

- Talk about what you feel like eating with the verb **apetecer** (*to be hungry for*).

    —¿Qué te **apetece** cenar esta noche?

    —¿Me **apetece** comida china. (Me **apetecen** camarones.)

- When used with food, the verb **picar** means *to nibble* or *snack* on something light.

    ¿Por qué no **picamos** algo antes de cenar?

- You already know how to express *to be hungry.* To say that you're starving, use these expressions.

  Me muero de hambre.   (lit.) *I'm dying of hunger.*
  Tengo un hambre de lobos.   (lit.) *I'm as hungry as a wolf.*

- To wish someone a pleasant dining experience, say **¡Buen apetito!** or **¡Buen provecho!**

NOTA CULTURAL: Meals in the Spanish-Speaking World

Hispanic eating habits are quite unlike those in the United States. Not only does the food itself differ somewhat, but the meals occur at different times.

There are three fundamental meals: **el desayuno, la comida / el almuerzo** (*midday meal*), and **la cena** (*supper*). Breakfast, which is eaten around 7:00 or 8:00, is a very simple meal, frugal by most U.S. standards: **café con leche** or **chocolate** (*hot chocolate*) with a plain or sweet roll or toast; that is all. The **café con leche** is heated milk with very strong coffee to add flavor and color.

The main meal of the day, **la comida / el almuerzo,** is frequently eaten as late as 2:00 P.M., and it is a much heartier meal than the average U.S. lunch. It might consist of soup, a meat or fish dish with vegetables and potatoes or rice, a green salad, and then dessert (often fruit or cheese). Coffee is usually served after the meal.

The evening meal, **la cena,** is somewhat lighter than the noon meal. It is rarely eaten before 8:00, and in Spain is commonly served as late as 10:00 or 11:00 P.M. Because the evening meal is served at such a late hour, it is customary to eat a light snack, or **merienda,** about 5:00 or 6:00 P.M. The **merienda** might consist of a sandwich or other snack with **café con leche** or **chocolate.** Similarly, a snack is often eaten in the morning between breakfast and the midday meal.

ESTRUCTURAS

17. Expressing Negation

Indefinite and Negative Words

▼ Imagine que Ud. vive en Lima este año. ¿Cómo contesta Ud. en estas situaciones?

SU AMIGO ALFONSO: Ya son las diez de la noche. Vamos a comer *algo* en El Cebiche. ¡Tengo hambre!

USTED: • No, gracias. Casi *nunca* ceno fuera.
• Pero... ¡*nadie* cena a estas horas!
• Sí, pero... ¿*no* hay *ningún* otro restaurante cerca de la universidad?

Los mejores Cebiches de Lima, estan en... EL CEBICHE

1 PISCO SOUR de cortesía

YOUR FRIEND ALFONSO: It's already ten at night. Let's eat something at El Cebiche. I'm hungry! YOU: • No, thanks. I almost never have dinner out. • But . . . nobody eats dinner at this hour! • OK, but . . . isn't there any other restaurant close to the university?

▼   EL CAMARERO: *También* tenemos cebiche, camarones...
▼   USTED: • Pues... creo que *no* voy a comer *nada,* gracias.
▼   • ¡Qué bien! Quiero probar *algunos* platos típicos.
▼   • Aquí *siempre* pido el cebiche.

Here is a list of the most common indefinite and negative words in Spanish. You have been using many of them since the first chapters of *¿Qué tal?*

algo	something, anything	**nada**	nothing, not anything
alguien	someone, anyone	**nadie**	no one, nobody, not anybody
algún (alguno/a/os/as)	some, any	**ningún (ninguno/a)**	no, none, not any
siempre	always	**nunca, jamás**	never
también	also	**tampoco**	neither, not either

Pronunciation hint: Remember to pronounce the **d** in **nada** and **nadie** as a fricative, that is, like a *th* sound: **na da, na die.**

¿**Siempre** cenas en la cafetería?
—No, casi **nunca** ceno aquí.

Queremos comer **algo** diferente esta noche.

¿**Alguien** viene hoy? —No, no viene **nadie.**

Do you always have dinner in the cafeteria? —No, I almost never have dinner here.

We want to have (eat) something different tonight.

Is someone coming today? —No, nobody's coming.

Pay particular attention to the following aspects of using negative words.

• When a negative word comes after the main verb, Spanish requires that another negative word—usually **no**—be placed before the verb. When a negative word precedes the verb, **no** is not used.

¿**No** estudia **nadie?**
¿**Nadie** estudia? }
Isn't anyone studying?

No estás en clase **nunca.**
Nunca estás en clase. }
You're never in class.

No quieren cenar aquí **tampoco.**
Tampoco quieren cenar aquí. }
They don't want to have dinner here, either.

• The adjectives **alguno** and **ninguno** shorten to **algún** and **ningún,** respectively, before a masculine singular noun—just as **uno** shortens to **un, bueno** to **buen,** and **malo** to **mal.** The plural forms **ningunos** and **ningunas** are rarely used.

¿Hay **algunos** recados para mí hoy? —Lo siento, pero hoy no hay **ningún** recado para Ud.

Are there any messages for me today? —I'm sorry, but there are no messages for you today. (There is not a single message for you today.)

WAITER: We also have ceviche (*marinated raw fish*), shrimp . . . YOU: • Well . . . I don't think I'll have anything, thank you. • Great! I want to try some typical dishes! • I always have the ceviche here.

Práctica

A ¡**Por eso no come nadie allí!** Exprese negativamente, usando la negativa doble.

1. Hay algo interesante en el menú.
2. Tienen algunos platos típicos.
3. El profesor cena allí también.
4. Mis amigos siempre almuerzan allí.

5. Preparan algo especial para grupos grandes.
6. Siempre hacen platos nuevos.
7. Y también sirven paella, mi plato favorito.

B **Rosa y Rodolfo**

Paso 1. Rosa es una persona muy positiva, pero su hermano Rodolfo tiene ideas muy negativas. Aquí hay unas oraciones que expresan las ideas de Rosa sobre varios temas. ¿Cuáles son las opiniones de Rodolfo?

SOBRE LAS CLASES Y LA VIDA UNIVERSITARIA

1. Hay algunos estudiantes excelentes en mi clase de sicología.
2. Hay algunas personas muy listas en la clase de español.
3. Por lo general, ¡me gusta muchísimo mi compañera de cuarto!
4. Salgo con mis amigos con frecuencia.

SOBRE LAS ACTIVIDADES DE ESTA NOCHE

5. Tengo hambre. ¿Por qué no comemos algo?
6. Vamos a beber algo antes de cenar.
7. Sirven algunos platos estupendos aquí.
8. Hay algo interesante en la tele esta noche.

Paso 2. Ahora invente Ud. algunos comentarios de Rodolfo sobre su familia y la ciudad donde vive. ¿Cómo reacciona Rosa?

C **¿Qué pasa esta noche en casa?** Tell whether the following statements about what is happening at this house are true (**cierto**) or false (**falso**). Then create as many additional sentences as you can about what is happening, following the model of the sentences.

1. No hay nadie en el baño.
2. En la cocina, alguien prepara la cena.
3. No hay ninguna persona en el patio.
4. Hay algo en la mesa del comedor.
5. Algunos amigos se divierten en la sala.
6. Hay algunos platos en la mesa del comedor.
7. No hay ningún niño en la casa.

Segundo paso

VOCABULARIO ▼▼▼▼▼▼▼▼▼▼▼▼▼▼▼▼▼▼▼▼▼▼▼▼▼

¿Qué sabe Ud. y a quién conoce?
Saber and conocer

¿**Conoce** al hombre de la foto? ¿**Sabe** su nombre?
Es el famoso cantante y actor Rubén Blades.
Es de Panamá. Sabe cantar muy bien, en inglés
y en español.

¿**Conoce** Ud. Panamá? Es un país muy bonito en
Centroamérica y tiene un canal importante.

la ciudad de Panamá

el canal de Panamá

saber *(to know)*		conocer *(to know)*	
sé	sabemos	cono**z**co	conocemos
sabes	sabéis	conoces	conocéis
sabe	saben	conoce	conocen

Two Spanish verbs express *to know*: **saber** and **conocer**.

- **Saber** means *to know* facts or pieces of information. When followed by an infinitive, **saber** means *to know how to do* something (or *to be able to do* something).

  No **sabemos** el teléfono de Alejandro. ¿**Saben** Uds. dónde vive Alejandro? ¿**Saben** llegar allí?

  We don't know Alejandro's phone number. Do you know where Alejandro lives? Do you know how to get there?

- **Conocer** means *to know* or *to be acquainted (familiar) with* a person, place, or thing. It can also mean *to meet*.

  No **conocen** a* la nueva estudiante todavía.

  They don't know the new student yet.

  ¿**Conocen** Uds. el restaurante mexicano en la calle Goya?

  Are you familiar with (Have you been to) the Mexican restaurant on Goya Street?

---

*Note the use of the word **a** in these examples. You will learn about this use of **a** in Grammar Section 18.

> ¿Quieres **conocer** a* aquel joven?
> —Ya lo **conocí.** Se llama Rafael.

> *Do you want to meet that young*
> *man? —I've already met him. His*
> *name is Rafael.*

Práctica

A ¿Qué saben hacer estas personas famosas?

Gloria Estefan			jugar al béisbol
Mikhail Baryshnikov			cantar (en español)
José Canseco	⎫		cocinar (*to cook*) bien
Stephen King	⎬ sabe		jugar al tenis
Julia Child	⎭		escribir novelas
Rubén Blades			bailar

B **Parejas famosas.** ¿A quién conoce... ?

Adán			Martha
Napoleón			Cleopatra
Romeo	⎫		Eva
Rhett Butler	⎬ conoce a		Julieta
Marco Antonio	⎭		Scarlett O'Hara
George Washington			Josefina

C **¿Saber o conocer?** Complete las siguientes oraciones con **conozco** o **sé.**

1. _____ al nuevo amigo de Marta pero no _____ de dónde es.
2. _____ un excelente restaurante chino pero no _____ en qué calle está.
3. Sí, sí, _____ a Julio pero no _____ su teléfono.
4. _____ jugar muy bien al tenis pero no _____ a ningún otro tenista (*tennis player*) en esta residencia.
5. No _____ muy bien la Ciudad de México pero _____ que quiero regresar.
6. ¡Qué problema! _____ que hay una prueba en esa clase mañana pero no _____ sobre qué capítulo es y no _____ a nadie de la clase.

D **¡Qué talento!**

Paso 1. Invente oraciones sobre tres cosas que Ud. sabe hacer.

MODELO: Sé tocar el acordeón.

Paso 2. Ahora, en grupos de tres estudiantes, pregúnteles a sus compañeros si saben hacer esas actividades. Escriba **sí** o **no,** según sus respuestas.

MODELO: ¿Sabes tocar el acordeón?

AMIGO/A 1: _____   AMIGO/A 2: _____

1. _____   _____
2. _____   _____
3. _____   _____

---

*Note the use of the word **a** in these examples. You will learn about this use of **a** in Grammar Section 18.

Paso 3. Ahora describa las habilidades de los estudiantes en su grupo.

MODELO: Marta y yo sabemos tocar el acordeón, pero Elena no. (En el grupo, sólo yo sé tocar el acordeón.) (En el grupo, nadie sabe tocar el acordeón.)

STUDY HINT: Practicing Spanish Outside of Class

The few hours you spend in class each week are not enough time for practicing Spanish. But once you have done your homework and gone to the language lab (if one is available to you), how else can you practice your Spanish outside of class?

1. Practice "talking to yourself" in Spanish. Have an imaginary conversation with someone you know, or simply practice describing what you see or what you are thinking about at a given moment. Write notes to yourself in Spanish.
2. Hold a conversation hour—perhaps on a regular basis—with other students of Spanish. Or make regular phone calls to practice Spanish with other students in your class.

3. See Spanish-language movies when they are shown on campus or in local movie theaters. Check local bookstores, libraries, and record stores for Spanish-language newspapers, magazines, and music. Read the radio and television listings. Are there any Spanish-language programs or any stations that broadcast partially or exclusively in Spanish?
4. Practice speaking Spanish with a native speaker—either a Hispanic American or a foreign student. Is there an international students' organization on campus? An authentic Hispanic restaurant in your town? Spanish-speaking professors at your university? Try out a few phrases—no matter how simple—every chance you get.

ESTRUCTURAS

18. Expressing *What* or *Whom*

Direct Objects and Personal *a*; Direct Object Pronouns

▼ **¿Dónde vamos a comer?**

AGUSTÍN: Empiezo a tener hambre. ¿Qué te parece si cenamos fuera esta noche?

MARIELA: ¡Buena idea! A propósito, ¿conoces *a* los Velázquez?

AGUSTÍN: Claro que sí. Hace años que *los* conozco. ¿Por qué me *lo* preguntas? Estamos hablando de comidas.

MARIELA: Pues acabo de oír que tienen un restaurante en la Avenida Bolívar.

AGUSTÍN: ¡Qué suerte! ¡A ver si *nos* invitan* a comer!

Where are we going to eat? AGUSTÍN: I'm getting hungry. What do you think about eating out tonight? MARIELA: Great! By the way, do you know the Velázquezes? AGUSTÍN? Of course I do. I've known them for years. Why do you ask? We're talking about food (meals). MARIELA: Well, I've just heard that they have a restaurant on Bolivar Avenue. AGUSTÍN: What luck! Let's see if they invite us to a free meal!

*¡OJO! **Invitar** is a cognate that has somewhat different connotations in Spanish and in English. In English, *to invite* someone is a request for that person's company. In Spanish, **te invito, nos invitan,** and similar phrases imply that the person who is inviting will also pay.

▼ 1. ¿Quién tiene hambre?   3. ¿Por qué habla Mariela de ellos?
▼ 2. ¿Quién conoce a los Velázquez? 4. ¿Quiere pagar la comida Agustín?

Direct Objects and Personal *a*

In English and in Spanish, the *direct object* (**el complemento directo**) of a sentence is the first recipient of the action of the verb.

> I see the *car*, but I don't see the *dog*.
> George is preparing *dinner* for the family.

Indicate the direct objects in the following sentences.

1. I don't see Betty.   3. Vamos a comprar un coche nuevo.
2. I need a new suit.   4. ¿Por qué no pones la sopa en la mesa?

In Spanish, the word **a** immediately precedes the direct object of a sentence when the direct object refers to a specific person or persons. This **a**, called the **a personal**, has no equivalent in English.*

Vamos a visitar **al profesor.**	*We're going to visit the professor.*
but	
Vamos a visitar **el museo.**	*We're going to visit the museum.*
Necesitan **a la camarera.**	*They need the waitress.*
but	
Necesitan **la cuenta.**	*They need the bill.*

The personal **a** is used before the interrogative words **¿quién?** and **¿quiénes?** when these words function as direct objects.

¿A quién llama?	*Whom are you calling?*
but	
¿Quién llama?	*Who is calling?*

The personal **a** is used before **alguien** and **nadie** when these words function as direct objects.

¿Vas a invitar **a alguien?**	*Are you going to invite someone?*
¿A quién llamas? —No llamo **a nadie.**	*Whom are you calling? —I'm not calling anyone.*

Direct Object Pronouns

¡OJO! The verbs **buscar** (*to look for*), **escuchar** (*to listen to*), **esperar** (*to wait for*), and **mirar** (*to look at*) include the sense of the English prepositions *for, to,* and *at*. These verbs take direct objects in Spanish (not prepositional phrases, as in English).

Busco **mi abrigo.**	*I'm looking for my overcoat.*
Espero **a mi hijo.**	*I'm waiting for my son.*

DIRECT OBJECT PRONOUNS			
me	me	**nos**	us
te	you (*fam. sing.*)	**os**	you (*fam. pl.*)
lo†	**you** (*form. sing.*), him, it (*m.*)	**los**	you (*form. pl.*), them (*m., m. + f.*)
la	you (*form. sing.*), her, it (*f.*)	**las**	you (*form. pl.*), them (*f.*)

---

*The personal **a** is not generally used with **tener: Tengo cuatro hijos.**

†In Spain and in some other parts of the Spanish-speaking world, **le** is frequently used instead of **lo** for the direct object pronoun *him*. This usage will not be followed in *¿Qué tal?*

A. Like direct object nouns, *direct object pronouns* (**los pronombres del complemento directo**) are the first recipient of the action of the verb. Direct object pronouns are placed before a conjugated verb and after the word **no** when it appears. Third person direct object pronouns are used only when the direct object noun has already been mentioned.

¿El libro? Diego no **lo** necesita.	*The book? Diego doesn't need it.*
¿Dónde están el libro y el periódico? **Los** necesito ahora.	*Where are the book and the newspaper? I need them now.*
Ellos **me** ayudan.	*They're helping me.*

[Práctica A–B]

B. The direct object pronouns may be attached to an infinitive.

Las tengo que leer. ⎫	
Tengo que leer**las**. ⎭	*I have to read them.*

[Práctica C]

C. Note that many verbs commonly used with reflexive pronouns can also be used with direct object nouns and pronouns when the action of the verb is directed at someone other than the subject of the sentence. The meaning of the verb will change slightly.

Generalmente me despierto a las ocho. El radio **me** despierta.	*I generally wake up at eight. The radio wakes me.*
En un restaurante, el camarero **nos** sienta.	*In a restaurant, the waiter seats us.*

[Práctica D–F]

D. Note that the direct object pronoun **lo** can refer to actions, situations, or ideas in general. When used in this way, **lo** expresses English *it* or *that*.

Lo comprende muy bien.	*He understands it (that) very well.*
No **lo** creo.	*I don't believe it (that).*
Lo sé.	*I know (it).*

Práctica

A ¿Qué come Ud.?

Paso 1. Para cada grupo, indique la respuesta que mejor represente sus preferencias en la comida.

1. las arvejas
☐ Las como con frecuencia.
☐ Las como de vez en cuando (*on occasion*).
☐ Nunca las como.

2. el queso
☐ Lo como con frecuencia.
☐ Lo como de vez en cuando.
☐ Nunca lo como.

3. la fruta
☐ La como con frecuencia.
☐ La como de vez en cuando.
☐ Nunca la como.

4. los dulces (*sweets*)
☐ Los como con frecuencia.
☐ Los como de vez en cuando.
☐ Nunca los como.

Paso 2. Ahora compare sus respuestas con las de sus compañeros de clase. ¿Tienen todos las mismas preferencias?

B **¿Qué come un vegetariano?** Aquí hay una lista de diferentes comidas. ¿Van a formar parte de la dieta de un vegetariano? Conteste según los modelos.

MODELOS: el bistec → No **lo** va a comer.
           la banana → **La** va a comer.

1. las papas
2. el arroz
3. las chuletas de cerdo
4. los huevos
5. la zanahoria
6. la manzana
7. los camarones
8. el pan
9. los frijoles
10. la ensalada

Si hay un estudiante vegetariano (una estudiante vegetariana) en la clase, pídale que verifique (*ask him or her to verify*) las respuestas de Ud.

C **Agustín y Mariela cenan fuera.** The following description of Agustín and Mariela's dinner out is very repetitive. Rephrase the sentences, changing direct object nouns to pronouns, as needed.

MODELO: El camarero tiene el menú y pone el menú delante de mí. →
           El camarero tiene el menú y **lo** pone delante de mí.

1. Agustín y Mariela toman el menú y leen el menú.
2. «¿Los platos del día? Voy a explicar los platos del día ahora.»
3. Agustín quiere comer un bistec y va a pedir un bistec.
4. Mariela prefiere el pescado fresco, pero hoy no tienen pescado fresco.
5. Agustín necesita pan y el camarero pone el pan en la mesa.
6. Mariela siempre prefiere comer la ensalada antes del plato principal. Por eso come la ensalada primero.
7. Los dos prefieren vino tinto. Por eso Agustín pide vino tinto.
8. «¿La cuenta (*check*)? Cómo no. Voy a preparar la cuenta para Uds. ahora mismo.»
9. Agustín quiere pagar con tarjeta de crédito, pero no tiene su tarjeta.
10. Por fin Mariela toma la cuenta y paga la cuenta.

D **¿Quién lo hace?** Indique a la persona o cosa que hace lo siguiente. Hay más de una respuesta posible.

Palabras útiles: el barbero, los (buenos) amigos, el camarero / la camarera, mi compañero/a, el despertador (*alarm clock*), el doctor / la doctora, mi esposo/a, los estudiantes, mi padre/madre, los profesores, el radio

1. Por la mañana, _____ me despierta.
2. En un restaurante, _____ nos sienta.
3. En una barbería, _____ nos afeita.
4. En un hospital, _____ nos examina.
5. _____ nos escuchan cuando necesitamos hablar.
6. _____ nos esperan cuando vamos a llegar tarde.
7. Generalmente los niños no se acuestan solos (*by themselves*). _____ los acuesta. _____ también los baña y los viste.
8. En una clase, _____ hacen las preguntas y _____ las contestan.

E **¿Quién ayuda?** Todos necesitamos la ayuda de alguien en diferentes circunstancias. ¿Quién los/las ayuda (a Uds.) con lo siguiente? Use **me** o **nos** en sus respuestas. Puede hablar del pasado, si quiere.

MODELOS: con las cuentas →
   Nuestros padres **nos** ayudan con las cuentas.
   Mis padres **me** ayudaron una vez.

Palabras útiles: mis/nuestros padres (compañeros, consejeros, amigos...)

1. con las cuentas
2. con la tarea (*homework*)
3. con la matrícula

4. con el horario de clases
5. con el español
6. con los problemas personales

F **Una encuesta sobre la comida.** Haga preguntas a sus compañeros de clase para saber si comen las comidas indicadas y con qué frecuencia. Deben explicar también por qué comen o **no** comen cierta comida.

MODELO: la carne → E1: ¿Comes carne?
   E2: No la como casi nunca. Tiene mucho colesterol. Pero la comí una vez la semana pasada.

Palabras útiles: la cafeína, las calorías, el colesterol, la grasa (*fat*)

Frases útiles: estar a dieta, ser alérgico/a a, ser bueno/a para la salud (*health*), me pone (*it makes me*) nervioso/a, me da asco (*it makes me sick*) / me dan asco (*they make me sick*), lo/la/los/las detesto

1. la carne
2. los mariscos
3. el yogur
4. la pizza

5. las hamburguesas
6. el pollo
7. el café
8. las habas (*lima beans*)

9. el alcohol
10. el atún
11. las espinacas
12. el hígado (*liver*)

A ¿Qué hace Roberto los martes?

Paso 1. Describa la rutina de Roberto, haciendo oraciones según las indicaciones.

1. martes / Roberto / nunca / salir / de / apartamento / antes de / doce
2. (*él*) esperar / su amigo Samuel / delante de / casa de Samuel
3. los dos / esperar / autobús (*m.*) / juntos
4. (*ellos*) llegar / a / universidad / a / una
5. (*ellos*) buscar / su amiga Ceci / en / cafetería

6. ella / empezar / estudios / allí / este año
7. (ella) no / conocer / mucha gente (*people*) / todavía
8. a veces / (ellos) hablar / con / profesora de historia
9. (ella) ser / persona / muy interesante / que / saber / mucho / de / ese / materia
10. a / dos / todos / tener / clase / de / sicología
11. siempre / (ellos) hacer / alguno / preguntas
12. a veces / (ellos) tener / oportunidad / de / conocer / conferenciante (*m., lecturer*)
13. a / cinco / Samuel y Roberto / volver / esperar / autobús
14. en / apartamento, / Roberto / siempre / buscar / su compañero Raúl / para / hablar / poco / con / él
15. los dos / preparar / cena / juntos / y / luego / mirar televisión

¿Quién habla?

1. Quiero conocer a más gente. ¡Casi no conozco a nadie todavía!
2. Algunos estudiantes hacen buenas preguntas.
3. ¡Acabo de llegar! ¿Dónde estás?
4. ¡Ay! Roberto ya está aquí y todavía tengo que buscar mis libros.

Paso 2. Ahora vuelva a contar la historia desde el punto de vista de Roberto, usando **yo** o **nosotros** como sujeto donde sea apropiado y los adjetivos posesivos apropiados.

B **¡Firma** (*Sign*) **aquí, por favor!** Find someone in the class about whom the following statements are true. Have that person sign his or her name. Don't forget to ask the question before they sign.

MODELO: E1: ¿Conoces a mucha gente latinoamericana?
          E2: Sí. Tengo amigos argentinos, bolivianos y mexicanos.
          E1: Firma aquí, por favor.

                                                                        FIRMA
1. Conozco a mucha gente latinoamericana.   _____
2. Sé hablar muy bien el español.   _____
3. Conozco a una persona famosa: _____ (nombre)   _____
4. Conozco un país donde se habla español _____ (nombre)   _____
5. Sé tocar un intrumento musical: _____.   _____
6. Sé jugar al ajedrez (*chess*).   _____
7. Sé quién es el cantante dominicano Juan Luis Guerra.   _____
8. Sé cantar una canción en español.   _____

SITUACIÓN Un nuevo restaurante

—Hay un nuevo restaurante en el barrio. Se llama El Charro. ¿Lo conoces?
—Sí, acabo de cenar allí con mis hijos.
—¿Y qué tal? ¿Qué tipo de comida tienen?
—Es un restaurante mexicano, y sirven muchos platos vegetarianos.

Un restaurante de San Antonio.

—¿Te gusta?
—Sí, me encanta.[a] Además[b] no es caro.
—Gracias por la recomendación, ¿eh?
—De nada.

[a]*me... I love it*   [b]*Besides*

NOTAS COMUNICATIVAS SOBRE EL DIÁLOGO

Use **acabar de** + [*inf.*] to express what you have just done.

Acabo de cenar con mis padres.	*I just had dinner with my parents*
Acabo de conocerlos.	*I just met them.*

Note that the infinitive must follow the preposition **de.**

Conversación

- Practique el diálogo con un compañero o una compañera. Luego adáptelo para hablar de algún restaurante nuevo en su ciudad.
- ¿Qué acaban de hacer Uds. cuando salen de los siguientes lugares?

  1. de un restaurante: Acabo de comer,...
  2. de un mercado: Acabo de...
  3. de una discoteca:
  4. de una biblioteca:
  5. de casa por la mañana:

¿POR O PARA?

Note in the preceding dialogue the use of **por** to thank someone for something.

gracias por + *noun*
   Gracias por el regalo.
   Gracias por la invitación.

gracias por + *infinitive*
   Gracias por llamarme.
   Gracias por invitarnos.

PARA ESCRIBIR

Think of your eating habits and the things that you like and don't like to eat. Then write two paragraphs.

- In the first one, summarize what you eat and don't eat: **Yo como... pero no como... Me gusta mucho comer... Como más... que...**

- In the second paragraph evaluate your diet: **En general, mi dieta es buena/ mala/regular porque... Debo comer más/menos...**

▼▼▼▼▼▼▼▼▼▼▼▼▼▼▼▼ **VOCABULARIO** ▼▼▼▼▼▼▼▼▼▼▼▼▼▼▼▼

Verbos

acabar de + (*inf.*) to have just (*done something*)
ayudar to help
cenar to have dinner
conocer (*irreg.*) to know (*people*); to be familiar with
desayunar to have breakfast
esperar to wait (for)
invitar to invite
saber (*irreg.*) to know (*information*)

Repaso: **almorzar (ue), pedir (i)**

La comida

el arroz rice
las arvejas peas
el atún tuna
el bistec steak
el bollo roll
los camarones shrimp
la carne meat
la chuleta (de cerdo) (pork) chop
el flan baked custard
los frijoles beans
la galleta cookie; cracker
el helado ice cream
el huevo egg
el jamón ham
la langosta lobster
la lechuga lettuce
la manzana apple
los mariscos shellfish
la naranja orange
el pan bread
el pan tostado toast

la papa potato
  al horno baked potato
  frita French fried potato
el pastel cake; pie
el pavo turkey
el pescado fish
el pollo chicken
el postre dessert
el queso cheese
la sopa soup
las verduras vegetables
la zanahoria carrot

Las bebidas

el agua (mineral) (mineral) water
el jugo juice
el vino blanco white wine
el vino tinto red wine

Repaso: **el café, la cerveza, la leche, el refresco**

Cognados (la comida, las bebidas): **la banana, la ensalada, los espárragos, la fruta, la hamburguesa, el salmón, el sándwich, el té, el tomate**

Las comidas

el almuerzo lunch
la cena dinner
el desayuno breakfast

Otros sustantivos

el/la camarero/a waitperson
la cuenta bill; check (*in a restaurant*)
el menú menú
el plato dish (*to eat*)

Adjetivos

ligero/a light (*in weight, content*)
rápido/a fast, quick

Palabras indefinidas y negativas

algo something
alguien someone, anyone
algún (alguno/a) some, any
jamás never
nada nothing, not anything
nadie nobody, no one
ningún (ninguno/a) no, none, not any
tampoco neither, not either

Repaso: **nunca, siempre, también**

Palabras adicionales

de vez en cuando on occasion, from time to time
fuera out (*not at home*)
gracias por thanks for
tener (mucha) hambre to be (very) hungry
tener (mucha) sed to be (very) thirsty
una vez once

Self-Test

Use the tape that accompanies this text to test yourself briefly on the important points of this chapter.

LECTURA
cultural

Antes de leer: Words with Multiple Meanings

It is easy to get "off the track" while reading if you assign the wrong meaning to a word that has multiple English equivalents. The word **como** can cause confusion because it can mean *how, like, the way that, as, since,* and *I eat,* depending on the context in which it occurs. Other common words with multiple meanings include **que** (*what, that, who*), **clase** (*class meeting, course, kind* or *type*), and **esperar** (*to wait for, to hope, to expect*).

You must rely on the context to determine which meaning is appropriate. Practice by telling what **como** means in each of the following sentences.

1. En España, como en Francia, se come mucho pescado.

2. No me gusta como habla el profesor; necesita hablar más despacio.

3. Como tú no deseas estudiar, ¿por qué no tomamos una cerveza?

Additional note: The readings in previous **Lectura cultural** sections were written especially for students like you, or they were simplified versions of authentic materials written for native speakers of Spanish. The following is the first truly authentic, unsimplified reading you have seen in *¿Qué tal?*. You should be able to get the gist of the reading easily, even though you will not understand every word. It is a good idea to scan the activities in the **Comprensión** section first, to get a sense for what is important in the article.

SABOR

Tapas^a y vinos, placer español

Las tapas no sustituyen una comida formal pero son ideales para una fiesta a la española o para disfrutar los deliciosos manjares de esa tierra

Calamares en su tinta, una tapa española típica que sirve el restaurante Barcelona Paradis en Nueva York

por Virginia Godoy

Irse de tapas es una divertida costumbre española que llegó a Estados Unidos durante la década de los ochenta. En las ciudades españolas, los mesones, tascas, cervecerías, bares, xampanyeries (champañerías catalanas), restaurantes y bodegones se convierten en centro de reunión donde estudiantes, banqueros y parroquianos[b] en general socializan, hablan del próximo examen universitario, de negocios o simplemente se relajan tomando tapas acompañadas de un buen vino o cerveza.

Aunque las tapas no sustituyen una comida formal, son ideales para una fiesta a la española a base de tapas y vinos. Se debe elegir una variación de tapas fritas, asadas u horneadas en el último minuto, otras con salsa, algunas frías o marinadas y otras servidas con pan o envueltas con masa.

Usualmente, las tapas con salsa como las angulas de Aguinaga, los champiñones al ajillo o los callos a la madrileña se sirven en cazuelitas de barro.[c] En cambio las ensaladas, arroces, pinchos, banderillas, queso y morcilla[d] se colocan en platos pequeños.

Una de las tapas más fáciles de preparar son las aceitunas[e] a la sevillana o las almendras[f] peladas y sofritas en aceite puro de oliva. Este tipo de tapas, junto con las de queso manchego (queso blanco duro español) y el jamón de Jabugo (similar al prosciutto de Parma) son ideales con una copa de jerez,[g] un scotch o cualquier otra bebida.

Existen tantas tapas como tipos de comida en las diferentes provincias españolas. Así por ejemplo los 'pescaítos'[h] fritos son típicos de Andalucía, los arroces de Valencia y las combinaciones de mariscos son de Galicia. Otras tapas como los riñones[i] al Jerez o los chorizos al cava reflejan la riqueza vinícola española en la cocina.

---

[a]*Appetizers* [b]*clientes* [c]*cazuelitas... clay bowls* [d]*blood sausage* [e]*olives* [f]*almonds* [g]*sherry* [h]*pescados* [i]*kidneys*

Comprensión

A Las siguientes palabras subrayadas tienen doble significado. ¿Entendió Ud. bien su significado?

1. « ...las tapas con salsa <u>como</u> las angulas de Aguinaga... »
   El significado apropiado de **como** es:
   - ☐ *I eat*
   - ☐ *such as*

2. « ...los champiñones al ajillo o los <u>callos</u> a la madrileña... »
   El significado apropiado de **callos** es:
   - ☐ *calluses*
   - ☐ *tripe*

3. « ...las ensaladas, arroces, pinchos, <u>banderillas</u>, queso... »
   El significado apropiado de **banderillas** es:
   - ☐ *barbed dart used in bullfighting*
   - ☐ *hors d'œuvres on a toothpick*

B ¿**Cierto o falso?** Conteste según la lectura.

1. La costumbre (*custom*) de las tapas viene de España.
2. En general, irse de tapas es una costumbre de la clase alta.
3. Hay gran variedad de tapas, aunque todas se sirven frías.
4. Muchas provincias tienen sus propias especialidades.
5. Las tapas son ideales porque reemplazan a la comida formal.

C En el artículo se menciona que las tapas se sirven en muchos lugares, como por ejemplo en las cervecerías y las champañerías. ¿Puede Ud. deducir el nombre de la bebida que se sirve en estos lugares?

En una cervecería sirven _____ .
En una champañería sirven _____ .

Primer paso

¡Buen provecho!^a

^a¡Buen… *Enjoy your meal!*

el cocinero

el dinero en efectivo

los Ramírez

la bandeja

la cuenta

el camarero

los González

la tarjeta de crédito

la botella

el menú

los Fuentes

el jarro

la cuchara

el vaso

la cucharita   el cuchillo   el mantel

la copa

la servilleta

el plato   el tenedor

En un
RESTAURANTE

Más vocabulario

el dueño/la dueña   owner

Práctica

A **Cuestiones de servicio.** ¿Qué objeto(s) se usa(n) para... ?

1. tomar agua o leche
2. llevar los platos a la mesa
3. llevar el vino a la mesa
4. indicar cuánto tienen que pagar los clientes
5. indicar todos los platos que se sirven en el restaurante
6. tomar vino o champán
7. tomar sopa
8. comer helado
9. pagar la cuenta

B **¿Quién habla?** ¿Habla el dueño del restaurante, el cocinero, el camarero o el cliente? A veces hay más de una respuesta posible.

1. Psst. En esa mesa necesitan una silla pequeña para un niño.
2. Otra servilleta, por favor, cuando pueda (*whenever you have a second*).
3. Aquí tienen Uds. el menú.
4. Señor, este tenedor está sucio.
5. ¡Imposible! No puedo preparar ese plato esta noche. No tengo todos los ingredientes...
6. No, señor, no puedo llevar esta bandeja con tantos platos.
7. La cuenta, por favor.
8. No tengo bastante (*enough*) dinero esta noche. Voy a usar mi tarjeta de crédito.
9. No aceptamos esa tarjeta de crédito.
10. Me gusta mucho este restaurante. Creo que debemos cenar aquí otra vez (*again*). Y tú, ¿qué crees?

EXPRESSING ACTIONS: *oír, traer,* and *ver*

oír *(to hear)*		traer *(to bring)*		ver *(to see)*	
oigo	oímos	traigo	traemos	veo	vemos
oyes	oís	traes	traéis	ves	veis
oye	oyen	trae	traen	ve	ven

- oír

  No **oigo** bien por el ruido.   *I can't hear well because of the noise.*

English uses *listen!* or *hey!* to attract someone's attention. In Spanish the command forms of **oír** are used: **oye (tú), oiga (Ud.), oigan (Uds.).**

  Oye, Juan, ¿vas a la fiesta así?   *Hey, Juan, are you going to the party (dressed) like that?*

  ¡Oiga Ud., por favor!   *Listen (Pay attention), please!*

- traer

  ¿Me **trae** la cuenta por favor?   *Would you bring the check, please?*

- ver

  No **veo** bien. ¿Qué pasa con la luz?   *I can't see well. What's wrong with the light?*

Práctica

A **¡Un restaurante desastroso!** At dinner with friends in a new restaurant, things are not working out. Describe what is happening by completing the following sentences in as many ways as you can, using forms of **oír, traer,** and **ver.**

Palabras útiles: mi cartera, la cuenta, la música, la conversación, a mis amigos, los platos, los platos del día (*specials*), el menú, el vino, la comida, el dinero

1. Hay mucho ruido. Por eso yo no...
2. Hay muy poca luz. Por eso yo no...
3. ¿Dónde está... ? El camarero debe...
4. ¡Qué desgracia! Aquí está la cuenta y yo no...

B **En la radio y en la televisión.** Complete las oraciones lógicamente.

1. Los jueves siempre veo _____ (programa).
2. Por la noche, después de ver las noticias (*news*), siempre veo _____ / me duermo en seguida.
3. Anoche vi (*I saw*) _____ (programa) en la televisión.
4. En la radio, siempre escucho _____ (estación).
5. Ayer oí _____ (programa, canción) en la radio.

DE AQUÍ Y DE ALLÁ

Just as mealtimes (and the actual foods eaten) vary throughout the Spanish-speaking world, so do the actual names for food. In fact, food vocabulary is one of the areas in which words most frequently differ from country to country. Here are some very common examples.

HISPANIC AMERICA:	la papa	los camarones	las arvejas
SPAIN:	la patata	las gambas	los guisantes

Another frequently used word means different things in different parts of the Hispanic world. You probably know what **una tortilla** is in Mexican cuisine (a type of flat bread made of corn or flour). In Spain, however, **una tortilla** is an omelette, and it can be **una tortilla francesa** (plain or with a light stuffing, such as ham or vegetables) or **una tortilla española** (with potatoes and onions).

ESTRUCTURAS

19. Expressing *To Whom* or *For Whom*

Indirect Object Pronouns; *dar* and *decir*

En un restaurante, antes de sentarse

HIJO: Mamá, tengo hambre. ¿*Me das* un caramelo?

MAMÁ: No, hijo. No *te* voy a *dar* dulces. Vamos a comer muy pronto.

HIJO: Bueno, pues entonces quiero leer. ¿*Me* compras una revista?

MAMÁ: No, no *te* voy a comprar otra revista. Acabo de comprar*te* una.

HIJO: Mamá...

MAMÁ: Oye, te quiero mucho, pero no *me* pidas más cosas, por favor.

HIJO: Pero mamá...

MAMÁ: ¡*Te dije* que no!

HIJO: Pero mamá, ¿no oíste? ¡Acaban de anunciar nuestro nombre!

▲ ▲ ▲

¿Qué dicen el niño y su mamá, **me** o **te**?

1. ¿_____ das un caramelo? No, no _____ doy más dulces.
2. ¿_____ compras una revista? No, no _____ voy a comprar nada más.
3. ¿_____ quieres mucho? ¡Claro que _____ quiero! Pero _____ pides demasiadas cosas.

At a restaurant, before sitting down.   SON: Mom, I'm hungry. Will you give me a piece of candy? MOM: No, son. I will not give you any sweets. We're going to eat very soon. SON: Okay, then, I want to read. Will you buy me a magazine? MOM: No, I'm not going to buy you another magazine. I just bought you one. SON: Mom . . . MOM: Listen, I love you a lot, but don't ask me for anything else, please. SON: But, Mom . . . MOM: I told you no! SON: But, Mom, didn't you hear? They've just called our name.

Indirect Object Pronouns

me	to/for me	**nos**	to/for us
te	to/for you (*fam. sing.*)	**os**	to/for you (*fam. pl.*)
le	to/for you (*form. sing.*), him, her it	**les**	to/for you (*form. pl.*), them

A. Indirect object nouns and pronouns are the second recipient of the action of the verb. They usually answer the questions *to whom?* or *for whom?* in relation to the verb. The word *to* is frequently omitted in English. Indirect object pronouns have the same form as direct object pronouns, except in the third person: **le, les.** Indicate the direct and indirect objects in the following sentences.

1. I'm giving her the present tomorrow.
2. Could you tell me the answer now?
3. El profesor nos va a hacer algunas preguntas.
4. ¿No me compras una revista ahora?

B. Like direct object pronouns, *indirect object pronouns* (**los pronombres del complemento indirecto**) are placed immediately before a conjugated verb. They may also be attached to an infinitive.

No, no **te** presto el coche.	*No, I won't lend you the car.*
Voy a guardar**te** el asiento. }	*I'll save your seat for you.*
Te voy a guardar el asiento. }	

C. Since **le** and **les** have several different equivalents, their meaning is often clarified or emphasized with the preposition **a** and the pronoun objects of prepositions.

Voy a mandar**le** un telegrama **a Ud. (a él, a ella).**	*I'm going to send you (him, her) a telegram.*
Les hago una comida **a Uds. (a ellos, a ellas).**	*I'm making you (them) a meal.*

D. When there is an indirect object noun in a sentence, the indirect object pronoun is almost always used in addition. This seemingly repetitive construction is very common in Spanish, especially with third person forms.

Vamos a decir**le** la verdad **a Juan.**	*Let's tell Juan the truth.*
¿**Les** guardo los asientos **a Jorge y Marta?**	*Shall I save the seats for Jorge and Marta?*

E. Verbs frequently used with indirect objects include **dar** (*to give*), **decir** (*to say; to tell*), **escribir, explicar, hablar, mandar** (*to send*), **ofrecer** (*to offer*), **pedir (i), preguntar** (*to ask*), **prestar** (*to lend*), **prometer** (*to promise*), **recomendar (ie), regalar** (*to give as a gift*), and **servir (i). ¡OJO!** ofrecer → yo ofrezco, like **conocer.**

Dar and *decir*

dar (*to give*)		**decir** (*to say; to tell*)	
d**oy**	damos	di**go**	decimos
das	dais	dices	decís
da	dan	dice	dicen

Dar and **decir** are almost always used with indirect object pronouns in Spanish.

¿Cuándo **me das** el dinero?   *When will you give me the money?*
¿Por qué no **me dice** Ud. la ver-   *Why don't you tell me the truth, sir?*
dad, señor?

¡OJO! In Spanish it is necessary to distinguish between the verbs **dar** (*to give*) and **regalar** (*to give as a gift*). Also, do not confuse **decir** (*to say* or *to tell*) with **hablar** (*to speak*) or **pedir** (*to ask for; to order*) with **preguntar** (*to ask [a question]*).

Práctica

A ¿Con qué frecuencia... ?

Paso 1. Indique con qué frecuencia Ud. hace las siguientes cosas.

	CON MUCHA FRECUENCIA	A VECES	NUNCA
1. Les escribo cartas a mis parientes.	☐	☐	☐
2. Les hago preguntas a mis profesores.	☐	☐	☐
3. Les presto dinero a mis amigos.	☐	☐	☐
4. Les ofrezco consejos (*advice*) a mis amigos.	☐	☐	☐
5. Les digo mentiras (*lies*) a mis padres.	☐	☐	☐
6. Les explico mis problemas a mis amigos.	☐	☐	☐
7. Le mando flores (*flowers*) y bombones a alguien.	☐	☐	☐
8. Le doy una cuenta a alguien.	☐	☐	☐

Paso 2. Ahora cambie (*change*) las oraciones para indicar con qué frecuencia las personas le hacen las mismas cosas a Ud.

MODELO: Mis padres me escriben cartas a veces.

B ¿Quién te... ? Who does the following things to or for you? Follow the model.

MODELO: En el restaurante: traer el menú (camarero) →
En el restaurante, el camarero **me** trae el menú.

1. En el restaurante: traer el menú (camarero), explicar los platos del día (camarero), preparar la comida (cocinero), servir la comida (camarero), dar la cuenta (dueño)
2. En clase: explicar la gramática (profesor[a]), hacer preguntas (otros estudiantes), dar exámenes (profesor[a]), prestar un lápiz o un papel (un compañero)

Now repeat the same items, using **nos: En el restaurante, el camarero *nos* trae el menú.**

C **En un restaurante.** Your four-year-old cousin Benjamín is not used to eating in restaurants. Explain to him what will happen, filling in the blanks with the appropriate indirect object pronoun.

Primero el camarero_____¹ indica (a ti) una mesa desocupada. Luego tú _____² pides el menú al camarero. También _____³ haces preguntas sobre los platos y las especialidades de la casa y _____⁴ dices tus preferencias. El camarero _____⁵ trae la comida. Por fin tu papá _____⁶ pide la cuenta al camarero. Si tú quieres pagar, _____⁷ pides dinero a tu papá y _____⁸ das el dinero al camarero.

D ¿Qué va a pasar? Dé varias respuestas.

Palabras útiles: medicinas, Santa Claus, tarjetas navideñas (*Christmas cards*), flores, juguetes (*toys*), portarse (*to behave*)

1. Su amiga Elena está en el hospital con un ataque de apendicitis. Todos le mandan... Le escriben... Las enfermeras (*nurses*) le dan... De comer, le sirven...
2. Es Navidad. Los niños les prometen a sus padres... Les piden... También le escriben... Le piden... Los padres les mandan... a sus amigos. Les regalan...
3. Mi coche no funciona hoy. Mi amigo me presta... Mis padres (hijos) me preguntan... Luego me dan...

E ¿Qué hacen estas personas? Complete las siguientes oraciones con un verbo lógico y un pronombre de complemento indirecto. Vea la lista de verbos en la página 186.

MODELO: El vicepresidente *le ofrece* consejos al presidente.

1. Romeo _____ flores a Julieta.
2. Snoopy _____ besos (*kisses*) a Lucy... ¡Y a ella no le gusta!
3. Eva _____ una manzana a Adán.
4. Ann Landers _____ consejos a sus lectores (*readers*).
5. Los bancos _____ dinero a las personas que quieren comprar una casa.
6. Los camareros _____ bebidas a los clientes.
7. George Washington _____ a su padre decir la verdad.
8. Los niños _____ la verdad a sus padres en diciembre.

Segundo paso

VOCABULARIO ▼▼▼▼▼▼▼▼▼▼▼▼▼▼▼▼▼▼▼▼▼▼▼▼

RECICLADO

You have already used forms of **gustar** to express your likes and dislikes (**Primeros pasos**). Review what you know by answering the following questions. Then use them, changing their form as needed, to interview your instructor.

1. ¿Te gusta el café (el vino, el té, ...)?
2. ¿Te gusta jugar al béisbol (al golf, al vólibol, al...)?
3. ¿Qué te gusta más, estudiar o ir a fiestas (trabajar o descansar, cocinar o comer)?

Expressing Likes and Dislikes: *gustar*

—¿Qué les parece este restaurante? ¿Les **gusta**?
—¡A mí me **gusta** mucho!
—Y a mí me **gustan** los postres que sirven.
—Bueno, ¿quién va a pagar hoy?
—¿Nadie contesta?
—Bueno, nos **gusta** mucho el restaurante... no nos **gustan** nada las cuentas.

You have been using the verb **gustar** since the beginning of *¿Qué tal?* to express likes and dislikes. However, **gustar** does not literally mean *to like,* but *to be pleasing.*

   Gustar is always used with an indirect object pronoun: someone or something is pleasing to someone else. The verb must agree with its subject, which is the person or thing that is pleasing. Note that an infinitive is viewed as a singular subject in Spanish.

Me **gusta** este **restaurante**.	*This restaurant is pleasing to me. I like this restaurant.*
Me **gusta** cocinar.	*Cooking is pleasing to me. I like to cook.*
Me **gustan** mis **compañeros** de clase.	*My classmates are pleasing to me. I like my classmates.*

Note that a phrase with **a** + a prepositional *pronoun* can be used for clarification or emphasis.

CLARIFICATION

¿**A Ud.** le gusta viajar?	*Do you like to travel?*
¿**A él** le gusta viajar?	*Does he like to travel?*

EMPHASIS

A mí me gustan las arvejas, pero **a ti** no te gustan, ¿verdad?	*I like peas but you don't, right?*

The indirect object pronoun *must* be used with **gustar** even when an indirect object noun is expressed. A common word order is as follows.

a + PRONOUN/NOUN	INDIRECT OBJECT PRONOUN	gustar + SUBJECT
A Juan	le	gustan las fiestas.
A mis tías	les	gusta cocinar.

Remember that the pronouns **mí** and **ti** (not the subject pronouns **yo** and **tú**) are used as the objects of prepositions.

Would Like / Wouldn't Like

What one *would* or *would not* like to do is expressed with the form **gustaría** + [*infinitive*] and the appropriate indirect objects.

A mí **me gustaría viajar** al Perú.	*I would like to travel to Peru.*
Nos gustaría cenar temprano esta noche.	*We would like to eat early tonight.*

Práctica

A Gustos y preferencias

Paso 1. Using the models as a guide, tell whether or not you like the following.

MODELOS: ¿el café? → (No) Me **gusta** el café.
¿los pasteles? → (No) Me **gustan** los pasteles.

1. ¿el vino?
2. ¿los niños pequeños?
3. ¿la música clásica?
4. ¿las canciones de Whitney Houston?
5. ¿cocinar?
6. ¿las clases que empiezan a las ocho de la mañana?
7. ¿la gramática?
8. ¿el invierno?
9. ¿el chocolate?
10. ¿las películas (*movies*) de horror?
11. ¿las clases de este semestre/trimestre?
12. ¿bailar en las discotecas?

Paso 2. Now share your reactions with a classmate. He or she will respond with one of the following reactions.

A mí también. (*So do I.*)
A mí tampoco. (*I don't either.* [*Neither do I.*])
Pues a mí, sí/no. (*Well . . . I do/don't.*)

How do your likes and dislikes compare? Keep track of them.

B Una cena en casa. The different members of the Soto family have their own opinions about eating in. Imagine that you are one of the Soto children and describe the family's preferences, following the model.

MODELO: madre / gustar / comer en restaurantes →
A mi madre le gusta comer en restaurantes.

1. pero / hermana Maripepa / gustar / cocinar
2. (*ella*) saber / preparar platos exóticos
3. padre / no / gustar / pagar la cuenta en en restaurante
4. por eso / (*él*) gustar / comer en casa
5. hermanos / gustar / ayudar en casa
6. (*ellos*) tener / traer los platos
7. ti / gustaría / lavar los platos esta noche / ¿verdad?

Now, remembering what you have learned about the Soto family, answer the following questions.

1. ¿A quién le gustaría comer en el Gran Hotel Colón?
2. ¿A quién no le gustaría comer allí?
3. ¿A quién le parecen buenos los platos exóticos?
4. ¿Quién va a poner la mesa?
5. ¿Quién va a cocinar?

C Entrevista: ¿Conoce bien a sus compañeros?

Paso 1. Piense en una persona de la clase de español que Ud. conoce un poco. En su opinión, ¿a esa persona le gustan o no las siguientes cosas?

		SÍ LE GUSTA(N)	NO, NO LE GUSTA(N)
1.	la música clásica	☐	☐
2.	el color negro	☐	☐
3.	las canciones de los años 60	☐	☐
4.	viajar en coche	☐	☐
5.	la comida mexicana	☐	☐
6.	tener clases por la mañana	☐	☐
7.	estudiar otras lenguas	☐	☐
8.	el arte surrealista	☐	☐
9.	las películas trágicas	☐	☐
10.	las casas viejas	☐	☐
11.	¿ ?	☐	☐

Paso 2. Ahora entreviste a su compañero/a para verificar si sus respuestas son correctas. ¿Cuántas respuestas correctas tiene Ud.? ¿Conoce bien a su compañero/a?

    MODELO: ¿Te gusta la música clásica?

▼▼▼▼▼▼▼▼▼▼▼▼▼▼▼▼▼▼▼▼▼▼▼▼▼▼▼▼▼ **ESTRUCTURAS**

RECICLADO

In **Capítulo 8** you learned some forms of the preterite, one of the past tenses in Spanish. Review those forms by completing the following:

hablar: (yo) habl-_____   (tú) habl-_____   (Ud.) habl-_____   ir: (yo) _____   hacer: (tú) _____

comer: (yo) com-_____   (tú) com-_____   (él) com-_____   ser: (yo) _____   tener: (tú) _____

vivir: (yo) viv-_____   (tú) viv-_____   (ella) viv-_____

20. Talking About the Past (2)

Preterite of Regular Verbs and of *dar*, *hacer*, *ir*, and *ser*

▼ **La noche del sábado**

▼   VIRGINIA: Por fin te encuentro. Ayer te *llamé* todo el día para salir por la noche.

▼   LIDIA: Lo siento. Ayer no te *llamé* porque *llegaron* mis tíos de Chicago y *pasamos* el día juntos.

▼   VIRGINIA: ¿Adónde los *llevaste*?

Saturday night. VIRGINIA: I've finally caught up with you. I called you all day yesterday to go out last night. LIDIA: I'm sorry. I didn't call you yesterday because my aunt and uncle arrived from Chicago and we spent the day together. VIRGINIA: Where did you take them?

▼   LIDIA: *Fuimos* al puerto y luego *paseamos* por el centro de la ciudad. Por la
▼   noche *cenamos* en un restaurante cubano que les *encantó. Comimos* ca-
▼   marones enchilados, arroz y frijoles negros y plátanos maduros. ¡*Fue*
▼   delicioso!
▼   VIRGINIA: ¡Qué bien! Y yo *me quedé* en casa sola toda la noche del sábado sin
▼   hacer nada. ¡*Fue* un aburrimiento total!
▼
▼   ▲ ▲ ▲
▼
▼ ¿Quién... ?

▼ 1. llamó a una amiga todo el día ayer   4. se quedó sola en casa anoche
▼ 2. cenó comida cubana   5. hizo de guía turístico
▼ 3. llegó de Chicago   6. salió el sábado por la noche

In **Capítulo 8** of *¿Qué tal?* you learned to use the singular forms of regular verbs in the preterite as well as the singular forms of the irregular verbs **dar, hacer, ir,** and **ser.** To talk about all aspects of the past in Spanish, you need to know how to use two *simple tenses* (tenses formed without an auxiliary or "helping" verb): the preterite and the imperfect. In this chapter, you will learn the plural forms of the preterite and practice more with the singular forms. In this and following chapters, you will learn more about preterite forms and their uses as well as about the imperfect and the ways in which it is used alone and with the preterite.

The *preterite* (**el pretérito**) has several equivalents in English. For example, **hablé** can mean *I spoke* or *I did speak.* The preterite is used to report finished, completed actions or states of being in the past. If the action or state of being is viewed as completed—no matter how long it lasted or took to complete—it will be expressed with the preterite.

Preterite of Regular Verbs

hablar		comer		vivir	
hablé	*I spoke (did speak)*	comí	*I ate (did eat)*	viví	*I lived (did live)*
hablaste	*you spoke*	comiste	*you ate*	viviste	*you lived*
habló	*you/he/she spoke*	comió	*you/he/she ate*	vivió	*you/he/she lived*
hablamos	*we spoke*	comimos	*we ate*	vivimos	*we lived*
hablasteis	*you spoke*	comisteis	*you ate*	vivisteis	*you lived*
hablaron	*you/they spoke*	comieron	*you/they ate*	vivieron	*you/they lived*

Note the accent marks on the first and third person singular of the preterite tense. These accent marks are dropped in the conjugation of **ver: vi, vio.**

Pronunciation hint: Some English words are distinguished from each other solely by the position of stress: *objéct (to express disagreement)* or *óbject (thing); súspect (one who is suspected)* or *suspéct (to be suspicious).* The same is true in Spanish: **tomas** (*you take*) or **Tomás** (*Thomas*). It is particularly important to pay attention to stress

---

LIDIA: We went to the harbor and then we walked around downtown. At night we had dinner at a Cuban restaurant that they loved. We ate shrimp in a pepper sauce, rice and black beans, and sweet (ripe) plantains. It was delicious! VIRGINIA: Great! And I stayed home alone all Saturday night doing nothing. It was a total bore!

in preterite verb forms, because many of them are identical—except for the written accent—to other forms you have learned: **hablo** (*I speak*) versus **habló** (*you/he/she spoke*), **hable** (*speak,* **Ud.** command) versus **hablé** (*I spoke*), and so on.

Also, note the following about regular preterite forms.

- The forms of the first person plural (**nosotros**) in the preterite of **-ar** and **-ir** verbs are identical to those of the present. You will know the difference because of the context.
- Verbs that end in **-car, -gar,** and **-zar** show a spelling change in the first person singular of the preterite.

      buscar: bus**qu**é, buscaste, ...   empezar: empe**c**é, empezaste, ...
      pagar: pa**gu**é, pagaste, ...

- **-Ar** and **-er** stem-changing verbs show no stem change in the preterite: **desperté, volví. -Ir** stem-changing verbs do show a change.*
- An unstressed **-i-** between two vowels becomes **-y-**.

      creer: cre**y**ó, cre**y**eron   leer: le**y**ó, le**y**eron

Irregular Preterite Forms

dar		hacer		ir/ser	
di	dimos	hice	hicimos	fui	fuimos
diste	disteis	hiciste	hicisteis	fuiste	fuisteis
dio	dieron	hizo	hicieron	fue	fueron

The preterite endings for **dar** are the same as those used for regular **-er/-ir** verbs in the preterite, except that the accent marks are dropped. The third person singular of **hacer**—**hizo**—is spelled with a **z** to keep the [s] sound of the infinitive. **Ser** and **ir** have identical forms in the preterite. Context will make the meaning clear.

Fui profesora.	*I was a professor.*
Fui al centro anoche.	*I went downtown last night.*

Práctica

A **¿Qué hicieron en clase ayer?** Un compañero de clase no asistió a clase ayer. Hoy quiere saber qué pasó en clase. Indique las oraciones apropiadas y añada algunas oraciones si puede.

1. Trabajamos en grupos. ☐
2. Escuchamos música. ☐
3. Escribimos en la pizarra. ☐
4. Conjugamos muchos verbos. ☐
5. Escribimos una composición. ☐
6. Leímos un artículo de una revista. ☐
7. Hablamos de la gramática. ☐
8. Hicimos y contestamos muchas preguntas. ☐
9. Vimos un vídeo. ☐
10. Practicamos el vocabulario. ☐

*You will practice the preterite of most stem-changing verbs in **Capítulo 13.**

B **El día de tres compañeras**

Paso 1. Teresa, Evangelina y Liliana comparten (*share*) un apartamento en un viejo edificio. Ayer Teresa y Evangelina fueron a la universidad mientras Liliana se quedó en casa. Describa lo que hicieron, según la perspectiva de cada una.

TERESA Y EVANGELINA:

1. (*nosotras*) salir / de / apartamento / a / nueve
2. llegar / biblioteca / a diez
3. estudiar / toda la mañana / para / examen
4. escribir / muchos ejercicios
5. almorzar / con / amigos / en / cafetería
6. ir / a / laboratorio / a / una
7. hacer / todos los experimentos / de / manual (*m.*)
8. tomar / examen / a / cuatro
9. ¡examen / ser / horrible!
10. regresar / a casa / después de / examen
11. ayudar / Liliana / a / preparar / cena
12. cenar / todas juntas / a / siete

LILIANA:

1. (*yo*) quedarse / en casa / todo el día
2. mirar / televisión / por / mañana
3. llamar / mi / padres / a / once
4. tomar / café / y / leer / periódico
5. estudiar / para / examen / de química
6. ir / a / garaje / para / buscar / algo
7. ir / a / supermercado / y / comprar / comida
8. empezar / a / preparar / cena / a / cinco

Paso 2. Ahora vuelva a contar cómo fue el día de Liliana, pero desde el punto de vista de sus compañeras de cuarto. Luego cuente cómo fue el día de Teresa y Evangelina según Liliana.

C **Un semestre en México.** Cuente la siguiente historia desde el punto de vista de la persona indicada, usando el pretérito de los verbos.

1. (*yo*) pasar un semestre en México
2. mis padres: pagarme el vuelo (*flight*)...
3. ... pero (*yo*) trabajar para ganar el dinero para la matrícula y los otros gastos (*expenses*)
4. vivir con una familia mexicana encantadora
5. aprender mucho sobre la vida y la cultura mexicanas
6. visitar muchos sitios de interés turístico e histórico
7. mis amigos: escribirme muchas cartas
8. (*yo*) mandarles muchas tarjetas postales
9. comprarles recuerdos a todos
10. volver a los Estados Unidos al final de agosto

D **El sábado por la tarde...** The following drawings depict what Julián did last Saturday night. Match the phrases with the individual drawings in the sequence. Then narrate what Julián did, using verbs in the preterite. Use adverbs such as **primero, luego,** etc. as much as possible.

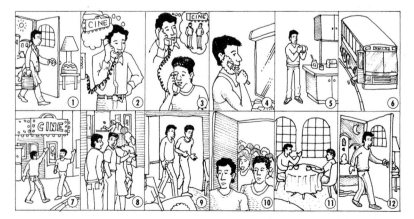

a. _____ comprar las entradas (*tickets*)
b. _____ regresar tarde a casa
c. _____ volver a casa después de trabajar
d. _____ ir a un café a tomar algo
e. _____ llegar al cine al mismo tiempo
f. _____ llamar a un amigo
g. _____ no gustarles la película
h. _____ comer rápidamente
i. _____ ducharse y afeitarse
j. _____ entrar en el cine
k. _____ ir al cine en autobús
l. _____ decidir encontrarse (*to meet up*) en el cine

Un paso más

UN POCO DE TODO

Tapas en un bar madrileño.

NOTA CULTURAL: Los aperitivos

Having something to eat or drink before dinner is a custom common to both U.S. and Hispanic cultures. The names for appetizers, however, vary considerably from one part of the Spanish-speaking world to another.

- In Spain, if someone invites you to have **un aperitivo,** you will probably order **un vermut**[a] or **un (vino) fino.**[b]
- In Latin America, **tomar un aperitivo** implies having a snack as well as a drink: olives, bits of cheese or sausage, and so on.
- In Spain, snacks of that kind are called **tapas,** a term also used in parts of the United States. There are many kinds of **tapas,** and people often make a full meal of them: **aceitunas,**[c] pieces of **chorizo,**[d] **tortilla española,**[e] **croquetas,** and many more.
- In Mexico, appetizers are called **antojitos, botanas,** or **bocadillos.**

[a]*vermouth* [b]*sherry* [c]*olives* [d]*sausage* [e]*tortilla... potato and onion omelette*

A **En un restaurante.** Complete the following conversation with the correct form of the words in parentheses, as suggested by the context. When two possibilities are given in parentheses, select the correct word.

CAMARERO: Buenas tardes, señor.

CLIENTE: Buenas tardes. ¿(Me/Mí[1]) trae (el/la[2]) menú, por favor?

CAMARERO: Cómo no. Ahora mismo[a] (le/la[3]) (*yo: traer*[4]) el menú y también agua. Mientras[b] decide lo que[c] desea para (almorzar/cenar[5]), ¿le (gusta/gustaría[6]) tomar (algo/nada[7]) de aperitivo?

CLIENTE: Pues... (un/una[8]) copa de vino tinto, por favor.

(Unos minutos más tarde)

CAMARERO: ¿Ya (conocer/saber[9]) Ud. lo que desea pedir?

CLIENTE: (Creer[10]) que sí. Para empezar, (me/le[11]) trae una sopa de tortillas, por favor. De segundo[d] plato, no (*yo: conocer/saber*[12])... ¿(Me/Te[13]) recomienda algo en especial?

CAMARERO: Pues los tacos (ser/estar[14]) la especialidad de la casa. Y personalmente, puedo decir(te/le[15]) que a (mí/mi[16]) me gusta (mucho/muy[17]) el pescado veracruzano que preparan aquí.

CLIENTE: Humm... A mí me (gustar[18]) los tacos. Voy a probar(les/los[19]).

CAMARERO: ¿Y de postre, señor?

CLIENTE: No (*yo: saber/conocer*[20]) todavía. ¿Puedo (ver[21]) el menú más tarde?

CAMARERO: Claro que sí.

[a]*Ahora... Right away* [b]*While* [c]*lo... what* [d]*main (second)*

B El fin de semana pasado

Paso 1. Haga una lista de diez cosas que Ud. hizo el fin de semana pasado. Pueden ser actividades que Ud. hizo solo/a o con los amigos.

> MODELOS: Me levanté tarde el sábado.
> Unos amigos y yo fuimos al cine el sábado.

Paso 2. Ahora entreviste a un compañero / una compañera para saber si hizo algunas de las mismas cosas. Debe hacerle preguntas basadas en su lista (**Paso 1**).

> MODELOS: ¿Te levantaste tarde el sábado? (¿A qué hora te levantaste el sábado?)
> ¿Fuiste al cine con unos amigos?

Paso 3. Ahora compare su fin de semana con el de (*that of*) su compañero/a.

> MODELO: Yo me levanté tarde, pero Juan se levantó temprano. Los dos fuimos al cine con unos amigos.

SITUACIÓN   Un problema en el restaurante

—¿Señora?
—Esta no es la sopa que yo pedí.
—¿No pidió Ud. gazpacho?
—No, yo le pedí sopa de tortillas. Además,[a] yo prefiero la ensalada antes de la sopa.
—Disculpe,[b] señora. Creo que esta sopa es de la otra mesa. Lo siento mucho.
—No hay problema. Pero tengo un poco de prisa.
—No se preocupe.[c] Ahora mismo le traigo su ensalada.

[a]*Besides*   [b]*Pardon me*   [c]*No... Don't worry.*

NOTAS COMUNICATIVAS SOBRE EL DIÁLOGO

Here are some useful words and expressions related to eating at home and in restaurants. You will be familiar with many of them already.

EL CAMARERO / LA CAMARERA	EL / LA CLIENTE
¿Qué desea Ud. de entremés? ¿de plato principal? ¿de postre? ¿para beber?	Favor de traerme un(a) _____.
¿Algo más?	¿Me trae un(a) _____, por favor?
	¿Qué recomienda Ud.?
	Un(a) _____ más, por favor.
	Oiga. Señor/Señorita.
	La cuenta, por favor.

Conversación

While having dinner in a restaurant, you have problems similar to those in the preceding dialogue. With a partner, alternate the roles of client and waitperson in the dialogue and substitute the following situations. Use the words and phrases in **Nota comunicativa sobre el diálogo,** as needed.

- You would like another napkin/knife/plate.
- Your soup is cold. (**¡OJO!** **estar**)

- Your knife/fork/spoon is dirty. (**¡OJO!** ¿**ser** o **estar**?)
- You need the check because you're in a hurry.

PARA ESCRIBIR

Write a brief paragraph about your eating preferences or those of your family. Use the following questions as a guide in developing your paragraph.

1. ¿Cuántas veces come(n) al día? ¿A qué hora?
2. ¿Comen juntos, a la misma hora y en la misma mesa? ¿Come Ud. solo/a (*alone*)?
3. ¿Quién(es) prepara(n) la comida?
4. ¿Qué prepara(n) con frecuencia? ¿Es excelente la comida? ¿buena? ¿mala? ¿regular?
5. ¿Conversa(n) mientras (*while*) comen? ¿Quién habla más? ¿menos? ¿Mira(n) la televisión mientras comen?
6. ¿Qué comida prefiere(n) cuando va(n) a un restaurante? ¿comida china? ¿mexicana? ¿italiana? ¿comida rápida? ¿En qué restaurantes comen?
7. ¿Come(n) allí con frecuencia? ¿Cuántas veces al año? ¿Cuándo va(n) a volver?

▼▼▼▼▼▼▼▼▼▼▼▼▼▼▼ **VOCABULARIO** ▼▼▼▼▼▼▼▼▼▼▼▼▼▼▼

Verbos

cocinar to cook
dar (*irreg.*) to give
decir (*irreg.*) to say; to tell
explicar to explain
gustar to like
mandar to send
ofrecer to offer
oír to hear
parecer to seem, appear
preguntar to ask (*questions*)
prestar to lend
prometer to promise
recomendar (ie) to recommend
regalar to give (as a gift)
traer to bring
ver (*irreg.*) to see

En el restaurante

la bandeja tray
la botella bottle
el/la cocinero/a cook, chef
la copa wine glass, goblet

el dinero en efectivo cash
el/la dueño/a owner
el jarro pitcher
el mantel tablecloth
la servilleta napkin
la tarjeta (de crédito) (credit) card
el vaso (drinking) glass

Repaso: **el/la camarero/a, la cuenta, el menú, el plato**

Utensilios de comer

la cuchara (soup)spoon
la cucharita teaspoon
el cuchillo knife
el tenedor fork

Otros sustantivos

el cine movies; movie theater
el consejo piece of advice
los dulces candy; sweets

la flor flower
la luz (*pl.* **luces**) light
la mentira lie
la película movie
el ruido noise

Palabras y expresiones útiles

buen provecho enjoy your meal
lo siento I'm sorry
me gustaría... I would like
otra vez again
pues... well

Self-Test

Use the tape that accompanies this text to test yourself briefly on the important points of this chapter.

VOCES

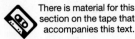There is material for this section on the tape that accompanies this text.

del mundo hispánico 5
Otras comunidades hispánicas en los Estados Unidos

Un 23% del total de los hispanos que viven en los Estados Unidos no son de origen mexicano, puertorriqueño o cubano. Los dominicanos son númericamente el cuarto[a] grupo hispánico en este país. Es un fenómeno reciente el gran aumento[b] de inmigrantes de Centroamérica, especialmente de El Salvador y Guatemala, debido a la inestable situación política y económica de esos países. También hay muchas personas del Perú, Colombia, el Ecuador, la Argentina, España y de otros países.

Estos grupos de hispanos son, por lo general, de inmigración reciente, y tien-

den[c] a establecerse en los grandes centros urbanos de la costa este y oeste. Por ejemplo, hay una importante población salvadoreña en Washington, D.C. Los dominicanos están en el nordeste, como los puertorriqueños. Los guatemaltecos usualmente van a California. Y muchos grupos hispanos no están localizados en centros de población bien definidos, como los españoles y los argentinos.

[a]fourth [b]increase [c]they tend

Lo mejor de la casa

L a mejor cocina caribeña es la casera.[a] Y el éxito de Sugar Reef, el restaurante pionero de la nueva onda caribeña en Nueva York, se debe a que sus platos representan la genuina tradición de esta región. El jefe de cocina, Pablo Rosado, aprendió a cocinar en su casa en la República Dominicana. En Nueva York, Rosado comenzó trabajando en la construcción del Sugar Reef y poco después fue contratado[b] como asistente de cocina. En un año había asumido la jefatura[c] de la misma, dominando no sólo los platos típicos dominicanos sino todas las tradiciones que distinguen el menú pancaribeño de Sugar Reef.

[a]homemade [b]hired [c]había... he had taken charge

Un chef dominicano trae el auténtico gusto caribeño a Nueva York

PABLO ROSADO

Jaime Escalante, profesor de matemáticas de escuela secundaria

Escalante, nacido[a] en Bolivia, enseña a los estudiantes de un barrio pobre de Los Ángeles, quienes consiguen[b] las calificaciones[c] más altas a nivel nacional en matemáticas y cálculo. Sus logros[d] con sus estudiantes son tan impresionantes que se hizo una película sobre él, *Stand and Deliver*, protagonizada por el actor mexicanoamericano James Edward Olmos.

[a]*born* [b]*achieve* [c]*grades* [d]*accomplishments*

Blades, la salsa de la política

Panamá pudo haber tenido[a] el presidente más melodioso del mundo. Rubén Blades, salsero[b] de profesión, decidió poner orden en su casa materna y presentarse a las elecciones presidenciales de 1994. «No vengo a buscar un carro ni una finca[c] ni a llenarme los bolsillos;[d] al contrario, estoy dejando[e] una situación muy favorable para venir aquí», afirma el también actor, que durante años ha vivido[f] en EE UU.[g] Los sondeos[h] antes de la elección demostraron su gran popularidad, sobre todo entre los más danzones.[i] Pero, al final, Blades quedó tercero,[j] y Ernesto Pérez Balladares fue elegido[k] presidente de Panamá.

adaptado de *Cambio 16*.

[a]*pudo... could have had* [b]*persona que toca o canta salsa, un ritmo caribeño* [c]*hacienda* [d]*llenarme... fill my pockets* [e]*leaving* [f]*durante... has lived for years* [g]EE UU. = Estados Unidos [h]*polls* [i]*los... people who like to dance.* [j]*third* [k]*fue... was elected*

Carolina Herrera, una mujer que está «de moda»

La venezolana Carolina Herrera es una de las diseñadoras de moda más famosas en los Estados Unidos e internacionalmente. Es propietaria[a] de su casa de diseño en Nueva York desde 1981. Han llevado[b] sus vestidos mujeres tan famosas como Jacquelyn Onassis y su hija Carolina y Nancy Reagan.

[a]*owner* [b]*Han... Have worn*

¡Qué interesante!

▼ En todos los casos, compare sus respuestas con las de otros compañeros.

▼ **1.** ¿Conoce Ud. a alguna persona original de los países que se mencionan en esta sección? ¿Sabe por qué esa persona vino (*came*) a los Estados Unidos?

▼ **2.** ¿Qué grupos étnicos, especialmente hispánicos, se representan entre los restaurantes de su ciudad?

▼ **3.** Rubén Blades quería (*wanted*) ser presidente de su país, Panamá. ¿Cree Ud. que eso es una cosa muy rara? ¿Hay alguna persona en los Estados Unidos que haya cambiado (*has exchanged*) una carrera artística por la política (*politics*)?

Primer paso

¡Vamos de vacaciones!

el avión

el aeropuerto

la estación del tren

el tren

el autobús

la estación de autobuses

el crucero

el agente de viajes

las montanas

el océano / el mar

la playa

la agencia de viajes

el hotel

el desierto

De VACACIONES

Más vocabulario

bajar de	to get off	viajar	to travel
esquiar*	to ski	volar (ue) en avión	to fly
estar/ir de vacaciones	to be/go on vacation	el boleto / el billete†	ticket
hacer *camping*	to go camping	el pasaje	plane/cruise ticket
nadar	to swim	de ida	one-way ticket
navegar en barco	to travel by boat	de ida y vuelta	round-trip ticket
pasarlo bien/mal	to have a good/bad time		
subir a	to get on	el/la agente de viajes	travel agent
tomar el sol	to sunbathe	el cheque de viajero	traveler's check

Práctica

A **Gustos y preferencias.** ¿Adónde prefieren ir de vacaciones las siguientes personas? Haga oraciones completas con una palabra o frase de cada grupo. Luego
explique cada respuesta con otra oración, según el modelo.

MODELO: A mí me gusta nadar. Por eso voy a la playa.

a mi familia	(no) me		navegar en barco
a mi (pariente)	le	} gusta	hacer *camping*
a mi mejor amigo/a	les		nadar, esquiar
a mí			hacer un crucero
a mis compañeros			estar en casa / en un gran hotel
a las personas ricas			pasar (un mes) en la playa / las montañas
			descansar (*to rest*)
			¿ ?

---

*Note the accentuation patterns in the forms of **esquiar: esquío, esquías, esquía, esquiamos, esquiáis,
esquían.**

†Throughout Spanish America, **boleto** is the word used for a ticket for travel. **Billete** is commonly used in
Spain. The words **entrada** and **localidad** are used to refer to tickets for movies, plays, and similar
functions.

B **Definiciones.** Defina Ud. los siguientes lugares según lo que (*what*) pasa allí. Siga el modelo.

MODELO: un aeropuerto →
          Subimos al avión en un aeropuerto (*allí*).

1. una estación del tren
2. el océano
3. un hotel

4. una estación de autobuses
5. el cielo (*sky*)
6. una playa

Nueva York.

Adivinanza

¿Qué es lo que se dice
una vez en un minuto
y dos en un momento?

NOTA LINGÜÍSTICA: Other Uses of *se* [for Recognition]

A Spanish phrase you have probably used a lot throughout the first weeks of the term is **¿Cómo se dice... en español?** (*How do you say . . . in Spanish?*). And it is likely that you have often seen and heard the phrase shown in the photo that accompanies this box: **Se habla español.** (*Spanish is spoken* [*here*]). Here are some additional examples of this use of **se** with Spanish verbs. Note how the meaning of the verb changes slightly.

Se venden billetes aquí.	*Tickets are sold here.*
Aquí no **se estaciona.**	*You don't (One doesn't) park here. Parking is forbidden here.*

Be alert to this use of **se** when you see it, because it will occur with some frequency in readings and in direction lines in **¿Qué tal?**

C **¿Dónde se hace esto?** Indique el lugar (o los lugares) donde se hacen las siguientes actividades.

Lugares: en casa, en la agencia de viajes, en el aeropuerto, en la playa...

1. Se planea el viaje.
2. Se compran los pasajes.
3. Se hace una reservación.
4. Se espera el avión.

5. Se espera el autobús.
6. Se nada y se toma el sol.
7. Se pide un cóctel.
8. Se mira una película.

D **Prueba cultural.** ¿Cierto o falso? Corrija las oraciones falsas.

1. Se habla español en el Brasil.
2. Se comen tacos en México.
3. Se dice «billete» en Panamá.
4. En España se cena después de las 9 de la noche.

5. La paella se prepara con lechuga.
6. Se dice «chau» en la Argentina.
7. Se puede esquiar en Chile en junio.
8. Se habla español en Miami.

E **Preguntas.**

Paso 1. Por lo general, ¿cuándo toma Ud. sus vacaciones? ¿en invierno? ¿en verano? En las vacaciones, ¿le gusta viajar o prefiere no salir de su ciudad? ¿Le gusta ir de vacaciones con su familia? ¿Prefiere ir solo/a, con un amigo / una amiga o con un grupo de personas?

Paso 2. Piense en el último viaje que Ud. hizo. ¿Cuándo hizo el viaje? ¿Adónde fue? ¿Con quién(es) viajó? ¿Lo pasó bien?

Paso 3. De los medios de transporte mencionados en **¡Vamos de vacaciones!**, ¿cuáles conoce Ud. por experiencia? Conteste usando esta oración: **He viajado** (*I have traveled*) **en avión (tren, autobús, barco, coche).** De estos medios de transporte, ¿cuál es el más rapido? ¿el más económico? ¿el más cómodo para un viaje largo? ¿Cómo prefiere Ud. viajar, por lo general?

DE AQUÍ Y DE ALLÁ

Here are some additional terms and expressions related to traveling.

- *to hitchhike* = hacer autostop (España)
  - hacer dedo (Latinoamérica)
  - pedir un aventón (México: ¿Me das un aventón?)
- en el tren   viajar en primera o en segunda
  - viajar en coche cama (*sleeping car*) o en litera (*berth*)
- el autobús = el autocar (España)
  - el camión (México)
  - la guagua (el Caribe, las Islas Canarias)

ESTRUCTURAS

21.   Influencing Others

Formal Commands

▼ **Un pasajero distraído**

AUXILIAR: *Pase* Ud., señor. Bienvenido a bordo.

PASAJERO: Gracias. Este es mi asiento, ¿verdad?

AUXILIAR: Sí, es el 5A. *Tome* asiento ahora mismo. Y, por favor, no *olvide* el cinturón de seguridad.

PASAJERO: ¿Puedo fumar?

AUXILIAR: Se puede fumar en esta sección, pero no *fume* ahora. Vamos a despegar pronto para Quito y...

PASAJERO: ¿Para Quito? Pero... el vuelo ciento doce va a Cuzco.

AUXILIAR: Sí, señor, pero este es el vuelo ciento dos. *¡Baje* Ud. ahora mismo!

An absent-minded passenger   FLIGHT ATTENDANT: Come in, sir. Welcome aboard. PASSENGER: Thank you. This is my seat, isn't it? FLIGHT ATTENDANT: Yes, it's 5A. Take your seat right now. And, please, don't forget your seat belt. PASSENGER: Can I smoke? FLIGHT ATTENDANT: Smoking is permitted (One can smoke) in this section, but don't smoke now. We're going to take off soon for Quito and . . . PASSENGER: For Quito? But . . . flight 112 goes to Cuzco. FLIGHT ATTENDANT: Yes, sir, but this is flight 102. Get off right now!

▲ ▲ ▲

▼ 1. ¿Qué dice la auxiliar cuando el pasajero entra en el avión?
▼ 2. ¿El pasajero encuentra (*finds*) su asiento? ¿Cuál es?
▼ 3. ¿Por qué no debe fumar ahora el pasajero?
▼ 4. ¿Cuál es el error del pasajero?
▼ 5. ¿Qué debe hacer el pasajero?

Formal Command Forms

You have seen commands throughout the direction lines in this text: **Haga...**, **Complete...**, **Conteste...**, and so on.

Commands (imperatives) are verb forms used to tell someone to do something in a very direct way. In Spanish, the *formal commands* (**los mandatos formales**) are used with people whom you address as **Ud.** or **Uds.** Study the command forms in the following chart, then read the explanation that follows.

	hablar	comer	escribir	volver	decir
Ud.	hable	coma	escriba	vuelva	diga
Uds.	hablen	coman	escriban	vuelvan	digan
English	*speak*	*eat*	*write*	*come back*	*tell*

• Almost all formal commands are based on the **yo** form of the present tense. Replace the **-o** with **-e** or **-en** for **-ar** verbs; replace the **-o** with **-a** or **-an** for **-er** and **-ir** verbs.

• Formal commands of stem-changing verbs will show the stem change.

  piense Ud.   **vue**lva Ud.   **pi**da Ud.

• Verbs ending in **-car, -gar,** and **-zar** have a spelling change to preserve the **-c-,** **-g-,** and **-z-** sounds.

  -car: c → qu   buscar: bus**que** Ud.
  -gar: g → gu   pagar: pa**gue** Ud.
  -zar: z → c   empezar: empie**ce** Ud.

• The **Ud./Uds.** commands for verbs that have irregular **yo** forms will reflect the irregularity.

  conocer: **conozca** Ud.   poner: **ponga** Ud.   venir: **venga** Ud.
  decir: **diga** Ud.   salir: **salga** Ud.   ver: **vea** Ud.
  hacer: **haga** Ud.   tener: **tenga** Ud.
  oír: **oiga** Ud.   traer: **traiga** Ud.

• A few verbs have irregular **Ud./Uds.** command forms.

  dar: **dé** Ud.   ir: **vaya** Ud.   ser: **sea** Ud.
  estar: **esté** Ud.   saber: **sepa** Ud.

Using **Ud.** or **Uds.** after the command forms makes the command somewhat more formal or more polite.

[Práctica A–D]

Position of Object Pronouns with Formal Commands

Direct and indirect object pronouns must follow affirmative commands and be attached to them. In order to maintain the original stress of the verb form, an accent mark is added to the stressed vowel if the original command has two or more syllables.

Léalo Ud.   *Read it.*
Búsquele el bolígrafo.   *Look for the pen for him.*

Direct and indirect object pronouns must precede negative commands.

No lo lea Ud.   *Don't read it.*
No le busque el bolígrafo.   *Don't look for the pen for him.*

[Práctica E–F]

Práctica

Conozca la zona más exótica de C.R.
LOS CANALES DE TORTUGUERO
a bordo del
MAWAMBA
Tour de 3 días · 2 noches
SALIDAS: TODOS LOS VIERNES

Haga sus reservaciones con anticipación para la temporada del desove de la Tortuga Verde.
O su Agencia de viajes favorita
El tour incluye: traslados, alojamiento, todas las comidas. Llámenos y consulte nuestro programa.

A Una excursión en Centroamérica.

Paso 1. Advertisements often use command forms in their attempt to encourage the reader to take immediate action. Scan the following ad for an excursion to see if you can locate the four formal commands it contains.

Paso 2. ¿Qué significan las siguientes palabras o frases?

1. C.R. (Es un país.)
2. la tortuga (Es un reptil que camina muy lento y que tiene una concha [*shell*].)
3. con anticipación

B Un viaje en avión.

Paso 1. La siguiente lista de mandatos describe los pasos más comunes para hacer un viaje en avión. Póngalos en orden cronológico, del 1 al 8.

PARA PLANEAR EL VIAJE
a. _____ Busque el número de la agencia de viajes.
b. _____ Déle al agente el número de su tarjeta de crédito.
c. _____ Decida cuándo y adónde quiere viajar.
d. _____ Hable con el agente.
e. _____ Espere la llegada de los boletos.
f. _____ Empiece a soñar con (*to dream about*) el viaje.
g. _____ Seleccione el plan más conveniente y barato.
h. _____ Llame a la agencia.

Paso 2. Ahora dé los mandatos anteriores (*preceding*) usando **Uds.** como sujeto.

Paso 3. ¿Qué se hace después? Dé algunos mandatos más.

C **El Sr. Casiano no está bien.** Lea la descripción que él da de algunas de sus actividades.

«**Trabajo** muchísimo—¡me gusta trabajar! En la oficina, **soy** impaciente y **critico** bastante (*a good deal*) a los otros. En mi vida personal, a veces **soy** un poco impulsivo. **Fumo** bastante y también **bebo** cerveza y otras bebidas alcohólicas, a veces sin moderación... **Almuerzo** y **ceno** fuerte, y casi nunca **desayuno**. Por la noche, con frecuencia **salgo** con los amigos—me gusta ir a las discotecas—y **vuelvo** tarde a casa.»

¿Qué **no** debe hacer el Sr. Casiano para estar mejor? Aconséjele sobre lo que no debe hacer, usando los verbos indicados o cualquier (*any*) otro, según los modelos.

MODELOS: **Trabajo** → Sr. Casiano, no trabaje tanto.
soy → Sr. Casiano, no sea tan impaciente.

D **Mandatos para la clase.** Imagine que Ud. es el profesor / la profesora hoy. ¿Qué mandatos debe dar a la clase?

MODELOS: hablar español → Hablen Uds. español.
hablar inglés → No hablen Uds. inglés.

1. llegar a tiempo
2. leer la lección
3. escribir una composición
4. abrir los libros
5. pensar en inglés
6. estar en clase mañana
7. traer los libros a clase
8. olvidar los verbos nuevos
9. ¿ ?

E **Situaciones.** El Sr. Casiano quiere adelgazar (*lose weight*). ¿Debe o no debe comer o beber las siguientes cosas? Con otro/a estudiante, haga y conteste preguntas según los modelos.

MODELOS: ensalada → —¿Ensalada?
—Cómala.

postres → —¿Postres?
—No los coma.

1. alcohol (*m.*)
2. verduras
3. pan
4. dulces
5. leche
6. hamburguesas con queso
7. frutas
8. refrescos dietéticos
9. pollo
10. carne
11. pizza
12. jugo de fruta

F **Consejos.** Su vecino (*neighbor*) Pablo es una persona muy perezosa y descuidada (*careless*). No estudia mucho y tampoco hace sus quehaceres (*tasks*) en el apartamento donde vive con un compañero. Déle consejos lógicos usando estos verbos, según el modelo.

MODELO: afeitarse → ¡Aféitese!

1. despertarse más temprano
2. levantarse más temprano
3. bañarse con frecuencia
4. quitarse esa ropa sucia
5. ponerse ropa limpia
6. vestirse mejor
7. estudiar más
8. no divertirse tanto con los amigos
9. ir más a la biblioteca
10. no acostarse tan tarde
11. ayudar con los quehaceres
12. ¿ ?

Segundo paso

▼ **VOCABULARIO**

Un vuelo a...

estar atrasado/a	to be late		
facturar el equipaje	to check one's bags		
guardar (un puesto)	to save (a place)		
hacer cola	to stand in line		
hacer las maletas	to pack		
aterrizar	to land		
despegar	to take off		
la demora	delay		
la puerta de embarque	gate	**el vuelo con/sin escalas**	flight with/without stops
la sala de espera	waiting area	**el vuelo directo**	direct flight

Este vocabulario no está traducido, pero es muy fácil de comprender. Indique la persona o el objeto con la letra apropiada.

_____ los asientos
_____ la azafata, el/la auxiliar de vuelo
_____ la clase turística
_____ los pasajeros
_____ el piloto
_____ la primera clase
_____ la sección de fumar
_____ la sección de no fumar

Práctica

A **Un viaje en avión.** Su vuelo sale a las siete de la mañana. Usando los números 1 a 10, indique en qué orden van a pasar las siguientes cosas.

_____ Subo al avión.
_____ Voy a la puerta de embarque y me siento en la sala de espera.
_____ Hago cola para comprar el boleto de ida y vuelta y facturo el equipaje.
_____ Por fin el avión despega. Va a aterrizar en dos horas.
_____ Llego al aeropuerto a tiempo (*on time*) y bajo del taxi.
_____ Por fin se anuncia el vuelo.
_____ Estoy atrasado/a. Salgo para el aeropuerto en taxi.
_____ La auxiliar me indica el asiento.
_____ Pido asiento en la sección de no fumar.
_____ Hay demora. Por eso todos tenemos que esperar el vuelo allí antes de subir al avión.

B **Decisiones.** ¿Qué va a hacer Ud. en estas situaciones?

1. Ud. no tiene mucho dinero. Si tiene que viajar, ¿qué clase de pasaje va a comprar?
   a. clase turística
   b. primera clase
   c. un pasaje en la sección de fumar
2. Ud. es una persona muy nerviosa y tiene miedo de viajar en avión. Necesita ir desde Nueva York a Madrid. ¿Qué pide Ud.?
   a. una cabina en un barco
   b. un vuelo sin escalas
   c. un boleto de tren
3. Ud. viaja en tren y tiene muchas maletas. Pesan (*They weigh*) mucho y no puede llevarlas. ¿Qué hace Ud.?
   a. Compro boletos.
   b. Guardo un asiento.
   c. Facturo el equipaje.
4. Su vuelo está atrasado, pero Ud. está tranquilo/a ¿Qué dice Ud.?
   a. Señorita, insisto en hablar con el capitán.
   b. Una demora más... no importa.
   c. Si no salimos dentro de diez minutos, bajo del avión.

C **En el aeropuerto.** ¿Cuántas cosas y acciones puede Ud. identificar o describir en este dibujo?

ESTRUCTURAS ▼▼▼▼▼▼▼▼▼▼▼▼▼▼▼▼▼▼▼▼▼▼▼▼▼▼

22. Expressing Desires and Requests

Present Subjunctive: An Introduction; Use of the Subjunctive: Influence

▼ **Al aeropuerto, por favor. ¡Tenemos mucha prisa!**

▼ ESTEBAN: ¡Más rápido, Carlota! *¡Quiero que lleguemos* al aeropuerto a tiempo!
▼ CARLOTA: *¿Quieres que* te *ayude* con las maletas?

▼ ESTEBAN: No. *Quiero que subas* al taxi. Estamos atrasados. *No quiero que perdamos*
▼   el vuelo, como la última vez.
▼ CARLOTA: ¡Y yo *no quiero que* esto te *dé* un ataque al corazón! Si el avión despega
▼   sin nosotros, ¿qué importa? Tomamos el próximo vuelo y llegamos
▼   unas horas más tarde.

▲ ▲ ▲

▼ Conteste según el diálogo.

▼ 1. Esteban quiere que (*ellos*)...
▼   a. lleguen a tiempo.   b. lleguen en dos horas.
▼ 2. Según Esteban, parece que Carlota...
▼   a. no tiene prisa.   b. no encuentra sus maletas.
▼ 3. Esteban quiere que Carlota...
▼   a. suba al taxi.   b. suba al autobús.
▼ 4. No quiere que Carlota...
▼   a. lo ayude con las maletas.   b. suba al taxi.
▼ 5. No quiere que (*ellos*)...
▼   a. pierdan el taxi.   b. pierdan el vuelo.
▼ 6. Según Carlota, es más importante...
▼   a. estar tranquilo.   b. estar en el aeropuerto a tiempo.

▼ Y Ud., ¿es como Carlota o como Esteban?

Present Subjunctive: An Introduction

A. The present tense forms you have learned so far in *¿Qué tal?* are part of a verb system called the *indicative mood* (**el modo indicativo**). In both English and Spanish, the indicative is used to state facts and to ask questions; it expresses actions and states that are considered "true" by the speaker.

¡Ya **estamos** aquí!	*We're here already!*
Yo **pienso** que el español **es** una lengua muy importante.	*I think that Spanish is a very important language.*

B. Both English and Spanish have another verb system called the *subjunctive mood* (**el modo subjuntivo**). The subjunctive is used to express actions or states that are not "just facts" according to the speaker. This includes things that the speaker wants to happen or wants others to do, events to which he or she reacts emotionally, things that are as yet unknown, and so on. The English subjunctive is in italics in the following examples.

I wish we *were* there already!
I prefer that you *be* home early.

To the airport, please. We're in a hurry! ESTEBAN: Faster, Carlota! I want us to get to the airport on time! CARLOTA: Do you want me to help you with the suitcases? ESTEBAN: No. I want you to get in the taxi. We're late. I don't want us to miss the flight, like last time. CARLOTA: And I don't want you to have a heart attack! If the plane takes off without us, so what? We take the next flight and get there a few hours later.

This section is the first presentation of the subjunctive in *¿Qué tal?* In it, you will learn the present tense forms of the subjunctive and some of the contexts in which it is used. More importantly, you will learn to recognize the subjunctive when you see it. Through the rest of *¿Qué tal?* there will be plenty of opportunities to learn more about the subjunctive as well as to practice using it.

Present Subjunctive: How to Use It and Its Meaning

A. Look back at the preceding examples of the English subjunctive. Each sentence has two clauses: a main or independent clause (*I wish . . .* , *I prefer . . .*) and a subordinate or dependent clause (*. . . we were there already, . . . that you be home early*). These subordinate clauses represent what the subject of the main clause (*I* in both cases) wants to have happen. That is, the action in the subordinate clause is not yet a fact. The subjunctive is used to express this not-yet-factual information in the subordinate clause, in English and in Spanish.

INDEPENDENT CLAUSE		DEPENDENT CLAUSE
Quiero	que	tú me **compres** el boleto.
La profesora **quiere**	que	sus estudiantes **lean** una revista en español.

Note two very important things about the preceding sentences.

- Each clause has a different subject: **yo/tú, la profesora / sus estudiantes.**
- The word **que** (*that*) must appear in the sentence. It is not optional, as it often is in English.

B. When there is no change of subject, the infinitive is used in Spanish and in English for the second verb. You have been using infinitives in this way since the beginning of *¿Qué tal?*

Quiero **comprar** el boleto.
La profesora quiere **leer** una revista en español.

C. Now reread the following sentences from the minidialogue and try to give their English equivalents.

—¿Quieres que te ayude con las maletas?
—No. Quiero que subas al taxi.

It's likely that you gave very literal English equivalents such as these: *Do you want that I help you with the suitcases? No, I want that you get in the taxi.* Keep in mind, however, that an infinitive is often used to express the Spanish subjunctive in English. The following translation sounds much more natural: *Do you want me to help you with the suitcases? No, I want you to get in the taxi.*

Forms of the Present Subjunctive

The Spanish formal commands, which you have just learned (Grammar Section 21), are part of the subjunctive mood. They are identical in form to the third person singular and plural of the present subjunctive. The command forms are highlighted in the following box. What you have already learned about forming **Ud.** and **Uds.** commands will help you learn the forms of the present subjunctive.

	hablar	comer	escribir	volver	decir
Singular	hable hables hable	coma comas coma	escriba escribas escriba	vuelva vuelvas vuelva	diga digas diga
Plural	hablemos habléis hablen	comamos comáis coman	escribamos escribáis escriban	volvamos volváis vuelvan	digamos digáis digan

- As with **Ud./Uds.** command forms, the personal endings of the present subjunctive are added to the first person singular of the present indicative minus its **-o** ending. **-Ar** verbs add endings with **-e**, while **-er/-ir** verbs add endings with **-a**.
- Verbs ending in **-car**, **-gar**, and **-zar** have a spelling change in all persons of the present subjunctive, in order to preserve the **-c-**, **-g-**, and **-z-** zounds.

    -car: c → **qu**   buscar: bus**qu**e, bus**qu**es, ...
    -gar: g → **gu**   pagar: pa**gu**e, pa**gu**es, ...
    -zar: z → **c**   empezar: empie**c**e, empie**c**es, ...

- Verbs with irregular **yo** forms show the irregularity in all persons of the present subjunctive.

    conocer: **conozca**, ...   poner: **ponga**, ...   venir: **venga**, ...
    decir: **diga**, ...   salir: **salga**, ...   ver: **vea**, ...
    hacer: **haga**, ...   tener: **tenga**, ...
    oír: **oiga**, ...   traer: **traiga**, ...

- A few verbs have irregular present subjunctive forms.

    dar: **dé, des, dé, demos, deis, den**   ir: **vaya**, ...
    estar: **esté**, ...   saber: **sepa**, ...
    haber (hay): **haya**   ser: **sea**, ...

- **-Ar** and **-er** stem-changing verbs follow the stem-changing pattern of the present indicative.

    pensar (ie): p**ie**nse, p**ie**nses, p**ie**nse, pensemos, penséis, p**ie**nsen
    poder (ue): p**ue**da, p**ue**das, p**ue**da, podamos, podáis, p**ue**dan

The only really new information you need to learn about the present subjunctive has to do with **-ir** stem-changing verbs. These verbs show a stem change in the four forms that have a change in the present indicative. In addition, however, they show a second stem change in the **nosotros** and **vosotros** forms.

    dormir (ue, u): d**ue**rma, d**ue**rmas, d**ue**rma, d**u**rmamos, d**u**rmáis, d**ue**rman
    pedir (i, i): p**i**da, p**i**das, p**i**da, p**i**damos, p**i**dáis, p**i**dan
    preferir (ie, i): pref**ie**ra, pref**ie**ras, pref**ie**ra, pref**i**ramos, pref**i**ráis, pref**ie**ran

> From this point on in *¿Qué tal?*, both stem changes for **-ir** verbs will be given with infinitives in vocabulary lists.

Use of the Subjunctive: Influence

A. So far, you have learned to identify the subjunctive by the following features:

- It appears in a subordinate (dependent) clause.
- Its subject is different from the one in the main (independent) clause.
- It is preceded by **que**.

B. In addition, the use of the subjunctive is also associated with the presence of a number of concepts or conditions that "trigger" the use of it in the dependent clause. The concept of influence is one of those "triggers." When the speaker wants something to happen, he or she tries to influence the behavior of others, as in these sentences. The main verbs in the Spanish sentences you have seen so far have been **querer** and **preferir,** both verbs of volition or influence.

INDEPENDENT CLAUSE		DEPENDENT CLAUSE
Yo **quiero**	**que**	tú **pagues** la cuenta.
La profesora **prefiere**	**que**	los estudiantes no **lleguen** tarde.

The verb in the main clause is, of course, in the indicative, since it is a fact that the subject of the sentence wants something. The subjunctive occurs in the dependent clause.

C. Querer and **preferir** are not, of course, the only verbs that can express the main subject's desire to influence what someone else thinks or does. There are many other verbs of influence, some very strong and direct, some very soft and polite.

desear	pedir (i, i)	prohibir (*to prohibit;*
insistir en	permitir (*to permit*)	*to forbid*)
mandar		recomendar (ie)

Note the accent marks on some of the forms of **prohibir: prohíbo, prohíbes, prohíbe(n).**

D. An impersonal generalization of influence or volition can also be the main clause that triggers the subjunctive. Here are some examples:

Es necesario que...	Es importante que...
Es urgente que...	Es mejor que...

Práctica

A **Preparándose para un viaje.** Ud. y un compañero / una compañera (un amigo o una amiga, su esposo/a, su hijo/a...) van a salir de viaje. Ud. quiere organizar el viaje muy bien para no tener problemas. ¿A quién le dice Ud. lo siguiente, a su compañero/a, al agente de viajes, al taxista o a su vecino (*neighbor*)?

1. Quiero que me mande los billetes en seguida.
2. Prefiero que no hagas la maleta a última hora.
3. Es necesario que venga a las ocho en punto para llevarnos al aeropuerto.
4. Quiero que nos llame si hay algún problema.
5. Es buena idea que lo tengas todo preparado la noche anterior.
6. Le pido que no le diga a nadie que no estamos en casa.
7. Deseo que nos cambie el vuelo para salir más temprano.

B **Cambios.** Haga oraciones según las indicaciones. **¡OJO!** Cambie sólo el infinitivo.

1. Quiero que (*tú*)... (bailar, cenar, mirar esto, llegar a tiempo, buscar a Anita)
2. ¿Quieres que el niño... ? (aprender, escribir, leer, responder, asistir a clases)
3. Es necesario que (*yo*)... ¿verdad? (empezar, jugar, pensarlo, servirlo, pedirlo)
4. Es buena idea que nosotros... (pedir eso, almorzar ahora, mandarlos, dormir allí, cerrarla)
5. Preferimos que Uds.... (conocerlo, hacerlo, traerlo, saberlo, decirlo)
6. Yo prohíbo que Ana... (venir, salir ahora, ponerlo, oírlo, ser su amiga)
7. ¿Recomiendas que (*yo*)... ? (tenerlo, verlo, estar allí, dar una fiesta, ir al cine)

C **En un aeropuerto.** Describa lo que desean las siguientes personas cuando están en el aeropuerto. Haga oraciones completas con frases de las dos columnas, usando el presente del subjuntivo del infinitivo. Hay más de una respuesta posible para cada persona.

los empleados de la línea aérea desean que
los pasajeros quieren que
el piloto prohíbe que
la azafata recomienda que

el día / terminar pronto
no haber una demora   **¡OJO!** haber = hay
el agente / darles un buen asiento
los pasajeros / (no) caminar mucho
los pasajeros / dormir la siesta
no haber mucho trabajo hoy
no haber problemas con la reservación
los pasajeros / (no) fumar en un vuelo nacional
¿ ?

D **La familia Soto.** Los miembros de esta familia planean unas vacaciones. Pero cada persona quiere que la familia vaya a un sitio diferente. ¡Qué lío! (*What a mess!*) Describa los planes de cada uno, según el modelo.

MODELO: papá / todos: ir a la playa →
          Papá quiere que todos vayan a la playa.

1. los niños / todos: ir a la playa también
2. Ernesto / todos: volver a hacer *camping* en las montañas
3. los abuelos / la familia: no salir de la ciudad en todo el verano
4. mamá / todos: hacer excursiones cortas
5. Elenita / la familia: visitar Nueva York

Y Ud., ¿va de vacaciones con su familia? ¿Adónde quiere que vaya su familia este verano? ¿Están todos los miembros de su familia de acuerdo?

E **Mandatos indirectos.** Working in groups, make a list of five things you would like someone else to do. Then present each request to someone in the class, who must either do it, promise to do it, or give a good excuse for not doing it.

MODELO: Queremos que Roberto nos traiga *donuts* mañana. →
          ROBERTO: No les voy a traer *donuts* porque no tengo dinero.

UN POCO DE TODO

A **Consejos para las vacaciones**

Paso 1. Lo que uno no debe hacer. The series of drawings on page 214 illustrates what one should not do when one is away during the summer. By matching up the statements below the drawings with the individual drawings, can you find the Spanish equivalent for the following words and phrases?

Lo que no debe hacer durante el verano: dejar que se le acumule el correo, mantener el garaje abierto, dejar cubos de basura vacíos a la puerta de su vivienda, dejar ventanas y persianas abiertas, fijar notas o avisos en la puerta de su domicilio, olvidar una escalera de mano fuera de la casa.

1. *mail*
2. *to keep*
3. *garbage cans*
4. *windows and blinds*
5. *to post or affix*
6. *ladder*

Paso 2. Lo que uno sí debe hacer. Now create a list of commands for what someone *should* do while on vacation. Here are some phrases to get you thinking.

1. hacer reservaciones con anticipación
2. comprar una buena cámara
3. descansar y comer mucho
4. tomar el sol... pero no demasiado (*too much*)
5. levantarse tarde y acostarse tarde

B **Recomendaciones para las vacaciones.** Complete the following vacation suggestion with the correct form of the words in parentheses, as suggested by the context. When two possibilities are given in parentheses, select the correct word.

(Les/Los[1]) quiero decir (algo/nada[2]) sobre (el/la[3]) ciudad de Machu Picchu. ¿Ya (lo/la[4]) (saber/conocer[5]) Uds.? (Ser/Estar[6]) situada en los Andes, a unos ochenta kilómetros[a] de la ciudad de Cuzco (Perú). Machu Picchu es conocida[b] como (el/la[7]) ciudad escondida[c] de los incas. Se dice que (ser/estar[8]) una de las manifestaciones (más/tan[9]) importantes de la arquitectura incaica. Era[d] refugio y a la vez ciudad de vacaciones de los reyes[e] (incaico[10]).

Uds. deben (visitarlo/visitarla[11]). (Le/Les[12]) gustaría porque (ser/estar[13]) un sitio inolvidable.[f] Es mejor (ir/van[14]) a Machu Picchu en primavera o verano—son las (mejor[15]) estaciones para visitar este lugar. Pero es necesario (comprar/compren[16]) los boletos con anticipación, porque (mucho[17]) turistas de todos los (país[18]) del mundo visitan este sitio extraordinario. ¡([Yo] Saber/Conocer[19]) que a Uds. (los/les[20]) va a gustar el viaje!

[a]ochenta... 50 millas [b]known [c]hidden [d]It was [e]kings [f]unforgettable

¿Cierto o falso? Conteste según la descripción.

1. Machu Picchu está en Chile.
2. Fue un lugar importante en el pasado.
3. Todavía es una atracción turística de gran interés.
4. Sólo los turistas latinoamericanos conocen Machu Picchu.

NOTA CULTURAL: Medios de transporte en el mundo hispano

Los países hispanos tienen una gran variedad de medios de transporte. De hecho,[a] el transporte público, como los trenes y autobuses, puede ser una manera muy eficiente de viajar. Además, puede resultar increíblemente económico para el turista norteamericano.

[a]De... *In fact*

El avión es muy rápido y eficiente si Ud. tiene pocos días disponibles[b] para su viaje y quiere visitar muchos sitios. Además, en Sudamérica la distancia entre las ciudades importantes es muy larga, así que[c] le conviene al viajero hacer el viaje de la manera más rápida posible. Pero si Ud. no tiene prisa, sea una persona aventurera y use el tren o el autobús. Así puede conocer mejor el territorio, su paisaje[d] y su gente. ¡En un viaje de esos puede aprender más español y conocer mejor la cultura del país que en muchas horas de estudio en la sala de clase!

Por fin, tenga en cuenta[e] que en el transporte público se usa con frecuencia el sistema militar de indicar la hora. Así, las 18:00 horas son las seis, las 22:30 son las diez y media, etcétera.

[b]*available* [c]*así... so*   [d]*landscape* [e]*tenga... keep in mind*

SITUACIÓN   Comprando un billete

EN UNA AGENCIA DE VIAJES

—Quiero un billete de ida y vuelta a Nueva York.
—¿Clase turística, negocios[a] o primera clase?
—Turística, el más barato que tenga, por favor.
—Con el pasaje más barato, Ud. tiene que hacer una escala de dos horas en Chicago. Pero puede facturar sus maletas directamente a Nueva York.
—Está bien.

[a]*business*

Bogotá, Colombia.

EN LA ESTACIÓN DE TRENES

The sentences in this dialogue are out of order. Read through all of the sentences, then put them in order. The first one is done for you.

_____ —¿A qué hora llega el tren de alta velocidad?
__1__ —¿Me da un billete para un tren a Sevilla para esta tarde, por favor?
_____ —El de alta velocidad vale[a] 2.000 pesetas más.
_____ —A las 22:30.
_____ —¿Cuál es la diferencia de precio?
_____ —¿Para qué tren? Hay uno normal que sale a las 18:00, y otro de alta velocidad que sale a las 20:00.

[a]*costs*

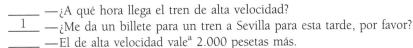

¿POR O PARA?

Note the use of **para** in the preceding dialogue to express *by* (*a certain time*).

¿Me da un billete para un tren a Sevilla **para** esta tarde?

Compare that use of **para** + [*time*] with the use of **por** + [*time*] that you have already learned.

Voy a escribir la composición **para** mañana **por** la tarde.

Para indicates the time by which something must be completed (**para el lunes, para esta tarde,** ...), while **por** expresses the time period *during which* the task will be done (**por la mañana/tarde/noche**).

Conversación

How would you go about getting the following information? Prepare a series of short statements and questions that will help you get all the information you need. Your instructor will play the role of ticket seller, travel agent, or flight attendant.

MODELO: You need to buy two first-class tickets on Tuesday's 10:50 A.M. train for Guanajuato. →
Dos boletos para Guanajuato, por favor. Para el martes, el tren de las once menos diez. De primera clase, por favor.

1. You need to buy two second-class (**segunda clase**) train tickets for today's 2:50 P.M. train for Barcelona.
2. You are at the train station and need to find out how to get to the university—which you understand is quite some distance away—by 10:00 A.M.
3. The flight you are on is arriving late, and you will probably miss your connecting flight to Mexico City. You want to explain your situation to the flight attendant and find out how you can get to Mexico City by 7:00 this evening.
4. You are talking to a travel agent and want to fly from Santiago, Chile, to Quito, Ecuador. You are traveling with two friends who prefer to travel first class, and you need to arrive in Quito by Saturday afternoon.

PARA ESCRIBIR

Escriba uno o dos párrafos recomendando un lugar de vacaciones que Ud. conozca. Dé todos los detalles posibles y diga por qué lo recomienda. Use las siguientes frases como guía.

Acabo de descubrir el lugar perfecto para pasar las vacaciones. Es... y está en...
Me gusta mucho el sitio porque...
Les recomiendo que visiten... en... (estación) porque...

▼ ▼ ▼ ▼ ▼ ▼ ▼ ▼ ▼ ▼ ▼ ▼ ▼ ▼ **VOCABULARIO** ▼ ▼ ▼ ▼ ▼ ▼ ▼ ▼ ▼ ▼ ▼ ▼ ▼ ▼

Verbos

fumar to smoke
haber *infinitive of* **hay**
insistir en to insist on
mandar to order
olvidar to forget
permitir to permit
prohibir to prohibit, forbid

Repaso: desear, pedir (i, i), recomendar (ie)

Actividades en los viajes

aterrizar to land (*an airplane*)
bajar (de) to get off (of), down (from)

descansar to rest
despegar to take off (*an airplane*)
esquiar to ski
estar/ir de vacaciones to be/go on vacation
facturar to check (*baggage*)
guardar to watch over; to save (*a place*)

hacer *camping* to go camping
hacer cola to stand/wait in line
hacer las maletas to pack one's bags
nadar to swim
navegar en barco to travel by boat
pasarlo bien/mal to have a good/ bad time
subir (a) to get (on) (*a vehicle*)
tomar el sol to sunbathe
viajar to travel
volar (ue) to fly

Los medios de transporte

el autobús bus
el avión plane
el barco boat; ship
el crucero cruise ship; cruise
el tren train

Los lugares

el aeropuerto airport
la agencia de viajes travel agency
el desierto desert
la estación station
   de autobuses bus station
   del tren train station
el hotel hotel

el mar sea
la montaña mountain
el océano ocean
la puerta de embarque departure gate
la sala de espera waiting area
la sección de (no) fumar (non)smoking section
Repaso: la playa

Las personas

el/la agente de viajes travel agent
el/la auxiliar de vuelo flight attendant
la azafata stewardess
el/la pasajero/a passenger
el/la piloto/a pilot

Otros sustantivos

el asiento seat
el billete/boleto ticket
   de ida one-way ticket
   de ida y vuelta roundtrip ticket
la clase turística tourist class
el cheque de viajero traveler's check
la demora delay
el equipaje luggage
el pasaje passage, ticket

la primera clase first class
el puesto place (*in line, etc.*)
el vuelo flight
   con/sin escalas flight with/ without stops
   directo direct flight

Adjetivos

atrasado/a late (*with* **estar**)
último/a last

Palabras adicionales

a tiempo on time
ahora mismo right now
lo que what/that which
para + [*time*] for/by (*future time*)

Self-Test

Use the tape that accompanies this text to test yourself briefly on the important points of this chapter.

LECTURA
cultural

Antes de leer: Obtaining Background Information

Before beginning a reading, consider what it might contain in order to review important background information you already know about the topic. For example, if you were reading a newspaper account of a traffic accident, what kinds of information and details would you expect to find in it? What kinds of information would you find in a magazine article about drugs? In a manual for the owner of a car or a computer?

Working with a partner, spend three minutes brainstorming about ideas and information you think will be presented in the following advertisements about vacation spots. You can talk in English or in Spanish. Then, working as a class, share your ideas and select the ten most frequently mentioned ideas. How many of the ideas actually appear in the reading?

¡Venga con nosotros a... !

L os siguientes anuncios son de revistas y periódicos sudamericanos y caribeños. Léalos para saber dónde y cómo la gente latinoamericana puede pasar sus vacaciones.

1.

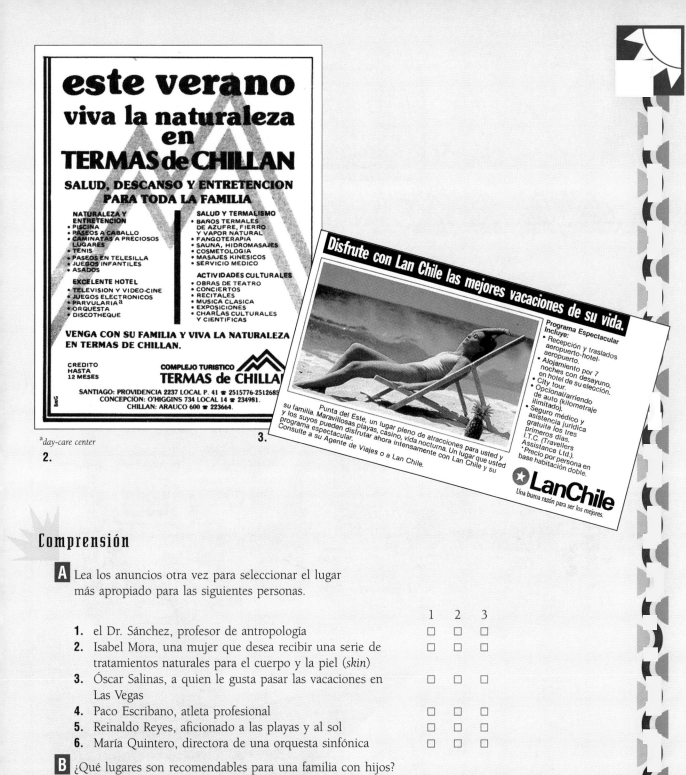

este verano
viva la naturaleza
en
TERMAS de CHILLAN

SALUD, DESCANSO Y ENTRETENCION
PARA TODA LA FAMILIA

NATURALEZA Y ENTRETENCION
- PISCINA
- PASEOS A CABALLO
- CAMINATAS A PRECIOSOS LUGARES
- TENIS
- PASEOS EN TELESILLA
- JUEGOS INFANTILES
- ASADOS

EXCELENTE HOTEL
- TELEVISION Y VIDEO-CINE
- JUEGOS ELECTRONICOS
- PARVULARIA[a]
- ORQUESTA
- DISCOTHEQUE

SALUD Y TERMALISMO
- BAÑOS TERMALES DE AZUFRE, FIERRO Y VAPOR NATURAL
- FANGOTERAPIA
- SAUNA, HIDROMASAJES
- COSMETOLOGIA
- MASAJES KINESICOS
- SERVICIO MEDICO

ACTIVIDADES CULTURALES
- OBRAS DE TEATRO
- CONCIERTOS
- RECITALES
- MUSICA CLASICA
- EXPOSICIONES
- CHARLAS CULTURALES Y CIENTIFICAS

VENGA CON SU FAMILIA Y VIVA LA NATURALEZA
EN TERMAS DE CHILLAN.

CREDITO
HASTA
12 MESES

COMPLEJO TURISTICO
TERMAS de CHILLAN

SANTIAGO: PROVIDENCIA 2237 LOCAL P. 41 ☎ 2515776-2512685
CONCEPCION: O'HIGGINS 734 LOCAL 14 ☎ 234981.
CHILLAN: ARAUCO 600 ☎ 223664.

[a]*day-care center*

2.

3.

Disfrute con Lan Chile las mejores vacaciones de su vida.

Punta del Este, un lugar pleno de atracciones para usted y su familia. Maravillosas playas, casino, vida nocturna. Un lugar que usted y los suyos pueden disfrutar ahora intensamente con Lan Chile y su programa espectacular. Consulte a su Agente de Viajes o a Lan Chile.

Programa Espectacular
Incluye:
- Recepción y traslados aeropuerto-hotel-aeropuerto.
- Alojamiento por 7 noches con desayuno, en hotel de su elección.
- City tour.
- Opcional/arriendo de auto (kilometraje ilimitado).
- Seguro médico y asistencia jurídica gratuita los tres primeros días. I.T.C. (Travellers Assistance Ltd.).
- Precio por persona en base habitación doble.

LanChile
Una buena razón para ser los mejores.

Comprensión

A Lea los anuncios otra vez para seleccionar el lugar más apropiado para las siguientes personas.

	1	2	3
1. el Dr. Sánchez, profesor de antropología	☐	☐	☐
2. Isabel Mora, una mujer que desea recibir una serie de tratamientos naturales para el cuerpo y la piel (*skin*)	☐	☐	☐
3. Óscar Salinas, a quien le gusta pasar las vacaciones en Las Vegas	☐	☐	☐
4. Paco Escribano, atleta profesional	☐	☐	☐
5. Reinaldo Reyes, aficionado a las playas y al sol	☐	☐	☐
6. María Quintero, directora de una orquesta sinfónica	☐	☐	☐

B ¿Qué lugares son recomendables para una familia con hijos?

	SÍ	NO
Cancún	☐	☐
Termas de Chillán	☐	☐
Punta del Este	☐	☐

Para los lugares recomendables, busque dos frases que confirman que es un buen sitio para la familia.

Primer paso

Los bienes personales[a]

[a]Los... Possessions

el pájaro

el cartel

el trofeo

el acuario

el pez

el equipo estereofónico
el *compact disc*

el televisor

la pintura

el *walkman*

el equipo fotográfico

la grabadora

el radio portátil

la videocasetera

el control remoto

la computadora / el ordenador*

el contestador automático

la impresora

la camioneta

la moto(cicleta)

el coche descapotable

la bici(cleta)

*__La computadora__ is the term most commonly used in Hispanic America. __El ordenador__ is used primarily in Spain.

Lo que tengo y LO QUE QUIERO

En la oficina

el aumento	raise	**el sueldo**	salary
el cheque	check	**el trabajo**	job, work; written
el *fax*	fax (machine)		work; (term) paper
el/la jefe/a	boss		

Note: This chapter of **¿Qué tal?** offers you a wide variety of vocabulary for talking about what you have . . . and about what you want or need. Learn in particular the vocabulary that is specific to your needs and interests.

Verbos útiles

cambiar (de canal,	to change (channels,	**funcionar**	to function,
de cuarto,	rooms, clothing . . .)		operate, work
de ropa...)		**ganar**	to earn; to win
conseguir (i, i)	to get, obtain	**sacar fotos**	to take photos
dejar	to leave (behind)		

Práctica

A ¿Qué utiliza Ud.? ¿Qué va a hacer Ud. en las siguientes situaciones? ¿Qué aparatos va a usar o poner?

1. Hay un programa muy interesante en la televisión esta noche, pero Ud. ya tiene planes para salir con unos amigos.
2. Hace muy buen tiempo y Ud. tiene ganas de visitar a un amigo que vive a unas cinco millas (*miles*) de su casa. Pero también quiere hacer un poco de ejercicio.
3. Ud. espera una llamada importante del banco, pero tiene que salir por unos minutos.
4. Después de estudiar todo el día en la biblioteca, Ud. está muy cansado/a. Cuando llega a casa, sólo quiere tumbarse (*drop down*) en el sofá y mirar la tele. No tiene la energía de levantarse para cambiar de canales.
5. Ud. necesita hacer un trabajo final para su clase de historia. El profesor exige (*demands*) 20 páginas como mínimo, con notas y bibliografía.
6. En el autobús, hay mucho ruido. Además, la persona sentada (*seated*) a su lado quiere hablar con Ud. ... pero a Ud. no le interesa. Ud. no quiere oír ruidos ni hablar con nadie.

B **El vehículo apropiado.** Unos amigos van a cambiar de trabajo. Por eso se trasladan (*they're moving*) a otra ciudad. Todos van a comprar un vehículo nuevo. ¿Qué tipo de vehículo les recomienda Ud.? Conteste completando esta oración: **Debe(n) comprarse...**

1. Marcos se va a vivir a Manhattan, donde el aparcamiento siempre es un problema.
2. Viviana se va a Los Ángeles, donde hace sol y buen tiempo gran parte del año.
3. Antonio se va a Key West, una isla soleada en el sur de la Florida. Es una comunidad muy informal.
4. Los Sres. Fuentes, con sus cinco hijos, se van a un suburbio de Chicago.

¿Qué tipo de vehículo tiene Ud.? ¿Es el más apropiado para la vida que Ud. lleva? ¿Qué vehículo le gustaría tener?

C **¿Necesidad o lujo (*luxury*)?**

Paso 1. Piense en las siguientes cosas. ¿Las considera Ud. un lujo o una necesidad de la vida moderna?

MODELO: el televisor → Para mí, el televisor es una necesidad.

1. el contestador automático
2. la videocasetera
3. el equipo estereofónico
4. el televisor

5. la computadora
6. el coche
7. la bicicleta
8. el *walkman* (la grabadora)

Ahora dé tres cosas más que Ud. considera necesarias en la vida moderna.

Paso 2. Ahora entreviste a un compañero / una compañera para saber si está de acuerdo con Ud.

MODELO: el televisor → E1: ¿El televisor?
                              E2: Yo lo considero un lujo.

Adivinanza

Habla por un tubo, pero no escucha;
tiene líneas, pero no es un cuaderno;
te la tragas,[a] pero no alimenta;[b]
tiene canales, pero no tiene agua.

[a]te... *you take it in (swallow it)*   [b]no... *it doesn't nourish*

¿POR O PARA?

Use the preposition **por** to express *per* (hour, day, week, month . . .) or *by* (the hour, the week, the month . . .).

Trabajo tres horas **por** día. Me pagan **por** hora.

I work three hours a day. They pay me by the hour.

D **¿Trabaja Ud. o sólo estudia?**

Paso 1. Lea la siguiente descripción de Lida, una estudiante típica de esta universidad.

Lida es estudiante de química, pero también trabaja para pagar sus gastos (*expenses*) personales y los de sus estudios en la universidad. Tiene un trabajo de tiempo parcial en un laboratorio de química. Trabaja veinte horas por semana y gana seis dólares por hora. ¡Necesita un aumento de sueldo! Su jefe le da un cheque cada semana.

Paso 2. Si Ud. trabaja, use el párrafo como modelo para describir su trabajo. Si Ud. busca trabajo, complete el siguiente párrafo. Si Ud. no tiene que trabajar, ¡enhorabuena (*congratulations*)!

No tengo trabajo, pero necesito conseguir uno. Me gustaría trabajar de (*as a*) ____ / en ____. Quiero trabajar ____ horas por semana como máximo. Quiero/ Busco un sueldo de ____ dólares por hora.

DE AQUÍ Y DE ALLÁ

Here are the words for some **bienes personales** that have become increasingly useful in recent years. Try to guess their meanings:

> el (teléfono) inalámbrico (*Hint:* el alambre = *wire*)
> el teléfono celular
> los juegos electrónicos

NOTA LINGÜÍSTICA: More About Describing Things

You already know that the verb **ser** can be used with **de** + [*noun*] to tell what something is made of:

Es una falda *de* algodón.   *It's a cotton skirt.*
Es una camisa *de* lana.   *It's a wool shirt.*

In English a noun can modify another noun to express the material that something is made of (*a gold watch*) or its make (*a Cross pen*). The same [*noun*] + [*noun*] structure is used in English to describe the nature of a place or thing: *the language lab, a summer day.* In Spanish, this structure can only be expressed by using a [*noun*] + **de** + [*noun*] phrase: **un reloj *de* oro, el laboratorio *de* lenguas, un día *de* verano.** Can you find any phrases in the **Vocabulario** section that use this structure?

IMPRESCINDIBLE. Alfredo Caral cuida el detalle hasta en los accesorios. Este llavero de cuero trenzado es de 3.000 pesetas.

DISTINCION. Este bolígrafo de Cross diseñado para BMW es un buen detalle a la hora de hacer un regalo y quedar siempre bien. Cuesta 18.369 pesetas.

E ¡Seamos lógicos! ¿De quiénes son los siguientes objetos? Explique su respuesta.

Objetos: la alarma de seguridad, las piezas de cerámica, el acuario de agua salada (*salt*), los trofeos de tenis, la tienda de campaña (*tent*), el saco de dormir

1. A Adela le encantan los deportes. Es campeona de golf, tenis y vólibol.
2. A Geraldo le gusta hacer *camping* en las montañas.
3. Los señores de Inza son muy ricos. Tienen una casa magnífica y una colección de pinturas de un valor incalculable.
4. Laura tiene una pequeña colección de figuras de animales.
5. A Ernestito le interesan mucho los peces. Tiene más de 100 peces tropicales.

F Tengo... Necesito... Quiero...

Paso 1. ¿Qué tiene Ud. en su cuarto (apartamento, casa) que es muy importante para Ud.? Nombre por lo menos tres cosas. ¿Qué necesita con urgencia? ¿Qué le gustaría tener algún día?

Paso 2. Ahora compare sus respuestas con las de (*those of*) otros estudiantes. ¿Son similares las respuestas de todos? ¿A qué se deben (*are due*) las diferencias?

ESTRUCTURAS

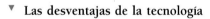

23. Expressing Feelings

Use of the Subjunctive: Emotion

▼ **Las desventajas de la tecnología**

CARLOS: ¿Marisa? *Me sorprende que estés* en casa a estas horas, pero... ¿qué pasa?

MARISA: Un desastre en la oficina. Otra vez me falló la computadora. Perdí dos días de trabajo en un proyecto importante.

CARLOS: *Me sorprende que no te compren* otra. Parece que la que tienes es imposible de arreglar...

MARISA: Tú sabes... Nunca hay dinero para nada. En fin. Ya que estoy en casa, puedo ver lo que hay en la tele. ¿Dónde está el control remoto?

CARLOS: Bueno... lo siento, pero... tengo malas noticias.

MARISA: ¿Sí?

CARLOS: Nuestro televisor no funciona tampoco.

MARISA: ¿Otra vez? Realmente debemos comprar otro.

CARLOS: ¡Vaya! *Me alegro de que* por fin *estés* de acuerdo en que necesitamos uno nuevo.

The disadvantages of technology CARLOS: Marisa? I'm surprised (that) you're home at this unusual time, but . . . what's up? MARISA: A mess at the office. My computer crashed again. I lost two days of work on an important project. CARLOS: I'm surprised that they don't buy you another one. It seems that the one you have is impossible to fix . . . MARISA: You know how it goes . . . . There's never money for anything. So . . . . Since I'm at home. I can see what's on TV. Where's the remote control? CARLOS: Well . . . I'm sorry, but . . . I have bad news. MARISA: Yeah? CARLOS: Our TV isn't working either. MARISA: Again? We really should buy another one. CARLOS: Well! I'm glad you finally agree that we need a new one.

▼ 1. Carlos se alegra de
▼   que _____.
▼ 2. A Marisa le molesta
▼   (*bothers*) que _____.
▼ 3. A Carlos le sorprende
▼   que _____.
▼
▼

a. no le compren una computadora nueva
b. no funcione el televisor
c. no haya mucho dinero para comprar cosas
d. le falle su computadora
e. su esposa esté en casa a estas horas
f. pierda trabajo en la computadora con frecuencia
g. Marisa quiera comprar otro televisor

INDEPENDENT CLAUSE		DEPENDENT CLAUSE
first subject + [*indicative*] (expression of emotion)	**que**	second subject + [*subjunctive*]

Esperamos que Ud. **pueda** asistir.	*We hope (that) you'll be able to come.*
Tengo miedo (de) que mi abuelo **esté** muy enfermo.	*I'm afraid (that) my grandfather is very ill.*
Es lástima que no **tengamos** más vacaciones este año.	*It's a shame we don't have more vacation this year.*

A. Expressions of emotion are those in which speakers express their feelings: *I'm glad you're here; It's good that they can come.* Such expressions of emotion are followed by the subjunctive mood in the dependent clause.

B. Some expressions of emotion are: **alegrarse de** (*to be happy about*), **esperar** (*to hope*), **sentir (ie, i)** (*to regret; to feel sorry*), **temer** (*to fear*), and **tener miedo (de)**. Some additional expressions of emotion used with indirect object pronouns include: **me (te, le, ...) gusta que, me (te, le, ...) molesta** (*it bothers me . . .*) **que**, and **me (te, le, ...) sorprende** (*it surprises me . . .*) **que.**

C. When a new subject is introduced after a generalization of emotion, it is followed by the subjunctive in the dependent clause. Some expressions of emotion are: **es terrible, es ridículo, es mejor/bueno/malo, es increíble** (*incredible*), **es extraño** (*strange*), **¡qué extraño!** (*how strange!*), **es lástima** (*a shame*), and **¡qué lástima!** (*what a shame!*).

Remember: When there is no new subject, the infinitive is used:

Es ridículo pasar todo el día en casa.

Práctica

A **Los aparatos y los demás** (*others*).

Paso 1. ¿Le gustan sus vecinos (*neighbors*)? Indique si las siguientes oraciones son ciertas o falsas.

	CIERTO	FALSO
1. No me gusta que fumen en mi casa (apartamento, cuarto).	☐	☐
2. Con frecuencia espero que bajen el volumen del estéreo / *compact disc.*	☐	☐
3. Me molesta que pongan el televisor a las tres de la mañana.	☐	☐
4. Espero que vengan a mis fiestas.	☐	☐

	CIERTO	FALSO

5. Temo que no devuelvan (*they won't return*) las cosas que me piden. ☐ ☐

6. Tengo miedo de que miren lo que yo hago en mi casa (apartamento, cuarto). ☐ ☐

7. Me sorprende que tengan tantas motocicletas. ☐ ☐

8. Siento que no pasemos más tiempo juntos. ☐ ☐

Paso 2. Ahora invente oraciones sobre lo que quiere, o no quiere, que hagan sus vecinos, según el modelo. Use las oraciones del **Paso 1** como base.

MODELO: 1. No quiero que fumen en mi casa.

B **Situaciones.** Complete las oraciones con la forma apropiada del verbo entre paréntesis.

1. Dicen en la tienda que esta videocasetera es fácil de usar. Por eso me sorprende que no (funcionar) bien. Temo que (ser) muy complicada. Me sorprende que ni (*not even*) mi compañera (entenderla).

2. ¡Qué desastre! El profesor dice que nos va a dar un examen. ¡Es increíble que (darnos) otro examen tan pronto! Es terrible que yo (tener) que estudiar este fin de semana. Espero que el profesor (cambiar) de idea.

3. Este año sólo tengo dos semanas de vacaciones. Es ridículo que sólo (tener) dos semanas. No me gusta que las vacaciones (ser) tan breves. Es lástima que yo no (poder) ir a ningún sitio.

C **Los valores de nuestra sociedad.** Express your feelings about the following situations by restating them, beginning with one of the following phrases or any others you can think of: **es bueno/malo que, es extraño/increíble que, es lástima que.**

1. Muchas personas viven para trabajar. No saben descansar.

2. Somos una sociedad de consumidores.

3. Siempre queremos tener el último modelo de todo... el coche de este año, la videocasetera que acaba de salir...

4. Juzgamos (*We judge*) a los otros por las cosas materiales que tienen.

5. Las personas ricas tienen mucho prestigio en esta sociedad.

6. Las mujeres generalmente no ganan tanto como los hombres cuando hacen el mismo trabajo.

7. Muchas personas no tienen con quién dejar a los niños cuando trabajan.

D **¿Qué le molesta más?** The following phrases describe aspects of university life. React to them, using phrases such as **Me gusta que..., Me molesta que..., Es terrible que...**

1. Se pone mucho énfasis en los deportes.

2. Pagamos mucho/poco por la matrícula.

3. Hay muchas/pocas reglas (*rules*) en la universidad.

4. Se ofrecen muchos/pocos cursos en mi especialización (*major*).

5. Es necesario estudiar ciencias/lenguas para graduarse.

6. Hay muchos/pocos requisitos (*requirements*) para graduarse.

7. En general, hay muchas/pocas personas en las clases.

NOTA COMUNICATIVA: Expressing Wishes with *ojalá*

¡**Ojalá** que yo **gane** la lotería   *I hope I win the*
algún día!   *lottery some day!*

The word **ojalá** is invariable in form and means *I wish* or *I hope*. It is used with the subjunctive to express wishes or hopes. The use of **que** with it is optional.

¡**Ojalá (que) haya** paz en el   *I hope (that) there will be peace*
mundo algún día!   *in the world some day!*

Ojalá que no **pierdan** su   *I hope (that) they don't lose your*
equipaje.   *luggage.*

Ojalá can also be used alone as an interjection in response to a question.

—¿Te va a ayudar Julio a estudiar para el examen?
—¡**Ojalá!**

E **Deseos para un vuelo feliz.** Ud. va de viaje en avión. Piense en todas las cosas que Ud. quiere que salgan bien y expréselas usando **ojalá.**

MODELO: (*nosotros*) / llegar / a tiempo / aeropuerto →
          Ojalá que lleguemos a tiempo al aeropuerto.

1. vuelo / salir a tiempo
2. la comida / estar buena
3. no haber / problemas / para despegar
4. vuelo / llegar / sin demora
5. no haber / escalas imprevistas (*unplanned*)
6. (*ellos*) / poner / película divertida
7. hacer / buen tiempo

NOTA CULTURAL: Palabras del idioma árabe en el español

El español es una lengua romántica, es decir que viene del latín, la lengua del Imperio Romano. Pero, en verdad, no todo el español viene exclusivamente de una lengua. Una de las fuentes[a] más importantes del vocabulario español es el árabe. Esto no es una casualidad.

Los árabes del norte de Africa invadieron la Península Ibérica a principios del siglo VIII[b] y se quedaron hasta 1492, año en que fueron expulsados de España por los Reyes Católicos (Fernando e Isabel).

En esos ocho siglos que estuvieron en España, los árabes dejaron muchos ejemplos de su avanzada cultura y de su lengua. **Ojalá** es una palabra que viene del árabe y significa «*may Allah grant*». Otras palabras de uso común y que también vienen del árabe son: **el álgebra, el aceite**[c] y **la almohada.**[d]

[a]*sources* [b]*principios... beginning of the 8th century* [c]*oil* [d]*pillow*

Los árabes también dejaron en España hermosos ejemplos de su arquitectura, como la Alhambra de Granada. «Alhambra» significa «palacio rojo».

Segundo paso

VOCABULARIO ▼▼▼▼▼▼▼▼▼▼▼▼▼▼▼▼▼▼▼▼▼▼▼

Los quehaceres[a] domésticos

[a]*tasks*

barrer (el suelo)	to sweep (the floor)	
hacer la cama	to make the bed	
lavar (las ventanas, los platos)	to wash (the windows, the dishes)	
limpiar la casa	to clean the house	
pasar la aspiradora	to vacuum	
pintar (las paredes)	to paint (the walls)	
planchar la ropa	to iron clothing	
poner la mesa	to set the table	
sacar la basura	to take out the trash	
sacudir los muebles*	to dust the furniture	

Algunos aparatos domésticos

el horno de microondas — el congelador — la tostadora — la cafetera — la estufa† — el lavaplatos — el refrigerador — la aspiradora — la secadora — la lavadora

Práctica

A **¿Dónde... ?** ¿En qué cuarto o parte de la casa se hacen las siguientes actividades? Hay más de una respuesta en muchos casos.

1. Se hace la cama en _____.
2. Se saca la basura de _____ y se deja en _____.
3. Se sacude los muebles de _____.
4. Uno se baña en _____. Pero es mejor que uno bañe al perro en _____.
5. Se barre el suelo de _____.
6. Se pasa la aspiradora en _____.
7. Se lava y se seca la ropa en _____. La ropa se plancha en _____.
8. Se usa la cafetera en _____.

---

*An alternative phrase used in some parts of the Spanish-speaking world is **quitar el polvo** (lit., *to remove the dust*).
†The word for *stove* varies in the Hispanic world. Many Spanish speakers use **la cocina**. *Oven* is generally **el horno**.

B **¡Manos a la obra!** (*Let's get to work!*) De los siguientes quehaceres, ¿cuáles le gustan más? Póngalos en orden de mayor (1) a menor (10) preferencia para Ud.

_____ barrer el suelo   _____ limpiar el garaje
_____ hacer la cama   _____ sacar la basura
_____ lavar los platos   _____ sacudir los muebles
_____ pasar la aspiradora   _____ pintar las paredes de un
_____ lavar la ropa   cuarto
_____ planchar la ropa

¿Hay un quehacer favorito entre todos? ¿Hay un quehacer que no le guste a la mayoría de los estudiantes? ¿Hay alguna diferencia entre las preferencias de los hombres y las de las mujeres?

C **Es un producto que sirve para...** Su amigo Arturo acaba de llegar de la Argentina y va por primera vez de compras a un supermercado. El pobre Arturo no conoce las marcas ni los productos y Ud. tiene que ayudarlo. Estas son algunas frases que Ud. puede usar en sus explicaciones:

> Es algo que se usa para... [+ *infinitive*]
> Es una cosa / un producto que se usa cuando... [+ *present indicative*]

1. Windex   **4.** Joy   **7.** disposable vacuum
2. Mr. Coffee   **5.** Tide   cleaner bags
3. Gladbags   **6.** furniture polish

NOTA LINGÜÍSTICA: Telling How Long Ago . . .

Tell how long ago something happened by using **hace** + [*period of time*].

> ¿Cuándo fuiste a Bogotá con   When did you go to Bogota with
>   tu familia? —**Hace tres**   your family? —*Three years*
> **años.**   *ago.*

The preterite is the verb form most commonly used with this **hace** expression. Note also the use of **que** when the **hace** phrase comes at the beginning of the sentence.

> **Fui** a Bogotá con mi familia **hace** tres años.
> **Hace** tres años **que fui** a Bogotá con mi familia.

D **¿Cuánto tiempo hace... ?** Dígales a sus compañeros cuándo fue la última vez que Ud. u (*or*) otra persona hizo los quehaceres domésticos del ejercicio **B** en su casa, apartamento o cuarto. Siga el modelo:

MODELO: barrer el suelo →
          Hace tres días que barrí el suelo. (Hace tres días que mi compañero
          barrió el suelo.)

Si hace mucho tiempo que Ud. hizo la limpieza y no quiere admitirlo públicamente, invente una respuesta o una explicación... ¡o mienta (*lie*)!

ESTRUCTURAS ▼▼▼▼▼▼▼▼▼▼▼▼▼▼▼▼▼▼▼▼▼▼▼

24. Talking About the Past (3)

Irregular Preterites

▼ **Un problema con un compañero de casa**

CECI: Oye, Graciela, *quise* ir a tu fiesta anoche, pero no *pude*... por el trabajo. ¿Qué tal *estuvo*?

GRACIELA: La fiesta *estuvo* estupenda. ¡Cuánta gente! Nos divertimos mucho. Pero, Ceci, Julio es un verdadero problema.

CECI: ¿Por qué, chica? ¿Qué *hizo*?

GRACIELA: No *hizo* nada. Y allí está el problema. Se acostó tan pronto como se *fueron* todos. No ayudó a recoger nada... y la verdad es que la casa quedó como un desastre, con vasos y platos en todas partes.

CECI: Cálmate, Graciela. Por lo menos es mejor que tu otro compañero de casa. ¿No lo recuerdas? ¡No te pagó el alquiler!

▲ ▲ ▲

¿Quién... ?

1. no pudo ir a una fiesta
2. no pagó una «cuenta» importante
3. dejó la casa hecha un desastre
4. calmó a una amiga
5. no hizo nada para arreglar la casa
6. tuvo que poner los platos en el lavaplatos

You have already learned the irregular preterite forms of **dar, hacer, ir,** and **ser.** The following verbs are also irregular in the preterite. Note that the first and third person singular endings, which are the only irregular ones, are unstressed, in contrast to the stressed endings of regular preterite forms.

estar:	**estuv-**	-e
poder:	**pud-**	-iste
poner:	**pus-**	-o
querer:	**quis-**	-imos
saber:	**sup-**	-isteis
tener:	**tuv-**	-ieron
venir:	**vin-**	

estar	
estuve	**estuvimos**
estuviste	**estuvisteis**
estuvo	**estuvieron**

decir:	**dij-**	-e, -iste, -o, -imos, -isteis, **-eron**
traer:	**traj-**	

A problem with a housemate   CECI: Hey, Graciela, I tried to get to the party last night, but I couldn't . . . because of work. How was it? GRACIELA: The party was wonderful. So many people (came)! We had a good time. But, Ceci, Julio is really a problem. CECI: Why, girl? What did he do? GRACIELA: He didn't do anything. And that's the problem. He went to bed as soon as everyone left. He didn't help to pick up anything . . . and the truth is that the house was a wreck, with glasses and plates everywhere. CECI: Calm down, Graciela. At least he's better than your other housemate. Don't you remember him? He didn't pay the rent!

When the preterite verb stem ends in **-j-**, the **-i-** of the third person plural ending is omitted: **dijeron, trajeron.**

The preterite of **hay** (**haber**) is **hubo** (*there was/were*).

Several of these Spanish verbs have an English equivalent in the preterite tense that is different from that of the infinitive.

saber:	Yo lo sé.	*I already know it.*
	Lo **supe** ayer.	*I found it out (learned it) yesterday.*
conocer:	Ya la conozco.	*I already know her.*
	La **conocí** ayer.	*I met her yesterday.*
querer:	Quiero hacerlo hoy.	*I want to do it today.*
	Quise hacerlo ayer.	*I tried to do it yesterday.*
	No quise hacerlo anteayer.	*I refused to do it the day before yesterday.*
poder:	Puedo leerlo.	*I can (am able to) read it.*
	Pude leerlo ayer.	*I could (and did) read it yesterday.*
	No pude leerlo anteayer.	*I couldn't (did not) read it the day before yesterday.*

Práctica

A **La semana pasada.**

Paso 1. Piense en las cosas que hizo la semana pasada. Indique si las siguientes oraciones se aplican a Ud.

	SÍ	NO
1. Tuve un examen muy importante.	☐	☐
2. Estuve en una fiesta hasta muy tarde.	☐	☐
3. Un pariente (Un amigo / Una amiga) vino a visitarme.	☐	☐
4. Conocí a alguien muy interesante.	☐	☐
5. No pude estudiar mucho porque estuve enfermo/a.	☐	☐
6. Puse mi cuarto y mis cosas en orden.	☐	☐
7. Alguien me dio un regalo.	☐	☐
8. Quise hacer algo imporante pero no pude.	☐	☐

Paso 2. Ahora use las oraciones del **Paso 1.** para entrevistar a un compañero / una compañera de clase. Su compañero debe dar algunos detalles, si puede.

MODELO: E1: ¿Tuviste un examen muy importante?
         E2: No, no tuve ningún examen. (Sí, tuve un examen importante en la clase de química.)

B **Una fiesta de cumpleaños.** Imagine que ayer hubo una fiesta de cumpleaños para Ud. en casa de su familia. Describa la fiesta, haciendo oraciones en el pretérito según las indicaciones.

1. todos / estar / en nuestra casa / antes de / nueve
2. nosotros / poner / mucho / regalos / encima / mesa
3. tíos y abuelos / venir / con / comida y refrescos
4. niños / querer / abrir / paquetes (*m.*) / pero / no / poder

5. yo / tener / que / ayudar / a / preparar / comida

6. más tarde / alguno / vecinos / venir / a / visitarnos

7. niños / pequeño / ir / a / su / alcobas / diez / y / acostarse

8. papá / sacar / basura / y / pasar / aspiradora

9. mamá / barrer / suelo / y / lavar / platos

10. al día siguiente / todos / decir / que / fiesta / estar / estupendo

¿Cierto, falso o no lo dice? Corrija las oraciones falsas.

1. Hubo muy poca gente en la fiesta.

2. Sólo vinieron los parientes.

3. Todos comieron bien... ¡y mucho!

4. Los niños abrieron los regalos.

C **Un sábado por la tarde.** Complete el siguiente diálogo con el pretérito de los infinitivos. Use el sujeto pronominal cuando sea necesario.

P1: Oye, ¿y dónde (*estar: tú*) toda la mañana?

P2: (*Tener: yo*) que ir a la oficina a terminar un trabajo.

P1: ¿Por qué no me lo (*decir: tú*) antes de irte?

P2: ¡Qué memoria! ¿Nunca recuerdas nada? Te lo (*decir: yo*) anoche.

P1: Puede ser, pero se me olvidó.[a]

P2: ¿(*Venir*) tus padres?

P1: Sí, y los chicos y yo (*tener*) que arreglar la sala. ¡Qué lata[b]!

P2: No te quejes.[c] Tú también puedes hacer algunos de los quehaceres.

P1: ¿Por qué? Nunca los (*hacer: yo*) en casa de mis padres y no quiero empezar ahora.

[a]se... *I forgot* [b]*pain* [c]No... *Don't complain.*

¿Quién lo dijo, la persona 1 o la persona 2?

1. Mañana tengo que regresar a la oficina, aunque es sábado.

2. Mis padres no me hicieron ayudar con los quehaceres.

3. No me gustan los quehaceres domésticos, pero los hago.

4. ¡Levántense, niños! Vienen los abuelos... ¡y la casa es un desastre!

Es probable que hablen dos esposos, pero... ¿quién es la persona 1 y quién es la persona 2? Conteste y explique su respuesta.

D **Hechos** (*Events*) **históricos.** Describa Ud. algunos hechos históricos, usando una palabra o frase de cada grupo. Use el pretérito de los verbos.

en 1957 los rusos	traer	en Valley Forge con sus soldados
en 1968 los esta-	saber	un hombre en la luna
dounidenses	conocer	un satélite en el espacio por primera vez
Adán y Eva	decir	«que coman (*let them eat*) pasteles»
George Washington	estar	el significado (*meaning*) de un árbol es-
los europeos	poner	pecial
los aztecas		a Livingston en África
Stanley		el caballo (*horse*) al Nuevo Mundo
María Antonieta		a Hernán Cortés en Tenochtitlán

Un paso más

UN POCO DE TODO

A **Entrevista.** Complete las oraciones lógicamente... ¡y sinceramente! Luego entreviste a otro/a estudiante para saber cómo él/ella completó las mismas oraciones.

MODELO: A mis padres les gusta que (*yo*) *los llame*. →
          E1: ¿Qué les gusta a tus padres que hagas?
          E2: Les gusta que yo estudie más. Y a tus padres, ¿qué les gusta que
              hagas?

1. A mis padres les gusta que (*yo*) _____.
2. Mi mejor amigo/a (esposo/a, novio/a, ...) siempre desea que (*yo*) _____.
3. Me gusta mucho que mis amigos _____.
4. No me gusta nada que mis amigos _____.
5. Es absolutamente ridículo que _____.
6. Una cosa que no tengo ahora pero que me gustaría mucho tener es _____.

B **¿Qué quiere o necesita Ud.?** Here is a series of answers to that question. Complete them with the correct form of each word in parentheses. When two possibilities are given in parentheses, select the correct word. **¡OJO!**   You will use the present indicative, present subjunctive, or preterite of the infinitives. And sometimes, the infinitive itself will be the appropriate form.

PERSONA A: Lo que yo deseo es que (haber[1]) paz[a] en (mí/mi[2]) país. Y espero que mi familia (estar[3]) bien. Para (mí/mi[4]), (*yo:* pedir[5]) muy poco.

PERSONA B: ¡Yo no (saber[6]) por dónde empezar la lista! Necesitamos una casa (tan/más[7]) grande, camas nuevas para los niños (pocos/pequeños[8]), (un/una[9]) televisor... Pero primero tenemos que (comprar[10]) (un/—[11]) otro coche, porque el que[b] tenemos (dejar[12]) de funcionar la semana pasada. ¡Ay! ¡Ojalá que (*nosotros:* ganar[13]) la lotería (este[14]) semana!

PERSONA C: Temo que (ser[15]) imposible tener todo lo que yo quiero. Deseo que no (haber[16]) hambre en el mundo y que los niños no (sufrir[c17]).

PERSONA D: ¡Uy! Muchas cosas para mi nuevo apartamento. Quiero (comprar[18]) (un/una[19]) sofá para la sala, y espero que mi madre me (comprar[20]) un horno de microondas. Es lástima que no (*yo:* poder[21]) comprar un televisor (este[22]) mes. Ojalá que mi hermana me (prestar[23]) el suyo. Además, me gustaría (comprar[24]) unas pinturas, (un/una[25]) *fax*...

PERSONA E: Yo quiero que mi papá me (llevar[26]) al circo. Mi amigo Enrique (ir[27]) la semana pasada y le (gustar[28]) mucho. También necesito (un/una[29]) bici. Y quiero que el bebé que va (a/de[30]) tener mi mamá (ser[31]) un hermanito. Si es una niña, es un rollo,[d] ¡porque no va a (querer[32]) jugar al básquetbol!

[a]*peace*   [b]*el... the one that*   [c]*to suffer*   [d]*pain*

SITUACIÓN Un problema con la computadora

EN UNA TIENDA DE COMPUTADORAS

DEPENDIENTE: Buenos días. ¿Qué desea Ud., señor?

CLIENTE: Buenos días. Mi computadora no funciona. No sé qué le pasa. Y la necesito con urgencia.

DEPENDIENTE: ¿La compró Ud. aquí?

CLIENTE: Sí, hace sólo dos meses. Aquí tengo la garantía y el recibo.[a]

[a]*receipt*

EN LA RESIDENCIA

Put the sentences in order, from 1 to 4.

_____ ANITA: Sí, cómo no. Sólo te pido que tengas un poco de cuidado[a] al[b] entrar y salir del cuarto.

_____ ANITA: Claro. Todos tienen trabajos que terminar esta semana.

_____ MARIBEL: Necesito trabajar con el ordenador y todos los terminales están ocupados.

_____ MARIBEL: Oye, tú tienes uno en tu cuarto, ¿verdad? ¿Me permites que lo use mientras estás en clase esta tarde?

[a]*care* [b]*as you*

Conversación

Think about things that you need to borrow from someone. Then, with a classmate, practice the second dialogue segment, substituting real information.

PARA ESCRIBIR

Write two short paragraphs about your living accomodations. The first paragraph should give information about where you live:

> a house, apartment, or dormitory
> the number of rooms
> a description of the furniture, appliances, and other possessions you have

In the second paragraph, write about what you like or do not like about your living arrangements. This can include the habits (**las costumbres**) of the people who live with you as well as your own: who gets up first, who smokes, and so on.

Verbos

alegrarse (de) to be happy (about)
cambiar (de) to change
conseguir (i, i) to get, obtain
dejar to leave (behind)
esperar to hope
funcionar to function, operate, work
ganar to earn; to win
sentir (ie, i) to regret; to feel sorry
temer to fear
terminar to end

Los bienes personales

el cartel poster
el contestador automático answering machine
el equipo equipment
la grabadora tape deck/recorder
la impresora printer
el ordenador computer (*Spain*)
la pintura painting
la videocasetera VCR

Cognados: el acuario, la bici(cleta), el *compact disc*, la computadora (L.A.), el control remoto, el equipo estereofónico/fotográfico, la moto(cicleta), el radio portátil, el trofeo, el *walkman*

Repaso: la camioneta, el coche, el pájaro, el pez, el televisor

Los quehaceres domésticos

barrer (el suelo) to sweep the floor
lavar to wash
limpiar to clean
pasar la aspiradora to vacuum
pintar (las paredes) to paint (the walls)
planchar to iron
sacar la basura to take out the trash
sacudir to dust

Repaso: hacer la cama, los muebles, el plato, poner la mesa, la ropa, la ventana

Algunos aparatos domésticos

la cafetera coffee pot
el congelador freezer
la estufa stove
el horno de microondas microwave oven
la lavadora washing machine
el lavaplatos dishwasher
la secadora dryer

Cognados: el refrigerador, la tostadora

En la oficina

el aumento raise, increase
el cheque check
el *fax* fax (machine)
el/la jefe/a boss

el sueldo salary
el trabajo job, work; written work; (term) paper

Otros sustantivos

el desastre disaster
la gente people
el lujo luxury
el/la vecino/a neighbor

Adjetivos

descapotable convertible (*with cars*)
increíble incredible

Palabras adicionales

es extraño it's strange
    ¡qué extraño! how strange!
es lástima it's a shame
    ¡qué lástima! what a shame!
hace + [*time*] (time) ago
me (te, le...) molesta it is bothersome to me (you, him . . .)
me (te, le...) sorprende it is surprising to me (you, him . . .)
ojalá (que) I hope (that)
por per, by
sacar fotos to take photographs

Self-Test

Use the tape that accompanies this text to test yourself briefly on the important points of this chapter.

VOCES

del mundo hispánico 6

México

Los Estados Unidos Mexicanos, nombre oficial de México, es un país con una cultura rica. Sus diversas culturas indígenas se mezclan con la tradición colonial española, ofreciendo un país de numerosos contrastes y extraordinaria belleza.

Para el turista, México lo tiene todo: clima templado, costas maravillosas, impresionantes ruinas arqueológicas, ciudades grandes y cosmopolitas, magníficos edificios, artesanías, etcétera. Su capital, Ciudad de México, en el Distrito Federal (o el D.F., como lo llaman los mexicanos), es probablemente la ciudad más grande del mundo, con aproximadamente 25.000.000 de habitantes.

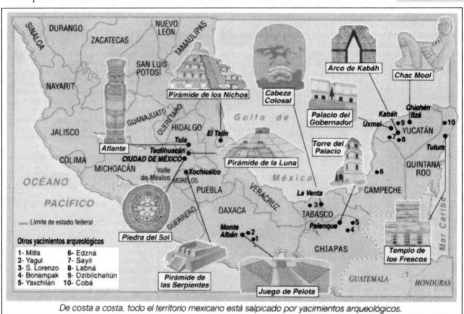

De costa a costa, todo el territorio mexicano está salpicado por yacimientos arqueológicos.

La capital del imperio azteca era[a] Tenochtitlán, una ciudad de 300.000 habitantes. Fue destruida por los españoles en 1521 y sobre sus ruinas se fundó la moderna Ciudad de México. Lo siguiente es parte de la descripción de Tenochtitlán por Hernán Cortés, en una carta al rey[b] de España.

[a]was [b]king

E sta gran ciudad de Tenochtitlán está fundada en esta laguna salada,[c] y desde[d] la tierra firme hasta el cuerpo[e] de la ciudad... hay dos leguas[f]... Es tan grande la ciudad como Sevilla y Córdoba. Son las calles[g] de ella muy anchas[h] y muy derechas[i] ... Tiene esta ciudad muchas plazas, donde hay continuos mercados y trato[j] de comprar y vender.

[c]salty [d]from [e]body [f]legua = 5572 meters [g]streets [h]wide [i]straight [j]dealings

La obra de Frida Kahlo es cada vez más famosa y reconocida a nivel artístico. Diego Rivera, su esposo, también es considerado como uno de los pintores más importantes de México y Latinoamérica. Es famoso por sus pinturas murales.

Autorretrato con mono.

Octavio Paz: Su premio nos honra[a]

Por dos años consecutivos el Premio Nobel de Literatura ha sido otorgado[b] a un escritor de nuestro idioma. El año pasado lo mereció el novelista español Camilo José Cela. Este año le ha correspondido[c] al gran poeta y ensayista[d] mexicano Octavio Paz, indiscutiblemente una de las figuras más importantes de las letras latinoamericanas y mundiales.

Para los latinos de los Estados Unidos, y para los mexicanoamericanos en particular, es importante recordar que Paz fue el primer gran intelectual que notó y analizó el significado[e] de la presencia latina en los Estados Unidos, en su libro más conocido *El laberinto de la soledad,*[f] un hermoso ensayo sobre la esencia del alma[g] mexicana.

Adaptado de *Más*

[a]nos... *honors us* [b]ha... *has been awarded* [c]le... *it was given* [d]*essayist* [e]*meaning* [f]*El... The Labyrinth of Solitude* [g]*soul*

Al iniciar mi vida en los Estados Unidos residí[a] algún tiempo en Los Ángeles, ciudad habitada por más de un millón de personas de origen mexicano. A primera vista sorprende al viajero—además de la pureza del cielo y de la fealdad[b] de las dispersas y ostentosas construcciones—la atmósfera vagamente mexicana de la ciudad, imposible de apresar[c] con palabras o conceptos. Esta mexicanidad—gusto por adornos, descuido y fausto,[d] negligencia, pasión y reserva—flota en el aire. Y digo que flota porque no se mezcla ni se funde[e] con el otro mundo, el mundo norteamericano, hecho[f] de precisión y eficacia. Flota, pero no se opone; se balancea, impulsada[g] por el viento, a veces desgarrada[h] como una nube, otras erguida[i] como un cohete[j] que asciende. Se arrastra, se pliega,[k] se expande, se contrae, duerme o sueña, hermosura harapienta.[l] Flota: no acaba de ser, no acaba de desaparecer.

Fragmento de *El laberinto de la soledad*, Fondo de cultura económica, España, 1988, p. 12.

[a]*viví* [b]*ugliness* [c]*to capture* [d]*descuido... carelessness and pomp* [e]*no... it doesn't mix or merge* [f]*made* [g]*propelled* [h]*torn* [i]*erected* [j]*rocket* [k]*Se... It crawls, it folds itself* [l]*hermosura... ragged beauty*

¡Qué interesante!

1. ¿Qué otras personalidades mexicanas conoce Ud.?
2. ¿Cuáles son los lugares mexicanos más famosos en este país? ¿Por qué son famosos? ¿Conoce personalmente alguno de estos lugares?
3. Tenochtitlán era (*was*) una ciudad azteca. La civilización azteca era una de las culturas indígenas más importantes de México. ¿Conoce otras culturas indígenas mexicanas? ¿Qué sabe de ellas?
4. ¿Qué implica Octavio Paz cuando dice que la «mexicanidad flota» en la ciudad de Los Ángeles? ¿Está Ud. de acuerdo? ¿Cree que ocurre algo similar en Nueva York, con los puertorriqueños, o en Miami, con los cubanos?

Primer paso

Hablando[a] de fiestas...

[a] *Talking*

el Día de los Muertos: el 2 de noviembre

la Nochebuena: el 24 de diciembre

el Día de los Reyes Magos: el 6 de enero

la Navidad: el 25 de diciembre

la Noche Vieja: el 31 de diciembre

Días FESTIVOS

Más vocabulario

¡felicidades!	wish for birthdays (lit. happiness!)	regalar	to give (as a gift)
¡felicitaciones!	congratulations!	reírse (i, i)	to laugh
¡feliz cumpleaños!	happy birthday!	sentirse (ie, i) feliz/triste	to feel happy/sad
la sorpresa	surprise	sonreír (i, i)	to smile

dar/hacer una fiesta — to give/have a party
despedirse (i, i) (de) — to say goodbye (to)
divertirse (ie, i) — to have a good time
faltar (a) — to be absent, lacking
llorar — to cry
pasarlo bien/mal — to have a good/bad time

ser + en + *place* — to take place at (*place*)
—**¿Dónde es la fiesta?** — Where is the party?
—**(Es) En casa de Julio.** — (It's) At Julio's house.

Don't confuse **ser + en** with **estar en** (*to be located in / at*).

Note the use of accent marks in the present tense forms of **reír** and **sonreír**: **(son)río, (son)ríes, (son)ríes, (son)reímos, (son)reís, (son)ríen.**

Estas fiestas también son muy importantes en el mundo hispano. ¿Puede Ud. relacionarlas con su equivalente en inglés?

el Día de Año Nuevo	el Día de Gracias	*birthday*	*Columbus Day*
el Día de la Raza (de la Hispanidad)	el cumpleaños	*New Year's Day*	*Thanksgiving*

Práctica

A **Definiciones.** ¿Qué palabra o frase corresponde a estas definiciones?

1. el día en que algunos cristianos celebran el nacimiento (*birth*) de Jesús
2. algo que alguien no sabe o no espera
3. lo que se le dice a la persona que cumple años
4. el día en que algunos hispanos visitan el cementerio para honrar la memoria de los difuntos (*deceased*)
5. reacción emocional cuando se reciben muy buenas noticias (*news*) (tres respuestas)
6. reacción emocional cuando se recibe la noticia de una tragedia (dos respuestas)

¿CUAL DE ESTAS FIESTAS ES MAS IMPORTANTE?		
	%	Total
Nochebuena		30,8
Navidad		19,4
Nochevieja		19,4
Año Nuevo		3,7
Reyes Magos		3,6
Todas por igual		21,2
NS/NC		2,0

ACTOS RELIGIOSOS		
Aparte de las celebraciones, ¿en estos días asiste usted a oficios religiosos navideños?		
	%	Total
Sí		42,7
No		55,2
NS/NC		2,2

239

7. la noche en que se celebra el fin de un año y el principio de otro
8. palabra que se dice para mostrar una reacción muy favorable, por ejemplo, cuando un amigo recibe un gran aumento de sueldo

B Algunos días festivos estadounidenses.

Paso 1. Diga a qué mes (o a qué día, si lo sabe) corresponde cada una de estas fiestas.

1. el Día de la Independencia
2. el Día de Gracias
3. el Día de San Patricio
4. el Día del Trabajo (**¡OJO!** Piense en el significado de la palabra **trabajo**.)

5. Janucá
6. el Día de San Valentín (de los Enamorados [*Lovers*])
7. la Pascua Florida (*Easter*)
8. la Pascua Judía (*Passover*)

Paso 2. Ahora, explíquele a un grupo de jóvenes hispanos qué se hace en este país en esos días.

Adivinanza

Somos los siete hermanitos,
sólo vivimos un día;
uno nace,[a] otro muere[b]
y así pasamos la vida.

[a]*is born* [b]*dies*

Vocabulary Library

el árbol	tree	**el pavo**	
la cesta	basket	**la sinagoga**	
el conejo	rabbit	**la tarjeta**	card
el corazón	heart	**el trébol**	four-leaf clover
el desfile	parade	**la vela**	candle
la fiesta del barrio	block party		
los fuegos artificiales	fireworks	**esconder**	to hide
la iglesia	church	**hacer un *picnic* / una barbacoa**	
la misa / el servicio religioso		**pintar**	to paint; to decorate

DE AQUÍ Y DE ALLÁ

In Spanish, *to toast* is **hacer un brindis.** Here are two common Spanish toasts.

- Salud (*Health*), amor y pesetas... y (el) tiempo para gozarlos (*to enjoy them*).
- Arriba, abajo, al centro y... ¡adentro!

Un brindis argentino.

ESTRUCTURAS

Review the direct (Grammar Section 18) and indirect (Grammar Section 19) object pronouns before beginning Grammar Section 25. Remember that direct objects answer the questions *what?* or *whom?* and that indirect objects answer the questions *to whom?* or *for whom?* in relation to the verb.

DIRECT

me   te   **lo/la**   nos   os   **los/las**

INDIRECT

me   te   **le**   nos   os   **les**

Identifique los complementos directo e (*and*) indirecto en las siguientes oraciones.

1. Nos mandan los libros mañana.
2. ¿Por qué no los vas a comprar?
3. ¿Me puedes leer el menú?
4. Hágalo ahora, por favor.

5. Juan no te va a dar el dinero hoy.
6. Quiero que lo tenga para mañana, por favor.
7. Sí, claro que te voy a invitar.
8. ¿Me escuchas?

25. Expressing Direct and Indirect Objects Together

Double Object Pronouns

[a] *Pedestrian!*

When both an indirect and a direct object pronoun are used in a sentence, the indirect object pronoun (**I**) precedes the direct (**D**): **ID.** Note that nothing comes between the two pronouns. The position of double object pronouns with respect to the verb is the same as that of single object pronouns.

¿La fecha del examen? ¡Claro que la sé! —¿Por qué no **nos la** dices?	*The date of the exam? Of course I know it! —Why don't you tell us?*

¿Tienes el trofeo? —Sí, acaban de dár**melo**.	*Do you have the trophy? —Yes, they just gave it to me.*
Mamá, ¿nos das el postre? —**Os lo** doy ahora mismo.	*Mom, will you give us dessert? —I'll give it to you right now.*

When both the indirect and the direct object pronouns begin with the letter **l,** the indirect object pronoun always changes to **se.** The direct object pronoun does not change.

Le compra unos zapatos. ↓	*He's buying her some shoes.*
Se los compra.	*He's buying them for her.*
Les mandamos la blusa. ↓	*We'll send you the blouse.*
Se la mandamos.	*We'll send it to you.*

Since **se** stands for **le** (*to/for you* [sing.], *him, her*) and **les** (*to/for you* [pl.], *them*), it is often necessary to clarify its meaning by using **a** plus the pronoun objects of prepositions.

Se lo escribo (**a Uds., a ellos, a ellas...**).	*I'll write it to (you, them . . .).*
Se las doy (**a Ud., a él, a ella...**)	*I'll give them to (you, him, her . . .).*

Práctica

A **Lo que se oye en casa.** ¿A qué se refieren las siguientes oraciones? Fíjese en (*Pay attention to*) los pronombres y en el sentido (*meaning*) de la oración.

el control remoto	una motocicleta	el televisor
la videocasetera	el canal	unas fotos

1. No quiero que se **lo** pongas a los niños. Miran demasiado la tele.
2. ¿Me **lo** das, por favor? Quiero cambiar el canal.
3. Es preferible que nos **la** arreglen pronto. Tengo un vídeo nuevo que quiero mirar.
4. No entiendo por qué no quieres prestárme**la**.
5. ¡Por favor! ¡No me **lo** cambies! Me gusta este programa.
6. ¿Por qué no se **las** mandas a los abuelos? Les van a gustar.

B **En la mesa.** Ud. acaba de comer pero todavía tiene hambre. Pida más comida, según el modelo. Fíjese en (*Note*) el uso del tiempo presente como sustituto del mandato.

MODELO: ensalada → ¿Hay más **ensalada**? Me **la** pasas, por favor.

1. pan 2. tortillas 3. tomates 4. fruta 5. vino 6. jamón

C **En la estación de trenes.** Cambie: sustantivos → pronombres, para evitar (*avoid*) la repetición.

1. ¿La hora de la salida? Acaban de decirnos la hora de la salida.
2. ¿El horario? Sí, quiero que me leas el horario, por favor.
3. ¿Los boletos? No, no tiene que darle los boletos aquí.

4. ¿El equipaje? Claro que le guardo el equipaje.

5. ¿Los pasajes? ¿No quieres que te compre los pasajes?

6. ¿El puesto? No te preocupes. Te puedo guardar el puesto.

7. ¿La clase turística? Sí, les recomiendo la clase turística, señores.

8. ¿Los boletos? El revisor (*conductor*) va a pedirnos los boletos en el tren.

D **¿Quién le regaló eso?**

Paso 1. Haga una lista de los cinco mejores regalos que Ud. ha recibido (*have received*) en su vida. Si no sabe alguna palabra, pregúntele a su profesor(a).

Paso 2. Ahora déle a un compañero / una compañera su lista. Él/Ella le va a preguntar: **¿Quién te regaló _____?** Use pronombres en su respuesta.

MODELO: —¿Quién te regaló **los pendientes**?
         —Mis padres me **los** regalaron.

RECICLADO

Before beginning **Vocabulario,** review Grammar Section 15, Comparisons. Then answer these questions.

1. ¿Cuál es el día festivo más interesante para Ud.?
2. ¿Cuál es mejor para el cumpleaños, un regalo caro o una fiesta de sorpresa?
3. ¿Cuál es peor, olvidar el cumpleaños de alguien o faltar a una cita (*appointment or date*)?
4. ¿En qué fiesta gasta la gente más dinero?

VOCABULARIO

Las emociones y los extremos

discutir (sobre)	to argue (about)	**ponerse** + *adj.*	to become + *adjective*
(con)	(with)	**portarse bien/mal**	to behave well/badly
enfermarse	to get sick	**quejarse (de)**	to complain (about)
enojarse (con)	to get mad (at)	**recordar (ue)**	to remember
olvidarse (de)	to forget (about)		

Cuidado especial en la época NAVIDEÑA

Durante la época de Navidad, nuestras mascotas están propensas a enfermarse o tener accidentes debido a todos los cambios que ocurren en nuestra rutina diaria. Hay árboles de Navidad, guirnaldas, cables eléctricos, fuegos artificiales, mucha fiesta, viajes y sobretodo, la comida típica de la navidad. Todas estas cosas presentan peligros inminentes que pueden afectar a nuestras mascotas.

Note in particular the use of **ponerse** with adjectives to indicate physical, mental, or emotional changes.

¿Por qué **te pusiste** tan **furioso**?	*Why did you get (become) so angry?*
El niño **se** va a **poner** muy **triste** si no le regalamos una bicicleta.	*The kid is going to be very sad if we don't give him a bicycle.*

The superlative (**el superlativo**) is formed in English by adding *-est* to adjectives or by using expressions such as *the most* and *the least* with the adjective. In Spanish this concept is expressed in the same way as the comparative (Grammar Section 15) but is always accompanied by the definite article.

el/la/los/las + *noun* + **más/menos** + *adjective* + **de**...	*the most/least* + *adjective -est* + *noun* + *of*
los días más largos **del** año	*the longest days in the year*
las personas más importantes **del** país	*the most important people in the country*
el/la/los/las + **mejor/peor** + *noun* + **de**...	*the best/worst* + *noun* + *of* . . .
¡Fue **el** peor día **de** mi vida!	*It was the worst day of my life!*
la mejor estudiante **de** la clase	*the best student in the class*

Práctica

A **Situaciones.** ¿Cómo reacciona o cómo se pone Ud. en estas situaciones? Use estos adjetivos o cualquier otro, y también los verbos que describen las reacciones emocionales.

serio/a	feliz/triste	avergonzado/a (*embarrassed*)
nervioso/a	furioso/a	contento/a

1. Es Navidad y alguien le regala a Ud. un reloj muy, muy caro.
2. Es Navidad y sus padres/hijos se olvidan de regalarle algo.
3. En una fiesta, alguien acaba de contarle (*to tell you*) un chiste (*joke*).
4. Ud. da una fiesta pero la gente no lo pasa bien; es decir, no se ríen, no sonríen, no cuentan chistes, están aburridos, etcétera.
5. Hay un examen importante esta mañana, pero Ud. no estudió nada anoche.
6. Ud. acaba de terminar un examen difícil/fácil y cree que lo hizo bien/mal.
7. En un examen de química, Ud. se olvida de una fórmula muy importante.
8. Sin querer, Ud. se portó de forma muy descortés con un buen amigo.

B **¿Está Ud. de acuerdo o no?**

Paso 1. Indique si Ud. está de acuerdo o no con las siguientes oraciones.

	SÍ	NO
1. El descubrimiento científico más importante del siglo XX es la vacuna contra la poliomielitis.	☐	☐
2. La persona más influyente (*influential*) del mundo es el presidente de los Estados Unidos.	☐	☐

	SÍ	NO
3. El estado menos atractivo de los Estados Unidos es Nevada.	☐	☐
4. El problema más serio del mundo es la desforestación de la región del Amazonas.	☐	☐
5. El día festivo más divertido del año es la Noche Vieja.	☐	☐
6. La mejor novela del mundo es *Lord of the Flies.*	☐	☐
7. La persona más generosa del mundo es la Madre Teresa.	☐	☐
8. El animal menos inteligente de todos es el avestruz (*ostrich*).	☐	☐
9. El peor mes del año es enero.	☐	☐
10. La ciudad más contaminada de los Estados Unidos es Los Ángeles.	☐	☐

Paso 2. Si alguna oración no refleja su opinión, haga otra oración.

MODELO: 5. No estoy de acuerdo. Creo que el día festivo más divertido del año es el Cuatro de Julio.

NOTA LINGÜÍSTICA: Being Emphatic

To be even more emphatic, use the ending **-ísimo** to add the idea *extremely* (*exceptionally, very very, super*) to the meaning of an adjective or adverb.

ADVERB

¿La Navidad? Me gusta **muchísimo.**

Christmas? I like it a whole lot.

ADJECTIVE

La comida tradicional del Día de Gracias es **dificilísima** de preparar, pero es **riquísima.** Durante la época navideña, los niños son **buenísimos.**

The traditional Thanksgiving dinner is very hard to prepare, but it's quite good. At Christmastime, kids are really really good.

If the adjective ends in a consonant, **-ísimo** is added to the singular form: **difícil → dificilísimo** (and any accents on the word are dropped). If the adjective ends in a vowel, the final vowel is dropped before adding **-ísimo: bueno → buenísimo.**

Note the spelling changes that occur when the final consonant of an adjective is **c, g,** or **z: riquísimo, larguísimo, felicísimo.**

C **Entrevista.** With another student, ask and answer questions based on the following phrases. Then report your opinions to the class. Report any disagreements as well.

1. la persona más guapa del mundo
2. la noticia más seria de esta semana
3. un libro interesantísimo y otro pesadísimo (*very boring*)
4. el mejor restaurante de la ciudad y el peor
5. el cuarto más importante de la casa y el menos importante
6. un plato riquísimo y otro malísimo
7. un programa de televisión interesantísimo y otro pesadísimo
8. un lugar tranquilísimo, otro animadísimo y otro peligrosísimo (*dangerous*)
9. la canción más bonita del año y la más fea
10. la mejor película del año y la peor

D **¿Diversión o aversión?** Los días festivos también son días difíciles para muchas personas. Para Ud., ¿son ciertas o falsas las siguientes oraciones? Cambie las oraciones falsas para que (*so that*) sean ciertas. Luego compare sus respuestas con las de sus compañeros de clase.

EN LAS FIESTAS FAMILIARES

1. Me gusta muchísimo asistir a las fiestas familiares.
2. Algunos parientes siempre discuten y se portan mal.
3. Sólo hablamos de los buenos momentos del pasado.
4. Hay un pariente que siempre se queja de la comida.
5. Alguien siempre come o bebe demasiado y luego se enferma.

NOTA CULTURAL: Una celebración muy importante

Para las señoritas, la fiesta de los quince años, **la quinceañera,** es una de las más importantes. Desde esa edad a la niña se le considera ya mujer. (Para los muchachos, la fiesta de los dieciocho o veintiún años representa la llegada a la mayoría de edad.[a])

Lea las respuestas de dos chicas hispanas a la siguiente pregunta:

¿Cuál fue el cumpleaños más inolvidable de su vida?

—Fue el de mis quince años. Es una costumbre[b] en la Argentina la celebración del día en que cumplen quince años las muchachas con una fiesta muy especial. Yo lo celebré rodeada de[c] mis amigos y mi familia, en una fiesta que duró hasta las siete de la mañana del día siguiente.

—Fue el de mis quince años, pues mis padres me hicieron mi fiesta Quinceañera, con catorce damas y catorce caballeros. Bailamos el tradicional vals y la fiesta duró toda la noche. Fue una fiesta inolvidable. Muchas personas estuvieron presentes y recibí muchos regalos.

[a]mayoría... *coming of age*

[b]*custom* [c]rodeada... *surrounded by*

ESTRUCTURAS ▼▼▼▼▼▼▼▼▼▼▼▼▼▼▼▼▼▼▼▼▼▼▼▼▼

26. Talking About the Past (4)

Preterite of Stem-changing Verbs

▼

▼ **El cumpleaños de Mercedes**

▼ Siguiendo las indicaciones, invente Ud. una descripción de la fiesta de sorpresa
▼ que se celebró para Mercedes el año pasado.

▼ 1. Todos llegaron a _____ (hora).

▼ 2. Mercedes llegó más tarde, a _____ (hora).

▼ 3. Mercedes
$$\begin{cases} \textbf{sonrió} \\ \textbf{se rió} \text{ mucho} \\ \text{empezó a llorar} \end{cases}$$
cuando vio a todos sus amigos.

▼

▼

▼ 4. Sus amigos le trajeron muchos regalos. Su amigo Raúl le regaló _____. Su

▼   prima Julita le regaló _____. Su hermano le trajo _____.

▼ 5. Su compañera de casa **sirvió** _____.

▼ 6. **Se despidieron** todos a _____ (hora).

▼ 7. Mercedes **se durmió,** muy contenta, a _____ (hora).

▼ Ahora repita Ud. algunos de los detalles, pero desde el punto de vista de

▼ Mercedes. Use los siguientes verbos: **sonreí, me reí, me dormí.**

As you learned in **Capítulo 10,** the **-ar** and **-er** stem-changing verbs have no stem change in the preterite.

recordar (ue)		perder (ie)	
rec**o**rdé	rec**o**rdamos	p**e**rdí	p**e**rdimos
rec**o**rdaste	rec**o**rdasteis	p**e**rdiste	p**e**rdisteis
rec**o**rdó	rec**o**rdaron	p**e**rdió	p**e**rdieron

The **-ir** stem-changing verbs do have a stem change in the preterite, but only in the third person singular and plural, where the stem vowels **e** and **o** change to **i** and **u** respectively. This is the same change that occurs in the **nosotros** and **vosotros** forms of the present subjunctive.

pedir (i, i)		dormir (ue, u)	
pedí	pedimos	dormí	dormimos
pediste	pedisteis	dormiste	dormisteis
p**i**dió	p**i**dieron	d**u**rmió	d**u**rmieron

These are the **-ir** stem-changing verbs that you already know or have seen.

conseguir (i, i)	morirse (ue, u)	reír(se) (i, i)*	sonreír (i, i)*
despedir(se) (i, i)	pedir (i, i)	sentir(se) (ie, i)	sugerir (ie, i)
divertir(se) (ie, i)	preferir (ie, i)	servir (i, i)	vestir(se) (i, i)
dormir(se) (ue, u)			

Práctica

A **¿Quién lo hizo?** ¿Ocurrieron algunas de estas cosas en clase la semana pasada? Conteste con el nombre de la persona apropiada. Si nadie lo hizo, conteste con **Nadie...** La persona nombrada debe confirmar la acción, según el modelo.

---

*Note the simplification: **ri-ió → rió; ri-ieron → rieron; son-ri-ió → sonrió; son-ri-ieron → sonrieron.**

MODELO: ____ se vistió muy elegante. →

ESTUDIANTE: Sara se vistió muy elegante.

SARA: Es verdad. Yo me vestí muy elegante el miércoles.

1. ____ se vistió muy elegante.
2. ____ se vistió de una manera rara (*strange*).
3. ____ se durmió en clase.
4. ____ le pidió al profesor / a la profesora más tarea.

5. ____ se sintió muy feliz.
6. ____ se divirtió muchísimo.
7. ____ no sonrió ni siquiera (*not even*) una vez.
8. ____ prefirió no contestar ninguna pregunta.

B **Historias.** Cuente las siguientes historias breves en el pretérito. Luego continúelas, si puede.

1. **En un restaurante:** Juan (sentarse) a la mesa. Cuando (venir) el camarero, le (pedir) una cerveza. El camarero no (recordar) lo que Juan (pedir) y le (servir) una Coca-Cola. Juan no (querer) beber la Coca-Cola. Le (decir) al camarero: «Perdón, señor. Le (pedir: *yo*) una cerveza.» El camarero le (contestar): ____.

2. **Un día típico:** Rosa (acostarse) temprano y (dormirse) en seguida. (Dormir) bien y (despertarse) temprano. (Vestirse) y (salir) para la universidad. En el autobús (ver) a su amigo José y los dos se (sonreír). A las nueve ____.

3. **Dos noches diferentes:** Yo (vestirse), (ir) a una fiesta, (divertirse) mucho y (volver) tarde a casa. Mi compañero de cuarto (decidir) quedarse en casa y (mirar) la televisión toda la noche. No (divertirse) nada. (Perder) una fiesta excelente y lo (sentir) mucho. Yo ____.

C **Las historias que todos conocemos.** Cuente algunos detalles de unas historias tradicionales, usando una palabra o frase de cada grupo y el pretérito de los verbos.

Drácula / el vampiro Lestat	conseguir	en un baile
el lobo (*wolf*)	perder	encontrar a la mujer misteriosa
Rip Van Winkle	divertirse	muchos años
Romeo	preferir	en la chimenea de los Tres Cochinitos (*Little Pigs*)
la Cenicienta (*Cinderella*)	morir	por el amor de Julieta
el Príncipe	sentir	durante el día
las hermanastras de la Cenicienta	vestirse	de (*as a*) abuela
	dormir	un zapato
		envidia (*envy*) de su hermanastra

¿POR O PARA?

Did you notice the use of **por** in the preceding activity?

Romeo murió **por** el amor de Julieta.

Por often expresses the motive or reason for something. In this sense, it is the equivalent of *because of* or *about*. It is often used with adjectives such as **preocupado, nervioso, furioso,** and so on, to give the reason why someone feels a particular way. It is also used with verbs like **enojarse, discutir,** and so on, to express the motive or reason for someone getting angry or arguing.

D **Entrevista.** With another student, ask and answer questions to determine the first or last time the following situations occurred. Answer using **hace** + *period of time.* If you have never done the thing mentioned, say **Nunca lo he hecho.**

MODELO: —¿Cuándo fue la última vez / la primera vez que tú **fuiste al cine**?
—Hace **una semana.**

1. decir algo estúpido en una clase
2. sentirse mal
3. enojarse con alguien
4. reírse mucho

5. tener que pedirle ayuda a alguien
6. vestirse elegantemente
7. enamorarse (*to fall in love*)
8. faltar a una clase

9. quejarse de algo
10. dormirse a las cuatro de la mañana
11. ¿ ?

Un paso más

UN POCO DE TODO

A **Situaciones y reacciones.** Imagine que ocurrieron las siguientes situaciones en algún momento en el pasado. ¿Cómo reaccionó Ud.? ¿Sonrió? ¿Lloró? ¿Se rió? ¿Se enojó? ¿Se puso triste, contento/a, furioso/a? ¿Qué hizo?

MODELO: Su compañero de cuarto hizo mucho ruido a las cuatro de la mañana.
¿Cómo reaccionó Ud.? →
Me enojé.
(Me puse furiosísimo/a.)
(Salí de casa y fui a dormir en casa de un amigo.)
(Hablé con él.)

SITUACIONES
1. Una amiga le regaló un libro pesadísimo que no le gustó nada.
2. El profesor le dijo que no hay clase mañana.
3. Ud. rompió las gafas (*eyeglasses*).
4. Su hermano perdió la cartera.
5. Su mejor amigo lo/la llamó a las seis de la mañana el día de su cumpleaños.
6. Nevó muchísimo y Ud. tuvo que hacer un viaje en auto.
7. Ud. recibió el aumento de sueldo más grande de la oficina.
8. Durante el último examen, Ud. no pudo recordar las formas del pretérito.
9. Ud. preparó una cena para algunos amigos y todo le salió horrible.

Ahora, usando las formas del pretérito, invente otras situaciones y pídales a sus compañeros de clase que le indiquen sus reacciones.

B **Más días festivos.** Complete the following paragraphs with the correct form of the words in parentheses, as suggested by the context. When two possibilities are given in parentheses, select the correct word. Use the preterite of infinitives in italics.

LA FIESTA DE LA VIRGEN DE GUADALUPE

En (alguno[1]) países hispánicos los días de (cierto[2]) santos (ser/estar[3]) fiestas nacionales. El día 12 (de/del[4]) diciembre se (conmemorar[5]) a la santa patrona de México, la Virgen de Guadalupe. (Mucho[6]) mexicanoamericanos celebran (este[7]) fiesta también. Se (creer[8]) que la Virgen María se le (*aparecer*[9]) (a/de[10]) Juan, un humilde pastor,[a] en el pueblo (a/de[11]) Guadalupe. La Virgen (*dejar*[12]) su imagen en un rebozo[b] que todavía se puede (ver[13]) en su Basílica en la Ciudad de México.

[a]*shepherd* [b]*shawl*

LA FIESTA DE SAN FERMÍN

No (todo[14]) las fiestas hispánicas (ser/estar[15]) religiosas. Esta fiesta de Pamplona (España) lleva (el/la[16]) nombre de un santo y (ser/estar[17]) de origen religioso, pero es esencialmente secular. Durante diez días—entre (el/la[18]) 7 y (el/la[19]) 17 de julio—se interrumpe la rutina diaria[c] (del / del la[20]) ciudad. (Llegar[21]) personas de todas partes de España e inclusive de (otro[22]) países para beber, cantar, bailar... y (pasarlo[23]) bien. Todas las mañanas se (permitir[24]) que algunos toros (correr[d][25]) sueltos[e] por (el/la[26]) calle de la Estafeta, en dirección (al / a la[27]) plaza de toros. (Alguno[28]) personas atrevidas[f] (correr[29]) delante de ellos. No (haber[30]) duda que (este[31]) demostración de valor[g] (ser/estar[32]) bastante peligrosa. Luego por (el/la[33]) tarde se celebra una corrida[h] en la famosa plaza de toros que (*describir*[34]) Ernest Hemingway en (su[35]) novela *The Sun Also Rises*. En Pamplona todavía (ser/estar[36]) posible (hablar[37]) con personas que (*saber/conocer*[38]) a este famoso escritor estadounidense.

[c]*daily* [d]*to run* [e]*free* [f]*daring* [g]*courage* [h]*bullfight*

☀ **SITUACIÓN** Frases útiles para una fiesta

The following brief dialogues are useful for gatherings of all kinds. As you read through them, try to determine whether they are most useful when you arrive (**a la llegada**), during the gathering (**durante la fiesta**), or when you are in the process of leaving (**a la despedida**).

1. —Muchas gracias por venir.
   —Gracias a ti. ¡Lo pasamos estupendamente!
2. —Otro año... y aquí estamos todos otra vez.
   —Somos más este año, abuela.
   —Eso está bien.
3. —¡Hola. ¡Por fin llegaron! Pasen,[a] pasen.
   —¡Hola! Perdona el retraso,[b] pero no sabes cómo está el tráfico.
4. —¿Qué quieren tomar?
   —Una bebida sin alcohol, por favor. Pero, primero, ¿dónde podemos dejar los abrigos?
   —En el cuarto de Antonio, por favor.
5. —Bueno, chica, tenemos que irnos.
   —¿Tan temprano?
   —Sí, yo trabajo mañana y Arturo también tiene varios compromisos.[c]

[a]*Come in* [b]*lateness* [c]*things to do*

Conversación

Put the brief dialogues into a logical order. Then, with one or two classmates, create a context in which to use them, such as a family celebration. Assign each person a role and vary or expand the exchanges to accommodate them to your particular context. Then, ask a member of another group how their celebration went: when it took place, what the occasion was, whether they had a good time, and so on.

PARA ESCRIBIR

Describa en una breve composición cómo se celebra el día festivo más importante para su familia. Empiece diciendo (*telling*) por qué es importante ese día. Después describa qué miembros de la familia lo celebran, qué hacen durante el día, qué comen, etcétera.

▼▼▼▼▼▼▼▼▼▼▼▼▼▼▼ VOCABULARIO ▼▼▼▼▼▼▼▼▼▼▼▼▼▼

Verbos

despedirse (i, i) (de) to say goodbye (to)
discutir (sobre) (con) to argue (about) (with)
enfermarse to get sick
enojarse (con) to get mad (at), angry (with)
faltar (a) to be absent, lacking
llorar to cry
morir(se) (ue, u) to die
olvidarse (de) to forget (about)
ponerse + *adj.* to become + *adjective*
portarse bien/mal to behave well/ badly
quejarse (de) to complain (about)
recordar (ue) to remember
reírse (i, i) to laugh
sentirse (ie, i) to feel
sonreír (i, i) to smile

Repaso: **dar/hacer una fiesta, divertirse (ie, i), pasarlo bien/ mal, regalar**

Los días festivos

el Día de Año Nuevo New Year's Day
el Día de Gracias Thanksgiving
el Día de la Raza (de la Hispani-dad) Hispanic Awareness Day
el Día de los Muertos All Souls' Day
el Día de los Reyes Magos Day of the Magi
la Navidad Christmas
la Nochebuena Christmas Eve
la Noche Vieja New Year's Eve

Repaso: **el cumpleaños**

Sustantivos

el principio beginning
la sorpresa surprise

Adjetivos

feliz (*pl.* **felices**) happy (*with* **ser**)
peligroso/a dangerous
pesado/a boring, a drag
rico/a rich, tasty (*with food*)

Repaso: **furioso/a**

Palabras adicionales

demasiado too; too much
¡felicidades! *wish for birthdays* (*lit.* happiness!)
¡felicitaciones! congratulations!
¡feliz cumpleaños! happy birthday!
por because of; about
ser + **en** + *place* to take place at (*place*)

Self-Test

Use the tape that accompanies this text to test yourself briefly on the important points of this chapter.

LECTURA
cultural

NAVIDAD CON SABOR A RANCHO

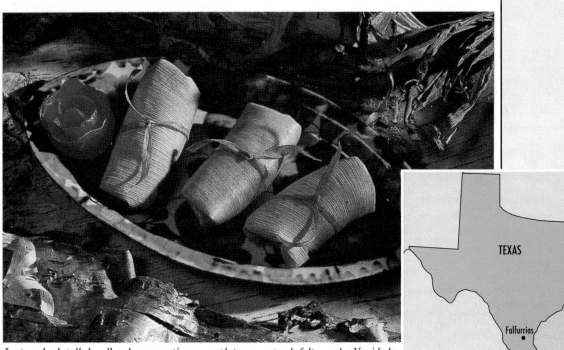

Los tamales de pollo han llegado a convertirse en un plato que no puede faltar en las Navidades

TEXAS

Falfurrias

Reinosa • • Matamoros

LOS RANCHEROS, GANADEROS, CAMPESINOS Y TRABA-Ljadores de la industria <u>petrolera</u> de Falfurrias aún mantienen las tradiciones navideñas traídas al Sur de Texas por sus <u>antepasados</u> españoles y mexicanos.

Situada a noventa millas al oeste de Corpus Christi, Falfurrias está muy cerca de las ciudades mexicanas de Matamoros y Reinosa.

Allí, los profesores del Falfurrias High School, Lucy Montalvo y Paul Garza, siguiendo estas costumbres, se reúnen con familiares y amigos el 24 de diciembre para preparar la comida y los postres que "esa noche disfrutaremos[a] durante la tamalada", señala Lucy.

En otra parte del rancho, los hermanos de Lucy cumplen con otra tradición de origen español: organizan una matanza de puercos. Durante ésta, hacen longani-

> *Las especias, el maíz y el puerco asado son ingredientes siempre presentes en las celebraciones navideñas del sur de Texas*

zas, morcillas[b] y chorizos con las <u>vísceras</u> y la sangre, y chicharrones[c] con la <u>grasa</u>.

Esa noche, celebran la cena de Nochebuena con tamales, chicharrones, guacamole con tortilla de masa, puerco asado o carne asada y quesadillas a la parrilla.[d] Todo esto se acompaña constantemente con margaritas, vino y cervezas. Cierran la velada con pan de polvo y leche quemada, dos postres navideños que Lucy aprendió de su madre Rafaela Cavazos de Montalvo.

A continuación van a la Misa del Gallo,[e] y al volver, toman champurrado con buñuelos. El Día de Navidad siguen comiendo, y no paran de hacerlo hasta Año Nuevo, que acostumbran a celebrarlo con turcos (empanadas), champurrado y té de canela.[g]

Aquí presentamos algunas <u>recetas</u> de *South Texas Mexican Cook Book*, de Lucy Garza, 1982, Eadkin Press, Austin, Texas.

[a]*we will enjoy* [b]*pork sausage* [c]*pork rinds* [d]*a... grilled* [e]*fiesta* [f]*Misa... Midnight Mass* [g]*cinnamon*

Celebración de una misa con mariachis en San Antonio

Comprensión

A **¿Cierto o falso?** Conteste según el artículo «Navidad con sabor a rancho».

1. Las celebraciones navideñas de Falfurrias duran dos días.
2. En Falfurrias la Navidad es una fiesta secular. Ya perdió el aspecto religioso.
3. En las costumbres navideñas de Falfurrias, se siente sólo la influencia española.
4. Las legumbres ocupan el sitio más importante en los platos navideños.

B **De origen español.** Una tradición navideña en la familia de Lucy Montalvo es «la matanza de puercos». ¿Entiende Ud. esta frase? Probablemente entiende la palabra **puerco**. (Ud. sabe un sinónimo de esta palabra. ¿Recuerda cuál es?) La palabra **matanza** es un poco más difícil de entender. Piense en la corrida de toros. ¿Cómo se llama la persona más importante que participa en la corrida? La palabra **matanza** y esta palabra se derivan del mismo verbo, **matar**, que describe un acto muy violento. ¿Ahora entiende en qué consiste esta tradición navideña?

C **Ideas clave.** Indique las ideas que Ud. pueda inferir de la lectura «Misa con mariachis».

1. Las misas en San Antonio son todavía en latín.
2. La gente prefiere las misas en latín.
3. El artículo se refiere a todas las comunidades cristianas de San Antonio.
4. Algunas parroquias católicas de San Antonio quieren unir el folklore tradicional con la religión.
5. Los texanos no van a misa desde el Concilio Vaticano II.
6. Los mariachis son sacerdotes (*priests*).
7. Los mariachis son conjuntos musicales tradicionales.
8. El propósito esencial de este cambio es que los parroquianos consideran a la iglesia como su casa.

MISA CON MARIACHIS

Hace 25 años, las misas en latín en las parroquias[a] católicas de San Antonio no se podían entender. Tras el Concilio Vaticano II todo empezó a cambiar. La misa <u>adquirió</u> el idioma español, las costumbres e incluso la música de México. Y las multitudes regresaron a los púlpitos.

Con los mariachis las parroquias que habían muerto[b] volvieron de repente a resucitar. Era lo que la teología debería ser—no sólo la buena música, sino la gente empezando a ver la iglesia como su casa. Era el retorno al hogar unido a un grato[c] sentimiento.

Hoy en día, por lo menos 20 parroquias se llenan todos los domingos con música de guitarras, bajo sextos y trompetas.

En la misión de San José, al sur de San Antonio, los turistas ocupan todos los asientos horas antes de que empiece la misa con los mariachis. Y la tradición se está <u>prolongando</u> al sur de Texas. "Nosotros no decimos que sólo las misas con mariachis son las buenas", dice el padre[d] Virgilio Elizondo, rector de la catedral de San Fernando. "Creo que lo que hacemos es tomar lo mejor de la cultura latinoamericana y <u>mez-clarla</u> con el cristianismo".

[a]*parishes* [b]*habían... had died* [c]*pleasant, nice* [d]*priest*

Primer paso

Me levanté con el pie izquierdo[a]

[a]con... *on the wrong side of the bed*

la cabeza

la mano

el brazo

Le duele la cabeza.

Se da con la puerta.

DAMAS

Se equivoca.

los dedos

la pierna

el pie

Se hace daño en el pie.

Se cae por la escalera.

Sufre muchas presiones.

Doler is used like **gustar:** Me duele la cabeza. Me duelen los dedos.

¡HUY, PERDÓN!

Más vocabulario

acordarse (ue) (de)	to remember
apagar	to turn off (*lights or an appliance*)
caerse (me caigo)	to fall down
equivocarse	to make a mistake
morir(se) (ue, u)	to die
pegar	to hit, strike
romper	to break

Discúlpeme.	Pardon me.
Fue sin querer.	It was unintentional; I (he, we . . .) didn't mean to do it.
¡Qué mala suerte!	What bad luck!
la aspirina	aspirin
la llave	key
distraído/a	absent-minded
torpe	clumsy

Práctica

A **Situaciones.** Indique una respuesta para cada pregunta o situación. Luego invente un contexto para cada diálogo. ¿Dónde están las personas que hablan? ¿en casa de un amigo? ¿en una oficina? ¿Qué van a decir después?

1. ¡Ay, sufro muchas presiones en el trabajo!
2. Anoche no me acordé de poner el despertador.
3. ¡Ay! ¡Me pegaste!
4. Nunca miro por donde camino (*I'm going*). Esta mañana me caí otra vez.
5. Lo siento, señores, pero esta no es la casa de Lola Pérez.
6. No cambié de lugar el coche y el policía me puso una multa (*fine*).
7. Anoche en casa de unos amigos rompí su lámpara favorita.
8. ¿Sabes? Ayer se murió nuestro perro.

a. ¿Vas a comprarles otra?
b. Perdón, señora. Nos equivocamos de casa.
c. ¿Otra vez? ¡Qué distraído eres! ¿Te hiciste daño?
d. ¡Huy, perdón! Fue sin querer.
e. ¿Te olvidaste otra vez? ¿A qué hora llegaste a la oficina?
f. ¡Qué triste! Lo siento.
g. ¡Qué mala suerte! ¿Cuánto tienes que pagar?
h. ¿Sí? ¿Por qué no te tomas unos días de vacaciones?

SEGURO ESPECIAL ACCIDENTES · *Puede ocurrirle esto...* · *O no ocurrirle nada...* · *...y suerte que está Asegurado*

255

B **Asociaciones.** ¿Qué verbos asocia Ud. con estas palabras?

1. la llave **3.** la mano **5.** la aspirina **7.** la luz **9.** el despertador
2. la pierna **4.** el brazo **6.** la cabeza **8.** los pies **10.** la escalera

Posibilidades: despedirse, doler, apagar, caminar, levantar, correr, preguntar, pegar, escribir, pensar, tomar, caerse, hacerse daño, poner, perder, dar(se)

C **¿Se refieren a Ud. estas oraciones?** Conteste según la siguiente escala:
1 = con frecuencia, 2 = algunas veces, 3 = nunca.

1. _____ Se me caen (*I drop*) las cosas.
2. _____ No me acuerdo de hacer la tarea para mis clases.
3. _____ Por la mañana apago el despertador y me duermo otra vez.
4. _____ Rompo los platos y los vasos cuando los lavo.
5. _____ Pierdo ciertos objetos, como las llaves, los cuadernos, la cartera...
6. _____ Me doy con los muebles y las puertas.
7. _____ Me olvido de los nombres de las personas.
8. _____ Les pego a otros sin querer.

Ahora sume (*add up*) sus respuestas y analice el total.

Adivinanza

Soy un animal que viajo
de mañana a cuatro pies,
a mediodía con dos,
y por la tarde con tres.
¿Quién soy?

8–12 puntos:	¡Quédese en cama y no salga de casa! Ud. es una persona realmente torpe y distraída.
13–19 puntos:	Ud. no es perfecto/a, pero es humano/a: hace cosas como todos.
20–24 puntos:	Ud. es una persona casi perfecta. Nunca se equivoca... pero... ¡qué vida más aburrida lleva!

D **Situaciones.** ¿Qué puede Ud. hacer o decir—o qué le puede pasar—en cada situación?

1. A Ud. le duele mucho la cabeza.
2. Ud. le pega a otra persona sin querer.
3. Ud. se olvida del nombre de otra persona.
4. Ud. está muy distraído/a y no mira por dónde camina.
5. Ud. se hace daño en la mano / en el pie.

STUDY HINT: False Cognates

Not all Spanish and English cognates are identical in meaning. Here are a few important "traps" to be aware of. These words are *false*, or misleading, *cognates* (**amigos falsos**).

sano = *healthy*	**una molestia** = *a bother*
la renta = *income*	**la sopa** = *soup*
el pariente = *relative*	**la ropa** = *clothing*
gracioso = *funny*	**real** = *real or royal*
actual = *current, up-to-date*	**sensible** = *sensitive*
la fábrica = *factory*	**el éxito** = *success*
el colegio = *elementary or secondary school*	**constipado** = *suffering from a head cold*

Occasionally such words can lead to communication problems. The American tourist who, feeling embarrassed, describes himself or herself as **embarazado/a** may find people chuckling at the remark, since **embarazada** means not *embarrassed* but *pregnant*.

DE AQUÍ Y DE ALLÁ

Here are some additional expressions to use when talking about occasions on which things don't go quite right for you or someone else.

meter la pata	to make a bad mistake; to stick one's foot (*lit.* paw) in one's mouth
ponerse colorado/a	to blush, turn red
¿Dónde llevas la cabeza?	Where's your head?
estar en las nubes	= **estar/ir distraído/a**

ESTRUCTURAS

27. Descriptions and Habitual Actions in the Past

Imperfect of Regular and Irregular Verbs

▼ **La nostalgia**

MATILDE: ...y todos los hijos *eran* chiquitos. *Entraban* y *salían* de casa como locos. ¡Qué ruido *había* siempre! ¿Te acuerdas?

ARMANDO: Sí, sí, sí, aquellos *eran* otros tiempos.

MATILDE: Y luego en verano *íbamos* siempre a la playa con todos los tíos y tus padres y dos criados y los amigos de los niños. *Teníamos* aquella casita tan linda...

ARMANDO: Sí, sí, sí, aquellos *eran* otros tiempos.

MATILDE: Dime una cosa, Armando. De verdad, ¿qué prefieres, aquella época o estos tiempos más tranquilos?

ARMANDO: Sí, sí, sí, aquellos *eran* otros tiempos.

MATILDE: Ay, querido, parece que las cosas nunca cambian. ¡Tampoco me *escuchabas* en aquel entonces!

Puerto Rico.

Nostalgia MATILDE: . . . and all the kids were little. They went in and out of the house like mad. There was always so much noise! Remember? ARMANDO: Yes, yes, yes, those were different times. MATILDE: And then in the summer we would go to the beach with all the uncles and aunts and your parents and two servants and the kids' friends. We used to have that pretty little house . . . ARMANDO: Yes, yes, yes, those were different times. MATILDE: Tell me something, Armando. Honestly, which do you prefer—those times or these more peaceful times? ARMANDO: Yes, yes, yes, those were different times. MATILDE: Well, dear, I guess things never change. You never used to listen to me back then, either!

▲ ▲ ▲

1. ¿Qué hacían los niños de Matilde y Armando?
2. ¿Su casa era muy tranquila?
3. ¿Adónde iban siempre en verano? ¿Iban solos?
4. ¿Qué le pregunta Matilde a Armando? ¿Cómo responde él?
5. ¿Armando escucha lo que Matilde dice? Y antes, ¿la escuchaba?

The *imperfect* (**el imperfecto**) is the second simple past tense in Spanish. In contrast to the preterite, which is used when you view actions or states of being as finished or completed, the imperfect tense is used when you view past actions or states of being as habitual or "in progress." The imperfect is also used for describing the past.

The imperfect has several English equivalents. For example, **hablaba**, the first person singular of **hablar**, can mean *I spoke, I was speaking, I used to speak,* or *I would speak* (when *would* implies a repeated action).

Most of these English equivalents indicate that the action was still in progress or was habitual, except for *I spoke,* which can correspond to either the preterite or the imperfect.

Forms of the Imperfect

-ar → -aba	-er/-ir → -ía	
hablar	**comer**	**vivir**
hablaba hablábamos	comía comíamos	vivía vivíamos
hablabas hablabais	comías comíais	vivías vivíais
hablaba hablaban	comía comían	vivía vivían

Stem-changing verbs do not show a change in the imperfect: **almorzaba, perdía, pedía.** The imperfect of **hay** (**haber**) is **había** (*there was, there were, there used to be*).

Only three verbs are irregular in the imperfect: **ir, ser,** and **ver.**

ir	ser	ver
iba íbamos	era éramos	veía veíamos
ibas ibais	eras erais	veías veías
iba iban	era eran	veía veían

Uses of the Imperfect

Note the following uses of the imperfect. If you have a clear sense for when and where the imperfect is used, understanding where the preterite is used will be easier: When talking about the past, it is used when the imperfect isn't. That is an oversimplification of the uses of these two past tenses, but at the same time it is a general rule of thumb that will help you out at first.

The imperfect is used . . .

- To describe *what used to happen* (*repeated habitual actions*) in the past

Siempre **nos quedábamos** en aquel hotel.	We always stayed (used to stay, would stay) at that hotel.
Todos los veranos **iban** a la costa.	Every summer they went (used to go, would go) to the coast.

- To describe an *action that was in progress* (*when something else happened*)

Pedía la cena.	She was ordering dinner.
Buscaba el carro.	He was looking for the car.

- To describe two *simultaneous past actions in progress*, with **mientras**

Tú **leías mientras** Juan **escribía** la carta.	You were reading while John was writing the letter.

- To describe ongoing *physical, mental,* or *emotional states* in the past

Estaban muy distraídos.	They were very distracted.
La **quería** muchísimo.	He loved her a lot.

- To tell *time* in the past and to express age with **tener**

Era la una.	It was one o'clock.
Eran las dos.	It was two o'clock.
Tenía dieciocho años.	She was eighteen years old.

Práctica

A **Mi niñez** (*childhood*).

Paso 1. Indique si las siguientes oraciones eran ciertas o falsas para Ud. cuando tenía diez años.

		CIERTO	FALSO
1.	Estaba en cuarto (*4th*) grado.	☐	☐
2.	Me acostaba a las nueve todas las noches.	☐	☐
3.	Me gustaba leer el suplemento para niños del periódico del domingo.	☐	☐
4.	Los sábados me levantaba a las ocho para mirar los dibujos animados.	☐	☐
5.	Era muy torpe en los deportes y me caía con frecuencia.	☐	☐
6.	Mis padres me pagaban por los quehaceres que hacía: cortar el césped (*grass*), lavar los platos...	☐	☐
7.	Me gustaba acompañar a mi madre/padre al supermercado.	☐	☐
8.	Le pegaba a mi hermano/a con frecuencia.	☐	☐
9.	Tocaba un instrumento musical en la orquesta de la escuela.	☐	☐
10.	Mis héroes eran personajes (*characters*) de las tiras cómicas, como Superman y Wonder Woman.	☐	☐

Paso 2. Ahora corrija las oraciones que son falsas para Ud.

MODELO: 2. Es falso. Me acostaba a las diez, no a las nueve.

B **Cuando Tina era niña...** Describa la vida de Tina cuando era muy joven, haciendo oraciones según las indicaciones.

La vida de Tina era muy diferente cuando tenía seis años.

1. todos los días / asistir / a / escuela primaria
2. por / mañana / aprender / a / leer / y / escribir / en / pizarra
3. a / diez / beber / leche / y / dormir / un poco
4. ir / a / casa / para / almorzar / y / regresar / a / escuela
5. estudiar / geografía / y / hacer / dibujos
6. jugar / con / compañeros / en / patio / de / escuela
7. camino de (*on the way*) casa / comprar / dulces / y / se los / comer
8. frecuentemente / pasar / por / casa / de / abuelos
9. cenar / con / padres / y / ayudar / a / lavar / platos
10. mirar / tele / un rato / y / acostarse / a / ocho

Ayer

C **Los tiempos cambian.** Muchas cosas y costumbres actuales son diferentes de las del pasado. Las oraciones siguientes describen algunos aspectos de la vida de hoy. Después de leer cada oración, invente Ud. otra, describiendo cómo eran las cosas antes, en otra época.

Hoy

MODELO: **Ahora** casi todos los bebés **nacen** en el hospital →
          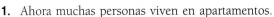
          Antes casi todos los bebés **nacían** en casa.

1. Ahora muchas personas viven en apartamentos.
2. Se come con frecuencia en los restaurantes.
3. Muchísimas mujeres trabajan fuera de casa.
4. Muchas personas van al cine y miran la televisión.
5. Ahora las mujeres—no sólo los hombres—llevan pantalones.
6. Ahora hay enfermeros y maestros—no sólo enfermeras y maestras.
7. Ahora tenemos coches pequeños que gastan (*use*) poca gasolina.
8. Ahora usamos más máquinas y por eso hacemos menos trabajo físico.
9. Ahora las familias son más pequeñas.
10. Muchas parejas viven juntas sin casarse (*to get married*).

D **¡Qué cambio! Una entrevista.** Hágale las siguientes preguntas a un compañero / una compañera de clase. Él/Ella va a pensar en las costumbres que tenía a los catorce años, es decir, cuando estaba en el noveno (*ninth*) o décimo (*tenth*) grado.

1. ¿Qué bebidas te gustaba beber antes? ¿Y ahora?
2. ¿Qué te gustaba comer? ¿Y ahora?
3. ¿Qué programa de televisión no te perdías nunca? ¿Y ahora?
4. ¿Qué te gustaba leer? ¿Y ahora?
5. ¿Qué hacías los sábados por la noche? ¿Y ahora?
6. ¿Qué deportes te gustaba practicar? ¿Y ahora?
7. ¿Con quién discutías mucho? ¿Y ahora?
8. ¿A quién te gustaba molestar (*annoy*)? ¿Y ahora?

▼▼▼▼▼▼▼▼▼▼▼▼▼▼▼▼▼▼▼▼▼▼▼▼▼▼ **VOCABULARIO**

Talking About How Things Are Done: Adverbs

Adverbs that end in -ly in English usually end in **-mente** in Spanish. The suffix **-mente** is added to the feminine singular form of adjectives. Adverbs ending in **-mente** have two stresses: one on the adjective stem and the other on **-mente.** The stress on the adjective stem is the stronger of the two.

ADJECTIVE	ADVERB	ENGLISH
rápido	**rápidamente**	rapidly
fácil	**fácilmente**	easily
valiente	**valientemente**	bravely

In Spanish, adverbs modifying a verb are placed as close to the verb as possible. When they modify adjectives or adverbs, they are placed directly before them.

Hablan **estupendamente** el español.	*They speak Spanish marvelously.*
Ese libro es **poco** interesante.*	*That book is not very interesting.*
Vamos a llegar **muy tarde.**	*We're going to arrive very late.*

Práctica

A **¡Seamos lógicos!** Complete estas oraciones lógicamente con adverbios basados en los siguientes adjetivos.

Adjetivos: constante, directo, fácil, inmediato, paciente, posible, puntual, rápido, total, tranquilo

1. La familia espera _____ en la cola.
2. Hay examen mañana y tengo que empezar a estudiar _____.
3. Se vive _____ en aquel pueblo en la montaña.
4. ¿Las enchiladas? Se preparan _____.
5. ¿El hombre va a vivir en la luna algún día? Mi hermana contesta, «_____».
6. ¿Qué pasa? Estoy _____ confundido.
7. Un vuelo que hace escalas no va _____ a su destino.
8. Cuando mira la tele, mi hermanito cambia el canal _____.
9. Es necesario que las clases empiecen _____.

---

*Note that in Spanish one equivalent of *not very* + *adjective* is **poco** + *adjective.*

B **Entrevista.** Con un compañero / una compañera, haga y conteste las siguientes preguntas.

MODELO: —¿Qué haces pacientemente?
—Espero a mi esposo pacientemente cuando se viste para salir. ¡Lo hace muy lentamente (*slowly*)!

1. ¿Qué haces rápidamente?
2. ¿Qué te toca hacer inmediatamente?
3. ¿Qué hiciste (comiste, ...) solamente una vez que no te gustó nada?
4. ¿Qué hiciste (comiste, ...) solamente una vez que te gustó muchísimo?
5. ¿Qué haces tú fácilmente que para los otros es difícil?
6. ¿Qué hace constantemente tu compañero/a (amigo/a, esposo/a, ...) que te molesta muchísimo?

ESTRUCTURAS ▼

28. Expressing Unplanned or Unexpected Events

Another Use of *se*

▼ Se me cayó **el florero.**   *I dropped the vase. (The vase fell*
▼   *from my hands.)*
▼ A Mario se le perdieron **las gafas.**   *Mario lost his glasses. (Mario's*
▼   *glasses were lost to him.)*

Unplanned or unexpected events (*I dropped . . . , We lost . . . , You forgot . . .*) are frequently expressed in Spanish with **se** and a third person form of the verb. In this structure, the occurrence is viewed as happening *to* someone—the unwitting performer of the action. Thus the victim is indicated by an indirect object pronoun, often clarified by **a** + *noun* or *pronoun*. In such sentences, the subject (the thing that is dropped, broken, forgotten, and so on) usually follows the verb.

(**a** + NOUN OR PRONOUN)	**se**	INDIRECT OBJECT PRONOUN	VERB	SUBJECT
(A mí)	Se	me	cayó	el florero.
(A ti)	Se	te	olvidó	la cartera.
A Mario	se	le	perdieron	las gafas.

The verb agrees with the grammatical subject of the Spanish sentence (**el florero, la cartera, las gafas**), not with the indirect object pronoun. **No** immediately precedes **se: A Mario** *no se* **le perdieron las gafas.**

As with **gustar,** the clarification of the indirect object pronoun is optional. But the indirect object pronoun itself is always necessary whether or not the victim is named: (*A la mujer*) **Se *le* rompió el plato.** Some verbs frequently used in this construction include the following.

acabar	to finish; to run out of	**perder (ie)**	to lose
caer	to fall	**quedar**	to remain, be left
olvidar	to forget	**romper**	to break

Note: The examples of this structure that you have seen so far use the indirect object pronouns **me, te,** and **le.** All of the indirect object pronouns can of course be used: **¿A Uds. se *les* perdió todo el dinero?, Se *nos* perdió el perro,** and so on. However, the exercises in this section will focus on sentences containing **se me...,** **se te...,** and **se le...** Emphasis will be on understanding this structure in context rather than on using it in original sentences.

Práctica

A **¡Qué mala memoria!** Hortensia se fue a España de vacaciones. Es una persona muy distraída y, claro, se le olvidó hacer muchas cosas antes de salir. Empareje (*Match*) los lapsos de Hortensia con las consecuencias.

LAPSOS

1. _____ Se le olvidó cerrar la puerta de su casa.
2. _____ Se le olvidó pagar las cuentas.
3. _____ Se le olvidó pedirle a alguien que le diera de comer (*feed*) a su perro.
4. _____ Se le olvidó cancelar la entrega (*delivery*) del periódico.
5. _____ Se le olvidó pedirle permiso a su jefa.
6. _____ Se le olvidó llevar el pasaporte.
7. _____ Se le olvidó hacer reserva en un hotel.

CONSECUENCIAS

a. Va a perder el trabajo.
b. No la van a dejar entrar en España.
c. Le van a suspender el servicio de la luz y el gas... ¡y cancelarle las tarjetas de crédito!
d. Alguien le va a robar el televisor.
e. ¡«King» se va a morir!
f. No va a tener dónde alojarse (*to stay*).
g. Todo el mundo va a saber que no está en casa.

B **¿Es Ud. torpe?**

Paso 1. Muchos niños son distraídos y torpes. ¿Cómo era Ud. de niño/a? Indique las oraciones que se le apliquen.

1. Se me caían los libros cuando iba para la escuela. ☐
2. Se me perdían la bufanda (*scarf*) y los guantes (*gloves*). ☐
3. Casi siempre se me olvidaba apagar las luces... ¡y mis padres me regañaban (*scolded*)! ☐
4. A veces se me rompían los platos cuando los lavaba. ☐
5. Muchas veces se me quedaban los juguetes en casa de mis amigos / amigas. ☐

Paso 2. ¿Y hoy? ¿Ha cambiado Ud. (*Have you changed*)? Conteste según el modelo. **¡OJO!** con el uso de **ya no** (*no longer*) y **todavía** (*still*).

MODELO: 1. Hoy todavía se me caen los libros.
(Hoy ya no se me caen los libros.)

C **¡Un día fatal!**

Paso 1. Pablo tuvo un día fatal ayer, porque estaba muy distraído. Lea la narración de los desastres de Pablo y—al mismo tiempo—mire los dibujos.

1. poner   2. ponerse   3. las llaves   4. la cartera

5. saludar   6. los papeles   7. una taza   8. tomar

1. Pablo no se levantó a las siete, como lo hace siempre.
2. Se vistió rápidamente y salió de casa descalzo (*barefoot*).
3. Entró en el garaje pero no pudo abrir la puerta de su coche.
4. Por eso tuvo que tomar el autobús para ir a la oficina. Pero cuando quiso pagarle al conductor, no tenía dinero.
5. Cuando llegó por fin a la oficina, su jefa se ofendió porque Pablo no la trató cortésmente.
6. Su primer cliente se enojó porque Pablo no tenía la información necesaria para su caso.
7. A las 10, Pablo tuvo una reunión con el vicepresidente de la compañía. Pablo le arruinó la chaqueta.
8. Por la tarde, Pablo volvió a casa con un terrible dolor de cabeza. Le dolía la cabeza desde las 11 de la mañana.

Paso 2. Ahora, con un compañero / una compañera, haga y conteste las preguntas para explicar por qué Pablo lo pasó tan mal ayer. La primera persona debe hacer una pregunta y la segunda persona debe contestar usando las sugerencias de los dibujos.

MODELO: —¿Por qué se levantó tarde Pablo?
          —Porque **se le olvidó** poner el despertador.

Frases útiles: se le cayó/cayeron...; se le olvidó/olvidaron...; se le perdió/perdieron...; se le quedó/quedaron...

Un paso más

UN POCO DE TODO

A **Blancanieves y los siete enanitos.** Complete the following familiar fairy tale with the correct form of the infinitives—preterite (**P**) or imperfect (**I**)—as indicated. When an adjective is given in parentheses, give the adverb derived from it. When two possibilities are given in parentheses, select the correct word.

The narrative starts with the Spanish equivalent of the words typically used to begin to tell a tale. Can you guess the meaning of the phrase and the meaning of the words glossed with question marks (¿ ?)? Use the context and your knowledge of the story.

1. Érase una vez una linda princesita blanca como la azucena,[a] hija de un rey casado por segunda vez.

2. Su madrastra,[b] la reina,[c] (tener: I[1]) un espejo[d] mágico. (Diario[2]) la reina le (preguntar: I[3]) al espejo: —¿Quién es la más hermosa?

[a]*lily*   [b]¿ ?   [c]¿ ?   [d]*mirror*

3. Un día el espejo le (contestar: P[4]): —¡Blancanieves! Llena[e] de envidia y de maldad,[f] la reina (mandar: P[5]) a un criado a que matara[g] a la princesa.

4. El criado la (llevar: P[6]) al bosque[h] y por compasión la (dejar: P[7]) abandonada. Una ardilla[i] la (llevar: P[8]) (alegre[9]) a una casita.

[e]*Full*   [f]¿ ?   [g]*que... to kill*   [h]¿ ?   [i]¿ ?

5. En la casita (vivir: I[10]) siete enanitos. Cuando (*ellos:* volver: P[11]) a casa por la noche, (encontrar: P[12]) a Blancanieves dormida[j] en sus camitas.

6. En el palacio, la madrastra (volver: P[13]) a consultar el espejo: —Y ahora, ¿quién es la más bella[k]? El espejo le (contestar: P[14]) sin vacilar: —¡Blancanieves!

[j]¿ ?   [k]¿ ?

7. Por eso la reina (planear: P[15]) matarla.[l] (Llegar: P[16]) a la casa de los enanitos una tarde, disfrazada[m] de vieja, y le (ofrecer: P[17]) a Blancanieves una manzana envenenada.[n]

8. Cuando (*ella:* morderla:[o] P[18]), Blancanieves (caer: P[19]) desvanecida.[p] Por la noche, los enanitos la (encontrar: P[20]) tendida[q] en el suelo.

[l]*to kill her*   [m]¿ ?   [n]¿ ?   [o]*to bite it*   [p]¿ ?   [q]*lying*

9. Un príncipe muy guapo, quien (enterarse:[r] P[21]) de lo que (ocurrir: I[22]), (ir: P[23]) a verla. Cuando el príncipe la (besar:[s] P[24]), Blancanieves (recobrarse: P[25]) (inmediato[26]).

10. Enamorados,[t] los dos (salir: P[27]) hacia el castillo del príncipe, donde (casarse: P[28]) con gran alegría de los enanitos.

[r]*to find out*   [s]¿ ?   [t]¿ ?

¿Quién lo dijo?

1. ¡Ay! ¿Qué vamos a hacer? ¡Parece que se murió!
2. No sabía que la manzana estaba envenenada.
3. Siento que no te guste mi nueva esposa.
4. ¡Te quiero desesperadamente! Quiero que te cases conmigo.
5. Yo estaba más contenta antes, cuando mamá estaba viva.
6. Ay, aquí viene otra vez a hacerme la misma pregunta... ¡Qué molestia!
7. No importa lo que me diga la reina. No lo puedo hacer.
8. ¿Cómo es posible que me conteste de la misma manera? Debe ser que todavía está viva...
9. En esta casita viven unos amigos míos que te van a gustar.
10. No hay nadie más linda que nuestra Blancanieves.

B **¿Quién es?** ¿Conoce Ud. a sus compañeros de clase? Vamos a ver. En otro papel, complete las siguientes oraciones.

1. De joven yo quería ser _____ (profesión) porque...
2. Cuando yo estaba en la escuela primaria, era _____ (adjetivo). Siempre...
3. En la secundaria, el animal que me simbolizaba mejor era _____ porque...

Entregue (*Hand in*) su papel a su profesor(a), pero sin firmarlo. Su profesor(a) va a leer las oraciones en clase. ¿Puede Ud. identificar a la persona descrita?

Vocabulary Library

Animales conocidos y cognados: el águila (*eagle*), **la cebra, el chimpancé, el elefante, el gato, el gorila, el hipopótamo, la jirafa, el león, el loro** (*parrot*), **el mono** (*monkey*), **el oso** (*bear*), **el pájaro, el perro, el pez, la rata, el ratón** (*mouse*), **el rinoceronte, la serpiente, el tigre**

SITUACIÓN Accidentes y tropiezos[a]

[a]*slip ups*

The following brief exchanges include a number of ways to make excuses.

SI LE PISA[a] EL PIE A UNA SEÑORA MAYOR EN EL AUTOBÚS

—Con permiso... perdón... ¿Me permite llegar a la puerta, por favor? Gracias.
—¡Ay! ¡Pero qué bruto[b]!
—Señora, lo siento muchísimo.

SI SE LE OLVIDA ALGO

—Oye, ¿me trajiste los apuntes[c] que te pedí?
—¡Uy, es que estoy en las nubes! Se me olvidó por completo. Espérame cinco minutos, que voy a casa y te los traigo ahora mismo.
—No, hombre (mujer). No vale la pena.[d] Mañana me los traes a clase.

SI LLEGA TARDE A UNA CITA[e]

—Disculpa. Lo siento muchísimo. Salí de casa a tiempo, pero es que el tráfico está imposible por el centro.
—¡Tranquilo/a, hombre (mujer)! No importa. Yo acabo de llegar también.

[a]*le... you step on*   [b]¿ ?   [c]*notes*   [d]*No... ¿ ?*   [e]*appointment, date*

Conversación

Con un compañero / una compañera practique los diálogos de las situaciones anteriores. Después hagan diálogos para las siguientes situaciones y practíquelas.

1. En el autobús, Ud. le pisa el pie a una viejecita. Ella grita, «¡Ay!» y todos los pasajeros se vuelven (*turn around*) para mirarlos.

2. Ud. bosteza (*yawn*), haciendo mucho ruido, en la clase de español.
3. En una fiesta, Ud. se da con una silla y se le cae la bebida encima del vestido nuevo de la anfitriona (*hostess*).
4. Se le olvidó el cumpleaños de su (novio/a, hermano/a, ...).

NOTA CULTURAL: Más sobre la cortesía

En español, «tener educación» significa no solamente tener preparación intelectual sino también ser cortés y tener buenos modales.[a] Una persona «mal educada» es alguien que no sabe comportarse en sociedad según las normas de cortesía y que no muestra[b] suficiente respeto por otras personas, sobre todo por las personas ancianas. Ser «bien educado» es una de las cualidades más apreciadas en el mundo hispano.

[a]*manners* [b]*no... doesn't show*

PARA ESCRIBIR

Escriba uno o dos párrafos sobre su vida infantil. Describa su familia, su casa y su rutina. No olvide hablar de sus sentimientos y emociones en esa época. Diga también si le gustaría ser niño/a otra vez.

VOCABULARIO

Verbos

acabar to finish; to run out of
acordarse (ue) (de) to remember
apagar to turn off (*lights or an appliance*)
caer(se) *irreg.* to fall
caminar to walk
darse (con) to bump (into)
doler (ue) to hurt
equivocarse to be wrong; to make a mistake
hacerse daño to hurt oneself
pegar to hit, strike
romper to break
sufrir to have, suffer

Repaso: **morirse (ue, u) olvidar, perder (ie), quedar**

Las partes del cuerpo

el brazo arm
la cabeza head

el dedo finger
la mano hand
el pie foot
la pierna leg

Sustantivos

la aspirina aspirin
el despertador alarm clock
la escalera staircase
las gafas eyeglasses
la niñez childhood
la presión pressure

Repaso: **la llave**

Adjetivos

distraído/a absent-minded
lento/a slow
torpe clumsy
tranquilo/a calm, tranquil

Palabras adicionales

de niño/a as a child
discúlpeme pardon me
en aquel entonces back then
fue sin querer it was unintentional; I (he, we . . .) didn't mean to do it
levantarse con el pie izquierdo to get up on the wrong side of the bed
¡qué mala suerte! bummer! what bad luck!

Self-Test

Use the tape that accompanies this text to test yourself briefly on the important points of this chapter.

VOCES

There is material for this section on the tape that accompanies this text.

del mundo hispánico 7
Centroamérica

Centroamérica es un área con graves problemas políticos, económicos y sociales. Quizás[a] Guatemala sea el ejemplo más claro de los problemas que confronta esta región. Este país, en el que[b] más del 50% (por ciento) de la población es indígena y un 87% de sus habitantes vive en la pobreza, continúa su larga guerra[c] civil. Guatemala tiene, además, el peor récord en cuanto a[d] la violación de los derechos[e] humanos de los indios en todo el Hemisferio norte.

Afortunadamente, se empieza a ver cierta mejoría[f] en la situación de los otros países centroamericanos. Nicaragua disfruta[g] actualmente[h] de un sistema democrático dirigido por[i] la presidenta Violeta Chamorro. En El Salvador el gobierno y el FMLN (Frente Farabundo Martí para la Liberación Nacional) firmaron[j] un acuerdo de paz en 1992. Panamá vive un período de frágil democracia, tras[k] el arresto del gobernante, el dictador Manuel Noriega, por los Estados Unidos. Por su parte, Honduras tiene el sistema de partidos[l] más antiguo de Latinoamérica.

Como un ejemplo democrático para toda la región centroamericana, es necesario mencionar a Costa Rica. Por[m] su larga tradición democrática, una paz estable y la ausencia de un aparato militar, Costa Rica es considerada como la «Suiza de Centroamérica».

Sólo en un país de Centroamérica, Belice, el español no es el idioma oficial.*

[a] *Perhaps* [b] *el... which* [c] *war* [d] *en... where . . . is concerned* [e] *rights* [f] *improvement* [g] *enjoys* [h] *currently* [i] *dirigido... led by* [j] *signed* [k] *since* [l] *political parties* [m] *Because of*

---

*Por ser un territorio ocupado, de hecho, por Inglaterra, el idioma oficial de Belice es el inglés.

Las 40 millas del canal de Panamá unen el océano Atlántico con el océano Pacífico.

Los premios del 92

PAZ
Rigoberta Menchú. India quiché de 33 años, nacida en Guatemala y descendiente de los indios mayas. El Quiché era el mayor reino indígena de Guatemala cuando los españoles llegaron a América. De empleada doméstica, Rigoberta pasó a ser líder y defensora de la libertad de los pueblos indígenas en 1980, cuando su padre Vicente Menchú fue quemado vivo por la policía gubernamental en la embajada de España durante una manifestación a favor de los derechos humanos. En ese mismo año, su madre y un hermano de 16 años fueron igualmente torturados y asesinados. Desde entonces vive exiliada en México.

«Mi tierra[a]»

Madre tierra, madre patria,[b]
aquí reposan[c] los huesos[d] y
memorias de mis antepasados[e]
en tus espaldas[f] se enterraron[g] los abuelos, los nietos y los hijos.
…
Tierra mía, madre de mis abuelos,
quisiera acariciar[h] tu belleza
contemplar tu serenidad y
acompañar tu silencio,
quisiera calmar tu dolor[i]
llorar tu lágrima[j] al ver
tus hijos dispersos por el mundo
regateando posada[k] en tierras
lejanas[l] sin alegría, sin paz,
sin madre, sin nada.

Rigoberta Menchú, Premio Nobel de la Paz en 1992

[a]*land* [b]*madre... motherland* [c]*rest* [d]*bones* [e]*ancestors* [f]*back* [g]*se... were buried*
[h]*quisiera... I would like to caress* [i]*pain* [j]*tear* [k]*regateando... bargaining for lodging*
[l]*far away*

Manifestación en Nicaragua.

Es imperdonable, y tal vez inmoral que los gobiernos del Tercer Mundo gasten tres veces más en equipos militares que en educación. Las naciones industrializadas deben de hacer más para que los países en vía de desarrollo[a] dejen de depender más en el aparato militar. Porque aunque se han visto[b] avances impresionantes[c] hacia la paz mundial en los últimos años, otras naciones están haciéndole daño[d] al Tercer Mundo, al continuar enviando[e] armas hacia esas regiones.»

Óscar Arias, ex Presidente de Costa Rica y Premio Nobel de la Paz en 1987

[a]*en... developing* [b]*se... have been made* [c]*avances... amazing steps* [d]*están... are doing damage* [e]*al... by continuing to send*

¡Qué interesante!

1. ¿Sabe Ud. el país de origen centroamericano de las siguientes personas, que no se mencionan en las lecturas de esta sección?
   a. Anastasio Somoza   **b.** Augusto César Sandino   **c.** Daniel Ortega
2. Óscar Arias denuncia el gasto excesivo de los países pobres en armas para el aparato militar. ¿Cómo se puede explicar que los países pobres gasten mucho más en armas que en educación?
3. Rigoberta Menchú compara su «tierra» con la figura de la madre. ¿Le parece a Ud. que es una asociación típica? ¿Por qué? ¿Con qué otros miembros de la familia identifica Ud. a su nación?

Primer paso

Más partes del cuerpo humano

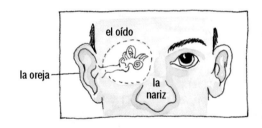

el oído

la oreja

la nariz

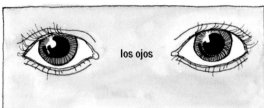

los ojos

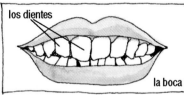

los dientes

la boca

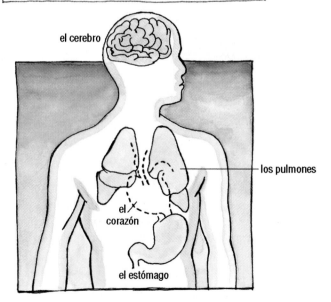

el cerebro

los pulmones

el corazón

el estómago

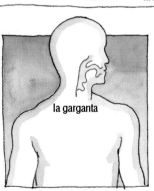

la garganta

La salud y el BIENESTAR FÍSICO[a]

[a]La... *Health and well being*

VOCABULARIO

Más vocabulario

caminar	to walk
correr	to run; to jog
hacer ejercicio	to exercise
practicar un deporte	to play a sport
cuidarse	to take care of oneself
dejar de + *inf.*	to stop (*doing something*)

dormir lo suficiente	to get enough sleep
llevar gafas/lentes (de contacto)	to wear glasses/(contact) lenses
llevar una vida sana	to lead a healthy life
tener buena salud	to be healthy

Práctica

A **Las partes del cuerpo.** ¿Cómo se llaman las partes del cuerpo indicadas en el dibujo?

B **Hablando claro.** ¿Qué significan, para Ud., las siguientes oraciones?

MODELO: Se debe comer equilibradamente. →
Eso quiere decir (*means*) que es necesario comer muchas verduras, que...

1. Se debe dormir lo suficiente todas las noches.
2. Hay que hacer ejercicio.
3. Es necesario llevar una vida tranquila.
4. En general, uno debe cuidarse mucho.

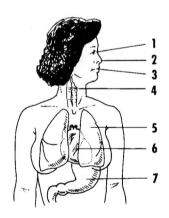

C **Entrevista.** Entreviste a un compañero / una compañera de clase para saber si él/ella cree que las siguientes acciones son buenas o malas para la salud.

MODELO: correr un poco todos los días →
E1: Correr un poco todos los días, ¿es bueno o malo para la salud?
E2: Es bueno. (Es malo.)
E1: ¿Por qué?

FRASES ÚTILES

Es bueno para _____ (parte del cuerpo).
Ayuda a fortalecer (*strengthen*) _____ (parte del cuerpo).
Hace daño a _____ (parte del cuerpo).

271

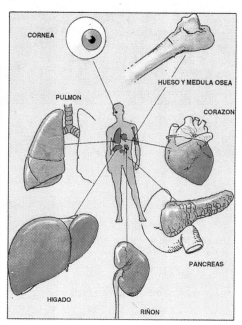

El trasplante de órganos y tejidos, a pesar de su complejidad y dificultades, está ya perfectamente introducido dentro del arsenal terapéutico de la Medicina. Su realización, en continua progresión, ha beneficiado ya a muchos pacientes que han podido salvar la vida y desarrollar una actividad normal en no pocos casos. En algunas enfermedades que producen fallo terminal e irreversible de determinados órganos es el único recurso final que puede ser eficaz. Para que todo ello sea posible es preciso contar, imprescindiblemente, con la generosidad de la donación

TRASPLANTES

1. fumar dos paquetes de cigarrillos al día
2. preocuparse mucho y no descansar
3. gritar (*to shout*) y enojarse con frecuencia
4. leer con poca luz
5. beber mucho café todos los días
6. salir sin chaqueta cuando hace frío
7. correr todos los días hasta el punto de quedar exhausto
8. beber uno o dos vasos de vino al día
9. dejar de comer por completo para adelgazar (*to lose weight*)

D **Asociaciones.** ¿Con qué parte(s) del cuerpo asocia Ud. las siguientes palabras? Trate de hacer asociaciones cómicas.

1. la digestión
2. escuchar
3. la respiración
4. el amor
5. una comida deliciosa
6. una película

BUSCA LA PAREJA

Busca en la columna de la derecha los órganos y partes estudiadas por las especialidades médicas citadas en la columna de la izquierda.

Oftalmología ■ ■ Aparato urogenital
Dermatología ■ ■ Los dientes
Cardiología ■ ■ Las articulaciones
Odontología ■ ■ Los riñones
Reumatología ■ ■ Los ojos
Urología ■ ■ El corazón
Pediatría ■ ■ La piel
Nefrología ■ ■ Enfermedades infantiles

NOTA LINGÜÍSTICA: The Good News . . . The Bad News

Use **lo** with the masculine singular form of an adjective to describe general qualities or characteristics.

lo bueno / lo malo   lo más importante
lo mejor / lo peor   lo mismo

This structure has a number of English equivalents, especially in colloquial speech.

lo bueno = the good thing/part/news, what's good

E **Lo positivo y lo negativo de todas las cosas.** ¿Sabe Ud. ver lo bueno y lo malo? Diga una cosa positiva y otra negativa de las siguientes situaciones. Use **se** + verbo.

MODELO: estar en la universidad →
         Lo mejor (Lo bueno) de estar en la universidad es que se aprende mucho.
         Lo peor (Lo malo) es que no se duerme mucho.

Palabras útiles: lo más/menos interesante, lo agradable/desagradable

1. estar en la universidad
2. ser una persona muy rica
3. ser presidente/a de los Estados Unidos
4. tener seis hermanos

5. asistir a la universidad en otro estado
6. tener un trabajo mientras se estudia una carrera
7. dejar de fumar

DE AQUÍ Y DE ALLÁ

Here are some more useful terms for talking about health-related problems and situations.

- **picar** to itch; to hurt (*colloquial*)

    Me pica la espalda (*back*).
    Me pica la garganta.

- **empastar una muela**   to fill a tooth

    el empaste filling

- **el SIDA** AIDS

ESTRUCTURAS

29. Recognizing *que, quien(es), lo que*

Relative Pronouns

▼ As you look at the
▼ following cartoon, try
▼ to guess the meaning
▼ of the sign (**el letrero**).

[a]¡Malditas... *It wasn't right for me to want to step on it*   [b]estén... *they're telling*

▼ Libertad es otro personaje de las tiras cómicas de Mafalda, la niña argentina que
▼ se ve en muchos capítulos de este libro. Complete las oraciones según la tira
▼ cómica.

▼   Libertad es una niña **que** _____.

▼   Ella ve un letrero **que** dice _____.

▼   Esto es **lo que** significa el letrero en inglés: _____.

There are four principal *relative pronouns* in English: *that, which, who,* and *whom.*
They are usually expressed in Spanish by the following relative pronouns, all of
which you already know.

que: refers to things and people
quien: refers only to people
lo que: refers to a situation

Learning to recognize the meaning of these words in context will make reading in
Spanish easier for you. See if you can understand the following sentences without
looking at the English equivalents.

que = *that, which, who*

Tuve una cita con el médico **que** duró una hora.	*I had an appointment with the doctor that lasted an hour.*
Es un buen médico **que** sabe mucho.	*He's a good doctor who knows a lot.*

quien(es) = *who/whom* after a preposition or as an indirect object

La mujer con **quien** hablaba era mi hermana.	*The woman with whom I was talking was my sister.*
Ese es el niño a **quien** no le gustan los helados.	*That's the boy who doesn't like ice cream.*

lo que = *what, that which*

No entiendo **lo que** dice.	*I don't understand what he is saying.*
Lo que no me gusta es su actitud.	*What I don't like is his attitude.*

The antecedent (*what it refers to*) of **lo que** is always a sentence, a whole situation,
or something that hasn't been mentioned yet.

Lo que necesito es <u>estudiar más</u>.

Práctica

A **Problemas médicos.** Complete las oraciones lógicamente, usando **que, quien** o
lo que.

EN LA SALA DE EMERGENCIAS

1. ¿Quién fue el hombre _____ la trajo aquí?
2. Desgraciadamente no podemos localizar a la mujer con _____ vive.

3. ¡_____ necesitamos es más tiempo!
4. Quiero saber el nombre de la medicina _____ Ud. tomaba.
5. ¿Dónde está el ayudante _____ empezó a trabajar ayer?

EN EL CONSULTORIO DEL MÉDICO (*DOCTOR'S OFFICE*)

—Pues _____[6] Ud. tiene es exceso de peso (*weight*). Debe perder por lo menos diez libras.

—Pero, doctor... Es cierto que como mucho, pero... no conozco a nadie a _____[7] no le guste comer.

—De ahora en adelante, Ud. puede comer todo _____[8] le guste... ¡y aquí está la lista de _____[9] le debe gustar!

B **El estrés, la condición humana.** Lea la siguiente tira cómica y conteste las preguntas.

1. Lo que quiere el padre de Libertad es _____.
2. Lo que tiene es _____.
3. Según el médico, lo que tiene su padre es _____.

¿Cuántos de esos malestares experimenta Ud.? ¿Son malestares crónicos o solamente los siente durante ciertas épocas del año? ¿En qué épocas?

Segundo paso

▼ **VOCABULARIO**

En el consultorio[a]

[a] *doctor's office*

el/la enfermero/a	nurse	**el antibiótico**	antibiotic
el/la médico/a	physician	**el jarabe**	(cough) syrup
el/la paciente	patient	**la medicina**	drug, medicine
		la pastilla	pill
		la receta	prescription
congestionado/a	congested, stuffed-up	**el resfriado**	cold
mareado/a	dizzy; nauseated	**la tos**	cough

doler (ue)	to hurt, ache
enfermarse	to get sick
guardar cama	to stay in bed
internarse (en)	to check in (to) (a hospital)
ponerle una inyección	to give (someone) a shot
resfriarse	to get/catch a cold
respirar	to breathe
sacar	to extract
sacar la lengua	to stick out one's tongue
sacar una muela	to extract a tooth (molar)
tener dolor (de)	to have a pain (in)
tener fiebre	to have a fever
tomarle la temperatura	to take (someone's) temperature
toser	to cough

—Pero ¿cómo quiere que le opere, si no tiene usted nada?

—Mejor, doctor. Así la operación le será más fácil...

NOTA CULTURAL: La medicina en los países hispánicos

FARMACIAS 4° turno
Abiertas de Sábado a Viernes de 8 a 22 hs.

Como regla general los hispanos tienen como costumbre consultar no sólo a los médicos sino[a] a otros profesionales cuando tienen problemas de salud. Por ejemplo, ya que[b] muchas drogas se venden sin receta en los países hispánicos, es posible que una persona enferma le explique sus síntomas a un farmacéutico, que le puede recomendar una medicina. Los farmacéuticos reciben un entrenamiento riguroso y están al tanto[c] en farmacología. También se puede consultar a un practicante. Estos tienen tres años de entrenamiento médico y pueden aplicar una serie de tratamientos, incluyendo inyecciones.

    Otra característica del sistema médico hispánico es que es fácil y barato conseguir los servicios de una enfermera particular[d] que cuide a un enfermo en casa. Las enfermeras no tienen que tener tantos conocimientos teóricos como las de los Estados Unidos, pero tienen mucha experiencia práctica en su campo.[e]

[a]*but*   [b]*ya... since*   [c]*al... up to date*   [d]*private*   [e]*field*

Práctica

A **Estudio de palabras.** Complete las siguientes oraciones con una palabra de la misma familia de la palabra en letras cursivas (*italics*).

1. Si me *resfrío*, tengo _____.
2. La *respiración* ocurre cuando alguien _____.
3. Si me _____, estoy *enfermo/a*. Un(a) _____ me toma la temperatura.
4. Cuando alguien *tose*, se oye una _____.
5. Si me *duele* el estómago, tengo un _____ de estómago.

B **Asociaciones.** ¿Qué partes del cuerpo asocia Ud. con las siguientes palabras?

1. la fiebre   3. sacar   5. congestionado   7. mareado
2. la tos   4. un resfriado 6. las inyecciones 8. el termómetro

C **Situaciones.** Describa Ud. la situación de estas personas. ¿Dónde y con quiénes están? ¿Qué síntomas tienen? ¿Qué deben hacer?

1. Anamari está muy bien de salud. Nunca le duele(n) _____. Nunca tiene _____. Siempre _____. Es bueno que _____.
2. A Martín le duele(n) _____. Debe _____. El dentista va a _____. Es necesario que _____.
3. Inés tiene apendicitis. Le duele(n) _____. Tiene _____. El médico y la enfermera quieren que _____. Es necesario que _____.

D **Entrevista.** Lea las siguientes preguntas sobre su última enfermedad y piense en las respuestas que Ud. daría (*would give*). Luego use las preguntas para entrevistar a un compañero / una compañera de clase, haciendo los cambios necesarios.

1. ¿Cuándo empezó Ud. a sentirse mal? ¿Dónde estaba Ud.? ¿Qué hacía?
2. ¿Cuáles eran sus síntomas? ¿Cómo se sentía? ¿Estaba mareado/a? ¿congestionado/a? ¿Le dolía alguna parte del cuerpo? ¿Tenía fiebre? ¿Se tomó la temperatura?
3. ¿Qué hizo? ¿Regresó a casa? ¿Se quitó la ropa? ¿Tosía mucho? ¿Se acostó?
4. ¿Fue al consultorio? ¿Lo/La examinó un médico? ¿Cuál fue su diagnóstico?
5. ¿Le puso una inyección el médico? ¿Le dio una receta? ¿Llevó Ud. la receta a la farmacia? ¿Cuánto le costó la medicina?
6. ¿Cuándo se sintió bien por fin? ¿Empezó a cuidarse más?

ESTRUCTURAS ▼▼▼▼▼▼▼▼▼▼▼▼▼▼▼▼▼▼▼▼▼▼▼▼▼

RECICLADO

Do you remember which past tense to use in each of the following contexts?

1. to tell what you did yesterday
2. to tell what you used to do when you were in grade school
3. to explain the situation or condition that caused you to do something
4. to tell what someone did as the result of a situation
5. to talk about the way things used to be
6. to describe an action that was in progress
7. to tell what time it was
8. to give someone's age in the past

If you understand those uses of the preterite and the imperfect, the following summary of their uses will not contain much that is new information for you.

30. Narrating in the Past

Using the Preterite and Imperfect

▼ **Un resfriado muy grave**

ENFERMERA: ¿Cuándo *empezó* a sentirse mal?

RODRIGO: Ayer por la noche *estaba* un poco congestionado. *Tosía* mucho y me *dolía* todo el cuerpo. Hoy, cuando *me desperté, me sentía* peor todavía. Por eso *llamé* para hacer una cita.

ENFERMERA: ¿Tiene otros síntomas?

RODRIGO: Creo que anoche *tenía* un poco de fiebre, pero no estoy seguro. No me *tomé* la temperatura. No *tenía* termómetro.

ENFERMERA: Pues... ¡nosotros sí tenemos! Abra la boca, por favor.

▲ ▲ ▲

In the preceding dialogue, locate all of the verbs that do the following.

1. indicate actions (or lack of action)
2. indicate conditions or descriptions

A very serious cold   NURSE: When did you begin to feel ill? RODRIGO: Yesterday evening I was a bit congested. I was coughing a lot and my whole body hurt. Today when I woke up, I was feeling even worse. That's why I called to make an appointment. NURSE: Do you have any other symptoms? RODRIGO: I think that I had a bit of a fever last night, but I'm not sure. I didn't take my temperature. I didn't have a thermometer. NURSE: Well, we do! Open your mouth, please.

When speaking about the past in English, you choose which past tense forms to use in a given context: *I wrote letters, I did write letters, I was writing letters, I used to write letters,* and so on. Usually only one or two of these options will convey exactly the idea you want to express. Similarly, in many Spanish sentences either the preterite or the imperfect can be used, but the meaning of the sentence will be different. The choice between the preterite and imperfect depends on your perspective: how do you view the action or state of being?

A. The preterite is used to report actions or states of being in the past as completed no matter how long they lasted or took to complete; focus may be on the beginning or end of the action or state. The imperfect is used, however, if the *ongoing* or *habitual nature* of the action is stressed, with no reference to its beginning or termination.

Escribí las cartas.	*I wrote (did write) the letters.*
Escribía las cartas cuando...	*I was writing the letters when . . .*
Anoche Carlos **comió** a las ocho.	*Last night Carlos ate at 8:00.*
Antes **comía** a cualquier hora.	*Before, he used to eat at any time.*
Anita **estuvo** allí a la una.	*Anita was (got) there at 1:00.*
Anita **estaba** allí a la una.	*Anita was there (already) at 1:00.*

B. *A series of completed actions that take place in sequence* will be expressed in the preterite (unless it refers to habitual actions).

Me **levanté,** me **vestí** y **desayuné.**	*I got up, got dressed, and ate breakfast.*

Actions or states *in progress* are expressed with the imperfect. The imperfect is also used to express most *descriptions; physical, mental,* and *emotional states* or *conditions; the time* (with **ser**); and *age* (with **tener**).

Yo **escribía** las cartas **mientras** Ana **leía.**	*I was writing letters while Ana was reading.*
Estaban cansados.	*They were tired.*
Eran las ocho.	*It was 8:00.*
Tenía ocho años.	*She was eight years old.*

C. Certain words and expressions are frequently associated with the preterite, others with the imperfect.

WORDS OFTEN ASSOCIATED WITH THE PRETERITE

ayer, anteayer, anoche	el año pasado, el lunes pasado, ...
una vez (*once*), dos veces (*twice*), ...	de repente (*suddenly*)

WORDS OFTEN ASSOCIATED WITH THE IMPERFECT

todos los días, todos los lunes, ...	*was _____ing, were _____ing* (in
siempre, frecuentemente	English)
mientras	*used to, would* (when *would* implies
de niño/a, de joven	*used to* in English)

¡OJO!   The words do not automatically cue either tense, however. The most important consideration is the meaning that the speaker wishes to convey.

Ayer cenamos temprano.	*Yesterday we had dinner early.*
Ayer cenábamos cuando Juan llamó.	*Yesterday we were having dinner when Juan called.*
De niño jugaba al fútbol.	*He played soccer as a child.*
De niño empezó a jugar al fútbol.	*He began to play soccer as a child.*

D. Remember the special English equivalents of the preterite forms of **saber, conocer, poder,** and **querer: supe** (*I found out*), **conocí** (*I met*), **pude** (*I could and did*), **no pude** (*I couldn't and didn't*), **quise** (*I tried*), **no quise** (*I refused*).

E. The preterite and the imperfect frequently occur in the same sentence.

Miguel **estudiaba** cuando **sonó** el teléfono.	*Miguel was studying when the phone rang.*
Olivia **comió** tanto porque **tenía** mucha hambre.	*Olivia ate so much because she was very hungry.*

In the first sentence the imperfect tells what was happening when another action—conveyed by the preterite—broke the continuity of the ongoing activity. In the second sentence, the preterite reports the action that took place because of a condition, described by the imperfect, that was in progress or in existence at that time.

F. The preterite and imperfect are also used together in the presentation of an event. The preterite narrates the action while the imperfect sets the stage, describes the conditions that caused the action, or emphasizes the continuing nature of a particular action.

Práctica

A **En el consultorio.** What did your doctor do the last time you had an appointment with him or her? Assume that you had the following conditions and match them with all the appropriate procedures.

CONDICIONES	ACCIONES
1. _____ Tenía mucho calor y temblaba.	**a.** Me hizo muchas preguntas.
2. _____ Me dolía la garganta.	**b.** Me puso una inyección.
3. _____ Tenía un poco de congestión en el pecho (*chest*).	**c.** Me tomó la temperatura.
4. _____ Creía que estaba anémico/a.	**d.** Me auscultó (*He/She listened to my*) los pulmones y el corazón.
5. _____ No sabía lo que tenía.	**e.** Me analizó la sangre (*blood*).
6. _____ Necesitaba medicinas.	**f.** Me hizo sacar la lengua.
7. _____ Sólo necesitaba un chequeo rutinario.	**g.** Me hizo toser.

B **¿Fue Ud. un niño o una niña precoz** (*precocious*)?

Paso 1. Con un compañero / una compañera, haga y conteste las siguientes preguntas.

¿Cuántos años tenías cuando... ?

1. aprendiste a pasear en bicicleta
2. hiciste tu primer viaje en avión
3. tuviste tu primera cita
4. empezaste a afeitarte
5. conseguiste tu licencia de manejar
6. abriste una cuenta corriente (*checking account*)

Paso 2. Con otro compañero / otra compañera, haga y conteste estas preguntas.

¿Cuántos años tenías cuando tus padres... ?

1. te dejaron cruzar la calle sin compañía
2. te permitieron ir de compras solo/a
3. te dejaron acostarte después de las nueve
4. te dejaron quedarte en casa sin niñero/a (*baby sitter*)
5. te permitieron usar la estufa
6. te dejaron ver una película prohibida para menores

Paso 3. Ahora, en grupos de cuatro, comparen sus respuestas. ¿Son muy diferentes las respuestas que dieron? ¿Quién del grupo tenía los padres más estrictos? ¿los menos estrictos?

C **Pequeñas historias.** Complete the following brief paragraphs with the appropriate phrases from the list. Before you begin, it is a good idea to look at the drawing that accompanies each paragraph and to scan through the complete paragraph to get the gist of it, even though you may not understand everything the first time you read it.

1. nos quedamos   íbamos   nuestra familia decidió
   nos quedábamos   nos gustó   vivíamos

   Cuando éramos niños, Jorge y yo _____[1] en la Argentina. Siempre _____[2] a la playa, a Mar del Plata, para pasar la Navidad. Allí casi siempre _____[3] en el Hotel Fénix. Un año, _____[4] quedarse en otro hotel, el Continental. No _____[5] tanto como el Fénix y por eso, al año siguiente, _____[6] en el Fénix otra vez.

2. leía   tenía   se nos apagaron
   había un problema   salí   me levanté
   estaban apagadas (*out*)

   Eran las once de la noche cuando ¡de repente _____[1] todas las luces de la casa! Puse el libro que _____[2] en la mesa y _____[3] para investigar la causa del incidente. La verdad es que _____[4] mucho miedo. _____[5] a la calle y vi que _____[6] las luces de todo el barrio. En ese momento me di cuenta[a] que _____[7] con la electricidad en toda la ciudad.

   [a]me... *I realized*

3. examinó   estaba   puso   dio
   le tomaba   esperaba   llegó   se sintió

   El niño tosía mientras que la enfermera _____[1] la temperatura. La madre del niño _____[2] pacientemente. Por fin _____[3] la doctora. Le _____[4] la garganta al niño, le _____[5] una inyección y le _____[6] a su madre una receta para un jarabe. La madre todavía _____[7] muy preocupada, pero después que la doctora le habló, _____[8] más tranquila.

D **Rubén y Soledad.** Read the following paragraph at least once to familiarize yourself with the sequence of events, and look at the drawing. Then reread the paragraph, giving the proper form of the verbs in parentheses in the preterite or the imperfect, according to the needs of each sentence and the context of the paragraph as a whole.

Rubén (estudiar[1]) cuando Soledad (entrar[2]) en el cuarto. Le (preguntar[3]) a Rubén si (querer[4]) ir al cine con ella. Rubén le (decir[5]) que sí porque se (sentir[6]) un poco aburrido con sus estudios. Los dos (salir[7]) en seguida para el cine. (Ver[8]) una película cómica y (reírse[9]) mucho. Luego, como (hacer[10]) frío, (entrar[11]) en su café favorito, El Gato Negro, y (tomar[12]) un chocolate. (Ser[13]) las dos de la mañana cuando por fin (regresar[14]) a casa. Soledad (acostarse[15]) inmediatamente porque (estar[16]) cansada, pero Rubén (empezar[17]) a estudiar otra vez.

Now answer the following questions based on the paragraph about Rubén and Soledad. **¡OJO!** A question is not always answered in the same tense as that in which it is asked. Remember this especially when you are asked to explain why something happened.

1. ¿Qué hacía Rubén cuando Soledad entró?
2. ¿Qué le preguntó Soledad a Rubén?
3. ¿Por qué dijo Rubén que sí?
4. ¿Les gustó la película? ¿Por qué?
5. ¿Por qué tomaron un chocolate?
6. ¿Regresaron a casa a las tres?
7. ¿Qué hicieron cuando llegaron a casa?

E **Caperucita Roja.**

Paso 1. Retell this familiar story, based on the drawings, sentences, and cues that accompany each drawing, using the imperfect or preterite of the infinitives, except for item 5. Add as many details as you can.

Palabras útiles: abalanzarse sobre (*to pounce on*), avisar (*to warn*), dispararle (*to shoot at someone/something*), esconderse (*to hide*), enterarse de (*to find out about*), huir (*to flee*), saltar (*to jump*)

1. Érase una vez una niña hermosa que (llamarse[1]) Caperucita Roja. Todos los animales del bosque (ser[2]) sus amigos y Caperucita Roja los (querer[3]) mucho.
2. Un día su mamá le (decir[4]): —Quiero que (llevar[5]) en seguida esta jarrita de miel[a] a casa de tu abuelita. Ten ciudado con el lobo[b] feroz.

   [a]*jarrita... jar of honey*   [b]¿ ?

3. En el bosque,[c] el lobo (salir[6]) a hablar con la niña. Le (preguntar[7]): —¿Adónde vas, Caperucita? Esta le (contestar[8]) dulcemente:[d] —Voy a casa de mi abuelita.
4. —Pues, si vas por este sendero,[e] vas a llegar antes,— (decir[9]) el malvado lobo, que (irse[10]) por otro camino más corto.

   [c]¿ ?   [d]*sweetly*   [e]*path*

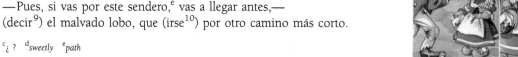

5. El lobo (llegar[11]) primero a la casa de la abuelita y (entrar[12]) silenciosamente. La abuelita (tener[13]) mucho miedo. (*Ella:* Saltar[14]) de la cama y (correr[15]) a esconderse.

6. Caperucita Roja (llegar[16]) por fin a la casa de la abuelita. (*Ella:* Encontrar[17]) a su «abuelita», que (estar[18]) en la cama, y le (decir[19]): —¡Qué
dientes tan largos tienes! —¡Son para comerte mejor!

7. Una ardilla[f] del bosque (enterarse[20]) del peligro que (correr[21]) Caperucita.
Por eso (avisar[22]) a un cazador.[g]

8. El lobo (saltar[23]) de la cama y (abalanzarse[24]) sobre Caperucita. Ella (salir[25])
de la casa corriendo y pidiendo socorro[h] desesperadamente.

[f]¿ ?   [g]¿ ?   [h]*help*

9. El cazador (ver[26]) lo que (ocurrir[27]). (*Él:* Dispararle[28]) al lobo y le (hacer[29])
huir.

10. Caperucita (regresar[30]) a la casa de su abuelita. La (abrazar: *ella*[31]) y le
(prometer[32]) escuchar siempre los consejos de su mamá.

Paso 2. Hay varias versiones del cuento de Caperucita Roja. La que Ud. acaba de
leer termina felizmente, pero otras no. Con otros dos compañeros, vuelva a contar
la historia, empezando por el dibujo número 7. Invente un diálogo más largo entre
Caperucita y el lobo y cambie por completo el final del cuento.

Más palabras útiles: comérselo/la (*to eat something up*), atacar, matar (*to kill*)

F **Mi primer día de universidad.** Dé Ud. sus impresiones de su primera clase el
primer día de universidad. Use estas preguntas como guía.

1. ¿Qué hora era cuando llegó Ud. a la universidad? ¿Por qué llegó a esa hora?
2. ¿Cuál fue la clase? ¿A qué hora era la clase y dónde era?
3. ¿Vino a clase con alguien? ¿Ya tenía su libro de texto o lo compró después?
4. ¿Qué hizo Ud. después de entrar en la sala de clase? ¿Qué hacía el profesor /
la profesora?
5. ¿A quién conoció Ud. aquel día? ¿Ya conocía a algunos miembros de la
clase? ¿A quiénes?
6. ¿Aprendió Ud. mucho durante la clase? ¿Ya sabía algo de esa materia?
7. ¿Le gustó el profesor / la profesora? ¿Por qué (no)? ¿Cómo era?
8. ¿Cómo se sentía durante la clase? ¿nervioso/a? ¿aburrido/a? ¿cómodo/a?
9. ¿Les dio tarea el profesor / la profesora? ¿Pudo Ud. hacerla fácilmente?
10. ¿Cuánto tiempo estudió Ud. la materia antes de la próxima clase?
11. Su primera impresión de la clase y del profesor / de la profesora, ¿fue válida
o cambió con el tiempo? ¿Por qué?

Un paso más

Un POCO DE TODO

A **Lo bueno de una enfermedad.** Form complete sentences based on the words given in the order given. Conjugate the verbs in the preterite or the imperfect and add or change words as needed. Use subject pronouns only when needed.

1. cuando / yo / ser / niño, / pensar / que / lo mejor / de / estar enfermo / ser / guardar cama
2. lo peor / ser / que / con frecuencia / yo / resfriarse / durante / vacaciones
3. una vez / yo / ponerme / muy / enfermo / durante / Navidad
4. mi / madre / llamar / a / médico / con / quien / tener / confianza
5. Dr. Matamoros / venir / casa / y / darme / antibiótico / porque / tener / mucho / fiebre
6. ser / cuatro / mañana / cuando / por fin / yo / empezar / respirar / sin dificultad
7. desgraciadamente / día / de / Navidad / yo / tener / tomar / jarabe / y / no / gustar / nada / sabor (*taste, m.*)
8. lo bueno / de / este / enfermedad / ser / que / mi / padre / tener / dejar / fumar / mientras / yo / estar / enfermo

Ahora vuelva a contar la historia desde el punto de vista de la madre del niño.

B **Un accidente tragicómico.** Complete the following paragraphs with the correct form of the words in parentheses—for verbs, the present, preterite, or imperfect—as suggested by the context. When two possibilities are given in parentheses, select the correct word.

Cuando mi hermana y yo (tener[1]) nueve y siete años respectivamente, (nuestro[2]) madre (tener[3]) un pequeño accidente. Papá (tener[4]) que pasar unos días fuera (por/para[5]) cuestiones de su trabajo. (Por/Para[6]) eso, (*nosotras:* ir[7]) a despedirlo al aeropuerto.

Cuando (*nosotras:* salir[8]), vimos que un perrito tenía la pata[a] atrapada[b] en una puerta. Las tres (correr[9]) a ayudarlo. Mamá (tomar[10]) al perrito en sus brazos y lo estaba (examinar[11]) mientras (*nosotras:* caminar[12]). Íbamos (tan/tanto[13]) preocupadas por la patita del perro que no (*nosotros:* ver[14]) un escalón.[c] (*Nosotras:* Caerse[15]) las tres... bueno, los cuatro. La situación (ser[16]) algo cómica. (*Nosotras:* Levantarse[17]) muertas de risa[d] y un poco avergonzadas.

Por fin (*nosotras:* dejar[18]) al perrito con (su[19]) dueños y (decidir[20]) irnos a casa. Nuestra madre (cojear[e21]) un poco. Esa misma tarde (*nosotras:* ir[22]) al hospital porque le (doler[23]) mucho todavía la pierna. No (haber[24]) duda. (*Ella:* Tener[25]) el tobillo roto.[f] Le escayolaron[g] el pie y la pierna y le (*ellos:* dar[26]) un par de muletas.[h] Además le (*ellos:* recomendar[27]) reposo absoluto.

[a]*paw* [b]*trapped* [c]*step* [d]*muertas... dying of laughter* [e]*to limp* [f]*el... a broken ankle* [g]*Le... They put a cast on* [h]*crutches*

Todavía hoy mi hermana y yo (acordarse[28]) de lo bien que (*nosotras:* pasarlo[29]) jugando a ser las enfermeras de mamá. Afortunadamente los abuelos (venir[30]) en nuestra ayuda.

¿Quién lo dijo?

1. Tenemos que ir a ayudar a las chicas. No pueden cuidar ellas solas a Marisa.
2. ¿Dónde está el perro? No lo veo por ningún sitio.
3. Siento decirle, señora, que tiene el tobillo fracturado.
4. ¡Qué torpes somos!, ¿verdad?
5. ¿Por qué no te llevamos a la sala de urgencia?

☀ SITUACIÓN En el consultorio

Este es un diálogo típico entre doctor y paciente. Note cómo la doctora da muchos mandatos, lo que es normal y aceptable en esta situación.

DOCTORA: Buenos días, David. ¿Qué le pasa?

DAVID: Tengo un resfriado fatal. Anoche tosía tanto que no pude dormir casi nada. Creo que también tengo algo de fiebre.

DOCTORA: Es que hay un virus muy infeccioso que está causando[a] muchos resfriados. Vamos a ver. Abra bien la boca. Saque la lengua y diga «a». Bueno, la garganta está un poco inflamada. Ahora voy a auscultarle. Respire profundamente y deje salir lentamente el aire. Los pulmones están bien. No tiene bronquitis, que es lo que me preocupaba.

DAVID: Pero yo toso mucho, incluso[b] cuando no estoy resfriado.

DOCTORA: Lo que le pasa es que Ud. fuma demasiado. ¿Cuándo va a dejar de fumar? Bueno, para este resfriado le voy a recetar un jarabe para la tos. Y si le duele la cabeza o tiene un poco de fiebre, tome aspirinas. Estará[c] bien en 2 ó 3 días.

DAVID: Gracias, doctora.

[a]está... *is causing*   [b]*even*   [c]*You'll be*

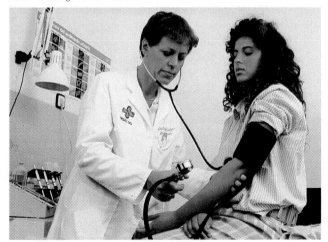

España.

NOTAS COMUNICATIVAS SOBRE EL DIÁLOGO

Here is some additional vocabulary to use if you need to consult a doctor or dentist.

¿Cuánto tiempo hace que Ud. está enfermo/a?	*How long have you been ill?*
Hace (dos días) que estoy enfermo/a.	*I've been sick for (two days).*
¿Cuándo se enfermó?	*When did you get sick?*
¿Padece de algo más?	*Is anything else wrong?*
Sí, padezco de _____.	*Yes, I'm also suffering from _____.*
¿Ha tenido Ud. _____?	*Have you had _____?*
Sí, he tenido _____. (No, no he tenido _____.)	*Yes, I've had _____. (No, I haven't had _____.)*
¿Toma Ud. alguna medicina?	*Are you taking any medicine?*
Vamos a sacar los rayos equis / las radiografías.	*We're going to take X-rays.*
Tenemos que sacarle el diente / la muela.	*We have to pull the tooth / molar.*

Remember that any temperature above 37 degrees Celsius (98.6 degrees Fahrenheit) constitutes a fever.

Conversación

Después de practicar el diálogo con un compañero o una compañera, con su profesor(a) o en parejas, escenifique (*act out*) las siguientes situaciones.

1. Ud. está en el consultorio del médico. Le duele mucho la garganta y tose con frecuencia. Espera una hora, pero el médico no lo/la atiende. Ud. habla con la enfermera. Por fin lo/la dejan pasar al consultorio.
2. Ud. va al médico porque tiene dolor de cabeza desde hace (*for*) una semana. También tiene problemas con la respiración; le es casi imposible bajar y subir las escaleras. Ud. fuma dos paquetes diarios de cigarrillos.
3. Ud. va al dentista porque hace varios días que le duele un diente. Pero Ud. es cobarde y no quiere que el dentista se lo saque.
4. Su perro tiene la pierna fracturada y Ud. lo lleva al veterinario. Hay varios gatos en la sala de espera y Ud. tiene que esperar una hora. Por fin lo/la atiende el veterinario.

PARA ESCRIBIR

Answer the following questions about your last visit to the doctor, adding as many details as possible.

PÁRRAFO A

1. ¿Cuándo fue la última vez que Ud. consultó con un médico?

2. ¿Por qué lo hizo? ¿Cuáles eran sus síntomas? ¿O era solamente un chequeo anual?

PÁRRAFO B

1. En el consultorio, ¿tuvo Ud. que esperar mucho tiempo? ¿Esperaban también otros pacientes?

2. Cuando por fin entró en el consultorio, ¿cuánto tiempo duró la consulta? ¿Qué actitud mostró el médico? ¿compasión? ¿humor? ¿preocupación? ¿indiferencia? ¿Por qué?

3. ¿Le recetó alguna medicina? ¿Qué otras recomendaciones le dio? ¿Las siguió Ud.? ¿Por qué sí o por qué no?

PÁRRAFO C

1. ¿Cuándo se mejoró Ud. por fin? ¿O cuándo va a tener otro chequeo anual?

2. ¿Qué hace ahora para mantenerse en buen estado de salud?

▼▼▼▼▼▼▼▼▼▼▼▼▼▼ **VOCABULARIO** ▼▼▼▼▼▼▼▼▼▼▼▼▼▼

Verbos

correr to run; to jog
practicar to play (*a sport*)

Repaso: caminar, hacer ejercicio

Más partes del cuerpo

la boca mouth
el cerebro brain
el corazón heart
el diente tooth
el estómago stomach
la garganta throat
la muela molar
la nariz* nose
el oído inner ear
el ojo eye
la oreja ear
los pulmones lungs

La salud

el bienestar well-being
los lentes (de contacto) (contact) lenses

lo suficiente enough

cuidarse to take care of oneself

---

*The plural of **nariz** (**narices**) means *nostrils.*

dejar de + *inf.* to stop (*doing something*)
llevar una vida sana to lead a healthy life

Repaso: dormir (ue, u), las gafas, llevar (to wear)

En el consultorio

el antibiótico antibiotic
el/la enfermero/a nurse
el jarabe (cough) syrup
la medicina drug, medicine
el/la médico/a physician
el/la paciente patient
la pastilla pill
la receta prescription
el resfriado cold
la tos cough

guardar cama to stay in bed
internarse (en) to check into (*a hospital*)
ponerle una inyección to give (someone) a shot
resfriarse to get/catch a cold
respirar to breathe
sacar la lengua to stick out one's tongue
sacar una muela to extract a tooth (molar)

tener dolor (de) to have a pain (in)
tener fiebre to have a fever
tomarle la temperatura to take (someone's) temperature
toser to cough

Repaso: doler (ue), enfermarse

Sustantivos

la cita appointment; date

Adjetivos

congestionado/a congested, stuffed-up
mareado/a dizzy; nauseated

Palabras adicionales

mientras (que) while

Repaso: lo que, que, quien

Self-Test

Use the tape that accompanies this text to test yourself briefly on the important points of this chapter.

LECTURA
cultural

Antes de leer: Predicting Content Before You Read

The following article is about an aspect of preventative medicine: the annual check-up. Based on that knowledge, what kinds of general recommendations would you expect to read about in the article? What recommendations do you think will be offered specifically for women? for men? Working with a partner, make a list of topics that you expect to be covered. After you have read the selection, compare its content with the items on your list.

CONSEJOS

Cuándo se deben realizar chequeos médicos. Prevenir es curar dice un viejo aforismo médico. Por eso es importante conocer cuándo se deben realizar los denominados chequeos, que no son otra cosa que exámenes de salud. Estos exámenes para ser efectivos deben de comenzar en la primera infancia, tal y como aconseja el doctor Miguel Renart en un artículo recientemente publicado en la *Revista de la Salud*. Las pautas[a] recomendables son:

- Revisiones anuales en ambos sexos, a partir del primer año de vida, de los ojos, oídos, dientes y crecimiento general.
- Cuando comience la pubertad, comprobar el desarrollo[b] del aparato genital, tanto en varones como en hembras, y realizar análisis de sangre y de orina. Estos análisis deben repetirse cada tres años.
- A partir de los 20 años se deben realizar los controles de peso, tensión arterial y niveles de colesterol con una frecuencia bianual.
- A partir de los 35 años se debe añadir un electrocardiograma y una radiografía de tórax repitiéndolos cada dos años hasta los 45, en que se deben realizar anualmente.
- Las mujeres tienen que hacerse una exploración ginecológica y mamaria, incluyendo citología, a partir de los 25 años.
- Todo hombre de más de 45 años debería someterse una vez al año a una exploración de la próstata.

[a]*guidelines* [b]comprobar... *check the development*

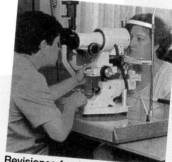
Revisiones fundamentales

Comprensión

A Un refrán español dice: «Prevenir es curar». ¿Cuál es el equivalente en inglés?

288

B De las siguientes recomendaciones, ¿cuáles aparecen en el artículo «Consejos»?

1. análisis de sangre y de orina cada tres años
2. examen ginecológico para mujeres a partir de los veinticinco años
3. examen bianual de los órganos internos para los dos sexos
4. revisión anual de los ojos y oídos
5. chequeo cardíaco anual a partir de los treinta y cinco años

C Según el artículo, ¿cuáles de las siguientes recomendaciones se aplican a Ud.?

1. análisis de sangre y de orina cada tres años
2. revisión anual de los ojos, oídos y dientes
3. revisión bianual para chequear el peso (*weight*), la tensión arterial y el nivel de colesterol
4. un electrocardiograma y una radiografía de tórax cada dos años
5. exploración ginecológica y mamaria
6. exploración anual de la próstata

D Busque en los anuncios palabras que puedan relacionarse con las siguientes personas, condiciones y definiciones

1. una persona muy vieja, especialmente las mujeres
2. beber demasiado alcohol
3. comer mucha grasa (*fat*)
4. comer demasiado
5. sufrir muchas presiones
6. lo que uno debe tener anualmente
7. estar distraído/a

16

Primer paso

¿Qué hace Ud. en su tiempo libre?

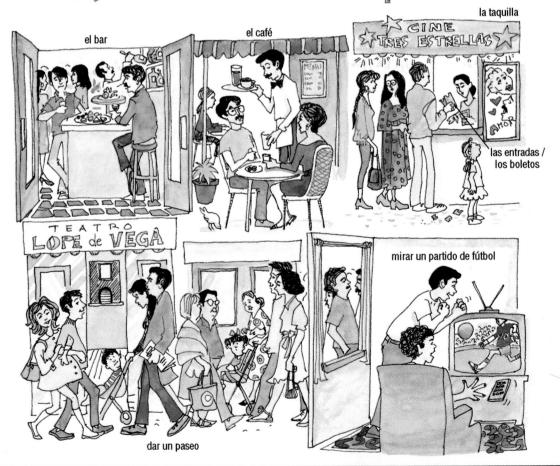

el bar

el café

la taquilla

CINE TRES ESTRELLAS

las entradas / los boletos

TEATRO LOPE de VEGA

mirar un partido de fútbol

dar un paseo

Los FINES DE SEMANA

Más pasatiempos

dar/hacer una fiesta	to have a party
hacer *camping*	to go camping
hacer planes para + *inf.*	to make plans to (*do something*)
ir al cine / al teatro	to go to the movies/theater
a una discoteca / un museo	to go to a disco / a museum
a un partido de...	to go to a . . . game
jugar (ue) a las cartas /	to play cards/chess
al ajedrez	
ser aficionado/a a...	to be a . . . fan
ser divertido/aburrido	to be fun/boring

Los deportes

el ciclismo	bicycling
correr	to run
esquiar	to ski
el fútbol	soccer
el fútbol americano	football
nadar	to swim
pasear en bicicleta	to ride a bicycle

Otros deportes: el básquetbol, el béisbol, el golf, el hockey, el tenis, el vólibol

Práctica

A **En el cine.** Ud. quiere ir al cine. Usando los números del **1** al **8,** indique en qué orden va a hacer las siguientes cosas.

_____ Llamo a mi amigo/a para ver si quiere acompañarme.

_____ Cuando hago planes para ir al cine, lo primero que hago es consultar el periódico.

_____ Compramos las entradas en la taquilla.

_____ Subo al autobús para ir al centro, donde está el cine.

_____ Buscamos buenas butacas (*seats*) para poder ver bien.

_____ Compramos refrescos para tomar durante la película.

_____ Espero a mi amigo/a delante de la taquilla.

_____ Después de la función, vamos a un café a tomar algo.

B **Gustos y preferencias.** Lea las siguientes descripciones de lo que les gusta hacer a unos estudiantes. Luego diga el nombre del pasatiempo más apropiado para cada uno en sus ratos libres. Hay más de una respuesta posible.

1. A Beatriz le gusta mucho estar al aire libre (*fresh air*).

2. A Julio y Juana les encanta el arte... moderno, medieval, del período que sea (*whatever the era*).

Adivinanzas

1. Dime qué deporte es oriundo de[a] Inglaterra, que se juega con los pies y también con la cabeza.

[a]oriundo... *originally from*

2. Tengo ruedas y pedales, cadena[b] y un manillar. Te ahorro[c] la gasolina aunque te haga sudar.[d]

[b]*chain*   [c]*I save*   [d]*sweat*

3. A Ramón le gusta que todos sus amigos vengan a su casa a pasarlo bien.
4. Ernesto y Magdalena siempre prefieren que sus hijos pasen su tiempo libre con ellos.
5. A Carmen y sus amigos les encanta bailar y cantar. En realidad les gusta la música en general.
6. Pepe tiene mucho interés en el cine, sobre todo en el cine español, argentino y mexicano.

C **¿Cierto o falso?** Corrija las oraciones falsas según su opinión.

1. Es aburrido quedarse en casa para leer.
2. Nunca lo paso bien con mi familia. De hecho (*In fact*), para divertirme, tengo que estar con mis amigos.
3. En cuanto a (*As for*) mis pasatiempos, soy mucho más intelectual (deportivo/a) que mis amigos (soy igual que mis amigos).
4. No soy aficionado/a a ningún deporte.
5. El fútbol americano es el deporte más violento de todos.
6. Tomar el sol con frecuencia es bueno para la salud.
7. Los estudiantes de esta universidad tienen muchos ratos libres porque los profesores no les piden que estudien mucho.
8. El pasatiempo favorito de los estudiantes de esta universidad es asistir a fiestas.

TIEMPO QUE DEDICAN A SUS AFICIONES	
(Media de minutos diarios)	
Ver la televisión	**120**
Tomar copas	**60**
Pasear	**22**
Leer libros	**15**
Escuchar música	**15**
Oír la radio	**8**
Hacer deporte	**9**
Practicar *hobbies*	**8**
Leer la prensa	**6**
«Juegos»	**4**

NOTA CULTURAL: La tertulia

Una costumbre muy común en muchas partes del mundo hispánico es la tertulia, que consiste en un grupo de amigos a quienes les gusta pasar el rato conversando.[a] Los participantes se reúnen periódicamente, por ejemplo, a la misma hora de la tarde todos los días. Generalmente la tertulia se celebra en un bar o café donde se puede tomar algo y hablar. Las conversaciones pueden abarcar[b] muchos temas, pero sin duda dos de los más comunes son los deportes y la política. Ya que la gente hispánica se muda[c] con menos frecuencia que en los Estados Unidos, muchos de estos grupos duran años y años, con los mismos amigos reuniéndose[d] en el mismo sitio y a la misma hora.

[a]*chatting* [b]*cover* [c]*se... move* [d]*getting together*

DE AQUÍ Y DE ALLÁ

Here are some additional words and phrases to use to describe what you do in your free time.

dar un paseo = pasear
dar una vuelta (con los compas [= compañeros])
estirar (*to stretch*) las piernas

mirar la tele = tumbarse a ver la tele
dormir un poco = echarse una siesta
ir a bailar = ir a la disco(teca)

ESTRUCTURAS

31.   ¿Qué estás haciendo?

Present Progressive: *estar* + *-ndo*

▼ **En sus ratos libres...**
▼ The sentences in the left-hand column tell what sports the following persons do or
▼ are able to do. Following the examples, tell what they are doing right now (**ahora**
▼ **mismo**).

Santiago esquía muy bien.   → Santiago **está esquiando** ahora
                                              mismo.

Soledad baila como una profe-   → Soledad **está bailando** ahora
sional.   mismo.

Jorge nada todos los días.   → Jorge _____ .

Ricardo pasea en bicicleta con fre-   → Ricardo _____ .
cuencia.

▲ ▲ ▲

Dolores   Vicente   Fabián   Nati

Now tell what *was happening* last night at this house.

▼   Dolores **estaba estudiando.** Nati **estaba** _____ . Vicente **estaba** _____ al
▼   ajedrez con la computadora. Y Fabián _____ , ¡como siempre!

Uses of the Progressive

As you saw in the drawings that open this section, you need to use special verb
forms in Spanish to describe an action in progress—that is, something actually
happening at the time of reference. These Spanish forms, called **el progresivo,**

correspond in form to the English *progressive: I am walking, we are driving*. But their use is not identical.

Here are some examples of the Spanish progressive. Note that they do correspond to the progressive in English.

Ramón no puede salir ahora porque **está estudiando**.	*Ramón can't go out now because he's studying.*
Ana no llamó ayer porque **estaba cuidando** a su mamá en el hospital.	*Ana didn't call yesterday because she was taking care of her mom at the hospital.*

However, English progressives are also used to tell what is going to happen in the future or what is happening over a long period of time. Spanish uses the simple present in these cases. Compare these sentences.

SPANISH SIMPLE PRESENT	ENGLISH PROGRESSIVE
Tenemos un examen mañana.	*We're having a test tomorrow.*
Ana **estudia** química este semestre/trimestre.	*Ana is studying chemistry this term.*

Formation of the Progressive Tenses

Spelling hint: Unaccented **i** represents the sound [y] in the participle ending **-iendo: comiendo, viviendo**. Unaccented **i** between two vowels becomes **y: leyendo, oyendo**.

The Spanish progressive is formed with **estar** plus the *present participle* (**el gerundio**), which is formed by adding **-ando** to the stem of **-ar** verbs and **-iendo** to the stem of **-er** and **-ir** verbs.* The present participle never varies; it always ends in **-o**.

tomar	→ **tomando**	*taking; drinking*
comprender	→ **comprendiendo**	*understanding*
abrir	→ **abriendo**	*opening*

The stem vowel in the present participle of **-ir** stem-changing verbs also shows a change. This change, the second of those shown in parentheses for stem-changing verbs, is the same one that occurs in the **nosotros** and **vosotros** forms of the present subjunctive.

preferir (ie, i)	→ prefiriendo	*preferring*
pedir (i, i)	→ pidiendo	*asking*
dormir (ue, u)	→ durmiendo	*sleeping*

The *present* progressive is formed of course with the present tense of **estar** plus the participle: **estoy (caminando, corriendo)**. The *past* progressive is most frequently formed with the imperfect of **estar: estaba (caminando, corriendo)**.†

Using Pronouns with the Progressive Tenses

Object pronouns may be attached to a present participle or precede the conjugated form of **estar**. Note the use of a written accent mark when pronouns are attached to the present participle.

---

*__Ir, poder__, and **venir** have irregular present participles: **yendo, pudiendo, viniendo**. These three verbs, however, are seldom used in the progressive.
†A progressive tense can also be formed with the preterite of **estar**: *Estuvieron* **cenando hasta las doce**. It is not used very often.

Pablo **le** está escribiendo. ⎫
Pablo está escribiéndo**le**. ⎭   *Pablo is writing to him.*

¿**Nos** estaban buscando? ⎫
¿Estaban buscándo**nos**? ⎭   *Were they looking for us?*

Práctica

A **Un sábado típico.** Indique lo que Ud. está haciendo a las horas indicadas en un sábado típico. En algunos casos hay más de una respuesta posible.

A las ocho de la mañana...   SÍ   NO

  1. estoy durmiendo   ☐   ☐
  2. estoy desayunando   ☐   ☐
  3. estoy mirando los dibujos animados en la tele   ☐   ☐
  4. estoy duchándome   ☐   ☐
  5. estoy trabajando   ☐   ☐
  6. estoy _____   ☐   ☐

Al mediodía (*noon*)...   SÍ   NO

  1. estoy durmiendo   ☐   ☐
  2. estoy almorzando   ☐   ☐
  3. estoy estudiando   ☐   ☐
  4. estoy practicando algún deporte   ☐   ☐
  5. estoy trabajando   ☐   ☐
  6. estoy limpiando la casa   ☐   ☐
  7. estoy _____   ☐   ☐

A las diez de la noche...   SÍ   NO

  1. estoy durmiendo   ☐   ☐
  2. estoy preparándome para salir   ☐   ☐
  3. estoy mirando algo en la tele   ☐   ☐
  4. estoy bailando en una fiesta o en una discoteca   ☐   ☐
  5. estoy trabajando   ☐   ☐
  6. estoy hablando por teléfono con un amigo / una amiga   ☐   ☐
  7. estoy _____   ☐   ☐

B **El sábado por la tarde.** Haga oraciones según las indicaciones.

Todos los amigos de Ud. están en el parque. Ud. quiere ir también. ¿Por qué?

todos ⎫   ⎧comer, beber
mi amigo/a _____ ⎭ estar ⎨hablar mucho
                           ⎪jugar al tenis, al vólibol, al béisbol, al ¿ ?
                           ⎩tomar el sol

Pero Ud. no puede ir. ¿Por qué no?

$$yo \Bigr\} \quad estar \quad \begin{cases} \text{trabajar (en \_\_\_\_\_)} \\ \text{estudiar (en \_\_\_\_\_)} \\ \text{leer la lección para el lunes, ¿ ?} \\ \text{aprender el vocabulario nuevo, ¿ ?} \\ \text{terminar una composición, ¿ ?} \end{cases}$$

C **Situaciones.** Julio is not working out as a roommate. What does Ceci have to do as a result of his sloppy habits? Answer following the model.

MODELO: Julio perdió la llave de la casa. (buscar) →
Ceci **la está buscando** en este momento.
(Ceci **está buscándola** en este momento.)

1. Julio dejó platos sucios en el comedor. (lavar)
2. También dejó su ropa sucia en el suelo de la sala. (recoger)
3. Dejó su ropa limpia en la lavadora. (poner en la secadora)
4. No sacó la basura de la cocina. (sacar)
5. Prometió pintar la puerta del garaje, pero no lo hizo. (pintar)

D **¡Ojo alerta!** Hay por lo menos siete diferencias entre los dos dibujos. ¿Las puede encontrar Ud.? Descríbalas usando el progresivo cuando sea necesario.

E **El trabajo de niñera** (*baby-sitter*). El trabajo de niñera puede ser simplemente pesado, pero cuando los niños son traviesos, puede ser hasta peligroso. ¿Qué estaba pasando cuando la niñera perdió por fin la paciencia? Describa todas las acciones que pueda, usando **estaba(n)** + **-ndo.**

Palabras útiles: discutir, ladrar (*to bark*), pelear (*to fight*), sonar (ue) (*to ring; to sound, play*)

Segundo paso

Las palabras interrogativas

Summary and Expansion

¿Cómo?	How?	¿Dónde?	Where?
¿Cuándo?	When?	¿De dónde?	From where?
¿A qué hora?	At what time?	¿Adónde?	Where (to)?
¿Qué?	What? Which?	¿Cuánto/a?	How much?
¿Cuál(es)?	What? Which one(s)?	¿Cuántos/as?	How many?
¿Por qué?	Why?	¿Quién(es)?	Who?
		¿De quién(es)?	Whose?

Remember: **ser en** + *place* = *to take place*

¿Cuántas preguntas puede Ud. hacer sobre las funciones de cine y ballet en estos anuncios?

MODELOS: ¿Cuándo dan la película *JFK*?
¿Quién fue JFK?
¿Dónde es el taller (*workshop*) de baile?

d a n z a

◆ **Ballet de San Juan-** 28 de octubre a las 7:30 PM en el Teatro del Colegio Universitario Tecnológico de Arecibo.
◆ **Taller de baile experimental con Viveca Vázquez-** 30 de octubre y 6, 13 y 20 de noviembre de 1:00 a 3:00 PM en el centro Dharma, al lado de la USC. Se invita a toda la comunidad a participar en estos talleres. Para más información llamar al 720-1793.

◆ **JFK-** 29 de octubre a las 10:30 AM y 6:00 PM en el Salón Buhomagia del Edificio de Letras del Colegio Universitario de Humacao.
◆ **El amante de Lady Chatterly-** 24 de noviembre a las 10:30 AM y 6:00 PM en Buhomagia del CUH.
◆ **Festival Internacional de Cine de Puerto Rico-** del 11 al 22 de noviembre en el Cinema Emperador de Ponce.

c i n e

You have been using interrogative words to ask questions and get information since the beginning of **¿Qué tal?** The preceding chart shows all of the interrogatives you have learned so far. Be sure that you know what they mean and how they are used. If you are not certain, the index will help you find where they are first introduced. Only the specific uses of **¿qué?** and **¿cuál?** represent "new" material.

Using ¿qué? and ¿cuál?

¿Qué? asks for a definition or an explanation.

¿Qué es esto?	*What is this?*
¿Qué quieres?	*What do you want?*
¿Qué tocas?	*What do you play?*

¿Qué? can be directly followed by a noun.

¿Qué traje necesitas?	*What (Which) suit do you need?*
¿Qué película te gusta más?	*What (Which) movie do you like most?*
¿Qué instrumento musical tocas?	*What (Which) musical instrument do you play?*

¿Cuál(es)? expresses *what?* or *which?* in all other cases.*

¿Cuál es el cine más grande?	*What (Which) is the biggest movie theater?*
¿Cuáles son tus actrices favoritas?	*What (Which) are your favorite actresses?*
¿Cuál es la capital del Uruguay?	*What is the capital of Uruguay?*
¿Cuál es tu teléfono?	*What is your phone number?*

Práctica

A ¿Qué? o ¿cuál(es)?

1. ¿_____ es esto? —Un peso mexicano.
2. ¿_____ es Sacramento? —Es la capital de California.
3. ¿_____ es tu clase preferida? —Pues, yo creo que es la de sicología.
4. ¿_____ guitarra vas a tocar? —La de Juanita.
5. ¿_____ son los cines más modernos? —Los del centro.
6. ¿_____ camisa debo llevar? —La azul.
7. ¿_____ es un «tambor»? —Es un instrumento musical.
8. ¿_____ es el novio de Alicia? —Es el hombre moreno.

---

*The **¿cuál(es)** + *noun* structure is not used by most speakers of Spanish: **¿Cuál de los dos libros quieres?** *Which of the two books do you want?* BUT **¿Qué libro quieres?** *Which book do you want?*

B **Datos personales.** Form the questions you would use to get the following information from another person. **¡OJO!** Each question will begin with **¿Cuál es/ fue... ?**

1. his/her telephone number (**teléfono**)
2. his/her address (**dirección**)
3. his/her birthday
4. his/her Social Security number (**número de seguro social**)
5. his/her nickname (**apodo**) as a child
6. his/her favorite TV cartoon (**dibujo animado**) as a child

C **Una encuesta.** Use questions that begin with **¿Qué... ?** to find out what a classmate prefers in the following categories.

MODELO: estaciones del año →
          ¿Qué estación del año prefieres (entre todos)?

1. tipos de música
2. pasatiempos o deportes
3. programas de televisión
4. materias este semestre/trimestre
5. colores
6. tipos de comida

ESTRUCTURAS

RECICLADO

Ud. and **Uds.** commands (Grammar Section 21) are the third persons (singular and plural) of the present subjunctive. Object pronouns (direct, indirect, reflexive) must follow and be attached to affirmative commands; they must precede negative commands.

AFFIRMATIVE:	Háblele Ud.	Duérmase.	Dígaselo Ud.
NEGATIVE:	No le hable Ud.	No se duerma.	No se lo diga Ud.

¿Cómo se dice en español?

1. Bring me the book. (**Uds.**)
2. Don't give it to her. (**Uds.**)
3. Sit here, please. (**Ud.**)
4. Don't sit in that chair! (**Ud.**)
5. Tell them the truth. (**Uds.**)
6. Tell it to them now! (**Uds.**)
7. Never tell it to her. (**Uds.**)
8. Take care of yourself. (**Ud.**)
9. Lead a healthy life. (**Ud.**)
10. Listen to me. (**Ud.**)

32. Influencing Others

Tú commands

▼ **Una barbacoa con la familia: Frases útiles para los padres**

—Maritere, *toma* tu leche; *no tomes* la de Carlos.
—Ramón, *bebe* más despacio; *no bebas* tan rápidamente.
—Cristina, *escucha; no grites* tanto.
—Joaquín, *siéntate* en el banco para comer; *no te sientes* en el suelo.
—Graciela, *dale* la hamburguesa a Ernesto; *no se la des* al perro.
—Ramón, *ten* cuidado; *no corras, no te caigas.*

▲ ▲ ▲

¿Qué están haciendo los niños, según los mandatos de los padres?

MODELO: Maritere está tomando la leche de Carlos.

Informal commands (**los mandatos informales**) are used with persons whom you address as **tú.** As you work with commands in this section, remember that these commands (and the **Ud.** and **Uds.** commands that you have already learned) are very direct commands. They can be softened by using expressions such as **por favor.**

Negative *tú* Commands

-ar VERBS		**-er/-ir** VERBS	
No hables.	*Don't speak.*	**No comas.**	*Don't eat.*
No cantes.	*Don't sing.*	**No escribas.**	*Don't write.*
No juegues.	*Don't play.*	**No pidas.**	*Don't order.*

Like **Ud.** commands (Grammar Section 21), the negative **tú** commands are expressed with the present subjunctive: **no hable Ud., no hables (tú).** The pronoun **tú** is used only for emphasis.

No cantes **tú** tan fuerte.   *Don't you sing so loudly.*

As with negative **Ud.** commands, object pronouns—direct, indirect, and reflexive— precede negative **tú** commands.

No lo mires.   *Don't look at him.*
No les escribas.   *Don't write to them.*
No te levantes.   *Don't get up.*

A family barbecue: Useful phrases for parents   Maritere, drink your milk; don't drink Carlos's. Ramón, drink more slowly; don't drink so fast. Cristina, listen; don't shout so much. Joaquín, sit on the picnic bench to eat; don't sit on the ground. Graciela, give the hamburger to Ernesto; don't give it to the dog. Ramón, be careful; don't run, don't fall.

Affirmative *tú* Commands*

-ar VERBS		**-er/-ir** VERBS	
Habla.	*Speak.*	**Come.**	*Eat.*
Canta.	*Sing.*	**Escribe.**	*Write.*
Juega.	*Play.*	**Pide.**	*Order.*

Unlike the other command forms you have learned, most affirmative **tú** commands have the same form as the third person singular of the present *indicative*. Some verbs have irregular affirmative **tú** command forms.

decir:	**di**	ir:	**ve**	salir:	**sal**	tener:	**ten**
hacer:	**haz**	poner:	**pon**	ser:	**sé**	venir:	**ven**

Sé puntual pero **ten** cuidado. — *Be there on time, but be careful.*

¡OJO! The affirmative **tú** commands for **ir** and **ver** are identical: **ve.** Context will clarify meaning.

¡**Ve** esa película! — *See that movie!*
Ve a casa ahora mismo. — *Go home right now.*

As in affirmative **Ud.** commands, object and reflexive pronouns follow affirmative **tú** commands and are attached to them. Accent marks are necessary except when a single pronoun is added to a one-syllable command.

Dile la verdad. — *Tell him the truth.*
Léela, por favor. — *Read it, please.*
Póntelos. — *Put them on.*

Práctica

A **Recuerdos de la niñez.** ¿Qué le decían siempre los adultos a Ud. cuando era niño/a?

Paso 1. Indique los mandatos afirmativos que Ud. oía con frecuencia. Después de leerlos todos, indique los dos que oía más. ¿Hay algún mandato que Ud. no oyó nunca?

1. _____ Limpia tu cuarto.
2. _____ Cómete las legumbres.
3. _____ Haz la tarea.
4. _____ Cierra la puerta.
5. _____ Bébete la leche.
6. _____ Lávate las manos.
7. _____ Dime la verdad.
8. _____ Quítate los zapatos.
9. _____ Guarda (*Put away*) tus juguetes.
10. _____ Haz la cama.

---

*Affirmative **vosotros** commands are formed by substituting **-d** for the final **-r** of the infinitive: **hablar** → **hablad; comer** → **comed; escribir** → **escribid.** There are no irregular affirmative **vosotros** commands. Negative **vosotros** commands are expressed with the present subjunctive: **no habléis / no comáis / no escribáis.** Placement of object pronouns is the same as with all other command forms: **Decídmelo; No me lo digáis.**

Los errores que no debes cometer en la mesa

- No comas con los codos apoyados en la mesa. En primer lugar, porque limitas tus movimientos. Y en segundo, porque los alimentos pueden caerse de los cubiertos. Tus brazos tienen que moverse libremente. Sin embargo, cuando no estés comiendo puedes apoyarlos sobre la mesa.
- No dejes las cucharas dentro de la taza del café, del té o de la sopa.
- No pongas alimentos en cantidades exageradas en tu boca. ¡Es de muy mal gusto!
- No mastiques con la boca abierta y no hagas ruido con los labios y la lengua, porque es muy antiestético.
- No hables con la boca llena, porque se saldrá la comida. Si quieres hablar mientras comes, hazlo cuando tengas una mínima cantidad de comida en la boca. De otra manera, habla después de haber tragado los alimentos.

Paso 2. Ahora indique los mandatos negativos que escuchaba con frecuencia. Debe indicar también los dos que oía más. ¿Hay uno que no oyó nunca?

1. _____ No cruces la calle solo/a.
2. _____ No juegues con cerillas (*matches*).
3. _____ No comas dulces antes de cenar.
4. _____ No pelees con tus amigos.
5. _____ No mastiques (*chew*) chicle en clase.
6. _____ No hables con desconocidos.
7. _____ No saltes (*jump*) en el sofá.
8. _____ No molestes al perro/gato.
9. _____ No digas tonterías (*dumb things*).
10. _____ No le pegues a tu hermano/a.

B **Julita.** Los señores Villarreal no están contentos con el comportamiento de su hija Julita. Continúe los comentarios de ellos con mandatos informales lógicos según cada situación. Siga los modelos.

MODELOS: **Hablaste** demasiado ayer. → No **hables** tanto hoy, por favor.
Dejaste tu ropa en el suelo anoche. → No la **dejes** allí hoy, por favor.

1. También **dejaste** tus libros en el suelo.
2. ¿Por qué **regresaste** tarde a casa hoy después de las clases?
3. Ayer **usaste** mi toalla (*towel*).
4. Tampoco quiero que **entres** en nuestro cuarto de baño para nada.
5. No es bueno que **corras** y **juegues** en la calle.
6. ¿Por qué **vas** al parque todas las tardes?
7. No es bueno que **mires** la televisión constantemente. ¿Y por qué quieres **ver** todos esos programas de detectives?
8. ¿Por qué le **dices** mentiras a tu papá?
9. Siempre **te olvidas** de sacar la basura, que es la única tarea que tienes que hacer.
10. Ay, hija, no te comprendemos. ¡**Eres** tan insolente!

C **Más sobre Julita.** La pobre Julita también escucha muchos mandatos de su maestra en clase. Invente Ud. esos mandatos según las indicaciones.

1. llegar / a / escuela / puntualmente
2. entrar / clase / sin / hacer tanto ruido
3. quitarse / abrigo / y / sentarse
4. sacar / libro de matemáticas / y / abrirlo / en / página diez
5. escribir / problema dos / en / pizarra
6. leer / nuevo / palabras / y / aprenderlas / para mañana
7. venir / aquí / a / hablar conmigo / sobre / este / composición
8. ayudar / Carlitos / con / su composición

D **Mandatos para unas vacaciones estupendas.** ¿Qué debe y **no** debe hacer su amigo Rigoberto para pasarlo muy bien durante sus vacaciones? Déle consejos en forma de mandatos informales. ¡**OJO!** Rigoberto no puede viajar; tiene que quedarse en esta ciudad.

A Situaciones.

Paso 1. Describa lo que está haciendo Ernesto ahora como resultado de lo que le pasó. Use el presente progresivo.

> MODELO: Los abuelos de Ernesto le regalaron una bicicleta. →
> Ahora Ernesto está paseando en bicicleta.

1. Un amigo le dio dos boletos para un partido de fútbol.
2. Una amiga le dio entradas para el teatro.
3. Una amiga le invitó a una discoteca.
4. Sus abuelos le mandaron mil dólares de (*as*) regalo.
5. Su novia le prestó su nuevo coche descapotable.
6. Ernesto dijo que le gustaría preparar una cena especial para su novia.

Paso 2. Algunos de los amigos de Ernesto le cuentan sus problemas. Invente los consejos que Ernesto les da, usando mandatos informales.

1. A Celia le encanta ir al cine, especialmente los viernes por la noche. Pero a su novio no le gusta salir mucho el viernes, porque está muy cansado después de una larga semana de trabajo. Celia, en cambio, tiene mucha energía.
2. Nati quiere vivir el año próximo en un apartamento con un grupo de amigos. Parece una situación ideal: apartamento económico y unos buenos amigos. Pero los padres de Nati son muy tradicionales y Nati sabe que no les va a gustar que ella viva con hombres en el mismo apartamento.

B Los fines de semana.

Complete the following paragraphs with the correct form of the words in parentheses, as suggested by the context. When two possibilities are given in parentheses, select the correct word. Use the preterite of the infinitives in italics.

Los fines de semana son como las burbujas[a] de oxígeno del calendario. Para muchos, son (los/las[1]) días más especiales. Casi todos los niños (*esperar*[2]) el sábado y el domingo con ansiedad. Quieren que papá, mamá o los abuelos los (*llevar*[3]) al cine o al parque el fin de semana. Sin duda los niños (*comer*[4]) más dulces y pasteles (ese[5]) días y, claro, ven (menos/más[6]) la televisión.

También para los mayores los fines de semana son días diferentes. Hay novios que (sólo/solo[7]) pueden (*reunirse*[8]) los fines de semana. Otras personas tienen (de/que[9]) hacer visitas o compras o ir al mercado... Algunas personas (*intentar*[b 10]) recuperar lo que no durmieron durante la semana. Hay gente que no (*querer*[11]) hacer absolutamente nada y personas que esperan (*hacer*[12]) todo lo

[a]*bubbles* [b]*to try*

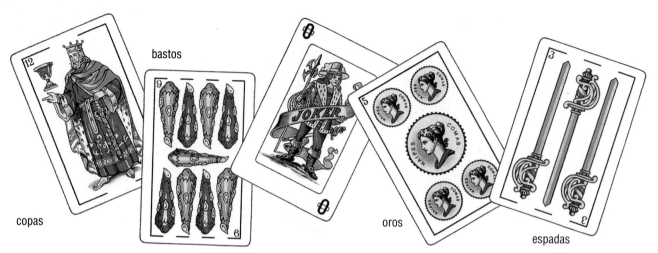

bastos

copas

oros

espadas

Los españoles usan la baraja (*deck*) de cartas que se usa en este país, pero en España también hay otra baraja que se usa para ciertos juegos de cartas. Esta baraja no tiene cartas de 8, 9 ni (*nor*) 10; tiene sólo 40 cartas. Los palos (*suits*) son diferentes también.

que no (hacer[13]) durante la semana. Quieren limpiar la casa, ir a la lavandería, estar con la familia, jugar (el/al[14]) tenis...

En el mundo moderno, parece que (hay/son[15]) cosas que sólo se pueden hacer los fines de semana porque (*nosotros:* ser/estar[16]) tan ocupados durante la semana. (Por/Para[17]) ejemplo: ver deportes en (el/la[18]) tele, ir al campo con los amigos o la familia, visitar museos...

También hay personas que (trabajar[19]) los fines de semana y que (descansar[20]) (los/las[21]) martes y miércoles. Y aunque parece increíble, hay personas a quienes no les (gustar[22]) los fines de semana... y también personas que (aburrirse[c23]) el sábado.

[c] *to be bored*

¿Cómo son los fines de semana para Ud.? Busque en los párrafos anteriores las palabras o frases que lo/la describen mejor a Ud. y úselas para completar una de las siguientes oraciones.

Para mí, los fines de semana son _____.
Soy una de esas personas que _____* los fines de semana.

☀ SITUACIÓN El fin de semana

HACIENDO PLANES PARA ESTE FIN DE SEMANA
—Oye, ¿tienes planes para este fin de semana?
—Aparte de estudiar, no. ¿Y tú? ¿En qué estás pensando?
—Bueno, yo también tengo mucho que estudiar y que hacer en la casa. Pero me gustaría divertirme un rato.
—¿Qué te parece si vamos en bicicleta hasta el lago el domingo? Podemos llevarnos un *picnic* y estudiar un poco allí.
—¡Me parece estupendo!

---

*Note that the verb form will be third person plural, since **esas personas** is the subject.

HABLANDO DEL FIN DE SEMANA PASADO

—¿Qué tal el fin de semana?

—Tranquilo. Vino mi hermana por el fin de semana y pasamos todo el tiempo en casa charlando y jugando a las cartas. ¿Y Uds.?

—Fuimos a la playa con unos compañeros de trabajo. Lo pasamos muy bien, pero me quemé[a] mucho.

[a]me... *I got sunburned*

Conversación

Invente conversaciones, siguiendo el modelo de los diálogos anteriores.

- Haga planes con un amigo / una amiga para pasar la tarde del sábado juntos.
- Pregunte a su profesor(a) cómo pasa los fines de semana.
- Pregunte a un amigo / una amiga cómo pasó el fin de semana pasado.

PARA ESCRIBIR

Escriba un párrafo o dos sobre lo que a Ud. le gusta hacer en su tiempo libre. ¿Cuáles son sus actividades favoritas? ¿Con quién las hace? ¿Adónde va? etcétera.

▼▼▼▼▼▼▼▼▼▼▼▼▼ VOCABULARIO ▼▼▼▼▼▼▼▼▼▼▼▼▼

Verbos

gritar to scream

Los pasatiempos

el ajedrez chess
el bar bar, neighborhood hang-out
el boleto ticket (*for a performance*)
las cartas cards
los dibujos animados cartoons (*on TV*)
la discoteca disco(theque)
la entrada ticket (*for a performance*)
la función show, showing (*of a movie or play*)
el museo museum
el partido game; match

los ratos libres leisure time
la taquilla ticket booth
el teatro theater

Repaso: el café, el cine

dar un paseo to stroll
hacer planes para + *inf.* to make plans to (*do something*)
ser aficionado/a a to be a . . . fan

Repaso: dar/hacer una fiesta, hacer *camping*, ir, jugar (ue)

Los deportes

el ciclismo bicycling
el fútbol soccer
el fútbol americano football
pasear en bicicleta to ride a bicycle

Otros deportes: el básquetbol, el béisbol, el golf, el hockey, el tenis, el vólibol

Repaso: correr, esquiar, nadar

Adjetivos

divertido/a fun, amusing

Self-Test

Use the tape that accompanies this text to test yourself briefly on the important points of this chapter.

del mundo hispánico 8
Colombia, Venezuela y dos islas del Caribe: Cuba y la República Dominicana

Colombia y Venezuela son países unidos por una frontera[a] común. Colombia es el tercer país más poblado de la América Latina. Es una nación próspera, con una posición geográfica única: es el único país sudamericano que tiene costa en dos océanos. Desde 1958 goza de[b] una democracia estable, pero desde la década de los 80 confronta una epidemia de violencia ocasionada por la producción y el tráfico de drogas.

Venezuela también vive un largo período de estabilidad política: sus presidentes han sido elegidos[c] en elecciones directas desde 1958. Es el país latinoamericano con mayor producto interno bruto[d] per cápita, gracias a su industria petrolera.

El petróleo, el «oro negro» del lago Maracaibo, Venezuela.

Personaje, Wilfredo Lam (Cuba). Esta figura, ¿es una madre con su niño o un curandero?

Cuba y la República Dominicana tienen (así como todos los países del Caribe) una cultura rica, resultado de la mezcla de sus raíces[e] indígenas, africanas y españolas. La herencia africana, que se manifiesta particularmente en la música y en el folclore, tiene gran influencia en su cultura.

Cuba consiguió su independencia de España en 1898, a consecuencia de la guerra entre España y los Estados Unidos. Desde la Revolución de 1959, vive bajo la dictadura de Fidel Castro, lo cual ha causado una gran ola[f] de inmigración a los Estados Unidos.

La República Dominicana ocupa los dos tercios orientales[g] de la antigua isla Hispaniola, la cual[h] comparte con Haití. Se independizó de España en 1821. Su último dictador, Héctor Bienvenido Trujillo, gobernó hasta 1960. Desde ese año, el país ha tenido períodos democráticos alternados con golpes[i] militares y levantamientos[j] civiles.

[a]*border* [b]*goza... it has enjoyed* [c]*han... have been elected* [d]*producto... gross national product* [e]*roots* [f]*wave* [g]*dos... Eastern two-thirds* [h]*la... which* [i]*coups d'etat* [j]*uprisings*

Cien años de soledad

Esta novela cuenta la historia de la familia Buendía a lo largo de[a] varias generaciones. El estilo que usa García Márquez en esta novela se llama «realismo mágico», porque cuenta hechos extraordinarios[b] de una manera que parece real. A continuación aparecen las primeras oraciones de la novela.

[a]a... through   [b]cuenta... he tells extraordinary events

Muchos años después, frente al pelotón de fusilamiento,[a] el coronel Aureliano Buendía había de recordar[b] aquella tarde remota en que su padre lo llevó a conocer el hielo.[c] Macondo era entonces una aldea[d] de veinte casas de barro y cañabrava[e] construidas a la orilla[f] de un río de aguas diáfanas que se precipitaban[g] por un lecho de piedras pulidas,[h] blancas y enormes como huevos prehistóricos. El mundo era tan reciente, que muchas cosas carecían de[i] nombre y había que señalarlas[j] con el dedo...»

[a]frente... in front of the firing squad   [b]había... would remember   [c]ice   [d]village   [e]de... of mud and reed   [f]a... on the banks
[g]se... rushed along   [h]lecho... bed of polished stones   [i]carecían... still didn't have   [j]había... it was necessary to point to them

Gabriel García Márquez, colombiano, Premio Nobel de Literatura, 1982; autor de *Cien años de soledad*.

Juan Luis Guerra: cantante dominicano

Este dominicano alto y calmado fue educado musicalmente en la tradición de su país y en la de los Estados Unidos. Pero también es amante[a] del flamenco y de la música africana, y ha estudiado la obra[b] de los grandes poetas de la lengua española, como Borges, Neruda, García Lorca y Vallejo.

En una época también le atraían[c] el rock y el jazz. Dice: «Nuestra sociedad... se apartaba de[d] la música folclórica. Se pensaba que lo nuestro no valía la pena[e]. Los cánones anglosajones eran los dominantes y por eso quise hacer rock. Pero luego me di cuenta de[f] que lo que tenía que hacer era tomar las cosas buenas del rock y transmitirlas a través del[g] merengue.»

Su último disco, Areíto, indaga en las raíces perdidas[h] de la población original de la isla, los tahínos, que fueron aniquilados[i] a la llegada de los españoles. «No quedó nada de ellos y menos de su música. Lo que yo hago es más un ejercicio de imaginación musical que una reconstrucción antropológica.»

Adaptado de *El País*.

[a]fan   [b]ha... he has studied the works   [c]le... he was attracted to   [d]se... was pulling away
from   [e]lo... ours [our music] wasn't worth anything   [f]me... I realized   [g]a... through   [h]indaga...
explores the lost roots   [i]annihilated

¡Qué interesante!

1. ¿Cuál es la situación actual política de estos cuatro países?
2. Imagine que Ud. trabaja en una galería de arte donde está esta pintura de Botero. Observe todos los detalles y luego describa la pintura, fijándose en (*noticing*) las formas, los colores y los temas.
3. Para hacer la presentación de Juan Luis Guerra en una emisora de radio de su universidad, haga una lista de las cosas más notables que puede decir de este cantante y de su país de origen.

«La familia presidencial»,* por Fernando Botero (Colombia). Botero es uno de los pintores y escultores americanos más famosos de este siglo.

*1967, oil on canvas, 80⅛" × 77¼" (204 × 196 cm)

17

Primer paso

Los Coches

Más vocabulario

los frenos	brakes	**chocar (con)**	to run into, collide (with)
la licencia (de manejar/ conducir)	(driver's) license	**doblar**	to turn (*a corner*)
		estacionar(se)	to park
una llanta desinflada	a flat tire	**gastar**	to use, expend
el parabrisas	windshield	**manejar, conducir (conduzco)**	to drive
arrancar	to start (*a motor*)		
arreglar	to fix, repair	**parar**	to stop
contener (*like* **tener**)	to contain, hold	**seguir (i, i) (todo derecho)**	to keep on going; to go (straight ahead)

Práctica

A Definiciones.

Paso 1. Busque Ud. la definición de las palabras de la columna de la derecha.

1. Se pone en el tanque.
2. Se llenan de aire.
3. Lubrica el motor.
4. Es necesaria para arrancar el motor.
5. Cuando se llega a una esquina hay que hacer esto o seguir todo derecho.
6. No contiene aire suficiente y por eso es necesario cambiarla.
7. Se usan para parar el coche.
8. Allí se revisan y se arreglan los carros.

a. los frenos
b. doblar
c. la batería
d. el taller
e. una llanta desinflada
f. la gasolina
g. las llantas
h. el aceite

Paso 2. Ahora, siguiendo el modelo de las definiciones anteriores, ¿puede Ud. dar una definición de las siguientes palabras?

1. el semáforo
2. la circulación
3. estacionarse
4. la licencia
5. la gasolinera
6. la autopista

B **En la gasolinera.** Describa Ud. las cosas y acciones que se ven en el dibujo.

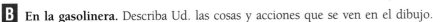

309

C **Entrevista: Un conductor responsable.**

Paso 1. Entreviste a un compañero / una compañera de clase para determinar con qué frecuencia hace las siguientes cosas.

1. dejar la licencia en casa cuando va a manejar
2. acelerar (*to speed up*) cuando ve a un policía
3. manejar después de beber alcohol
4. respetar o exceder el límite de velocidad
5. estacionar el coche donde dice «Prohibido estacionarse»
6. revisar el aceite y la batería
7. seguir todo derecho a toda velocidad cuando no sabe llegar a su destino
8. adelantar (*to pass*) tres carros a la vez (*at the same time*)

Paso 2. Ahora, con el mismo compañero, haga una lista de diez cosas que hace—o no hace—un conductor responsable. Pueden usar frases del Paso 1, si quieren.

DE AQUÍ Y DE ALLÁ

Languages often have several words to express one concept, especially when the concept is important to the society in which the language is spoken. It should come as no surprise that there are various ways to say *traffic* and *traffic jam* in Spanish.

la circulación, el tráfico, el tránsito	traffic
el atasco, el embotellamiento, el barullo (de tráfico)	traffic jam

The *pedestrian crosswalk* is **el cruce/paso para peatones.**

LOS SEMAFOROS
Son dispositivos de control para regular el tránsito automotor y permitir el paso seguro de los peatones.

ESTRUCTURAS ▼▼▼▼▼▼▼▼▼▼▼▼▼▼▼▼▼▼▼▼▼▼▼▼▼▼▼▼▼

RECICLADO

You have been using forms of the present subjunctive since **Capítulo 11** of *¿Qué tal?* Review what you know about them by completing the following sentences.

1. Quiero que tú... doblar aquí / recibir un servicio completo / seguir todo derecho / conducir con cuidado.
2. Es bueno que tu coche... no gastar mucha gasolina / siempre arrancar en invierno / ser económico / no tener serios problemas.

33. Expressing Uncertainty

Use of the Subjunctive: Doubt and Denial

▼ **Problemas de los peatones**

En este capítulo se habla mucho de conductores y de coches. Pero los peatones también tienen sus derechos (*rights*). Para empezar, ¿qué cree Ud. que significa este letrero?

Ahora que tiene idea de lo que significa ese letrero, puede interpretar el significado del letrero en el siguiente dibujo. Escoja el significado correcto.

- Prohibido cruzar esta calle entre las ocho y las trece o entre las quince y las diecinueve horas del día
- Prohibido atropellar (*to run over*) peatones durante esas horas

▲ ▲ ▲

Ahora conteste estas preguntas sobre el dibujo.

1. ¿Quién es el hombre? Es posible que sea... profesor / hombre de negocios (*business*).
2. ¿Dónde está? Es posible que esté... en un pueblo pequeño / en el centro de una gran ciudad.
3. ¿Por qué va a pie este hombre en vez de ir en coche? Es posible que... no tenga coche / no le guste conducir.
4. ¿Qué espera el hombre? Espera que sea... hora de regresar a casa / hora de cruzar la calle sin peligro.

INDEPENDENT CLAUSE		DEPENDENT CLAUSE
first subject + *indicative* (expression of doubt or denial)	**que**	second subject + *subjunctive*

No creo que **sean** estudiantes.	*I don't believe they're students.*
Es imposible que ella **esté** con él.	*It's impossible for her to be with him.*

A. Expressions of doubt and denial are those in which speakers express uncertainty or negation: *I doubt he's right. It's not possible for her to be here.* Such expressions, however strong or weak, are followed by the subjunctive in the dependent clause in Spanish.

B. Expressions of doubt and denial include **no creer, dudar** (*to doubt*), **no estar seguro/a,** and **negar (ie)** (*to deny*). Not all Spanish expressions of doubt are given here. Remember that any expression of doubt is followed by the subjunctive in the dependent clause.

Niego que **sea** simpático.	*I deny that he's nice.*
No creemos que el examen **sea** hoy.	*We don't believe that the exam is today.*

¡OJO! The expressions **creer, no dudar, estar seguro/a** and **no negar** are usually followed by the indicative.

C. When a new subject is introduced after a generalization of doubt, the subjunctive is used in the dependent clause. Some generalizations of doubt and denial are **es posible, es imposible, es probable, es improbable, no es verdad, no es cierto** (*certain*), and **no es seguro** (*a sure thing*).*

Práctica

A ¿Qué opina Ud.?

Paso 1. Lea las siguientes oraciones e indique lo que opina de cada uno.

	ES CIERTO.	NO ES CIERTO.
1. Todos los mecánicos **son** honrados.	☐	☐
2. Los coches siempre **arrancan** en invierno.	☐	☐
3. El semáforo siempre **está** en verde cuando yo tengo prisa.	☐	☐
4. **Salgo** muy guapo/a en la foto de mi licencia de conducir.	☐	☐
5. Siempre **están** haciendo reparaciones en las calles de esta ciudad.	☐	☐
6. **Hay** muchas llantas desinfladas cuando llueve.	☐	☐
7. Una gasolinera siempre **está** muy cerca cuando se me acaba la gasolina.	☐	☐

Paso 2. Ahora diga las oraciones del Paso 1, empezando con **Es cierto que...** o **No es cierto que...** según sus respuestas. **¡OJO!** Hay que usar el subjuntivo de los verbos indicados con **No es cierto que...**

B ¡El coche no funciona! Esta es una conversación que ocurrió ayer en el taller cuando Ud. llevó allí su «nuevo coche viejo». Haga oraciones según las indicaciones. Use el pretérito de los verbos indicados.

Habla Ud.

1. es verdad / que / (*yo*) sólo / pagar / mil / dólar / por / coche
2. es cierto / que / coche / funcionar / bien / al principio (*at first*)
3. ahora / dudo / que / carro / arrancar / otra vez
4. (*yo*) creer / que / ser / transmisión

Habla el mecánico.

5. es mejor / que / Ud. / dejarlo / aquí / hasta / mañana
6. (*yo*) no / estar / seguro / de que / (*yo*) poder / arreglarlo
7. (*yo*) creer / que / es probable / Ud. / tener / que / comprar / otro / coche
8. es posible / que / en / agencia / (*ellos*) darle / ciento / dólar / por / coche

¿Cierto, falso o no lo dice? Corrija las oraciones falsas.

1. Es verdad que Ud. tiene un coche nuevo.
2. Es seguro que Ud. tiene que comprar otro coche.
3. Ud. manejó el coche a casa ayer.

---

*Generalizations that express certainty are not followed by the subjunctive but by the indicative: *Es verdad* que *cocina* bien. *No hay duda* de que *Julio lo* paga.

SEÑALES REGLAMENTARIAS
Son aquellas que limitan, prohíben o restringen el uso de las vías, desobedecerlas constituye una infracción de tránsito.

SEÑALES PREVENTIVAS
Son aquellas que advierten sobre la existencia de un peligro, especificando su naturaleza.

SEÑALES INFORMATIVAS
Son aquellas que indican la proximidad de sitios necesarios para el usuario de la vía.

C **Un coche usado.** Ud. y su esposo/a (amigo/a) buscan «un nuevo coche viejo», es decir, un coche usado. Esto es lo que dicen en la agencia sobre este coche. ¿Qué creen Uds.?

¡UNA GANGA ESTUPENDA!
* Sólo $10.000
* En excelentes condiciones
* Batería nueva
* Sólo 40.000 millas
* Interior en buenas condiciones

Expresen sus reacciones empezando con estas frases.

1. ¡Es imposible que... !	**4.** Estoy seguro/a que...
2. No creo/creemos que...	**5.** Estamos seguros/as que...
3. Dudo/Dudamos que...	**6.** ¡No es posible que... !

D **Ud. y los coches.** Diga «Es cierto» si Ud. está de acuerdo con las siguientes oraciones. Corrija las oraciones «falsas» con frases como **No creo que...**, **No es cierto que...**, **No es verdad que...** y **Dudo que...** Si no tiene opinión, diga «No tengo opinión».

1. El coche más prestigioso hoy en los Estados Unidos es el Rolls Royce.
2. El mejor coche es el Honda, sin duda.
3. El coche más deportivo es el Miata.
4. El coche con más «personalidad» es el Volkswagen Bug.
5. El coche más práctico es el Jeep.
6. El coche más rápido es el Porsche.
7. El coche más bonito y elegante es el Jaguar.
8. Los coches japoneses son más económicos que los norteamericanos. ¡Y dan menos problemas!

¿Qué tipo de persona es el padre de Mafalda? ¿Y Miguelito? ¿Tienen los coches alguna importancia para él?

[a]*brag*

VOCABULARIO ▼▼▼▼▼▼▼▼▼▼▼▼▼▼▼▼▼▼▼▼▼▼▼▼▼

Putting Things in Rank Order: Ordinals

primer(o)	first	**séptimo**	seventh
segundo	second	**octavo**	eighth
tercer(o)	third	**noveno**	ninth
cuarto	fourth	**décimo**	tenth
quinto	fifth	**último**	last
sexto	sixth		

Ordinal numbers are adjectives and must agree in number and gender with the nouns they modify.* Ordinals usually precede the noun: **la cuarta lección, el octavo ejercicio.**

Like **bueno,** the ordinals **primero** and **tercero** shorten to **primer** and **tercer** before masculine singular nouns: **el primer niño, el tercer mes.**

Práctica

A **La Indi 500.** Imagine que este año todos los conductores de esta carrera (*race*) son hispánicos... ¡y que hay varias conductoras! ¿En qué lugar llegaron las siguientes personas?

1. Manuel Gutiérrez: 5°
2. Teresa Gómez: 3er
3. Eduardo Cabrera: 7°
4. Jesús Alonso: 1er
5. Pablo Valencia: 10°
6. Evangelina Ramírez: 2°

B **¿Cuáles son sus prioridades?** Ordene de primero a octavo los siguientes factores, según lo más o menos importante para Ud.

1. **En la selección de cursos:** la hora de la clase, el profesor / la profesora, la materia, la posibilidad de sacar una buena nota, el costo de los libros y otros materiales, si tiene laboratorio o no, el lugar donde se da la clase, el número de estudiantes en clase

---

*Ordinal numbers are frequently abbreviated with superscript letters that show the adjective ending: **las 1as lecciones, el 1er grado, el 5° estudiante, la 2ª lección.**

2. En la selección de un trabajo: el prestigio de la compañía, la posibilidad de un ascenso (*promotion*), la ciudad o el país donde esté el trabajo, el sueldo, la personalidad del jefe / de la jefa, las condiciones físicas del lugar de trabajo, si Ud. tiene una oficina privada o no, si el trabajo requiere viajar

▼▼▼▼▼▼▼▼▼▼▼▼▼▼▼▼▼▼▼▼▼▼▼▼  **ESTRUCTURAS**

34. Expressing Influence, Emotion, Doubt, and Denial

Uses of the Subjunctive: A Summary

▼ **En el taller**

CLIENTE: *Temo* que mi carro *tenga* algo serio. ¿Podría revisarlo, por favor?

EMPLEADO: Sí, señor. Entre por aquí y apague el motor, por favor.

CLIENTE: Esta mañana tuve dificultad en hacerlo arrancar.

EMPLEADO: Puede ser la batería.

CLIENTE: Pues... la verdad... *me sorprende* que *sea* la batería. Es nueva; la cambié hace dos semanas, ¿sabe?

EMPLEADO: En ese caso, le *recomiendo* que lo *deje* para poder revisarlo con cuidado.

CLIENTE: Está bien. También *quiero* que le *revise* las llantas delanteras y las bujías.

EMPLEADO: Sí, señor. Eso es parte de nuestro servicio normal.

CLIENTE: ¿Por cuánto tiempo debo dejar el carro aquí?

EMPLEADO: Lo puede venir a buscar en dos horas. *No creo* que *sea* nada que requiera más tiempo.

▲ ▲ ▲

1. ¿Qué teme el dueño del carro?
2. ¿Está de acuerdo el empleado del taller?
3. ¿Qué posibilidad sugiere el empleado?
4. ¿Cuál es la reacción del dueño?
5. ¿Qué recomienda el empleado?
6. ¿Cuánto tiempo se requiere para revisar el coche?

At the shop   CLIENT: I'm afraid there is something seriously wrong with my car. Could you take a look at it, please? EMPLOYEE: Yes, sir. Come in through here and shut off the motor, please. CLIENT: I had trouble getting it to start this morning. EMPLOYEE: It may be the battery. CLIENT: Well, the truth is . . . I'll be surprised if it is (*lit.* that it could be) the battery. It's new; I changed it two weeks ago, you know? EMPLOYEE: In that case, I recommend that you leave it to be checked out carefully. CLIENT: OK. I also want you to check the front tires and the spark plugs. EMPLOYEE: Yes, sir. That's part of our normal service. CLIENT: How long should I leave the car here? EMPLOYEE: You can come to get it in two hours. I don't think it will take any longer.

INDEPENDENT CLAUSE		DEPENDENT CLAUSE
first subject + *indicative*	**que**	second subject + *subjunctive*

expression of { influence / emotion / doubt, denial }

A. Remember that, in Spanish, the subjunctive occurs primarily in two-clause sentences with a different subject in each clause. If there is no change of subject, an infinitive follows the first verb. Compare the following.

Quiero } que **él revise** el carro.
Es necesario }

I want } him to check the car.
It's necessary for }

Quiero } **revisar** el carro.
Es necesario }

I want } to check the car.
It's necessary }

The independent clause, in addition to fulfilling the preceding condition, must contain an expression of influence, emotion, or doubt in order for the subjunctive to occur in the dependent clause. If there is no such expression, the indicative is used.* Compare the following.

Dicen que maneje Julio.
Dicen que Julio **maneja** muy mal; por eso quieren que maneje Carlota.

They say that Julio should drive.
They say that Julio drives very badly; that's why they want Carlota to drive.

Note that **decir** is an expression of influence in the first sentence (and is followed by the subjunctive in the dependent clause). However, in the second sentence, **decir** simply conveys information (and is followed by the indicative).

B. Some verbs of influence are frequently used with indirect object pronouns.

Nos dicen }
Nos piden } que vayamos.
Nos recomiendan }

They tell us to }
They ask us to } go.
They recommend that we }

The indirect object indicates the subject of the dependent clause, as in the preceding sentences: **nos** → **vayamos.**

C. All of the uses of the subjunctive that you have learned so far fall into the general category of the subjunctive in *noun clauses*. The clause in which the subjunctive appears functions like a noun in the sentence as a whole. That is, it is the subject or the direct object of the verb.

¿Qué quiere el dueño del coche? Quiere que el mecánico le arregle el carro.

Here, the dependent clause (**que el mecánico...**) is the direct object of the verb **quiere.**

¿Qué no les gusta a los clientes? No les gusta que los precios sean muy altos.

Here, the dependent clause (**que los precios...**) is the subject of the verb **gusta.**

---

*See Grammar Sections 22, 23, and 33 for a more detailed presentation of the uses of the subjunctive in noun clauses.

Práctica

A **Un coche: ¿Una compra esencial?** Si Ud. quiere comprar un coche para su uso personal, tiene que ir a una agencia de automóviles. Allí va a ver todos los nuevos modelos.

1. ¿Qué quiere Ud. que pase en la agencia? —Quiero que el vendedor...

   - enseñarme los últimos modelos
   - explicarme las opciones que tengo
   - decirme cuáles son las ventajas y las desventajas de cada modelo

2. Claro está que Ud. va a aprender mucho. ¿Qué es lo que le va a sorprender? —Me va a sorprender que...

   - costar tanto los coches hoy día
   - ser tan fáciles de manejar
   - haber tantos modelos distintos

3. Después de examinar muchos coches, es probable que Ud. por fin decida comprar uno. Si no puede pagar al contado (*in cash*), es posible que le hagan unas sugerencias en la agencia. —Es posible que el vendedor...

   - proponerme un plan para pagar a plazos (*in installments*)
   - pedirme mi tarjeta de crédito
   - decirme que espere hasta el mes que viene, pues va a haber unas rebajas

B **El mejor aparato doméstico.** Imagine que Ud. tiene en casa un robot de último modelo que va a hacer todo lo que Ud. le diga, especialmente las cosas que a Ud. no le gusta hacer. ¿Qué le va a mandar al robot que haga?

Le voy a decir que...
Le voy a pedir que...

lavarme los platos, hacerme las camas, mantener el carro en buenas condiciones, cambiarle el aceite al carro cada tres meses, escribirme todos los cheques, ¿ ?

C **En un taller.** Usando las siguientes frases como guía, invente oraciones para una conversación entre un mecánico y un cliente que tiene problemas con su coche.

Quiero que
Temo que
Recomiendo que
Me sorprende que
¿Cómo es posible que... ?

revisar _____
su _____ estar roto/a (*broken*)
no funcionar bien _____
poner un(a) _____ nuevo/a
arreglar _____
ir a costar _____
usar un(a) _____ reconstruido/a (*rebuilt*)
no hay _____ en _____
¿ ?

Bogotá, Colombia.

Un paso más

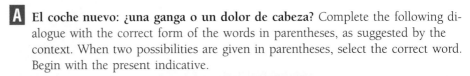

UN POCO DE TODO

A **El coche nuevo: ¿una ganga o un dolor de cabeza?** Complete the following dialogue with the correct form of the words in parentheses, as suggested by the context. When two possibilities are given in parentheses, select the correct word. Begin with the present indicative.

Margarita, (un/una[1]) joven de veinticinco años que (acabar[2]) (de/que[3]) comprarse un carro nuevo
Alberto, un amigo de Margarita (quien/que[4]) sabe (mucho/muchos[5]) de coches

Camino a[a] una fiesta en casa de unos amigos

A: (Al volante[b]) Margarita, perdona (que / lo que[6]) te interrumpa, pero a sólo 3 kilómetros de tu casa, no es posible que el termómetro (marcar[7]) una temperatura (tan/tanto[8]) alta en el motor. Ya (ser/estar[9]) en la zona roja.

M: No te (preocupar[10]); debe (que/—[11]) estar roto como el cuentakilómetros y (el/la[12]) reloj, que tampoco (funcionar[13]).

A: Pronto te vas a (quedas/quedar[14]) sin coche. Mira, en cosa de pocos minutos se (poder[15]) localizar (el/la[16]) problema. En (ese[17]) estación de servicio (haber[18]) un mecánico y un electricista. ¿Quieres que (yo: parar[19])?

M: ¡Ay, Alberto! Ahora no vamos a (un/una[20]) taller sino[c] a una fiesta. Conduce más (rápido[21]), por favor, o vamos a (llegamos/llegar[22]) tarde.

[a]Camino... *On the way to* [b]*wheel* [c]*but rather*

Ahora, con un compañero / una compañera, invente el resto de la conversación entre Margarita y Alberto.

B Las siguientes oraciones mencionan temas de vital importancia en el mundo de hoy. ¿Qué cree Ud.? Exprese sus reacciones a estas oraciones, empezando con una de estas expresiones.

Dudo que...   Es bueno/malo que...
(No) Es verdad que...   Es lástima que...
No hay duda que...   Es increíble que...
Es probable que...   (No) Me gusta que...

1. Los niños miran la televisión seis horas al día.
2. Hay mucha pobreza (*poverty*) en el mundo.
3. En los Estados Unidos gastamos mucha energía.
4. Hay mucho sexo y violencia en la televisión y en el cine.
5. Se come poco y mal en muchas partes del mundo.
6. Los temas de la música *rap* son demasiado violentos.
7. Hay mucho interés en la exploración del espacio.
8. No se permite el uso de la marihuana.

Indique Ud. soluciones para algunos de los problemas. Empiece las soluciones con estas frases.

Es urgente que...   Es necesario que...
Es preferible que...   Es importante que...
Quiero que...   Insisto en que...

SITUACIÓN   Dando y pidiendo direcciones

The following dialogue shows how to ask for and give directions. Try to guess the meaning of the words you don't know, then verify their meaning in **Notas comunicativas sobre el diálogo.**

TURISTA: Perdone. ¿Podría decirme dónde queda la Plaza de Armas?

POLICÍA: Cómo no. Doble en la primera calle a la derecha y siga todo derecho por esa calle hasta la Avenida Dos de Mayo. No puede perderse, porque es una avenida muy grande. Al llegar[a] allí doble a la izquierda y ya va a ver la Plaza al final de la avenida.

TURISTA: Bien. Una pregunta más, si no le importa. ¿Hay aparcamiento fácil allí?

POLICÍA: A esta hora, lo dudo. Es mejor que aparque por aquí y vaya caminando hasta la Plaza de Armas. Está muy cerca.

TURISTA: Muchísimas gracias.

POLICÍA: A su servicio.

[a]Al... *When you arrive*

NOTAS COMUNICATIVAS SOBRE EL DIÁLOGO

Here are some frequently used variations for some of the phrases that occur in the dialogue.

perdón, perdone = disculpe
¿Podría decirme... ? = ¿Puede decirme... ?
¿Dónde queda... ? = ¿Dónde está...?
doblar = girar
todo derecho = todo seguido, todo recto
el aparcamiento = el estacionamiento

¿POR O PARA?

In the preceding dialogue, note the use of **por** to express *along.* **Por** can also mean *through:* **Pase Ud. por ese pueblo.** Note also the idiomatic expression **por aquí/allí** (*around here/there*).

Conversación

Practique el diálogo con un compañero / una compañera. Después, seleccionen unos puntos de interés turístico en su ciudad y pidan y den direcciones para llegar allí. Uds. están en la universidad, claro, pero pueden imaginarse que están en otro sitio, como el centro.

PARA ESCRIBIR

En español hay un refrán que dice: «Mujer al volante, peligro constante» (*lit.* "Woman at the wheel, constant danger"). ¿Está Ud. de acuerdo? Escriba una breve composición para expresar y justificar su opinión.

Primer párrafo:	Evaluación general del refrán
Segundo párrafo:	Su opinión personal: **Yo (no) pienso que... , Yo dudo que...** etcétera
Tercer párrafo:	Defensa de su posición
Cuarto párrafo:	Una nueva versión del refrán, reafirmando o atacando sus implicaciones

NOTA CULTURAL: Variaciones lingüísticas

Las palabras que se usan para hablar de caminos y vehículos y de la acción de manejar varían en las diferentes partes del mundo de habla española. Aquí hay algunos ejemplos.

car = el coche, el auto, el automóvil (uso generalizado)
el carro (el Caribe, Centroamérica y los Estados Unidos)

¡OJO! el carro = *cart* en España

bus = el autobús (uso generalizado)
el bus (Hispanoamérica)
la guagua (Cuba, Puerto Rico)
el camión (México)

¡OJO! el camión = *truck* en la mayor parte del mundo de habla española

tire = la llanta (uso generalizado)
la rueda (España)

▼ ▼ ▼ ▼ ▼ ▼ ▼ ▼ ▼ ▼ ▼ ▼ ▼ ▼ ▼ VOCABULARIO ▼ ▼ ▼ ▼ ▼ ▼ ▼ ▼ ▼ ▼ ▼ ▼ ▼ ▼ ▼

Verbos

costar (ue) to cost
dudar to doubt
negar (ie) to deny

Hablando de coches

arrancar to start (a motor)
arreglar to fix, repair
contener (*like* **tener**) to contain, hold
gastar to use, expend
llenar to fill (up)
mantener (*like* **tener**) to maintain, keep up
revisar to check

Repaso: limpiar

el aceite oil
la batería battery
la estación de gasolina gas station
los frenos brakes
la gasolina gas
la gasolinera gas station

la llanta (desinflada) (flat) tire
el/la mecánico/a mechanic
el parabrisas windshield
el servicio service
el taller (repair) shop
el tanque tank

En el camino

conducir (conduzco) to drive
chocar (con) to run (into), collide (with)
doblar to turn
estacionar(se) to park
manejar to drive
parar to stop
seguir (i, i) to keep on going

la autopista freeway
la calle street
la carretera highway
la circulación traffic
el/la conductor(a) driver
la esquina corner
el letrero sign
la licencia license

el semáforo traffic signal
el tráfico traffic
la velocidad speed

Otros sustantivos

el peatón (la peatona) pedestrian

Los adjetivos ordinales

segundo/a, tercer(o/a), cuarto/a, quinto/a, sexto/a, séptimo/a, octavo/a, noveno/a, décimo/a

Repaso: **primer(o/a), último/a**

Palabras adicionales

no es cierto it's not certain
no es seguro it's not certain
por along; through
todo derecho straight ahead

Self-Test

Use the tape that accompanies this text to test yourself briefly on the important points of this chapter.

LECTURA
cultural

Antes de leer: Recognizing Derivative Adjectives

A large group of Spanish adjectives is derived from verbs. The adjectives end in **-ado** or **-ido**. You can often guess the meaning of these adjectives if you know the related verb. For example: **conocer** (*to know*) → **conocido** (*known, famous*); **preparar** (*to prepare*) → **preparado** (*prepared*). Can you guess the meaning of the following italicized adjectives based on verbs you already know?

1. unas ideas bien *explicadas*
2. una mujer *desconocida*
3. su libro *preferido*

In the following reading there are a number of **-do** adjectives. Try to guess their meaning from context. Knowing the meaning of these verbs will help you.

callar	*to silence*
lesionar	*to wound, hurt*
mojar	*to wet, dampen*
pavimentar	*to pave*
resbalar	*to slip*

Manual para el conductor

Las normas generales de seguridad, dictadas por el sentido común al conducir, son universales. Estos ejemplos son de un manual de conductores de Nicaragua.

Monterrey, México.

SIETE CONSEJOS PARA CONDUCIR BIEN

1. Saber, cuidar y mantener el vehículo en condiciones mecánicas seguras y excelentes: Lubricación, frenos, llantas, volante, luces y amortiguadores.[a]

2. Saber manipular el vehículo diestramente.

3. Conocer y usar las reglas y prácticas de conducir vehículos.

4. Saber usar correctamente sus ojos.

5. Saber conducir en toda clase de caminos, rectos, con curvas, pendiente, ascendente y descendente, secos, mojados, resbaladizos, con hojas mojadas, aceitosos.

6. Conocer los peligros y evitar el beber y conducir.

7. Sea un conductor que conduce a la defensiva; tenga buena actitud; asuma responsabilidad de conducir sin accidentes.

[a]*mufflers*

EL ACCIDENTE INEVITABLE

La gran mayoría de los accidentes que le ocurran a los vehículos de motor podrían llamarse colisiones-choques y los pocos restantes podrían considerarse más correctamente como accidentes. En este último grupo se incluyen los que realmente son accidentes por su naturaleza, los que son casi <u>inevitables</u>. En otras palabras, la inmensa mayoría de los choques son evitables, son innecesarios y reflejan errores o faltas de parte de los conductores afectados.

FALTA DE ATENCION AL CONDUCIR SU VEHICULO.

Invitando al enterrador

"Mira Juan, que bonita está aquella tumba"

EL CAMINO HACIA EL INFIERNO ESTA PAVIMENTADO CON FALTA DE ATENCION

BUSCANDO LA DIRECCION MIENTRAS SE GUIA EL AUTO

Los conductores están sujetos a sufrir muchas distracciones mientras guían. Ellos son responsables, sin embargo, de no permitir que estas distracciones les hagan apartar la atención y descuidar su obligación fundamental: guiar dentro de las normas de seguridad.

1. Hable poco cuando vaya guiando y no vuelva nunca la cabeza para hablar con un pasajero.

2. Cuando los reglamentos permitan fumar, tenga el mayor cuidado al <u>encender</u> un cigarrillo, especialmente si es de noche, porque ello puede producirle una ceguera momentánea.

3. Saliéndose de la carretera hacia el <u>hombrillo</u>, detenga el auto siempre que vaya a consultar los mapas o su libreta de direcciones.

Pasajeros en el asiento posterior. Los estudios sobre las causas de accidentes revelan claramente que los conductores que llevan pasajeros que saben manejar en el asiento posterior sufren más accidentes que los conductores que llevan pasajeros silenciosos. ¿Puede haber una razón mejor para que los conductores en el asiento posterior permanezcan callados? ¡No sólo es desagradable, es peligroso!

No levante caminantes. Levantar personas que van por las carreteras ha resultado en atracos y en otras experiencias desagradables para el conductor. Estos transeúntes tienen derecho a exigir también compensación si resultaren lesionados. Por esto es que muchas compañías advierten a los conductores de autos o camiones que "NO LEVANTEN CAMINANTES"

Comprensión

A De los «Siete consejos para conducir bien», ¿cuál trata de (*deals with*)... ?

_____ el alcohol
_____ el estado del vehículo
_____ la necesidad de ser un
      conductor responsable
_____ la vista (*vision*)

_____ el acto de manejar
_____ el conocimiento del
      reglamento de tránsito
_____ la condición del camino

B Según el manual, ¿cuál es la diferencia entre colisiones-choques y accidentes? Explique brevemente, en sus propias palabras, esta diferencia.

C Busque el equivalente español de las siguientes frases en inglés.

1. Don't pick up hitchhikers.
2. Don't turn your head.
3. backseat driver

4. temporary blindness
5. the shoulder (of the road)

Primer paso

¿La ciudad o el campo?

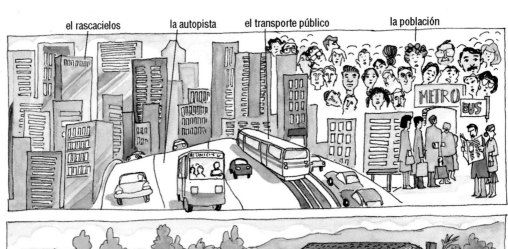

el rascacielos   la autopista   el transporte público   la población

el árbol

la flor

los campesinos   el rancho / la finca   montar a caballo

El Mundo de Hoy

Más vocabulario

Las siguientes palabras se relacionan con la vida en la ciudad o en el campo. ¿Con cuál las asocia Ud.?

bello/a	beautiful	**la naturaleza**	nature
denso/a	dense	**el ritmo acelerado de la vida**	fast pace of life
puro/a	pure	**los servicios públicos**	public service
la agricultura	agriculture	**la soledad**	solitude
el aislamiento	isolation	**la violencia**	violence
el delito	crime		

Práctica

A **¿El campo o la ciudad?** De las siguientes oraciones, ¿cuáles se asocian con el campo? ¿con la ciudad?

1. El aire es más puro y hay menos contaminación.
2. La naturaleza es más bella.
3. El ritmo de la vida es más acelerado.
4. Hay menos autopistas y menos tráfico.
5. Los delitos son más frecuentes.
6. Hay pocos medios de transporte público.
7. La población es menos densa.
8. Hay más árboles y más vegetación.

B **Definiciones.** Dé Ud. una definición de estas palabras.

MODELO: ranchero → Es el dueño de una finca (un rancho).

1. campo
2. campesino
3. delito
4. finca
5. naturaleza
6. población
7. soledad
8. rascacielos

C Ventajas y desventajas.

Paso 1. Pancho cree que la vida del campo es ideal. Gabriela, la amiga de Pancho, es una mujer muy cosmopolita. ¿Quién dijo las siguientes oraciones? ¿Qué desventaja puede citar la otra persona en cada caso?

1. No hay buenos servicios públicos.
2. Hay más actividades culturales—teatro, conciertos y museos.
3. Allí es posible vivir en paz y tranquilidad.
4. No me gusta levantarme temprano para empezar el trabajo del día.
5. Me encanta manejar en las autopistas de la ciudad por la noche.
6. Necesito vivir en contacto con la naturaleza.
7. Cuando la nieve cubre las calles, las ciudades están paralizadas.

Paso 2. Ahora adopte el punto de vista de Pancho o de Gabriela. ¿Qué va Ud. a decir sobre los siguientes temas?

1. el ritmo de la vida
2. la explotación de la tierra
3. la gente / los vecinos
4. los delitos

 **ESTRUCTURAS**

35. Más descripciones

Past Participle Used As an Adjective

▼ **Unos refranes y dichos en español**

1. En boca *cerrada* no entran moscas.

2. *Aburrido* como una ostra.

3. Cuando está *abierto* el cajón, el más *honrado* es ladrón.

▲ ▲ ▲

Empareje (*Match*) estas oraciones con el refrán o dicho que explican.

1. Es posible que una persona honrada caiga en la tentación de hacer algo malo si la oportunidad se le presenta.
2. Hay que ser prudente. A veces es mejor no decir nada para evitarse (*to avoid*) problemas.

A few Spanish proverbs and sayings 1. Into a closed mouth no flies enter. 2. As bored as an oyster.
3. When the (cash) drawer is open, the most honest person is (can become) a thief.

▼ 3. Las ostras ejemplifican el aburrimiento (*boredom*) porque llevan una vida
▼   tranquila... siempre igual.

Forms of the Past Participle

hablar	comer	vivir
habl**ado** (*spoken*)	com**ido** (*eaten*)	viv**ido** (*lived*)

The past participle of most English verbs ends in *-ed:* for example, *to walk →
walked; to close → closed.* Many English past participles, however, are irregular: *to
sing → sung; to write → written.*

   In Spanish the *past participle* (**el participio pasado**) is formed by adding **-ado** to
the stem of **-ar** verbs, and **-ido** to the stem of **-er** and **-ir** verbs. An accent mark is
used on the past participle of **-er/-ir** verbs with stems ending in **-a, -e,** or **-o.**

    caído   **creído**   **leído**   **oído**   **(son)reído**   **traído**

The following Spanish verbs have irregular past participles.

abrir:	**abierto**	morir:	**muerto**
cubrir (*to cover*):	**cubierto**	poner:	**puesto**
decir:	**dicho**	romper (*to break*):	**roto**
escribir:	**escrito**	ver:	**visto**
hacer:	**hecho**	volver:	**vuelto**

The Past Participle Used As an Adjective

In both English and Spanish, the past participle can be used as an adjective to
modify a noun. Like other Spanish adjectives, the past participle must agree in
number and gender with the noun modified.

Tengo una bolsa **hecha** en El Salvador.	*I have a purse made in El Salvador.*
El español es una de las lenguas **habladas** en los Estados Unidos.	*Spanish is one of the languages spoken in the United States.*

The past participle is frequently used as an adjective with **estar** to describe conditions that are the result of a previous action.

La puerta **está abierta.**	*The door is open.*
Todos los lápices **estaban rotos.**	*All the pencils were broken.*

¡OJO!   English past participles often have the same form as the past tense: *I **closed**
the book. The thief stood behind the **closed** door.* The Spanish past participle is never
identical in form or use to a past tense. Compare the following.

Cerré la puerta. Ahora la puerta está **cerrada.**	*I **closed** the door. Now the door is **closed.***

Práctica

A ¡Rápidamente! Dé Ud. el nombre de...

1. algo contaminado
2. una persona muy/poco organizada
3. un edificio bien/mal construido
4. un grupo humano explotado
5. algo que pueda estar cerrado o abierto
6. un servicio necesitado por (*by*) muchas personas
7. un tipo de transporte usado por muchas personas
8. algo deseado por muchas personas

¿POR O PARA?

In the preceding activity, note the use of **por** to express *by*.

B En este momento...

Paso 1. En este momento, ¿son ciertas o falsas las siguientes oraciones con relación a su sala de clase? ¡OJO! **colgar** = *to hang;* **enchufar** = *to plug in;* **prender** = *to turn on* (*lights or an appliance*).

1. La puerta está abierta.
2. Las luces están prendidas.
3. Las ventanas están cerradas.
4. Algunos libros están abiertos.
5. Los estudiantes están sentados.
6. Hay algo escrito en la pizarra.
7. Una silla está rota.
8. Hay carteles y anuncios colgados en la pared.
9. Un aparato está enchufado.

Paso 2. Ahora describa el estado de las siguientes cosas de su casa (cuarto, apartamento).

MODELO: Cuando estudio, las luces están prendidas.

Sugerencias: Cuando estudio / duermo / ceno / me relajo... Por la mañana/tarde/noche...

1. las luces
2. la cama
3. el televisor
4. las ventanas
5. la puerta
6. las cortinas (*curtains*)

C **Cosas sin hacer.** ¿Cuál es la situación del momento presente? Conteste, siguiendo el modelo.

MODELO: Natalia les tiene que **escribir** una carta a sus abuelos. →
La carta no está **escrita** todavía.

1. Los Sres. García deben **abrir** la tienda más temprano. ¡Ya son las nueve!
2. Pablo tiene que **cerrar** las ventanas; entra un aire frío.
3. Los niños siempre esperan que la tierra se **cubra** de nieve para la Navidad.
4. Delia debe **poner** la mesa. Los invitados llegan a las nueve y ya son las ocho y media.
5. La contaminación va a contribuir a la **contaminación** del medio ambiente (*environment*).

D **Comentarios sobre el mundo de hoy.** Complete el siguiente párrafo con los participios pasados de los verbos apropiados de la lista.

La conservación de la energía: acostumbrar, agotar (*to use up*), apagar (*to turn off*), bajar, cerrar, limitar

Las fuentes[a] de energía no están _____[1] todavía. Pero estas fuentes son _____.[2] Desgraciadamente, todavía no estamos _____[3] a conservar energía diariamente. ¿Qué podemos hacer? Cuando nos servimos la comida, la puerta del refrigerador debe estar _____[4] Cuando miramos la televisión, algunas luces de la casa deben estar _____.[5] El termómetro debe estar _____[6] cuando nos acostamos.

[a]*sources*

Consuma electricidad como si quedara poca.

Queda poca.
Es increíble. Dá la sensación de que el interruptor es una fuente inagotable de energía, ¿no es verdad?

No es verdad. Porque las fuentes de producción de energía eléctrica son limitadas. Bien es cierto que estamos aún muy lejos de un agotamiento, de una insuficiencia eléctrica. Pero prevenir es curar. Y prevenir es fácil en este caso.

Segundo paso

▼ **VOCABULARIO**

El medio ambiente[a]

[a]*medio... environment*

la capa de ozono	ozone layer
la contaminación (del aire)	(air) pollution
la energía	energy
la escasez	lack, shortage
la fábrica	factory
la falta	lack, absence
el gobierno	government
los recursos naturales	natural resources
acabar	to run out, use up completely
conservar	to save, conserve
construir*	to build
contaminar	to pollute
desarrollar	to develop
destruir*	to destroy
proteger (protejo)	to protect

NO CONTAMINES A NUESTRA COSTA

*Note the present indicative conjugation of **construir**: construyo, construyes, construye, construimos, construís, construyen. **Destruir** is conjugated like **construir**.

Práctica

A **¿Le afecta a Ud.?** Indique si los siguientes problemas del mundo de hoy tienen importancia en la vida de Ud. o no.

	SÍ	NO
1. la contaminación del aire	☐	☐
2. la destrucción de la capa de ozono	☐	☐
3. la escasez de energía	☐	☐
4. la desforestación del Amazonas	☐	☐
5. la falta de casas para todos	☐	☐
6. el abuso de los recursos naturales	☐	☐

B **Opiniones.** ¿Está Ud. de acuerdo con las ideas siguientes? Defienda sus opiniones.

1. Para conservar energía debemos bajar el termostato en invierno y usar menos el aire acondicionador en verano.

2. Es mejor calentar la casa con una estufa de leña (*wood stove*) que con gas o electricidad.

3. Debemos proteger nuestras «zonas verdes» y crear (*create*) más parques públicos para las futuras generaciones.

4. Es más importante explotar los recursos naturales que proteger el medio ambiente.

5. Para gastar menos gasolina, debemos tomar el autobús, caminar más y viajar con otras personas en el coche para ir al trabajo.

6. No debemos importar petróleo de otros países a menos que (*unless*) se acaben nuestras propias reservas.

7. El gobierno debe poner multas muy fuertes a las compañías y a los individuos que contaminen el aire.

C **¿Qué piensa Ud. de la tecnología?** Express your opinions about this topic by completing the following sentences in a logical manner, selecting topics from the right-hand column and adding appropriate information. Then ask other students how they responded (**¿Qué esperas de... ?** etc.) until you find some who share your hopes and/or uncertainties.

MODELO: Espero que la tecnolgía ayude a resolver el problema del hambre mundial. Y tú, ¿qué esperas de la tecnología?

1. Espero que _____.
2. Estoy seguro/a de que _____.
3. Dudo que _____.
4. Me alegro de que _____.
5. Tengo miedo de que _____.
6. Creo que _____.

las computadoras
el progreso científico
la tecnología
la energía nuclear
la escasez de energía
la comunicación instantánea
los robots
¿ ?

DE AQUÍ Y DE ALLÁ

The vocabulary of ecology changes quickly and is often closely related to English terms. Can you guess the meaning of the following words and phrases?

los verdes
la comida natural
las especies protegidas

el efecto invernadero
el parque natural

ESTRUCTURAS

36. ¿Qué has hecho?

Perfect Forms: Present Perfect Indicative and Present Perfect Subjunctive

▼ **¿Cambio de ritmo?**

RAFAEL: Como tú sabes, Aurelia, yo siempre *he vivido* en grandes ciudades. Siempre *he usado* el carro para todo. Nunca *he tenido* tiempo de apreciar la naturaleza. ¡Y nunca *he madrugado* con regularidad! Por eso me extraña tanto la vida que Uds. llevan aquí.

AURELIA: Pues... como yo siempre *he vivido* en una finca, no *he conocido* otro estilo de vida. Nunca *he estado* en esos rascacielos en que tú siempre *has trabajado*. Y nunca *he conocido* la vida cultural de que me hablas tanto. Por eso no la echo de menos.

▲ ▲ ▲

A change of pace? RAFAEL: As you know, Aurelia, I've always lived in big cities. I've always used the car for everything. I've never had time to appreciate nature. And I've never gotten up at dawn on a regular basis! That's why the life you people lead here is so strange to me. AURELIA: Well . . . since I've always lived on a ranch, I've never know another lifestyle. I've never been in those skyscrapers where you have always worked. And I've never known the cultural life that you talk about so much. That's why I don't miss it.

▼ Exprese las opiniones de Rafael y Aurelia, completando las siguientes oraciones.

▼
   RAFAEL: 1. Siento que Aurelia siempre haya... (vivir en una finca)
▼
            2. Es raro que no haya... (conocer otro estilo de vida)
▼
            3. Me parece increíble que nunca haya... (trabajar en un rascacielos)
▼ AURELIA: 1. Es extraño que Rafael siempre haya... (vivir en ciudades grandes)
▼
            2. Es imposible que siempre haya... (usar el coche para todo)
▼
            3. No creo que haya... (madrugar con regularidad)

Present Perfect Indicative

Even though **haber** is the equivalent of English *to have* in these verb forms, **haber** does not express English *to have* in any other context and is not interchangeable with **tener.**

he hablado	*I have spoken*	**hemos** hablado	*we have spoken*
has hablado	*you have spoken*	**habéis** hablado	*you (pl.) have spoken*
ha hablado	*you have spoken, he/ she has spoken*	**han** hablado	*you (pl.)/they have spoken*

Look for the past participle used as an adjective in this cartoon and for the past participle that is part of a present perfect form.

In English, the *present perfect* is a compound tense consisting of the present tense form of the verb *to have* plus the past participle: *I have written, you have spoken,* and so on. In Spanish, the present perfect (**el presente prefecto**) is formed with the present tense forms of **haber** plus the past participle. In general, the use of the Spanish present perfect parallels that of the English present perfect.

No **hemos estado** aquí antes.	*We haven't been here before.*
Me **he divertido** mucho.	*I've had a very good time.*

The form of the past participle never changes when it is used with **haber,** regardless of the gender or number of the subject. The past participle always appears immediately after the appropriate form of **haber** and is never separated from it. Object pronouns and **no** are always placed directly before the form of **haber.**

The present perfect form of **hay** is **ha habido** (*there has/have been*).

¡OJO! Remember that **acabar** + **de** + *infinitive*—not the present perfect tense—is used to state that something *has just* occurred.

Acabo de mandar la carta.	*I've just mailed the letter.*

[Práctica A–C]

[a]¡Todas... *All my courses passed in Bs and As!*   [b]¡He... *I have failed as a child!*

Present Perfect Subjunctive

haya hablado	**hayamos** hablado
hayas hablado	**hayáis** hablado
haya hablado	**hayan** hablado

The *present perfect subjunctive* (**el perfecto del subjuntivo**) is formed with the present subjunctive of **haber** plus the past participle. It is used to express *I have spoken* (*written,* and so on) when the subjunctive is required.

Es posible que lo **haya hecho.**	*It's possible (that) he may have done (he did) it.*
Me alegro de que **hayas venido.**	*I'm glad (that) you have come (you came).*
Es bueno que lo **hayan construido.**	*It's good that they built (have built) it.*

Note that the English equivalent of the present perfect subjunctive can be expressed as a simple or as a compound tense: *did / have done; came / have come; built / have built.*

[Práctica D]

Práctica

A **El pasado y el futuro.**

Paso 1. Indique las actividades que Ud. ha hecho en el pasado.

1. _____ He hecho un viaje a Europa.
2. _____ He montado a camello (*camel*).
3. _____ He tomado una clase de informática.
4. _____ He buceado (*gone scuba diving*).
5. _____ He ido de safari a África.
6. _____ He comprado un coche.
7. _____ He preparado una comida italiana.
8. _____ He ocupado un puesto (*position*) político.
9. _____ He tenido una mascota.
10. _____ He escrito un poema.

Paso 2. Ahora, entre las cosas que Ud. no ha hecho, ¿cuáles le gustaría hacer? Conteste, siguiendo los modelos.

MODELOS: Nunca he montado a camello, pero me gustaría hacerlo.
Nunca he montado a camello y no me interesa hacerlo.

B **Un aparato nuevo.** Aurelia y Rafael han comprado una nueva computadora. Describa lo que les ha pasado, según el modelo.

MODELO: comprar una nueva computadora →
Han comprado una nueva computadora.

1. llevarla a casa
2. enchufarla
3. limpiar la pantalla (*screen*)
4. leer el manual de instrucciones
5. llamar a un amigo
6. pedirle ayuda al amigo
7. volver a su escritorio
8. escribir sus cartas a mano... ¡pero sólo por hoy!

C **Entrevista.** Con un compañero / una compañera, haga y conteste preguntas con estos verbos. La persona que contesta debe decir la verdad.

MODELO: visitar México →
—¿Has visitado México?
—Sí, he visitado México una vez.
(No, no he visitado México nunca.)
(Sí, he visitado México durante las últimas vacaciones.)

1. comer en un restaurante hispánico
2. estar en Nueva York
3. manejar un Alfa Romeo
4. correr en un maratón
5. escribir un poema
6. actuar en una obra teatral
7. conocer a una persona famosa
8. romperse la pierna alguna vez

D **¡No lo creo!** ¿Tienen espíritu aventurero sus compañeros de clase? ¿Llevan una vida interesante?¿O están tan aburridos como una ostra? ¡A ver!

Paso 1. De cada par de oraciones, indique la que (*the one that*) expresa la opinión de Ud. acerca de los estudiantes de esta clase.

1. ☐ Creo que alguien en esta clase ha visto las pirámides de Egipto.
   ☐ Es dudoso que alguien haya visto las pirámides de Egipto.
2. ☐ Estoy seguro/a que por lo menos uno de mis compañeros ha escalado (*climbed*) una montaña alta.
   ☐ No creo que nadie haya escalado una montaña alta.
3. ☐ Creo que alguien ha viajado haciendo *autostop* (*hitchhiking*).
   ☐ Dudo que alguien haya hecho *autostop* en un viaje.
4. ☐ Creo que alguien ha practicado el paracaidismo (*skydiving*).
   ☐ Es improbable que alguien haya practicado el paracaidismo.
5. ☐ Estoy seguro/a de que alguien ha tomado el metro en Nueva York a medianoche (*midnight*).
   ☐ No creo que nadie haya tomado el metro neoyorquino a medianoche.

Paso 2. Ahora escuche mientras el profesor / la profesora pregunta si alguien ha hecho estas actividades. ¿Tenía Ud. razón en el Paso 1?

Un paso más

UN POCO DE TODO

A **Dos dibujos, un punto de vista.** Un español hizo el dibujo de la izquierda, un argentino, el de abajo. Pero los dos comentan el mismo tema.

Palabras útiles: el arado (*plow*), la deshumanización, la gente, la mecanización, la mula, el tractor

Paso 1. Conteste estas preguntas sobre el dibujo a la izquierda.

1. Describa la ciudad que se ve en el dibujo.
2. ¿Qué ha descubierto la gente? ¿Por qué mira con tanto interés?
3. Para construir esta ciudad, ¿qué han hecho? ¿Qué han destruido?

Paso 2. Conteste estas preguntas sobre el otro dibujo.

1. ¿Qué se ha comprado el agricultor a la izquierda? ¿Qué ha vendido?'
2. ¿Qué es «más moderno», según el otro agricultor?
3. ¿Qué desventaja tiene el tractor?

Paso 3. Ahora explique su reacción personal a estos dos dibujos. ¿Le gusta este tipo de humor o le parece muy serio?

B **«El Yunque».** Complete the following paragraphs about a forest (**un bosque**) in Puerto Rico with the correct form of the words in parentheses, as suggested by the context. When two possibilities are given in parentheses, select the correct word. Use the preterite or the imperfect of the verbs in italics.

El Bosque Nacional del Caribe es (conocer[1]) local-mente como «El Yunque». (Ser/Estar[2]) situado a 25 millas al este de San Juan, Puerto Rico. Originalmente (*ser*[3]) segregado[a] en 1876 por el rey de España. Por esa razón (ser/estar[4]) una de las reservas más antiguas del hemisferio occidental. Cuando Puerto Rico (*pasar*[5]) a manos de los Estados Unidos en 1898, (*haber*[6]) 12.400 cuerdas[b] en la reserva. En 1903 el Presidente Theodore Roosevelt las (*declarar*[7]) la Reserva Forestal de Luquillo. Ahora su nombre legal (ser/estar[8]) Bosque Nacional del Caribe.

La alta precipitación, con un promedio[c] de 140 pulgadas[d] anuales de lluvia, y su clima tropical durante todo el año (haber[9]) producido un bosque denso y siempre verde que (contener[10]) 225 especies de árboles y plantas. La vida silvestre que se (encontrar[11]) en el bosque consiste en muchas especies de pájaros, lagartos, ranas, murciélagos[e] y de (alguno[12]) peces. También hay dos especies, la Cotorra[f] Puertorriqueña y la Boa Puertorriqueña, (amenazar[13]) y (considerar[14]) en peligro de extinción por leyes federales.

Aunque (ser/estar[15]) pequeño en comparación con otros bosques nacionales, la importancia de este Bosque Nacional del Caribe (ser/estar[16]) más grande de lo que su tamaño[g] pueda sugerir. Constituye el área forestal más extensa en Puerto Rico y es el único bosque tropical en (el/la[17]) Sistema de Bosques Nacionales.

[a]*set aside* [b]*measure of land* [c]*average* [d]*inches* [e]*lagartos... lizards, frogs, bats* [f]*Parrot* [g]*size*

El Yunque, Puerto Rico.

¿Cierto o falso?

1. El Yunque es una reserva relativamente moderna.
2. Es una de las reservas forestales más grandes del Sistema de Bosques Nacionales.
3. Hay pocos animales en El Yunque.

☼ SITUACIÓN   Reciclar es cosa de todos

—Hombre, ¡no tires el periódico en ese cesto[a]

—¡Pero si ya lo he leído!

—Sí, pero aquí lo reciclamos todo. El papel de oficina aquí, y los periódicos aquí. En la cocina están los cestos para los objetos de plástico, vidrio y aluminio.

—No sabía que podíamos reciclar todas estas cosas. Me parece una idea estupenda. No te preocupes; no vuelvo a tirar un periódico en la basura.

[a]*wastebasket*

Conversación

Después de practicar el diálogo con un compañero o una compañera, hagan otros de acuerdo con las siguientes circunstancias. ¿Cómo sería la conversación entre uno de los «ecologistas» y una de las siguientes personas?

1. Una persona está bebiendo café en un vaso de plástico.
2. Una persona siempre deja las luces de la casa encendidas.
3. Alguien siempre deja los grifos (*faucets*) abiertos mientras se cepilla los dientes.

☼ PARA ESCRIBIR

Lea los siguientes anuncios de una revista «ecologista». Estas personas buscan trabajo y vivienda (*housing*) relacionados con sus intereses ecológicos.

TENGO MUCHAS GANAS DE TRABAJAR, ya sea en el campo o en alguna casa o restaurante vegetariano. Tengo nociones sobre cocina y sé algo de francés. Mari Ripollés. c/. San Fernando, 12. Oliva (Valencia).

DESEARÍA TRABAJAR en un restaurante vegetariano (preferible en Barcelona o Valencia). No tengo ninguna experiencia, razón por la cual quiero aprender. Merçè Vallès Figueres. Pza. de la Estación, 6. Santa Bárbara (Tarragona). Tel. (977) 41 81 19.

NECESITO LUGAR con buena agua y buen aire para vivir con mi hija de 5 años. Haría cualquier trabajo campestre, artesanal, doméstico, docente, musical, administrativo o sanitario. Tengo carnet de conducir. M.ª Luz Gil. Sta. Otilia, 28. 08032 Barcelona. Tel. 358 03 99.

DESEO CONTACTO CON PERSONAS que quieran vivir en el campo. Tengo casa y tierra. Damián Carrasco. Lista de Correos. Mogón (Jaén).

LLEVAMOS 6 AÑOS VIVIENDO en el campo. Poseemos cabras, colmenas y huerta. Venden cerca de nosotros, en Guadalupe (Cáceres), 110 ha. de monte y algo de llano con mucha agua. Nos podríamos asociar y crear una cooperativa de quesos. José Luis Martín Martín. Navatrasierra (Cáceres).

DESEO CONOCER MÁS DE CERCA España, el país, su vida y su gente, por lo cual me interesaría poder trabajar en el campo durante un tiempo a fin de profundizar mis impresiones. Tengo 22 años, experiencia en el manejo de caballos y en trabajos de cestería. Renate Ginhold. Schyrenstr. 10, 8000 Munchen. Rep. Fed. de Alemania.

SOMOS UN MATRIMONIO con cuatro hijos de 8 a 13 años. Nos ofrecemos para llevar granja y huerta en Catalunya o trabajar como cocineros en una casa de colonias (durante todo el año). Tenemos experiencia como granjeros. Ignacio Vilaseca. c/. San Pedro, 13, Artés (Barcelona). Tel. 873 57 58 (dejar recado).

SÓC MESTRA I VEGETARIANA, vull treballar en qualsevol cosa. Angela Buj i Alfara. c/. Campanar, 2. Alcanar. Montsià; Tel. (977) 73 09 10 (dilluns).

ME GUSTARÍA TRABAJAR con gente sana y sincera en alguna granja-escuela en el extranjero, preferiblemente en Inglaterra y a ser posible después del verano. No tengo experiencia. Jesús María Sarries Napal. c/. Maruguete, 9. Navascues (Navarra).

¿Qué le interesa a Ud.? Imagínese que Ud. busca trabajo y un lugar para vivir también. Escriba un breve anuncio, como los de la revista. Ofrézcase para trabajar en un puesto (*job*) específico y para vivir en algún tipo de lugar. (Ud. no tiene que expresar un punto de vista «ecologista» ... a menos que [*unless*] lo tenga.)

NOTA CULTURAL: Las otras lenguas de España

You have probably noticed that, among the preceding ads, there is one that is not in Spanish. It's written in **catalán,** one of three other languages spoken in Spain. **El catalán** is spoken primarily in the region of Spain called **Cataluña.** The other two languages are **el gallego,** spoken in the region of **Galicia,** and **el vascuence** (Basque—also called **el vasco**), spoken in the region known as **el País Vasco** (or **la Vascongada**).

Spanish, Catalan, and Galician are all romance languages, that is, languages that evolved from Latin. But Basque, called **euskera** in the Basque language, is not, which makes it unique . . . and very difficult! No one knows exactly when or from which language Basque was originally derived.

▼▼▼▼▼▼▼▼▼▼▼▼▼▼ VOCABULARIO ▼▼▼▼▼▼▼▼▼▼▼▼▼▼

Verbos

colgar (ue) to hang
cubrir to cover
encender (ie) to turn on (*lights or an appliance*)
enchufar to plug in

¿La ciudad o el campo?

la agricultura agriculture
el aislamiento isolation
el árbol tree
el/la campesino/a peasant, farm worker
el delito crime
la finca farm
la naturaleza nature
la población population
el rancho ranch
el rascacielos skyscraper
el ritmo acelerado de la vida fast pace of life
los servicios públicos public services

la soledad solitude
el transporte público public transportation
la violencia violence

montar a caballo to ride horseback

Repaso: **la autopista, la flor**

El medio ambiente

la capa de ozono ozone layer
la contaminación (del aire) (air) pollution
la energía energy
la escasez (*pl.* **escaseces**) lack, shortage
la fábrica factory
la falta lack, absence
el gobierno government
los recursos naturales natural resources

conservar to save, conserve
construir to build
contaminar to pollute
desarrollar to develop

destruir to destroy
proteger (protejo) to protect

Repaso: **acabar**

Adjetivos

bello/a beautiful
denso/a dense
puro/a pure

Palabras adicionales

por by

Self-Test

Use the tape that accompanies this text to test yourself briefly on the important points of this chapter.

VOCES

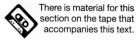
There is material for this section on the tape that accompanies this text.

del mundo hispánico 9
La región andina: el Ecuador, el Perú, Bolivia y Chile

La cordillera de los Andes cruza el continente sudamericano de norte a sur, desde Venezuela hasta Chile. Es el sistema de montañas más largo del mundo (6.400 km.) Entre más de 50 montañas de más de 6.000 metros de altura destaca[a] el pico Aconcagua (7.000 metros).

Cuatro países andinos, el Ecuador, el Perú, Bolivia y Chile, también tienen en común el hecho de haber sido parte del territorio del Imperio inca.

Antes de la llegada de los españoles, había diversos pueblos indígenas por toda la zona de los países andinos: los araucanos (en Chile); los naszca, los chimú, los tiahuanaquenses y los aymarás (desde el Ecuador hasta la Argentina). Estos pueblos fueron dominados por los quechuas, formando lo que hoy llamamos el Imperio inca. Inca era el título del gobernante supremo de los quechuas, que tenían una sociedad teocrática y politeísta. Eran excelentes arquitectos y su conocimiento de las matemáticas y la astronomía era muy alto. Sin embargo, no conocían el uso industrial de la rueda[b] ni tenían animales de carga.[c]

Los españoles, dirigidos[d] por Pizarro en 1532, encontraron débil resistencia cuando intentaron conquistar el Imperio inca. Cuando llegó la expedición de Pizarro, el imperio estaba dividido por luchas de sucesión entre los hermanos Atahualpa y Huáscar. Este enfrentamiento interno facilitó la caída del imperio en manos de los españoles.

De estos cuatro países andinos, Chile es el que disfruta[e] actualmente del más alto nivel de vida y mejor situación política. Su presidente, Eduardo Frei, fue elegido[f] democráti-

Una niña quechua, El Cuzco, Perú.

camente en 1994. La situación es menos favorable en el Perú, donde el presidente Fujimori, elegido democráticamente en 1990, dio un «autogolpe» de estado en 1992 y gobierna ahora de manera dictatorial. El Ecuador depende de su industria petrolera y tiene un pasado político inestable. Finalmente, Bolivia, en donde el 60% de la población es indígena y el 30% es mestiza, vive un período democrático desde 1982, totalmente dominado por la minoría blanca.

[a]*stands out* [b]*wheel* [c]*animales... beasts of burden* [d]*led* [e]*enjoys* [f]*elected*

Una tortuga de las islas Galápagos. Las islas pertenecen al Ecuador, y sirvieron a Darwin para desarrollar sus teorías de la evolución.

Simón Bolívar (Caracas, 1783–1830).

El libertador de Sudamérica

Conocido en América Latina como el Libertador, Bolívar es el George Washington de Latinoamérica. Consiguió la independencia de cinco países andinos: Colombia, el Ecuador, el Perú, Bolivia y Chile. Su sueño[a] fue crear una gran federación de estados latinoamericanos, similar a la de los Estados Unidos en Norteamérica. Sólo pudo lograr[b] la unión de Colombia, Venezuela, el Ecuador y Panamá, constituyendo así la República de la Gran Colombia, que duró nueve años (1821–1830). Bolívar murió desilusionado por el separatismo de los países que él soñó[c] unir.

[a]*dream* [b]*achieve* [c]*dreamed of*

Meciendo[a]

El mar sus millares de olas[b]
mece,[c] divino.
Oyendo a los mares amantes,[d]
mezo a mi niño.

El viento errabundo[e] en la noche
mece los trigos.[f]
Oyendo a los vientos amantes,
mezo a mi niño.

Dios Padre sus miles de mundos
mece sin ruido.
Sintiendo su mano en la sombra[g]
mezo a mi niño.

[a]*Rocking* [b]*millares... thousands of waves* [c]*(the sea) rocks* [d]*loving* [e]*wandering* [f]*wheat* [g]*shadow*

Gabriela Mistral, poeta chilena (1889–1957), fue la primera persona hispanoamericana que recibió el Premio Nobel de Literatura, en 1945. (*Ternura*, 1924).

Machu Picchu.

¡Qué interesante!

1. Mire un mapa de Sudamérica y fíjese en el tipo de geografía y clima de los países andinos. ¿Qué otros tipos de clima y geografía tienen estos países? ¿Se puede hablar de homogeneidad geográfica en esta región?
2. En los países hispánicos sólo se usa el sistema métrico decimal para medir (*measure*). Por eso la longitud (*length*) y la altura de los Andes está en metros y kilómetros. ¿Cuál es la equivalencia de esas medidas en pies y millas?
3. Gabriela Mistral escribió poemas para madres y niños. ¿En qué momento del día podríamos recitarle este poema a un niño? Explique por qué.

1 metro = 3,1 pies aproximadamente / 1,09 yardas
1 kilómetro = 0,6 milla

19

Primer paso

Las relaciones sentimentales

la amistad

la cita

la cita

el amor

el noviazgo

la luna de miel

el matrimonio

la boda

el divorcio

Las relaciones Humanas

Más vocabulario

el/la amigo/a	friend
el/la esposo/a	husband/wife
el/la novio/a	boyfriend/girlfriend; fiancé(e); groom/bride
la pareja	(married) couple; partner
amistoso/a	friendly
cariñoso/a	affectionate
casado/a	married
celoso/a	jealous
soltero/a	single, not married

casarse (con)	to marry
divorciarse (de)	to get divorced (from)
enamorarse (de)	to fall in love (with)
llevarse bien/mal (con)	to get along well/badly (with)
pasar tiempo (con)	to spend time (with)
querer (ie)	to love
salir (con)	to go out (with)
separarse	to separate

You may wish to review the additional vocabulary you have already learned for expressing family relationships. The vocabulary in **Capítulo 4** and especially in **De aquí y de allá** in that chapter will be useful to you.

Práctica

A **Definiciones.** Empareje (*Match*) las palabras con sus definiciones. Luego, para cada palabra definida, dé un verbo y también el nombre de una persona asociada con esa relación social. Hay más de una respuesta posible en cada caso.

1. el matrimonio
2. el amor
3. el divorcio
4. la boda
5. la amistad

a. Es una relación cariñosa entre dos personas. Se llevan bien y se hablan con frecuencia.

b. Es el posible resultado de un matrimonio, cuando los esposos no se llevan bien.

c. Es una relación sentimental, apasionada, muy especial entre dos personas. Puede llevar al (*lead to*) matrimonio.

d. Es una ceremonia religiosa o civil en la que la novia a veces lleva un vestido blanco.

e. Es una relación legal entre dos personas que viven juntas y que a veces tienen hijos.

B ¡**Seamos lógicos!** Complete las oraciones lógicamente.

1. Mi abuelo es el _____ de mi abuela.
2. Muchos novios tienen un largo _____ antes de la boda.
3. María y Julio tienen _____ el viernes para comer en un restaurante. Luego van a bailar.
4. La _____ de Juan y Marta es el domingo a las dos de la tarde, en la iglesia (*church*) de San Martín.
5. En una _____, ¿quién debe pagar o comprar los boletos, el hombre o la mujer?
6. La _____ entre los ex esposos es imposible. No pueden ser amigos.
7. ¡El _____ es ciego (*blind*)!
8. Para algunas personas, _____ es un concepto anticuado. Prefieren vivir juntos, sin casarse.
9. Algunas parejas modernas no quieren gastar su dinero en _____.
10. Algunas personas creen que es posible _____ a primera vista.

¿POR QUE SE CASARIAN LOS CHICOS?

1.° Por amor.
2.° Para formar una familia.
3.° Para compartir su vida con la chica a la que aman.
4.° Para no quedarse solo de viejo.
5.° Para entregarse totalmente a ella.
6.° Para legalizar su situación.
7.° Porque no halla otra solución.
8.° Por educación.
9.° Por imposiciones familiares.
10.° Por dinero o similar.

¿POR QUE SE CASARIAN LAS CHICAS?

1.° Por amor.
2.° Por compartir su vida con el chico al que aman.
3.° Porque es una forma de demostrar su amor.
4.° Por legalizar la relación.
5.° Para tener a alguien en quien depositar toda su confianza.
6.° Para formar una familia.
7.° Por tradición.
8.° Por causas morales, éticas y religiosas.
9.° Por imposición de los padres.
10.° Por dinero o similar.

DE AQUÍ Y DE ALLÁ

Hispanics use a number of affectionate terms to refer to loved ones, and there are many regional differences. People from Spain do not use as many terms of affection as Spanish speakers from other areas of the world. In contrast, people from Mexico and the Caribbean use these expressions frequently, even with people who are just good friends. **Mi amor** and **mi hijo/a** (**m'hijo/a**) are examples of terms of affection that are often used with friends.

The following expressions are commonly used among boyfriends and girlfriends, spouses, or parents and children.

mi vida   mi cielo (*heaven*)
(mi) corazón   mi amor, amorcito/a
negrito/a (Cuba)

The term **viejo/a** is often used to refer to one's spouse, and children sometimes use it to refer to their parents.

▼▼▼▼▼▼▼▼▼▼▼▼▼▼▼▼▼▼▼▼▼▼▼▼▼ **ESTRUCTURAS**

37. Expressing *Each Other*

Reciprocal Actions with Reflexive Pronouns

▼ 1. ¿Dónde se encuentran los dos pulpos?
▼ 2. ¿Cómo se saludan (*do they greet each other*)?
▼ 3. ¿Se conocen? ¿Cómo se sabe?

The plural reflexive pronouns, **nos, os,** and **se,** can be
used to express *reciprocal actions* (**las acciones recíprocas**).
Reciprocal actions are usually expressed in English with
each other or *one another.*

—¿Tú crees que cada vez que
nos encontramos tenemos que
saludarnos dándonos la mano?

Nos queremos.	*We love each other.*
¿**Os** ayudáis?	*Do you help one another?*
Se miran.	*They're looking at each other.*

Nos queremos.

Se miran.

Práctica

A **Buenos amigos.** Indique las cinco oraciones que describen lo que hacen Ud. y
un buen amigo / una buena amiga para mantener su amistad.

1. Nos vemos con frecuencia. ☐
2. Nos conocemos muy bien. No hay secretos entre nosotros. ☐
3. Nos respetamos mucho. ☐
4. Nos ayudamos con cualquier (*any*) problema. ☐
5. Nos escribimos cuando no estamos en la misma ciudad. ☐
6. Nos hablamos por teléfono con frecuencia. ☐
7. Nos decimos la verdad siempre, sea esta (*be it*) bonita o fea. ☐
8. Cuando estamos muy ocupados, no importa que no nos hablemos ☐
   por algún tiempo.

B **La triste historia de amor de Orlando y Patricia.** Descríbala, usando el pretérito de los siguientes verbos.

1. verse en clase
2. mirarse
3. saludarse
4. hablarse mucho
5. empezar a llamarse por teléfono
   constantemente
6. darse regalos
7. escribirse durante las vacaciones
8. ayudarse con sus problemas
9. casarse
10. no llevarse bien
11. ella: quejarse de él
12. él: quejarse de la familia de ella
13. separarse
14. divorciarse

C **Relaciones familiares o sociales.** Describa las siguientes relaciones haciendo oraciones completas con una palabra o frase de cada columna.

los buenos amigos	(no) verse (con frecuencia, en clase, en...)
los parientes	quererse, tratarse con cariño, respetarse
los esposos	necesitarse, tolerarse, perdonarse
los padres y los hijos	abrazarse (*to hug*), besarse (*to kiss*)
los amigos que no viven en la misma ciudad	llamarse por teléfono, escribirse
los profesores y los estudiantes	ayudarse (con...)
los compañeros de cuarto/casa	mirarse (con cariño)

Segundo paso

VOCABULARIO ▼▼▼▼▼▼▼▼▼▼▼▼▼▼▼▼▼▼▼▼▼▼▼▼▼

¿Dónde vive Ud.? ¿Dónde quiere vivir?

Creamos ciudades dentro de las ciudades:
metrópolis
Otra ciudad dentro de la ciudad

alquilar	to rent	**las afueras**	outskirts; suburbs
el alquiler	rent		
la dirección	address	**el barrio**	neighborhood
el/la dueño/a	owner; landlord, landlady	**el *campus***	university campus
		el centro	downtown
el gas	gas; heat	**la casa**	house; home
el/la inquilino/a	tenant, renter	**la casa de**	apartment house;
la luz	light; electricity	**apartamentos**	highrise building
el/la portero/a	building manager; doorman		
el/la vecino/a	neighbor	**el cuarto**	room
la vista	view	**la residencia**	dorm

In English the phrases *ground floor* and *first floor* are sometimes used interchangeably. In Spanish, however, there are separate expressions for these concepts. **La planta baja** means the *ground floor*. **El primer piso** (literally, *the first floor*) refers to to the floor *above* the ground floor. **El segundo piso** (literally, *the second floor*) refers to what American English calls the *third floor,* and so on.

Práctica

A **¿Qué prefiere Ud.?** Indique su preferencia en cada caso. ¿Coincide lo que Ud. prefiere con la realidad?

1. ¿vivir en una residencia, en una casa o en una casa de apartamentos?
2. ¿vivir en el *campus,* cerca del *campus,* o en el centro o en las afueras de la ciudad? ¿o tal vez en el campo?
3. ¿alquilar un cuarto / una casa / un apartamento o ser el dueño / la dueña?
4. ¿pagar el gas y la luz aparte o pagar un alquiler más alto con el gas y la luz incluidos?
5. ¿vivir en la planta baja o en un piso más alto?
6. ¿tener un apartamento pequeño en un barrio elegante o un apartamento grande en un barrio de la clase media?
7. ¿tener un apartamento con vista aunque pague un alquiler muy alto, o un apartamento sin vista pero pagar un alquiler bajo?
8. ¿tener amistad con sus vecinos o mantenerse a distancia?

B Definiciones.

MODELO: la piscina → Allí nadamos. (Se nada en una piscina.)

1. el inquilino	3. el alquiler	5. el vecino	7. la criada
2. el centro	4. el portero	6. el dueño	8. las afueras

▼▼▼▼▼▼▼▼▼▼▼▼▼▼▼▼▼▼▼▼▼▼▼▼ **ESTRUCTURAS**

38. ¿Hay alguien que... ? ¿Hay un lugar donde... ?

Subjunctive After Nonexistent and Indefinite Antecedents

▼ **En la plaza central**

Describa lo que pasa y lo que **no** ocurre en esta escena de la plaza principal de un pueblo mexicano.

- *Hay personas que* conversan *con los amigos, que* se ven *aquí siempre, que* pasan *aquí sus ratos libres todos los días, que...* (jugar al ajedrez, vender/comprar periódicos/comida, tomar el sol, ¿ ?)
- *Hay niños que* toman *helados, que...* (jugar al fútbol, dar un paseo con sus padres, ¿ ?)
- *No hay nadie que* lleve *ropa de invierno, que* pasee *en bicicleta, que...* (ser aficionado al golf, ser de los Estados Unidos, escuchar la radio, ¿ ?)

In English and Spanish, statements or questions that give or ask for information about a person, place, or thing often contain two clauses.

> I have a **car** that gets good mileage.
> Is there a **house for sale** that is closer to the city?

Each of the preceding sentences contains a main clause (*I have a car . . . ; Is there a house for sale . . .*). In addition, each sentence also has a dependent clause (*. . . that gets good mileage; . . . that is closer to the city?*) that modifies a noun in the main clause: *car, house.* The noun (or pronoun) modified is called the *antecedent* (**el antecedente**) of the dependent clause, and the clause itself is called an adjective clause, since—like an adjective—it modifies a noun (or pronoun).

Sometimes the antecedent of an adjective clause can be something that, in the speaker's mind, does not exist or whose existence is indefinite or uncertain:

NONEXISTENT ANTECEDENT:	There is *nothing* that you can do.
INDEFINITE ANTECEDENT:	We need *a car* that will last us for years. (We don't have one yet.)

In these cases, the subjunctive must be used in the adjective (dependent) clause in Spanish.

EXISTENT ANTECEDENT:	**Hay algo** aquí que me **interesa.**	*There is something here that interests me.*
NONEXISTENT ANTECEDENT:	**No veo nada** que me **interese.**	*I don't see anyting that interests me.*
DEFINITE ANTECEDENT:	**Hay muchos restaurantes** donde **sirven** comida mexicana auténtica.	*There are a lot of restaurants where they serve authentic Mexican food.*
INDEFINITE ANTECEDENT:	**Buscamos un restaurante** donde **sirvan** comida salvadoreña auténtica.	*We're looking for a restaurant where they serve authentic Salvadoran food.*

Note in the preceding examples that adjective clauses of this type can be introduced with **donde...** rather than **que...**

¡OJO!   The dependent adjective clause structure is often used in questions to find out information about someone or something the speaker does not know much about. Note, however, that the indicative is used to answer the question if the antecedent is known to the person who answers.

INDEFINITE ANTECEDENT:	**¿Hay algo** aquí que te **guste?**	*Is there anything here that you like?*
DEFINITE ANTECEDENT:	Sí, **hay varias bolsas** que me **gustan.**	*Yes, there are several purses that I like.*

¡OJO!   The personal **a** is not used with direct object nouns that refer to hypothetical persons.* Compare the use of the indicative and the subjunctive in the following sentences.

NONEXISTENT ANTECEDENT:	Busco **un señor** que lo **sepa.**	*I'm looking for a man who knows that (it).*
EXISTENT ANTECEDENT:	Busco **al señor** que lo **sabe.**	*I'm looking for the man who knows that (it).*

Estos señores tienen una hija que va a la escuela. Sin embargo (*Nevertheless*), ¿hay algo que les preocupe? (Les preocupa que...)

---

*Remember that **alguien** and **nadie** always take the personal **a** when they are used as direct objects: **Busco a alguien que lo sepa. No veo a nadie que sea norteamericano.**

Práctica

A **Hablando de la familia.** En su familia, ¿hay personas que tengan las siguientes características? Indique la oración apropiada en cada par de oraciones.

TENGO UN PARIENTE...	NO TENGO NINGÚN PARIENTE...
1. ☐ que habla español	☐ que hable español
2. ☐ que vive en el extranjero	☐ que viva en el extranjero
3. ☐ que es dueño de un restaurante	☐ que sea dueño de un restaurante
4. ☐ que sabe tocar el piano	☐ que sepa tocar el piano
5. ☐ que es médico/a	☐ que sea médico/a
6. ☐ que fuma	☐ que fume
7. ☐ que trabaja en la televisión	☐ que trabaje en la televisión
8. ☐ que colecciona monedas (*coins*)	☐ que coleccione monedas
9. ☐ ¿ ?	☐ ¿ ?

B **Las preguntas de Carmen.** Carmen acaba de llegar aquí de otro estado. Quiere saber algunas cosas sobre la universidad y la ciudad. Haga las preguntas de Carmen según el modelo.

MODELO: restaurantes / sirven comida latinoamericana →
         ¿Hay restaurantes que sirv**an** (donde sirv**an**) comida latinoamericana?

1. librerías / venden libros usados
2. tiendas / se puede comprar revistas de Latinoamérica
3. cafés cerca de la universidad / se reúnen muchos estudiantes
4. parques / la gente corre o da paseos
5. cines / pasan (*they show*) películas en español
6. un gimnasio en la universidad / se juega al ráquetbol
7. apartamentos cerca de la universidad / son buenos y baratos
8. museos / hacen exposiciones de arte latinoamericano

Según las preguntas que le ha hecho Carmen, ¿son ciertas o falsas las siguientes declaraciones?

1. A Carmen no le interesa la cultura hispánica.
2. Carmen es deportista.
3. Es posible que sea estudiante.
4. Este año piensa vivir con unos amigos de sus padres.

Ahora conteste las preguntas de Carmen con información verdadera sobre la ciudad donde Ud. vive y su universidad. **¡OJO!** Use el indicativo si los lugares existen en su ciudad.

C **Una encuesta.** Las habilidades o características de un grupo de personas pueden ser sorprendentes. ¿Qué sabe Ud. de los compañeros de su clase de español? Por turno, pregunte a la clase quién sabe hacer lo siguiente o a quién le ocurre lo siguiente. Luego la persona que hizo la pregunta debe hacer un comentario apropiado. Siga el modelo. No olvide inventar su propia pregunta en el número 8.

MODELO: hablar chino →
         En esta clase, ¿hay alguien que hable chino? (Nadie levanta la mano.)
         No hay nadie que hable chino.

1. hablar ruso
2. saber tocar la viola
3. conocer a un actor / una actriz
4. saber preparar comida vietnamita
5. tener el cumpleaños hoy
6. escribir poemas
7. vivir en las afueras
8. ¿ ?

Un paso más

UN POCO DE TODO

A **Buscando un nuevo apartamento.** Complete the following paragraphs with the correct form of the words in parentheses, as suggested by the context. When two possibilities are given in parentheses, select the correct word.

(Este[1]) semana mi compañero de casa y yo (ir[2]) a buscar un nuevo lugar para (vivir[3]). Ya (ser/estar[4]) cansados de vivir en el apartamento que (tener[5]) ahora. Primero, el (alquiler/inquilino[6]) es muy alto, y la dueña quiere que (*nosotros: pagar*[7]) más dinero (este[8]) año. Segundo, nuestro apartamento (ser/estar[9]) en la planta (bajo[10]), en (uno[11]) calle con mucho tráfico. Hay (tan/tanto[12]) ruido que no podemos (dormimos/dormir[13]). Y además, están los vecinos de la (primero[14]) planta. ¡Ay, (ese[15]) horribles vecinos! Ellos hacen mucho ruido por la noche antes de (acostarse[16]), cuando nosotros necesitamos estudiar. El (portero/inquilino[17]) habló con ellos, pero las cosas no cambian.

(Ser/Estar[18]) decididos. ¡(Se/Nos[19]) vamos! Queremos un apartamento que (tener[20]) buena vista y que (estar[21]) en un lugar (tranquilo[22]). No importa que no (esté/está[23]) en el centro: en (esta/esa/aquella[24]) ciudad hay (bueno[25]) transportes urbanos. Y si el apartamento está en las afueras, (*nosotros: ser/estar*[26]) seguros que el (alquiler/gas[27]) va a ser más barato (que/de[28]) aquí en el centro.

¡Y si además tenemos buenos vecinos, (ese/eso[29]) será[a] el apartamento perfecto!

[a]*will be*

¿Cuáles son las razones por las que (*for which*) el narrador va a buscar otro apartamento?

1. Primero,...
2. Después, tiene el problema de que... y por eso...
3. Finalmente están...
4. Vivir en las afueras no es un problema porque...
5. En resumen, el narrador y su compañero necesitan un apartamento que...

B **Experiencias sentimentales.** En esta actividad, Ud. va a describir algunas citas románticas (o algunas amistades) que Ud. ha tenido y también va a expresar sus preferencias personales. ¿Ha salido Ud. alguna vez con una persona cómica? ¿o con una persona nerviosa? ¿o tal vez con una persona ultra elegante? ¿Busca Ud. un novio / una novia que sea súper cultivado/a? ¿que le guste la música clásica?

Paso 1. Haga oraciones sobre los siguientes tipos de personas, si puede. (No tiene que hacer oraciones sobre todos los tipos.) Explique lo que la persona hizo, usando principalmente el pretérito.

MODELO: una persona cómica →
Una vez salí con una persona que contó chistes toda la noche. En el restaurante imitó al camarero. Nos hizo reír a todos. (*He/She made everyone laugh.*)

1. una persona cómica
2. una persona nerviosa
3. una persona súper elegante
4. una persona torpe

5. un empollón / una empollona (*bookworm*)
6. una persona maleducada (*impolite*)
7. ¿ ?

Paso 2. Ahora Ud. tiene la oportunidad de expresar sus preferencias. Complete las siguientes oraciones.

MODELO: Me atrae una persona que **sea atlética y que tenga buen sentido del humor.**

1. Me atrae una persona que _____.
2. Pero no me atrae una persona que _____.

SITUACIÓN   Cita para el fin de semana

ESTELA: ¡Por fin es viernes! ¡Qué alegría![a]

ALFONSO: ¿Qué vas a hacer este fin de semana?

ESTELA: El sábado Luisa y yo vamos a la playa, pero regresamos temprano. Ven con nosotras, si quieres.

ALFONSO: Gracias, pero no puedo. Hace tiempo que tengo ganas de ir a la playa, pero tengo varias cosas que hacer mañana. Tal vez otro fin de semana.

ESTELA: ¿Por qué no cenas con nosotras por lo menos? Tenemos mesa en el restaurante La Olla. ¿Sabes dónde está?

ALFONSO: Sí, y es una gran idea. ¿A qué hora?

ESTELA: Entre las siete menos cuarto y las siete. La mesa está reservada en mi nombre.

ALFONSO: Muy bien y... muchas gracias por insistir. Hasta mañana, ¿eh?

[a] ¡Qué... *Great!*

Madrid, España.

NOTAS COMUNICATIVAS SOBRE EL DIÁLOGO

Here are some additional useful phrases for extending and accepting or rejecting invitations. You should be able to recognize the meaning of all of them.

¿Estás libre { esta tarde / hoy?
para + (*infinitivo*)?

Ven a + (*infinitivo*) con nosotros.

Claro. Perfecto.

Lo siento, pero...
Es una lástima, pero...

Es imposible porque...
tengo (que)...
ya tengo planes
estoy invitado/a a (comer en casa de un amigo, salir con unos amigos,...)

Conversación

With your instructor, use the preceding phrases—or variations on them—to accept or decline an invitation that he or she will extend to you. Then, with another student, create a dialogue illustrating one or more of the following situations.

1. Una persona quiere ir al cine (tomar un café), pero la otra declina la invitación.
2. Dos personas que no se conocen están en un museo, mirando una pintura muy famosa. Él quiere hablar con ella y ella con él. Uno de ellos inicia la conversación y luego invita a la otra persona a tomar café.
3. Un joven de catorce años invita a una chica de trece años a una fiesta. Los dos están muy nerviosos.
4. Dos personas van a una fiesta. Tienen que arreglar todos los detalles: ¿a qué hora van, qué ropa van a llevar, cómo van, etcétera?

PARA ESCRIBIR

Escriba una pequeña composición sobre su mejor amigo/a, su novio/a o su esposo/a. En el primer párrafo cuente cómo se conocieron y llegaron a ser (*became*) amigos o novios. En el segundo párrafo explique cómo es esa persona y todo lo que él/ella significa en su vida.

¿Qué opina Ud. de los resultados de esta encuesta, que se realizó en Puerto Rico?

LAS PRIMERAS CINCO PRIORIDADES DEL HOMBRE

Mantener una buena relación familiar 27.60%

Vivir con tranquilidad 20.54%

Ser respetado 16.43%

Conseguir el éxito profesional 16.43%

Ser amado 15.92%

Otras 3.08%

LO QUE MAS ADMIRAN EN LA MUJER

La honestidad y la inteligencia corren parejas como las dos cualidades que los hombres admiran más en las mujeres con 31.60% ambos renglones, para un total de 63.20%. La autosuficiencia es la tercera característica que más le interesa a ellos con 20.07%. Un 16.73% de los encuestados prefirió otras características como la belleza y la laboriosidad.

NOTA CULTURAL: Los apellidos hispánicos

En español, generalmente, las personas tienen dos apellidos: el apellido paterno y también el materno. Cuando un individuo usa solamente uno de sus apellidos, casi siempre es el paterno.

Imagine que Ud. tiene una amiga, Gloria Gómez Pereda. El **nombre** de esta persona es «Gloria» y sus **apellidos** son «Gómez» y «Pereda». «Gómez» es el apellido paterno y «Pereda» es el materno. En situaciones oficiales o formales, ella usa los dos apellidos. En ocasiones informales, usa solamente el paterno. Cuando uno habla con ella, la llama «Señorita Gómez» o «Señorita Gómez Pereda», pero nunca «Señorita Pereda».

Ahora imagine que su amiga Gloria va a casarse con un señor que se llama Eduardo Cabrera Meléndez. El nombre de casada de Gloria será[a] Gloria Gómez de Cabrera, pues ella va a usar su apellido paterno (Gómez) y el apellido paterno de su esposo (Cabrera). En ocasiones formales Gloria será «la señora Gómez de Cabrera» o «la señora de Cabrera», pero nunca «la señora Gómez».

[a]*will be*

Madrid, España.

VOCABULARIO

Verbos

saludarse to greet each other

Las relaciones sentimentales

casarse (con) to marry
divorciarse (de) to get divorced (from)
enamorarse (de) to fall in love (with)
llevarse bien/mal (con) to get along well/badly (with)
pasar tiempo (con) to spend time (with)
querer (ie) to love
separarse to separate

Repaso: **salir (con)**

la amistad friendship
el amor love
la boda wedding
el cariño affection
el divorcio divorce

la luna de miel honeymoon
el matrimonio marriage
el noviazgo engagement
la pareja married couple; partner

Repaso: el/la amigo/a, la cita, el/la esposo/a, el/la novio/a

¿Dónde vive Ud.? ¿Dónde quiere vivir?

alquilar to rent

las afueras outskirts; suburbs
el alquiler rent
el barrio neighborhood
el *campus* university campus
la casa de apartamentos apartment house
la dirección address
el/la dueño/a owner; landlord, landlady
el/la inquilino/a tenant, renter
el piso floor

la planta baja ground floor
el/la portero/a building manager; doorman
la vista view

Repaso: la casa, el centro, el cuarto, el gas, la luz, la residencia, el/la vecino/a

Adjetivos

amistoso/a friendly
cariñoso/a affectionate
celoso/a jealous

Repaso: **casado/a, soltero/a**

Self-Test

Use the tape that accompanies this text to test yourself briefly on the important points of this chapter.

LECTURA cultural

Una de las relaciones sociales presentadas en este capítulo es la amistad. Antes de leer el artículo de esta sección, escriba tres adjetivos que describen qué clase de amigo/a es Ud.

1. _____ 2. _____ 3. _____

Según el artículo que Ud. va a leer, cada signo del zodíaco tiene su propia personalidad con respecto a la amistad. ¿Qué opina Ud.? ¿Existe una relación entre el horóscopo y la amistad? Lea el artículo y luego decida.

El horóscopo

ARIES En este momento los planetas favorecen tu salud y tu actitud es positiva. Aunque tienes un temperamento impulsivo, ahora posees la disciplina para trabajar de forma ordenada, haciendo cada cosa a su debido tiempo. En la amistad eres el general del zodíaco. Tus amistades saben que siempre que les suceda algo malo tú estarás ahí para ofrecer consuelo y ayuda.

TAURO Aprovecha este tiempo para disfrutar los frutos de tu propia cosecha. Es el momento de apreciar el resultado exitoso de todos los esfuerzos de los últimos meses. Descansa un poco, organiza una cena o una fiesta y prepárate para la próxima etapa. En la amistad eres fiel y das cariño, pero también quieres poseer. Aunque tengas pocas amistades, las que tienes son profundas y duraderas.

GÉMINIS Este otoño vas a pasar horas hojeando revistas de hogar y diseño, imaginando cómo se vería tu casa con una nuevee cocina o cambiando el comedor. Es el momento perfecto para hacer todo tipo de renovaciones en tu casa. Cambia los colores de las paredes, compra cuadros o simplemente pon flores por todas partes. Te sientes bien haciendo cualquier cosa relacionada con tu hogar. Tus amistades te dicen que eres muy difícil de conocer, pero que vale la pena intentarlo.

CÁNCER Pensaste que la mentira que dijiste a tu pareja o socio el mes pasado era una broma inocente. Pero esas palabras van a meterte en un verdadero lío[a] a principios de octubre. Lo mejor es confesar tu error y tratar de comenzar de nuevo. Eres propenso a la timidez, por eso te resulta difícil hacer nuevas amistades. Pero una vez que tienes confianza en una persona, das mucho cariño a tus amigos.

LEO Sientes una gran pereza; sólo te apetece ver la televisión o leer en la cama. Por el momento, descansar no te va a venir mal. Pero no pierdas la oportunidad y la suerte que las estrellas te brindan durante este otoño. Juega a la lotería o vete a una fiesta donde haya gente nueva que puedas conocer. Puedes ganar mucho más de lo que tú te imaginas. En la amistad a veces te comportas de forma un poco egoísta, pero siempre eres fiel y todos te quieren y te aprecian.

VIRGO En esta época de tu cumpleaños te esperan muchas actividades, nuevas personas e invitaciones inesperadas. Además, en octubre puedes recibir un golpe de fortuna. Por ahora no te preocupes por buscar una pareja, todo el mundo estará buscándote a ti. Reconoces la importancia de las amistades, por eso te dedicas a cuidar tu jardín de amigos como si fueran orquídeas. Nunca te olvidas de las fechas de cumpleaños de tus amigos.

LIBRA Presta atención a todo lo que hagas a principios de octubre. Aunque estés pensando en planes e ideas puedes darte un tropezón.[b] El símbolo de tu signo es el balance, pero en este momento no te sientes equilibrado. Lo mejor que puedes hacer es mirar bien en todas las direcciones antes de tomar una decisión. Tus amigos

[a]*mess*

[b]darte... *stumble, trip*

siempre te buscan para recibir un consejo, porque tienes la capacidad de ver y analizar todos los aspectos de un problema.

ESCORPIÓN Si estabas esperando el momento perfecto para lanzar un proyecto nuevo o para presentar una idea a tu jefe, hazlo ahora. Realmente, el sol brilla para ti; cualquier cosa que hagas en el ámbito público va a resultar exitosa hasta finales de septiembre. Eres una gran amistad, y tus amigos saben que siempre pueden depender de ti. Pero te resulta difícil dejarlos entrar en tu vida privada.

SAGITARIO No debes preocuparte por los asuntos financieros, pero al mismo tiempo debes cuidar tus pequeños ahorros. No prestes tu dinero ni tus posesiones porque alguien puede aprovecharse de tu generosidad. Para ti la amistad es tan natural como respirar. Atraes

muchos amigos por tu optimismo y alegría. Pero lo que ellos te achacan es tu costumbre de decir siempre la verdad, lo cual a veces puede resultar hiriente.[c]

CAPRICORNIO Este otoño tu camino se hace un poco menos duro. Se acaban las lluvias de las indecisiones y llega el sol. En este momento sabes muy bien lo que eres y lo que tienes que hacer, y nadie te puede confundir. Así que tus metas[d] están más claras. Te vas a encontrar con un nuevo círculo de amigos o un nuevo trabajo. Tienes la capacidad de atraer amigos para toda la vida. La amistad para ti es una cosa muy seria y quieres que tus amigos piensen lo mismo de ti.

ACUARIO En estos meses empieza una etapa nueva en tu vida, como una especie de renacimiento. Vas a limpiar tu vida de todas las cosas, perso-

nas y emociones que no te sirven. Este proceso es difícil, y a veces doloroso, pero cuando termines te vas a sentir mejor que nunca. Tienes muchos amigos, pero te resulta difícil transformar la amistad en intimidad. Casi siempre tu pareja es tu mejor amigo.

PISCIS Siempre estás ayudando a tus amigos y amantes. Y en varias ocasiones te has preguntado, ¿dónde está la persona que me va a cuidar a mí? Es verdad que hay pocas personas en el mundo capaces de querer con la intensidad y entrega con que tú lo haces. Pero este otoño las estrellas indican que vas a encontrar a esta persona tan esperada. Y si ya la conoces, tu relación va a ponerse tan al rojo vivo que ni siquiera las estrellas son capaces de predecir lo que va a pasar.

[c]*stinging*   [d]*objetivos*

Comprensión

A Indique a qué signo se refiere cada oración.

1. La persona nacida (*born*) bajo este signo es capaz de dar consejos para resolver problemas.
   a. Acuario   **b.** Géminis   **c.** Libra

2. La persona nacida bajo este signo es impulsiva, pero siempre ayuda a sus amistades.
   a. Sagitario   **b.** Aries   **c.** Tauro

3. La persona nacida bajo este signo es bastante tímida pero muy cariñosa con sus amigos.
   a. Leo   **b.** Cáncer   **c.** Acuario

4. La persona nacida bajo este signo a veces es egoísta, pero es un amigo fiel y muy apreciado.
   a. Géminis   **b.** Piscis   **c.** Leo

5. La persona nacida bajo este signo siempre ayuda a sus amigos, pero al mismo tiempo prefiere mantenerse a distancia.
   a. Capricornio   **b.** Escorpión   **c.** Tauro

B ¿Cuál es su signo? Como amigo/a, ¿cuáles son los adjetivos que lo/la describen a Ud. en el artículo?

Primer paso

En el banco

la ventanilla

BANCO NACIONAL

el cajero

la cajera

depositar

el talonario de cheques

sacar

la cuenta corriente

VISA
9094 60770 2224

la tarjeta de crédito

la cuenta de ahorros

la libreta de ahorros

El DINERO

Más vocabulario

el alquiler	rent	**devolver (ue)**	to return (*something*)
la cuenta/factura	bill	**disminuir (disminuyo)**	to decrease
el presupuesto	budget	**economizar**	to economize
		gastar	to spend (*money*)
ahorrar	to save (*money*)	**pagar a plazos / en**	to pay in installments /
aumentar	to increase	**efectivo / con cheque**	in cash / by check
cargar (a la cuenta de	to charge (to someone's	**prestar**	to lend
uno)	account)	**quejarse (de)**	to complain (about)
cobrar	to cash (*a check*); to		
	charge (*someone for an*		
	item or service)		

Práctica

A **Diálogos.** Empareje (*Match*) las preguntas de la izquierda con las respuestas de la derecha. ¿Dónde están las personas? ¿Quiénes son?

1. ¿Cómo prefiere Ud. pagar?
2. ¿Hay algún problema?
3. Me da su pasaporte, por favor. Necesito verlo para que pueda cobrar su cheque.
4. ¿Quisiera usar su tarjeta de crédito?
5. ¿Va a depositar este cheque en su cuenta corriente o en su cuenta de ahorros?
6. ¿Adónde quiere Ud. que mandemos la factura?

a. En la cuenta de ahorros, por favor.
b. Me la manda a la oficina, por favor.
c. No, prefiero pagar al contado.
d. Sí, señorita, Ud. me cobró demasiado por el jarabe.
e. Aquí lo tiene Ud. Me lo va a devolver pronto, ¿verdad?
f. Cárguelo a mi cuenta, por favor.

B **Definiciones.** Dé una definición de estas palabras en español.

1. el presupuesto
2. economizar
3. prestar
4. la factura
5. el alquiler
6. pagar a plazos

Ahora explique la diferencia entre una cuenta corriente y una cuenta de ahorros; entre un talonario de cheques y una libreta de ahorros; entre depositar dinero en una cuenta y sacarlo.

355

C **Situaciones.** Describa lo que pasa en los siguientes dibujos, contestando por lo menos estas preguntas: ¿Quiénes son estas personas? ¿Dónde están? ¿Qué van a comprar? ¿Cómo van a pagar? ¿Qué van a hacer después?

1.

2.

3.

4.

DE AQUÍ Y DE ALLÁ

Spanish, like English, has a number of colloquial terms that refer to money.

generalized usage	la plata	*Mexico*	la lana
Spain	la pasta	*Central America and Peru*	el pisto
Puerto Rico	los chavos		

Adivinanza

Es tanto lo que me quiere
el hombre en su necio orgullo,[a]
que hasta crímenes comete,
sólo por hacerme suyo.[b]

[a]*necio... foolish pride* [b]*his*

NOTA CULTURAL: Using Foreign Currency

Using foreign currency when traveling outside the United States can be confusing. Often tourists have no concrete sense of what foreign currency is worth or how much they are paying for an item or a service, even though they know the current conversion factor used to exchange money at the bank.

Here are the current exchange rates (**cambios**) for the currencies of several Spanish-speaking countries. These rates of exchange fluctuate; they may be different by the time you read this.

México: 1 peso = $.32 U.S.A. (100 pesos = $32; $1.00 = 3.122 pesos; $10.00 = 31.22 pesos)

España: 1 peseta = $.0075 U.S.A. (100 pesetas = $.75; $1.00 = 133 pesetas; $10.00 = 1,330 pesetas)

Colombia: 1 peso = $.0015 U.S.A. (100 pesos = $.15; $1.00 = 678 pesos; $10.00 = 6,780 pesos)

If you are traveling in Puerto Rico, the U.S. dollar is the unit of currency; it is called **un peso,** however. And, in Mexico, be aware of the recent devaluation of the currency and the creation of the **nuevo peso** (**NP**), which is the unit of currency in which prices are now quoted.

▼▼▼▼▼▼▼▼▼▼▼▼▼▼▼▼▼▼▼▼▼▼▼▼▼▼ **ESTRUCTURAS**

39.   Talking About the Future

Future Verb Forms

▼ **¡Hay que reducir los gastos! ¿Qué vamos a hacer?**

▼
▼ MADRE: *Tomaré* el autobús en vez de usar el carro.
▼ ANDRÉS: *Comeremos* más ensalada y menos carne y pasteles.
▼ PADRE: Los niños no *irán* al cine con tanta frecuencia.
▼ JULIETA: Yo *dejaré* de fumar.
▼ MADRE: Los niños *gastarán* menos en dulces.
▼ PADRE: Y yo no *cargaré* nada a nuestras cuentas. Lo *pagaré*
▼   todo en efectivo.
▼ JULIETA: *Bajaremos* el termostato por la noche.
▼ GABRIELA: Y yo me *iré* a vivir con los abuelos. Allí todo *será* como
▼   siempre, ¿verdad?
▼
▼   ▲ ▲ ▲
▼
▼ 1. ¿Quién dejará de usar el carro? ¿de fumar?
▼ 2. ¿Qué comerá la familia? ¿Qué no comerá?
▼ 3. ¿Cómo gastará menos dinero el padre? ¿y los niños?
▼ 4. ¿Adónde irá a vivir Gabriela? ¿Por qué?

You have already learned to talk about the future in a number of ways. The forms
of the **ir** + **a** + *infinitive* construction and of the present are commonly used to express future actions. The future can also be expressed, however, with future verb
forms.

hablar		comer		vivir	
hablar**é**	hablar**emos**	comer**é**	comer**emos**	vivir**é**	vivir**emos**
hablar**ás**	hablar**éis**	comer**ás**	comer**éis**	vivir**ás**	vivir**éis**
hablar**á**	hablar**án**	comer**á**	comer**án**	vivir**á**	vivir**án**

In English, the future is formed with the auxiliary verbs *will* or *shall: I **will**/**shall**
speak.* In Spanish, the *future* (**el futuro**) is a simple verb form (only one word). It is
formed by adding the future endings (the same for **-ar,** **-er,** and **ir** verbs) **-é, -ás, -á,
-emos, -éis, -án** to the infinitive. No auxiliary verbs are needed.

It's necessary to cut down on expenses! What are we going to do?   MOTHER: I'll take the bus instead of using
the car. ANDRÉS: We'll eat more salad and less meat and cake. JULIETA: I'll stop smoking. MOTHER: The kids will spend less on candy. FATHER: And I won't charge
anything. I'll pay for everything in cash. JULIETA: We'll turn down the thermostat at night. GABRIELA: And
I'll go to live with our grandparents. There everything will be as usual, right?

The following verbs add the future endings to irregular stems.

decir:	**dir-**
hacer:	**har-**
poder:	**podr-**
poner:	**pondr-**
querer:	**querr-**
saber:	**sabr-**
salir:	**saldr-**
tener:	**tendr-**
venir:	**vendr-**

-é
-ás
-á
-emos
-éis
-án

decir	
diré	diremos
dirás	diréis
dirá	dirán

The future of **hay** (**haber**) is **habrá** (*there will be*).*

¡OJO!   Remember that indicative and subjunctive present tense forms can be used to express the immediate future. Compare the following.

Llegaré a tiempo.	*I'll arrive on time.*
Llego a las ocho mañana. ¿Vienes a buscarme?	*I arrive at 8:00 tomorrow. Will you pick me up?*
No creo que Pepe **llegue** a tiempo.	*I don't think Pepe will arrive on time.*

Práctica

A **Pensando en mañana...** Durante una entrevista, es común que le pregunten a uno, «¿Dónde espera estar dentro de diez años?» ¿Sabe Ud. dónde estará o cómo será su vida en diez años? Piénselo un momento. Luego indique las oraciones que le parezcan posibles.

1. _____ Estaré casado/a. (Estaré divorciado/a.)
2. _____ Tendré más de un hijo. (Tendré por lo menos un nieto.)
3. _____ Viviré en un pueblo pequeño.
4. _____ Trabajaré en una compañía internacional.
5. _____ Ganaré por lo menos $100.000 al año.
6. _____ Usaré gafas. (Usaré gafas bifocales.)
7. _____ Llevaré una vida más sana.
8. _____ Estaré en contacto con los amigos que tengo hoy.

B **Mi amigo Gregorio.** Describa Ud. las siguientes cosas que hará su compañero Gregorio. Luego indique si Ud. hará lo mismo (**Yo también..., Yo tampoco...**) u otra cosa.

MODELO: no / gastar / menos / mes →
Gregorio no gastará menos este mes. Yo tampoco gastaré menos.
(Yo sí gastaré menos este mes. ¡Tengo que ahorrar!)

---

*The future forms of the verb **haber** are used to form the *future perfect tense* (**el futuro perfecto**), which expresses what *will have* occurred at some point in the future.

Para mañana, ya **habré hablado** con Miguel.   *By tomorrow, I will have spoken with Miguel.*

You will find a more detailed presentation of these forms in Appendix 2, Additional Perfect Forms (Indicative and Subjunctive).

1. pagar / tarde / todo / cuentas
2. tratar / adaptarse a / presupuesto
3. volver / hacer / presupuesto / próximo mes
4. no / depositar / nada / en / cuenta de ahorros
5. quejarse / porque / no / tener / suficiente dinero
6. usar / tarjetas / crédito / con frecuencia
7. pedirles / dinero / a / padres
8. buscar / trabajo / de tiempo parcial

¿Cuál de las siguientes oraciones describe mejor a su amigo?

1. Gregorio es muy responsable en cuanto a asuntos de dinero. Es un buen modelo para imitar.
2. Gregorio tiene que aprender a ser más responsable con su dinero.

C **Ventajas y desventajas.** What can you do to get extra cash or to save money? Some possibilities are shown in the following drawings. What are the advantages and disadvantages of each suggestion?

MODELO: dejar de tomar tanto café →
Dejaré de tomar tanto café. Así (*In that way*) ahorraré sólo un poco de dinero. Estaré menos nervioso/a, pero creo que será más difícil despertarme por la mañana.

1. pedirles dinero a mis amigos o parientes
2. cometer un robo
3. alquilar unos cuartos de mi casa a otras personas
4. dejar de fumar (beber cerveza, tomar tanto café...)
5. buscar un trabajo de tiempo parcial
6. vender mi videocasetera (coche, televisor...)
7. comprar muchos billetes de lotería
8. ¿ ?

D **El mundo en el año 2500.** ¿Cómo será el mundo del futuro? Haga una lista de temas o cosas que Ud. cree que van a ser diferentes en el año 2500. Por ejemplo: el transporte, la comida, la vivienda... Piense también en temas globales: la política, los problemas que presenta la capa de ozono...

Ahora, a base de su lista, haga una serie de predicciones para el futuro.

MODELO: La gente comerá (Nosotros comeremos) comidas sintéticas.

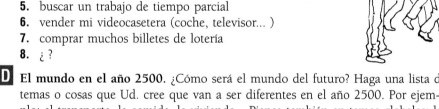

Vocabulary Library

la colonización	el robot
la energía nuclear/solar	el satélite
el espacio	
la galaxia	conquistar
el planeta	eliminar

Segundo paso

VOCABULARIO ▼▼▼▼▼▼▼▼▼▼▼▼▼▼▼▼▼▼▼▼▼▼▼▼

Más sobre los asuntos económicos

¿Puede Ud. entender el significado de las palabras de la segunda columna?

gastar	→	**los gastos**
depositar	→	**el depósito**
prestar	→	**el préstamo**
el cajero	→	**el cajero automático**
el cheque	→	**el cheque de viajero**

Ahora, con ayuda del contexto, adivine (*guess*) el significado de las palabras indicadas.

- ¡Hoy es el 15 de abril, el último día para pagar los **impuestos,** y yo todavía no he llenado los formularios! Creo que voy a pedir una extensión de la fecha límite.
- Mis abuelos ya no (*no longer*) trabajan, pero afortunadamente viven bien. Sus pensiones de **jubilación** son muy buenas.
- He usado mis tarjetas de crédito mucho este mes. Por eso les **debo** mucho dinero a los bancos. ¡Ojalá que los **intereses** no suban demasiado. También tengo muchas **deudas** con los amigos que me han prestado dinero.
- Mi hijo colecciona **monedas** de todos los países. ¡A su padre le interesan más los **billetes,** porque valen más!

Práctica

A **La hija de Eva.** Evita va a ir a la universidad el próximo semestre. Por eso Eva, su madre, habla de su situación económica actual y futura. Empareje una frase de la primera columna con otra de la segunda.

1. Cuando yo compre* una casa nueva
2. Cuando Evita ya tenga un trabajo
3. Cuando yo gane más dinero
4. Cuando Evita necesite un poco de dinero
5. Cuando Evita necesite comprar ropa
6. Cuando Evita vaya a España
7. Cuando me jubile

a. la dejaré usar mi tarjeta de crédito.
b. llevará cheques de viajero.
c. podrá pagar algunos de sus gastos universitarios, como la matrícula.
d. podrá sacarlo de un cajero automático.
e. podré pagar algunas de mis deudas.
f. tendré una buena pensión de jubilación.
g. pediré un préstamo al banco.

B Preguntas.

1. Antes de venir a la universidad, ¿había usado Ud. un cajero automático alguna vez? ¿una tarjeta de crédito? ¿Ha usado Ud. cheques de viajero alguna vez? ¿Cuándo?

2. ¿Ha pedido Ud. un préstamo alguna vez? ¿A quién? ¿Para qué? ¿Lo ha terminado de pagar? ¿A cómo estaban los intereses? (% = por ciento) ¿Ha comprado algo a plazos? ¿Qué ha comprado?

3. ¿Ha presentado Ud. una declaración de impuestos alguna vez? ¿Tuvo que pagar o le devolvieron dinero?

4. ¿Tiene una cuenta de ahorros? ¿Pagan buenos intereses en su banco?

5. ¿Conoce a alguna persona jubilada? ¿Tiene una buena o una mala pensión?

6. ¿Colecciona Ud. monedas? ¿Alguno de sus amigos las colecciona? ¿Qué tipo de monedas?

▼▼▼▼▼▼▼▼▼▼▼▼▼▼▼▼▼▼▼▼▼▼▼▼▼▼▼ **ESTRUCTURAS**

40. Expressing Future or Pending Actions

Subjunctive and Indicative After Conjunctions of Time

[a]eres [b]salir... decir que

Complete la oración según el dibujo.

Cuando Mafalda sea grande...

- no le va a hacer preguntas a su padre.
- su padre no le va a contestar las preguntas.
- su padre le va a decir que los grandes no entienden las cosas de los ancianos.

*Note the use of the subjunctive after **Cuando...** in these sentences. You will learn about this use of the subjunctive in Grammar Section 40.

The subjunctive is often used in Spanish in adverbial clauses, which function like adverbs, telling when the action of the main verb takes place. Such adverbial clauses are introduced by *conjunctions* (**las conjunciones**).

> Lo veré **mañana.** (adverb)
> Lo veré **cuando venga mañana.** (adverbial clause)

Future events are often expressed in Spanish in two-clause sentences that include conjunctions of time such as the following.

antes (de) que	before	**en cuanto**	as soon as
cuando	when	**hasta que**	until
después (de) que	after	**tan pronto como**	as soon as

In a dependent clause after these conjunctions of time, the subjunctive is used to express a future action or state of being, that is, one that is still pending or has not yet occurred from the point of view of the main verb. This use of the subjunctive is very frequent in conversation in phrases such as the following.

Cuando sea grande/mayor...	*When I'm older . . .*
Cuando tenga tiempo...	*When I have the time . . .*
Cuando me gradúe...	*When I graduate . . .*

The events in the dependent clause are imagined—not real-world—events. They haven't happened yet.

When the present subjunctive is used in this way to express pending actions, the main-clause verb is in the present indicative or future.

PENDING ACTION (SUBJUNCTIVE)

Pagaré las cuentas **en cuanto reciba** mi cheque.	*I'll pay the bills as soon as I get my check.*
Debo depositar el dinero **tan pronto como** lo **reciba.**	*I should deposit money as soon as I get it.*

However, the indicative (not the present subjunctive) is used after conjunctions of time to describe a habitual action or a completed action in the past. Compare the following.

HABITUAL ACTIONS (INDICATIVE)

Siempre pago las cuentas **en cuanto recibo** mi cheque.	*I always pay bills as soon as I get my check.*
Deposito el dinero **tan pronto como** lo **recibo.**	*I deposit money as soon as I receive it.*

COMPLETED PAST ACTION (INDICATIVE)

El mes pasado pagué las cuentas **en cuanto recibí** mi cheque.	*Last month I paid my bills as soon as I got my check.*
Deposité el dinero **tan pronto como** lo **recibí.**	*I deposited the money as soon as I got it.*

¡OJO! The subjunctive is always used with **antes (de) que.** See Grammar Section 41.

Práctica

A Decisiones económicas.

Paso 1. Lea las siguientes oraciones sobre Rigoberto y decida si se trata de una acción habitual o de una acción que no ha pasado todavía. Luego indique la frase que mejor complete la oración.

1. Rigoberto se va a comprar una computadora en cuanto...
   a. el banco le dé el préstamo.   **b.** el banco le da el préstamo.
2. Siempre usa su tarjeta de crédito cuando...
   a. no tenga efectivo.   **b.** no tiene efectivo.
3. Cada mes balancea su cuenta corriente después de que...
   a. el banco le envíe el estado de cuentas (*statement*).
   b. el banco le envía el estado de cuentas.
4. Piensa abrir una cuenta de ahorros tan pronto como...
   a. consiga un trabajo.   **b.** consigue un trabajo.
5. No puede pagar sus cuentas este mes hasta que...
   a. su hermano le devuelva el dinero que le prestó.
   b. su hermano le devuelve el dinero que le prestó.
6. Este mes va a pagar sus cuentas con cheque...
   a. antes de que se le olvide.
   b. antes de que se le olvida.

Un cajero automático en Buenos Aires, Argentina.

Paso 2. Ahora describa cómo lleva Ud. sus propios asuntos económicos, completando las siguientes oraciones semejantes.

1. Voy a comprarme _____ en cuanto el banco me dé un préstamo.
2. Cuando no tengo efectivo, siempre uso _____ .
3. Después de que el banco me envía el estado de cuentas, yo siempre _____ .
4. Tan pronto como consiga un trabajo, voy a _____ .
5. No te presto más dinero hasta que tú me _____ el dinero que me debes.
6. Este mes, voy a _____ antes de que se me olvide.

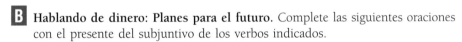

B Hablando de dinero: **Planes para el futuro.** Complete las siguientes oraciones con el presente del subjuntivo de los verbos indicados.

1. Voy a ahorrar más en cuanto... (tener [*yo*] un trabajo [mejor]; dejar de gastar tanto; graduarme)
2. Pagaré todas mis cuentas tan pronto como... (tener el dinero para hacerlo; ser absolutamente necesario; recibirlas)
3. El semestre/trimestre que viene, pagaré la matrícula después de que... (cobrar mi cheque en el banco; mandarme [mis padres, ¿ ?] un cheque; llegar la factura)
4. No podré pagar el alquiler hasta que... (sacar dinero de mi cuenta de ahorros; depositar el dinero en mi cuenta corriente; darme mi compañero/a su parte del alquiler)
5. No voy a jubilarme antes de que mis hijos... (terminar sus estudios universitarios; casarse; comprarse una casa)

DISFRUTE UN NUEVO SERVICIO.... AGIL, EFECTIVO Y SEGURO

Reciba ahora oportunamente su dinero desde cualquier ciudad del país donde el BIC posea sucursales.

Controle ahora con mayor facilidad sus cuentas por cobrar y disminuya los costos de cobranza.

Elimine ahora riesgos en el traslado de su dinero.

Deposite ahora sus ahorros sin presentar su libreta.

Los depósitos realizados en efectivo serán fondos disponibles rápidamente.

C **Dos momentos en la vida.** Las siguientes oraciones describen algunos aspectos de la vida de Mariana en el pasado, en el presente y en el futuro. Lea cada grupo de oraciones para tener una idea general del contexto. Luego dé la forma apropiada de los infinitivos.

1. Hace cuatro años, cuando Mariana (graduarse) en la escuela secundaria, sus padres (darle) un reloj. El año que viene, cuando (graduarse) en la universidad, (darle) un coche.
2. Cuando (ser) niña, Mariana (querer) ser enfermera. Luego, cuando (tener) 18 años, (decidir) que quería estudiar computación. Cuando (terminar) su carrera este año, yo creo que (poder) encontrar un buen trabajo como programadora.
3. Generalmente Mariana no (escribir) cheques hasta que (tener) los fondos en su cuenta corriente. Este mes tiene muchos gastos, pero no (ir) a pagar ninguna cuenta hasta que le (llegar) el cheque.

D **Descripciones.** Describa Ud. los dibujos, completando la oraciones e inventando un contexto para las escenas. Luego describa Ud. su propia vida.

1.
2.
3.

1. Pablo va a estudiar hasta que _____.
    Esta noche yo voy a estudiar hasta que _____.
    Siempre estudio hasta que _____.
    Anoche estudié hasta que _____.
2. Los señores Castro van a cenar tan pronto como _____.
    Esta noche voy a cenar tan pronto como _____.
    Siempre ceno tan pronto como _____.
    Anoche cené tan pronto como _____.
3. Lupe va a viajar al extranjero en cuanto _____.
    En cuanto gane la lotería, yo voy a _____.
    En cuanto tengo el dinero, siempre _____.
    De niño/a, _____ en cuanto tenía el dinero.

Un paso más

UN POCO DE TODO

A **Los planes de la familia Alonso.** Es necesario que los Alonso ahorren más. Haga oraciones completas según las indicaciones. Use el futuro del primer verbo.

1. ser / necesario / que / (*nosotros*) ahorrar / más
2. yo / no / usar / tanto / tarjetas / crédito
3. mamá / buscar / trabajo / donde / (*ellos*) pagarle / más
4. (*nosotros*) pedir / préstamo / en / banco
5. nos / lo / dar, / ¿no / creer (*tú*)?
6. papá / estar / tranquilo / cuando / nosotros / empezar / economizar
7. (*tú*) deber / pagar / siempre / al contado
8. no / haber / manera / de que / (*nosotros*) poder / ir / de vacaciones / este verano

B **El presupuesto.**

Paso 1. ¿Cómo es su presupuesto mensual? Explíquele a la clase cuánto dinero gasta Ud. por mes por cada categoría en el siguiente presupuesto. Si no gasta nada, ponga un cero.

1. ropa   _____
2. casa (alquiler, hipoteca [*mortgage*])   _____
3. gas, luz, agua, teléfono   _____
4. comida   _____
5. diversiones (cine, fiestas, restaurantes, etcétera)   _____
6. gastos médicos   _____
7. seguros (*insurance*) (automóvil, casa, etcétera)   _____
8. automóvil (préstamos, reparaciones, gasolina, aceite, etcétera)   _____
9. educación (matrícula, libros, etcétera)   _____
10. ahorros   _____

TOTAL: _____

> LO ÚNICO QUE ME CONSUELA DE GANAR UN MAL SUELDO[a] ES SABER QUE UN BUEN SUELDO TAMPOCO ALCANZA[b] PARA NADA

[a]*salary*   [b]*tampoco... isn't enough either*

Paso 2. Ahora, con un compañero / una compañera de clase, imagine que juntos ganan $1.500,00 al mes. ¿Cómo será su presupuesto? ¿Cómo gastarán el dinero? Conteste, usando las siguientes preguntas como guía.

1. ¿Cuánto gastarán por cada categoría?
2. ¿Les será fácil o difícil ahorrar dinero? Expliquen.
3. Imaginen que alguien les da cinco mil dólares y Uds. pueden hacer cualquier cosa con ese dinero. ¿Qué harán con él? ¿Lo ahorrarán? ¿Comprarán algo? ¿Pagarán sus facturas? Expliquen.
4. ¿Qué harán para economizar? ¿En qué categoría podrán gastar menos?

⁂ **SITUACIÓN** Cambiando dinero en un banco

Before you read the dialogue, complete the following sentences. Then check your answers in the dialogue.

1. Para cambiar moneda en España, es necesario darle al cajero (la licencia de manejar / el pasaporte) de uno.

2. El cambio (*rate of exchange*) (no varía según el billete / varía según el billete).

EN LA VENTANILLA DE CAMBIO

CLIENTE: Quiero cambiar estos dólares en pesetas y también estos cheques de viajero.

CAJERO: Bien. ¿Ya firmó[a] los cheques?

CLIENTE: Los firmaré ahora mismo. ¿A cuánto está el cambio?

CAJERO: Depende. El dólar en billetes grandes está a ciento cuarenta y dos pesetas, y el billete pequeño, a ciento dos. ¿Me permite su pasaporte, por favor?

CLIENTE: Sí, aquí lo tiene.

CAJERO: En total, Ud. quiere cambiar cuatrocientos dólares, ¿verdad?

CLIENTE: Sí, eso es.

CAJERO: Firme allí abajo y pase por la Caja.[b] Allí le darán el dinero, su pasaporte y el recibo.[c]

[a]*did you sign . . . ?* [b]*Cashier's Window* [c]*receipt*

¿Qué ventaja de esta tarjeta de crédito le interesa más a Ud.? ¿Por qué?

Conversación

Invente las siguientes conversaciones, siguiendo el modelo del diálogo anterior. Busque en el periódico la tasa de cambio (*exchange rate*) actual de la moneda indicada e incluya en el diálogo la cantidad en moneda nacional que el/la turista va a recibir.

- Un(a) turista quiere cambiar 500 dólares a pesetas (España).
- Un(a) turista quiere cambiar 100 dólares a pesos mexicanos.
- Un(a) turista quiere cambiar 200 dólares a pesos colombianos.

PARA ESCRIBIR

¿Qué le aconsejaron sus padres con respecto al dinero cuando Ud. iba a venir a la universidad por primera vez? Seguro que sus padres le dieron algunos consejos sobre lo que debía y no debía hacer con el dinero, los gastos, etcétera. Pensando en esos consejos, escriba todos los consejos que Ud. le daría (*would give*) a su hijo/a antes de que él/ella saliera (*left*) para la universidad. Use el mandato informal cuando sea apropiado.

▼▼▼▼▼▼▼▼▼▼▼▼▼▼ **VOCABULARIO** ▼▼▼▼▼▼▼▼▼▼▼▼▼▼

Verbos

graduarse (en) to graduate (from)
jubilarse to retire

En el banco

ahorrar to save (*money*)
aumentar to increase
cargar (a la cuenta de uno) to charge (to someone's account)
cobrar to cash (*a check*); to charge (*someone for an item or service*)
deber to owe
depositar to put in, deposit
devolver (ue) to return (something)
disminuir (*like* **construir**) to decrease
economizar to economize

Repaso: **gastar, pagar, prestar, quejarse (de), sacar**

el billete bill (*money*)
el cajero automático automatic teller machine
el/la cajero/a bank teller
la cuenta corriente checking account
la cuenta de ahorros savings account
el cheque check
el depósito deposit
la deuda debt
la factura bill
los gastos expenses
los impuestos taxes
el interés interest
la libreta de ahorros savings passbook
la moneda coin; currency
el préstamo loan
el presupuesto budget
el talonario de cheques checkbook
la ventanilla teller's window

Repaso: **el alquiler, la cuenta, el cheque de viajero, la tarjeta de crédito**

Otros sustantivos

la jubilación retirement

Conjunciones

antes (de) que before
después (de) que after
en cuanto as soon as
hasta que until
tan pronto como as soon as

Repaso: **cuando**

Palabras adicionales

a plazos in installments
así in that way, so, thus
en efectivo in cash

Self-Test

Use the tape that accompanies this text to test yourself briefly on the important points of this chapter.

There is material for this section on the tape that accompanies this text.

del mundo hispánico 10
Al este de los Andes: La Argentina, el Paraguay y el Uruguay

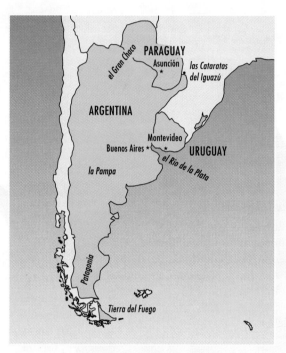

Estos países, al igual que la mayoría de los países hispanos, comparten una triste historia de dictadores y golpes de estado[a] militares. La Argentina es el país de habla hispana más grande. Su historia política está llena de dictadores como Perón (1946–1955), pero desde 1983, tiene una democracia estable a pesar de los graves problemas económicos y sociales que enfrenta.[b]

El Paraguay tiene dos lenguas oficiales: el castellano y el guaraní, una lengua indígena. El guaraní se habla más que el castellano y cuenta con[c] su propia literatura. El actual presidente paraguayo, el general Andrés Rodríguez, es un excolaborador del dictador previo, Stroessner. Rodríguez se apoderó del gobierno[d] en un golpe de estado en 1989, pero en ese mismo año convocó unas elecciones que ganó masivamente.

El Uruguay tiene un pasado notable de paz y democracia en comparación con sus países vecinos, además de tener el mejor récord, en el área de reformas sociales, de toda Latinoamérica. Desgraciadamente el costo de esas reformas causó un descontento social que acabó en un golpe de estado en 1973, lo cual[e] llevó al país a doce años de dictadura, que terminó en 1985.

El Uruguay y el Paraguay tienen un nivel muy bajo de analfabetismo (8% y 4% respectivamente).

[a]golpes... *coups d'etats*   [b]*it is facing*   [c]cuenta... *tiene*
[d]*se... took over the government*   [e]*lo... which*

Jorge Luis Borges, argentino (1899–1986), es considerado uno de los más grandes escritores y eruditos de este siglo.

Las cataratas del Iguazú.

El dios de las moscas[a]

Las moscas imaginaron a su dios. Era otra mosca. El dios de las moscas era una mosca, ya[b] verde, ya negra y dorada, ya rosa, ya blanca, ya purpúrea, una mosca inverosímil,[c] una mosca bellísima, una mosca monstruosa, una mosca terrible, una mosca benévola, una mosca vengativa, una mosca justiciera,[d] una mosca joven, una mosca vieja, pero siempre una mosca. Algunos aumentaban su tamaño[e] hasta volverla enorme como un buey,[f] otros la ideaban[g] tan microscópica que no se la veía. En algunas religiones carecía de alas[h] («Vuela, sostenían,[i] pero no necesita alas»), en otras tenía infinitas alas. Aquí disponía de[j] antenas como cuernos,[k] allá los ojos le comían[l] toda la cabeza. Para unos zumbaba[m] constantemente, para otros era muda pero se hacía entender lo mismo.[n] Y para todos, cuando las moscas morían, las conducía en un vuelo arrebatado[o] hasta el paraíso. Y el paraíso era un trozo de carroña,[p] hediondo[q] y putrefacto, que las almas[r] de las moscas muertas devoraban por toda la eternidad y que no se consumía nunca, pues aquella celestial bazofia[s] continuamente renacía y se renovaba bajo el enjambre[t] de las moscas. De las buenas.[u] Porque también había moscas malas y para estas había un infierno. El infierno de las moscas condenadas era un sitio sin excrementos, sin desperdicios,[v] sin basura, sin hedor,[w] sin nada de nada, un sitio limpio y reluciente[x] y para colmo[y] iluminado por una luz deslumbradora[z] es decir, un lugar abominable.

Mario Denevi, escritor argentino (1922–). De *Falsificaciones*.

[a] El... *The God of the Flies* [b] *now* [c] *unreal* [d] *just* [e] *size* [f] *ox* [g] *imaginaban* [h] carecía... *she didn't have wings* [i] *they maintained* [j] disponía... *tenía* [k] *horns* [l] *ocupaban* [m] *she buzzed* [n] lo... *just the same* [o] *frantic* [p] trozo... *piece of carrion* [q] *foul smelling* [r] *souls* [s] *refuse, garbage* [t] *swarming* [u] De... *De las buenas moscas*. [v] *waste matter* [w] *foul odors* [x] *shining* [y] para... *to top it off* [z] *blinding*

LA HISTORIA OFICIAL

En 1986 obtuvo el Oscar a la Mejor Película Extranjera y recibió veintisiete premios internacionales. Quizás esta presentación baste para referirse al filme del argentino Luis Puenzo, quien, en casi dos horas, retrata[a] un período traumático de la vida de su país.

A través de la vida de "Alicia" (Norma Aleandro) –una profesora de historia estricta y conservadora– se va descubriendo lo que aconteció[b] en Argentina durante los regímenes militares. La maestra, casada con un próspero hombre de negocios. "Roberto" (Héctor Alterio), vive feliz junto a "Gaby", a quien adoptaron al verse impedida ella de tener hijos. Hasta ese momento, su situación es ideal. Los tres conforman un hogar[c] armónico, donde la niña es lo principal.

Sus angustias irrumpen cuando en la prensa abundan las informaciones respecto a menores, cuyos[d] padres por razones políticas han desaparecido, que fueron entregados en adopción. Desde ese momento, "Alicia" no descansará. Quiere llegar a la verdad, y una vez que la obtiene ya no puede vivir con ella. La dramática trama se combina con lo que acontece[e] en esos momentos en Buenos Aires, adquiriendo esta "Historia oficial" un carácter documental.

Argentina (1985)
Protagonistas: Norma Aleandro y Héctor Alterio
Director: Luis Puenzo
Censura: Mayores de 18 años
Duración: 112 minutos
Distribuidora: Villarrica Films Video
Hablada: En español

[a] *portrays* [b] *pasó* [c] *casa* [d] *whose* [e] *pasa* *Videograma*, Santiago (Chile).

¡Qué interesante!

1. ¿Con qué zona de los Estados Unidos se puede comparar las tierras ganaderas (*for raising cattle*) de la Argentina y del Uruguay? ¿Con qué figuras de la vida y el folclore de los Estados Unidos se pueden comparar los gauchos?

2. En un mundo tan diverso como el nuestro, ¿cuál es el mensaje del cuento de Denevi?

3. Siguiendo la pista (*clue*) del artículo sobre la película «La historia oficial», ¿sabe Ud. algo de las manifestaciones de «las madres de la Plaza de Mayo»?

4. Proyecto de investigación: ¿Cuáles son las principales fuentes de ingreso (*income sources*) de estos tres países? ¿Cómo es su situación política y económica?

Los gauchos se dedican a cuidar y criar (*raise*) ganado (*cattle*). La Argentina (la Pampa) y el Uruguay tienen grandes extensiones de terreno donde se cría ganado. Los gauchos son figuras representativas de su folclore.

369

Primer paso

Ir al extranjero

cruzar la frontera

BIENVENIDOS A MÉXICO
CONTROL DE ADUANA

BIENVENIDOS A MÉXICO

el inspector de aduanas

declarar las compras

ADUANA

pagar los derechos de aduana / una multa

registrar el equipaje

el viajero

Hotel Internacional

HOTEL de la PAZ

el huésped

PENSIÓN GÓMEZ

el botones / el mozo

la huéspeda

el hotel de lujo

los huéspedes

el hotel de dos (tres) estrellas

la pensión

En el EXTRANJERO[a]

[a]En... Abroad

En un viaje al extranjero

el formulario de inmigración
la nacionalidad
el pasaporte
el/la turista

You should be able to guess the meaning of all of the words listed under **En un viaje al extranjero.**

El alojamiento

alojarse/quedarse	to stay (*in a place*)
hacer/confirmar las reservas/ reservaciones*	to make / to confirm reservations
la habitación individual/doble con/sin baño	single/double room with/without a bathroom

la pensión	boardinghouse
pensión completa	room and full board
media pensión	room with breakfast and one other meal
la propina	tip (to an employee)
la recepción	front desk
con anticipación	ahead of time

Práctica

A ¿Quiénes son? Empareje (*Match*) las personas con la descripción apropiada.

1. el huésped
2. la recepcionista
3. el botones
4. la turista
5. la inspectora de aduanas
6. el extranjero

a. la persona que nos ayuda con el equipaje en un hotel
b. la persona que se aloja en un hotel o una pensión
c. una persona que nació en otro país
d. alguien que viaja para ver otros lugares
e. la persona que nos registra las maletas y toma la declaración en la aduana
f. la persona que nos atiende en la recepción de un hotel

Adivinanza

Estudiante que estudiaste en el libro de Salomón,[a] dime, ¿cuál es el ave[b] que no tiene corazón?

[a]*King Solomon*   [b]pájaro

---

*The word **reserva** is used in Spain to express *reservation* (for accommodations). **La reservación** is widely used in other parts of the Spanish-speaking world.

B **Pasando por la aduana.** ¿Qué dice o pregunta el inspector en este diálogo?

BIENVENIDO A LOS ESTADOS UNIDOS

DEPARTMENTO DEL TESORO
SERVICIO DE ADUANAS DE LOS ESTADOS UNIDOS

DECLARACION DE ADUANAS

FORM APPROVED
OMB NO. 1515-0041

Todo viajero o jefe de familia que llega a los Estados Unidos debe facilitar la información siguiente (basta con una declaración por familia):

1. Nombre: _____
   Apellido   Nombre   Inicial del segundo nombre

2. Número de familiares que viajan con usted _____

3. Fecha de nacimiento: ____|____|____   4. Línea aérea y
   Mes   Día   Año   número del vuelo: _____

INSPECTOR: ¿_____¹?
  VIAJERA: Soy española, de Toledo.
INSPECTOR: _____.²
  VIAJERA: Aquí lo tiene, señor.
INSPECTOR: ¿_____³?
  VIAJERA: Solamente estos libros y estos cigarrillos para uso personal.
INSPECTOR: ¿_____⁴?
  VIAJERA: Espere Ud. un momento. Mi esposo trae la llave.
INSPECTOR: _____.⁵
  VIAJERA: ¡Oh, no! ¡No sabía que { tenía que declararlos! era ilegal!
INSPECTOR: _____.⁶
  VIAJERA: ¿Cuánto tengo que pagar, pues?
INSPECTOR: _____.⁷

EL INSPECTOR:

a. ¿Me permite registrar su maleta?
b. ¿Nacionalidad?
c. La multa es de 3.300 pesos.
d. Lo siento, pero tiene que pagar una multa.
e. Su pasaporte, por favor.
f. ¿Tiene algo que declarar?
g. Señora, hay que declarar los objetos de arte.

C **Cuando Ud. viaja...**

Paso 1. A continuación hay una lista de las acciones típicas de los viajeros. ¿Hace Ud. lo mismo cuando viaja? Indique las acciones que son verdaderas para Ud.

1. _____ Hago una reserva en un hotel (motel) con un mes de anticipación.
2. _____ Confirmo la reserva antes de salir de viaje.
3. _____ Voy al banco a conseguir cheques de viajero.
4. _____ Alquilo un coche.
5. _____ Me alojo en un hotel de lujo.
6. _____ Pido que el mozo me suba las maletas.
7. _____ Llamo al servicio de cuartos en vez de comer en el restaurante.
8. _____ Le dejo una propina a la criada o al mozo el último día de mi estancia (*stay*) en la habitación.

Paso 2. Ahora piense en su último viaje. ¿Hizo Ud. las acciones del **Paso 1**? Conteste según el modelo y cambie los detalles de esas oraciones por los que en realidad ocurrieron en su viaje.

MODELO: La última vez que hice un viaje... →
Hice una reserva en un hotel de lujo, pero con sólo dos días de anticipación.

PARA QUIEN LLEVA EL MUNDO DE LA MANO.

Viajan continuamente. Hablan el lenguaje del éxito. Están habituados a lo mejor que el mundo les puede ofrecer. Y no se conforman con cualquier hotel. Necesitan uno que por sus prestaciones, calidad y confort, alcance el más alto nivel. El nivel del Hotel Castellana Inter-Continental Madrid.

Para los que llevan el mundo de la mano.

HOTEL
**CASTELLANA
INTER·CONTINENTAL**
MADRID

D **Situaciones.** Con un compañero / una compañera, hagan los papeles de un viajero / una viajera y el de el/la recepcionista del Hotel Crillón.

Paso 1. El/La recepcionista le pregunta al viajero / a la viajera, que acaba de llegar:

- si tiene una reserva
- cuánto tiempo piensa quedarse
- el tipo de habitación reservada (o deseada)
- la forma de pago

Paso 2. El huésped / La huéspeda pide los siguientes servicios:

- el desayuno en su cuarto
- la ayuda de un botones
- información sobre _____

Paso 3. Por fin, el huésped / la huéspeda pasa por la recepción para pagar la cuenta. Encuentra los siguientes errores en su cuenta.

- Le cobraron por un desayuno que no tomó.
- Le cobraron por cuatro noches en vez de tres.

DESAYUNO Crillón

Café americano / American coffee	Jugo naranja / Orange juice	Fritos / Fried
Café express / Express coffee	Jugo pomelo / Grapefruit juice	Revueltos / Scrambled
Café con leche / Coffee with milk	Jugo tomate / Tomato juice	Omelette
Te / Tea	Jugo anana / Pineapple juice	Con: / With:
Chocolate	Yoghurt	Panceta / Bacon
Cereales / Corn flakes	Huevos / Eggs	Jamón / Ham
Ensalada de frutas / Fruit salad	Pasados por agua / Boiled	Salchicha / Sausage

Incluye: faturas, tostadas, manteca y mermelada
Rolls, toast, butter and marmalade included.
CON ESTE DESAYUNO SE SABOREA EL RICO CAFE "MARTINEZ"

Pedido especial / Special request ....

N° Hab. .... Firma del cliente: ....
ROOM NUMBER: .... Guest's signature: ....
Aclaración de firma: ....

ESTRUCTURAS

41. Antes de que sea muy tarde

Subjunctive After Conjunctions of Contingency and Purpose

▼ **En la recepción de un hotel**

RECEPCIONISTA: Lo siento, pero sólo nos queda una habitación individual con cama de matrimonio... *a menos que no lleguen* los señores de la 320.

MUJER: ¡Dios mío! ¡Otra noche en el coche! ¡Mi pobre hija!

RECEPCIONISTA: No se preocupe, señora; *en caso de que* la habitación 320 *no esté* libre, podemos poner una cama suplemento en la habitación individual *para que duerma* la pequeña, si Uds. quieren.

HOMBRE: ¡Eso sería estupendo! No importa que estemos apretados en la habitación, *con tal que podamos* dormir en una cama esta noche.

▲ ▲ ▲

▼ Busque en el diálogo el equivalente de las siguientes oraciones.

At the front desk of a hotel RECEPTIONIST: I'm sorry, but we only have a single room with a double bed left . . . unless the people in 320 don't arrive. WOMAN: My goodness! Another night in the car! My poor daughter! RECEPTIONIST: Don't worry, madam. In case room 320 isn't free, we can bring in an extra bed, so that your daughter can sleep in it, if you want. MAN: That would be great! It doesn't matter if we're crowded in the room as long as we can sleep in a bed tonight.

▼ 1. Cualquier (*Any*) habitación está bien si podemos dormir en una cama esta
▼   noche.
▼ 2. La habitación 320 está libre si no vienen las personas que hicieron la reserva.
▼ 3. Ponemos una camita extra y la niña puede dormir allí.

▼ ¿Por qué cree Ud. que esta familia tuvo que dormir anoche en su coche? ¿Por
▼ qué cree que el hotel está lleno?

When one action or condtion is related to another—X will happen provided that Y
occurs; we'll do Z unless A happens—a relationship of *contingency* is said to exist:
one thing is contingent, or depends, on another.

     The following Spanish conjunctions express relationships of contingency or pur-
pose. The subjunctive always occurs in dependent clauses introduced by these
conjunctions.

a menos que	unless	**en caso de que**	in case
antes (de) que	before	**para que**	so that
con tal (de) que	provided (that)		

Voy **con tal que** ellos me acompañen.	*I'm going, provided (that) they go with me.*
En caso de que llegue Juan, dile que ya salí.	*In case Juan arrives, tell him that I already left.*

Note that these conjunctions introduce dependent clauses in which the events have
not yet materialized; the events are imagined, not real-world, events. When there is
no change of subject in the dependent clause, Spanish more frequently uses the
prepositions **antes de** and **para**, plus an infinitive, instead of the corresponding
conjunctions plus the subjunctive. Compare the following.

PREPOSITION:	Estoy aquí **para aprender.**	*I'm here (in order) to learn.*
CONJUNCTION:	Estoy aquí **para que Uds. aprendan.**	*I'm here so that you will learn.*
PREPOSITION:	Voy a comer **antes de salir.**	*I'm going to eat before leaving.*
CONJUNCTION:	Voy a comer **antes (de) que salgamos.**	*I'm going to eat before we leave.*

> You have already seen the use of the subjunctive with **antes (de) que,** which is also considered to be a conjunction of time.

Práctica

A **Ud. y las vacaciones.** Indique si las siguientes oraciones son ciertas o falsas
para Ud.

	CIERTO	FALSO
1. Voy a viajar al extranjero algún día con tal que tenga dinero suficiente.	☐	☐
2. Siempre compro cheques de viajero a menos que el viaje sea muy breve.	☐	☐
3. Cuando viajo, me gusta ir acompañado/a de una o dos personas solamente, para que no haya demasiadas diferencias de opinión.	☐	☐

	CIERTO	FALSO

4. Normalmente tengo reservado mi alojamiento antes de llegar al lugar de destino. ☐ ☐

5. Siempre le digo a mi familia dónde voy a alojarme en caso de que haya alguna emergencia. ☐ ☐

6. Me gusta mandar tarjetas postales de mis vacaciones, a menos que sólo esté fuera por un fin de semana. ☐ ☐

7. Me encanta tomar muchas fotos para que mis amigos puedan ver donde estuve y lo que hice durante las vacaciones. ☐ ☐

8. Me gustaría viajar a un país de habla española para practicar mi español. ☐ ☐

B **Un fin de semana en las montañas.** Hablan Manuel y su esposa Marta. Use la conjunción entre paréntesis para unir las oraciones, haciendo todos los cambios necesarios.

1. No voy. Dejamos a los niños en casa. (a menos que)
2. Yo también prefiero que vayamos solos. Pasamos un rato libre sin ellos. (para que)
3. Esta vez voy a aprender a esquiar. Tú me enseñas. (con tal que)
4. Quiero que salgamos temprano por la mañana. Nieva mucho. (a menos que)
5. Es importante que lleguemos a la cabaña. Empieza a nevar en las montañas. (antes de que)
6. Compra leña (*firewood*) aquí. No hay leña en la cabaña. (en caso de que)
7. Deja un recado (*message*). Tus padres nos llaman. (en caso de que)

¿Cierto, falso o no lo dice?

1. Manuel y Marta acaban de casarse.
2. Casi siempre van de vacaciones con los niños.
3. Los dos son esquiadores excelentes.
4. Son dueños de una cabaña que está en las montañas.

C **Es buena idea llegar temprano.** Su amigo Julio, quien va al cine con Ud. esta tarde, no quiere salir con un poco de anticipación. Trate de convencerle de que Uds. deben salir pronto.

JULIO: No entiendo por qué quieres que lleguemos al teatro tan temprano.
UD.: Pues, para que (nosotros)...

Sugerencias: poder estacionar el coche, no perder el principio de la función, poder comprar los boletos, conseguir buenas butacas (*seats*), no tener que hacer cola, comprar palomitas (*popcorn*) antes de que empiece la película, hablar con los amigos.

DE AQUÍ Y DE ALLÁ

The concept of being a tourist in a foreign country is not new. Centuries ago, Miguel de Cervantes had this advice for travelers: **«Allí donde fueres haz lo que vieres.»** What English saying makes the same recommendation? If you are not able to follow Cervantes' advice, people may say this about you: **Tiene pinta (= aspecto) de turista.**

VOCABULARIO ▼▼▼▼▼▼▼▼▼▼▼▼▼▼▼▼▼▼▼▼▼▼▼

Cosas y lugares necesarios en el extranjero

Las cosas		Los lugares	
el papel para cartas	stationery	el café	café
el paquete	package	el correo	post office
el sello	stamp	la estación del metro	subway stop
el sobre	envelope	el estanco	tobacco stand/shop
la tarjeta postal	postcard	la farmacia	pharmacy, drugstore
		la papelería	stationery store
		la parada del autobús	bus stop
		la pastelería	pastry shop
		el quiosco	kiosk (*small outdoor stand selling a variety of items*)

Práctica

A **Preguntas.** Lea primero la Nota cultural, página 383.

1. ¿Dónde se compra el champú?
2. ¿Cuál es la diferencia entre una farmacia de los Estados Unidos y una farmacia en el extranjero?
3. ¿Dónde se puede comprar sellos? (dos lugares)
4. Si Ud. necesita cigarrillos o fósforos, ¿adónde va?
5. ¿Qué es un quiosco? ¿Qué cosas se venden allí?
6. ¿Qué venden en una papelería?

B **¿Cierto o falso?** Corrija las oraciones falsas.

1. Se puede comprar galletas en una pastelería.
2. Si yo quiero tomar una cerveza, voy a un quiosco.
3. Se va a un quiosco para mandar paquetes.
4. Es más rápido ir a pie que tomar el metro.
5. Se va a un café a comprar champú.
6. Si yo necesito pasta dental, voy al correo.
7. Se puede comprar cigarrillos en un estanco.

ESTRUCTURAS

42. Perdón, ¿pudiera Ud.* decirme... ?

Different Ways of Requesting

—Atención. *Abran* los libros
en la página 254.
—Perdón, ¿*puede* repetir
el número de la página?

—¿Estás muy ocupado hoy? ¿*Pudieras*
ayudarme a ordenar el apartamento?
Mi madre viene mañana y me
gustaría impresionarla.
—¡Claro, cómo no!

—¿Me *pasas* la sal, por favor?
—Aquí la tienes.

In Spanish, as in English, direct commands are not always an acceptable way to make a request. They can often sound too sharp or abrupt.

The preceding dialogues show a variety of ways to make requests. Some are more formal, others informal. Your relationship with the person to whom you are making the request will determine which form is most appropriate.

- DIRECT COMMANDS
  These are used to give orders or advice. The speaker occupies a position of some authority with the person he or she is speaking to.

> Un cliente al camarero: **Tráigame** sopa de tortilla y una cerveza, por favor.
> Un médico a un paciente: **No fume** Ud.
> Un anuncio publicitario: Si bebe, no **conduzca.**
> Una madre a su hijo: **No** le **pegues** a tu hermanita.

- QUESTIONS WITH THE PRESENT INDICATIVE
  Very often used in informal situations, these are equivalent to English *Would you . . . ?*

> En la mesa: ¿Me **pasas** el pan, por favor?
> A una compañera de cuarto: ¿Me **prestas** tu camiseta roja?

- THE VERBS **poder** AND **querer**
  Poder is used in a variety of tenses to make requests. The present tense is the most direct. The imperfect subjunctive (**pudiera**) and the conditional (**podría**)† are more formal, like English *Could you . . . ?* The imperfect subjunctive of **querer** expresses English *I would like . . . .*

¡OJO! Don't use the future to make requests in Spanish.

---

*¿**Pudiera Ud.?** *Could/Would you please?* You will learn about this imperfect subjunctive form in Grammar Section 43. For now, just learn the polite form **pudiera.**
†You have been using the conditional of **gustar** (**me gustaría**) for some time. **Podría** (**poder**) is a conditional verb form. You will learn about the conditional in Grammar Section 45.

> A un profesor: Por favor, ¿**puede** (**¿pudiera**) repetir la última pregunta?
>
> A alguien en la calle: Perdón, ¿me **podría/pudiera** decir la hora?
>
> A un camarero: **Quisiera** un café, por favor.

- OTHER POLITE FORMS

  Here are other phrases to use to make very polite requests.

¿**Le/Te importaría***... ?	*Would you mind . . . ?*
¿**Sería*** **tan amable de**... ?	*Would you be so kind as to . . . ?*

  Use these forms to ask for a really big favor or to make a request of someone you don't know very well and with whom you wish to err on the side of politeness.

Práctica

A **Preguntas y respuestas.** Match the requests and commands in the first column with the responses in the second column. Then see if you can invent the context. Who is speaking and to whom? Where are they? **¡OJO!** There is one extra answer.

PREGUNTAS

1. Perdone. ¿Pudiera decirme dónde está la estación de trenes?
2. ¡No comas tantos dulces!
3. ¿Me invitas a un café? Olvidé mi cartera en casa hoy.
4. ¿Sería tan amable de explicarme esta fórmula otra vez?
5. ¿Podría decirme con quién debo hablar para solucionar mi problema?
6. Como vas a la cocina, ¿me traes un vaso de agua, por favor?

RESPUESTAS

a. Pero, profesora, ¡mañana tenemos un examen!
b. Por supuesto. Debe hablar con la decano (*dean*) de ciencias.
c. Cómo no. ¿Quieres venir a mi oficina esta tarde?
d. ¡Tú nunca te levantas para nada!
e. Pero, papá, son un regalo de mi cumpleaños.
f. Sí, siga por esta calle y va a verla muy pronto.
g. ¡Claro que sí! ¡Tú siempre me invitas a mí!

B **Situaciones.** What might one say in the following situations?

1. You want your instructor to give you an extension to hand in your composition.
2. An instructor wants students to close their books.
3. A doctor tells a patient to eat a little more.
4. A mother tells her young children to be quiet.
5. At the table, someone needs the water, which is on the other side of the table.
6. You are taking a message by phone, and could not hear the phone number.
7. You are talking in Spanish to an older Guatemalan lady who speaks very fast. You cannot understand most of what she says.
8. You are writing an ad for teenagers' parents to make them aware of the possible problems of their children.

¡Mamá, papá! Mire el dibujo y lea lo que le dice el niño a su papá. ¿Por qué tenía sed antes pero ahora ya no tiene? ¿Por qué le habla de una manera tan cortés a su padre? ¿Por qué dice «quisiera» y no «quiero»?

—Verás, quisiera un vaso de agua. Pero no te molestes, porque ya no tengo sed. Sólo quisiera saber si, en el caso de que tuviese otra vez sed, podría (*I could*) venir a pedirte un vaso de agua.

***Importaría** (**importar**), and **sería** (**ser**) are all conditional verb forms. You will learn about the conditional in Grammar Section 45.

Un paso más

UN POCO DE TODO

En busca de alojamiento. Complete the following dialogue with the correct form of the words in parentheses, as suggested by the context. When two possibilities are given in parentheses, select the correct words.

ALFONSO: Yo no (saber/conocer[1]) cómo vamos a encontrar alojamiento. No tenemos (mucho/muy[2]) dinero, y ya (ser/estar[3]) un poco tarde.

ELENA: Y (el/la[4]) equipaje pesa[a] mucho. No podemos (ir[5]) muy lejos.

ALFONSO: (Mirar: *tú*[6]), en esa oficina parece que dan información sobre alojamientos. Vamos.

EMPLEADO: ¿Qué (desear: *Uds.*[7])?

ALFONSO: Pues quisiéramos una habitación (por/para[8]) los dos. Sólo (por/para[9]) esta noche, pues solamente estamos (hacer[10]) escala aquí y mañana (*nosotros:* seguir[11]) con nuestro viaje.

ELENA: (Por/Para[12]) favor, no queremos que (ser/estar[13]) muy cara. Hemos (cambiar[14]) muy poca moneda. Tampoco queremos que (ser/estar[15]) muy lejos.

EMPLEADO: Bien, (esperar: *Uds.*[16]) un momento. Voy a llamar a una pensión (mucho/muy[17]) agradable que no (ser/estar[18]) muy lejos de la estación.

Pocos minutos después...

EMPLEADO: Sí, me dicen que (haber[19]) una habitación doble disponible[b] todavía.

ALFONSO: ¡Qué bien! ¿Pagamos ahora?

EMPLEADO: No (ser/estar[20]) necesario. Aquí tienen los datos. (Este/Esta[21]) papel sirve como reserva. También (los/les[22]) he anotado el precio. Pero no tarden mucho en (llegar[23]).

ELENA: Muy bien. ¿Podría Ud. indicarnos cómo llegar allí?

EMPLEADO: (Mirar: *Uds.*[24]). Estamos aquí y la pensión (ser/estar[25]) en esta plaza. Se lo marco en (el/la[26]) mapa. Caminando, puede tomarles unos quince o veinte minutos. Si (tomar[27]) el metro, sólo son dos estaciones.

ELENA: ¡Ah! ¿Sabe si (ser/estar[28]) incluido el desayuno en el precio?

EMPLEADO: Sí, lo que Uds. (llamar[29]) desayuno continental.

ALFONSO: Y otra cosa. ¿(Ser/Estar[30]) posible dejar parte de nuestro equipaje en la estación? Mañana tenemos (de/que[31]) volver a la estación.

EMPLEADO: Sí. Cuando salgan de la oficina, a mano derecha (*Uds.:* ver[32]) la consigna.[c] Pueden dejar(lo/la[33]) allí.

ALFONSO: Adiós y gracias (por/para[34]) todo.

[a]*weighs* [b]*available* [c]*baggage check room*

¿Quién lo dice?

1. Sí, todavía tenemos una habitación para esta noche.

2. ¡Qué suerte hemos tenido! Una habitación barata y cerca de la estación.

3. A ver qué quieren estos dos jóvenes.
4. Sí, señor. El empleado de la estación nos dio este papel como reserva para una habitación.

SITUACIÓN   En el control de inmigración

EN LA FILA[a] DE INMIGRACIONES, URUGUAY

AGENTE: Pasaporte, por favor.
VIAJERO: Aquí lo tiene.
AGENTE: ¿Cuánto tiempo piensa quedarse?
VIAJERO: Dos semanas.
AGENTE: Está bien. Le doy treinta días. Puede pasar.
VIAJERO: Gracias.

ENTRANDO EN UN PAÍS EXTRANJERO

AGENTE: Pasaporte. ¿En qué vuelo llegó? ¿Cuánto tiempo piensa permanecer[b] en el país?
VIAJERO: El número de vuelo está aquí, en el billete. Voy a quedarme cinco semanas.
AGENTE: ¿Tiene una dirección aquí en la que se le pueda localizar[c]?
VIAJERO: En casa de mis primos. Aquí tengo las señas.[d]
AGENTE: ¿Cuenta con dinero suficiente para cubrir sus gastos durante el tiempo que permanezca en el país?
VIAJERO: Sí, señor. Aquí tiene los recibos[e] de los cheques de viajero que traigo conmigo.
AGENTE: Está bien. Eso es todo.

[a]cola   [b]¿ ?   [c]¿ ?   [d]las... la dirección   [e]*receipts*

Conversación

Con un compañero / una compañera, practiquen los papeles de oficial de inmigración y viajero/a. Después tomen los papeles de inspector(a) de aduanas y extranjero/a. A continuación hay una serie de preguntas y comentarios típicos de un oficial de aduanas.

1. ¿Algo que declarar?
2. Hummm. ¡Ud. trae muchos cigarrillos / una computadora / muchas botellas de licor!
3. ¿Cuáles son sus maletas?
4. ¿Qué lleva en la pequeña/grande?
5. Abra la maleta, por favor.
6. Es necesario que pague derechos de aduana por...
7. Doscientos pesos / Tres mil pesetas / ...

PARA ESCRIBIR

Imagine que está entrando en la Argentina. Trate de (*Try to*) llenar este formulario sin mirar las traducciones en inglés.

ENTRADA ARRIVAL ARRIVEE	USO OFICIAL OFFICIAL USE RESERVE A L'ADMINISTRATION	SALIDA DEPARTURE DEPART
Empresa y N° de vuelo o viaje Company and N° of flight or voyage Compagnie et N° de vol		**Empresa y N° de vuelo o viaje** Company and N° of flight or voyage Compagnie et N° de vol

Tarjeta internacional de entrada-salida · International card of arrival departure · Carte internationale d'arrivee depart

Para ser completado con letra de imprenta · Complete in block letters · Completer en lettres capitales

REPUBLICA ARGENTINA

Apellidos Family Name Nom

Nombres Name Prénom

Fecha de Nacimiento Date of Birth Date de Naissance — Día/Day/Jour — Mes/Month/Mois — Año/Year/Annee — Sexo/Sex M F — Uso oficial Official use Reserve a l'Administ

Nacionalidad Nationality Nationalite

Ocupación Occupation Profession

Pais de residencia habitual Usual residence country Domicile

Dirección en Argentina Address in Argentina Adresse en Argentina

Tipo y N° de documento Type and number of document Clase et N° de document

Expedido por - Issued by · Delivré par

▼▼▼▼▼▼▼▼▼▼▼▼▼▼▼▼ VOCABULARIO ▼▼▼▼▼▼▼▼▼▼▼▼▼▼▼▼

En un viaje al extranjero

cruzar to cross
declarar to declare
registrar to search, examine

los derechos (de aduana) (customs) duty
el formulario de inmigración immigration form
la frontera border
el/la inspector(a) (de aduanas) (customs) inspector
la multa fine
la nacionalidad nationality
el/la turista tourist
el/la viajero/a traveler

Repaso: las compras, la maleta, el pasaporte, pagar

El alojamiento

alojarse to stay (*at lodgings*)
confirmar to confirm

el botones bellhop
la habitación individual/doble single/double room
  con/sin baño with/without a bathroom

el hotel de dos (tres) estrellas two- (three-)star hotel
el hotel de lujo luxury hotel
el/la huésped(a) hotel guest
el mozo bellhop
la pensión boardinghouse
  media pensión room with breakfast and one other meal
  pensión completa room and full board
la recepción front desk
la reserva/reservación reservation

Repaso: la propina, quedarse

Cosas y lugares en el extranjero

el correo post office
la estación del metro subway station
el estanco tobacco shop/stand
el papel para cartas stationery
la papelería stationery store
el paquete package
la parada del autobús bus stop
la pastelería pastry shop
el quiosco kiosk
el sello stamp

el sobre envelope

Repaso: el café, la farmacia, la tarjeta postal

Las conjunciones

a menos que unless
con tal (de) que provided that
en caso de que in case
para que so that

Repaso: antes (de) que

Palabras útiles

con anticipación ahead of time
¿Le/Te importaría... ? Would you mind . . . ?
¿Podría(s)/Pudiera(s)... ? Could you . . . ?
Quisiera... I would like
¿Sería tan amable de... ? Would you be so kind as to . . . ?

Self-Test

Use the tape that accompanies this text to test yourself briefly on the important points of this chapter.

LECTURA
cultural

Imagine que Ud. va a alojarse en un hotel de Madrid. Aquí hay tres formularios que Ud. puede o tiene que llenar durante su estancia en el hotel. ¿Puede Ud. entenderlos? ¿Sabe lo que son? **¡OJO!** La palabra **matrícula** no sólo significa *registration fees* en español.

1.

ENTRADA DE EXTRANJEROS Nº. 674604

APELLIDOS 1.º.............. NOMBRE ....
(Nom/Name)   2.º...... (Prénom/First name/Vorname)

FECHA DE NACIMIENTO ....
(Date de naissance/Birth date/Geburtsdatum)

NACIONALIDAD ACTUAL ....
(Nationalité actuelle/Present nationaliti/Gegenwartige staatangehongkeit)

LUGAR DE NACIMIENTO ....
(Lieu de naissance/Place of birth/Geburtsort)

PASAPORTE N.º............... EXP. EN ....
(N.º du passeport/Passport number/Reisepassnummer)

.... de .... de 19........

ESTABLECIMIENTO .... Firma,
DOMICILIO .... Signature/Unterschrft

APELLIDOS 1.º.............. NOMBRE ....
Nom   Prénom
Name   2.º...... First name
               Vorname

DOMICILIO ....

.... de .... de 19........

Mod. 1.020-E   El encargado,

DIRECCION GENERAL DE LA POLICIA   Nº 674604
Precio: 3 pesetas

2.

Matrícula ....

Modelo ....

Color ....

Habitación ....

Nombre ....

....

....

Fecha ....

HOTEL NH PRINCIPE DE VERGARA

3.

Reserva	SÍ	No
¿Fue su reserva de habitación atendida cortés y rápidamente?	—	—
Comentarios: _____		

Recepción	SÍ	No
¿Recibió un trato amable y eficaz a su llegada y salida del Hotel?	—	—
Comentarios:_____		

Atenciones y servicios	SÍ	No
¿Ha sido la telefonista cortés y eficaz?	—	—
¿Recibió sus mensajes detallados y a tiempo?	—	—
¿Fue el servicio de lavandería óptimo y puntual?	—	—
Comentarios: _____		

Habitaciones	SÍ	No
Encontró su habitación:		
¿Limpia?		
¿Confortable?	—	—
¿Instalaciones en buenas condiciones? (T.V., lámparas, aire acondicionado, calefacción, etc...)	—	—

Comentarios Generales

¿Cómo valora usted el servicio y presentaciones recibidos?

Excelente	Bien	Medio	Pobre

¿Cómo ha encontrado usted la actitud del personal a su servicio?

Excelente	Bien	Medio	Pobre

¿Volvería a utilizar nuestros servicios para futuras estancias en esta ciudad? SÍ ___ No ___

Comentarios: _____

¿Algún empleado en particular ha demostrado una eficacia remarcable?_____

Número habitación _____ Fecha llegada _____ Fecha salida_____

SR. / SRA.
Nombre y apellidos _____
Empresa _____
Dirección _____
Ciudad _____
País _____
Distrito _____
Teléfono_____

NOTA CULTURAL: De compras en el mundo hispano

Aunque los nombres de muchos lugares y tiendas del mundo hispánico se parecen a los de los Estados Unidos, no siempre son iguales los productos que en ellos se venden. Tomen en cuenta sobre todo las siguientes diferencias.

Barcelona, España.

- En las farmacias no venden la variedad de cosas—dulces, tarjetas postales, etcétera—que se venden en las farmacias de los EE.UU.* Sólo se venden, por lo general, medicinas y productos para la higiene personal como pasta dental, champú...

- En los estancos, además de productos tabacaleros, se venden sellos, así que[a] uno no tiene que ir a los correos para comprarlos. También se venden sobres y tarjetas postales en los estancos.

- En los quioscos se vende una gran variedad de cosas: periódicos, revistas, libros, etcétera, pero también caramelos, cigarrillos...

[a]así... *so*

Comprensión

A Identifique los tres formularios.

1. El formulario número 1 es _____.
2. El formulario número 2 es _____.
3. El formulario número 3 es _____.

a. una solicitud para conseguir crédito
b. un minicuestionario sobre su estancia (*stay*) en el hotel
c. una tarjeta que todo extranjero tiene que llenar cuando se aloja en un hotel en España
d. un mensaje para otra persona
e. un sobre para las llaves de su coche

B Ahora busque la siguiente información en los formularios.

1. el nombre del hotel
2. el equivalente de las siguientes palabras inglesas
   average   messages
   license number   laundry

---

*EE. UU. is one way to abbreviate **Estados Unidos**. E.U. and USA are also used.

22

Primer paso

Las noticias

Y ahora, el canal 45 les ofrece a Uds. el Noticiero 45.

Asesinato de un dictador

Huelga de obreros

Guerra en el Oriente Medio

Erupción de un volcán en Centroamérica

Choque de trenes

Bombas en un avión

Las últimas
NOVEDADES

Más vocabulario

la prensa	press; print medium	**el desastre**	disaster
el/la reportero/a	reporter	**la esperanza**	hope
el/la testigo	witness	**la paz**	peace
el acontecimiento	event	**enterarse (de)**	to find out, learn (about)
el barrio	neighborhood	**informar**	to inform
		ofrecer (ofrezco)	to offer

DE AQUÍ Y DE ALLÁ

Words for talking about news and people who work in the news media also vary from country to country. Here are a few.

journalist: el reportero / la reportera, el/la periodista, el/la corresponsal de prensa (*correspondent*)

news program: las noticias, el telediario, el noticiero

spokesperson: el/la portavoz (España), el vocero / la vocera (México, EE.UU)

Práctica

A   **Definiciones.** ¿Qué palabra se asocia con cada definición?

1. un programa que nos informa de lo que pasa en nuestro mundo
2. la persona que está presente durante un acontecimiento y lo ve todo
3. un medio importantísimo de comunicación
4. la persona que nos informa de las novedades
5. la persona que gobierna un país de una forma absoluta
6. una persona que emplea la violencia para cambiar el mundo según sus deseos
7. cuando los obreros se niegan a (*refuse to*) trabajar
8. la frecuencia en que se transmiten y se reciben los programas de televisión
9. la confrontación armada entre dos o más países

a. el noticiero
b. la guerra
c. el/la terrorista
d. el/la dictador(a)
e. el canal
f. el/la testigo
g. el/la reportero/a
h. la huelga
i. la prensa

385

B **Ud. y las noticias.** Indique el interés que tienen para Ud. los siguientes aconte-cimientos: 1 = de poco o ningún interés, 2 = de interés, 3 = de gran interés.

1. _____ el asesinato de un político estadounidense
2. _____ el asesinato del dictador de otro país
3. _____ las noticias del continente africano
4. _____ un accidente de coches en una carretera que está cerca de su barrio
5. _____ una huelga de obreros en algún país europeo
6. _____ una huelga de obreros en el suroeste de los Estados Unidos
7. _____ una guerra en el Oriente Medio
8. _____ una guerra en Centroamérica o en Sudamérica
9. _____ una guerra en Europa
10. _____ el precio de la gasolina

Ahora compare las respuestas de los miembros de la clase. ¿Qué indican sus res-puestas sobre su interés en los acontecimientos mundiales?

C **El mundo de hoy.** Algunos creen que las siguientes declaraciones describen el estado del mundo actual. ¿Qué cree Ud.? Dé su opinión, empezando con una de estas expresiones.

(No) Dudo que...   Es lástima que...
(No) Es verdad que...   Es increíble que...
Es probable que...   (No) Me gusta que...
Es bueno/malo que...

1. En los Estados Unidos seguimos usando demasiado petróleo.
2. Debemos concederles todo lo que pidan a los terroristas que tienen rehenes (*hostages*).
3. Hay más catástrofes naturales actualmente que hace 50 años.
4. Es una buena idea asesinar a todos los dictadores del mundo.
5. No hay esperanza de una paz mundial.
6. Los policías, los bomberos (*firefighters*), los médicos y los enfermeros no tienen el derecho de declararse en huelga.
7. La guerra es un buen medio de resolver los conflictos internacionales.

Ahora invente una oración a la que van a responder sus compañeros de clase.

ESTRUCTURAS ▼▼▼▼▼▼▼▼▼▼▼▼▼▼▼▼▼▼▼▼▼▼▼▼▼

RECICLADO

In Grammar Section 43, you will learn about and begin to use the forms of the past subjunctive. To learn the forms of the past subjunctive, you will need to know the forms of the preterite well, especially the third person plural (Grammar Sections 20 and 24).

Give the third person plural of the preterite for these infinitives.

1. hablar	4. jugar	7. reír	10. tener	13. traer	16. vestirse	19. ir
2. comer	5. perder	8. leer	11. destruir	14. dar	17. decir	20. poder
3. vivir	6. dormir	9. estar	12. mantener	15. saber	18. creer	

43. ¡Ojalá que pudiéramos hacerlo!

Past Subjunctive

▼ **Aquellos eran otros tiempos...**
▼
▼   DON JORGE: ¡Parece imposible que yo *dijera* eso! ¡Qué egoísmo!
▼ DON GUSTAVO: ¡No es posible que *lucháramos* tanto!
▼
▼ Hace treinta años, era difícil que don Jorge y don Gustavo *hablaran*
▼ de las elecciones sin pelearse. Era imposible que *se pusieran* de
▼ acuerdo en política. ¡Qué lástima que *hubiera* tanta enemistad entre
▼ ellos en aquel entonces!
▼   Ahora es probable que no se acuerden de todas las peleas del
▼ pasado. También es posible que sus convicciones políticas sean menos
▼ fuertes... o simplemente que ahora tengan otras cosas de que hablar.
▼
▼   ▲ ▲ ▲
▼
▼ Hace diez años...
▼
▼ 1. ¿de qué era difícil que Ud. hablara con sus padres?
▼ 2. ¿con quién era imposible que Ud. se pusiera de acuerdo?
▼ 3. ¿con quién era imposible que Ud. se comunicara?
▼
▼ Cuando Ud. era niño/a...
▼
▼ 4. ¿dónde le prohibían sus padres que jugara?
▼ 5. ¿qué era obligatorio que comiera o bebiera?
▼ 6. ¿qué temía que sus padres supieran?

—VIEJOS VOTANTES. ¿Recuerda cuánto tuvimos que discurrir (*to discuss*) usted y yo antes de votar hace treinta años?

Although Spanish has two simple indicative past tenses (preterite and imperfect), it has only one simple subjunctive past tense, **el imperfecto del subjuntivo** (*past subjunctive*). Generally speaking, this tense is used in the same situations as the present subjunctive but, of course, when talking about past events. The exact English equivalent depends on the context in which it is used.

Forms of the Past Subjunctive

PAST SUBJUNCTIVE OF REGULAR VERBS*					
habar: hablar*ón*		**comer: comier*ón***		**vivir: vivier*ón***	
hablar**a**	hablár**amos**	comier**a**	comiér**amos**	vivier**a**	viviér**amos**
hablar**as**	hablar**ais**	comier**as**	comier**ais**	vivier**as**	vivier**ais**
hablar**a**	hablar**an**	comier**a**	comier**an**	vivier**a**	vivier**an**

In the old days . . .   DON JORGE: It seems impossible that I said that! How selfish! DON GUSTAVO: It's not possible that we fought that much!

Thirty years ago it was difficult for don Jorge and don Gustavo to talk about elections without fighting. It was impossible for them to come to any agreement about politics. What a shame that there was so much bad feeling between them back then!

Now it's probable that they don't remember all the fights of the past. It's also possible that their political convictions are less intense . . . or just that they have other things to discuss now.

*An alternative form of the past subjunctive (used primarily in Spain) ends in **-se: hablase, hablases, hablase, hablásemos, hablaseis, hablasen.** This form will not be practiced in *¿Qué tal?*

The past subjunctive endings **-a, -as, -a, -amos, -ais, -an** are identical for **-ar, -er,** and **-ir** verbs. These endings are added to the third person plural of the preterite indicative, minus its **-on** ending. For this reason, the forms of the past subjunctive reflect the irregularities of the preterite.

STEM-CHANGING VERBS

-Ar and **-er** verbs: no change

> **empezar (ie):**   empezar*ón* → **empezara, empezaras,** etc.
> **volver (ue):**   volvier*ón*   → **volviera, volvieras,** etc.

-Ir verbs: all persons of the past subjunctive reflect the vowel change that appears in the third person plural of the preterite.

> **dormir (ue, u):**   durmier*ón* → **durmiera, durmieras,** etc.
> **pedir (i, i)**   pidier*ón* → **pidiera, pidieras,** etc.

SPELLING CHANGES

All persons of the past subjunctive reflect the change from **i** to **y** between two vowels.

> **i** → **y** (caer, construir, creer, destruir, leer, oír)

> **creer:** creyer*ón* → **creyera, creyeras,** etc.

VERBS WITH IRREGULAR PRETERITES

> **dar:** dier*ón* → **diera, dieras, diera, diéramos, dierais, dieran**

decir:	dijer*ón* → **dijera**	**poner:**	pusier*ón* → **pusiera**
estar:	estuvier*ón* → **estuviera**	**querer:**	quisier*ón* → **quisiera**
haber:	hubier*ón* → **hubiera**	**saber:**	supier*ón* → **supiera**
hacer:	hicier*ón* → **hiciera**	**ser:**	fuer*ón* → **fuera**
ir:	fuer*ón* → **fuera**	**tener:**	tuvier*ón* → **tuviera**
poder:	pudier*ón* → **pudiera**	**venir:**	vinier*ón* → **viniera**

Uses of the Past Subjunctive

The past subjunctive usually has the same applications as the present subjunctive, but is used for past events. Compare these pairs of sentences.

Quiero que **jueguen** ahora.	*I want them to play now.*
Quería que **jugaran** ayer por la tarde.	*I wanted them to play yesterday afternoon.*
Siente que no **estén** allí ahora.	*He's sorry (that) they aren't there now.*
Sintió que no **estuvieran** allí anoche.	*He was sorry (that) they weren't there last night.*
Dudamos que lo **sepan.**	*We doubt that they know it.*
Dudábamos que lo **supieran.**	*We doubted that they knew it.*

Remember that the subjunctive is used in independent clauses after (1) expressions of *influence, emotion,* and *doubt;* (2) *nonexistent* and *indefinite antecedents;* and (3) certain *conjunctions.*

1.   **¿Era necesario** que **regatearas**?   *Was it necessary for you to bargain?*
2.   **No había nadie** que **pudiera**   *There wasn't anyone who could*
     resolverlo.   *(might have been able to) solve it.*
3.   Los padres **trabajaron para que**   *The parents worked so that their*
     sus hijos **asistieran** a la   *children could (might) go to the*
     universidad.   *university.*

Práctica

A **Mi vida en la escuela secundaria.** Lea las siguientes oraciones e indique las que son verdaderas para Ud. Cambie las oraciones falsas para que expresen su propia experiencia.

En la escuela secundaria...

   1. _____ era obligatorio que yo asistiera a todas mis clases.
   2. _____ mis padres insistían en que yo estudiara mucho.
   3. _____ era necesario que yo trabajara para que pudiera asistir a la universidad algún día.
   4. _____ no había ninguna clase que me interesara.
   5. _____ tenía que sacar buenas notas para que mis padres me dieran dinero.
   6. _____ mis amigos querían que los llevara en coche a todas partes.
   7. _____ era necesario que volviera a casa a una hora determinada, aun los fines de semana.
   8. _____ mis padres me exigían que limpiara mi cuarto cada semana.

¿Era mejor la vida en la escuela secundaria? ¿Le gustaría regresar a esa época? ¿Por qué sí o por qué no?

B **Y ahora, la niñez.** ¿Qué quería Ud. de la vida cuando era niño/a? ¿Y qué querían los demás que Ud. hiciera? Conteste, haciendo oraciones con una frase de cada grupo.

   1. Mis padres (no) querían que yo...
   2. Mis maestros me pedían que...
   3. Yo buscaba amigos que...
   4. Me gustaba mucho que nosotros...

   ir a la iglesia (al templo) con ellos
   portarse bien, ser bueno/a
   estudiar mucho, hacer la tarea todas las noches, sacar buenas notas
   ponerse ropa vieja para jugar, jugar en las calles, pelear con
     mis amigos, recoger animales en la calle y traerlos a casa
   mirar mucho la televisión, leer muchas tiras cómicas, comer muchos
     dulces
   vivir en nuestro barrio, asistir a la misma escuela, tener muchos
     juguetes, ser aventureros
   ir de vacaciones en verano, pasar todos juntos los días feriados,
     tener un árbol de Navidad muy alto

FALTA DE LATINOS EN LA PRENSA AMERICANA

Extra! ¡Extra! ¡Los latinos estamos mal representados en la prensa americana! A esta conclusión han arribado tanto la Asociación Nacional de Periodistas Hispanos (National Association of Hispanic Journalists) como el servicio de noticias Hispanic Link. Sólo 2.8% del personal de los 56 periódicos más importantes de los Estados Unidos es hispano, según la NAHJ. Y una encuesta de Hispanic Link muestra que cuatro de cada cinco dirigentes hispanos creen que los periódicos no hacen lo suficiente para mejorar la información sobre, y la comunicación con, nuestras comunidades.

C **El noticiero de las seis.** Lea las siguientes oraciones y cámbialas al pasado. Debe usar el imperfecto del primer verbo en cada oración y luego el imperfecto del subjuntivo en la segunda parte.

1. «Los obreros quieren que les den un aumento de sueldo.»
2. «Es posible que los trabajadores sigan en huelga hasta el verano.»
3. «Es lástima que no haya espacio para todos allí.»
4. «Los terroristas piden que los oficiales no los persigan.»
5. «Parece imposible que el gobierno acepte sus demandas.»
6. «Es necesario que el gobierno informe a todos los ciudadanos del desastre.»
7. «Dudo que la paz mundial esté fuera de nuestro alcance (reach).»
8. «Los políticos temen que el número de votantes sea muy bajo en las elecciones.»

D **El comienzo y el fin del delito perfecto.** Combine las oraciones, usando las conjunciones entre paréntesis y haciendo otros cambios necesarios.

1. El ladrón (thief) no pensaba entrar en la casa. No oía ningún ruido. (a menos que)
2. No iba a molestar a los dueños. Encontraba dinero y objetos de valor. (con tal que)
3. Un amigo lo acompañaba. Había alguna dificultad. (en caso de que)
4. El amigo rompió la ventana. El ladrón pudo entrar. (para que)
5. El ladrón entró silenciosamente. Los dueños no se despertaron. (para que)
6. Salió. Los dueños pudieron llamar a la policía. (antes de que)

E **Los consejos se dan gratis.** Sin duda, varias personas le dieron a Ud. muchos consejos o recomendaciones antes de que Ud. empezara a estudiar en la universidad. ¿Qué le recomendaron las siguientes personas? Indique las oraciones que son apropiadas para Ud. Luego dé por lo menos otro consejo o recomendación más que cada persona o grupo de personas le ofreció a Ud.

Frases útiles: tomar muchas clases diferentes, hacerme socio/a (member) de un(a) fraternity/sorority, graduarme dentro de cuatro años, participar en muchas actividades extracurriculares, llamar con frecuencia, evitar el alcohol y las drogas

1. Mis amigos me recomendaron que viviera en una residencia en vez de en un apartamento.
2. Mis padres me aconsejaron que estudiara mucho.
3. Mi mejor amigo/a me pidió que le escribiera de vez en cuando.
4. Mi consejero/a me recomendó que me especializara en una carrera práctica y útil.

Segundo paso

▼▼▼▼▼▼▼▼▼▼▼▼▼▼▼▼▼▼▼▼▼▼▼▼▼▼▼   **VOCABULARIO**

El gobierno y la responsabilidad cívica

comunicarse (con)	to communicate (with)
durar	to last, endure
obedecer (obedezco)	to obey
votar	to vote
el/la ciudadano/a	citizen
la constitución	constitution
el deber	responsibility, obligation
los demás	others, other people
el derecho	right
la (des)igualdad	(in)equality
la dictadura	dictatorship
la discriminación	discrimination
la ley	law
el rey / la reina	king/queen

HONOR A DENNIS CHAVEZ

Una querida y admirada figura hispana de la política nacional ha recibido una de las más altas distinciones conferidas a los servidores públicos: su propio sello postal. El honor fue otorgado a Dennis Chávez, el primer senador hispano en la historia del país. Durante más de tres décadas, Chávez representó al estado de Nuevo México en Washington hasta su muerte, en 1962.

El sello forma parte de la colección Grandes Series Americanas de 1991, con la cual el servicio postal pretende reconocer la labor de figuras, eventos o lugares como motivos ilustrativos de la presencia hispana en el país. ◆

El senador Chávez

Práctica

A **Asociaciones.** ¿Qué cosas, personas o ideas asocia Ud. con las siguientes palabras?

1. el deber
2. el derecho
3. la ley
4. la discriminación
5. la monarquía
6. la dictadura

B ¡**Peligro** (*Jeopardy*)! ¿Cuánto sabe Ud. de historia y política? Conteste rápidamente con la información necesaria.

1. Fue un dictador argentino que tenía una esposa famosa.
2. Se llama Elizabeth y vive en Buckingham Palace.
3. Es una famosa película de Orson Welles, y su protagonista se llama Kane.
4. Fue un presidente estadounidense que se opuso a (*opposed*) la esclavitud de los negros.
5. En este documento se especifican los derechos de los ciudadanos de un país.
6. Es la forma de gobierno que existe en España.
7. Existe cuando muchas personas no tienen los mismos derechos que los demás.
8. Es un deber de los ciudadanos en una democracia.

NOTA CULTURAL: Formas de gobierno

No es por casualidad que los hispanoamericanos llaman a España la «madre patria». Cuando los españoles llegaron a América, instalaron un sistema de gobierno, controlado directamente desde España, que duró casi trescientos años. Pero a pesar de los vínculos[a] culturales, sociales y religiosos que existen entre estos países y España, ha habido también muchas diferencias entre ellos, sobre todo en el área de la política.

España tiene una larga tradición monárquica. La unificación política de la península ocurrió cuando se casaron la reina Isabel y el rey Fernando en 1469. Esta tradición ha sido interrumpida sólo por dos períodos republicanos, una Guerra Civil (1936–1939) y la dictadura del general Francisco

Franco (1939–1975). Según la Constitución Española de 1978, «La forma política del Estado español es la Monarquía parlamentaria.» El monarca actual es el rey don Juan Carlos I.

En Hispanoamérica, el siglo XIX es la época de las guerras de independencia y de los libertadores. Se destaca[b] entre todos la figura de Simón Bolívar, quien es para Sudamérica lo que George Washington es para los norteamericanos: el verdadero padre de la independencia. En la actualidad todavía continúan las luchas[c] en Hispanoamérica. Ha habido—y sigue habiendo[d]—guerras de guerrillas en algunos países y verdaderas revoluciones en otros. El objetivo de estas es lograr[e] cambios políticos, económicos y sociales.

[a]*a... in spite of the ties* [b]*Se... Stands out* [c]*struggles* [d]*sigue... there continue to be* [e]*to achieve*

ESTRUCTURAS ▼▼▼▼▼▼▼▼▼▼▼▼▼▼▼▼▼▼▼▼▼

44. ¿Por o para?

A Summary of Their Uses

▼ **En un museo**

GUÍA: Pasen *por* aquí, *por* favor. Dejen espacio *para* todos. Y bien. *Por fin* estamos delante del Guernica, la obra maestra pintada *por* Picasso *para* representar los horrores de la guerra. Picasso pintó este cuadro como reacción al bombardeo de la ciudad de Guernica durante la Guerra Civil Española. *Por* razones políticas, durante la dictadura de

Guernica, por Pablo Picasso.

Franco, el cuadro estuvo muchos años en el Museo de Arte Moderno de Nueva York. Pero *por* deseo expreso del pintor, fue trasladado a España después de la muerte del dictador...

VISITANTE 1: *Para* mí, este cuadro no es bonito. ¡Si *por lo menos* tuviera color... !

VISITANTE 2: ¿*Por* qué tiene que ser bonito? *Para* mí, la falta de color sirve *para* expresar el dolor y el desastre... *Por eso* puedo sentir el mensaje de horror y destrucción en este cuadro.

▲ ▲ ▲

Busque el equivalente de las siguientes oraciones en el diálogo.

1. Yo prefiero los cuadros en colores.
2. Picasso pintó una obra que representa la guerra.
3. Yo entiendo el propósito (*purpose*) del uso de blanco y negro.
4. Quiero que todos me sigan y que se pongan delante del cuadro.
5. Picasso quería que el Guernica se trasladara a España.

You have been using the prepositions **por** and **para** from the beginning of *¿Qué tal?* as they have been presented to you gradually throughout the chapters in boxes called *¿**Por** o **para**?* Thus, most of the information in this section will be a review.

Por

The preposition **por** has the following English equivalents.

- *by, by means of*

    Vamos **por** avión (tren, barco,...).   *We're going by plane (train, ship, . . .).*

In a museum   GUIDE: Step through here, please. Leave room for everyone. O.K. At last, we are in front of Guernica, the masterpiece painted by Picasso to represent the horrors of war. Picasso painted this picture as a reaction to the bombing of the city of Guernica during the Spanish Civil War. For political reasons during Franco's dictatorship, the painting was at the Museum of Modern Art of New York for many years. But, because of the painter's explicit wish, it was moved to Spain after the dictator's death... VISITOR 1: For me, this painting is not pretty. If it had some color at least! VISITOR 2: Why does it have to be pretty? For me, the lack of color serves to express pain and disaster . . . That's why I can sense a message of horror and destruction in this painting.

Nos hablamos **por** teléfono mañana.	*We'll talk by (on the) phone tomorrow.*

- *through, along*

Me gusta pasear **por** el parque y **por** la playa.	*I like to stroll through the park and along the beach.*

- *during, in* (time of day)

Trabajo **por** la mañana.	*I work in the morning.*

- *because of, due to*

Estoy nervioso **por** la entrevista.	*I'm nervous because of the interview.*

- *for = in exchange for*

Piden 1.000 dólares **por** el coche.	*They're asking $1,000 for the car.*
Gracias **por** todo.	*Thanks for everything.*

- *for = for the sake of, on behalf of*

Lo hago **por** ti.	*I'm doing it for you (for your sake).*

- *for = duration* (often omitted)

Vivieron allí (**por**) un año.	*They lived there for a year.*

Por is also used in a number of fixed expressions.

por Dios	for heaven's sake	**por lo general**	generally, in general
por ejemplo	for example	**por lo menos**	at least
por eso	that's why	**por primera/última vez**	for the first/last time
por favor	please	**por si acaso**	just in case
por fin	finally	**¡por supuesto!**	of course!

Para

Although **para** has many English equivalents, including *for,* the basic underlying meaning refers to a goal or destination.

- *in order to* + infinitive

Regresaron pronto **para** estudiar.	*They returned soon (in order) to study.*
Estudian **para** conseguir un buen trabajo.	*They're studying (in order) to get a good job.*

- *for = destined for, to be given to*

Todo esto es **para** ti.	*All this is for you.*
Le di un libro **para** su hijo.	*I gave her a book for her son.*

- *for = by* (deadline, specified future time)

Para mañana, estudien **por** y **para.**	*For tomorrow, study **por** and **para.***
La composición es **para** el lunes.	*The composition is for Monday.*

- *for = toward, in the direction of*

  Salió **para** el Ecuador ayer.   *She left for Ecuador yesterday.*

- *for = to be used for*

  El dinero es **para** la matrícula.   *The money is for tuition.*
  Es un vaso **para** agua.   *It's a water glass.*

  ¡OJO!   Compare this to **un vaso de agua** = *a glass (full) of water.*

- *for = as compared with others, in relation to others*

  Para mí, el español es fácil.   *For me, Spanish is easy.*
  Para (ser) extranjera, habla muy   *For a foreigner, she speaks English*
  bien el inglés.   *very well.*

- *for = in the employ of*

  Trabajan **para** el gobierno.   *They work for the government.*

Práctica

A **¿Por** or **para?** Complete los siguientes diálogos y oraciones con **por** o **para.**

1. Los señores Arana salieron _____ el Perú ayer. Van _____ avión, claro, pero luego piensan viajar en coche _____ todo el país. Van a estar allí _____ dos meses. Va a ser una experiencia extraordinaria _____ toda la familia.

2. —Buscamos un regalo de boda _____ nuestra nieta. ¿No tienen Uds. unas copas de cristal _____ vino?
   —Claro que sí, señora. Tenemos estas _____ quince dólares cada una y también estas _____ veinte.

3. Mi prima Graciela quiere estudiar _____ (ser) doctora. _____ eso trabaja _____ un médico _____ la mañana; tiene clases _____ la tarde.

4. —No dejes la tarea _____ mañana, ¿eh?
   —No te preocupes, mamá. Hoy _____ la noche voy a estudiar _____ el examen.

5. —¿_____ qué están Uds. aquí todavía? Yo pensaba que iban a dar un paseo _____ el parque.
   —Íbamos a hacerlo, pero _____ fin no fuimos, _____ la nieve.

6. Este cuadro fue pintado _____ Picasso _____ expresar los desastres de la guerra. _____ muchos críticos de arte, es la obra maestra de este artista.

B **Entre abuelo y nieta.** Complete el siguiente diálogo con **por** o **para.**

NIETA: Abuelito, ¿_____[1] qué vivimos aquí en Nueva York?

ABUELO: Porque perdí mi finca,[a] hija, y entre la falta de trabajo en Puerto Rico y la oportunidad de trabajar _____[2] el negocio de la familia de un amigo aquí, tu abuela y yo decidimos emigrar.

NIETA: Entonces, ¿_____[3] qué dices a veces que preferirías vivir allí todavía?

ABUELO: Mira, es que somos de otra cultura, hablamos otra lengua... Pero tú has nacido aquí; _____[4] ti todo es diferente. _____[5] nosotros la Isla es nuestra patria. No salimos _____[6] gusto sino[b] _____[7] necesidad.

NIETA: ¿Es _____[8] eso que les gusta regresar todos los años?

ABUELO: Claro, _____[9] estar con los nuestros, en nuestro ambiente...

[a]*farm*   [b]*but rather*

Ahora complete las oraciones según el diálogo.

1. Los abuelos salieron porque _____.
2. Regresan todos los años porque _____.
3. La nieta está a gusto en los Estados Unidos porque _____.

C **Cada oveja con su pareja.** (*Every sheep with its mate.*) Escoja una respuesta para cada pregunta o situación. Luego invente un contexto para cada diálogo. ¿Dónde están las personas que hablan? ¿Quiénes son? ¿Por qué dicen lo que dicen?

1. ¡Huy! Acabo de jugar al básquetbol por dos horas.
2. ¿Por qué quieres que llame a Pili y Adolfo? Nunca están en casa por la noche, sobre todo a estas horas.
3. ¿No vas a comer nada? ¿Por qué no comes un sándwich?
4. ¡Cuánto lo siento, don Javier! Sé que he llegado con una hora de retraso. No fue mi intención hacerle esperar.
5. Es imposible que tome el examen hoy, por muchas razones.
6. ¿No has oído? Juana acaba de tener un accidente horrible.
7. ¡Pero, papá, quiero ir!
8. Ay, Mariana, pensaba que sabías lo del terremoto. Murieron más de cien personas.

a. ¡Por Dios! ¡Qué desgracia!
b. Te digo que no, por última vez.
c. No se preocupe. Lo importante es que por fin está aquí.
d. ¡Por Dios! ¿Qué le pasó?
e. No, gracias. No tengo mucha hambre y además tengo que salir en seguida.
f. ¿Por ejemplo? Dígame...
g. Ah, por eso tienes tanto calor.
h. Llámalos de todas formas, por si acaso...

D **Un dibujo vale más de mil palabras.** Empareje cada dibujo con la frase adecuada.

1. Le da 1.000 pesetas para las revistas.   3. Van para las montañas.
2. Le da 1.000 pesetas por las revistas.   4. Van por las montañas.

a.   b.   c.   d.

E **Entrevista.** Hágale preguntas a su profesor(a) para saber la siguiente información.

1. la tarea para mañana y para la semana que viene
2. lo que hay que estudiar para el examen final
3. si para él/ella son interesantes o aburridas las ciencias
4. la opinión que tiene de la pronunciación de Uds., para ser principiantes
5. cuál es el mejor curso de español para Ud. para el semestre/trimestre que viene

Un paso más

Un POCO DE TODO

A Escenas históricas.

Paso 1. La gente emigra por varias razones. Complete las siguientes oraciones con la forma correcta del infinitivo. Luego, si puede, nombre un grupo que emigró por la razón citada.

1. Las leyes de su país de origen no permitían que este grupo (practicar) libremente su religión.
2. Algunas personas esperaban que (haber) oro y plata en América.
3. El rey no quería que estos criminales (seguir) viviendo en su país.
4. Estos inmigrantes buscaban un país donde (haber) paz y esperanza y seguridad (*safety*) personal.
5. Los miembros de este grupo buscaban un país donde no (tener) que pasar hambre.

Paso 2. Dé una breve descripción del pasado histórico de los Estados Unidos, haciendo oraciones según las indicaciones.

1. indios / temer / que / colonos / quitarles / toda la tierra
2. colonos / no / gustar / que / ser necesario / pagarle / impuestos / rey
3. parecía imposible / que / joven república / tener éxito (*success*)
4. los del sur / no / gustar / que / gobernarlos / los del norte
5. abolicionistas / no / gustar / que / algunos / no / tener / mismo / libertades

B ¿Qué lees? Complete the following dialogue with the correct form of the words in parentheses, as suggested by the context. When two possibilities are given in parentheses, select the correct word.

EDUARDO: ¿De quién (ser/estar[1]) esta revista?
LINDA: Yo la (comprar[2]) ayer. Te (lo/la[3]) puedo prestar, si quieres.
EDUARDO: Pues me gustaría que me la (dejar[4]). La he (hojear[a5]) y me ha gustado.
LINDA: Para (yo/mí[6]) también ha sido una sorpresa. No pensaba que (ser/estar[7]) (tan/tanto[8]) buena. Tiene un poco de todo. Aunque yo temía que (resultar[b9]) superficial, no es así.
EDUARDO: (*Yo*: Ser/Estar[10]) de acuerdo. Trae artículos de política internacional (muy/mucho[11]) interesantes. Quiero terminar de (leer[12]) ese artículo sobre la situación de las antiguas[c] repúblicas soviéticas.
LINDA: (Leer: *Tú*[13]) también el reportaje sobre África. Hace un análisis muy interesante sobre (el/la[14]) relación entre el hambre, la guerra y (el/la[15]) desertización. Pero también habla de la política nacional, de ciencia...
EDUARDO: Sí y ya (ver: yo[16]) que además trae (un/una[17]) reportaje sobre mi actor favorito.

[a]*to look over*   [b]*to turn out*   [c]*former*

LINDA: (Es/Está[18]) cierto. Trae bastantes comentarios sobre el cine. También puedes (enterarse[19]) de las últimas novedades, tanto sobre libros (que/como[20]) sobre música.

EDUARDO: Y también me imagino[d] (que / lo que[21]) tiene secciones sobre viajes, salud, deportes...

LINDA: Tienes (suerte/razón[22]). Es una buena forma de enterarse de todo lo actual.

[d]me... *I imagine*

¿Cierto o falso? Corrija las oraciones falsas.

1. A Linda le gusta leer más que a Eduardo.
2. La revista de que hablan es superficial.
3. Es posible que tenga también una sección sobre viajes.

✹ SITUACIÓN   Discutiendo de política

The following discussion contains some patterns useful for disagreeing with others. How many can you find?

PERSONA 1: Ese Ramírez... Sólo habla de los trabajadores y el medio ambiente. Y toda la violencia que hay en las calles de esta ciudad, ¿qué?

PERSONA 2: La culpa de todo eso la tiene este gobierno. El presidente no ha hecho nada en los últimos cuatro años.

PERSONA 3: ¿Qué estás diciendo, hombre? La mayoría de la gente vive mucho mejor ahora. Y mira todo el desarrollo urbano...

PERSONA 4: ¡Pero eso es una postura[a] muy egoísta! Es que a ti sólo te importa tu vida, tu barrio, tu trabajo. Pero hay mucha gente que se muere de hambre, que no tiene dónde vivir...

[a]*position*

NOTAS COMUNICATIVAS SOBRE EL DIÁLOGO

The Spanish word **discusión** is not really an exact equivalent of the English *discussion*. A Spanish **discusión** can be an argument, and the verb **discutir** does mean *to argue,* not *to discuss.*

The Hispanic style of debating politics is much livelier than corresponding discussions in the English-speaking world. Aggressive remarks are more acceptable, and it is also acceptable to break in with remarks while someone else is speaking. Good friends and relatives will not hesitate to tell each other that what the other is saying is **una tontería** (*a stupid thing*), all in the spirit of having a good time over coffee or drinks.

Here are some "safe" phrases that will help you disagree and jump into a discussion.

> Sí, pero...
> Bueno, pero yo creo que...
> Yo no sé, pero...
> Eso suena (*sounds*) bien, pero la realidad es diferente.

[a]*portside*

Los españoles tienen fama de discutir mucho. ¿Es por eso que el capitán sabe que el barco es español?

Conversación

With a partner, choose one of the following topics and prepare several position statements about it. Then, with another pair of classmates, take turns reacting to each other's statements. Play "devil's advocate," even if you agree with what the others have said.

Sugerencias: la pena de muerte (*death penalty*), la legalización de la marihuana, el récord del actual presidente, las próximas elecciones locales o nacionales, el medio ambiente

PARA ESCRIBIR

Escríbale una carta al editor de un periódico o revista o al presidente de una de las redes (*networks*) principales de televisión (NBC, CBS, ABC, CNN, etcétera) o de un canal local para expresar su opinión sobre la clase de reportaje que ofrece. En su carta, puede hacer una crítica negativa o una crítica favorable en la que elogie (*praise*) el reportaje.

Antes de escribirla, lea un artículo o mire las noticias en la televisión y tome apuntes (*take notes*) para formarse una opinión. Luego escriba la carta, explicando por qué le gusta el reportaje o por qué no. Incluya recomendaciones para mejorar el reportaje.

VOCABULARIO

Verbos

discutir to argue, disagree
pelear to fight

Las noticias

enterarse (de) to find out, learn (about)
informar to inform

el acontecimiento event
el asesinato assasination
la bomba bomb
el canal (TV) channel
el choque crash, collision
la esperanza hope
la guerra war
la huelga strike
el noticiero newscast
el/la obrero/a worker, laborer
la paz (*pl.* **paces**) peace
la prensa press; print medium

el/la reportero/a reporter
el/la testigo witness

Repaso: el barrio, el desastre

El gobierno y la responsabilidad cívica

comunicarse (con) to communicate (with)
durar to last
obedecer (obedezco) to obey
votar to vote

el/la ciudadano/a citizen
la constitución constitution
el deber responsibility, obligation
los demás others, other people
el derecho right
la (des)igualdad (in)equality
el/la dictador(a) dictator
la dictadura dictatorship

la discriminación discrimination
la ley law
el rey / la reina king/queen

Palabras adicionales

por Dios for heaven's sake
por lo menos at least
por si acaso just in case
¡por supuesto! of course!

Repaso: por ejemplo, por eso, por favor, por fin, por lo general

Self-Test
Use the tape that accompanies this text to test yourself briefly on the important points of this chapter.

VOCES

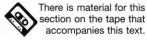

There is material for this
section on the tape that
accompanies this text.

del mundo hispánico 11
España

El nombre **España** viene del latín **Hispania**, y
de ahí los términos **hispano** e **hispánico** que
se aplican a los países americanos de lengua
española a sus habitantes.

La historia de España es tan turbulenta
como la de sus antiguas[a] colonias. En este
siglo España sufrió numerosos conflictos
sociopolíticos que culminaron con la Guerra
Civil (1936–1939) y la dictadura de Francisco
Franco, que duró hasta su muerte en 1975.
Desde entonces, el país ha establecido una
democracia bien consolidada, en forma de
monarquía parlamentaria (similar al sistema
británico).

España es hoy un país desarrollado y moderno, que forma parte de la Comunidad Europea y la OTAN (Organización del Tratado del Atlántico Norte). Geopolítica-
mente, el país está dividido en 17 comunidades autónomas.

Aunque el español es la lengua oficial de la nación y se habla en todas partes,
existen otras tres lenguas, que son oficiales en sus respectivas comunidades: el catalán, el gallego y el vasco o euskera.

[a]*former*

La transición democrática española es un
capítulo excepcional en la historia de
nuestro país y una experiencia singular en
el contexto nacional. Los últimos diez años de
la política española han representado un giro[a]
radical en el itinerario de nuestra vida colectiva
en la época contemporánea. En el plano internacional el modelo español de transición pací-
fica a la democracia por su originalidad ejerce
una profunda influencia en los complejos pro-
cesos de cambio por los que atraviesan[b] las sociedades iberoamericanas en la actualidad.»

[a]*turn* [b]*por... through which are passing*

Felipe González, presidente del gobierno socialista de España.

El Alcázar, Sevilla. La larga presencia árabe (711–1492)
ha dejado una gran influencia en España, que la hace
diferente del resto de Europa.

400

El niño al que se le murió el amigo

U na mañana se levantó y fue a buscar al amigo, al otro lado de la valla.[a] Pero el amigo no estaba, y cuando volvió, le dijo la madre: «El amigo se murió. Niño, no pienses más en él y busca otros para jugar.» El niño se sentó en el quicio[b] de la puerta, con la cara entre las manos y los codos[c] en las rodillas. «Él volverá», pensó. Porque no podía ser que allí estuviesen[d] las canicas,[e] el camión y la pistola de hojalata,[f] y el reloj aquel que ya no andaba,[g] y el amigo no viniese[h] a buscarlos. Vino la noche, con una estrella muy grande, y el niño no quería entrar a cenar. «Entra, niño, que llega el frío[i]», dijo la madre. Pero, en lugar de entrar, el niño se levantó del quicio y se fue en busca del amigo, con las canicas, el camión, la pistola de hojalata y el reloj que no andaba. Al llegar a la cerca,[j] la voz del amigo no le llamó, ni le oyó en el árbol, ni en el pozo.[k] Pasó buscándole toda la noche. Y fue una larga noche casi blanca, que le llenó de polvo[l] el traje y los zapatos. Cuando llegó el sol, el niño, que tenía sueño y sed, estiró[m] los brazos, y pensó: «Qué tontos y pequeños son esos juguetes. Y ese reloj que no anda, no sirve para

nada.» Lo tiró todo al pozo, y volvió a la casa, con mucha hambre. La madre le abrió la puerta, y dijo: «Cuánto ha crecido este niño.[n]» Y le compró un traje de hombre, porque el que llevaba le venía muy corto.[o]

Familia de saltimbancos (acrobats) *con mono*, pintado por Pablo Picasso (1881–1973), uno de los pintores españoles más famosos del mundo.

[a] *al... on the other side of the fence* [b] *frame* [c] *elbows* [d] *estuvieran* [e] *marbles* [f] *tin* [g] *funcionaba* [h] *viniera* [i] *que... it's getting cold*
[j] *fence* [k] *well* [l] *le... covered with dust* [m] *stretched* [n] Cuánto... *How this child has grown up!* [o] *le... was too small for him*

Ana María Matute (1926–), escritora española de la post-guerra. Sus cuentos tienen con frecuencia protagonistas infantiles. (De *El árbol de oro y otros relatos*. Edición de Julián Moreiro. Editorial Bruño: 1991.)

¡Qué interesante!

▼ **1.** Mirando un mapa de España, ¿puede identificar las regiones en que se hablan el gallego, el catalán y el vasco? ¿Con qué regiones asocia Ud. las siguientes cosas?

la capital del país, Madrid
las naranjas
Don Quijote
los Juegos Olímpicos de 1992

la Expo '92 (exposición internacional para conmemorar los 500 años de la llegada de Colón a América)

El actual rey Juan Carlos I.

▼ **2.** España es tierra de notables artistas. ¿Qué otros artistas españoles conoce Ud.? Recuerde: hay españoles famosos en todas las áreas del arte, desde la pintura hasta la música y el cine.

▼ **3.** ¿Por qué la transición democrática española resulta un modelo tan atractivo para muchos países iberoamericanos (latinoamericanos)?

▼ **4.** Según Ana María Matute: «El niño no es un proyecto de hombre, sino que (*but rather*) el hombre es lo que queda del niño que fue.» ¿Cómo se refleja esta idea en el cuento «El niño al que se le murió el amigo»?

23

Primer paso

Profesiones y oficios[a]

[a]trades

la abogada

el dentista

la enfermera

la mujer de negocios

la veterinaria

el cocinero

el plomero

la peluquera

la obrera

la contadora

el soldado

el ama de casa

Hablando de CARRERAS

Más vocabulario

¿Reconoce los siguientes oficios y profesiones? Ud. ya las conoce casi todas. Y es seguro que puede reconocer las nuevas también.

el/la analista de sistemas
el/la bibliotecario/a
el/la cajero/a
el/la comerciante
el/la electricista
el/la fotógrafo/a
el/la ingeniero/a
el/la maestro/a (de primaria o secundaria)
el/la mecánico/a

el/la médico/a
el/la periodista
el/la secretario/a
el/la sicólogo/a
el/la siquiatra
el/la técnico/a
el/la trabajador(a) social
el/la traductor(a)
el/la vendedor(a)

> Learn to use the new terms for professions and trades that are important or interesting to you. Not all of these words will be considered "active vocabulary" that you will be expected to say or write spontaneously.

Práctica

A **¿A quién necesita Ud.?** ¿A quién llamará o con quién consultará en estas situaciones? Hay más de una respuesta posible en algunos casos.

1. La tubería (*plumbing*) de su cocina no funciona bien.
2. Ud. acaba de tener un accidente con el coche; el otro conductor dice que Ud. tuvo la culpa (*blame*).
3. Por las muchas tensiones y presiones de su vida profesional y personal, Ud. tiene serios problemas afectivos (*emotional*).
4. Ud. está en el hospital y quiere que alguien le dé una aspirina.
5. Ud. quiere que alguien le ayude con un asunto legal.
6. Ud. quiere que alguien le construya una pared en el jardín.
7. Ud. conoce todos los detalles de un escándalo en el gobierno de su ciudad y quiere divulgarlos.

B **Asociaciones.** ¿Qué profesiones u oficios asocia Ud. con estas frases? Consulte la lista de **Profesiones y oficios** y use las siguientes palabras también. Haga asociaciones rápidas. ¡No lo piense demasiado!

403

1. creativo/rutinario
2. muchos/pocos años de preparación
3. mucho/poco salario
4. mucha/poca responsabilidad
5. mucho/poco prestigio
6. flexibilidad/«de nueve a cinco»
7. mucho/poco tiempo libre
8. peligroso/seguro
9. en el pasado, sólo para hombres/mujeres
10. todavía, sólo para hombres/mujeres

actor/actriz
arquitecto/a
asistente de vuelo
barman
camarero/a
carpintero/a
consejero/a
cura / pastor(a) / rabino/a

chófer
detective
niñero/a
pintor(a)
poeta
policía / mujer policía
político/a
presidente/a
senador(a)

C ¿**Qué preparación se necesita para ser...** ? Imagine que Ud. es consejero universitario / consejera universitaria. Explíquele a un estudiante los cursos que debe tomar para prepararse para las siguientes carreras. Consulte la lista de cursos académicos del **Capítulo 2**. Recomiéndele también lo que debe hacer durante los veranos y los trabajos de tiempo parcial que debe buscar para ganar experiencia en su campo.

1. traductor(a) en la ONU (Organización de las Naciones Unidas)
2. reportero/a en la televisión, especializado/a en los deportes
3. contador(a) para un grupo de abogados
4. periodista en la redacción (*editorial staff*) de una revista de ecología
5. maestro/a de primaria, especializado/a en la educación bilingüe

D **Entrevista.** Con un compañero / una compañera, haga y conteste preguntas para saber la siguiente información.

1. lo que hacían sus abuelos
2. la profesión u oficio de sus padres
3. si tiene un amigo o pariente que tenga una profesión extraordinaria o interesante y el nombre de esa profesión
4. lo que sus padres (su esposo/a) quiere(n) que él/ella sea
5. lo que él/ella quiere ser
6. la carrera para la cual (*which*) se preparan muchos de sus amigos

DE AQUÍ Y DE ALLÁ

Career decisions have an enormous impact on our lives. Here are two ways to comment on them.

- ¿La medicina? Es **una carrera** { **con muchas salidas (opciones).** / **con mucho futuro.**

- Quiero ser programadora para { **hacerme un porvenir.** / **hacerme un futuro.**

When you get a job, express it in these ways.

Por fin { **conseguí un trabajo.** / **me coloqué. (colocarse)**

▼▼▼▼▼▼▼▼▼▼▼▼▼▼▼▼▼▼▼▼▼▼▼▼▼ **ESTRUCTURAS**

45. Expressing What You Would Do

Conditional Verb Forms

▼ **La fantasía de la maestra de Mafalda**

«¡Ya no aguanto este puesto! Creo que me *gustaría* ser abogada... *Pasaría* todo el día con tipos interesantes... *Ganaría* mucho dinero... *Viajaría* mucho, pues *tendría* clientes en todas partes del país... Me *llamarían* actores, actrices, políticos,

hombres y mujeres de negocios para consultar conmigo... También *haría* viajes internacionales para investigar casos en el extranjero... Todo el mundo me *respetaría* y me *escucharía*... »

▲ ▲ ▲

Y Ud., siendo la maestra / el maestro de Mafalda, ¿cómo sería? Use **no** cuando sea necesario.

MODELO: estar contento/a → *Estaría* contento/a.

1. ser un tipo / una tipa coherente
2. desorientar a los estudiantes
3. mirarlos con ojos furiosos
4. hacerlos morir de miedo y llorar de lástima (**¡OJO!** har-)
5. ponerles cara de poco sueldo (**¡OJO!** pondr-)

You have been using the phrase **me gustaría...** for some time to express what you *would like* (to do, say, and so on). **Gustaría** is a conditional verb form, part of a system that will allow you to talk about what you and others would do (say, buy, and so on) in a given situation.

hablar		comer		vivir	
hablar**ía**	hablar**íamos**	comer**ía**	comer**íamos**	vivir**ía**	vivir**íamos**
hablar**ías**	hablar**íais**	comer**ías**	comer**íais**	vivir**ías**	vivir**íais**
hablar**ía**	hablar**ían**	comer**ía**	comer**ían**	vivir**ía**	vivir**ían**

The fantasy of Mafalda's teacher   I can't take this job anymore! I think I would like to be a lawyer . . . I would spend all day with interesting people . . . I would earn a lot of money . . . I would travel a lot, since I would have clients all over the country . . . Actors, actresses, politicians, businesspeople would call to consult with me . . . I would also take international trips to investigate cases abroad . . . Everyone would respect me and listen to me . . .

Like the English future, the English conditional is formed with an auxiliary verb: *I would speak, I would write*. The Spanish *conditional* (**el condicional**), like the Spanish future, is a simple verb form (only one word). It is formed by adding the conditional endings **-ía, -ías, -ía, -íamos, -íais, -ían** to the infinitive. No auxiliary verbs are needed.

Verbs that form the future on an irregular stem use the same stem to form the conditional.

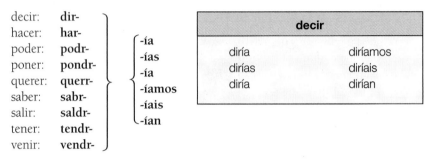

decir:	dir-
hacer:	har-
poder:	podr-
poner:	pondr-
querer:	querr-
saber:	sabr-
salir:	saldr-
tener:	tendr-
venir:	vendr-

| -ía |
| -ías |
| -ía |
| -íamos |
| -íais |
| -ían |

decir	
diría	diríamos
dirías	diríais
diría	dirían

The conditional of **hay** (**haber**) is **habría** (*there would be*).*

The conditional expresses what you would do in a particular situation, given a particular set of circumstances.

| ¿**Hablarías** español en el Brasil? | *Would you speak Spanish in Brazil?* |
| —No. **Hablaría** portugués. | *—No. I would speak Portuguese.* |

¡OJO!   When *would* implies *used to* in English, Spanish uses the imperfect.

| **Íbamos** a la playa todos los veranos. | *We would go (used to go) to the beach every summer.* |

Práctica

A **Estereotipos en las profesiones.** Complete cada oración con la palabra más lógica... ¡y también más estereotípica!

1. Un (plomero/secretario/dentista) me causaría mucho dolor.
2. Una (abogada/maestra/médica) tendría una manzana en su escritorio.
3. Un (profesor/peluquero/soldado) tendría el pelo bastante corto.
4. Un (contador/periodista/fotógrafo) sería una persona pesada y aburrida.
5. Una (comerciante/trabajadora social/plomera) cobraría mucho dinero por su servicio.
6. Una (vendedora/bibliotecaria/mecánica) sería tímida y solterona (*spinsterish*).
7. Un (veterinario/ingeniero/cocinero) sería gordo.

---

*The conditional forms of the verb **haber** are used to form the *conditional perfect tense* (**el condicional perfecto**), which expresses what *would have* occurred at some point in the past.

| **Habríamos tenido** que buscarla en el aeropuerto. | *We would have had to pick her up at the airport.* |

You will find a more detailed presentation of these forms in Appendix 2, Additional Perfect Forms (Indicative and Subjunctive).

B **¿Es posible escapar?** Cuente Ud. la fantasía de esta trabajadora social, dando la forma condicional de los verbos.

Necesito salir de todo esto... Creo que me (gustar[1]) ir a Puerto Rico o a algún otro lugar exótico del Caribe... No (trabajar[2])... (Poder[3]) nadar todos los días... (Tomar[4]) el sol en la playa... (Comer[5]) platos exóticos... (Ver[6]) bellos lugares naturales... El viaje (ser[7]) ideal...

     Pero..., tarde o temprano, (tener[8]) que volver a lo de siempre... a los rascacielos de la ciudad... al tráfico... al medio ambiente contaminado... al mundo del trabajo... (Poder[9]) usar mi tarjeta de crédito, como dice el anuncio—pero ¡(tener[10]) que pagar después!

¿Cierto, falso o no lo dice? Corrija las oraciones falsas.

1. Esta persona trabaja en una ciudad grande.
2. No le interesan los deportes acuáticos.
3. Puede pagar este viaje de sueños al contado.
4. Tiene un novio con quien quisiera hacer el viaje.

C **¿Qué haría si pudiera?** Con un compañero / una compañera, haga y conteste preguntas según el modelo. Cambie los detalles, si quiere.

MODELO: estudiar árabe / japonés →
          E1: ¿Estudiarías árabe?
          E2: No, estudiaría japonés.

1. estudiar italiano / chino
2. hacer un viaje a España / a la Argentina
3. salir de casa sin apagar el estéreo / las luces
4. seguir un presupuesto rígido / uno flexible
5. gastar menos en ropa / en libros
6. poner el aire acondicionado en invierno / en verano
7. alquilar un coche de lujo / uno económico
8. alojarse en una pensión / un hotel de tres estrellas

D **Entrevista.** ¿Cómo será su futuro? ¿Qué hará? ¿Qué haría? Con otro/a estudiante, haga y conteste las siguientes preguntas.

MODELO: —¿Dejarás de fumar algún día? →
          —No. No dejaré de fumar nunca. No puedo.
            (Creo que sí. Dejaré de fumar algún día.)

PREGUNTAS CON EL FUTURO
1. ¿Te graduarás en esta universidad (o en otra)?
2. ¿Vivirás en esta ciudad después de graduarte?
3. ¿Buscarás un puesto aquí?
4. ¿Te casarás (¿Te divorciarás) después de graduarte?
5. ¿Cuántos niños (nietos) crees que tendrás algún día?
6. ¿Serás famoso/a algún día?

PREGUNTAS CON EL CONDICIONAL
1. ¿Te casarías con una persona de otro país?
2. ¿Podrías estar contento/a sin la televisión?
3. ¿Serías capaz de (*capable of*) ahorrar el diez por ciento de tu salario?
4. ¿Te gustaría ayudar a colonizar otro planeta?
5. ¿Podrías vivir sin las tarjetas de crédito?
6. ¿Renunciarías a tu trabajo para viajar por el mundo?

Segundo paso

VOCABULARIO ▼▼▼▼▼▼▼▼▼▼▼▼▼▼▼▼▼▼▼▼▼▼▼▼▼

En busca de un puesto[a]

[a]*job, position*

caerle (caigo) bien/mal a alguien	to make a good/bad impression on someone
dejar	to quit
llenar	to fill out (*a form*)
renunciar (a)	to resign (from)
el/la aspirante	candidate, applicant
el currículum	resumé
la dirección de personal	personnel office
la empresa	corporation, business
la solicitud	application (form)

Labels in illustration: graduarse; caerle bien a la entrevistadora; ¡renunciar al puesto!; DIRECCIÓN DE PERSONAL; llenar las solicitudes; escribir a máquina y contestar el teléfono todo el día

Práctica

Un puesto nuevo. Imagine que Ud. solicitó un puesto recientemente. Usando los números del 1 al 14, indique en qué orden ocurrió lo siguiente. El número 1 ya está indicado.

a. _____ Se despidió de Ud. cordialmente, diciendo que lo/la iba a llamar en una semana.

b. _____ Fue a la biblioteca para informarse sobre la empresa: su historia, dónde tiene sucursales (*branches*), etcétera.

c. _____ Ud. llenó la solicitud tan pronto como la recibió y la mandó, con el currículum, a la empresa.

d. _____ Por fin, el secretario le dijo que Ud. se iba a entrevistar con la directora de personal.

e. __1__ En la oficina de empleos de su universidad, Ud. leyó un anuncio para un puesto en su especialización.

f. _____ Le dijo que le iba a mandar una solicitud para llenar y también le pidió que mandara su currículum.

g. _____ Mientras esperaba en la Dirección de Personal, Ud. estaba nerviosísimo/a.

h. _____ La directora le hizo una serie de preguntas: cuándo se iba a graduar, qué cursos había tomado, etcétera.

i. _____ Cuando por fin lo/la llamó la directora, ¡fue para ofrecerle el puesto!

j. _____ Llamó al teléfono que daba el anuncio y habló con un secretario en la Dirección de Personal.

k. _____ La mañana de la entrevista, Ud. se levantó temprano, se vistió con cuidado y salió temprano para la empresa para llegar puntualmente.

l. _____ Al entrar en la oficina de la directora, Ud. la saludó con cortesía, tratando de caerle bien desde el principio.

m. _____ También le pidió que hablara un poco en español, ya que la empresa tiene una sucursal en Santiago, Chile.

n. _____ En una semana lo/la llamaron para arreglar una entrevista.

▼▼▼▼▼▼▼▼▼▼▼▼▼▼▼▼▼▼▼▼▼▼▼▼▼▼  **ESTRUCTURAS**

46. Hypothetical Situations: What If . . . ?

Si Clause Sentences

▼ **Si yo fuera...**

▼
▼ **¿Qué profesión tendría si... ?**

▼ **1.** Si yo fuera _____, entrevistaría a personas famosas y sabría los
▼ detalles de muchos escándalos.

▼ **2.** Si fuera _____, pasaría todo el día con niños y haría muchas excursiones.

▼ **3.** Si fuera _____, volaría mucho en avión y tendría mucho cuidado con
▼ todos los detalles de mi trabajo.

Both English and Spanish use clauses with *if* (**si**) to speculate or hypothesize about situations that are possible or contrary to fact. In Spanish, when the **si** clause is about the present, the present indicative is used after **si** and in the main clause.

Si le **interesa** el puesto, **llenará** la solicitud.

If she's interested in the job, she'll fill out the application.

To express a contrary-to-fact situation, **si** is followed by the past subjunctive. The conditional is used in the other clause.

Si le **interesara** el puesto, **llenaría** la solicitud.
If she were interested in the job, she would fill out the application.

Si yo **fuera** tú, no **haría** eso.
If I were you, I wouldn't do that.*

Podría hacerse médica si **estudiara** más.
She could become a doctor if she studied more.

---

*The contary-to-fact situations in these sentences express speculations about the present. The perfect forms of the conditional and the past subjunctive are used to speculate about the past: what *would have* happened if a particular event *had* or *had not* occurred.

Si **hubiera tenido** el dinero, **habría hecho** el viaje.
If I had had the money, I would have made the trip.

You will find a more detailed presentation of this structure in Appendix 2, Additional Perfect Forms (Indicative and Subjunctive).

When the **si** clause sentence is in the past tense but is not contrary to fact, the indicative is used. This is especially true when habitual actions or situations are expressed.

Si le **interesaba** el puesto, llenaba la solicitud.

If (When) she was interested in the job, she would (used to) fill out the application.

Práctica

A ¿Qué haría Ud.? ¿Adónde iría? Complete las oraciones lógicamente.

1. Si yo quisiera comprar comida, iría a _____.
2. Si necesitara comprar un libro, iría a _____.
3. Si necesitara usar un libro, iría a _____.
4. Si tuviera sed en este momento, tomaría _____.
5. Si tuviera que emigrar, iría a _____.
6. Si quisiera ir a _____, viajaría en avión.
7. Si quisiera tomar _____, lo esperaría en la estación.
8. Si no funcionara(n) _____, compraría un coche nuevo.

B Si buscara un puesto... ¿Qué haría Ud. si necesitara un puesto? Haga oraciones según el modelo.

MODELO: si / necesitar / puesto, / leer / anuncios / en / periódico →
Si necesitara un puesto, leería los anuncios en el periódico.

1. si / encontrar / anuncio / interesante, / llamar / a / empresa
2. si / empresa / mandarme / solicitud, / llenarla
3. si / (ellos) pedirme / currículum, / mandárselo
4. si / interesarme / salario, / pedir / entrevista
5. si / (ellos) darme / entrevista, / tratar / caerle / bien / entrevistador
6. si / él / hacerme / mucho / preguntas, / contestar / honestamente
7. si / yo / tener / preguntas que hacer / sobre / empresa, / hacerlas / durante / entrevista
8. si / (ellos) ofrecerme / puesto, / estar / muy / contento/a

C El horario de todos los días. ¿Tiene Ud. un horario bastante fijo y rutinario? A ver si puede contestar las siguientes preguntas.

¿Dónde estaría Ud. ... ?

1. si fuera miércoles a las tres de la tarde
2. si fuera jueves a las diez de la mañana
3. si fuera viernes a las nueve de la noche
4. si fuera domingo a las nueve de la mañana
5. si fuera lunes a la una de la tarde

D Situaciones. ¿Qué haría Ud. en estas situaciones? Explique su respuesta.

1. Los señores Medina están durmiendo. De repente se oye un ruido. Un hombre con máscara y guantes (*gloves*) entra silenciosamente en la alcoba.

MODELO: **Si yo fuera** el señor (la señora) Medina, _____.
Si yo fuera el hombre, _____.

2. Celia está estudiando para un examen muy importante. Su compañera de cuarto se pone enferma y la tiene que llevar al hospital. No puede seguir estudiando y, a la mañana siguiente, no está lista para tomar el examen.

MODELO: **Si yo fuera** Celia, _____.
Si yo fuera su compañera, _____.

3. Los padres de Ana no quieren que se case con su novio Antonio, que vive en otro estado. Un día, Ana recibe una carta de Antonio, la lee y de repente sale de la casa. Deja la carta, abierta, en la mesa.

MODELO: **Si yo fuera** Ana, _____ .

   Si yo fuera el padre / la madre, _____ .

E **Entrevista: ¿Bajo qué circunstancias... ?** Entreviste a otro/a estudiante según el modelo.

MODELO: comprar un coche nuevo →

   —¿En qué circunstancias comprarías un coche nuevo?

   —Compraría un coche nuevo si tuviera más dinero.

1. dejar de estudiar
2. emigrar a otro país
3. estudiar otro idioma
4. no obedecer a los padres / al jefe
5. no decirle la verdad a un amigo
6. ir al extranjero este verano
7. desobedecer una ley
8. pelear con un amigo

^aalgún... *a bribe capable of making me desert my principles* ^b*pancakes* ^c¡Qué... *Sometimes I even disgust myself!*

A Mafalda no le gusta para nada la sopa. Pero, bajo ciertas circunstancias, todo es posible, ¿no?

Un paso más

UN POCO DE TODO

A **Si el mundo fuera diferente...** Adaptarse a un nuevo país o a nuevas circunstancias es difícil, pero también es una aventura interesante. ¿Qué ocurriría si el mundo fuera diferente?

MODELO: Si yo fuera la última persona en el mundo... →

   tendría que aprender a hacer muchas cosas.

   sería la persona más importante—y más ignorante—del mundo.

   me adaptaría fácilmente/difícilmente.

   los animales y yo seríamos buenos amigos.

1. Si yo pudiera tener solamente un amigo / una amiga, _____ .
2. Si yo tuviera que pasar un año en una isla desierta, _____ .
3. Si yo fuera (otra persona), _____ .
4. Si el presidente fuera presidenta, _____ .
5. Si yo viviera en la Argentina, _____ .
6. Si fuera el año 2080, _____ .
7. Si yo viviera en el siglo XIX (XV, etcétera), _____ .
8. Si yo fuera la persona más poderosa (*powerful*) del mundo, _____ .
9. Si los estudiantes fueran profesores y los profesores fueran estudiantes,

   _____ .

B **Un exiliado cubano.** Complete the following story with the correct form of the words in parentheses, as suggested by the context. When two possibilities are given in parentheses, select the correct word.

Miguel García es un médico excelente que vive y trabaja en Miami. Emigró de Cuba (después de / después de que[1]) la revolución de Fidel Castro. Miguel (querer[2]) mucho a su patria, pero no le (gustar[3]) el nuevo sistema político. Así (salir: él[4]) de Cuba en 1963 y (llegar[5]) con su familia a los Estados Unidos. El gobierno cubano no permitió que (traer: ellos[6]) muchos bienes[a] personales; (también/tampoco[7]) les (dejar[8]) sacar dinero del país.

Ser un refugiado político es como empezar una nueva vida. Al[b] establecerse en los Estados Unidos, Miguel (experimentar[c][9]) muchos cambios difíciles. (El/ La[10]) idioma, (por/para[11]) ejemplo, (representar[12]) un obstáculo para él. Ya (saber[13]) bastante[d] gramática (inglés[14]) porque la (haber estudiar[15]) en el colegio en Cuba. Pero nunca (haber aprender[16]) a hablarlo con facilidad, y (también/ tampoco[17]) tuvo muchos problemas en comprender (al / a la[18]) gente. Aunque Miguel (haber ser[19]) médico en Cuba, fue difícil encontrar trabajo. Tuvo que trabajar en una fábrica (por/para[20]) mantener[e] a su mujer[f] y a sus tres hijos. Mientras tanto,[g] hizo la residencia en un hospital y (tomar[21]) el examen en el estado de Florida. (Por/Para[22]) fin (conseguir[23]) un (bueno[24]) puesto en un hospital de Miami.

Además, era necesario que los García (acostumbrarse[25]) a una vida y a una cultura completamente diferentes. (Decidir: ellos[26]) adoptar una vida bilingüe: el español es (que / lo que[27]) usan en la casa, pero hablan inglés en el trabajo y en (el/la[28]) calle.

Hoy, después de muchos años de exilio, Miguel y su familia se (haber acostumbrar[29]) a la forma de vida en los Estados Unidos. (Ser/Estar: ellos[30]) ciudadanos de (este/esto[31]) país, aunque muchas veces añoran[h] su tierra natal. Sin embargo, saben que si todavía (estar[32]) en Cuba, su vida (ser[33]) muy diferente.

[a]*goods, belongings* [b]*Upon* [c]*to experience* [d]*a fair amount of* [e]*support* [f]*esposa* [g]*Mientras... Meanwhile* [h]*they miss*

¿Cierto, falso o no lo dice?

1. Miguel tuvo que salir de Cuba; no pudo escoger.
2. Miguel y su familia sufrieron más al principio que ahora.
3. A Miguel no le gustó trabajar en la fábrica.
4. Tuvo que estudiar mucho para aprobar sus exámenes.
5. Los hijos de los Sres. García son bilingües.
6. No extrañan (*They don't miss*) nada de la cultura cubana.

SITUACIÓN   Los trabajos, una preocupación universal

En los siguientes diálogos, una persona tiene un puesto que no le gusta y otra no tiene puesto todavía. ¿Quién tiene el peor problema?

—¿Cuánto tiempo hace que estás en tu nuevo empleo?
—Casi dos meses.
—¿Y cómo te va?
—No muy bien. Me piden que trabaje los fines de semana..., y el salario no es muy bueno. Voy a cambiar de trabajo en cuanto pueda.

—Te digo que de verdad estoy preocupada. No he podido encontrar empleo todavía.
—¿No viste el anuncio en el Departamento de Lenguas? En dos semanas habrá puestos en la Compañía Palacios.
—¡No me digas! ¿Crees que pagarán bien?
—No lo dicen, pero piden varias lenguas y ofrecen la oportunidad de progresar y de viajar.

Buenos Aires, Argentina.

Conversación

Hágale preguntas a un compañero / una compañera de clase que tiene un trabajo (de tiempo completo o de tiempo parcial) para saber la siguiente información. Si su compañero/a no tiene trabajo, hágale preguntas sobre un amigo / una amiga o un miembro de su familia que sí trabaja. También puede entrevistar a su profesor(a).

- el nombre exacto del trabajo que tiene
- la carrera que hizo en la universidad
- el tiempo que tardó en colocarse
- la experiencia que tenía en ese campo cuando se colocó
- el tiempo que lleva en el empleo

PARA ESCRIBIR

Describa su trabajo actual, o el último trabajo que tuvo. ¿Cómo supo de ese trabajo? ¿Qué hizo para conseguirlo? ¿Qué hace durante las horas de trabajo? ¿Le gusta? ¿Por qué? ¿Piensa cambiar pronto de colocación (*job*)? Si Ud. no ha trabajado nunca, describa su trabajo ideal.

MODELO: Me gustaría tener un trabajo que fuera...

VOCABULARIO

Profesiones y oficios

el/la abogado/a lawyer
el amo/a de casa housekeeper
el/la contador(a) accountant
el/la peluquero/a hairdresser
el/la plomero/a plumber
el soldado / la mujer soldado soldier
el/la veterinario/a veterinarian

Repaso: el/la cocinero/a, el/la dentista, el/la enfermero/a, el hombre / la mujer de negocios, el/la obrero/a

En busca de un puesto

caerle (caigo) bien/mal to make a good/bad impression
dejar to quit (*a job*)
llenar to fill out (*a form*)
renunciar (a) to resign (from)

Repaso: escribir a máquina, graduarse (en)

el/la aspirante candidate, applicant
el currículum resumé
la dirección de personal personnel office

la empresa corporation, business
el/la entrevistador(a) interviewer
la solicitud application (form)

Self-Test

Use the tape that accompanies this text to test yourself briefly on the important points of this chapter.

LECTURA
cultural

El breve artículo siguiente es de una revista española. En el artículo, una serie de personas que ejercen varias profesiones contestan la pregunta que da título a esta lectura.

¿CREES EN LO QUE HACES?

ENCUESTA

1.

VIRGINIA MATAIX
(ACTRIZ)

Si no creyera no lo haría. Estoy muy satisfecha de mi trabajo como actriz y, ahora, como presentadora, donde también tengo que actuar. Soy muy entusiasta de lo que hago porque está muy relacionado con las emociones y la creatividad.

2.

AMANDO DE MIGUEL
(SOCIOLOGO)

Qué pregunta más abstracta. Si no creyera sería como para volverse loco. Mi trabajo es muy apetecible[a] y, como no aspiro al poder, procuro hacer las cosas yo mismo y no delegar en los otros. Como sociólogo asimilo información, la digiero y luego la emito, procurando eliminar lo que me viene impuesto e imponer lo que me gusta.

[a]*tempting, attractive*

3.

ESPERANZA ROY
(ACTRIZ)

Absolutamente. Si no creyera en lo que estoy haciendo buscaría otra forma de creer, porque no me sentiría bien realizada.[b] Pienso que hay varias formas de realizarse en la vida, y una de ellas es creer en tu aportación personal.

[b]*fulfilled*

4.

FELIPE CAMPUZANO
(CANTANTE)

Hombre, claro que creo, porque sería absurdo no hacerlo, aunque fuera equivocadamente. Soy un Sagitario empedernido[c] y estoy seguro de que mi éxito se debe, en cierta forma, a creer en lo que hago.

5.

MAGDA ORANICH
(ABOGADA)

Sí, creo y mucho. A veces, demasiado. Pero no le veo un mérito especial, porque me resultaría muy difícil hacer algo si no creyera en ello. Tanto en el aspecto profesional, político, como en la vida cotidiana, mi actitud es tan importante para la sociedad como para mí misma. A veces me crea problemas pasajeros, pero la satisfacción de haber obrado[d] según mis convicciones supera cualquier otro inconveniente.

6.

MONCHO ALPUENTE
(PERIODISTA)

Creo en lo que hago, entre otras cosas, porque no tengo otro remedio. Nunca he cuestionado mi facultad fundamental, que es la de escribir, y lo hago instintivamente. Lo que sí me planteo[e] es su comercialización: qué escribo y para qué medio de comunicación.

[c]*stubborn*

[d]*acted*

[e]*me... I ask myself about*

414

NOTA CULTURAL: Los nombres de las profesiones

En el mundo de habla española hay poco acuerdo sobre las palabras que deben usarse para referirse a las mujeres que ejercen ciertas profesiones. En gran parte, eso se debe al hecho de que,[a] en muchos de estos países, las mujeres acaban de empezar a ejercer esas profesiones; por eso el idioma todavía está cambiando para acomodarse a esa nueva realidad. En la actualidad se emplean, entre otras, las siguientes formas:

- Se usa el artículo **la** con los sustantivos que terminan en **-ista.**

  el dentista → **la** dent**ista**

- En otros casos se usa una forma femenina.

  el médico → **la** médic**a**
  el trabajador → **la** trabajador**a**

- Se usa la palabra **mujer** con el nombre de la profesión.

  el policía → **la mujer** policía
  el soldado → **la mujer** soldado

Escuche lo que dice la persona con que Ud. habla para saber las formas que él o ella usa. No se trata de[b] formas correctas o incorrectas, sólo de usos y costumbres locales.

[a]al... *to the fact that* [b]No... *It's not a question of*

Comprensión

A ¿**Cierto o falso?** Corrija las oraciones falsas.

1. Todas las personas entrevistadas creen en lo que hacen.
2. Algunas personas creen en su profesión, pero no creen en sus propias habilidades.
3. Algunas personas ven una relación entre su trabajo y su vida personal y emotiva.

B Dé el número correspondiente. De las personas del artículo, ¿quién... ?

a. _____ atribuye su satisfacción profesional a las características de su signo astrológico
b. _____ cree que contribuye al bienestar general de la sociedad con su trabajo
c. _____ cree que hace su trabajo casi sin pensar
d. _____ estaría loca si no creyera en lo que hace
e. _____ pone énfasis en la necesidad de poder contribuir con algo en esta vida
f. _____ pone énfasis en lo emocional y no en lo intelectual

¡Enhorabuena! (*Congratulations!*) Ud. ha llegado al final de *¿Qué tal?* Esperamos que esta haya sido una «excursión» muy agradable para Ud. Metafóricamente, Ud. ha viajado muchas millas para llegar a este lugar, y ha trabajado mucho. Pero en vez de considerar esta sección como el punto final de su viaje, preferimos que Ud. la considere como otro punto de partida (*point of departure*). Ojalá que las horas que Ud. ha pasado en esta clase le hayan inspirado a tomar otra clase de español o a visitar algún país de habla española.

Como preparativo para tales experiencias futuras, en esta sección Ud. va a planear un viaje. La actividad debe considerarse no sólo como la culminación de todos los meses anteriores sino como el comienzo del mañana.

Paso 1. Como Ud. ha podido ver en las fotos de los capítulos anteriores y como puede verlo también en estas páginas, el mundo hispano le ofrece al turista una gran variedad de sitios de interés.

¿Hay algún país hispanohablante que Ud. siempre haya querido visitar? ¿Le parece interesante algún lugar que su profesor(a) haya mencionado durante el año? ¿Le atrae en particular algún lugar que ha visto en las fotos de este libro? Antes de planear el viaje, debe decidir primero adónde ir. Consulte los mapas de este libro y vuelva a mirar las fotos del libro, si quiere.

Paso 2. Una vez que ha seleccionado el lugar de su destino, tiene que decidir qué es lo que va a llevar. Y para hacerlo, tiene que contestar una serie de preguntas.

Las playas de Cancún (México) tienen fama en el mundo hispánico. Desde Cancún se hacen fácilmente excursiones a las ruinas mayas de Yucatán.

Caminar por las calles de Toledo (España) es como regresar a la época medieval. Aproveche su visita a esta ciudad para ver las obras de El Greco.

Planeando un viaje al
MUNDO HISPÁNICO

¿Cuándo piensa viajar? Es decir, ¿en qué mes del año y en qué estación? ¿Cómo es el clima del lugar que piensa visitar durante esta estación? (**¡OJO!** ¿Está el país en el hemisferio sur?) Si es necesario, consulte una enciclopedia o una guía turística.

Paso 3. También tiene que saber algo sobre los varios sitios de interés turístico. Es decir, ¿qué es lo que le gustaría ver o hacer durante su viaje? Haga una lista de por lo menos cinco cosas que quisiera hacer.

Paso 4. Ahora haga una lista, por categorías, de lo que Ud. va a poner en su(s) maleta(s), según el clima y según lo que piensa hacer. Las siguientes categorías le pueden ser útiles: Ropa, Artículos de uso personal, Miscelánea.

Paso 5. Ahora piense en las cosas que Ud. tiene que hacer antes de salir de viaje. ¿Tiene que comprar el billete? ¿conseguir un pasaporte? ¿comprar una cámara especial? ¿Qué más tiene que hacer para que todo le vaya bien en el viaje?

Paso 6. Por fin, con toda la información que Ud. apuntó en los **Pasos 1–5,** escriba una serie de párrafos breves que describan su viaje y los preparativos que va a hacer. Debe terminar la composición con un párrafo de despedida (*farewell*) a su profesor(a) de español. Puede agradecerle su ayuda durante el año y mencionar el día o el momento más inolvidable de la clase. También debe recordar las actividades que lo/la han preparado para hacer su viaje al mundo hispano. ¡Buen viaje!

Las metrópolis de Latinoamérica y de España le ofrecen al turista todos los atractivos de las grandes capitales del mundo: bulevares espaciosos, tiendas elegantes, hoteles y rascacielos ultramodernos. Aquí se ve una vista del centro de Buenos Aires, Argentina.

En las calles del Viejo San Juan (Puerto Rico) hay de todo: boutiques, museos, restaurantes y cafés con un ambiente muy agradable. Muy cerca están las famosas playas del Condado.

CALLE
DE
SAN SEBASTIAN

▼ ▼

USING ADJECTIVES AS NOUNS

Nominalization means using an adjective as a noun. In Spanish, adjectives can be nominalized in a number of ways, all of which involve dropping the noun that accompanies the adjective, then using the adjective in combination with an article or other word. One kind of adjective, the demonstrative, can simply be used alone. In most cases, these usages parallel those of English, although the English equivalent may be phrased differently from the Spanish.

Article + Adjective

Simply omit the noun from an *article + noun + adjective* phrase.

> el **libro** azul → **el azul** (*the blue one*)
> la **hermana** casada → **la casada** (*the married one*)
> el **señor** mexicano → **el mexicano** (*the Mexican one*)
> los **pantalones** baratos → **los baratos** (*the inexpensive ones*)

You can also drop the first noun in an *article + noun + de + noun* phrase.

> la **casa** de Julio → **la de Julio** (*Julio's*)
> los **coches** del Sr. Martínez → **los del Sr. Martínez** (*Mr. Martínez's*)

In both cases, the construction is used to refer to a noun that has already been mentioned. The English equivalent uses *one* or *ones*, or a possessive without the noun.

> —¿Necesitas el libro grande?
> —No. Necesito **el pequeño.**
> —*Do you need the big book?*
> —*No. I need the small one.*

> —¿Usamos el coche de Ernesto?
> —No. Usemos **el de Ana.**
> —*Shall we use Ernesto's car?*
> —*No. Let's use Ana's.*

Note that in the preceding examples the noun is mentioned in the first part of the exchange (**libro, coche**) but

not in the response or rejoinder.

Note also that a demonstrative can be used to nominalize an adjective: **este rojo** (*this red one*), **esos azules** (*those blue ones*).

Lo + Adjective

As seen in **Capítulo 15, lo** combines with the masculine singular form of an adjective to describe general qualities or characteristics. The English equivalent is expressed with words like *part* or *thing*.

> lo mejor   *the best thing (part), what's best*
> lo mismo   *the same thing*
> lo cómico   *the funny thing (part), what's funny*

Article + Stressed Possessive Adjective

There are two kinds of possessive adjectives in Spanish: stressed and unstressed. In *¿Qué tal?* you will learn to use only the unstressed forms (Grammar Section 8). The forms of the stressed possessive adjectives are as follows:

mío/a (míos/as)	nuestro/a (nuestros/as)
tuyo/a (tuyos/as)	vuestro/a (vuestros/as)
suyo/a (suyos/as)	suyo/a (suyos/as)

Forms of the stressed possessive adjectives agree with the noun they modify in number and gender. They follow the modified noun: **la casa mía, el libro suyo.**

The stressed possessive adjectives—but not the unstressed possessives—can be used as possessive pronouns: **la maleta suya → la suya.** The article and the possessive form agree in gender and number with the noun to which they refer.

> Este es mi **banco.** ¿Dónde está **el suyo?**
> *This is my bank. Where is yours?*

> Sus **bebidas** están preparadas; **las nuestras,** no.
> *Their drinks are ready; ours aren't.*

> No es la **maleta** de Juan; es **la mía.**
> *It isn't Juan's suitcase; it's mine.*

Note that the definite article is frequently omitted after forms of **ser: ¿Esa maleta? Es suya.**

Demonstrative Pronouns

The demonstrative adjective can be used alone, without a noun.

> Necesito este diccionario y **ese.**
> *I need this dictionary and that one.*

> Estas señoras y **aquellas** son las hermanas de Sara, ¿no?

These women and those (over there) are Sara's sisters, aren't they?

It is acceptable (though not always the norm) in modern Spanish, per the **Real Academia de la Lengua,** not to use an accent on demonstrative pronouns when context makes the meaning clear and no ambiguity is possible.

 # APPENDIX 2

▼ ▼

ADDITIONAL PERFECT FORMS (INDICATIVE AND SUBJUNCTIVE)

Some indicative verb tenses have corresponding perfect forms in the indicative and subjunctive moods. Here is the present tense system.

el presente:	yo hablo, como, pongo
el presente perfecto:	yo he hablado, comido, puesto
el presente perfecto del subjuntivo:	yo haya hablado, comido, puesto

Other indicative forms that you have learned also have corresponding perfect indicative and subjunctive forms. Here are the most important ones, along with examples of their use. In each case, the tense or mood is formed with the appropriate form of **haber.**

El pluscuamperfecto del subjuntivo

yo:	hubiera hablado, comido, vivido, *etc.*
tú:	hubieras hablado, comido, vivido, *etc.*
Ud./él/ella:	hubiera hablado, comido, vivido, *etc.*
nosotros:	hubiéramos hablado, comido, vivido, *etc.*
vosotros:	hubierais hablado, comido, vivido, *etc.*
Uds./ellos/ellas:	hubieran hablado, comido, vivido, *etc.*

These forms correspond to **el presente perfecto del indicativo (Capítulo 18).** These forms are most frequently used in **si** clause sentences, along with the conditional perfect. See examples on page A–3.

El futuro perfecto

yo:	habré hablado, comido, vivido, *etc.*
tú:	habrás hablado, comido, vivido, *etc.*
Ud./él/ella:	habrá hablado, comido, vivido, *etc.*
nosotros:	habremos hablado, comido, vivido, *etc.*
vosotros:	habréis hablado, comido, vivido, *etc.*
Uds./ellos/ellas:	habrán hablado, comido, vivido, *etc.*

These forms correspond to **el futuro (Capítulo 20)** and are most frequently used to tell what *will have already happened* at some point in the future. (In contrast, the future is used to tell what *will happen.*)

> Mañana **hablaré** con Miguel.
> *I'll speak with Miguel tomorrow.*

> Para las tres, ya **habré hablado** con Miguel.
> *By 3:00, I'll already have spoken to Miguel.*

> El año que viene **visitaremos** a los nietos.
> *We'll visit our grandchildren next year.*

> Para las Navidades, ya **habremos visitado** a los nietos.
> *We'll already have visited our grandchildren by Christmas.*

El condicional perfecto

yo:	habría hablado, comido, vivido, *etc.*
tú:	habrías hablado, comido, vivido, *etc.*
Ud./él/ella:	habría hablado, comido, vivido, *etc.*
nosotros:	habríamos hablado, comido, vivido, *etc.*
vosotros:	habríais hablado, comido, vivido, *etc.*
Uds./ellos/ellas:	habrían hablado, comido, vivido, *etc.*

These forms correspond to **el condicional (Capítulo 23).** These forms are frequently used to tell what *would have happened* at some point in the past. (In contrast, the conditional tells what one *would do.*)

Yo **hablaría** con Miguel.
I would speak with Miguel (if I were you, at some point in the future).

Yo **habría hablado** con Miguel.
I would have spoken with Miguel (if I were you, at some point in the past).

Si Clause: Sentences About the Past

You have learned **(Capítulo 23)** to use the past subjunctive and conditional to speculate about the present in **si** clause sentences: what *would happen* if a particular event *were* (or *were not*) to occur.

Si **tuviera** el tiempo, **aprendería** francés.
If I had the time, I would learn French (in the present or at some point in the future).

The perfect forms of the past subjunctive and the conditional are used to speculate about the past: what *would have happened* if a particular event *had* (or *had not*) occurred.

En la escuela superior, si **hubiera tenido** el tiempo, **habría aprendido** francés.
In high school, if I had had the time, I would have learned French.

APPENDIX 3

VERBS

A. Regular Verbs: Simple Tenses

Infinitive Present Participle Past Participle	INDICATIVE					SUBJUNCTIVE		IMPERATIVE
	Present	Imperfect	Preterite	Future	Conditional	Present	Imperfect	
hablar hablando hablado	hablo hablas habla hablamos habláis hablan	hablaba hablabas hablaba hablábamos hablabais hablaban	hablé hablaste habló hablamos hablasteis hablaron	hablaré hablarás hablará hablaremos hablaréis hablarán	hablaría hablarías hablaría hablaríamos hablaríais hablarían	hable hables hable hablemos habléis hablen	hablara hablaras hablara habláramos hablarais hablaran	habla tú, no hables hable Ud. hablemos hablen
comer comiendo comido	como comes come comemos coméis comen	comía comías comía comíamos comíais comían	comí comiste comió comimos comisteis comieron	comeré comerás comerá comeremos comeréis comerán	comería comerías comería comeríamos comeríais comerían	coma comas coma comamos comáis coman	comiera comieras comiera comiéramos comierais comieran	come tú, no comas coma Ud. comamos coman
vivir viviendo vivido	vivo vives vive vivimos vivís viven	vivía vivías vivía vivíamos vivíais vivían	viví viviste vivió vivimos vivisteis vivieron	viviré vivirás vivirá viviremos viviréis vivirán	viviría vivirías viviría viviríamos viviríais vivirían	viva vivas viva vivamos viváis vivan	viviera vivieras viviera viviéramos vivierais vivieran	vive tú, no vivas viva Ud. vivamos vivan

B. Regular Verbs: Perfect Tenses

INDICATIVE				
Present Perfect	Past Perfect	Preterite Perfect	Future Perfect	Conditional Perfect
he has ha hemos habéis han } hablado comido vivido	había habías había habíamos habíais habían } hablado comido vivido	hube hubiste hubo hubimos hubisteis hubieron } hablado comido vivido	habré habrás habrá habremos habréis habrán } hablado comido vivido	habría habrías habría habríamos habríais habrían } hablado comido vivido

SUBJUNCTIVE	
Present Perfect	Past Perfect
haya hayas haya hayamos hayáis hayan } hablado comido vivido	hubiera hubieras hubiera hubiéramos hubierais hubieran } hablado comido vivido

C. Irregular Verbs

Infinitive Present Participle Past Participle	INDICATIVE						SUBJUNCTIVE		IMPERATIVE
	Present	Imperfect	Preterite	Future	Conditional		Present	Imperfect	
andar andando andado	ando andas anda andamos andáis andan	andaba andabas andaba andábamos andabais andaban	anduve anduviste anduvo anduvimos anduvisteis anduvieron	andaré andarás andará andaremos andaréis andarán	andaría andarías andaría andaríamos andaríais andarían		ande andes ande andemos andéis anden	anduviera anduvieras anduviera anduviéramos anduvierais anduvieran	anda tú, no andes ande Ud. andemos anden
caer cayendo caído	caigo caes cae caemos caéis caen	caía caías caía caíamos caíais caían	caí caíste cayó caímos caísteis cayeron	caeré caerás caerá caeremos caeréis caerán	caería caerías caería caeríamos caeríais caerían		caiga caigas caiga caigamos caigáis caigan	cayera cayeras cayera cayéramos cayerais cayeran	cae tú, no caigas caiga Ud. caigamos caigan
dar dando dado	doy das da damos dais dan	daba dabas daba dábamos dabais daban	di diste dio dimos disteis dieron	daré darás dará daremos daréis darán	daría darías daría daríamos daríais darían		dé des dé demos deis den	diera dieras diera diéramos dierais dieran	da tú, no des dé Ud. demos den
decir diciendo dicho	digo dices dice decimos decís dicen	decía decías decía decíamos decíais decían	dije dijiste dijo dijimos dijisteis dijeron	diré dirás dirá diremos diréis dirán	diría dirías diría diríamos diríais dirían		diga digas diga digamos digáis digan	dijera dijeras dijera dijéramos dijerais dijeran	di tú, no digas diga Ud. digamos digan
estar estando estado	estoy estás está estamos estáis están	estaba estabas estaba estábamos estabais estaban	estuve estuviste estuvo estuvimos estuvisteis estuvieron	estaré estarás estará estaremos estaréis estarán	estaría estarías estaría estaríamos estaríais estarían		esté estés esté estemos estéis estén	estuviera estuvieras estuviera estuviéramos estuvierais estuviera	está tú, no estés esté Ud. estemos estén
haber habiendo habido	he has ha hemos habéis han	había habías había habíamos habíais habían	hube hubiste hubo hubimos hubisteis hubieron	habré habrás habrá habremos habréis habrán	habría habrías habría habríamos habríais habrían		haya hayas haya hayamos hayáis hayan	hubiera hubieras hubiera hubiéramos hubierais hubieran	
hacer haciendo hecho	hago haces hace hacemos hacéis hacen	hacía hacías hacía hacíamos hacíais hacían	hice hiciste hizo hicimos hicisteis hicieron	haré harás hará haremos haréis harán	haría harías haría haríamos haríais harían		haga hagas haga hagamos hagáis hagan	hiciera hicieras hiciera hiciéramos hicierais hicieran	haz tú, no hagas haga Ud. hagamos hagan

C. Irregular Verbs (continued)

Infinitive / Present Participle / Past Participle	INDICATIVE Present	Imperfect	Preterite	Future	Conditional	SUBJUNCTIVE Present	Imperfect	IMPERATIVE
ir / yendo / ido	voy / vas / va / vamos / vais / van	iba / ibas / iba / íbamos / ibais / iban	fui / fuiste / fue / fuimos / fuisteis / fueron	iré / irás / irá / iremos / iréis / irán	iría / irías / iría / iríamos / iríais / irían	vaya / vayas / vaya / vayamos / vayáis / vayan	fuera / fueras / fuera / fuéramos / fuerais / fueran	ve tú, no vayas / vaya Ud. / vayamos / vayan
oír / oyendo / oído	oigo / oyes / oye / oímos / oís / oyen	oía / oías / oía / oíamos / oíais / oían	oí / oíste / oyó / oímos / oísteis / oyeron	oiré / oirás / oirá / oiremos / oiréis / oirán	oiría / oirías / oiría / oiríamos / oiríais / oirían	oiga / oigas / oiga / oigamos / oigáis / oigan	oyera / oyeras / oyera / oyéramos / oyerais / oyeran	oye tú, no oigas / oiga Ud. / oigamos / oigan
poder / pudiendo / podido	puedo / puedes / puede / podemos / podéis / pueden	podía / podías / podía / podíamos / podíais / podían	pude / pudiste / pudo / pudimos / pudisteis / pudieron	podré / podrás / podrá / podremos / podréis / podrán	podría / podrías / podría / podríamos / podríais / podrían	pueda / puedas / pueda / podamos / podáis / puedan	pudiera / pudieras / pudiera / pudiéramos / pudierais / pudieran	
poner / poniendo / puesto	pongo / pones / pone / ponemos / ponéis / ponen	ponía / ponías / ponía / poníamos / poníais / ponían	puse / pusiste / puso / pusimos / pusisteis / pusieron	pondré / pondrás / pondrá / pondremos / pondréis / pondrán	pondría / pondrías / pondría / pondríamos / pondríais / pondrían	ponga / pongas / ponga / pongamos / pongáis / pongan	pusiera / pusieras / pusiera / pusiéramos / pusierais / pusieran	pon tú, no pongas / ponga Ud. / pongamos / pongan
querer / queriendo / querido	quiero / quieres / quiere / queremos / queréis / quieren	quería / querías / quería / queríamos / queríais / querían	quise / quisiste / quiso / quisimos / quisisteis / quisieron	querré / querrás / querrá / querremos / querréis / querrán	querría / querrías / querría / querríamos / querríais / querrían	quiera / quieras / quiera / queramos / queráis / quieran	quisiera / quisieras / quisiera / quisiéramos / quisierais / quisieran	quiere tú, no quieras / quiera Ud. / queramos / quieran
saber / sabiendo / sabido	sé / sabes / sabe / sabemos / sabéis / saben	sabía / sabías / sabía / sabíamos / sabíais / sabían	supe / supiste / supo / supimos / supisteis / supieron	sabré / sabrás / sabrá / sabremos / sabréis / sabrán	sabría / sabrías / sabría / sabríamos / sabríais / sabrían	sepa / sepas / sepa / sepamos / sepáis / sepan	supiera / supieras / supiera / supiéramos / supierais / supieran	sabe tú, no sepas / sepa Ud. / sepamos / sepan
salir / saliendo / salido	salgo / sales / sale / salimos / salís / salen	salía / salías / salía / salíamos / salíais / salían	salí / saliste / salió / salimos / salisteis / salieron	saldré / saldrás / saldrá / saldremos / saldréis / saldrán	saldría / saldrías / saldría / saldríamos / saldríais / saldrían	salga / salgas / salga / salgamos / salgáis / salgan	saliera / salieras / saliera / saliéramos / salierais / salieran	sal tú, no salgas / salga Ud. / salgamos / salgan
ser / siendo / sido	soy / eres / es / somos / sois / son	era / eras / era / éramos / erais / eran	fui / fuiste / fue / fuimos / fuisteis / fueron	seré / serás / será / seremos / seréis / serán	sería / serías / sería / seríamos / seríais / serían	sea / seas / sea / seamos / seáis / sean	fuera / fueras / fuera / fuéramos / fuerais / fueran	sé tú, no seas / sea Ud. / seamos / sean

Infinitive / Present Participle / Past Participle	Present	Imperfect	Preterite	Future	Conditional	Subjunctive Present	Subjunctive Imperfect	Imperative
tener teniendo tenido	tengo tienes tiene tenemos tenéis tienen	tenía tenías tenía teníamos teníais tenían	tuve tuviste tuvo tuvimos tuvisteis tuvieron	tendré tendrás tendrá tendremos tendréis tendrán	tendría tendrías tendría tendríamos tendríais tendrían	tenga tengas tenga tengamos tengáis tengan	tuviera tuvieras tuviera tuviéramos tuvierais tuvieran	ten tú, no tengas tenga Ud. tengamos tengan
traer trayendo traído	traigo traes trae traemos traéis traen	traía traías traía traíamos traíais traían	traje trajiste trajo trajimos trajisteis trajeron	traeré traerás traerá traeremos traeréis traerán	traería traerías traería traeríamos traeríais traerían	traiga traigas traiga traigamos traigáis traigan	trajera trajeras trajera trajéramos trajerais trajeran	trae tú, no traigas traiga Ud. traigamos traigan
venir viniendo venido	vengo vienes viene venimos venís vienen	venía venías venía veníamos veníais venían	vine viniste vino vinimos vinisteis vinieron	vendré vendrás vendrá vendremos vendréis vendrán	vendría vendrías vendría vendríamos vendríais vendrían	venga vengas venga vengamos vengáis vengan	viniera vinieras viniera viniéramos vinierais vinieran	ven tú, no vengas venga Ud. vengamos vengan
ver viendo visto	veo ves ve vemos veis ven	veía veías veía veíamos veíais veían	vi viste vio vimos visteis vieron	veré verás verá veremos veréis verán	vería verías vería veríamos veríais verían	vea veas vea veamos veáis vean	viera vieras viera viéramos vierais vieran	ve tú, no veas vea Ud. veamos vean

D. Stem-Changing and Spelling Change Verbs

Infinitive / Present Participle / Past Participle	INDICATIVE					SUBJUNCTIVE		IMPERATIVE
	Present	Imperfect	Preterite	Future	Conditional	Present	Imperfect	
pensar (ie) pensando pensado	pienso piensas piensa pensamos pensáis piensan	pensaba pensabas pensaba pensábamos pensabais pensaban	pensé pensaste pensó pensamos pensasteis pensaron	pensaré pensarás pensará pensaremos pensaréis pensarán	pensaría pensarías pensaría pensaríamos pensaríais pensarían	piense pienses piense pensemos penséis piensen	pensara pensaras pensara pensáramos pensarais pensaran	piensa tú, no pienses piense Ud. pensemos piensen
volver (ue) volviendo vuelto	vuelvo vuelves vuelve volvemos volvéis vuelven	volvía volvías volvía volvíamos volvíais volvían	volví volviste volvió volvimos volvisteis volvieron	volveré volverás volverá volveremos volveréis volverán	volvería volverías volvería volveríamos volveríais volverían	vuelva vuelvas vuelva volvamos volváis vuelvan	volviera volvieras volviera volviéramos volvierais volvieran	vuelve tú, no vuelvas vuelva Ud. volvamos vuelvan

D. Stem-Changing and Spelling Change Verbs (continued)

Infinitive / Present Participle / Past Participle	INDICATIVE					SUBJUNCTIVE		IMPERATIVE
	Present	Imperfect	Preterite	Future	Conditional	Present	Imperfect	
dormir (ue, u) durmiendo dormido	duermo duermes duerme dormimos dormís duermen	dormía dormías dormía dormíamos dormíais dormían	dormí dormiste durmió dormimos dormisteis durmieron	dormiré dormirás dormirá dormiremos dormiréis dormirán	dormiría dormirías dormiría dormiríamos dormiríais dormirían	duerma duermas duerma durmamos durmáis duerman	durmiera durmieras durmiera durmiéramos durmierais durmieran	duerme tú, no duermas duerma Ud. durmamos duerman
sentir (ie, i) sintiendo sentido	siento sientes siente sentimos sentís sienten	sentía sentías sentía sentíamos sentíais sentían	sentí sentiste sintió sentimos sentisteis sintieron	sentiré sentirás sentirá sentiremos sentiréis sentirán	sentiría sentirías sentiría sentiríamos sentiríais sentirían	sienta sientas sienta sintamos sintáis sientan	sintiera sintieras sintiera sintiéramos sintierais sintieran	siente tú, no sientas sienta Ud. sintamos sientan
pedir (i, i) pidiendo pedido	pido pides pide pedimos pedís piden	pedía pedías pedía pedíamos pedíais pedían	pedí pediste pidió pedimos pedisteis pidieron	pediré pedirás pedirá pediremos pediréis pedirán	pediría pedirías pediría pediríamos pediríais pedirían	pida pidas pida pidamos pidáis pidan	pidiera pidieras pidiera pidiéramos pidierais pidieran	pide tú, no pidas pida Ud. pidamos pidan
reír (i, i) riendo reído	río ríes ríe reímos reís ríen	reía reías reía reíamos reíais reían	reí reíste rió reímos reísteis rieron	reiré reirás reirá reiremos reiréis reirán	reiría reirías reiría reiríamos reiríais reirían	ría rías ría riamos riáis rían	riera rieras riera riéramos rierais rieran	ríe tú, no rías ría Ud. riamos rían
seguir (i, i) (g) siguiendo seguido	sigo sigues sigue seguimos seguís siguen	seguía seguías seguía seguíamos seguíais seguían	seguí seguiste siguió seguimos seguisteis siguieron	seguiré seguirás seguirá seguiremos seguiréis seguirán	seguiría seguirías seguiría seguiríamos seguiríais seguirían	siga sigas siga sigamos sigáis sigan	siguiera siguieras siguiera siguiéramos siguierais siguieran	sigue tú, no sigas siga Ud. sigamos sigan
construir (y) construyendo construido	construyo construyes construye construimos construís construyen	construía construías construía construíamos construíais construían	construí construiste construyó construimos construisteis construyeron	construiré construirás construirá construiremos construiréis construirán	construiría construirías construiría construiríamos construiríais construirían	construya construyas construya construyamos construyáis construyan	construyera construyeras construyera construyéramos construyerais construyeran	construye tú, no construyas construya Ud. construyamos construyan
producir (zc) produciendo producido	produzco produces produce producimos producís producen	producía producías producía producíamos producíais producían	produje produjiste produjo produjimos produjisteis produjeron	produciré producirás producirá produciremos produciréis producirán	produciría producirías produciría produciríamos produciríais producirían	produzca produzcas produzca produzcamos produzcáis produzcan	produjera produjeras produjera produjéramos produjerais produjeran	produce tú, no produzcas produzca Ud. produzcamos produzcan

VOCABULARIES

▼ ▼

The **Spanish–English Vocabulary** contains all the words that appear in the text and in its functional and decorative realia, with the following exceptions: (1) most close or identical cognates that do not appear in the chapter vocabulary lists; (2) most conjugated verb forms; (3) diminutives in **-ito/a**; (4) absolute superlatives in **-ísimo/a**; (5) most adverbs in **-mente**; (6) most vocabulary that is glossed in the text; and (7) much vocabulary from realia and authentic readings. Active vocabulary is indicated by the number of the chapter in which a word or given meaning is first listed (**P = Primeros pasos**); vocabulary that is glossed in the text is not considered to be active vocabulary and is not numbered. Only meanings that are used in the text are given. The **English–Spanish**

Vocabulary is based on the chapter lists of active vocabulary. It includes all words and expressions necessary to do the translation exercises in the **Workbook** that accompanies the text.

The gender of nouns is indicated, except for masculine nouns ending in **-o** and feminine nouns ending in **-a**. Stem changes and spelling changes are indicated for verbs: **dormir (ue, u)**; **llegar (gu)**; **seguir (i, i) (g)**.

Words beginning with **ch, ll,** and **ñ** are found under separate headings, following the letters **c, l,** and **n,** respectively. Similarly, **ch, ll,** and **ñ** within words follow **c, l,** and **n,** respectively. For example, **coche** follows **coctel, callado/a** follows **calzado,** and **añadir** follows **anuncio.**

The following abbreviations are used:

adj.	adjective	*inf.*	infinitive	*poss.*	possessive
adv.	adverb	*inv.*	invariable in form	*prep.*	preposition
approx.	approximately	*irreg.*	irregular	*pron.*	pronoun
col.	colloquial	*L.A.*	Latin America	*refl. pron.*	reflexive pronoun
conj.	conjunction	*m.*	masculine	*s.*	singular
d.o.	direct object	*Mex.*	Mexico	*Sp.*	Spain
f.	feminine	*n.*	noun	*sub. pron.*	subject pronoun
fam.	familiar	*obj. (of prep.)*	object (of a preposition)	*subj.*	subjunctive
form.	formal	*p.p.*	past participle	*v.*	verb
gram.	grammatical term	*pl.*	plural	*var.*	variation
i.o.	indirect object				

SPANISH – ENGLISH VOCABULARY

▼ ▼

A

a to (P); at (*with time*) (P); **a la(s)...** at (hour) (P)
abajo *adv.* below
abalanzarse (c) (sobre) to pounce (on)
abanderar to join, take up someone's cause
abandonar to abandon
abarcar (qu) to cover (*a topic*)
abarrotado/a crowded, completely full
abierto/a *p.p.* open(ed) (4)
abogado/a lawyer (23)
abolicionista *m., f.* abolitionist
abrazar (c) to hug
abrigo coat (5); **abrigo de pieles** fur coat
abril *m.* April (7)
abrir (*p.p.* **abierto/a**) to open (4)

absoluto/a absolute
abstracto/a abstract
absurdo/a absurd
abuelo/a grandfather/grandmother (4); *pl.* grandparents (4)
aburrido/a bored (4); boring; **estar** (*irreg.*) **aburrido/a** to be bored; **ser** (*irreg.*) **aburrido/a** to be boring
aburrimiento boredom
aburrir to bore
abuso abuse
acabar to finish (14); to run out of (14); **acabar de** + *inf.* to have just (*done something*) (9)
academia: Real Academia de la Lengua Spanish Royal Academy (of the Language)

académico/a academic
acampada camping
acariciar to caress
acaso perhaps; **por si acaso** just in case (22)
acceso access
accesorio accessory
accidente *m.* accident
acción *f.* action
aceite *m.* oil (17)
aceitoso/a oily, greasy
aceituna olive
acelerado/a fast, accelerated; **ritmo acelerado de la vida** fast pace of life (18)
acelerar to accelerate, speed up
acelga Swiss chard
acento accent

aceptar to accept

acerca de *prep.* about, concerning

aclaración (*f.*) **de firma** printed name (*to clarify signature*)

acogedor(a) welcoming, friendly

acomodar to accommodate

acompañado/a accompanied

acompañar to accompany

acondicionado/a: aire (*m.*) **acondicionado** air conditioning

acondicionador *m.* air conditioner

aconsejable advisable

aconsejar to advise

acontecer (zc) to happen

acontecimiento event (22)

acordarse (ue) (de) to remember (14)

acordeón *m.* accordion

acostar (ue) to put to bed; **acostarse** to go to bed (7)

acostumbrar(se) (a) to get used, accustomed (to); to be accustomed (to)

actitud *f.* attitude

actividad *f.* activity

activo/a active

acto act, action

actor *m.* actor

actriz *f.* (*pl.* **actrices**) actress

actual current, present day, up-to-date

actualidad *f.* present time

actuar (actúo) to act

acuario aquarium (12); **Acuario** Aquarius

acuático/a aquatic

acuerdo agreement; **de acuerdo** agreed; **de acuerdo con** according to; **(no) estar** (*irreg.*) **de acuerdo** to (dis)agree (3); **ponerse** (*irreg.*) **de acuerdo** to reach an agreement

acumularse to accumulate

acusado/a marked, pronounced

acústico/a acoustic

achacar (qu) to attribute

adaptar to adapt; **adaptarse** to adapt oneself

adecuado/a adequate

adelantar to pass (*a vehicle*)

adelante: de ahora en adelante from now on

adelanto advance

adelgazar (c) to make thin, slender

además *adv.* besides; **además de** *prep.* in addition (to)

adentro *adv.* inside

adicional additional

adiós good-bye (P)

adivinanza riddle

adivinar to guess

adjetivo adjective (3)

administración *f.* administration; **administración de empresas** business (*school subject*) (2)

administrativo/a administrative

admiración *f.* admiration

admirar to admire

admitir to admit; to accept

¿adónde? where (to)?

adopción *f.* adoption

adoptar to adopt

adornar to adorn

adorno decoration

adquirir (ie) to acquire

aduana customs; **derechos** (*pl.*) **de aduana** customs duty; **inspector(a) de aduanas** customs inspector (21)

adulto/a adult

adverbio adverb

advertir (ie, i) to warn, advise

aéreo/a: línea aérea airline

aeróbico/a aerobic

aeropuerto airport (11)

afectar to affect

afectivo/a affective, emotional

afectuoso/a affectionate

afeitada shave

afeitar to shave; **afeitarse** to shave (oneself) (7)

aficionado/a *n.* fan, enthusiast; **ser** (*irreg.*) **aficionado/a a...** to be a . . . fan (16); *adj.* fond (of)

afín connected, related

afirmar to affirm

afirmativo/a affirmative

aforismo aphorism

afortunado/a fortunate, lucky

africano/a African

afuera *adv.* outside (7)

afueras *n. pl.* outskirts, suburbs (19)

agencia agency; **agencia de viajes** travel agency (11)

agente *m., f.* agent; **agente de viajes** travel agent (11)

ágil agile

agobiado/a overwhelmed

agosto August (7)

agotador(a) exhausting, tiring

agotamiento exhaustion

agotar to deplete; **agotarse** to exhaust oneself

agradable agreeable, pleasant

agradecer (zc) to thank

agresivo/a aggressive

agricultor(a) farmer

agricultura agriculture (18)

agua *f.* (*but* **el agua**) water (9); **agua mineral** mineral water (9); **agua salada** salt water; **cama de agua** water bed (8)

aguantar to put up with, endure, tolerate

aguar to spoil (*a party*)

águila *f.* (*but* **el águila**) eagle

ahí there

ahora now (4); **ahora mismo** right now (11); **de ahora en adelante** from now on

ahorrar to save (*money*) (20)

ahorros *pl.* savings; **cuenta de ahorros** savings account (20); **libreta de ahorros** savings passbook (20)

aire *m.* air; **aire acondicionado** air conditioning; **contaminación** (*f.*) **del aire** air pollution (18); **mercado al aire libre** outdoor marketplace (6)

aislamiento isolation (18)

ajedrez *m.* chess (16)

ajillo: al ajillo in garlic sauce

ajo garlic

ajustar to fit

al (*contraction of* **a** + **el**) to the; **al** + *inf.* upon; **al (mes, año, etcétera)** per (month, year, etc.)

ala *f.* (*but* **el ala**) wing

alambre *m.* wire

alarma alarm; **alarma de seguridad** security alarm

albóndiga meatball

albor *m.* beginning; dawn

álbum *m.* album

alcalde *m.* mayor

alcance *m.* reach; range

alcanzar (c) to get up to; to reach

alcázar *m.* fortress; castle

alcoba bedroom (8)

alcohol *m.* alcohol

alcohólico/a alcoholic

aldea village

alegrarse (de) to be happy (about) (12)

alegre happy

alegría happiness, joy

alemán *m.* German (*language*) (2)

alemán, alemana German

Alemania Germany

alergia allergy

alérgico/a allergic; **ser** (*irreg.*) **alérgico/a (a)** to be allergic (to)

alerta: ojo alerta be alert, watch out

alfabeto alphabet

alfombra rug (8)

alfombrado/a carpeted

algo *pron.* something, anything (9); *adv.* somewhat

algodón *m.* cotton (5)

alguien someone, anyone (9)

algún, alguno/a some, any (9); **algún día** some day; **alguna vez** once; ever

alimentación *f.* food

alimento food

aliviar to alleviate

alma *f.* (*but* **el alma**) soul

almacén *m.* department store (6)

almacenar to store

almendra almond

almohada pillow

almorzar (ue) (c) to have lunch (6)

almuerzo lunch (9)

alojamiento lodging (21)

alojarse to stay (*at lodgings*) (21)

alquilar to rent (19)

alquiler *m.* rent (19)

alrededor de *prep.* around

alternar to alternate

alternativa alternative

alto/a tall (3); high; **en voz alta** out loud

altura height

aluminio aluminum

allá there

allí there

amable kind, nice (3); **¿sería tan amable de... ?** would you be so kind as to . . . ? (21)

amante *m., f.* lover; sweetheart

amar to love

amarillo/a yellow (5)

Amazonas *m. s.* Amazon

ambiente *m.* environment; atmosphere; **medio ambiente** environment (18)

ámbito environment; place

ambos/as both

amenaza threat

amenazar (c) to threaten

América Central Central America; **América Latina** Latin America
americano/a American; **fútbol** (*m.*) **americano** football (16)
amigo/a friend (1)
amistad *f.* friendship (19); *pl.* friends
amistoso/a friendly
amo, ama *f.* (*but* **el ama**) **de casa** housekeeper (23)
amor *m.* love (19)
amortiguador *m.* muffler
amparo shelter, protection
ampliación *f.* expansion
amplio/a large, ample, spacious
anales *m. pl.* annals
analfabetismo illiteracy
analgésico analgesic, pain reliever
análisis *m. inv.* analysis
analista (*m., f.*) **de sistemas** systems analyst
analizar (c) to analyze
ananá *m.* pineapple
anaranjado/a *adj.* orange (5)
anciano/a *n.* elderly person; *adj.* old, aged
ancho/a wide
andar *irreg.* to go; to function; to walk; to be; **anda** come on, now; **andar en bicicleta** to ride a bicycle
andino/a Andean
anécdota anecdote
anémico/a anemic
anfitrión, anfitriona host, hostess
ángel *m.* angel
anglosajón, anglosajona Anglo-Saxon
angula eel
ángulo angle
angustia anxiety
animado/a animated; **dibujos** (*pl.*) **animados** cartoons (*on TV*)
animal *m.* animal; **animal de carga** pack animal
animar a + *inf.* to encourage to (*do something*)
ánimo: estado de ánimo mood
aniquilado/a annihilated
aniversario anniversary
anoche *adv.* last night (8)
anotar to jot down
ansiedad *f.* anxiety
ansioso/a anxious
ante *prep.* before; **ante todo** above all
anteayer *adv.* (the) day before yesterday
antecedente *m.* antecedent
anteojos *pl.* (eye)glasses
antepasado/a ancestor
anterior previous, preceding
antes *adv.* sooner; before; **antes de** *prep.* before (6); **antes de Cristo (a.C.)** before Christ (B.C.); **antes (de) que** *conj.* before (20)
antibiótico antibiotic (15)
anticipación: con anticipación ahead of time (21)
anticipar to pay in advance
anticuado/a antiquated, out-of-date
antiguo/a old, ancient (8); antique (8)
antipático/a unpleasant (3)

antipatriótico/a unpatriotic
antojito appetizer; hors d'oeuvre
antónimo antonym
antropología anthropology
antropológico/a anthropological
anunciar to announce
anuncio ad; announcement; **anuncio publicitario** ad(vertisement)
añadir to add
año year; **el año pasado** last year; **cumplir años** to have a birthday; **Día** (*m.*) **de Año Nuevo** New Year's Day (13); **tener** (*irreg.*)**... años** to be . . . years old (4)
añorar to miss, long for
apagar to turn off (*lights or an appliance*) (14)
aparato apparatus, appliance; **aparato doméstico** home appliance (12)
aparcamiento parking
aparcar (qu) to park
aparecer (zc) to appear
apartamento apartment; **casa de apartamentos** apartment house (19)
apartar to turn away; **apartarse** to move away
aparte apart
apasionado/a passionate
apellido last name (3)
apenado/a sorry, sad
apendicitis *f.* appendicitis
aperitivo appetizer; before-dinner drink
apertura opening
apetecer (zc) to crave, feel like (*food or drink*)
apetecible appealing
apetito: buen apetito enjoy your meal
apio celery
aplicación *f.* application
aplicar (qu) to apply
apoderarse de to seize, take control of
apodo nickname
aportación *f.* contribution
aporte *m.* contribution
apoyar to support
apreciar to appreciate, esteem, value; to notice
aprender to learn (4)
apresar to capture
aprobar (ue) to pass (*an exam, a class*)
apropiado/a appropriate
aprovechar to make good use (of); **aprovecharse de** to profit from/by, take advantage of
aproximadamente approximately
aproximarse (a) to approach
apuntar to take notes, make a note of
apuntes *m. pl.* notes
aquel, aquella *adj.* that (*over there*) (8); (*var.* **aquél, aquélla**) *pron.* that one (*over there*); **en aquel entonces** back then (14)
aquello *pron.* that, that thing, fact, idea (*over there*) (8)
aquellos/as *adj.* those (*over there*); (*var.* **aquéllos/as**) *pron.* those (ones) (*over there*)
aquí here
árabe *m.* Arabic (*language*); *n. m., f.* Arab; *adj.* Arabic, Arabian

Arabia Saudita Saudi Arabia
araña spider
árbol *m.* tree; **árbol de Navidad** Christmas tree
archipiélago archipelago
archivos *pl.* archives
ardilla squirrel
arduo/a arduous, hard
área *f.* (*but* **el área**) area
arena sand
aretes *m. pl.* earrings (5)
argentino/a Argentine, Argentinian
arma *f.* (*but* **el arma**) weapon, arm; **llevar armas** to bear arms
armado/a armed
armamentismo arms proliferation
armamento weaponry
armario closet (8)
arqueología archaeology
arqueológico/a archaeological
arquitecto/a architect
arquitectura architecture
arrancar (qu) to start (*a motor*) (17)
arrasar to raze, destroy
arrastrar to drag
arrebatado/a *col.* crazy
arrebatador(a) captivating, charming
arreglar to fix, repair; to arrange (17)
arresto arrest
arriba up
arribar to arrive
arriendo renting
arrogante arrogant
arrojar to throw, toss
arroz (*pl.* **arroces**) rice (9)
arrugar (gu) to wrinkle
arruinar to ruin
arrullar to lull to sleep
arsenal *m.* storehouse, arsenal
arte *m., f.* (*but* **el arte**) art (2); **las artes liberales** liberal arts
arterial: tensión (*f.*) **arterial** blood pressure
artesanía *s.* crafts
articulación *f.* joint (*anatomy*)
artículo article
artificial artificial; **fuegos** (*pl.*) **artificiales** fireworks
artista *m., f.* artist
artístico/a artistic
arveja pea (9)
asado/a roasted (*meat*)
ascendente ascending
ascender (ie) to go up, rise, ascend
asco: me da(n) asco it (they) make me sick; I can't stand it (them)
asegurado/a insured
asentarse (ie) to settle down; to establish oneself
asesinar to murder, assassinate
asesinato assassination (22)
así in that way, so, thus (20); **así como** as well as; **así que** therefore, consequently
asiento seat (11); **asiento posterior** back seat
asignatura course, subject
asimilar to assimilate

asimismo likewise, also
asistencia aid, assistance
asistente *m., f.* assistant; **asistente de vuelo** flight attendant
asistir (a) to attend, go (to) (*a class, function*) (4)
asociación *f.* association
asociar to associate; **asociarse (con)** to be associated (with)
asombrar to amaze, astonish
aspecto aspect, appearance
aspereza harshness
áspero/a harsh
aspiración *f.* aspiration, desire
aspiradora vacuum cleaner (12); **pasar la aspiradora** to vacuum (12)
aspirante *m., f.* candidate, applicant (23)
aspirar to aspire
aspirina aspirin (14)
astrología astrology
astrológico/a astrological
astronomía astronomy
asumir to assume
asunto matter
asustado/a frightened
atacar (qu) to attack
ataque *m.* attack; **ataque al corazón** heart attack
atasco traffic jam
atención *f.* attention; **prestar atención** to pay attention
atender (ie) to attend to; to serve
aterrizar (c) to land (*an airplane*) (11)
atlántico/a Atlantic; **Océano Atlántico** Atlantic Ocean
atleta *m., f.* athlete
atlético/a athletic
atmósfera atmosphere
atómico/a: bomba atómica atomic bomb
atracción *f.* attraction; *pl.* entertainment
atraco robbery
atractivo/a attractive
atraer (like traer) to attract
atrapar to catch, trap
atrás *adv.* behind
atrasado/a: estar (irreg.) atrasado/a to be late (11)
atravesar (ie) to cross, go through
atrevido/a bold, daring
atribuir (y) to attribute; to credit
atropellar to run over (*with a vehicle*)
atún *m.* tuna (9)
aumentar to increase (20)
aumento raise; increase (20)
aun *adv.* even
aún *adv.* still, yet
aunque although
auscultar to listen (*medical*)
ausencia absence
auspiciar to back, support
auténtico/a authentic
autobús *m.* bus (11); **estación (f.) de autobuses** bus station (11); **parada del autobús** bus stop (21)
autocar *m.* bus (*Sp.*)
automático/a automatic; **cajero automático**

automatic teller machine (20); **contestador** (*m.*) **automático** answering machine (12)
automotor(a) automotive
auto(móvil) *m.* car, auto(mobile)
autónomo/a autonomous
autopista freeway (17)
autor(a) author
autoridad *f.* authority
autostop *m.* hitchhiking; **hacer (irreg.) autostop** to hitchhike
autosuficiencia self-sufficiency
auxiliar (*m., f.*) **de vuelo** flight attendant (11)
avance *m.* advance
avanzado/a advanced
ave *f.* (*but* **el ave**) bird, fowl
avenida avenue
aventón *m.* ride, lift (*Mex.*)
aventura adventure
aventurero/a adventurous
avergonzado/a embarrassed
avestruz *m.* (*pl.* **avestruces**) ostrich
avión *m.* airplane (11)
avisar to advise, warn
aviso announcement, advertisement
¡ay! oh my!; ouch!
ayer yesterday (8)
ayuda help, assistance
ayudar to help (9)
azafata stewardess (11)
azotea rooftop
azteca *m., f.* Aztec
azúcar *m.* sugar (7)
azucena lily
azufre *m.* sulfur
azul blue (5)
azulejo tile

B

babor *m.*: **a babor** on the port side (*maritime*)
bacalao codfish
bachillerato *course of studies equivalent to high school, junior college*
bahía bay
bailador(a) dancer
bailar to dance (2)
bailarín, bailarina dancer
baile *m.* dance
bajar (de) to get off (of) (11); to get down (from) (11); to lower
bajo *prep.* under
bajo/a short (*in height*) (3); low; **planta baja** ground floor
balance *m.* balance; **hacer (irreg.) el balance** to balance (*an account*)
balancear to balance (*an account*); to rock
balcón *m.* balcony
Baleares: Islas Baleares Balearic Islands
banana banana (9)
banca *n.* banking
bancario/a *adj.* banking
banco bank (20)

bandeja tray (10)
banderilla *type of appetizer* (*Sp.*)
banquero/a banker
banquete *m.* banquet
bañar to bathe; **bañarse** to bathe (7); to take a bath
bañera bathtub (8)
baño bath; bathroom (8); **con/sin baño** with/without a bathroom (21); **traje** (*m.*) **de baño** swimsuit (5)
bar *m.* bar
baraja deck of cards
barato/a inexpensive, cheap (6)
barbacoa barbecue
bárbaro/a *n.* barbarian; *adj.* barbaric; great, impressive
barbería barbershop
barco boat, ship (11); **navegar (gu) en barco** to travel by boat (11)
barra bar (*of metal, wood*)
barrer (el suelo) to sweep (the floor) (12)
barrio neighborhood (19); **fiesta de barrio** block party
barro mud; clay
bártulos *pl.* household goods
barullo *col.* confusion
basar to base; **basarse en** to be based on
base *f.* base, basis; **a base de** based on; **en base** basic
básico/a basic
básquetbol *m.* basketball (16)
bastante rather, quite; sufficient, enough; a lot
bastar to be enough
basto club (*suit of cards*)
basura trash; **sacar (qu) la basura** to take out the trash (12)
bata robe, housecoat
batería battery (17); drums
bazofia refuse, garbage
bebé *m.* baby
beber to drink (4)
bebida drink, beverage (9)
beca scholarship
béisbol *m.* baseball (16)
belga *adj. m., f.* Belgian
Bélgica Belgium
bélico/a warlike, bellicose
belleza beauty
bello/a beautiful (18)
beneficiarse to benefit
benévolo/a benevolent, kind
besar to kiss
beso kiss
bibliografía bibliography
biblioteca library (1)
bibliotecario/a librarian
bicicleta bicycle (12); **andar (irreg.) en bicicleta** to ride a bicycle; **bicicleta de montaña** mountain bike (12); **pasear en bicicleta** to ride a bicycle (16)
bicolor *adj. m., f.* two-colored
bien *n. m.* good; *adv.* well (P); **caerle (irreg.) bien** to make a good impression (23); **estar (irreg.) bien** to be comfortable (*temperature*) (7); **llevarse bien (con)** to get

along well (with) (19); **muy bien** very well (P); **pasarlo bien** to have a good time (11); **portarse bien** to behave well (13)

bienes *m. pl.* possessions, property (12)

bienestar *m.* well-being (15)

bienvenida: dar (*irreg.*) **la bienvenida** to welcome

bienvenido/a *adj.* welcome

bifocal: gafas (*pl.*) **bifocales** bifocal glasses

bilingüe bilingual

billete *m.* ticket (11); bill (money) (20); **billete de ida** one-way ticket (11); **billete de ida y vuelta** round-trip ticket (11)

biográfico/a biographical

biología biology

biopsia biopsy

bioterapia biotherapy

bistec *m.* steak (9)

Blancanieves *f. s.* Snow White

blanco/a white (5); **vino blanco** white wine (9)

bluejeans *m. pl.* jeans (5)

blusa blouse (5)

boca mouth (15)

bocadillo snack

boda wedding (19)

bodegón *m.* tavern

boleto ticket (*for a performance*) (16); **boleto de ida** one-way ticket (11); **boleto de ida y vuelta** round-trip ticket (11)

bolígrafo (ballpoint) pen (1)

bolillo bread roll (*Mex.*)

bolívar *m. monetary unit of Venezuela*

boliviano/a Bolivian

bolsa purse (5)

bolsillo pocket

bolso purse; bag

bollo roll (9)

bomba bomb (22); **bomba atómica** atomic bomb

bombardeo bombardment, bombing

bombero/a firefighter

bombón *m.* bonbon

bonito/a pretty (3)

bordear to border on

bordo: a bordo on board

Borinquen *aboriginal and poetic name of Puerto Rico*

borinqueño/a Puerto Rican

bosque *m.* forest

bostezar (c) to yawn

bota boot (5)

botella bottle (10)

botones *m. s.* bellhop

boutique *f.* boutique

Brasil *m.* Brazil

bravura courage

brazo arm (14)

brécol *m.* broccoli

Bretaña: Gran Bretaña Great Britain

breve short, brief

brillar to shine

brillo brilliance; shine

brindar to drink a toast; to offer

brindis *m. inv.* toast

británico/a British

broma joke

bronquitis *f. inv.* bronchitis

bruto stupid, boorish; **producto interno**

bruto gross national product

bucear to skin-dive, scuba dive

buen, bueno/a good (3); **buen apetito** enjoy your meal; **buen provecho** enjoy your meal; **buena suerte** good luck; **buenas noches** good night (P); **buenas tardes** good afternoon (P); **buenos días** good morning (P); **hace (muy) buen tiempo** it's (very) good weather (7)

bueno *adv.* well

buey *m.* ox

bufanda scarf

bujía spark plug

bulevar *m.* boulevard

buñuelo doughnut, fritter

burbuja bubble

burócrata *m., f.* bureaucrat

burro donkey

bus *m.* bus

busca: en busca de in search of

buscar (qu) to look for (2)

butaca seat (*in a theater*)

C

caballero gentleman

caballo horse; **montar a caballo** to ride horseback

cabaña cabin

caber *irreg.* to fit

cabeza head (14); **dolor** (*m.*) **de cabeza** headache

cabida: tener (*irreg.*) **cabida en** to be acceptable

cabina cabin (*in a ship*)

cable *m.* cable

cabra goat

cacatúa cockatoo

cacerola casserole

cacto cactus

cada *inv.* each, every; **cada uno** each one

cadena chain

caer(se) *irreg.* to fall (14); **caerle bien/mal** to make a good/bad impression (23)

café *m.* coffee (2); café, coffee shop (6)

cafeína caffeine

cafetera coffee pot (12)

cafetería cafeteria, café (1)

caída *n.* fall

caído/a fallen

caja box; case; cashier

cajero/a bank teller (20); **cajero automático** automatic teller machine (20)

cajón *m.* drawer

calado/a drenched

calamar *m.* squid

calcetines *m. pl.* socks (5)

calculadora calculator (1)

calcular to calculate

cálculo calculus

calefacción *f.* heating, heat

calendario calendar

calentar (ie) to heat

calidad *f.* quality

calidez *f.* heat, warmth

cálido/a warm, hot (*climate*)

caliente hot (*temperature*)

calificación *f.* evaluation

calificar (qu) to qualify

calma *n.* calm

calmar to calm, soothe; **calmarse** to calm down

calor *m.* heat; **hace (mucho) calor** it's (very) hot (*weather*); **tener** (*irreg.*) **calor** to be (feel) warm/hot (*person*)

caloría calorie

calzado footwear

callado/a quiet

calle *f.* street (17)

callos a la madrileña *tripe specialty of Madrid*

cama bed (8); **cama de agua** water bed (8); **cama de matrimonio** double bed; **guardar cama** to stay in bed (15); **hacer** (*irreg.*) **la cama** to make the bed (12)

cámara camera

camarero/a waiter, waitress (9)

camarones *m. pl.* shrimp

cambiar (de) to change (12); to exchange; **cambiar de canal** to change the channel; **cambiar de idea** to change one's mind

cambio change; (rate of) exchange (*currency*); **cambio de ritmo** change of pace; **en cambio** on the other hand

camello camel

caminante *m., f.* hitchhiker

caminar to walk (14)

camino road (17); path; way

camión *m.* truck; bus (*Mex.*)

camioneta station wagon (3)

camisa shirt (5)

camiseta T-shirt (5)

campamento camp

campaña camping; campaign; **tienda de campaña** tent

campeón, campeona champion

campesino/a peasant, farm worker (18)

campestre *adj.* rural, country

camping: hacer (*irreg.*) **camping** to go camping (11)

campo *n.* country(side) (18); field (*professional*)

campus *m.* university campus (19)

canal *m.* canal; (TV) channel (22); **cambiar de canal** to change the channel (12)

Canarias: Islas Canarias Canary Islands

canario canary

cancelar to cancel

cáncer *m.* cancer

canción *f.* song

cancha de tenis tennis court

candidato/a candidate

candidatura candidacy

canela cinnamon

cangrejo crab

canica marble

canoa canoe

cansado/a tired (4)

cansancio tiredness, weariness

cansar to make tired; *col.* to annoy; **cansarse** to become tired

cantante *m., f.* singer

cantar to sing (2)

cántaros: llueve a cántaros (*col.*) it's raining cats and dogs

cantidad *f.* quantity

caña cane

cañabrava *kind of reed*

capa coating; **capa del ozono** ozone layer (18)
capacidad *f.* capacity
caparra deposit
capaz (*pl.* **capaces**) capable
Caperucita Roja Little Red Riding Hood
capital *f.* capital (city)
capitán *m.* captain
capítulo chapter
cara face
caracol *m.* snail
carácter *m.* character
característica *n.* characteristic
caramelo candy
carbohidrato carbohydrate
cardíaco/a: chequeo cardíaco heart checkup
cardiología cardiology
carecer (zc) to lack
carga: animal (*m.*) **de carga** pack animal
cargar (gu) to load; **cargar (a la cuenta de uno)** to charge (to someone's account) (20)
cargo charge, debit
Caribe *m.* Caribbean
caribeño/a *adj.* Caribbean
cariño affection
cariñoso/a affectionate (4)
carismático/a charismatic
carmín *m.* crimson
carne *f.* meat (9)
carnet (*m.*) **de conducir** driver's license
caro/a expensive (6)
carpintero/a carpenter
carrera race; course of study; career, profession
carretera highway (17)
carro car
carroña carrion
carta letter (4); (playing) card; **jugar (ue) (gu) a las cartas** to play cards; **papel** (*m.*) **para cartas** stationery (21)
cartel *m.* poster (12)
cartelera billboard; entertainment listing
cartera wallet (5)
casa house, home; **amo, ama** (*f. but* **el ama**) **de casa** housekeeper (23); **casa de apartamentos** apartment house (19); **limpiar la casa** to clean the house (12); **regresar a casa** to go home (2)
casado/a married (3)
casarse (con) to marry (19)
cascada waterfall
caserío hamlet
casero/a homemade
casi almost (9); **casi nunca** almost never (4)
caso case; **en caso de que** in case (21)
castellano Castilian; Spanish
castellano/a Castilian
castillo castle
casualidad *f.* coincidence; **por casualidad** by chance
catalán *m.* Catalan (*language of Catalonia*)
catalán, catalana *person from Catalonia*
catarata waterfall
catástrofe *f.* catastrophe
catedral *f.* cathedral
catedrático/a university professor

categoría category; class
catolicismo Catholicism
católico/a *n., adj.* Catholic
catorce fourteen (P)
causa cause; **a causa de** because of, on account of
causar to cause
cauteloso/a cautious, careful
cautivante captivating
cava sparkling wine; champagne
cayo key, islet
cazador(a) hunter
cazuela casserole (*dish*)
cebiche *m.* spiced dish of raw fish marinated in lemon juice
cebolla onion
cebra zebra
ceda el paso yield
ceguera blindness
celebración *f.* celebration
celebrar to celebrate
celoso/a jealous
celular cellular; **teléfono celular** cellular telephone (12)
cementerio cemetery
cena dinner (9)
cenar to have dinner (9)
Cenicienta Cinderella
censo census
censura censorship
centenario *n.* centennial
centígrado/a centigrade
central central; **América Central** Central America
céntrico/a central
centro center; downtown (6); **centro comercial** (shopping) mall (4)
Centroamérica Central America
centroamericano/a Central American
cepillarse los dientes to brush one's teeth
cerámica ceramic, tile
cerca *n.* fence, wall; *adv.* nearby, close; **cerca de** *prep.* close to (7), near
cercanía closeness
cercano/a close by
cerco siege
cerdo pork; **chuletas de cerdo** pork chops (9)
cereal *m.* cereal
cerebro brain (15)
ceremonia ceremony
cerilla match (*for lighting things*)
cero zero (P)
cerrado/a closed (4)
cerrar (ie) to close (6)
certificado/a certified
cervecería beer hall
cerveza beer (2)
césped *m.* lawn, grass
cesta basket
cestería basketmaking
cesto basket
ciclismo bicycling (16)
ciclón *m.* cyclone
ciego/a blind
cielo sky; heaven
cien, ciento one hundred (3) (6); **por ciento** percent

ciencia science; *pl.* sciences (2); **ciencia ficción** science fiction; **ciencias naturales** natural sciences (2); **ciencias políticas** *pl.* political science (2)
científico/a scientific
cierto/a certain; true; **(no) es cierto** it's (not) true (17)
ciervo deer, stag, buck
cifra figure, number
cigarrillo cigarette
cigarro cigar, cigarette
cinco five (P)
cincuenta fifty (3)
cine *m.* movie theater (10); movies (10)
cinta tape (3)
cinturón *m.* belt (5); **cinturón de seguridad** seatbelt
circo circus
circuito circuit
circulación *f.* traffic (17)
círculo circle
circunstancia circumstance
cita appointment, date (15)
citar to cite
citología cytology (*the study of cells*)
ciudad *f.* city (3)
ciudadanía citizenship
ciudadano/a citizen (22)
cívico/a civic (22)
civil: estado civil marital or civic status; **guardia civil** Civil Guard (*Sp.*)
civilización *f.* civilization
clarinete *m.* clarinet
claro/a clear; **claro (que sí)** of course
clase *f.* class; kind; **clase** (*f.*) **turística** tourist class (11); **compañero/a de clase** classmate (1); **primera clase** first class (11); **sala de clase** classroom
clásico/a classic; classical
clasificar (qu) to classify
clausurar to close, bring to a close
clave *f.* key; *adj.* key, important
cliente *m., f.* client, customer (1)
clima *m.* climate (7)
clínica clinic
club *m.* club
cobarde *m., f.* coward
cobranza collection
cobrar to cash (a check) (20); to charge (*someone for an item or service*) (20); to acquire
cocina kitchen (8); cuisine, cooking
cocinar to cook (10)
cocinero/a cook, chef (10)
coctel *m.* cocktail
coche *m.* car (3); **coche deportivo** sports car; **coche descapotable** convertible car (12); **teléfono del coche** car (tele)phone (12)
cochino pig
codo elbow
coger (j) to take, take hold of
cognado cognate
cohete *m.* rocket
coincidir to coincide; to agree
cojear to limp

cola line; **hacer** (*irreg.*) **cola** to stand/wait in line (11)
colección *f.* collection
coleccionar to collect
coleccionista *m., f.* collector
colectivo/a collective
colegio elementary or secondary (high) school
colesterol *m.* cholesterol
colgar (**ue**) (**gu**) to hang (18)
colilla cigarette butt
colisión *f.* collision
colmena beehive
colmo: para colmo to top it all off
colocación *f.* job, position
colocar (**qu**) to place; **colocarse** to find a job
colombiano/a Colombian
colonia colony; camp
colonización *f.* colonization
colonizar (**c**) to colonize, settle
colono colonist
color *m.* color (5)
colorado/a: ponerse (*irreg.*) **colorado/a** to blush
columna column
comandante *m.* commander
combativo/a aggressive
combinación *f.* combination
combinar to combine
combustible *m.* fuel
comedia play (*theater*); comedy
comedor *m.* dining room (8)
comensal *m.* fellow diner
comentar to comment on; to discuss
comentario comment, commentary
comenzar (**ie**) (**c**) to begin
comer to eat (4); **utensilios** (*pl.*) **de comer** eating utensils (10)
comercial *adj.* commercial, business; **centro comercial** (shopping) mall (4)
comercialización *f.* commercialization
comerciante *m., f.* merchant, shopkeeper
comercio commerce, business
cometer to commit
cómico/a comic(al), funny, amusing; **tira cómica** comic strip
comida food (9); meal (9); midday meal
comienzo *n.* beginning
comisión *f.* commission
como as (a); like; since; **así como** as well as; **como si** + *past subj.* as if . . . ; **como si nada** as if nothing were wrong; **tan... como** as . . . as; **tan pronto como** as soon as; **tanto/a... como** as much . . . as (8) **tantos/as... como** as many . . . as (8)
¿cómo? how (P)?; what? I didn't catch that; **¿cómo es usted?** what are you (*form. s.*) like? (P); **¿cómo está(s)?** how are you? (P); **¡cómo no!** of course!; **¿cómo que... ?** what do you mean . . . ?; **¿cómo se dice... ?** how do you say . . . ?; **¿cómo se llama usted?, ¿cómo te llamas?** what is your name? (P)
cómoda bureau, dresser (8)
comodidad *f.* comfort

cómodo/a comfortable (8)
compact disc *m.* compact disc (*player*) (12)
compacto/a: disco compacto compact disc
compañero/a companion; friend; **compañero/a de clase** classmate (1); **compañero/a de cuarto** roommate (1)
compañía company
comparación *f.* comparison (8)
comparar to compare
comparativo *gram.* comparative
compartir to share
compasión *f.* compassion
compendio compendium
compensación *f.* compensation
complacerse (**zc**) (**en**) to take pleasure (in)
complejidad *f.* complexity
complejo *n.* complex
complejo/a *adj.* complex
complemento *gram.* object
completar to complete
completo/a complete; full; **pensión** (*f.*) **completa** full room and board (21); **por completo** completely; **trabajo de tiempo completo** full-time job
complicado/a complicated
comportamiento behavior
comportarse to behave oneself
composición *f.* composition
compra *n.* purchase; **de compras** shopping (6); **ir** (*irreg.*) **de compras** to go shopping (6)
comprador(a) buyer, purchaser; shopper, customer
comprar to buy (2)
comprender to understand (4)
comprensión *f.* comprehension
comprensivo/a *adj.* understanding
comprobar (**ue**) to prove; to confirm
compromiso commitment, appointment
computación *f.* computer science (2)
computadora computer (12)
común common, usual, ordinary; **sentido común** common sense
comunicación *f.* communication; *pl.* communications (2)
comunicarse (**qu**) (**con**) to communicate (with) (22)
comunicativo/a communicative
comunidad *f.* community
comunismo communism
comunista *n. m., f.; adj.* communist
comunitario/a *adj.* community
con with; **con anticipación** ahead of time (21); **con baño** with a bathroom (21); **con frecuencia** frequently (4); **con permiso** pardon me, excuse me (P); **con tal (de) que** provided that (21)
conceder to grant
concentración *f.* concentration
concentrado *n.* concentrate
concentrar to concentrate
concepto concept
concertar (**ie**) to arrange
concierto concert
concilio council
concluir (**y**) to conclude

conclusión *f.* conclusion
concreto/a *adj.* concrete
concha shell
condado county
condena condemnation
condenar to condemn
condición *f.* condition
condicional *m. gram.* conditional (*tense*)
conducir *irreg.* to drive (*a vehicle*) (17); **carnet** (*m.*) **/ licencia de conducir** driver's license
conducta conduct, behavior
conductor(a) driver (17); conductor
conexión *f.* connection
confección *f.* garment industry
conferenciante *m., f.* lecturer, speaker
conferir (**ie, i**) to confer, award
confesar (**ie**) to confess
confianza confidence, trust
confiar (**confío**) to trust
confirmar to confirm (21)
conflicto conflict
conformar to form; **conformarse con** to be content with
confort *m.* comfort
confortable comfortable
confrontación *f.* confrontation
confrontar to confront
confundir to confuse
congelador *m.* freezer (12)
congestión *f.* congestion
congestionado/a congested, stuffed-up (15)
congreso congress
conjugar (**gu**) *gram.* to conjugate
conjunción *f. gram.* conjunction (20)
conjunto group
conmemorar to commemorate, remember
conmigo with me
conocer (**zc**) to know (*people*) (9); to be familiar with (9); to meet
conocimiento(s) knowledge
conquistar to conquer
consagrar to consecrate
consecuencia consequence
consecutivo/a consecutive
conseguir (**i, i**) (**g**) to get, obtain (12)
consejero/a advisor (1)
consejo (piece of) advice (10)
conservación *f.* conservation
conservador(a) *adj.* conservative
conservar to save, conserve (18)
considerar to consider, think
consigna baggage check
consigo with him, with her, with you (*form.*)
consistir (**en**) to consist (of)
consolar (**ue**) to console
consolidar to consolidate
constancia evidence, proof
constante constant
constelación *f.* constellation
constipado head cold
constitución *f.* constitution (22)
constituir (**y**) to constitute, make up
construcción *f.* construction
constructivo/a constructive

construir (y) to build (18)
consuelo comfort, consolation
consulta consultation
consultar to consult
consultorio (medical) office (15)
consumidor(a) consumer
consumir to consume
consumista *adj.* consumer
consumo consumption
contabilidad *f.* accounting
contacto contact; **lentes** (*m. pl.*) **de contacto** contact lenses (15); **llevar lentes de contacto** to wear contact lenses
contado: pagar (gu) al contado to pay cash
contador(a) accountant
contaminación *f.* pollution (7); **contaminación del aire** air pollution (18); **hay contaminación** there's pollution, smog (7)
contaminar to pollute (18)
contar (ue) to count; to tell (about); **contar con** to have; to count on
contemplar to contemplate
contemporáneo/a contemporary
contener (*like* **tener**) to contain, hold (17)
contento/a happy (4)
contestador (*m.*) **automático** answering machine (12)
contestar to answer
contexto context
contigo with you (*fam.*)
continente *m.* continent
continuación *f.*: **a continuación** immediately after, next
continuar (continúo) to continue
continuidad *f.* continuity
continuo/a continuous
contra against
contraer (*like* **traer**) to contract
contrario: al contrario on the contrary
contraste *m.* contrast
contratar to hire
contrato contract
contribuir (y) to contribute
control *m.* control; **control remoto** remote control (12)
controlar to control
convención *f.* convention
conveniente convenient
convenir (*like* **venir**) to suit; to be convenient
conversación *f.* conversation
conversar to converse
convertirse (ie, i) (en) to become
convicción *f.* conviction, belief
convocar (qu) to convoke, call together
cónyuge *m., f.* spouse
cooperación *f.* cooperation
cooperativa *n.* cooperative society
copa wine glass, goblet (10); drink
copia copy
copiar to copy
coquí *m.* small tree frog indigenous to Puerto Rico
coraje *m.* courage
corazón *m.* heart (15); **ataque** (*m.*) **al corazón** heart attack
corbata tie (*clothing*) (5)

cordero lamb
cordialmente cordially, warmly
cordillera mountain range
corista *m., f.* member of the chorus
cornudo cuckold
coro chorus, choir
coronel *m.* colonel
corral *m.* corral
correcto/a correct, right
corregir (i, i) (j) to correct
correo mail; post office (21); **correo electrónico** electronic mail (12)
correr to run, jog (15)
corresponder to correspond
correspondiente *adj.* corresponding
corresponsal *m., f.* correspondent
corrida (de toros) bullfight
corriente: cuenta corriente checking account (20)
cortar to cut; to cut off
cortés courteous
cortesía courtesy (P)
cortina curtain
cortisona cortisone
corto/a short (*in length*) (3); **pantalones** (*m. pl.*) **cortos** shorts
cosa thing (1)
cosecha harvest
cosmético *n.* cosmetic
cosmetología cosmetology
cosmopolita *adj. m., f.* cosmopolitan
costa coast
costar (ue) to cost (6)
costo cost
costumbre *f.* custom, habit; **por costumbre** out of habit
cotidiano/a *adj.* daily
cotillón *m.* cotillion (*dance*)
cotorra parrot
COU: Curso de Orientación Universitaria *one-year course of study similar to preparatory school (Sp.)*
creación *f.* creation
crear to create
creatividad *f.* creativity
creativo/a creative
crecer (zc) to grow
crecimiento growth
credenciales *f. pl.* credentials
crédito credit; **tarjeta de crédito** credit card (10)
creencia belief
creer (y) (en) to think, believe (in) (4); **creo que sí/no** I (don't) think so
criada maid
criado/a servant
crianza breeding
criar to raise, bring up
crimen *m.* crime
criminal *m., f.* criminal
criminología criminology
cristal *m.* crystal
cristalería crystalware
cristianismo Christianity
cristiano/a *n.; adj.* Christian
Cristo: antes de Cristo (a.C.) before Christ (B.C.); **después de Cristo (d.C.)** after

Christ (A.D.)
crítica criticism
crítico/a *n.* critic; *adj.* critical
crónico/a chronic
cronológico/a chronological
croqueta croquette, fritter
cruce (*m.*) **para peatones** pedestrian walkway
crucero cruise ship, cruise (11)
cruciletras *m. inv.* crossword puzzle
crudo/a raw
cruzar (c) to cross (21)
cuaderno notebook (1)
cuadrado/a *adj.* square
cuadro painting; picture; **de cuadros** plaid (5)
cual which; **lo cual** which; **por lo cual** because of which
¿cuál? what?, which? (P); **¿cuál(es)?** which one(s)?; **¿cuál es la fecha?** what is the date? (7)
cualidad *f.* quality
cualquier(a) *adj.* any
cuando when; **de vez en cuando** from time to time
¿cuándo? when? (2)
cuanto: en cuanto *conj.* as soon as (20); **en cuanto a** *prep.* with regard to, regarding
¿cuánto/a? how much?
¿cuántos/as? how many? (P)
cuarenta forty (3)
cuarto room (1); **compañero/a de cuarto** roommate (1); **menos cuarto** a quarter to (*with time*) (P); **y cuarto** quarter past (*with time*) (P)
cuarto/a *adj.* fourth (17)
cuatro four (P)
cuatrocientos/as four hundred (6)
cubano/a *n.; adj.* Cuban
cubanoamericano/a *n., adj.* Cuban American
cubierto/a *p.p.* covered
cubiertos *m. pl.* silverware, flatware
cubo pail, bucket
cubrir (*p.p.* **cubierto/a**) to cover (18)
cuchara (soup)spoon (10)
cucharita teaspoon (10)
cuchillo knife (10)
cuenta bill, check (*in restaurant*) (9); account; **cargar (gu) (a la cuenta de uno)** to charge (to someone's account) (20); **cuenta corriente** checking account (20); **cuenta de ahorros** savings account (20); **darse** (*irreg.*) **cuenta de** to realize; **tener** (*irreg.*)/**tomar en cuenta** to keep/have in mind, take into account
cuentakilómetros *m. inv.* odometer
cuento story
cuerda rope
cuerno horn
cuero leather
cuerpo body (14)
cuestión *f.* question, matter
cuestionar to question
cuestionario questionnaire
cuidado care; **con cuidado** carefully; **tener** (*irreg.*) **cuidado (de)** to be careful (about)
cuidar to take care of; **cuidarse** to take care

of oneself (15)
culinario/a culinary
culminación *f.* culmination
culpa fault, blame
culpable guilty
cultivado/a cultivated
cultura culture
cumbre *f.* summit
cumpleaños *m. inv.* birthday (7); **¡feliz cumpleaños!** happy birthday! (13)
cumplimiento fulfillment
cumplir to accomplish; to fulfill; **cumplir años** to have a birthday; **cumplir con** to fulfill (*an obligation*)
cuna cradle
cuñado/a brother-in-law/sister-in-law
cuota fee
cura *m.* priest; *f.* cure
curandero/a healer; witch doctor
curar to heal, cure
curiosidad *f.* curiosity
currículum *m.* résumé (23)
cursivo/a: letras cursivas italics
curso course (2)
curva curve
cuyo/a whose

CH

champán *m.* champagne
champañería champagne bar
champiñón *m.* mushroom
champú *m.* shampoo
champurrado chocolate-flavored atole (*cornmeal drink*) (*Mex.*)
chaperón, chaperona chaperone
chaqueta jacket (5)
charla *n.* chat, talk
charlar to chat, talk
¡chau! ciao!, good-bye!
chavo cent (*L.A.*)
cheque *m.* check (12); **cheque de viajero** traveler's check (11); **talonario de cheques** checkbook (20)
chequear to check
chequeo check; checkup; **chequeo cardíaco** heart checkup
chévere terrific, great
chicano/a *n.; adj.* Chicano
chicle *m.* chewing gum
chico/a *n.* boy/girl; *pl.* children; *adj.* small
chicharrón *m.* cracklings, crisp pork rind
chichimeca *m., f.* Indian of a nomadic group belonging to the Otomi linguistic stock
chileno/a Chilean
chimenea chimney; fireplace
chimpancé *m.* chimpanzee
chino *n.* Chinese (*language*)
chino/a *n.; adj.* Chinese
chismear to gossip
chiste *m.* joke
chistoso/a funny
chivo kid, goat
chocar (qu) (con) to run (into), collide (with) (17)

chocolate *m.* chocolate
chofer *m.* chauffeur, driver
choque *m.* crash, collision (22)
chorizo sausage
chubasco shower (*weather*)
chuleta *f.* chop (9); **chuleta de puerco/ cerdo** pork chop (9)
chulo/a pretty

D

dama lady, woman
danza dance
daño: hacerse (*irreg.*) **daño** to hurt oneself (14)
dar *irreg.* to give (10); **dar la bienvenida** to welcome; **dar miedo** to frighten; **dar un paseo** to stroll, take a walk (16); **dar una fiesta** to give a party (13); **dar una vuelta** to take a walk; **darse (con)** to bump (into) (14); **darse cuenta de** to realize; **(eso) me da igual** it's (that's) all the same to me; **me da(n) asco** it (they) make me sick; I can't stand it (them)
datar de to date from
dato fact; *pl.* data, information
de *prep.* of (P); from (P); **de compras** shopping (6); **de la mañana/tarde/noche** in the morning/afternoon/evening, at night (P); **de nada** you're welcome (P); **de repente** suddenly; **de todas formas** anyway; **de todo** everything; **de verdad** real; really; **de vez en cuando** on occasion, from time to time
debajo de *prep.* below (7)
debate *m.* debate
deber *n. m.* responsibility, obligation (22)
deber *v.* to owe (20); **deber** + *inf.* should, must, ought to (*do something*) (4)
debido/a proper; **debido/a a** due to
débil weak
debilidad *f.* weakness
década decade
decano/a dean
decidir to decide
décimo/a *adj.* tenth (17)
decir *irreg.* to say, tell (10); **es decir** that is to say; **eso quiere decir (que)** that means (that)
decisión *f.* decision
declaración *f.* declaration, statement
declarar to declare (21)
declinar to decline
decoración *f.* (interior) decoration
decorado scenery (*theater*)
dedicación *f.* dedication
dedicar (qu) to dedicate
dedo finger (14); **hacer** (*irreg.*) **dedo** to hitchhike (*L.A.*)
defecto defect, fault
defenderse (ie) to defend oneself
defensa defense
defensiva: a la defensiva on the defensive
defensor(a) defender, protector
definición *f.* definition

definido/a definite; defined
definir to define
definitiva: en definitiva in short
dejar to leave (behind) (12); to quit (*a job*) (23); to let, allow; **dejar de** + *inf.* to stop (*doing something*) (15)
del (*contraction of* **de** + **el**) of, from the
delante *adv.* in front, ahead; **delante de** *prep.* in front of (7)
delantero/a *adj.* front
delegar (gu) (en) to delegate (to)
delgado/a thin, slender (3)
delicado/a delicate
delicioso/a delicious
delito crime (18)
demanda demand
demás *adj. inv.* other, rest of; **los/las demás** others, other people (22)
demasiado *adv.* too; too much
demasiado/a *adj.* too much
democracia democracy
democrático/a democratic
demonio devil, demon; **¿qué demonios... ?** what the heck . . . ?
demora delay (11)
demostración *f.* demonstration
demostrar (ue) to demonstrate
demostrativo/a *gram.* demonstrative (8)
denominado/a called; so-called
denominar to name, call
denso/a dense (18)
dental: pasta dental toothpaste
dentista *m., f.* dentist
dentro de *prep.* inside; within
denunciar to denounce
departamento department
dependencia dependency
depender (de) to depend (on)
dependiente/a clerk (1)
deporte *m.* sport (2); **practicar (qu) deportes** to play sports (15)
deportista *m., f.* sportsman/sportswoman; *adj.* sports-minded
deportivo/a sports-loving; **coche** (*m.*) **deportivo** sports car
depositar to put in, deposit (20)
depósito deposit (20)
depredador *m.* predator
deprimente *adj.* depressing
deprimido/a depressed
derecha *n.* right (*direction*); **a la derecha de** to the right of (7); **de la derecha** at (the) right
derecho *n.* law; right (22); (custom's) duty (21); **derechos** (*pl.*) **de aduana** customs duty; *adv.* straight; **todo derecho** straight ahead (17)
derecho/a *adj.* straight; right; **salir** (*irreg.*) **a derechas** to turn out correctly
derivar to derive
dermatología dermatology
desagradable disagreeable, unpleasant
desaparecer (zc) to disappear
desaparición *f.* disappearance
desarraigo uprooting, eradication

desarrollar to develop (18)
desarrollo development
desastre *m.* disaster (12)
desastroso/a disastrous, miserable
desayunar to have breakfast (9)
desayuno breakfast (9)
descalzo/a barefoot
descansar to rest (11)
descanso rest
descapotable: coche (*m.*) **descapotable** convertible car (12)
descendente *adj.* descending, downward
descender (ie) to go down, descend
descendiente *m., f.* descendant
desconocido/a unknown
descontento/a discontent
descortés impolite, discourteous
describir (*p.p.* **descrito/a**) to describe
descripción *f.* description
descubierto/a *p.p.* discovered
descubrimiento discovery
descubrir (*p.p.* **descubierto/a**) to discover
descuento discount
descuidado/a careless
descuidar to neglect
descuido *n.* carelessness, neglect
desde *prep.* from, since; **desde que** *conj.* since
desdentado/a *adj.* toothless
desear to want (2)
desembocar (**qu**) to lead, go (*one street to another*)
deseo *n.* desire, wish
desequilibrio imbalance
desertar to desert, abandon
desertización *f.* (*process of*) turning into a desert
desesperación *f.* desperation
desesperado/a desperate
desfile *m.* parade
desforestación *f.* deforestation
desgarrado/a torn, ripped
desgracia: ¡qué desgracia! what a shame!
desgraciadamente unfortunately
desierto *n.* desert (11)
desierto/a *adj.* deserted
designar to designate, appoint
desigualdad inequality (22)
desilusionar to disillusion, disappoint
desinflado/a: llanta desinflada flat tire (17)
desintegrar to disintegrate
desintoxicación *f.* detoxification
desleal disloyal
deslumbrador(a) brilliant, glaring
deslumbrante *adj.* brilliant, dazzling
desmayarse to faint
desnudo/a bare, naked
desobedecer (**zc**) to disobey
desocupado/a vacant, unoccupied
desordenado/a messy (4)
desorientación *f.* disorientation
desorientar to confuse, mislead
desove *m.* spawning season
despacio *adv.* slowly
despedida good-bye, farewell
despedir (i, i) to say good-bye to, see off;

despedirse (de) to say good-bye (to), take leave of (13)
despegar (gu) to take off (*airplane*) (11)
despejado/a clear, cloudless
despensa pantry
desperdicio waste
despertador *m.* alarm clock
despertar (ie) to wake (*someone*) up; **despertarse** to wake up (7)
desplazamiento *n.* removal; shifting
desplazar (c) to displace
después *adv.* later, afterwards; **después de** *prep.* after (6); **después de Cristo (d.C.)** after Christ (A.D.); **después (de) que** *conj.* after (20)
destacado/a outstanding, prominent
destacar (qu) to stand out
destinar to allot, earmark (*money*)
destino destination
destrucción *f.* destruction
destruir (y) to destroy (18)
desventaja disadvantage
detallado/a detailed
detalle *m.* detail
detectar to detect
detective *m.* detective
detener (*like* **tener**) to detain
determinado/a determined; specific
determinar to determine
detestar to detest
detractor(a) detractor
detrás de *prep.* behind (7)
deuda debt (20)
devastar to desolate
devolver (ue) (*p.p.* **devuelto/a**) to return (*something*) (20); to refund, give back
devorar to devour, consume
día *m.* day (1); **algún día** some day; **buenos días** good morning (P); **Día de Año Nuevo** New Year's Day (13); **Día de Gracias** Thanksgiving (13); **Día de la Hispanidad** Hispanic Awareness Day (13); **Día de la Raza** Hispanic Awareness Day (13); **Día de los Enamorados** Valentine's Day; **Día de los Muertos** All Soul's Day (November 2) (13); **Día de los Reyes Magos** Day of the Magi, Epiphany (13); **Día del Santo** Saint's Day (*of the saint for whom one is named*); **día feriado** holiday; **día festivo** holiday (13); **hoy (en) día** nowadays; **todos los días** every day (2)
diabetes *f.* diabetes
diáfano/a transparent, diaphanous
diagnosticar (qu) to diagnose
diagnóstico diagnosis
diálogo dialogue
diamante *m.* diamond
diario/a daily (7)
dibujo drawing, sketch; cartoon; **dibujos animados** cartoons (*on TV*) (16)
diccionario dictionary (1)
diciembre *m.* December (7)
dictado dictation
dictador(a) dictator (22)
dictadura dictatorship (22)

dictar to dictate
dicho *n.* saying, proverb
diecinueve nineteen (P)
dieciocho eighteen (P)
dieciséis sixteen (P)
diecisiete seventeen (P)
diente *m.* tooth
diestramente skillfully
dieta diet; **estar** (*irreg.*) **a dieta** to be on a diet
dietético/a *adj.* diet, dietetic
diez ten (P)
diferencia difference
diferente different
difícil difficult
dificultad *f.* difficulty
difunto/a dead, deceased
digerir (ie, i) to digest
digestión *f.* digestion
dignidad *f.* dignity
digno/a worthy
Dinamarca Denmark
dineral *m.* fortune
dinero money (2); **dinero en efectivo** cash (10)
dios *m.* god; **Dios** God; **por Dios** for heaven's sake (22)
diplomático/a diplomat
diptongo *gram.* diphthong
diputado/a representative
dirección *f.* address (19); **Dirección de Personal** personnel office (23); **libreta de direcciones** address book
directo/a direct; **vuelo directo** direct (*nonstop*) flight (11)
director(a) director, manager
dirigente *m.* manager
dirigir (j) to direct; to lead; **dirigirse** to address (*someone*)
disc *m.*: **compact disc** compact disc (*player*) (12)
disciplina discipline
disco computer diskette (12); record (12); **disco compacto** compact disc
disco(teca) disco(theque) (16)
discreto/a discreet
discriminación *f.* discrimination (22)
discriminar to discriminate, distinguish
disculpa excuse, apology
disculparse to excuse oneself, apologize; **discúlpame** pardon me (14)
discurrir to discuss
discurso speech
discusión *f.* discussion
discutir (sobre/con) to argue (about/with) (13); to argue, disagree (22)
diseñador(a) designer
diseñar to design
diseño design
disfrazado/a disguised
disfrutar (de) to enjoy
disgusto annoyance, displeasure
disminuir (*like* **construir**) to decrease (20)
disparar to fire, shoot
disperso/a spread out, dispersed
disponer (*like* **poner**) (**de**) to have at one's

disposal
disponible available
disposición *f.* disposition
dispositivo device
distancia distance; **mantenerse** (*like* **tener**) **a distancia** to stay away
distante distant
distinción *f.* distinction
distinguir (g) to distinguish, differentiate
distinto/a different
distracción *f.* distraction
distraído/a absent-minded (14); distracted
distribución *f.* distribution
distribuidor(a) distributor
distrito district
diversidad *f.* diversity
diversión *f.* diversion, entertainment, amusement
diverso/a diverse; *pl.* various
divertido/a fun, amusing (16)
divertirse (ie, i) to have a good time, enjoy oneself (7)
dividir to divide
divino/a divine
divorciado/a divorced
divorciarse (de) to get divorced (from)
divorcio *n.* divorce
divulgar (gu) to divulge, disclose
doblar to turn (17)
doble double; **habitación** (*f.*) **doble** double room (21)
doce twelve (P)
docente *adj.* teaching, educational
doctor(a) doctor
documentación *f.* documentation
documental *m.* documentary
documento document
dólar *m.* dollar
doler (ue) to hurt, ache (14)
dolor *m.* pain; **dolor de cabeza** headache; **dolor de garganta** sore throat; **tener** (*irreg.*) **dolor (de)** to have a pain (in) (15)
doloroso/a painful
doméstico/a domestic; **aparato doméstico** home appliance (12); **quehacer** (*m.*) **doméstico** (household) chore (12)
domicilio residence, home
dominado/a dominated
dominanate *adj.* prevailing
domingo Sunday (2)
dominicano/a Dominican (*from the Dominican Republic*); **República Dominicana** Dominican Republic
dominó *s.* dominoes (*game*)
don *m.* ability; *title of respect used with a man's first name*
donación *f.* donation
donde where
¿dónde? where? (P); **¿adónde?** where (to)?; **¿de dónde es Ud.?** where are you from?; **¿dónde quiere vivir?** where do you (*form. s.*) want to live? (19); **¿dónde vive Ud.?** where do you (*form. s.*) live? (19)
dondequiera wherever
donut *m.* doughnut
doña *title of respect used with a woman's first*

name
dorado/a golden
dormido/a asleep
dormilón, dormilona sleepy-head
dormir (ue, u) to sleep (6); **dormir la siesta** to take a nap; **dormir lo suficiente** to get enough sleep; **dormirse** to fall asleep (7); **saco de dormir** sleeping bag
dormitorio bedroom
dos two (P)
doscientos/as two hundred (6)
drama *m.* drama, play
dramático/a dramatic
drenar to drain
droga drug
ducha shower
ducharse to take a shower (7)
duda doubt: **no hay duda** there's no doubt; **sin duda** without a doubt
dudar to doubt (17)
dudoso/a doubtful
dueño/a owner (10); landlord, landlady (19)
dulce *adj.* sweet
dulces *m. pl.* candy, sweets
duración *f.* duration
duradero/a durable, lasting
durante during
durar to last (22); to endure
duro/a hard

E

e and (*used instead of* **y** *before words beginning with* **i** *or* **hi**)
ecología ecology
ecológico/a ecological
ecologista *n. m., f.; adj.* ecologist
economía *s.* economics (2); economy
económico/a economical; economic
economizar (c) to economize (20)
echar to put; to throw; to throw out, expel; to put out, sprout (*roots*); **echar de menos** to miss; **echarse una siesta** to take a nap
edad *f.* age; **mayoría de edad** full legal age; **tercera edad** senior citizens
edificio *n.* building (1)
editorial *f.* publishing company
educación *f.* education
educado/a polite; **mal educado/a** rude, poorly behaved
educar (qu) to educate
educativo/a educational
efectivo cash; **dinero en efectivo** cash (10); **en efectivo** in cash (20)
efecto effect, result; **efecto invernadero** greenhouse effect
efectuar (efectúo) to carry out, perform
eficacia effectiveness
eficaz (*pl.* **eficaces**) efficient, effective
eficiente efficient
Egipto Egypt
egocéntrico/a egocentric, self-centered
egoísmo selfishness, egotism
egoísta *m., f.* egotist; *adj.* egotistical, selfish

¿eh? okay? (*confirmation*)
ejecutivo/a executive
ejemplar *m.* specimen
ejemplificar (qu) to exemplify, illustrate
ejemplo example; **por ejemplo** for example
ejercer (z) to practice (*a profession*); to exert
ejercicio exercise (3); **hacer** (*irreg.*) **ejercicio** to exercise
ejército army
el the (*m. definite article*)
él *sub. pron.* he; *obj.* (*of prep.*) him
elección *f.* election; choice
electricidad *f.* electricity
electricista *m., f.* electrician
eléctrico/a electric
electrocardiograma *m.* electrocardiogram
electrónico/a electronic; **correo electrónico** electronic mail (12)
elefante *m.* elephant
elegancia elegance
elegante elegant, formal
elegir (i, i) (j) to select, choose
elemento element
elevar to raise, elevate
eliminar to eliminate
elitista *m., f.* elitist
elogiar to praise
ella *sub. pron.* she; *obj.* (*of prep.*) her
ello it, that; **todo ello** all that
ellos/as *sub. pron.* they; *obj.* (*of prep.*) them
embajada embassy
embarazada pregnant
embarazo pregnancy
embargo: sin embargo however, nevertheless
embarque *m.*: **puerta de embarque** departure gate (11); **tarjeta de embarque** boarding pass
embotellado/a bottled
embotellamiento traffic jam
emergencia emergency; **sala de emergencias** emergency room
emigrar to emigrate
emisión *f.* emission
emisora broadcasting station (*radio*)
emitir to issue; to utter, declare
emoción *f.* emotion
emocional emotional
emocionar to move (*emotionally*)
emotivo/a emotional
empanada turnover
empapelado/a wallpapered
emparejar to match
empastar to fill a tooth
empaste filling (*tooth*)
empedernido/a diehard, confirmed
emperador, emperatriz (*pl.* **emperatrices**) emperor, empress
empezar (ie) (c) to begin (6); **empezar (a)** to begin to (*do something*) (6)
emplazamiento site
empleado/a employee
emplear to use
empleo job, employment; **oficina de empleos** employment office
empollón, empollona bookworm

empresa corporation, business (23); **administración** (*f.*) **de empresas** business (*school subject*) (2)

empresario/a *adj.* business

en in (P); at (P); on; **en aquel entonces** back then (14); **en cambio** on the other hand; **en efectivo** in cash (20); **en fin** in short; **en seguida** right away, immediately (8)

enamorado/a *n.* sweetheart, lover; *adj.* in love; **Día** (*m.*) **de los Enamorados** Valentine's Day

enamorarse (de) to fall in love (with) (19)

enanito/a dwarf

encajar to fit

encantado/a delighted; pleased to meet you (P)

encantador(a) charming

encantar to love; to like very much

encanto charm, enchantment

encargado/a manager, person in charge

encender (ie) to turn on (*lights or an appliance*) (18); to light

enciclopedia encyclopedia

encima de *prep.* on top of (7)

encontrar (ue) to find; **encontrarse** to meet (*someone somewhere*); to find oneself (*in a state of being*)

encrucijada crossroads

encuentro *n.* encounter; meeting

encuesta survey, poll

encuestado/a person polled

enchilada enchilada (*rolled tortilla with meat, cheese, etc., covered with a chili sauce*)

enchilar to season with chili pepper

enchufar to plug in (18)

endémico/a endemic

enemigo enemy

enemistad *f.* animosity

energía energy (18)

enero January (7)

énfasis *m. inv.* emphasis

enfático/a emphatic

enfermarse to get sick (13)

enfermedad *f.* illness

enfermero/a nurse (15)

enfermo/a sick, ill (4)

enfrentamiento confrontation

enfrentar to confront

enfrente *adv.* in front, opposite

¡enhorabuena! congratulations!

enjambre *m.* swarm

enlace *m.* union, connection

enloquecido/a crazed, crazy

enojarse (con) to get mad (at) (13)

enorme enormous

enriquecer (zc) to enrich

ensalada salad (9)

ensayista *m., f.* essayist

ensayo essay

enseñar to teach (2)

entender (ie) to understand (6)

enterarse (de) to find out, learn (about) (22)

entero/a whole, entire

entonces then, next (6); in that case; **en**

aquel entonces back then (14)

entrada ticket (*for a performance*) (16); entry, entrance; entrée

entrar (en) to enter, go (into)

entre *prep.* between, among (7); **entre paréntesis** in parentheses

entrega delivery; devotion

entregar (gu) to hand in, over; to deliver; **entregarse a** to dedicate oneself to

entremés *m.* appetizer

entrenador(a) trainer, coach

entrenamiento *n.* training

entrevista interview

entrevistador(a) interviewer

entrevistar to interview

entusiasta enthusiastic

envenenado/a poisoned

enviar (envío) to send

envidia envy

envoltura wrapper

envuelto/a *p.p.* wrapped

epidemia epidemic

época era, time (*period*)

equilibrado/a well-balanced

equipado/a equipped

equipaje *m.* luggage (11); **facturar el equipaje** to check one's bags (11)

equipamiento equipment

equipo equipment (12); team; appliance; **equipo estereofónico** stereo equipment (12); **equipo fotográfico** photographic equipment (12)

equis: rayos (*pl.*) **equis** X-rays

equivalente *n. m.* equivalence; *adj.* equivalent

equivocado/a mistaken

equivocarse (qu) to be wrong (14); to make a mistake (14)

érase una vez once upon a time

eres you (*fam.*) are (P)

erguir *irreg.* to raise, straighten

erial *m.* untilled land

errabundo/a wandering

error *m.* error

erudito/a *n.* scholar

erupción *f.* eruption

es you (*form. s.*) are (P); he/she/it is (P); **es decir** that is to say; **es extraño** it's strange (12); **es la...** it's _____ o'clock (P); **es lástima** it's a shame (12)

escala stopover; scale; **sin escalas** nonstop (*flight*); **vuelo con escalas** flight with stops (11)

escalar to scale, climb

escalera stepladder, ladder; stairs, staircase (14)

escalón *m.* step, stair

escándalo scandal

escapar(se) to escape

escasez *f.* (*pl.* **escaseces**) lack, shortage (18)

escayolar to put in a plaster cast

escena scene

escenario stage

escenificar (qu) to stage, dramatize

esclavitud *f.* slavery

escoger (j) to choose, select

esconder(se) to hide

Escorpión *m.* Scorpio

escribir (*p.p.* **escrito/a**) to write (4); **escribir a máquina** to type

escrito/a *p.p.* written

escritor(a) writer

escritorio desk (1)

escrúpulo scruple

escuchar to listen (to) (2)

escuela school; **escuela primaria** elementary school; **escuela secundaria** high school

ese/a *adj.* that (8); (*var.* **ése/a**) *pron.* that one

esencia essence

esencial essential

esfuerzo effort

eso *pron.* that, that thing, fact, idea (8); **eso quiere decir (que)** that means (that)

esos/as *adj.* those (8); (*var.* **ésos/as**) *pron.* those (ones)

espacio space, room

espacioso/a spacious

espada sword; *pl.* spades (*suit of cards*); **pez** (*m.*) (*pl.* **peces**) **espada** swordfish

espalda *n.* back

espantoso/a frightening

España Spain

español *m.* Spanish (*language*)

español(a) *m., f.* Spaniard; *adj.* Spanish; **de habla española** Spanish-speaking

espárragos *pl.* asparagus (9)

especia spice

especial *adj.* special

especialidad *f.* specialty

especialización *f.* specialization; major (*academic*); **segunda especialización** minor (*academic*)

especializarse (c) (en) to specialize (in)

especialmente especially

especie *f.* species, kind, class, type

especificar (qu) to specify; to state

específico/a specific

espectacular spectacular

espectáculo spectacle; show

especulador(a) speculator

espejo mirror

espera: sala de espera waiting area (11)

esperanza hope (22)

esperar to wait (for) (9); to expect; to hope

espinacas *pl.* spinach

espiral *f.* spiral

espíritu *m.* spirit

espléndido/a splendid, magnificent

esplendor *m.* splendor

esposo/a husband/wife (4)

esquiador(a) skier

esquiar (esquío) to ski (11)

esquina corner (17)

está is (located) (P)

estabilidad *f.* stability

estable *adj.* stable

establecer (zc) to establish; **establecerse** to establish oneself establecimiento establishment

estación *f.* season (7); station; **estación de autobuses** bus station (11); **estación de gasolina** gas station (17); **estación de metro** subway station (21); **estación del tren** train station (11)

estacionar(se) to park (17); **prohibido estacionarse** no parking

estadística statistic

estado state; condition; **estado civil** marital or civil status; **Estados Unidos** United States; **golpe** (*m.*) **de estado** coup d'etat

estadounidense *m., f.* person from the United States; *adj.* of or pertaining to the United States

estancia stay

estanco tobacco shop/stand (21)

estante *m.* bookshelf (8)

estar *irreg.* to be (1); **¿cómo está(s)?** how are you? (P); **está de moda** it's in style (5); **está nublado** it's cloudy, overcast (7); **estar a dieta** to be on a diet; **estar atrasado/a** to be late (11); **estar bien** to be comfortable (*temperature*) (7); **estar de vacaciones** to be on vacation (11); **estar sujeto a** to be subject to; **(no) estar de acuerdo** to (dis)agree (3); **sala de estar** living room

estatua statue

este *m.* east

este/a *adj.* this; **en este momento** right now, at this very moment (5); **esta noche** tonight; **esta tarde** this afternoon (4); (*var.* **éste/a**) *pron.* this one

estéreo stereo

estereofónico/a: **equipo estereofónico** stereo equipment (12)

estereotípico/a stereotypical

estereotipo stereotype

estilo style; **estilo de vida** lifestyle

estimar to estimate

estirar to stretch

esto *pron.* this, this thing, fact, idea (8)

estómago stomach (15)

estornudo *n.* sneeze

estos/as *adj.* these; (*var.* **éstos/as**) *pron.* these (ones)

estoy I am (1)

estrecho/a narrow

estrella star; **hotel** (*m.*) **de dos/tres estrellas** two-/three-star hotel (21)

estrés *m.* stress

estricto/a strict

estructura structure

estudiante *m., f.* student (1)

estudiantil *adj.* student

estudiar to study (2)

estudio *n.* study; *pl.* studies, schoolwork

estudioso/a studious

estufa stove (12)

estupendo/a wonderful, marvelous

estúpido/a stupid

etapa stage

etcétera et cetera

eternidad *f.* eternity

ético/a ethical

étnico/a ethnic

eugenesia eugenics (*study of genetic control*)

Europa Europe

europeo/a *n.; adj.* European

euskera *m.* Basque (*language*)

evacuación *f.* evacuation

evacuado/a evacuated

evaluación *f.* evaluation

evaluar (evalúo) to evaluate

evento event

evidenciar to make evident, clear

evitable avoidable

evitar to avoid

evocación *f.* evocation

evocar (qu) to evoke

evolución *f.* evolution

exacto/a exact

exagerar to exaggerate

examen *m.* test, exam (3)

examinar to examine

exceder to exceed

excelencia: **por excelencia** par excellence, superlative

excelente excellent

excepcional exceptional

excesivo/a excessive

exceso excess

exclamar to exclaim

excluir (y) to exclude

exclusivo/a exclusive

excolaborador(a) ex-collaborator

excremento excrement

excursión *f.* excursion, trip

exhausto/a exhausted

exhibición *f.* exhibition

exhibir to show

exigencia requirement

exigente *adj.* demanding

exigir (j) to demand

exiliado/a *n.* exile, expatriate; *adj.* exiled

exilio exile

existencia existence

existir to exist

éxito success; **tener** (*irreg.*) **éxito** to be successful

exitoso/a successful

exótico/a exotic

expandir to expand

expedición *f.* expedition

expedido/a sent; issued

experiencia experience; **por experiencia** personally

experimentar to experience

experimento experiment

experto/a *n.* expert

explicación *f.* explanation

explicar (qu) to explain (10)

exploración *f.* exploration; scanning

explorador(a) explorer

explosión *f.* explosion

explotación *f.* exploitation

explotar to exploit

exponer (*like* **poner**; *p.p.* **expuesto/a**) to exhibit, show

exportación *f.* export

exposición *f.* show, exhibit

expresar to express

expresión *f.* expression; **libertad** (*f.*) **de expresión** freedom of speech

expreso express, exact

expuesto/a *p.p.* on display

expulsar to expel, drive out

exquisito/a exquisite

extático/a ecstatic

extensión *f.* extension

extenso/a extensive

exterior *m.* exterior; *adj.* foreign

externo/a external

extinción *f.* extinction

extraído/a taken (from)

extranjero *n.* abroad (21); **ir** (*irreg.*) **al extranjero** to go abroad; **viajar al/en el extranjero** to travel abroad

extranjero/a *n.* foreigner; *adj.* foreign; **lengua extranjera** foreign language (2)

extrañar to surprise; to miss

extraño strange; **es extraño** it's strange (12)

extraordinario/a extraordinary

extravagancia extravagance

extrovertido/a outgoing, extroverted (8)

F

fábrica factory (18)

fabuloso/a fabulous

fácil easy

facilidad *f.* facility; ease

facilitar to facilitate

factor *m.* factor

factura bill, invoice (20)

facturar to check (*baggage*) (11); **facturar el equipaje** to check one's bags (11)

facultad *f.* campus; department (*of a university*); ability

fachada facade

fajitas *thin strips of marinated and grilled meat, served with tortillas and salsa*

falda skirt (5)

falsificación *f.* falsification

falso/a false

falta lack, absence (18)

faltar (a) to be absent, lacking (13)

fallar to "crash" (*computer*) (12)

fallo failure

fama fame; reputation

familia family (4)

familiar *n. m.* relation, member of the family; *adj.* family-related, of the family (4)

famoso/a famous

fangoterapia mud therapy

fantasía fantasy

fantástico/a fantastic

farmacéutico/a pharmacist

farmacia pharmacy, drugstore

farmacología pharmacology

fascinante fascinating

fatal terrible, bad; fatal

fausto magnificence

favor *m.* favor; **por favor** please (P)
favorecer (zc) to favor
favorito/a favorite
fax *m.* fax machine (12)
fealdad *f.* ugliness
febrero February (7)
fecha date; **¿cuál es la fecha?** what is the date? (7); **fecha límite** deadline
federación *f.* federation
felicidades *f. pl.* congratulations (13)
felicitaciones *f. pl.* congratulations (13)
feliz (*pl.* **felices**) happy (13); **¡feliz cumpleaños!** happy birthday! (13); **sentirse (ie, i) feliz** to feel happy (13)
femenino/a feminine
fenomenal phenomenal
fenómeno phenomenon
feo/a ugly (3)
feria fair, exhibition
feriado/a: día (*m.*) **feriado** holiday
feroz (*pl.* **feroces**) ferocious
ferrocarril *m.* railway, railroad
ferruginoso/a containing iron
festival *m.* festival
festivo/a: día (*m.*) **festivo** holiday (13)
ficción *f.* fiction; **ciencia ficción** science fiction
fiebre *f.* fever; **tener** (*irreg.*) **fiebre** to have a fever (15)
fiel honest, faithful; loyal
fierro iron
fiesta party (2); **dar** (*irreg.*) / **hacer** (*irreg.*) **una fiesta** to give/have a party (13); **fiesta de barrio** block party
figura figure; figurine
figurilla figurine
fijar to attach; **fijarse (en)** to take notice (of), pay attention (to)
fijo/a fixed; **precio fijo** fixed (set) price (6)
fila line
filarmónico/a philharmonic
filatelia philately, stamp collecting
filatélico/a philatelic
filme *m.* film
filosofía philosophy (2)
filtro filter
fin *m.* end; **a fin de** in order to, so as to; **al fin** at last; in the end; **en fin** in short; **fin de semana** (on) the weekend (2); **por fin** finally, at last (8)
final *n. m.* final; end; **a finales de** at the end of (*with time*); **al final de** at the end of
finalmente finally (6)
financiamiento *n.* financing
financiero/a financial
finca farm (18)
Finlandia Finland
fino/a fine; refined
firma signature; **aclaración** (*f.*) **de firma** printed name (*to clarify signature*)
firmar to sign
firme *adj.* firm
física *s.* physics
físico/a physical
flan *m.* baked custard (9)
flauta flute

flexibilidad *f.* flexibility
flor *f.* flower (10)
florero flower vase
florido/a flowery, ornate; **Pascua Florida** Easter
flota fleet
flotar to float
foco focal point
folklore *m.* folklore
folklórico/a folk, folkloric
folleto pamphlet
fondo *s.* bottom, depth(s); *pl.* funds
forestal *adj.* pertaining to forests or forestry
forma form, manner; **de todas formas** anyway
formar to form
fórmula formula
formulario form; **formulario de inmigración** immigration form (21)
fortalecer (zc) to fortify, strengthen
fortalecimiento fortification, strengthening
fortaleza fortress
fortuna fortune
fósforo match (*for lighting things*)
foto(grafía) *f.* photo(graph); photography; **sacar (qu) fotos** to take photos (12)
fotográfico/a photographic; **equipo fotográfico** photographic equipment (12)
fotógrafo/a photographer
fracasar to fail
fracturado/a fractured, broken
frágil fragile
fragmento fragment
francés *m.* French (*language*) (2)
francés, francesa French
frase *f.* phrase; sentence
fray *m.* Brother (*used before the name of clerics of certain religious orders*)
frecuencia frequency; **con frecuencia** frequently (4); **¿con qué frecuencia?** how frequently? (4)
frecuente frequent
frenos *pl.* brakes (17)
frente *m.* front; **frente a** facing
fresco/a fresh; **hace fresco** it's cool (*weather*) (7)
frijol *m.* bean (9)
frío/a *adj.* cold; **hace frío** it's cold (*weather*) (7); **tener** (*irreg.*) **frío** to be cold (*person*) (7)
frito/a fried; **papa frita** (*L.A.*) French fried potato (9); **patata frita** (*Sp.*) French fried potato
frondoso/a leafy
frontera border, frontier (21)
frontón *m.* court for playing jai alai (*a type of handball*)
frustrado/a frustrated
fruta fruit (9)
frutal *adj.* fruit
fue sin querer it was unintentional (14)
fuego fire; **fuegos** (*pl.*) **artificiales** fireworks
fuente *f.* source; fountain
fuera *adv.* out, outside; **fuera de** *prep.* out of
fuerte strong; heavy, large (*meal*); **plato fuerte** main course

fuerza strength
fugaz (*pl.* **fugaces**) brief, transitory
fumar to smoke (11); **sección** (*f.*) **de (no) fumar** (non)smoking section (11)
función *f.* show, performance, showing (*movie or play*) (16)
funcionar to function, operate, work (12)
fundar to found
fundir to join, merge
furioso/a angry, furious (4)
fusilamiento shooting, execution; **pelotón** (*m.*) **de fusilamiento** firing squad
fútbol *m.* soccer (16); **fútbol americano** football (16)
futuro *n.* future
futuro/a *adj.* future

G

gafas *pl.* (eye)glasses (14); **gafas bifocales** bifocal glasses; **llevar gafas** to wear glasses
galante gallant
galaxia galaxy
galeón *m.* galleon
galería gallery
gallego language of Galicia (*in northwestern Spain*)
galleta cookie (9); cracker (9)
gallinero henhouse
gallo rooster; **misa del gallo** Midnight Mass (*Christmas Eve*)
gambas *pl.* shrimp (*Sp.*)
ganadero cattleman
ganadero/a *adj.* cattle
ganado livestock, cattle
ganador(a) winner
ganar to earn (12); to win (12)
ganas *f. pl.:* **tener ganas de** + *inf.* to feel like (*doing something*) (5)
ganga bargain
ganso goose
garaje *m.* garage (8)
garantía guarantee
garantizar (c) to guarantee
garganta throat (15); **dolor** (*m.*) **de garganta** sore throat
gas *m.* gas; heat (19)
gasolina gasoline (17); **estación** (*f.*) **de gasolina** gas station (17); **gastar mucha gasolina** to use a lot of gas
gasolinera gas station (17)
gastar to use, expend (17); to spend (money); **gastar mucha gasolina** to use a lot of gas
gasto expense (20)
gastronomía gastronomy
gastronómico/a gastronomic
gato/a cat (3)
gelatinado/a: capa gelatinada gel cap
gemelo/a twin
generación *f.* generation
general *n. m.* general; *adj.* general, usual; **en general** generally, in general; **por lo general** in general (3)

generalizado/a generalized
género *gram.* gender
generosidad *f.* generosity
generoso/a generous
genial wonderful
genio genius
gente *f. s.* people (12)
gentil kind, pleasant
genuino/a genuine
geografía geography
geográfico/a geographical
geopolítico/a geopolitical
geranio geranium
gerundio *gram.* gerund
gigante *n. m.; adj.* giant
gigantesco/a gigantic
gimnasio gymnasium
ginecológico/a gynecological
girar to turn
giro *n.* turn
glorioso/a glorious
gobernante *m., f.* ruler
gobernar (ie) to govern, rule
gobierno government (18)
golf *m.* golf (16)
golpe *m.* blow; strike; **golpe de estado** coup d'etat
gordo/a fat (3)
gorila *m.* gorilla
gorra cap (5)
gozar (c) to enjoy
grabación *f.* recording
grabadora tape deck/recorder (12)
grabar to record; to tape
gracias thanks (P); **Día** (*m.*) **de Gracias** Thanksgiving (13); **muchas gracias** thank you very much; many thanks (P)
gracioso/a funny
grado degree (*temperature*); grade (*in school*)
graduación *f.* graduation
graduado/a *adj.* graduate
graduarse (en) to graduate (from) (20)
gramática grammar
gran, grande large, big (3); great (3)
Gran Bretaña Great Britain
grandeza greatness, magnificence
granja farm
granjero/a farmer
grasa grease; fat
gratis *inv.* free, gratis
grato/a pleasant
gratuito/a free
grave grave, important; serious
gravoso/a onerous; costly
Grecia Greece
griego/a Greek
grifo faucet, tap
gris gray (5)
gritar to shout, scream (16)
grito *n.* shout, cry
grupo group
guagua bus (*Cuba, Puerto Rico*)
guajolote *m.* turkey (*Mex.*)
guante *m.* glove
guapo/a handsome, good-looking (3)
guardar to watch over (11); to save (*a place*)

(11); to keep (*a secret*); **guardar cama** to stay in bed (15); **guardar un puesto** to save a place (11)
guardarropa *m.* wardrobe
guardia civil Civil Guard (*Sp.*)
guayabera loose-fitting, embroidered shirt
gubernamental *adj.* government
guerra war (22)
guerrero warrior, soldier
guía *m., f.* guide (*person*); *f.* guidebook; **guía** (*f.*) **telefónica** telephone book
guiar (guío) to drive
guiñar to wink
guirnalda garland, wreath
guisante *m.* pea
guitarra guitar
gustar to like (10); **¿le gusta... ?** does he/she like . . . ?; do you (*form. s.*) like . . . ? (P); **me gustaría** I would like (10); **no, no me gusta...** no, I don't like . . . (P); **sí, me gusta...** yes, I like . . . (P); **¿te gusta... ?** do you (*fam. s.*) like . . . ? (P)
gusto *n.* like, preference (P); taste; flavor; pleasure; **a gusto** comfortable; **mucho gusto** pleased to meet you (P)

H

haba *f.* (*but* **el haba**) bean
haber (*irreg.*) *infinitive of* **hay** (11); to have (*auxiliary*); **va a haber** there's going to be
habilidad *f.* ability
habitación *f.* room; **habitación individual/ doble** single/double room (21)
habitante *m., f.* inhabitant
habitar to inhabit; to live
hábito habit
habituado/a accustomed
habla *f.* (*but* **el habla**) speech (*language*); **de habla española** Spanish-speaking
hablar to speak (2); to talk (2)
hace + *time* ago (12); **hace** + *period of time* + **que** + *present tense* to have been (*doing something*) for (*period of time*)
hacer *irreg.* (*p.p.* **hecho/a**) to do; to make; **hace (muy) buen/mal tiempo** it's (very) good/bad weather (7); **hace (mucho) calor** it's (very) hot (*weather*); **hace fresco** it's cool (*weather*) (7); **hace frío** it's cold (*weather*) (7); **hace sol** it's sunny (7); **hace viento** it's windy (7); **hacer auto-stop** to hitchhike; **hacer camping** to go camping (11); **hacer cola** to stand/wait in line (11); **hacer dedo** to hitchhike (*L.A.*); **hacer ejercicio** to exercise; **hacer el balance** to balance (*an account*); **hacer la cama** to make the bed (12); **hacer las maletas** to pack one's bags (11); **hacer planes para** + *inf.* to make plans to (*do something*) (16); **hacer un picnic** to have a picnic; **hacer una fiesta** to have a party (13); **hacer una pregunta** to ask a question (7); **hacerse daño** to hurt oneself (14); **¿qué tiempo hace?** what's the weather like? (7)

hacia toward; about
hacienda farm, ranch
hallar to find
hamaca hammock
hambre *f.* (*but* **el hambre**) hunger; **tener** (*irreg.*) (**mucha**) **hambre** to be (very) hungry (9)
hamburguesa hamburger (9)
harapiento/a unkempt
hasta *prep.* until; *adv.* even; **hasta luego** see you later (P); **hasta mañana** until tomorrow, see you tomorrow (P); **hasta pronto** see you soon; **hasta que** *conj.* until (20)
hay there is/are (P); **hay contaminación** there's pollution, smog (7); **no hay** there is not/are not (P); **no hay de qué** you're welcome (P); **no hay duda** there's no doubt
hebreo/a Hebrew
hectárea hectare (*approx. 2.5 acres*)
hecho *n.* fact, event; **de hecho** in fact
hecho/a *p.p.* made, done
hediondo/a *adj.* stinking
hedor *m.* stink, stench
helado ice cream (9)
helado/a freezing, very cold
hembra female
hemisferio hemisphere
heredero/a heir
herencia inheritance; heritage
herido/a wounded
hermanastro/a stepbrother/stepsister
hermano/a brother (3) / sister (4); **medio hermano / media hermana** half brother / half sister
hermoso/a beautiful
hermosura beauty
héroe *m.*, **heroína** *f.* hero, heroine
hervido/a boiled
hidromasaje *m.* water massage
hielo ice (7)
hígado liver
higiene *f.* hygiene
hijastro/a stepson/stepdaughter
hijo/a son/daughter (4); *pl.* children (4)
himno hymn
hinchar to fill, stuff
hipopótamo hippopotamus
hipoteca mortgage
hiriente *adj.* wounding
hispánico/a *n.; adj.* Hispanic
hispanidad *f.*: **Día** (*m.*) **de la Hispanidad** Hispanic Awareness Day (13)
hispano/a *n.; adj.* Hispanic
Hispanoamérica Latin America
hispanoamericano/a Latin American
hispanohablante Spanish-speaking
histérico/a hysterical
historia history (2); story
histórico/a historic
historieta comic strip; cartoon
hockey *m.* hockey (16)
hogar *m.* home, house
hoguera bonfire
hoja leaf
hojalata tin

hojear to leaf through
hola hello (P)
Holanda Holland
holandés, holandesa Dutch
hombre *m.* man (1); **¡hombre!** well!, man!;
  hombre de negocios businessman
hombrillo shoulder (*of road*)
homeopatía homeopathy
homogeneidad *f.* homogeneity
homosexualidad *f.* homosexuality
honestidad *f.* honesty
honesto/a honest
honor *m.* honor
honrar to honor
hora hour; **¿a qué hora?** (at) what time? (P);
  hora de + *inf.* time to (*do something*);
  hora punta rush hour; **por hora** per
  hour; **¿qué hora es?** what time is it? (P)
horario schedule (8); timetable
horizonte *m.* horizon
horneado/a baked
horno oven; **horno de microondas** microwave oven (12); **papa al horno** baked
  potato (9)
horóscopo horoscope
horrible horrible, awful
horror *m.* horror
hospital *m.* hospital
hotel *m.* hotel (11); **hotel de dos/tres estrellas** two-/three-star hotel (21); **hotel de
  lujo** luxury hotel (21)
hoy today (2); **hoy (en) día** nowadays; **hoy
  es viernes** today is Friday (2)
huelga strike (*labor*) (22)
huerta orchard; garden
hueso bone
huésped(a) (hotel) guest (21)
huevo egg (9)
huir (y) to flee
humanidad *f.* humanity
humano/a *adj.* human; **ser** (*n. m.*) **humano**
  human being
humilde humble
humor *m.* humor; **sentido del humor** sense
  of humor
humorista *m., f.* humorist
huracán *m.* hurricane

I

ibérico/a Iberian
iberoamericano/a Ibero-American
ida: billete/boleto de ida one-way ticket
  (11); **billete** (*m.*) **/ boleto de ida y vuelta**
  round-trip ticket (11)
idea idea; **cambiar de idea** to change one's
  mind
idealista *m., f.* idealist
idear to imagine
idéntico/a identical
identidad *f.* identity
identificación *f.* identification
identificar (qu) to identify

ideología ideology
idioma *m.* language
iglesia church
ignorante ignorant
igual equal, same; **(eso) me da igual** it's
  (that's) all the same to me; **igual que** the
  same as; **por igual** equally
igualdad *f.* equality (22)
igualmente likewise (P)
ilegal illegal
iluminado/a illuminated
ilustración *f.* illustration
ilustrativo/a illustrative
imagen *f.* image
imaginación *f.* imagination
imaginar to imagine
imaginario/a imaginary
imitar to imitate
impaciente impatient
impar odd (*with numbers*)
impedir (i, i) to impede, hinder
imperdonable unpardonable, unforgivable
imperfecto *gram.* imperfect (*tense*)
imperfecto/a imperfect
imperio empire
impermeable *m.* raincoat (5)
implicación *f.* implication
implicar (qu) to imply
imponer (*like* **poner**) to impose
importación *f.* import, importation
importancia importance
importante important
importar to be important, matter; to import;
  ¿le/te importaría... ? would you mind
  . . . ? (21); **no (me) importa** it doesn't
  matter (to me)
imposición *f.* imposition
impráctico/a impractical
imprenta: letra de imprenta print(ing)
imprescindible indispensable
impresión *f.* impression
impresionante impressive
impresionar to impress
impresora printer (12)
imprevisto/a unforeseen, unexpected
improductivo/a unproductive
impuesto tax (20)
impulsar to drive, force
impulsivo/a impulsive
inagotable inexhaustible
inalámbrico/a wireless
inca *m.* Inca
incaico/a *adj.* Inca, Incan
incendio fire
incentivo incentive
incidencia incidence
incidente *m.* incident
incierto/a unstable
inclinado/a inclined
incluir (y) to include
inclusive *adj.* including
incluso *adv.* even, including
inconveniente *m.* drawback
incorporar to incorporate
incorrecto/a incorrect
increíble incredible (12)

indagar (gu) to investigate
indecisión *f.* indecision
indefinido/a indefinite (9)
independencia independence
independiente independent
independizarse (c) to become independent
indicación *f.* instruction; direction
indicado/a indicated
indicar (qu) to indicate, point out
indicativo *gram.* indicative (*mood*)
índice *m.* index
indiferencia indifference
indiferente indifferent
indígeno/a indigenous
indio/a *n.; adj.* Indian
indirecto/a indirect
indiscreto/a indiscreet
indiscutible indisputable
individual: habitación (*f.*) **individual** single
  room (21)
individuo individual, person
industria industry
industrializado/a industrialized
inesperado/a unexpected
inestable unstable
infancia infancy
infantil *adj.* children's
infeccioso/a infectious
inferior inferior; lower
inferir (ie, i) to infer
infierno hell
infinitivo *gram.* infinitive
infinito/a infinite
inflamado/a inflamed
influencia influence
influyente influential
información *f.* information
informar to inform (22); **informarse** to inquire, find out
informática data processing
informativo/a informative
informe *m.* report
infracción *f.* infraction
ingeniería engineering
ingeniero/a engineer
ingente enormous
ingenuo/a innocent; naive
Inglaterra England
inglés *m.* English (*language*) (2)
inglés, inglesa *n.* English person; *adj.*
  English
ingrediente *m.* ingredient
ingresar to put in, deposit
ingresos *m. pl.* income; revenue
inicial initial
iniciar to initiate
iniciativa initiative
injusto/a unjust, unfair
inmediato/a immediate
inmenso/a immense
inmigración *f.* immigration; **formulario de
  inmigración** immigration form (21)
inmigrante *n. m., f.; adj.* immigrant
inminente imminent
inmoral immoral
innecesario/a unnecessary

inocente innocent
inolvidable unforgettable
inquilino/a tenant, renter (19)
inscribirse (*p.p.* inscrito/a) to enroll, register
inscripción *f.* enrollment
inscrito/a *p.p.* recorded
insensible insensitive
insistir (en) to insist (on) (11)
insolente insolent
insoportable unbearable
inspector(a) inspector; inspector(a) de aduanas customs inspector (21)
inspirar to inspire, stimulate
instalación *f.* installation
instalar to install
instantáneo/a instantaneous
instintivo/a instinctive
institución *f.* institution
instituto institute; secondary school
instrucción *f.* instruction
instrumento instrument
insuficiencia insufficiency, scarcity
insulto insult
intacto/a intact
integridad *f.* integrity
inteligencia intelligence
inteligente intelligent
intención *f.* intention
intensidad *f.* intensity
intensivo/a intensive
intenso/a intense
intentar to try
interés *m.* interest (20)
interesante interesting
interesar to interest, be interesting
interior *n. m.; adj.* interior; inside
internarse (en) to check in(to) (*a hospital*) (15)
interno/a internal; producto interno bruto gross national product
interpretar to interpret
intérprete *m., f.* interpreter
interrogativo/a interrogative (P)
interrumpir to interrupt
interruptor *m.* (electrical) switch
intimidad *f.* intimacy
intranquilidad *f.* uneasiness, restlessness
introducción *f.* introduction
introducir *irreg.* to bring in
introvertido/a introverted
inundación *f.* flood
inútil useless
invadir to invade
invasivo/a invasive
inventar to invent
invernadero/a: efecto invernadero greenhouse effect
inverosímil fantastic, unimaginable
invertir (ie, i) to invest (*funds*)
investigación *f.* research
investigar (gu) to investigate; to research
invierno winter (7)
invitación *f.* invitation
invitado/a guest (8)

invitar to invite (9)
involucrar to involve
inyección *f.* shot, injection; ponerle (*irreg.*) una inyección to give (*someone*) a shot (15)
ir *irreg.* to go; ir a + *inf.* to be going to (*do something*); ir al extranjero to go abroad; ir al teatro to go to the theater; ir de compras to go shopping (6); ir de vacaciones to go on vacation (11); irse to leave, go away
Irlanda Ireland
ironía irony
irracional irrational
irreligioso/a unreligious
irreverente irreverent
irrumpir to burst in
isla island
Islandia Iceland
Islas Baleares Balearic Islands
Islas Canarias Canary Islands
isleño/a of or pertaining to an island
Italia Italy
italiano *n.* Italian (*language*) (2)
italiano/a Italian
itinerario itinerary
izquierda *n.* left (*direction*) a la izquierda (de) to the left (of) (7)
izquierdo/a *adj.* left; levantarse con el pie izquierdo to get up on the wrong side of the bed (14)

J

jactarse to boast, brag
jamás never (9)
jamón *m.* ham
Jánuca Hannukah
Japón *m.* Japan
japonés *m.* Japanese (*language*) (2)
japonés, japonesa *n.* Japanese person; *adj.* Japanese
jarabe *m.* (cough) syrup (15)
jardín *m.* garden
jardinero/a gardener
jarra jug
jarro pitcher (10)
jefatura leadership
jefe/a boss (12)
jerez *m.* sherry
jersey *m.* sweater
jirafa giraffe
jornada occasion
joven *n. m., f.* young person; *adj.* young (3); de joven as a youth
joya jewel
joyería jewelry; jewelry store
jubilación *f.* retirement (20)
jubilarse to retire (*from work*) (20)
judía green bean
judío/a *adj.* Jewish
juego game; Juegos Olímpicos Olympic Games
jueves *m. inv.* Thursday (2)
jugar (ue) (gu) (al) to play (*a sport*) (6); jugar a las cartas to play cards

jugo juice (9)
jugoso/a juicy
juguete *m.* toy
juicio judgment
julio July (7)
junio June (7)
junto/a together
jurado jury
jurídico/a legal, juridical
justicia justice
justiciero/a just, fair
justificar (qu) to justify
justo/a just, fair
juvenil youthful
juventud *f.* youth
juzgar (gu) to judge

K

karate *m.* karate
kilometraje *m.* mileage (distance in kilometers)
kilómetro kilometer (*approx .62 mile*)
kinésico/a kinesthetic

L

la the (*f. definite article*); *d.o.* you (*form. s.*), her, it (*f.*)
laberinto labyrinth
labio lip
labor *f.* work
laboral *adj. pertaining to work or labor*
laboratorio lab, laboratory
laboriosidad *f.* industriousness
lácteo/a *adj.* dairy
lado side; al lado de alongside of (7); por otro lado on the other hand
ladrar to bark
ladrón, ladrona thief
lagarto lizard
lago lake
lágrima tear
laguna lagoon
lamento moan, wail
lámpara lamp (8)
lana wool (5)
langosta lobster (9)
lanzamiento launching (*new product*)
lanzar (c) to throw; to launch
lápiz *m.* (*pl.* lápices) pencil (1)
lapso lapse
largo/a long (3)
las the (*f. pl. definite article*); *d.o.* you (*form. pl.*), them (*f.*)
lástima *n.* pity; es lástima it's a shame (12); ¡qué lástima! what a shame! (12)
lata (tin) can; ¡qué lata! what a bore!
latín *m.* Latin (*language*)
latino/a *n.* Latin person, Latino; América Latina Latin America
Latinoamérica Latin America
latinoamericano/a *n.; adj.* Latin American
lavabo (bathroom) sink (8)

lavadora washer (12)
lavandería laundry; laundromat
lavaplatos m. inv. dishwasher (12)
lavar to wash; **lavar las ventanas** to wash the windows (12); **lavar los platos** to wash the dishes (12); **lavar(se)** to wash (oneself); to get washed
le i.o. to/for you (form. s.), him, her, it
leal loyal
lección f. lesson
lector(a) reader (person)
lectura n. reading
leche f. milk (7)
lechuga lettuce (9)
leer (y) to read (4)
legado legacy
legalización f. legalization
legalizar (c) to legalize
legendario/a legendary
legua league (approx. 3.5 miles)
legumbre f. vegetable
lejano/a distant
lejos adv. far away; **lejos de** prep. far from (7)
lengua language; tongue; **lengua extranjera** foreign language (2); **Real Academia de la Lengua** Spanish Royal Academy (of the Language); **sacar (qu) la lengua** to stick out one's tongue (15)
lenguaje m. language; speech
lenteja lentil
lentes (m. pl.) **de contacto** contact lenses (15); **llevar lentes de contacto** to wear contact lenses
lento/a slow (14)
leña (fire)wood
león m. lion
les i.o. to/for you (form. pl.), them
lesionado/a hurt
letra letter (alphabet); **letra de imprenta** print(ing); **letras cursivas** italics
letrero sign (17)
levantar to lift, raise; **levantarse** to get up, stand up (7); **levantarse con el pie izquierdo** to get up on the wrong side of the bed (14)
ley f. law (22)
liberación f. liberation
liberal liberal; **artes** (f. pl.) **liberales** liberal arts
libertad f. liberty, freedom; **libertad de expresión** freedom of speech
libertador(a) liberator
libra pound
libre free; **mercado al aire libre** outdoor marketplace (6); **ratos** (pl.) **libres** leisure time (16); **tiempo libre** free time
librería bookstore (1)
libreta de ahorros savings passbook (20); **libreta de direcciones** address book
libro book (1); **libro de texto** textbook (1)
licencia license (17); **licencia de manejar/ conducir** driver's license
licenciatura degree (university)
liceo high school
licor m. liquor

líder m. leader
ligar (gu) to link
ligero/a light (in weight, content) (9)
limitar to limit
límite m. limit; **fecha límite** deadline; **límite de velocidad** speed limit
limón m. lemon
limonada lemonade
limpiar to clean (12); **limpiar la casa** to clean the house (12)
limpieza n. cleaning
limpio/a clean (4)
lindo/a pretty
línea line; **línea aérea** airline
lingüístico/a linguistic
lío mess
líquido liquid
liso/a smooth
lista list
listo/a smart, clever (3); ready
litera berth (in boat or train)
literatura literature (2)
lo d.o. you (form. s.), him, it (m.); **lo cual** which; **lo que** what, that which; **lo siento** I'm sorry; **lo suficiente** enough (15); **por lo cual** for which reason, because of which
lobo wolf
local m. building, place
localizar (c) to find, locate
loco/a crazy, "nuts"; **volverse (ue) loco/a** to go crazy
lógico/a logical
lograr to achieve; to obtain
logro achievement
longaniza pork sausage
longitud f. length
loro parrot
los the (m. pl. definite article); d.o. you (form. pl.), them (m.)
lotería lottery
lubricación f. lubrication
lubricar (qu) to lubricate
lucir (zc) to show
lucha fight
luchar to fight
luego then, afterward (6); **hasta luego** see you later (P)
lugar m. place (1)
lujo luxury; **hotel** (m.) **de lujo** luxury hotel (21)
lujoso/a luxurious
luna moon; **luna de miel** honeymoon
lunes m. inv. Monday (2); **el/los lunes** on Monday(s) (2)
luz f. (pl. **luces**) light, electricity (19)

LL

llamada call
llamado/a called; so-called
llamar to call; **¿cómo se llama usted?** what is your (form.) name? (P); **¿cómo te llamas?** what is your (fam.) name? (P); **llamar por teléfono** to telephone; **llamarse**

to be named, called; **me llamo...** my name is . . . (P)
llanta tire (17); **llanta desinflada** flat tire (17)
llave f. key (6)
llavero key ring
llegada arrival (11)
llegar (gu) to arrive (6); **llegar a tiempo** to arrive on time
llenar to fill (up) (17); to fill out (a form) (23)
lleno/a full
llevar to wear (5); to carry (5); to take (5); **llevar armas** to bear arms; **llevar gafas** to wear glasses; **llevar lentes de contacto** to wear contact lenses; **llevar una vida sana** to lead a healthy life (15); **llevarse bien/ mal (con)** to get along well/badly (with) (19)
llorar to cry (13)
llover (ue) to rain (7); **llueve a cántaros** (col.) it's raining cats and dogs
llovizna drizzle
lluvia rain (7)
lluvioso/a rainy

M

maceta flowerpot
madrastra stepmother
madre f. mother (4)
madrileño/a from Madrid; **callos** (pl.) **a la madrileña** tripe specialty of Madrid
madrugador(a) early riser
madrugar (gu) to get up early
maduro/a mature; ripe
maestro/a n. grade school teacher; adj. superlative; **obra maestra** masterpiece
magia magic
mágico/a adj. magic, magical
magnífico/a magnificent, wonderful
mago: Día (m.) **de los Reyes Magos** Day of the Magi, Epiphany (13)
maíz m. corn
mal adv. badly (2); **caerle (irreg.) mal** to make a bad impression (23); **llevarse mal (con)** to get along badly (with) (19); **pasarlo mal** to have a bad time (11); **portarse mal** to behave badly (13)
mal, malo/a bad (3); **hace (muy) mal tiempo** it's (very) bad weather (7); **¡qué mala suerte!** what bad luck! (14)
maldad f. wickedness
maldito/a cursed, damned
maleducado/a rude, ill-mannered
malestar m. malaise, indisposition
maleta suitcase; **hacer (irreg.) las maletas** to pack one's bags (11)
malicioso/a malicious, nasty
maltratar to mistreat, abuse
malvado/a evil, wicked
mamá mom (4)
mamario/a mammary
mamífero mammal
manchego/a of or from La Mancha (region of

Spain)
mandar to send (10); to order (11)
mandatario agent
mandato command
manejar to drive; to use (*a machine*); **licencia de manejar** driver's license
manera manner, way
manifestación *f.* demonstration; manifestation
manifestar (ie) to express, show
manillar *m. s.* handlebars (*bicycle*)
manipular to manipulate, handle
manjar *m.* food; dish
mano *f.* hand (14)
manta blanket
manteca butter
mantel *m.* tablecloth (10)
mantener (*like* **tener**) to maintain, keep up (17); **mantenerse a distancia** to stay away
manual *m.* manual
manzana apple (9)
mañana *n.* morning; **de la mañana** in the morning (P); *adv.* tomorrow; **hasta mañana** until tomorrow, see you tomorrow (P); **mañana es viernes** tomorrow is Friday (2); **pasado mañana** day after tomorrow (2)
mapa *m.* map
maqueta model
máquina machine; **escribir a máquina** to type
mar *m.* sea (11)
maratón *m.* marathon
maravilloso/a wonderful, marvelous
marca brand, make
marcar (qu) to mark; to stamp
marchar to go
mareado/a dizzy, nauseated (15)
marejada *n.* groundswell
margen *m.* margin
marido husband (4)
marihuana marijuana
mariscos *pl.* shellfish
Marruecos *m.* Morocco
martes *m. inv.* Tuesday
marzo March
más more; most; **más tarde** later
masa dough
masaje *m.* massage
máscara mask
mascota pet (4)
masculino/a masculine
masivo/a massive
masticar (qu) to chew
mata shrub
matanza *n.* slaughtering
matar to kill
matemáticas *pl.* mathematics (2)
materia subject (*in school*) (2); material
material *n. m.; adj.* material (5)
materno/a maternal
matrícula tuition; registration (2)
matrimonial *adj.* matrimonial, marriage
matrimonio marriage; married couple; **cama de matrimonio** double bed

máximo/a *adj.* maximum
maya *n. m., f.; adj.* Maya, Mayan
mayo May (7);
mayor older (8); greatest, greater
mayoría majority; **mayoría de edad** full legal age
me *d.o.* me; *i.o.* to/for me; *refl. pron.* myself
mecánica *s.* mechanics
mecánico/a *n.* mechanic (17); *adj.* mechanical
mecedor(a): silla mecedora rocking chair
mecer (z) to rock, move to and fro
mediano/a middle; average
medianoche *f.* midnight
medias *pl.* stockings (5)
medicina medicine
médico/a *n.* physician (15); (medical) doctor; *adj.* medical; **seguro médico** medical insurance
medida: a medida que as, at the same time as
medio *n.* means; medium; **medio ambiente** environment (18); **medio de transporte** means of transportation (11)
medio/a *adj.* half; middle; **y media** _____ thirty, half past (*with time*) (P); **media pensión** room with breakfast meal (21); **medio hermano / media hermana** half brother / half sister; **Oriente** (*m.*) **Medio** Middle East
mediodía *m.* noon; midday
medir (i, i) to measure
mediterráneo/a Mediterranean
médula marrow
mejor best (3); better (8)
mejorar to improve
mejoría improvement
melodioso/a melodious, tuneful
melodrama *m.* melodrama
memoria memory
mencionar to mention
menor younger (8); least; lower
menos less; minus; least; **a menos que** unless (21); **echar de menos** to miss; **menos cuarto** a quarter to (*with time*) (P); **menos que** less than (8)
mensaje *m.* message
mensual monthly
mensualidad *f.* monthly installment
mentir (ie, i) to lie, tell lies
mentira lie (10)
menú *m.* menu (9)
mercado market(place) (6); **mercado al aire libre** outdoor marketplace (6)
merecer (zc) to deserve
merienda snack
mérito merit; worth
mermelada jam; marmalade
mes *m.* month (7); **...al mes** . . . a month
mesa table (1); **poner** (*irreg.*) **la mesa** to set the table (12)
meseta plain (*geographic*)
mesita end table (8)
mesón *m.* inn; tavern
mestizo/a *n.; adj.* mestizo, of mixed blood
meta goal

metafóricamente metaphorically
meteorológico/a meteorological
meteorólogo/a meteorologist
meter to put in; **meter la pata** to put one's foot in one's mouth
método method
métrico/a metric
metro subway; meter; **estación** (*f.*) **de metro** subway station (21)
metrópolis *m.* metropolis
mexicanidad *f.* Mexicanism, Mexican spirit
mexicano/a Mexican
mexicanoamericano/a Mexican American
mexicoamericano/a Mexican American
mezcla mixture
mezclar to mix, blend
mezcolanza *col.* mixture, hodgepodge
mi *poss.* my
mí *obj. (of prep.)* me (7)
microondas *m. s.:* **horno de microondas** microwave oven (12)
microscópico/a microscopic
miedo fear; **dar** (*irreg.*) **miedo** to frighten; **tener** (*irreg.*) **miedo (de)** to be afraid (of) (5)
miel *f.* honey; **luna de miel** honeymoon
miembro member
mientras (que) *conj.* while (15); **mientras tanto** *adv.* meanwhile
miércoles *m. inv.* Wednesday (2)
migratorio/a migratory
mil *m.* thousand, one thousand (6)
militar *adj.* military
milla mile
millares *m. pl.* thousands
millón (*m.*) **(de)** million (6)
millonario/a millionaire
mineral: agua (*f. but* **el agua**) **mineral** mineral water (9)
minicuestionario miniquestionnaire
minidiálogo minidialogue
minifalda miniskirt
mínimo *n.* minimum
mínimo/a *adj.* minimum
ministro minister
minoría minority
minuciosamente *adv.* meticulously
minuto *n.* minute (*time*)
mío/a *poss.* my, (of) mine
mirar to look (at) (2); to watch
misa Mass; **misa del gallo** Midnight Mass (*Christmas Eve*)
miscelánea miscellany, assortment
misión *f.* mission
mismo/a self; same; **ahora mismo** right now (11)
misterio mystery
misterioso/a mysterious
mitad *f.* half
mítico/a mythic
mochila backpack (1)
moda fashion; **está de moda** it's in style (5)
modales *m. pl.* manners
modelo model
moderación *f.* moderation
modernidad *f.* modernity
moderno/a modern

modesto/a modest
módico/a moderate, reasonable
modismo idiom
modo manner, way; mood (*gram.*)
mojado/a wet
mole *m. Mexican dish prepared with meat, chili sauce, and chocolate*
molestar to bother; **me/te/le molesta** it bothers me/you/him (12); **molestarse** to get upset
molestia *n.* bother
momentáneo/a momentary, temporary
momentito just a minute, second
momento moment; **en este momento** right now, at this very moment (5)
monarca *m.* monarch, king
monarquía monarchy
monárquico/a monarchical
moneda coin, currency (20); money
mono monkey
mono/a cute, pretty
monopatín *m.* skateboard (12)
monótono/a monotonous
monstruoso/a monstrous
montaña mountain (11); **bicicleta de montaña** mountain bike (12)
montar to ride; **montar a caballo** to ride horseback
monte *m.* mountain
montón *m.* heap, pile
monumento monument
morado/a purple (5)
morcilla blood sausage
morder (ue) to bite
moreno/a *n.; adj.* brunette (3)
morir(se) (ue, u) (*p.p.* **muerto/a**) to die (13)
moro/a *n.* Moor; *adj.* Moorish
mosca fly
mostrar (ue) to show, exhibit
motel *m.* motel
motivo motive, reason
moto(cicleta) motorcycle (12)
motor *m.* motor
mover (ue) to move
móvil *adj.* mobile
movimiento movement
mozo bellhop (21)
muchacho/a young man/woman; boy/girl
mucho *adv.* much, a lot (5)
mucho/a *adj.* a lot of; *pl.* many (5); **muchas gracias** thank you very much, many thanks (P); **mucho gusto** pleased to meet you (P)
mudarse to move (*from one residence to another*)
mudo/a mute, silent
muebles *m. pl.* furniture (8); **sacudir los muebles** to dust the furniture (12)
muela molar; **sacar (qu) una muela** to extract a molar (*tooth*) (15)
muerte *f.* death; **pena de muerte** death sentence
muerto/a *n.* dead person; *p.p.* dead; died; killed; **Día** (*m.*) **de los Muertos** All Soul's Day (November 2) (13)
muestra sample; demonstration

mujer *f.* woman (1); wife (4); **mujer de negocios** businesswoman; **mujer policía** female police officer; **mujer soldado** female soldier (23)
multa fine, penalty; **poner** (*irreg.*) **una multa** to give a fine/ticket
multitud *f.* multitude
mundial *adj.* world
mundo world (5)
mural *m.* mural
murciélago bat
museo museum (16)
música music
músico/a musician
muy very (P); **muy bien** very well (P)

N

nacer (zc) to be born
nacimiento birth
nación *f.* nation
nacional national; domestic
nacionalidad *f.* nationality (21)
nada nothing, not anything (9); **de nada** you're welcome (P)
nadar to swim (11)
nadie no one, nobody, not anybody (9)
naranja *n.* orange (*fruit*) (9)
nariz *f.* nose (15)
narración *f.* narration, account
narrador(a) narrator
narrar to narrate
nata cream
natación *n. f.* swimming
natal *adj.* native, of birth
nativo/a *adj.* native
natural natural; **ciencias** (*pl.*) **naturales** natural sciences (2); **recursos** (*pl.*) **naturales** natural resources (18)
naturaleza nature (18)
navegar (gu) en barco to travel by boat (11)
Navidad *f.* Christmas (13); **árbol** (*m.*) **de Navidad** Christmas tree
navideño/a *adj.* Christmas
necesario/a necessary
necesidad *f.* necessity; need
necesitar to need (2)
necio/a foolish; stubborn
nefrología nephrology (*study of the kidney*)
negar (ie) (gu) to deny (17)
negativo/a negative (9)
negligencia negligence
negligente negligent
negociante *m., f.* dealer, merchant
negocio(s) business; **hombre** (*m.*)/**mujer** (*f.*) **de negocios** businessman/ businesswoman
negro/a black (5)
neoyorquino/a *of or pertaining to New York*
nervioso/a nervous (4)
nevado/a snow-covered
nevar (ie) to snow (7)
ni neither; nor; **ni siquiera** not even

nicaragüense *n. m., f.; adj.* Nicaraguan
niebla fog
nieto/a grandson/granddaughter (4); *pl.* grandchildren
nieve *f.* snow
ningún, ninguno/a no, none, not any (9)
niñero/a baby-sitter
niñez *f.* childhood (14)
niño/a boy, girl (3); *pl.* children; **de niño/a** as a child
nivel *m.* level
no no (P); not; **¿no?** right?, don't they (you, *etc.*)? (5)
nociones *f. pl.* rudimentary knowledge
nocturno/a *adj.* night, nocturnal
noche *f.* night (1); **buenas noches** good night (P); **de la noche** in the evening, at night (P); **esta noche** tonight; **Noche Vieja** New Year's Eve (13); **por la noche** in the evening, at night (2); **todas las noches** every evening, night
Nochebuena Christmas Eve (13)
nombrado/a named
nombre *m.* (first) name (3)
nordeste *m.* northeast
noreste *m.* northeast
norma norm; rule
normalidad *f.* normality
norte *m.* north; **al norte de** to the north of (7)
Norteamérica North America
norteamericano/a *n.; adj.* North American; from the United States (3); **fútbol** (*m.*) **norteamericano** football
norteño/a northern
nos *d.o.* us; *i.o.* to/for us; *refl. pron.* ourselves
nosotros/as *sub. pron.* we; *obj.* (*of prep.*) us
nota grade (*in a class*); note
notar to note, notice
noticia piece of news; *pl.* news (22)
noticiero newscast (22)
novecientos/as nine hundred (6)
novedad *f.* new thing; *pl.* news
novela novel (4)
novelista *m., f.* novelist
noveno/a *adj.* ninth (17)
noventa ninety (3)
noviazgo engagement
noviembre *m.* November (7)
novio/a boyfriend/girlfriend (8); fiancé(e); groom/bride
nube *f.* cloud
nublado/a cloudy, overcast; **está nublado** it's cloudy, overcast (7)
núcleo nucleus
nuera daughter-in-law
nuestro/a *poss.* our; (of) ours
nueve nine (P)
nuevo/a new (3); **Día** (*m.*) **de Año Nuevo** New Year's Day (13)
numérico/a numerical
número number (P); size; **número de teléfono** telephone number
numeroso/a numerous
nunca never (4); **casi nunca** almost never (4)

O

o or (P)
obedecer (zc) to obey (22)
obelisco obelisk
objetivo *n.* objective
objeto object
obligación *f.* obligation
obligar (gu) to oblige, compel
obligatorio/a obligatory
obra work (*of art, literature, etc.*); **obra de teatro** play; **obra maestra** masterpiece
obrar to work
obrero/a worker, laborer (22)
observar to observe, watch
obsesión *f.* obsession
obstáculo obstacle; limitation
obtener (*like* tener) to get, obtain
obvio/a obvious
ocasión *f.* occasion
ocasionar to cause
occidental occidental, western
océano ocean (11); **Océano Atlántico** Atlantic Ocean; **Océano Pacífico** Pacific Ocean
octavo/a *adj.* eighth (17)
octubre *m.* October
ocupación *f.* occupation
ocupado/a busy (4)
ocupar to occupy; **ocuparse (de)** to be in charge (of); to attend (to)
ocurrir to happen, occur
ochenta eighty (3)
ocho eight (P)
ochocientos/as eight hundred (6)
odiar to hate
odontología odontology (*study of the teeth*)
oeste *m.* west; **al oeste de** to the west of (7)
ofender to offend, insult
oferta offer
oficial *n. m.* official, officer; *adj.* official
oficina office (1); **oficina de empleos** employment office
oficio trade, job (23)
ofrecer (zc) to offer (10)
oftalmología opthalmology (*study of the eye*)
oído inner ear (15)
oír *irreg.* to hear (10)
ojalá (que) I hope, wish (that) (12)
ojo eye (15); **¡ojo!** watch out!; **ojo alerta** be alert, watch out
ola wave (*ocean*)
olímpico/a: Juegos Olímpicos Olympic Games
oliva olive
olvidar to forget (11); **olvidarse (de)** to forget (about) (13)
olla pot
once eleven (P)
onda wave, craze (*fashion, etc.*); **en onda** in style
opaco/a opaque
opción *f.* option
opcional optional
operar to operate
operario/a operator

opinar to think, have an opinion
oponerse (*like* poner) (a) to oppose, be opposed (to)
oportunidad *f.* opportunity, chance
oportuno/a opportune; suitable
optimismo optimism
optimista *n. m., f.* optimist; *adj.* optimistic
óptimo/a excellent
opulento/a opulent
oración *f. gram.* sentence
orden *m.* order (*sequence*); *f.* order, command
ordenado/a neat, orderly (4)
ordenador *m.* computer (*Sp.*) (12)
ordenar to arrange; to order
ordinal ordinal (17)
ordinario/a ordinary
oreja ear (15)
organización *f.* organization
organizar (c) to organize
órgano organ
orgullo pride
oriental eastern
Oriente (*m.*) Medio Middle East
origen *m.* origin
originalidad *f.* originality
originar to create
orilla shore, bank
orina urine
oriundo/a native, originating
oro gold; **Ricitos de Oro** Goldilocks
orquesta orchestra
orquídea orchid
os *d.o.* you (*fam. pl. Sp.*); *i.o.* to/for you (*fam. pl. Sp.*); *refl. pron.* yourselves (*fam. pl. Sp.*)
oscilar to oscillate; to fluctuate
oscuridad *f.* darkness
oscuro/a dark
óseo/a *adj.* bone
oso bear
ostentoso/a ostentatious
ostra oyster
otoño autumn, fall (*season*) (7)
otorgar (gu) to award
otro/a other, another (3); **otra vez** again (10); **por otro lado** on the other hand
oveja sheep, ewe
oxígeno oxygen
oye hey, listen (*to get someone's attention*) (*fam.*)
ozono: capa del ozono ozone layer (18)

P

paciencia patience
paciente *n. m., f.* patient (15); *adj.* patient
pacífico/a peaceful; **Océano Pacífico** Pacific Ocean
padecer (zc) to suffer, feel deeply
padrastro stepfather
padre *m.* father (4); *pl.* parents
paella paella (*Spanish dish of rice, shellfish, and chicken, flavored with saffron*)
pagar (gu) to pay (for) (2); **pagar a plazos**

to pay in installments; **pagar al contado** to pay cash
página page
pago payment
país *m.* country, nation
paisaje *m.* landscape
pájaro bird (4)
palabra word (P)
palacio palace
paladar *m.* palate, taste
palma palm tree
palmera palm tree
palo stick
pampa pampa, grassland
pan *m.* bread (9); **pan de polvo** *Mexican Christmas dessert;* **pan tostado** toast (9)
panameño/a *n.; adj.* Panamanian
pancaribeño/a Pan-Caribbean
panceta bacon
páncreas *m.* pancreas
pandilla group of friends
panqueque *m.* pancake
pantalón *m. s.* pants; *pl.* pants (5); **pantalones cortos** shorts
pantalla screen
papa potato (9); **papa al horno** baked potato (9); **papa frita** (*L.A.*) French fried potato (9)
papá *m.* dad (4)
papel *m.* (piece of) paper (1); role; **papel para cartas** stationery (21)
papelería stationery store (21)
paquete *m.* package (21); pack, packet
paquistaní *adj. m., f.* Pakistani
par *m.* pair (5); *adj.* even (*numbers*)
para *prep.* (intended) for (3); in order to (5); **para** + *time* for/by (*future time*) (11); **para colmo** to top it all off; **para la cual** for which; **para que** so that (21)
parabrisas *m. s.* windshield (17)
paracaidismo parachute jumping
parada del autobús bus stop (21)
paraguas *m. s.* umbrella
paraguayo/a Paraguayan
paraíso paradise
paraje *m.* place, spot
paralizado/a paralyzed
parar to stop (17)
parcial partial; **trabajo de tiempo parcial** part-time job (12)
pardo/a brown (5)
parecer (zc) to seem, appear; **parecerse (a)** to look like, resemble
pared *f.* wall (8); **pintar las paredes** to paint the walls (12)
pareja married couple; pair; partner
paréntesis *m. inv.* parenthesis; **entre paréntesis** in parentheses
pariente *m.* relative (4)
parlamentario/a parliamentary
parque *m.* park
párrafo paragraph
parrilla grill
parroquia parish
parroquiano/a parishioner

parte *f.* part; place; **de parte de** on behalf of; **por todas partes** everywhere
participante *m., f.* participant
participar to participate
participio *gram.* participle
particular particular; private
partida: punto de partida point of departure
partido game (*in sports*), match (16); (political) party
partir: a partir de starting from
parvulario nursery school
pasado *n.* past
pasado/a *adj.* past, former (*with time*); **el año pasado** last year; **pasado mañana** day after tomorrow (2)
pasaje *m.* passage, ticket (11)
pasajero/a *n.* passenger (11); *adj.* passing; fleeting
pasaporte *m.* passport
pasar to spend (*time*); to pass (*someone, something*); to happen; **pasar la aspiradora** to vacuum (12); **pasar tiempo (con)** to spend time (with) (19); **pasarlo bien/mal** to have a good/bad time (11)
pasatiempo hobby, pastime, diversion (16)
Pascua Passover; **Pascua Florida** Easter
pasear to take a walk, stroll; **pasear en bicicleta** to ride a bicycle (16)
paseo stroll, promenade; avenue; **dar** (*irreg.*) **un paseo** to stroll, take a walk (16)
pasillo aisle (11); hall, corridor
pasión *f.* passion
pasivo/a passive
pasmado/a astounded, stunned
paso step; pace; **ceda el paso** yield
pasta pasta; paste; **pasta dental** toothpaste
pastel *m.* cake (9); pie (9)
pastelería pastry shop (21)
pastilla pill (15)
pastor(a) pastor, shepherd
pata paw; **meter la pata** to put one's foot in one's mouth
patata potato (*Sp.*); **patata frita** (*Sp.*) French fried potato
paterno/a paternal
patinar to skate
patio patio; yard (8)
patria homeland, native land
patriótico/a patriotic
patrocinador(a) sponsor
patrón, patrona patron; *m.* pattern, model
patronímico patronymic (*name derived from a paternal ancestor*)
paulatinamente little by little
pauta guideline
pavimentado/a paved
pavo turkey (9)
paz *f.* (*pl.* **paces**) peace (22)
peatón, peatona pedestrian (17); **cruce** (*m.*)**/paso para peatones** pedestrian walkway
pecado sin
pecho chest
pedal *m.* pedal
pediatría *s.* pediatrics

pedido *n.* request
pedir (**i, i**) to ask for, order (6)
pegar (**gu**) to hit, strike (14)
pelar to peel
pelear to fight (22)
película movie
peligro danger
peligroso/a dangerous (13)
pelo hair; **tomarle el pelo a alguien** to pull someone's leg
pelota vasca jai alai (*a type of handball*)
pelotón (*m.*) **de fusilamiento** firing squad
peluquero/a hairdresser (23)
pena trouble; punishment; **pena de muerte** death sentence; (**no**) **valer la pena** to (not) be worth the effort
pendiente *m.* earring
penicilina penicillin
península peninsula
pensar (**ie**) to think (6); **pensar** + *inf.* to intend, plan to (*do something*) (6); **pensar de** to think of, have an opinion about; **pensar en** to think about
pensión *f.* boardinghouse (21); pension; **media pensión** room with breakfast meal (21); **pensión completa** room and full board (21)
peor worse (8); worst
pequeño/a small (3)
perder (**ie**) to lose (6); to miss (*a bus, plane, social function, etc.*); **perderse** to get lost
pérdida loss
perdón pardon me, excuse me (P)
perdonar to pardon, forgive
perdone pardon me
perdurar to last
peregrinar to wander, journey
pereza laziness
perezoso/a lazy (3)
perfecto/a perfect, fine
perfil *m.* profile
perfume *m.* perfume
periódico *n.* newspaper (4)
periódico/a *adj.* periodic(al)
periodista *m., f.* journalist
período period
perla pearl
permanecer (**zc**) to stay, remain
permiso permission; permit; **con permiso** pardon me, excuse me (P)
permitir to permit, allow (11)
pero *conj.* but (4)
perro/a dog (3)
perseguir (*like* **seguir**) to pursue, chase
persiana Venetian blind
persona person (1)
personaje *m.* character (*of a story, play*)
personal *n. m.* personnel; *adj.* personal; **Dirección** (*f.*) **de Personal** personnel office (23)
personalidad *f.* personality
personalizar (**c**) to personalize
perspectiva perspective
pertenecer (**zc**) to belong
pesadilla nightmare
pesado/a boring, a drag (13); heavy
pesar to weigh; **a pesar de** in spite of

pesca *n.* fishing
pescado fish (*cooked*) (9)
peseta *monetary unit of Spain*
pesimista *n. m., f.* pessimist; *adj.* pessimistic
peso weight; *monetary unit of Mexico and several other Latin American countries*
petróleo petroleum, oil
petrolero/a *adj.* petroleum
pez *m.* (*pl.* **peces**) fish (*live*) (4); **pez espada** swordfish
picante hot, spicy
picar (**qu**) to itch; to nibble
picnic *m.* picnic; **hacer** (*irreg.*) **un picnic** to have a picnic
pico (mountain) peak
pie *m.* foot (14); **a pie** on foot; **levantarse con el pie izquierdo** to get up on the wrong side of the bed (14)
piedra rock, stone
piel *f.* skin; *pl.* furs; **abrigo de pieles** fur coat
pierna leg (14)
pieza piece
pigmeo/a pygmy
píldora pill
piloto/a pilot (11)
pincho *broiled snack served on a skewer*
pingüino penguin
pinta look, appearance
pintar to paint; **pintar las paredes** to paint the walls (12)
pintor(a) painter
pintura painting (12)
piña pineapple
pionero/a pioneer
pirámide *f.* pyramid
pirata *m.* pirate
pirómano/a pyromaniac
pisar to step on
piscina (swimming) pool (8)
piso floor
pista track, trail
pisto *col.* money, cash
pistola pistol, gun
pizarra chalkboard (1)
placer *m.* pleasure
plan *m.* plan; **hacer** (*irreg.*) **planes para** + *inf.* to make plans to (*do something*) (16)
planchar (**la ropa**) to iron (clothing) (12)
planeación *f.* planning
planear to plan
planeta *m.* planet
plano plane; **primer plano** foreground
planta plant; floor (*of a building*); **planta baja** ground floor
plantear to pose (*a question*)
plástico plastic
plata silver (*metal*); *col.* money, cash
plátano banana
platicar (**qu**) to chat, discuss
plato plate, dish (8); dish (*to eat*) (9); **lavar los platos** to wash the dishes (12); **plato fuerte** main dish; **plato principal** main course
playa beach (7)
plaza square; place, space; **plaza de toros** bullring

plazos *pl.*: **a plazos** in installments (20)
plegar **(ie) (gu)** to fold
pleno/a full
plomero/a plumber (23)
población *f.* population (18)
poblado/a populated
poblador(a) founder
poblano/a: **mole** (*m.*) **poblano** *Mexican dish prepared with meat, chili sauce, and chocolate*
pobre poor (3)
pobreza poverty
poco *adv.* not much, little (5); **poco a poco** little by little
poco/a *adj.* little, few (5)
poder *n. m.* power
poder *v. irreg.* to be able, can (5); **¿podría(s)... ?** could you . . . ? (21)
poderoso/a powerful
poema *m.* poem
poeta *m., f.* poet
poético/a poetic
policía *m.* police officer; *f.* police force; **mujer** (*f.*) **policía** female police officer
policíaco/a *of or pertaining to the police*
policial *of or pertaining to the police*
poliomielitis *f.* poliomyelitis
politeísta *adj.* polytheistic
política *s.* politics
político/a *n.* politician; *adj.* political; in-law; **ciencias políticas** *pl.* political science (2)
polvo dust; **pan** (*m.*) **de polvo** *Mexican Christmas dessert*
pollo chicken (9)
pomelo grapefruit
poner *irreg.* to put, place (7); to turn on (*a light or appliance*); **poner la mesa** to set the table (12); **poner término a** to put an end to; **poner una multa** to give a fine/ ticket; **poner(le) una inyección** to give (someone) a shot (15); **ponerse** to put on (*clothing*) (7); to become (13); **ponerse colorado/a** to blush; **ponerse de acuerdo** to reach an agreement
popularidad *f.* popularity
por *prep.* in exchange for (6); because of; around; for; per (12); in, during (2); by (18); along, through; on account of; for the sake of; **por casualidad** by chance; **por ciento** percent; **por completo** completely; **por costumbre** out of habit; **por Dios** for heaven's sake (22); **por ejemplo** for example (22); **por eso** that's why (3); **por excelencia** par excellence, superlative; **por experiencia** personally; **por favor** please (P); **por fin** finally, at last (8); **por hora** per hour; **por igual** equally; **por la mañana/tarde/noche** in the morning/ afternoon/evening (2); **por lo cual** for which reason, because of which; **por lo general** in general (3); **por otro lado** on the other hand; **por si acaso** just in case (22); **por supuesto** of course (22); **por teléfono** by telephone (2); **por todas partes** everywhere; **por última vez** for the last time

porcelana porcelain
porcentaje *m.* percentage
porque because (3)
¿por qué? why? (4)
portada facade
portarse to behave; **portarse bien/mal** to behave well/badly (13)
portátil *adj.* portable; **radio portátil** portable radio (12)
portavoz (*pl.* **portavoces**) *m., f.* spokesperson
portero/a building manager, doorman (19)
portugués *m.* Portuguese (*language*)
posada lodging
pose *f.* pose, affectation
poseer **(y)** to possess
posesión *f.* possession
posesivo/a possessive (4)
posguerra postwar period
posibilidad *f.* possibility
posible possible
posición *f.* position
positivo/a positive
postal postal; **tarjeta postal** postcard
posterior: **asiento posterior** back seat
posteriormente afterwards, subsequently
postre *m.* dessert
postura position
potasio potassium
pozo *n.* well
práctica practice
practicante *m., f.* internist
practicar **(qu)** to practice (2); **practicar deportes** to play sports (15)
práctico/a practical (3)
precaución *f.* precaution
precio price (6); **precio fijo** fixed (set) price (6)
precioso/a precious; lovely
precipitación *f.* precipitation
precipitar to precipitate
precisión *f.* precision
precolombino/a pre-Columbian, before Columbus
precoz (*pl.* **precoces**) precocious
predecir (*like* **decir**) to predict
predicción *f.* prediction
predominante predominant
preferencia preference (P)
preferible preferable
preferido/a favorite
preferir **(ie, i)** to prefer (5)
pregunta question; **hacer** (*irreg.*) **una pregunta** to ask a question (7)
preguntar to ask (*a question*) (10)
prehistórico/a prehistoric
premio prize
prenda article of clothing
prender to switch on (*a light or appliance*)
prensa press, print medium (22)
preocupación *f.* preoccupation, worry, care, concern
preocupado/a worried (4)
preocuparse **(por)** to worry (about)
preparación *f.* preparation
preparar to prepare

preparativo preparation
preparatorio preparatory school
preposición *f., gram.* preposition (7)
presencia presence
presentación *f.* presentation
presentador(a) presenter
presentar to introduce; to present
presente *n. m.* present (*time*); *gram.* present (*tense*); *adj.* present, current
preservar to preserve, keep
preservativo condom
presidencial presidential
presidente/a president
presidir to preside over
presión *f.* pressure (14); **sufrir muchas presiones** to be under a lot of pressure
prestación *f.* service
préstamo loan (20)
prestar to lend (10); **prestar atención** to pay attention
prestigio prestige
prestigioso/a prestigious
presupuesto budget (20)
pretender to try, endeavor
pretérito *gram.* preterite
prevenir (*like* **venir**) to prevent
preventivo/a preventive; warning
previo/a previous
primario/a primary; **escuela primaria** elementary school
primavera spring (7); **vacaciones** (*f. pl.*) **de primavera** spring break
primer, primero/a *adj.* first (8); **el primero de...** the first of (*month*); **por primera vez** for the first time; **primer plano** foreground; **primera clase** first class (11)
primero *adv.* first (6)
primo/a cousin (4)
princesa princess
principal main; **plato principal** main course
príncipe *m.* prince
principiante *m., f.* beginner
principio beginning; **al principio (de)** at the beginning (of)
prioridad *f.* priority
prisa haste, hurry; **tener** (*irreg.*) **prisa** to be in a hurry
privado/a private
probador *m.* fitting room
probar **(ue)** to taste, try
problema *m.* problem (1)
problemólogo problem finder
procedimiento procedure
proceso process
procurar to try
producción *f.* production
producir *irreg.* to produce
producto product; **producto interno bruto** gross national product
profesión *f.* profession (23)
profesional *n. m., f.; adj.* professional
profesionalizar **(c)** to make professional
profesor(a) professor (1)
profesorado faculty
profundizar **(c)** to deepen
profundo/a profound; deep

programa *m.* program
programación *f.* programming
programador(a) programmer
progresar to progress
progresión *f.* progression
progresivo *gram.* progressive (*tense*)
progreso progress
prohibido/a prohibited, forbidden; **prohibido estacionarse** no parking
prohibir (prohíbo) to prohibit, forbid (11)
prolongar (gu) to prolong, extend
promedio average
prometer to promise (10)
pronombre *m. gram.* pronoun; **pronombre reflexivo** reflexive pronoun
pronto soon; **hasta pronto** see you soon; **tan pronto como** as soon as (20)
pronunciación *f.* pronunciation
pronunciar to pronounce
propaganda advertising
propenso/a inclined, prone
propietario/a owner
propina tip
propio/a *adj.* own, one's own
proponer (*like* **poner**) to propose
proporcionar to furnish, provide
propósito aim, object, purpose; **a propósito** by the way
prosperar to prosper
próspero/a prosperous
próstata prostate
protagonista *m., f.* protagonist; hero, heroine
protagonizar (c) to play the main role
protección *f.* protection
proteger (j) to protect (18)
proteína protein
protestar to protest
provecho: buen provecho enjoy your meal
provincia province
provisión *f.* provision
provocar (qu) to provoke; to cause
proximidad *f.* proximity
próximo/a next
proyecto project
prudente prudent
prueba quiz (8)
pubertad *f.* puberty
publicar (qu) to publish
publicidad *f.* advertising
publicitario/a *adj.* advertising; **anuncio publicitario** ad(vertisement)
público/a *adj.* public; **servicios** (*pl.*) **públicos** public services (18); **transporte** (*m.*) **público** public transportation (18)
pueblo town
puente *m.* bridge
puerco pork
puerro leek, scallion
puerta door (1); **puerta de embarque** departure gate (11)
puerto port
puertorriqueño/a *n.; adj.* Puerto Rican
pues well
puesto place (in line) (11); job, position (23); **guardar un puesto** to save a place (11)

pulgada inch
pulido/a polished
pulmón *m.* lung (15)
púlpito pulpit
pulpo octopus
punta: hora punta rush hour
punto point; **en punto** exactly, on the dot (*time*) (P); **punto de partida** point of departure; **punto de vista** point of view
puntual punctual
pureza purity
puro/a pure (18)
purpúreo/a purple
putrefacto/a rotten, putrid

Q

que that (P); which (P); who; **así que** therefore, consequently; **lo que** what, that which (11); **que** + *subj.* I hope + *verb form*
qué what, which; **¿qué?** what?; which? (P); **¿a qué hora?** (at) what time? (P); **¡qué** + *noun!* what a . . . !; **¡qué demonios... ?** what the heck . . . ?; **¡qué desgracia!** what a shame!; **¡qué hora es?** what time is it? (P); **¡qué lástima!** what a shame! (12); **¡qué lata!** what a bore!; **¡qué mala suerte!** what bad luck! (14); **¿qué tal?** how are you (doing)? (P)
quedar to remain, be left; **quedarse** to stay, remain (7)
quehacer *m.* task, chore; **quehacer doméstico** (household) chore (12)
quejarse (de) to complain (about) (13)
quemar to burn
querer *irreg.* to want (5); to love (*with people*) (19); **¿dónde quiere vivir?** where do you (*form. s.*) want to live? (19); **eso quiere decir (que)** that means (that); **fue sin querer** it was unintentional (14)
querido/a dear, beloved
quesadilla *cornmeal pie filled with cheese*
queso cheese (9)
quetzal *m. monetary unit of Guatemala*
quicio doorframe
quien who
¿quién? who? whom? (1); **¿de quién?** whose?
química chemistry
quince fifteen (P)
quinceañera *young woman's fifteenth birthday party*
quinientos/as five hundred (6)
quinto/a *adj.* fifth (17)
quiosco kiosk (*small outdoor stand where a variety of items are sold*) (21)
quitar to remove, take away; **quitarse** to take off (*clothing*); to take out, withhold
quizá(s) perhaps

R

rábano radish
rabino/a rabbi
rabioso/a furious, angry

racional rational
racismo racism
radical *n. m. gram.* stem, radical; *adj.* radical
radio *m.* radio (set); *f.* radio (*medium*); **radio portátil** portable radio (12)
radiografía X-ray
rail *m.* rail, track
raíz *f.* (*pl.* **raíces**) root; *gram.* stem, radical
rama branch
rana frog
rancio/a rancid; old
ranchera *type of Mexican music*
ranchero/a rancher
rancho ranch (18)
rápido/a fast, quick (9)
ráquetbol *m.* racquetball
raro/a strange; rare
rascacielos *m. s.* skyscraper (18)
rasgo characteristic
rata rat
rato a while (8); **ratos** (*pl.*) **libres** leisure time (16)
ratón *m.* mouse (12)
rayas: de rayas striped (5)
rayos (*pl.*) **equis** X-rays
raza race (*of people*); **Día** (*m.*) **de la Raza** Columbus Day, Hispanic Awareness Day (13)
razón *f.* reason; **(no) tener** (*irreg.*) **razón** to be right (wrong) (5)
razonable reasonable
reacción *f.* reaction
reaccionar to react
reactor *m.* reactor
reafirmar reaffirm
real real; royal; **Real Academia de la Lengua** Spanish Royal Academy (of the Language)
realidad *f.* reality
realismo realism
realista *n. m., f.* realist; *adj.* realistic
realización *f.* realization
realizar (c) to bring about, realize; to fulfill
rebajas *pl.* sales, reductions (6)
rebelde *n. m., f.* rebel; *adj.* rebellious
rebozo shawl, cloak
recado message
recámara bedroom (*Mex.*)
recepción *f.* front desk (21); reception
recepcionista *m., f.* receptionist
receta prescription (15)
recetar to prescribe
recibir to receive (4)
recibo receipt
reciclar to recycle
recién recently
reciente recent
recinto area
recíproco/a reciprocal
recital *m.* recital
reclamar to demand
reclutamiento recruitment
recobrarse to recover, recuperate
recoger (j) to pick up (*from a place*)
recomendación *f.* recommendation
recomendar (ie) to recommend (10)
reconocer (zc) to recognize

reconstrucción f. reconstruction
reconstruir (y) to reconstruct
récord m. record (sports)
recordar (ue) to remember (13); to bring to mind
recorte m. clipping
recreación f. recreation
recto/a straight
rector(a) (university) president
recuerdo memory; recollection; souvenir
recuperación f. recovery
recuperar to recover, recuperate
recurso resource; recursos (pl.) naturales natural resources (18)
red f. network
redecorado/a redecorated
reducción f. reduction
reducido/a small
reducir (like producir) to reduce, cut down
referéndum m. referendum
referirse (ie, i) (a) to refer (to)
refinado/a refined
reflejar to reflect
reflexivo/a gram. reflexive; pronombre (m.) reflexivo reflexive pronoun
reforma n. reform
refrán m. proverb
refresco soft drink (7)
refrigerador m. refrigerator (12)
refugiado/a refugee
refugio refuge
regalar to give (a gift) (10)
regalo gift (3)
regañar to scold
regatear to haggle, bargain
régimen m. regime
región f. region
registrar to search, examine (21)
registro register; record
regla rule
reglamentario/a prescribed by regulation
reglamento s. regulations
regresar to return (to a place) (2); regresar a casa to go home (2)
regreso: de regreso adj. return
regular v. to regulate
regular adj. okay, so-so (P)
regularidad f.: con regularidad regularly
rehén m. hostage
reina queen (22)
reino kingdom; Reino Unido United Kingdom
reírse (i, i) (de) to laugh (at, about) (13)
reivindicar (qu) to recover
relación f. relation; relationship (19)
relacionar to relate, connect, associate
relajar to relax
relativo/a adj. relative
relato story
religión f. religion
religiosidad f. religiosity
religioso/a religious
reloj m. watch (5); clock
reluciente shining
remarcable remarkable
remedio: no tener (irreg.) otro remedio to

be unavoidable
remodelado/a remodeled
remontarse to go back to (a date in the past)
remoto/a remote; control (m.) remoto remote control (12)
remunerar to pay
renacer (zc) to be reborn
renacimiento rebirth; renaissance
renegar (ie) (gu) to renounce one's faith
renglón m. line; item
renovación f. renovation
renovar (ue) to renovate; to renew
renta income
renunciar (a) to resign (from) (23)
reparación f. repair
reparar to repair
repasar to review
repaso n. review
repente: de repente suddenly
repetición f. repetition
repetir (i, i) to repeat
reportaje m. article, report
reportero/a reporter (22)
reposo rest
representación f. representation
representante n. m., f. representative
representar to represent
representativo/a adj. representative
reproducción f. reproduction
reptil m. reptile
república republic; República Dominicana Dominican Republic
republicano/a adj. republican
repuesto n. spare
repugnante repugnant; disgusting
requerir (ie, i) to require
requisito requirement
resbaladizo/a slippery
reseco/a dry
reserva reservation (21)
reservación f. reservation
reservado/a reserved
reservar to reserve
resfriado cold (illness) (15)
resfriarse (me resfrío) to get/catch a cold (15)
residencia dormitory (1); residence
residir to reside
resistencia resistance
resistir to endure, bear
resolver (ue) (p.p. resuelto/a) to solve, resolve
respectivo/a respective
respecto: con respecto a with respect to
respetar to respect
respeto respect
respetuoso/a respectful
respiración f. breathing
respirar to breathe (15)
responder to answer, respond
responsabilidad f. responsibility (22)
respuesta answer
restante adj. remaining
restaurado/a restored
restaurante m. restaurant (10)
resto rest, remainder

restringir (j) to restrict, limit
resucitar to bring/come back to life
resultado n. result
resultar to result, turn out
resumen m. summary
resumir to summarize
retorno return
retraso delay
retratar to portray, describe
reunión f. reunion; meeting
reunir (reúno) to unite; to reunite; reunirse (con) to get together (with)
revelar to reveal
reverente reverent
revisar to check, examine, inspect (17)
revisión f. revision, examination
revisor(a) conductor
revista magazine (8)
revitalización f. revitalization
revolución f. revolution
revolucionar to revolutionize
revuelta n. revolt, revolution
revuelto/a p.p. scrambled (eggs)
rey m. king (22); Día (m.) de los Reyes Magos Day of the Magi, Epiphany (13)
Ricitos de Oro Goldilocks
rico/a rich (3); tasty (food) (13)
ridículo/a ridiculous
riesgo risk
rígido/a rigid
riguroso/a rigorous
rimar to rhyme
rinoceronte m. rhinocerous
riñón m. kidney
río river
riqueza wealth; abundance
risa laughter
ritmo rhythm, pace; cambio de ritmo change of pace; ritmo acelerado de la vida fast pace of life (18)
robar to steal
robo robbery
robot m. robot
rodear to surround
rodilla knee
rojo/a red (5); Caperucita Roja Little Red Riding Hood
rollo col. bore
romano/a Roman
romántico/a romantic
romper (p.p. roto/a) to break (14)
ropa clothing (5); planchar la ropa to iron clothing (12)
rosa n. rose; de color rosa pink
rosado/a pink (5)
roto/a p.p. broken
rozar (c) to scrape, graze
rubio n. cigarette made of light tobacco
rubio/a blond(e) (3)
rueda wheel
ruido noise (10)
ruidoso/a noisy
ruina ruin
rumbo direction
ruso m. Russian (language) (2)

ruso/a *n.; adj.* Russian
rutina routine, habit (7)
rutinario/a *adj.* routine

S

sábado Saturday (2)
saber *irreg.* to know (*information*) (9); **saber + inf.** to know how to (*do something*)
sabiduría wisdom; knowledge
sabor *m.* taste; flavor
sacar (qu) to take out, remove, extract; to get, receive (*grades*); to take out (*money*); **sacar fotos** to take photos (12); **sacar la basura** to take out the trash (12); **sacar la lengua** to stick out one's tongue (15); **sacar una muela** to extract a molar (tooth) (15)
sacerdote *m.* priest
saco de dormir sleeping bag
sacrificio sacrifice
sacudir (los muebles) to dust (the furniture) (12)
sagrado/a sacred, holy
sajón, sajona Saxon
sal *f.* salt
sala room; living room (8); **sala de clase** classroom; **sala de emergencias/urgencia** emergency room; **sala de espera** waiting area (11); **sala de estar** living room
salado/a *adj.* salt; **agua** (*f. but* **el agua**) **salada** salt water
salario salary, wages
salchicha sausage
salida departure (11)
saliente salient; prominent
salir *irreg.* to leave (*a place*), go out (7); **salir a derechas** to turn out right; **salir (con)** to go out (with), date (*someone*) (7); **salir para** to leave for (*a place*) (7)
salmón *m.* salmon (9)
salón *m.* room, reception room
salsa sauce; salsa music
salsero/a member of a salsa band
saltar to jump
saltimbanco acrobat
salud *f.* health (15)
saludarse to greet each other (19)
saludo greeting (P)
salvadoreño/a *n., adj.* Salvadoran
salvar to save
san saint (*contraction of* **santo** *used before most masculine names*)
sandalia sandal (5)
sándwich *m.* sandwich (9)
sangre *f.* blood
sanitario/a sanitary
sano/a healthy; wholesome; **llevar una vida sana** to lead a healthy life (15)
santo/a *n. m., f.* saint; *adj.* holy, blessed; **Día** (*m.*) **del Santo** Saint's Day (*of the saint for whom one is named*)
Satanás *m. s.* Satan
satélite *m.* satellite
satisfacción *f.* satisfaction

satisfacer (*like* **hacer**) to satisfy
Saudita: Arabia Saudita Saudi Arabia
saxofón *m.* saxophone
se (*impersonal*) one; *refl. pron.* yourself (*form. s.*), himself, herself, yourselves (*form. pl.*), themselves
sea: o sea in other words
secadora clothes dryer (12)
sección *f.* section; **sección de (no) fumar** (non)smoking section (11)
seco/a dry
secretario/a secretary (1)
secreto secret
sector *m.* sector
secuencia sequence, series
secundaria secondary; **(escuela) secundaria** high school
sed *f.* thirst; **tener** (*irreg.*) **sed** to be thirsty (9)
seda silk (5)
sedentario/a sedentary
segregado/a segregated
seguida: en seguida right away, immediately (8)
seguido/a straight; in a row
seguir (i, i) (g) to continue; **seguir (todo derecho)** to keep on going (17)
según according to
segundo *n.* second (*time*)
segundo/a *adj.* second (17); **segunda especialización** minor (*academic*)
seguridad *f.* security; **alarma de seguridad** security alarm; **cinturón** (*m.*) **de seguridad** seatbelt
seguro *n.* insurance; **seguro médico** medical insurance
seguro/a sure, certain; **estar** (*irreg.*) **seguro/a** to be sure, certain; **(no) es seguro** it's (not) certain (17); **seguro que** of course
seis six (P)
seiscientos/as six hundred (6)
seleccionar to choose
selectividad *f.* selection (for university acceptance)
selva jungle
sellado/a stamped
sello stamp (21)
semáforo traffic signal (17)
semana week (2); **...a la semana** ... a week; **(el) fin** (*m.*) **de semana** (on the) weekend (2)
semejante similar
semestre *m.* semester
seminario seminar
senador(a) senator
sencillo/a simple
sendero path
sensación *f.* sensation
sensible sensitive; sentimental
sentar (ie) to seat, lead to a seat; **sentarse** to sit down (7)
sentido *n.* sense; meaning; **sentido común** common sense; **sentido del humor** sense of humor
sentimental sentimental (19)
sentimiento feeling, emotion, sentiment
sentir (ie, i) to regret, feel sorry (12); **lo siento** I'm sorry; **sentirse** to feel (13);

sentirse feliz/triste to feel happy/sad (13)
señal *f.* signal; sign
señalar to point out
señas *pl.* directions; address
señor (Sr.) *m.* Mr., sir; gentleman (P)
señora (Sra.) Mrs.; lady (P)
señores (Sres.) *m. pl.* Mr. and Mrs.; gentlemen
señorita (Srta.) Miss; young lady (P)
separar(se) to separate (19)
separatismo separatism
septiembre *m.* September
séptimo/a *adj.* seventh (17)
sequía drought
ser *irreg.* to be (3); **fue sin querer** it was unintentional (14); **ser aburrido/a** to be boring; **ser aficionado/a a** to be a ... fan (16); **ser alérgico/a (a)** to be allergic (to); **ser en...** to take place at ... (13); **¿sería tan amable de... ?** would you be so kind as to ... ? (21)
ser (*n. m.*) **humano** human being
serenidad *f.* serenity
serie *f.* series
serio/a serious
serpiente *f.* snake
servicio service (17); **estación** (*f.*) **de servicio** service station; **servicios públicos** public services (18)
servidor(a) servant
servilleta napkin (10)
servir (i, i) to serve (6)
sesenta sixty (3)
sesión *f.* session
setecientos/as seven hundred (6)
setenta seventy (3)
severo/a severe; strict
sexo sex
sexto/a *adj.* sixth (17)
si if; **como si + past subj.** as if + *verb form*; **como si nada** as if nothing were wrong; **por si acaso** just in case (22)
sí yes (P); **claro (que sí)** of course
sicología psychology
sicólogo/a psychologist
SIDA *m.* AIDS
siempre always
siesta nap, siesta; **dormir (ue, u) la siesta** to take a nap; **echarse una siesta** to take a nap
siete seven (P)
siglo century
significado *n.* meaning
significar (qu) to mean; to signify
significativo/a significant
signo sign
siguiente following, next
sílaba syllable
silencio silence
silencioso/a silent
silvestre wild; rustic
silla chair (1); **silla mecedora** rocking chair
sillón *m.* armchair
simbólico/a symbolic
simbolizar (c) to symbolize

símbolo symbol
simbología symbolism
simpático/a nice, likable (3)
sin *prep.* without (4); **fue sin querer** it was unintentional (14); **sin baño** without a bathroom (21); **sin duda** without a doubt; **sin embargo** however, nevertheless; **sin escalas** nonstop (*flight*); **sin vacilar** without hesitation
sinagoga synagogue
sincero/a sincere
sinfonía symphony
sinfónico/a symphonic
siniestro/a sinister
sino but (rather)
sinónimo synonym
sintético/a synthetic
síntoma *m.* symptom
siquiatra *m., f.* psychiatrist
siquiera even; **ni siquiera** not even
sísmico/a seismic
sistema *m.* system; **analista** (*m., f.*) **de sistemas** systems analyst
sitio place; room
situación *f.* situation
situado/a located
soborno bribe
sobre *n. m.* envelope (21); *prep.* about, above, on; **sobre todo** above all, especially
sobresaliente outstanding
sobrevivir to survive
sobrino/a nephew/niece (4)
social: trabajador(a) social social worker (23)
socialista *adj.* socialist
socializar (c) to socialize
sociedad *f.* society
socio/a member; partner
sociología sociology
sociólogo/a sociologist
socorro *n.* help
sofá *m.* sofa (8)
sofocante stifling
sofrito/a sautéed
sol *m.* sun; **hace sol** it's sunny (7); **tomar el sol** to sunbathe (11)
solar *n. m.* plot, ground, lot
soldado soldier; **mujer** (*f.*) **soldado** female soldier (23)
soleado/a sunny
soledad *f.* solitude (18)
soler (ue) + *inf.* to tend to, be in the habit of (*doing something*)
solicitar to solicit, ask for
solicitud *f.* application (*form*) (23)
solidarista *adj.* solidarity
solitario/a solitary
sólo *adv.* only (2)
solo/a *adj.* alone (4)
soltero/a single, unmarried
solterón, solterona old bachelor / spinster, old maid
solución *f.* solution
solucionar to solve
solucionólogo/a problem-solver

sollozo sob
sombra shadow
sombrero hat (5)
someter to submit
son las... it's _____ o'clock (P)
sonar (ue) to ring; to sound, play
sondeo (opinion) poll
sonido sound
sonreír (i, i) to smile (13)
soñar (ue) (con) to dream (about)
sopa soup (9)
sorprendente surprising
sorprender to surprise, be surprising; **me (te, le,** *etc.*) **sorprende** it's surprising to me (you, him, *etc.*) (12)
sorpresa surprise (13)
sos you (*fam. s.*) are (*Arg.*)
sospechoso/a suspicious
sostener (*like* **tener**) to support
soviético/a *adj.* Soviet
soy I am (P)
su *poss.* his, her, its, your (*form. s., pl.*), their
subir (a) to go up; to get (on) (*a vehicle*) (11); to carry up; to raise
subjuntivo *gram.* subjunctive (*mood*)
suburbio suburb
subvencionado/a subsidized
suceder to happen
sucesión *f.* succession
sucio/a dirty (4)
suculento/a succulent, juicy
sucursal *f.* branch (office)
Sudáfrica South Africa
Sudamérica South America
sudar to sweat
sudoeste *m.* southwest
suegro/a father-in-law/mother-in-law
sueldo salary (12)
suelo floor; **barrer el suelo** to sweep the floor (12)
suelto/a loose
sueño sleepiness; dream; **tener** (*irreg.*) **sueño** to be sleepy
suerte *f.* luck; **buena suerte** good luck; **¡qué mala suerte!** what bad luck! (14); **tener** (*irreg.*) **suerte** to be lucky
suéter *m.* sweater (5)
suficiente sufficient, enough; **dormir (ue, u) lo suficiente** to get enough sleep; **lo suficiente** enough (15)
sufijo *gram.* suffix
sufrimiento *n.* suffering
sufrir to have, suffer (from) (14); **sufrir muchas presiones** to be under a lot of pressure
sugerencia suggestion
sugerir (ie, i) to suggest
Suiza Switzerland
suizo/a Swiss
sujeto *gram.* subject; *adj.* subject, liable; **estar** (*irreg.*) **sujeto a** to be subject to
suma amount
sumamente *adv.* extremely
sumar to add; to total
superar to exceed
superlativo/a *gram.* superlative

supermercado supermarket (6)
superpoblación *f.* overpopulation
superpoblado/a overpopulated
supervisor(a) supervisor
supervivencia survival
suplementario/a supplementary
suplemento supplement
suponer (*like* **poner**) to suppose, assume
supuesto: por supuesto of course (22)
sur *m.* south; **al sur de** to the south of (7)
surcado/a furrowed
surgir (j) to spring up, arise
suroeste *m.* southwest
surrealista *adj.* surrealistic
suscripción *f.* subscription
suspender to suspend, hang
suspenso failing grade
sustantivo *gram.* noun (1)
sustituir (y) to substitute
sustituto *n.* substitute
susto scare, fright
suyo/a, *poss.* your, (of) yours (*form. s., pl.*); (of) his; her, (of) hers; (of) its; their, (of) theirs

T

tabacalero/a related to tobacco
tabaco tobacco
tabú *m. taboo*
taco taco (*tortilla filled with meat and vegetables*)
tailandés, tailandesa *adj.* Thai
tal such (a); **con tal (de) que** provided that (21); **¿qué tal?** how are you (doing)? (P); **tal vez** perhaps, maybe
talento talent
talonario de cheques checkbook (20)
talla size
taller *m.* (repair) shop (17)
tamal *m.* tamale (*cornmeal, chicken or meat, and chili wrapped in banana leaves or corn husk*)
tamalada tamale-making party
tamaño size
también also (P)
tambor *m.* drum
tampoco neither, not either (9)
tan as, so; **¿sería tan amable de... ?** would you be so kind as to . . . ? (21); **tan... como** as . . . as (8); **tan pronto como** as soon as (20)
tanque *m.* tank (17)
tanto *adv.* as, so much; **mientras tanto** *adv.* meanwhile
tanto/a as much; *pl.* as many; **al tanto** up-to-date; **tanto/a... como** as much . . . as (8); **tantos/as... como** as many . . . as (8)
tapa snack, hors d'oeuvre (*Sp.*)
taquilla ticket booth (16)
tardar (en + *inf.*) to take a long time (*to do something*)
tarde *f.* afternoon, evening (1); **buenas tardes** good afternoon/evening (P); **de la tarde** in the afternoon/evening (P); **esta**

tarde this afternoon (4); **por la tarde** in the afternoon/evening (20); **todas las tardes** every afternoon

tarde *adv.* late (7); **más tarde** later; **tarde o temprano** sooner or later

tarea homework; task

tarifa tariff, rate; fare

tarjeta card; **tarjeta de crédito** credit card (10); **tarjeta de embarque** boarding pass; **tarjeta postal** postcard

tasa tax; rate

tasca bar, tavern

taxi *m.* taxi (11)

taxista *m., f.* taxi driver

taza cup

te *d.o.* you (*fam. s.*); *i.o.* to/for you (*fam. s.*); *refl. pron.* yourself (*fam. s.*)

té *m.* tea

teatral theatrical

teatro theater (16); **ir** (*irreg.*) **al teatro** to go to the theater; **obra de teatro** play

técnico/a technician

tecnología technology

tecnológico/a technological

techo roof; ceiling

tejano/a Texan

tejido tissue; fabric

telediario newscast

telefónico/a *adj.* telephone; **guía telefónica** telephone book

telefonista *m., f.* telephone operator

teléfono telephone; **llamar por teléfono** to telephone; **número de teléfono** telephone number; **por teléfono** by telephone; **teléfono celular** cellular telephone (12); **teléfono del coche** car (tele)phone (12)

teleserie *f.* (TV) series

telesilla *m.* chair lift

tele(visión) *f.* television, TV

televisor *m.* television (set) (7)

tema *m.* theme, topic

temblar (ie) to tremble, shake

temer to fear (12)

temperamento temperament

temperatura temperature; **tomarle la temperatura** to take someone's temperature (15)

tempestad *f.* storm

templado/a cool, temperate

templo temple

temporada season

temprano *adv.* early (7); **tarde o temprano** sooner or later

temprano/a *adj.* early; young (*age*)

tendencia tendency

tender (ie) to tend to; to make (*a bed*)

tendido/a lying down

tenedor *m.* fork

tener *irreg.* to have; **no tener otro remedio** to be unavoidable; **(no) tener razón** to be right (wrong) (5); **tener... años** to be . . . years old (4); **tener cabida (en)** to be acceptable; **tener calor** to be (feel) warm/hot (*person*); **tener cuidado (de)** to be careful (about); **tener dolor (de)** to

have a pain (in) (15); **tener en cuenta** to keep/have in mind, take into account; **tener éxito** to be successful; **tener fiebre** to have a fever (15); **tener frío** to be cold (*person*) (7); **tener ganas de** + *inf.* to feel like (*doing something*); **tener miedo (de)** to be afraid (of) (5); **tener (mucha) hambre** to be (very) hungry (9); **tener prisa** to be in a hurry; **tener sed** to be thirsty (9); **tener sueño** to be sleepy; **tener suerte** to be lucky

tengo I have (4)

tenis *m.* tennis (16); **cancha de tenis** tennis court; **zapato de tenis** tennis shoe (5)

tenista *m., f.* tennis player

tensión *f.* tension, pressure; **tensión arterial** blood pressure

tentación *f.* temptation

teocrático/a theocratic

teología theology

teoría theory

teórico/a theoretical

terapéutico/a therapeutic

terapia therapy

tercer, tercero/a third (17); **tercera edad** senior citizens

tercio *n.* third

termal *adj.* thermal

termalismo *n.* thermal treatment

terminación *f.* ending

terminal *m.; adj.* terminal

terminar to end

término: poner (*irreg.*) **término a** to put an end to

termómetro thermometer

termostato thermostat

ternera veal

terraza terrace, veranda

terremoto earthquake

terreno land, ground, terrain; piece or plot of land

territorio territory

terrorista *m., f.* terrorist

tersura smoothness

tertulia social gathering

tesoro treasure; treasury

testigo *m., f.* witness (22)

testimonio testimony

texano/a Texan

texto text (1); **libro de texto** textbook (1)

ti *obj. (of prep.)* you (*fam. s.*)

tiempo time (7); weather (7); *gram.* (verb) tense; **a tiempo** on time (11); **hace (muy) buen/mal tiempo** it's (very) good/bad weather (7); **llegar (gu) a tiempo** to arrive on time; **pasar tiempo (con)** to spend time (with) (19); **¿qué tiempo hace?** what's the weather like? (7); **tiempo libre** free time; **trabajo de tiempo completo** full-time job; **trabajo de tiempo parcial** part-time job

tienda shop (5); store (5); **tienda de campaña** tent

tienes you have (4)

tierno/a tender; sensitive

tierra land, earth

tigre *m.* tiger

timbre *m.* bell, buzzer

timidez *f.* timidity; shyness

tímido/a timid, shy

tinto: vino tinto red wine (9)

tío/a uncle/aunt (4)

típico/a typical

tipo *n.* kind; type

tipo/a guy/gal; character

tira cómica comic strip

tirar to throw

titulado/a *adj.* holding an academic degree

titular *m.* holder (*of a post; of a credit card*)

título title; degree

toalla towel

tobillo ankle

tocar (qu) to touch; to play (*a musical instrument*) (2); to be someone's turn

todavía still, yet

todo *n.* all, everything; **ante todo** first of all; **de todo** everything; **sobre todo** above all, especially

todo/a *adj.* all, every; **de todas formas** anyway; **por todas partes** everywhere; **todas las tardes/noches** every afternoon/evening, night; **todo derecho** straight ahead (17); **todos los días** every day (2)

tolerante tolerant

tomar to take (2); to drink (2); to eat; **tomar el sol** to sunbathe (11); **tomar en cuenta** to keep/have in mind, take into account; **tomarle el pelo a alguien** to pull someone's leg; **tomarle la temperatura** to take someone's temperature (15)

tomate *m.* tomato (9)

tontería silly, foolish thing

tonto/a silly, foolish (3)

topar con to run into

tórax *m. inv.* thorax

torcer (ue) (z) to twist

toreo bullfighting

torero/a bullfighter

tormenta storm

toro bull; **corrida de toros** bullfight; **plaza de toros** bullring

tortilla omelette (*Sp.*); tortilla (*round, flat bread made of corn or wheat flour*) (*Mex., Central America*)

tortuga turtle

tortura torture

torturar to torture

tos *f.* cough (15)

toser to cough (15)

tostada *n.* (piece of) toast

tostado/a toasted; **pan** (*m.*) **tostado** toast (9)

tostadora toaster (12)

total *m.* total; *adj.* total; **en total** in all

trabajador(a) *n.* worker; *adj.* hard-working; **trabajador(a) social** social worker (23)

trabajar to work (2)

trabajo job (12); work (12); written work (12); (term) paper (12); **trabajo de tiempo completo** full-time job; **trabajo de tiempo parcial** part-time job

tractor *m.* tractor

tradición *f.* tradition
tradicional traditional
traducción *f.* translation
traducir (*like* **producir**) to translate
traductor(a) translator
traer *irreg.* to bring (10)
tráfico traffic (17)
tragar (gu) to swallow
tragedia tragedy
trágico/a tragic
tragicómico/a tragicomic
traicionar to betray
traje *m.* suit (5); **traje de baño** swimsuit (5)
trama plot
tranquilidad *f.* peace, tranquility
tranquilo/a calm, tranquil (14)
transeúnte *m., f.* passer-by
transformar to transform, change
transición *f.* transition
tránsito traffic
transmisión *f.* transmission
transmitir to transmit; to broadcast
transportación *f.* transportation
transporte *m.* transportation; **medio de transporte** means of transportation (11); **transporte público** public transportation (18)
tras *prep.* after, behind
trasladar to transfer, move
traslado *n.* transfer
trasplante *n. m.* transplant
tratado treaty
tratamiento treatment
tratar to treat, give treatment to; **tratar de +** *inf.* to try to (*do something*)
traumático/a traumatic
través: a través (de) through, by means of
travieso/a mischievous
trébol *m.* club (*suit of cards*)
trece thirteen (P)
treinta thirty (P)
tremendo/a tremendous; terrible
tren *m.* train (11); **estación** (*f.*) **del tren** train station (11)
trenzar (c) to braid
tres three (P)
trescientos/as three hundred (6)
trigo wheat
trimestre *m.* trimester
triste sad (4); **sentirse (ie, i) triste** to feel sad (13)
triunfar to be successful
triunfo triumph; victory
trofeo trophy (12)
trompeta trumpet
tropezón *m.* stumble, trip; mistake
tropiezo stumble, trip
trozo piece
tu *poss.* your (*fam. s.*)
tú *sub. pron.* you (*fam. s.*); **¿y tú?** and you? (P)
tubería pipes
tumba tomb
tumbarse to lie down
turbulento/a turbulent
turismo tourism

turista *m., f.* tourist (21)
turístico/a *adj.* tourist; **clase** (*f.*) **turística** tourist class (11)
turno turn; shift
tuyo/a *poss.* your, (of) yours (*fam. s.*)

U

u or (*used instead of* **o** *before words beginning with* **o** *or* **ho**)
ubicuo/a omnipresent; ubiquitous
último/a last (11); latest; final; **por última vez** for the last time
un, uno/a one, a, an (*indefinite article*); one (*number*) (P); **cada uno/a** each one
único/a only; unique
unidad *f.* unity
unido/a united; **Estados** (*pl.*) **Unidos** United States; **Reino Unido** United Kingdom
unificación *f.* unification
unión *f.* union
unir to unite
universidad *f.* university (1)
universitario/a *n.* university student; *adj.* university, of the university
unos/as some, several; a few
urbanismo city planning
urbanístico/a *adj.* city-planning, housing
urbano/a urban
urbe *m.* metropolis
urgencia urgency; **sala de urgencia** emergency room
urgente urgent
urología urology
usar to use (5); to wear (5)
uso use
usted (Ud., Vd.) *sub. pron.* you (*form. s.*); **¿cómo es usted?** what are you like? (P) **¿y usted?** and you? (P); *obj.* (*of prep.*) you (*form. s.*)
ustedes (Uds., Vds.) *sub. pron.* you (*form. pl.*); *obj.* (*of prep.*) you (*form. pl.*)
usuario/a user
utensilios (*pl.*) **de comer** eating utensils (10)
útil useful; helpful
utilizar (c) to use, make use of
uva grape

V

vacaciones *f. pl.* vacation (11); **estar** (*irreg.*) **de vacaciones** to be on vacation (11); **ir** (*irreg.*) **de vacaciones** to go on vacation (11); **vacaciones de primavera** spring break
vacilar: sin vacilar without hesitation
vacío/a empty
vacuna shot, vaccination
vago/a vague
valer *irreg.* to be worth; **(no) valer la pena** to (not) be worthwhile
válido/a valid
valiente brave, courageous
valor *m.* value

valorar to appraise, calculate
vals *m.* waltz
valla fence, barricade
valle *m.* valley
vapor *m.* steam
vaquero cowboy; *pl.* jeans
vara rod
variación *f.* variety, variation
variado/a varied
variar (varío) to vary
variedad *f.* variety
varios/as *pl.* various, several
varón *m.* male
vasco Basque (*language*)
vasco/a *n.; adj.* Basque; **pelota vasca** jai alai (*type of handball*)
vascuence *m.* Basque (*language*)
vasija vase
vaso (drinking) glass (10)
Vaticano Vatican
vecindario neighborhood
vecino/a neighbor (12)
vegetación *f.* vegetation
vegetariano/a *n.; adj.* vegetarian
vehículo vehicle
veinte twenty (P)
veinticinco twenty-five
veinticuatro twenty-four
veintidós twenty-two
veintinueve twenty-nine
veintiocho twenty-eight
veintiséis twenty-six
veintisiete twenty-seven
veintitrés twenty-three
veintiún, veintiuno/a twenty-one
vela candle
velada evening
velocidad *f.* speed (17); **límite** (*m.*) **de velocidad** speed limit
vencer (z) to overcome, conquer
vendedor(a) salesperson, seller (6)
vender to sell (4)
venezolano/a Venezuelan
vengativo/a vindictive
venir *irreg.* to come (5)
venta sale
ventaja advantage
ventana window (1); **lavar las ventanas** to wash the windows (12)
ventanilla (airplane) window (11); teller's window (2)
ventilador *m.* fan
ver *irreg.* to see (10); **a ver** let's see
veraneo summer holiday(s)
verano summer (7)
verbo *gram.* verb (1)
verdad *f.* truth; **de verdad** real; really; **¿verdad?** right? don't they (you, etc.)? (5)
verdadero/a true, real
verde green (5)
verdura vegetable (9)
vergonzoso/a embarrassing
verificar (qu) to verify
vermut *m.* vermouth
versión *f.* version
verso verse; poem

vestíbulo hall, foyer
vestido dress (5)
vestigio vestige, trace
vestir (i, i) to dress; to wear; **vestirse** to get dressed (7)
veterinario/a veterinarian (23)
vez *f.* (*pl.* **veces**) time, occasion; **a su vez** at the same time; **a veces** at times, sometimes (4); **alguna vez** once; ever; **de vez en cuando** on occasion, from time to time (9); **en vez de** instead of; **érase una vez** once upon a time; **otra vez** again (10); **por primera vez** for the first time; **por última vez** for the last time; **tal vez** perhaps, maybe; **una vez** once (9)
vía road, way
viajar to travel (11); **viajar al/en el extranjero** to travel abroad
viaje *m.* trip, voyage; **agencia de viajes** travel agency (11); **agente** (*m., f.*) **de viajes** travel agent (11)
viajero/a traveler (21); **cheque** (*m.*) **de viajero** traveler's check (11)
vibrar to vibrate; to quiver
vicepresidente/a vice president
vida life; **estilo de vida** lifestyle; **llevar una vida sana** to lead a healthy life (15); **ritmo acelerado de la vida** fast pace of life (18)
videocámara video camera
videocasetera videocassette recorder (VCR) (12)
vidrio glass
viejo/a old (3); **Noche** (*f.*) **Vieja** New Year's Eve (13)
viento wind; **hace viento** it's windy (7)
viernes *m. inv..* Friday (2); **hoy es viernes** today is Friday (2)
vietnamita *n. m., f.; adj.* Vietnamese
vikingo Viking
villa town, village
vínculo bond, tie, link
vinícola *of or pertaining to wine, wine-making*
vino (blanco/tinto) (white/red) wine (9)

violación *f.* violation
violencia violence (18)
violento/a violent
violín *m.* violin
violoncelista *m., f.* cellist
violoncelo cello
virgen *f.* virgin
virus *m.* virus
visado visa (*Sp.*)
vísceras *pl.* viscera, innards
visita *n.* visit
visitante *m., f.* visitor
visitar to visit
vislumbrar to catch a glimpse of
vista view (19); sight; **punto de vista** point of view
vitamina vitamin
vivienda housing
vivir to live (4); **¿dónde quiere vivir?** where do you (*form. s.*) want to live? (19); **¿dónde vive Ud.?** where do you (*form. s.*) live? (19)
vivo/a alive, living; bright (*of colors*)
vocabulario vocabulary
vocal *f. gram.* vowel
vocero/a spokesperson
volante *m.* steering wheel
volar (ue) to fly (11)
volcán *m.* volcano
volcánico/a volcanic
vólibol *m.* volleyball (16)
volumen *m.* volume
voluntario/a volunteer
volver (ue) (*p.p.* **vuelto/a**) to return (*to a place*) (6); **volver a** + *inf.* to (*do something*) again (6); **volverse loco/a** to go crazy
vos *sub. pron.* you (*fam. s.*) (*Argentina*)
vosotros/as *sub. pron.* you (*fam. pl. Sp.*); *obj.* (*of prep.*) you (*fam. pl. Sp.*)
votante *m., f.* voter
votar to vote (22)
voz *f.* (*pl.* **voces**) voice; **en voz alta** out loud
vuelo flight (11); **asistente** (*m., f.*) **de vuelo**

flight attendant; **auxiliar** (*m., f.*) **de vuelo** flight attendant (11); **vuelo con escalas** flight with stops (11); **vuelo directo** direct (nonstop) flight (11)
vuelta return; stroll, walk; **billete** (*m.*)/**boleto de ida y vuelta** round-trip ticket (11); **dar** (*irreg.*) **una vuelta** to take a walk
vuelto/a *p.p.* returned
vuestro/a *poss.* your (*fam. pl. Sp.*); (of) yours (*fam. pl. Sp.*)

W

walkman *m.* Walkman (12)

Y

y and (P); **y cuarto** quarter past (*with time*) (P); **y media** _____ thirty, half-past (*with time*) (P)
ya already, now; **ya no** no longer; **ya que** since, considering that
yacimiento bed, deposit (*geology*)
yarda yard
yate *m.* yacht
yerno son-in-law
yo *sub. pron.* I
yogur(t) *m.* yogurt

Z

zanahoria carrot (9)
zapatería shoe store
zapato shoe (5); **zapato de tenis** tennis shoe (5)
zarza bramble
zodíaco zodiac
zona zone
zumbar to buzz, hum

A

able: to be able **poder** (*irreg.*) (5)
about **por** (13)
abroad **al extranjero** (20)
absence **falta** (18)
absent: to be absent **faltar (a)** (13)
absent-minded **distraído/a** (14)
according to **según** (4)
account: checking account **cuenta corriente** (20); savings account **cuenta de ahorros** (20)
accountant **contador(a)** (23)
ache *v.* **doler (ue)** (15)
activity **actividad** *f.* (11)
additional **adicional** (P)
address **dirección** *f.* (19)
adjective **adjetivo** (3)
advice: piece of advice **consejo** (10)
advisor **consejero/a** (1)
affection **cariño** (19)
affectionate **cariñoso/a** (19)
afraid: to be afraid (of) **tener** (*irreg.*) **miedo (de)** (5)
after *prep.* **después de** (6); *conj.* **después (de) que** (20)
afternoon **tarde** *f.* (1); good afternoon **buenas tardes** (P); in the afternoon **de la tarde** (P); **por la tarde** (2)
afterward **luego** (6)
again **otra vez** (10); to (*do something*) again **volver (ue) a** + *inf.* (6)
agency: travel agency **agencia de viajes** (11)
agent: travel agent **agente** (*m., f.*) **de viajes** (11)
ago: (*time*) ago **hace** (+ *time*) (12)
agree **estar** (*irreg.*) **de acuerdo** (3)
agriculture **agricultura** (18)
ahead: ahead of time **con anticipación** (21); straight ahead **todo derecho** (17)
air **aire** *m.*; air pollution **contaminación** (*f.*) **del aire** (18)
airport **aeropuerto** (11)
alarm clock **despertador** *m.* (14)
all **todo/a** (3); All Souls' Day **Día** (*m.*) **de los Muertos** (13)
almost never **casi nunca** (4)
alone **solo/a** (4, 11)
along **por** (17); to get along well/badly (with) **llevarse bien/mal (con)** (19)
alongside of **al lado de** (7)
already **ya**
also **también** (P)
although **aunque**
always **siempre** (4)
am: I am **soy** (P); **estoy** (1)
American: North American **norteamericano/a** (3)

among **entre** (7)
amusing **divertido/a** (16)
ancient **antiguo/a** (8)
and **y** (P)
angry **furioso/a** (4, 13)
another **otro/a** (3)
answering: automatic answering machine **contestador** (*m.*) **automático** (12)
antibiotic **antibiótico** (15)
antique **antiguo/a** (8)
any **algún, alguno/a** (9); not any **ningún, ninguno/a** (9)
anyone **alguien** (9)
anything: not anything **nada** (9)
apartment house **casa de apartamentos** (19)
apple **manzana** (9)
appliance: home appliance **aparato doméstico** (12)
applicant **aspirante** *m., f.* (23)
application (form) **solicitud** *f.* (23)
appointment **cita** (15)
April **abril** *m.* (7)
aquarium **acuario** (12)
are: there are **hay** (P); you are **eres** *fam. s.* (P); **es** *form. s.* (P); **estás** *fam. s.* (1); **está** *form. s.* (1)
area: waiting area **sala de espera** (11)
argue **discutir** (22); to argue (about, with) **discutir (sobre, con)** (13)
arm **brazo** (14)
armchair **sillón** *m.* (8)
arrive **llegar (gu)** (6)
art **arte** *f.* (*but* **el arte**) (2)
as: as a child **de niño/a** (14); as . . . as **tan... como** (8); as much/many . . . as **tanto/a/os/as... como** (8); *conj.* as soon as **en cuanto** (20); **tan pronto como** (20)
ask (questions) **preguntar** (10); to ask a question **hacer** (*irreg.*) **una pregunta** (7); to ask for **pedir (i, i)** (6)
asleep: to fall asleep **dormirse (ue, u)** (7)
asparagus **espárragos** *pl.* (9)
aspirin **aspirina** (14)
assassination **asesinato** (22)
at **en** (P); (*with time*) **a** (P); **a la(s)...** (P); at home **en casa** (2); at least **por lo menos** (22); at this very moment **en este momento** (5); at times **a veces** (4)
attend **asistir** (4)
attendant: flight attendant **auxiliar** (*m., f.*) **de vuelo** (11)
August **agosto** (7)
aunt **tía** (4)
automatic: automatic answering machine **contestador** (*m.*) **automático** (12); automatic teller machine **cajero automático** (20)
autumn **otoño** (7)

awareness: Hispanic Awareness Day **Día** (*m.*) **de la Raza** (13); **Día** (*m.*) **de la Hispanidad** (13)

B

back then **en aquel entonces** (14)
backpack **mochila** (1)
bad **mal, malo/a** (3); it's (very) bad weather **hace (muy) mal tiempo** (7); to have a bad time **pasarlo mal** (11); to make a bad impression **caerle** (*irreg.*) **mal** (23); what bad luck! **¡qué mala suerte!** (14)
badly **mal** (2); to get along badly (with) **llevarse mal (con)** (19)
bags: to pack one's bags **hacer** (*irreg.*) **las maletas** (11)
baked: baked custard **flan** *m.* (9); baked potato **papa al horno** (9)
ballpoint pen **bolígrafo** (1)
banana **banana** (9)
bank **banco** (20); bank teller **cajero/a** (20)
bar **bar** *m.* (16)
bargain *v.* **regatear** (6)
baseball **béisbol** *m.* (16)
basketball **básquetbol** *m.* (16)
bathe **bañarse** (7)
bathroom **baño** (8); bathroom sink **lavabo** (8); room with/without a bathroom **habitación** (*f.*) **con/sin baño** (21)
bathtub **bañera** (8)
battery **batería** (17)
be **estar** (*irreg.*) (1, 2), **ser** (*irreg.*) (3); to be . . . years old **tener** (*irreg.*)... **años** (4); to be afraid (of) / in a hurry / right **tener** (*irreg.*) **miedo (de)** / **prisa** / **razón** (5); to be cold / warm, hot / sleepy **tener frío** / **calor** / **sueño** (7); to be hungry / thirsty **tener hambre** / **sed** (9); to be on vacation **estar de vacaciones** (11); to be wrong **no tener** (*irreg.*) **razón** (5)
beach **playa** (7)
beans **frijoles** *m. pl.* (9)
beautiful **bello/a** (18)
because **porque** (3); because of **por** (13)
become: to become + *adj.* **ponerse** (*irreg.*) + *adj.* (13)
bed **cama** (8); to get up on the wrong side of the bed **levantarse con el pie izquierdo** (14); to go to bed **acostarse (ue)** (7); to stay in bed **guardar cama** (15); water bed **cama de agua** (8)
bedroom **alcoba** (8)
beer **cerveza** (2)
before *prep.* **antes de** (6); *conj.* **antes (de) que** (20)
begin **empezar (ie) (c)** (6); to begin to (*do something*) **empezar a** + *inf.* (6)

beginning **principio** (13)

behave: to behave well/badly **portarse bien/ mal** (13)

behind **detrás de** (7)

believe: to believe (in) **creer (y) (en)** (4)

bellhop **botones** m. s. (21)

below **debajo de** (7)

belt **cinturón** m. (5)

better **mejor** (8)

between **entre** (7)

beverage **bebida** (9)

bicycle **bici(cleta)** (12); to ride a bicycle **pasear en bicicleta** (16)

bicycling **ciclismo** (16)

big **gran(de)** (3)

bill **cuenta** (9); **factura** (20); (money) **billete** m. (20)

bird **pájaro** (4)

birthday **cumpleaños** m. s. (7); happy birthday! **¡feliz cumpleaños!** (13); wish for birthdays **¡felicidades!** (13)

bit: a little bit **un poco**

black **negro/a** (5)

blond(e) **rubio/a** (3)

blouse **blusa** (5)

blue **azul** (5)

board: room and full board **pensión** (f.) **completa** (21)

boardinghouse **pensión** f. (21)

boat **barco** (11); to travel by boat **navegar (gu) en barco** (11)

body **cuerpo** (14)

bomb **bomba** (22)

book **libro** (1)

bookshelf **estante** m. (8)

bookstore **librería** (1)

boot **bota** (5)

booth: ticket booth **taquilla** (16)

border **frontera** (21)

bored **aburrido/a** (4)

boring **pesado/a** (13)

boss **jefe/a** (12)

bothersome: it is bothersome to me (you, him . . .) **me (te, le...) molesta** (12)

bottle **botella** (10)

boutique **boutique** m. (6)

boy **niño** (3)

boyfriend **novio** (8)

brain **cerebro** (15)

brakes **frenos** pl. (16)

bread **pan** m. (9)

break **romper** (p.p. **roto/a**) (14, 18)

breakfast **desayuno** (9); room with breakfast meal **media pensión** (21); to have breakfast **desayunar** (9)

breathe **respirar** (15)

bring **traer** (irreg.) (10)

brother **hermano** (3)

brown **pardo/a** (5)

brunette **moreno/a** (3)

budget **presupuesto** (20)

build **construir (y)** (18)

building **edificio** (1); building manager **portero/a** (19)

bummer! **¡qué mala suerte!** (14)

bump (into) **darse** (irreg.) **con** (14)

bureau (furniture) **cómoda** (8)

bus **autobús** m. (11); bus station **estación** (f.) **de autobuses** (11); bus stop **parada del autobús** (21)

business (corporation) **empresa** (23); business (academic course) **administración** (f.) **de empresas** (2)

busy **ocupado/a** (4)

but **pero** (4)

buy **comprar** (2)

by **por** (12, 18); by (future time) **para +** time (11); by telephone **por teléfono** (2)

C

cafeteria **cafetería** (1)

cake **pastel** m. (9)

calculator **calculadora** (1)

calm **tranquilo/a** (14)

camping: to go camping **hacer** (irreg.) **camping** (11)

campus: university campus **campus** m. (19)

can v. **poder** (irreg.) (5)

candidate **aspirante** m., f. (23)

candy **dulces** m. pl. (10)

cap **gorra** (5)

car **coche** m. (3)

card **tarjeta** (10); credit card **tarjeta de crédito** (10); (playing) cards **cartas** f. pl. (16)

care: to take care of oneself **cuidarse** (15)

carrot **zanahoria** (9)

carry **llevar** (5)

cartoons (on TV) **dibujos** (pl.) **animados** (16)

case: in case **en caso de que** (21); just in case **por si acaso** (22)

cash v. (a check) **cobrar** (20); n. **dinero en efectivo** (10); in cash **en efectivo** (20)

cat **gato** (3)

catch a cold **resfriarse** (15)

certain: it's not certain **no es cierto** (17); **no es seguro** (17)

chair **silla** (1)

chalkboard **pizarra** (1)

change v. **cambiar (de)** (12)

channel (TV) **canal** m. (22)

charge v. (someone for an item or service) **cobrar** (20); (to someone's account) **cargar (gu)** (20)

check v. **revisar** (17); (baggage) **facturar** (11); n. (in a restaurant) **cuenta** (9); **cheque** m. (20); to check in(to) (a hospital) **internarse (en)** (15); traveler's check **cheque** (m.) **de viajero** (11)

checkbook **talonario de cheques** (20)

checking account **cuenta corriente** (20)

cheese **queso** (9)

chef **cocinero/a** (10)

chemistry **química** (2)

chess **ajedrez** m. (16)

chicken **pollo** (9)

child: as a child **de niño/a** (14)

childhood **niñez** f. (14)

children **hijos** pl. (4)

Chinese (language) **chino** (2)

chop: (pork) chop **chuleta** (pl.) **(de puerco)** (9)

chores: household chores **quehaceres** (m. pl.) **domésticos** (12)

Christmas **Navidad** f. (13); Christmas Eve **Nochebuena** (13)

citizen **ciudadano/a** (22)

city **ciudad** f. (3)

civic responsibility **responsabilidad** (f.) **cívica** (22)

class **clase** f. (1); first class **primera clase** (11); tourist class **clase turística** (11)

classmate **compañero/a de clase** (1)

clean v. **limpiar** (12); adj. **limpio/a** (4)

clerk **dependiente/a** (1)

clever **listo/a** (3)

client **cliente** m., f. (1)

climate **clima** m. (7)

clock: alarm clock **despertador** m. (14)

close v. **cerrar (ie)** (6); prep. close to **cerca de** (7)

closed **cerrado/a** (4)

closet **armario** (8)

clothes **ropa** s. (5)

cloudy: it's (very) cloudy **está (muy) nublado** (7)

clumsy **torpe** (14)

coffee **café** m. (2, 7); coffee pot **cafetera** (12)

coin **moneda** (20)

cold (illness) **resfriado** (14); it's (very) cold (weather) **hace (mucho) frío** (7); to be cold (person) **tener** (irreg.) **frío** (7); to catch a cold **resfriarse** (15)

collide (with) **chocar (qu) (con)** (17)

collision **choque** m. (22)

color **color** m. (5)

come **venir** (irreg.) (5)

comfortable **cómodo/a** (8); to be comfortable (temperature) **estar** (irreg.) **bien** (7)

communicate (with) **comunicarse (qu) (con)** (22)

communications **comunicaciones** f. (2)

compact disc (player) **compact** (m.) **disc** (12)

comparison **comparación** f. (8)

complain (about) **quejarse (de)** (13)

computer **computadora** (L.A.) (12); **ordenador** m. (Sp.) (12); computer science **computación** f. (2)

confirm **confirmar** (21)

congested **congestionado/a** (15)

congratulations! **¡felicitaciones!** (13)

conjunction **conjunción** f. (20)

conserve **conservar** (18)

constitution **constitución** f. (22)

contact lenses **lentes** (m.) **de contacto** (15)

contain **contener** (like **tener**) (17)

control: remote control **control** (m.) **remoto** (12)

convertible adj. (with cars) **descapotable** (12)

cook v. **cocinar** (10); n. **cocinero/a** (10)

cookie **galleta** (9)

cool: it's cool (weather) **hace fresco** (7)

corner **esquina** (17)

corporation **empresa** (23)

cost v. **costar (ue)** (6, 17)

cotton **algodón** m. (5)

cough *v.* **toser** (15); *n.* **tos** *f.* (15); cough syrup **jarabe** *m.* (15)
could you . . . ? **¿podría(s)... ?** (21)
country **país** *m.* (7); country(side) **campo** (18)
couple: married couple **pareja** (19)
course **curso** (2); of course **claro que sí** (1); **¡por supuesto!** (22)
courtesy **cortesía** (P)
cousin **primo/a** (4)
cover *v.* **cubrir** (*p.p.* **cubierto/a**) (18)
cracker **galleta** (9)
crash **choque** *m.* (22)
cream: ice cream **helado** (9)
credit card **tarjeta de crédito** (10)
crime **delito** (18)
cross *v.* **cruzar** (c) (21)
cruise **crucero** (11); cruise ship **crucero** (11)
cry *v.* **llorar** (13)
currency **moneda** (20)
custard: baked custard **flan** *m.* (9)
customs: customs duty **derechos** (*pl.*) **de aduana** (21); customs inspector **inspector(a) de aduana** (21)

D

dad **papá** *m.* (4)
daily **diario/a** (7)
dance *v.* **bailar** (2)
dangerous **peligroso/a** (13)
date *v.* (*someone*) **salir** (*irreg.*) **con** (7); *n.* **cita** (15); what's the date? **¿cuál es la fecha?** (7)
daughter **hija** (4)
day **día** *m.* (1); day after tomorrow **pasado mañana** (2); every day **todos los días** (2)
debt **deuda** (20)
December **diciembre** *m.* (7)
deck: tape deck **grabadora** (12)
declare **declarar** (21)
decrease *v.* **disminuir** (*like* **construir**) (20)
delay *n.* **demora** (11)
demonstrative **demostrativo/a** (8)
dense **denso/a** (18)
deny **negar** (ie) (gu) (17)
department store **almacén** *m.* (6)
departure gate **puerta de embarque** (11)
deposit *v.* **depositar** (20); *n.* **depósito** (20)
desert **desierto** (11)
desk **escritorio** (1); front desk **recepción** *f.* (21)
dessert **postre** *m.* (9)
destroy **destruir** (y) (18)
develop **desarrollar** (18)
dictator **dictador(a)** (22)
dictatorship **dictadura** (22)
dictionary **diccionario** (1)
die **morir(se)** (ue, u) (13)
dining room **comedor** *m.* (8)
dinner **cena** (9); to have dinner **cenar** (9)
direct flight **vuelo directo** (11)
dirty **sucio/a** (4)
disagree **discutir** (22)
disaster **desastre** *m.* (12, 22)
disc: compact disc **compact** (*m.*) **disc** (12)

disco(theque) **discoteca** (16)
discrimination **discriminación** *f.* (22)
dish **plato** (8); (*to eat*) **plato** (9)
dishwasher **lavaplatos** *m. s.* (12)
divorce *n.* **divorcio** (19)
divorced: to get divorced (from) **divorciarse (de)** (19)
dizzy **mareado/a** (15)
do **hacer** (*irreg.*) (*p.p.* **hecho/a**) (7); to (*do something*) again **volver** (ue) **a** + *inf.* (6)
doctor's office **consultorio** (15)
dog **perro** (3)
door **puerta** (1)
doorman **portero/a** (19)
dormitory **dormitorio** (1)
dot: on the dot **en punto** (P)
double room **habitación** (*f.*) **doble** (21)
doubt *v.* **dudar** (17)
down: to sit down **sentarse** (ie) (7)
downtown **centro** (6)
drag: a drag **pesado/a** (13)
dress *n.* **vestido** (5)
dressed: to get dressed **vestirse** (i, i) (7)
dresser **cómoda** (8)
drink *v.* **tomar** (2); **beber** (4); *n.* **bebida** (9); soft drink **refresco** (7)
drive **conducir** (*irreg.*) (17); **manejar** (17)
driver **conductor(a)** (17)
dryer **secadora** (12)
during **por** (*with time of day*) (2); **durante** (6)
dust *v.* **sacudir** (12)
duty: (customs) duty **derechos** (*pl.*) **de aduana** (21)

E

each **cada** (*inv.*)
ear **oreja** (15); inner ear **oído** (15)
early **temprano** (7)
earn **ganar** (12)
earrings **aretes** *m. pl.* (5)
east: to the east of **al este de** (7)
eat **comer** (4)
eating utensils **utensilios** (*pl.*) **de comer** (10)
economics **economía** *s.* (2)
economize **economizar** (c) (20)
egg **huevo** (9)
eight **ocho** (P); eight hundred **ochocientos/as** (6)
eighteen **dieciocho** (P)
eighth **octavo/a** (17)
eighty **ochenta** (3)
either: not either **tampoco** (9)
eleven **once** (P)
end *v.* **terminar** (12)
end table **mesita** (8)
energy **energía** (18)
engagement (*betrothal*) **noviazgo** (19)
English (*language*) **inglés** *m.* (2)
enjoy oneself **divertirse** (ie, i) (7); enjoy your meal **buen provecho** (10)
enough **lo suficiente** (15)
envelope **sobre** *m.* (21)
environment **medio ambiente** (18)

equality **igualdad** *f.* (22)
equipment **equipo** (12); photographic equipment **equipo fotográfico** (12); stereo equipment **equipo estereofónico** (12)
Eve: Christmas Eve **Nochebuena** (13); New Year's Eve **Noche** (*f.*) **Vieja** (13)
evening **tarde** *f.* (1); good evening **buenas tardes/noches** (P); in the evening **de la tarde/noche** (P); **por la tarde/noche** (2)
event **acontecimiento** (22)
every **todo/a** (3); **cada** *inv.*; every day **todos los días** (2)
everything **de todo** (6)
exactly **en punto** (*with time*) (P)
examine **registrar** (21)
example: for example **por ejemplo** (8)
excuse me **con permiso** (P)
exercise *v.* **hacer** (*irreg.*) **ejercicio** (7)
expend **gastar** (17)
expenses **gastos** *pl.* (20)
expensive **caro/a** (6)
explain **explicar** (qu) (10)
expression **expresión** *f.* (P)
extract a tooth (*molar*) **sacar** (qu) **una muela** (15)
extroverted **extrovertido/a** (8)
eye **ojo** (15)
eyeglasses **gafas** *pl.* (14)

F

factory **fábrica** (18)
fall *v.* **caer(se)** (*irreg.*) (17); *n.* (*season*) **otoño** (7); to fall asleep **dormirse** (ue, u) (7); to fall in love (with) **enamorarse (de)** (19)
familiar: to be familiar with **conocer** (*irreg.*) (9)
family **familia** (3); family-related, of the family **familiar** (4)
fan: to be a . . . fan **ser** (*irreg.*) **aficionado/a a...** (16)
far from **lejos de** (7)
farm **finca** (18); farm worker **campesino/a** (18)
fast **rápido/a** (9); fast pace of life **ritmo acelerado de la vida** (18)
fat **gordo/a** (3)
father **padre** *m.* (4)
fax **fax** *m.* (12)
fear *v.* **temer** (12)
February **febrero** (7)
feel **sentirse** (ie, i) (13); to feel like (*doing something*) **tener** (*irreg.*) **ganas de** + *inf.* (5); to feel sorry **sentir** (ie, i) (12)
fever: to have a fever **tener** (*irreg.*) **fiebre** (15)
few **pocos/as**
fifteen **quince** (P)
fifth **quinto/a** (17)
fifty **cincuenta** (3)
fight *v.* **pelear** (22)
fill out (*a form*) **llenar** (23); to fill (up) **llenar** (17)
finally **finalmente** (6); **por fin** (8)
find out (about) **enterarse (de)** (22)
fine *n.* **multa** (21); *adv.* (**muy**) **bien** (P)

finger **dedo** (14)
finish **acabar** (14)
first *adv.* **primero** (6); *adj.* **primer, primero/a** (8, 17); first class **primera clase** (11); the first of . . . (date) **el primero de...** (7)
fish (*live*) **pez** *m.* (*pl.* **peces**) (4, 12); (*cooked*) **pescado** (9)
five **cinco** (P); five hundred **quinientos/as** (6)
fix **arreglar** (17)
fixed price **precio fijo** (6)
flat tire **llanta desinflada** (17)
flight **vuelo** (11); direct flight **vuelo directo** (11); flight attendant **auxiliar** (*m., f.*) **de vuelo** (11); flight with/without stops **vuelo con/sin escalas** (11)
floor **suelo** (12)
flower **flor** *f.* (10)
fly *v.* **volar (ue)** (11)
following *adj.* **siguiente**
food **comida** (9)
foolish **tonto/a** (3)
foot **pie** *m.* (14)
football **fútbol** (*m.*) **americano** (16)
for (*intended*) **para** (3); (*in exchange*) **por** (6); (*destination*) **para** (7); (*future time*) **para + time** (11); for heaven's sake **por Dios** (22)
forbid **prohibir** (11)
foreign **extranjero/a** (2)
forget **olvidar** (11); to forget (about) **olvidarse (de)** (13)
fork **tenedor** *m.* (10)
form: immigration form **formulario de inmigración** (21)
forty **cuarenta** (3)
four **cuatro** (P); four hundred **cuatrocientos/as** (6)
fourteen **catorce** (P)
fourth **cuarto/a** (17)
freeway **autopista** (17)
freezer **congelador** *m.* (12)
French (*language*) **francés** *m.* (2); French fried potato **papa frita** (9)
frequently **con frecuencia** (4); how frequently? **¿con qué frecuencia?** (4)
Friday **viernes** *m. inv.* (1)
fried: French fried potato **papa frita** (9)
friend **amigo/a** (1)
friendly **amistoso/a** (19)
friendship **amistad** *f.* (19)
from **de** (P); from time to time **de vez en cuando** (9)
front: front desk **recepción** *f.* (21); in front of **delante de** (7)
fruit **fruta** (9)
full: room and full board **pensión** (*f.*) **completa** (21)
fun *adj.* **divertido/a** (16)
function *v.* **funcionar** (12)
furious **furioso/a** (13)
furniture **muebles** *m. pl.* (8)

G

game **partido** (16)
garage **garaje** *m.* (8)

garden **jardín** *m.* (8)
gas **gasolina** (17); gas station **estación** (*f.*) **de gasolina** (17); **gasolinera** (17)
gate: departure gate **puerta de embarque** (11)
general: in general **por lo general** (3)
German (*language*) **alemán** *m.* (2)
get **conseguir (i, i) (ga)** (12); to get a cold **resfriarse** (15); to get along well/badly (with) **llevarse bien/mal (con)** (19); to get down (from) **bajar (de)** (11); to get dressed **vestirse (i, i)** (7); to get mad (at) **enojarse (con)** (13); to get off (of) **bajar (de)** (11); to get on (*a vehicle*) **subir (a)** (11); to get sick **enfermarse** (13); to get up **levantarse** (7); to get up on the wrong side of the bed **levantarse con el pie izquierdo** (14)
gift **regalo** (3); to give (*as a gift*) **regalar** (10)
girl **niña** (3)
girlfriend **novia** (8)
give **dar** (*irreg.*) (10); to give (*as a gift*) **regalar** (10); to give (*someone*) a shot **poner(le)** (*irreg.*) **una inyección** (15)
glass (*for drinking*) **vaso** (10); wine glass **copa** (10)
go **ir** (*irreg.*) (6); to be going to (*do something*) **ir a + inf.** (6); to go camping **hacer** (*irreg.*) **camping** (11); to go home **regresar a casa** (2); to go on vacation **ir de vacaciones** (11); to go shopping **ir de compras** (6); to go to (*a class, function*) **asistir a** (4); to go to bed **acostarse (ue)** (7); to keep on going **seguir (i, i) (ga)** (17)
goblet **copa** (10)
golf **golf** *m.* (16)
good *adj.* **buen, bueno/a** (3); *n.* goods **bienes** *m.* (12); it's (very) good weather **hace (muy) buen tiempo** (7); to have a good time **divertirse (ie, i)** (7); **pasarlo bien** (11); to make a good impression **caerle** (*irreg.*) **bien** (23)
good-bye **adiós** (P); to say good-bye (to) **despedirse (i, i) (de)** (13)
good-looking **guapo/a** (3)
government **gobierno** (18)
graduate (from) **graduarse (en)** (20)
granddaughter **nieta** (4)
grandfather **abuelo** (4)
grandmother **abuela** (4)
grandparents **abuelos** *pl.* (4)
grandson **nieto** (4)
gray **gris** (5)
great **gran, grande** (3)
green **verde** (5)
greet each other **saludarse** (19)
greeting **saludo** (P)
guest **invitado/a** (8); hotel guest **huésped(a)** (21)

H

haggle **regatear** (6)
hairdresser **peluquero/a** (23)
half: it's half past . . . **es la... / son las... y media** (P)

ham **jamón** *m.* (9)
hamburger **hamburguesa** (9)
hand **mano** *f.* (14)
handsome **guapo/a** (3)
hang **colgar (ue) (ga)** (18)
hang-out: neighborhood hang-out **bar** *m.* (16)
happiness! **¡felicidades!** (13)
happy **contento/a** (4); **feliz** (*pl.* **felices**) (*with ser*) (13); happy birthday! **¡feliz cumpleaños!** (13); to be happy (about) **alegrarse (de)** (12)
hardworking **trabajador(a)** (3)
hat **sombrero** (5)
have **tener** (*irreg.*) (5); (*suffer from*) **sufrir** (14); I have **tengo** (4); to have a fever **tener fiebre** (15); to have a good time **divertirse (i, i)** (7); **pasarlo bien** (11); to have a pain (in) **tener dolor (de)** (15); to have just (*done something*) **acabar de + inf.** (9); to have to (*do something*) **tener que + inf.** (5); you have **tienes** (*fam. s.*) (4); you have **tiene** (*form. s.*) (4)
he **él**
head **cabeza** (14)
health **salud** *f.* (15)
healthy: to lead a healthy life **llevar una vida sana** (15)
hear **oír** (*irreg.*) (10)
heart **corazón** *m.* (15)
heaven: for heaven's sake **por Dios** (22)
hello **hola** (P)
help *v.* **ayudar** (9)
her *poss.* **su(s)** (4)
here **aquí** (2)
hi **hola** (P)
highway **carretera** (17)
his *poss.* **su(s)** (4)
Hispanic Awareness Day **Día** (*m.*) **de la Raza** (13)
history **historia** (2)
hit **pegar (gu)** (14)
hockey **hockey** *m.* (16)
hold **contener** (*like tener*) (17)
holiday **día** (*m.*) **festivo** (13)
home: at home **en casa** (2); home appliance **aparato doméstico** (12); to go home **regresar a casa** (2)
honeymoon **luna de miel** (19)
hope: I hope (that) **ojalá (que)** (12); *n.* **esperanza** (22)
hot: it's (very) hot (*weather*) **hace (mucho) calor** (7); to be hot (*person*) **tener** (*irreg.*) **calor** (7)
hotel **hotel** *m.* (11); hotel guest **huésped(a)** (21); luxury hotel **hotel de lujo** (21); two- (three-)star hotel **hotel de dos (tres) estrellas** (21)
house **casa** (3); apartment house **casa de apartamentos** (19)
household chores **quehaceres** (*m. pl.*) **domésticos** (12)
housekeeper **amo, ama** (*f. but el ama*) **de casa** (23)
how? **¿cómo?** (P); how are you? **¿cómo está(s)?** (P); how are you doing? **¿qué**

tal? (P); how many? **¿cuántos/as?** (P); how often? **¿con qué frecuencia?** (4)
hundred: one hundred **cien, ciento** (3, 6)
hungry: to be (very) hungry **tener** (*irreg.*) **(mucha) hambre** (9)
hurry: to be in a hurry **tener** (*irreg.*) **prisa** (5)
hurt *v.* **doler (ue)** (14, 15); to hurt oneself **hacerse** (*irreg.*) **daño** (14)
husband **esposo** (4); **marido** (4)

I

ice **hielo** (7); ice cream **helado** (9)
if **si** (2)
ill **enfermo/a** (4)
immediately **en seguida** (8)
immigration form **formulario de inmigración** (21)
impression: to make a good/bad impression **caerle** (*irreg.*) **bien/mal** (23)
in **en** (P); **por** (*with time of day*) (2); in case **en caso de que** (21); in front of **delante de** (7); in general **por lo general** (3); in order to (*do something*) **para** + *inf.* (5); in that way **así** (20); in the morning/afternoon/evening **por la mañana/tarde/ noche** (2)
increase *v.* **aumentar** (20); *n.* **aumento** (12)
incredible **increíble** (12)
indefinite **indefinido/a** (9)
inequality **desigualdad** *f.* (22)
inexpensive **barato/a** (6)
inform **informar** (22)
inner ear **oído** (15)
insist: to insist on **insistir en** (11)
inspector: customs inspector **inspector(a) de aduana** (21)
installments: in installments **a plazos** (20)
instead of **en vez de**
intend: to intend to (*do something*) **pensar (ie)** + *inf.* (6)
interest **interés** *m.* (20)
interrogative **interrogativo/a** (P)
interviewer **entrevistador(a)** (23)
invite **invitar** (9)
iron *v.* **planchar** (12)
is (*located*) **está** (P); he/she is **es** (P, 1); there is **hay** (P)
isolation **aislamiento** (18)
Italian (*language*) **italiano** (2)

J

January **enero** (7)
Japanese (*language*) **japonés** (2)
jealous **celoso/a** (19)
jeans **bluejeans** (5)
jewelry store **joyería** (6)
job **trabajo** (12); **puesto** (23)
jog **correr** (15)
juice **jugo** (9)
July **julio** (7)
June **junio** (7)

just: just in case **por si acaso** (22); to have just (*done something*) **acabar de** + *inf.* (9)

K

keep: to keep on going **seguir (i, i) (ga)** (17); to keep up (*maintain*) **mantener** (*like* **tener**) (17)
key **llave** *f.* (6)
kind **amable** (3); would you be so kind as to . . . ? **¿sería tan amable de... ?** (22)
king **rey** *m.* (22)
kiosk **quiosco** (21)
kitchen **cocina** (8)
knife **cuchillo** (10)
know (*information*) **saber** (*irreg.*) (9); (*people*) **conocer** (*irreg.*) (9)

L

laborer **obrero/a** (22)
lack **falta** (18); **escasez** *f.* (*pl.* **escaseces**) (18)
lacking: to be lacking **faltar (a)** (13)
lamp **lámpara** (8)
land (an airplane) **aterrizar (c)** (11)
landlady **dueña** (19)
landlord **dueño** (19)
language **lengua** (2)
large **gran, grande** (3)
last *v.* **durar** (22); *adj.* **último/a** (11, 17); last night **anoche** (8)
late *adv.* **tarde** (7); *adj.* **atrasado/a** (*with* **estar**) (11)
later: see you later **hasta luego** (P)
latest (most recent) **último/a**
laugh *v.* **reírse (i, i)** (13)
law **ley** *f.* (22)
lawyer **abogado/a** (23)
layer: ozone layer **capa de ozono** (18)
lazy **perezoso/a** (3)
lead: to lead a healthy life **llevar una vida sana** (15)
learn **aprender** (4); to learn (about) **enterarse (de)** (22)
least: at least **por lo menos** (22)
leave (*a place*) **salir** (*irreg.*) **(de)** (7); to leave (behind) **dejar** (12)
left: to the left of **a la izquierda de** (7)
leg **pierna** (14)
leisure time **ratos** (*pl.*) **libres** (16)
lend **prestar** (10)
lenses: (contact) lenses **lentes** (*m. pl.*) **(de contacto)** (15)
less than **menos que** (8)
letter **carta** (4)
lettuce **lechuga** (9)
library **biblioteca** (1)
license **licencia** (17)
lie **mentira** (10)
life: fast pace of life **ritmo acelerado de la vida** (18); to lead a healthy life **llevar una vida sana** (15)
light *n.* **luz** *f.* (10); *adj.* (*in weight, content*) **ligero/a** (9)
likable **amable** (3)

like **gustar** (10); do you like . . . ? **¿te gusta... ?** *fam. s.* (P); **¿le gusta... ?** *form. s.* (P); I would like . . . **me gustaría...** (10); no, I don't like . . . **no, no me gusta...** (P); to feel like (*doing something*) **tener** (*irreg.*) **ganas de** + *inf.* (5); yes, I like . . . **sí, me gusta...** (P)
line: to stand/wait in line **hacer** (*irreg.*) **cola** (11)
listen: to listen (to) **escuchar** (2)
literature **literatura** (2)
little *adv.* **poco** (5); *adj.* **poco/a** (5); a little bit **un poco**
live *v.* **vivir** (4); where do you (*form. s.*) live? **¿dónde vive Ud.?** (19); where do you (*form. s.*) want to live? **¿dónde quiere vivir?** (19)
living room **sala** (8)
loan *n.* **préstamo** (20)
lobster **langosta** (9)
lodging **alojamiento** (21)
long **largo/a** (3)
look: to look (at) **mirar** (2); to look for **buscar (qu)** (2)
lose **perder (ie)** (6)
lot: a lot *adv.* **mucho** (5); *adj.* **mucho/a** (5)
love *v.* **querer** (*irreg.*) (19); *n.* **amor** *m.* (19); to fall in love (with) **enamorarse (de)** (19)
luck: what bad luck! **¡qué mala suerte!** (14)
luggage **equipaje** *m.* (11)
lunch **almuerzo** (9); to have lunch **almorzar (ue) (c)** (6)
lung **pulmón** *m.* (15)
luxury **lujo** (12); luxury hotel **hotel** (*m.*) **de lujo** (21)

M

machine: automatic answering machine **contestador** (*m.*) **automático** (12); automatic teller machine **cajero automático** (20); washing machine **lavadora** (12)
mad: to get mad (at) **enojarse (con)** (13)
made: it is made of . . . **es de...** (5)
magazine **revista** (8)
Magi: Day of the Magi **Día** (*m.*) **de los Reyes Magos** (13)
maintain **mantener** (*like* **tener**) (17)
make **hacer** (*irreg.*) (*p.p.* **hecho/a**) (7); to make a good/bad impression **caerle** (*irreg.*) **bien/mal** (23); to make a mistake **equivocarse (qu)** (14); to make plans to (*do something*) **hacer planes para** + *inf.* (16)
mall **centro comercial** (4)
man **hombre** *m.* (1)
manager: building manager **portero/a** (19)
many **muchos/as** (5); as many . . . as **tantos/ as... como** (8); how many? **¿cuántos/as?** (P)
March **marzo** (7)
market(place) **mercado** (6); outdoor market(place) **mercado al aire libre** (6)
marriage **matrimonio** (19)
married **casado/a** (3); married couple **pareja** (19)
marry **casarse (con)** (19)

match (game) **partido** (16)
material **material** (5)
mathematics **matemáticas** *pl.* (2)
May **mayo** (7)
me *obj. of prep.* **mí** (7)
meal **comida** (9); enjoy your meal **buen provecho** (10); room with breakfast and one other meal **media pensión** (21)
mean: I (he, we . . .) didn't mean to do it **fue sin querer** (14)
means of transportation **medios** (*pl.*) **de transporte** (11)
meat **carne** *f.* (9)
mechanic **mecánico/a** (17)
medium: print medium **prensa** (22)
meet: pleased to meet you **mucho gusto** (P); **encantado/a** (P); **igualmente** (P)
menu **menú** *m.* (9)
messy **desordenado/a** (4)
microwave oven **horno de microondas** (12)
milk **leche** *f.* (7)
million **millón** (*m.*) (**de**) (6)
mind: would you mind . . . ? **¿le/te importaría... ?** (22)
mineral water **agua** (*f. but* **el agua**) **mineral** (9)
miss (*a function*) **perder** (**ie**) (6)
Miss **señorita** (**Srta.**) (P)
mistake: to make a mistake **equivocarse** (**qu**) (14)
molar **muela** (15); to extract a molar **sacar** (**qu**) **una muela** (15)
mom **mamá** (4)
moment: at this very moment **en este momento** (5)
Monday **lunes** *m. inv.* (2)
money **dinero** (2)
month **mes** *m.* (7)
more **más** (2); more than **más que** (8)
morning: good morning **buenos días** (P); in the morning **de la mañana** (P); **por la mañana** (2)
mother **madre** *f.* (4)
motorcycle **moto(cicleta)** (12)
mountain **montaña** (11)
mouth **boca** (15)
movie **película** (10); *pl.* **cine** *m.* (10); movie theater **cine** *m.* (10)
Mr. **señor** (**Sr.**) *m.* (P)
Mrs. **señora** (**Sra.**) (P)
much: as much . . . as **tanto/a... como** (8); not much *adv.* **poco** (5); *adj.* **poco/a** (5); to like very much **encantar** (10); too much **demasiado** (13)
museum **museo** (16)
must (*do something*) **deber** + *inf.* (4)
my *poss.* **mi(s)** (4); my name is . . . **me llamo...** (P)

N

name: my name is . . . **me llamo...** (P); what's your name? **¿cómo te llamas?** *fam. s.* (P); **¿cómo se llama usted?** *form. s.* (P)
napkin **servilleta** (10)

nationality **nacionalidad** (21)
natural: natural resources **recursos** (*pl.*) **naturales** (18); natural sciences **ciencias** (*pl.*) **naturales** (2)
nature **naturaleza** (18)
nauseated **mareado/a** (15)
near *prep.* **cerca de**
neat **ordenado/a** (4)
need *v.* **necesitar** (2)
negative **negativo/a** (9)
neighbor **vecino/a** (12)
neighborhood **barrio** (19); neighborhood hang-out **bar** *m.* (16)
neither **tampoco** (9)
nephew **sobrino** (4)
nervous **nervioso/a** (4)
never **nunca** (4); **jamás** (9); almost never **casi nunca** (4)
new **nuevo/a** (3); New Year's Day **Día** (*m.*) **de Año Nuevo** (13); New Year's Eve **Noche** (*f.*) **Vieja** (13)
news **noticias** *pl.* (22)
newscast **noticiero** (22)
newspaper **periódico** (4)
next **entonces** (6)
nice **amable** (3); **simpático/a** (3)
niece **sobrina** (4)
night **noche** *f.* (1); at night **de la tarde/ noche** (P); **por la noche** (2); good night **buenas tardes/noches** (P)
nine **nueve** (P); nine hundred **novecientos/ as** (6)
nineteen **diecinueve** (P)
ninety **noventa** (3)
ninth **noveno/a** (17)
no **no** (P); **ningún, ninguno/a** (9); no one **nadie** (9)
nobody **nadie** (9)
noise **ruido** (10)
none **ningún, ninguno/a** (9)
nonsmoking section **sección** (*f.*) **de no fumar** (11)
normal **regular** (P)
north: to the north of **al norte de** (7)
North American **norteamericano/a** (3)
nose **nariz** *f.* (*pl.* **narices**) (15)
not: not any **ningún, ninguno/a** (9); not anything **nada** (9); not either **tampoco** (9); there is not / are not **no hay** (P)
notebook **cuaderno** (1)
nothing **nada** (9)
noun **sustantivo** (1)
November **noviembre** (7)
now **ahora** (4); right now **en este momento** (5); **ahora mismo** (11)
number **número** (P)
nurse **enfermero/a** (15)

O

obey **obedecer** (**zc**) (22)
obligation **deber** *m.* (22)
obtain **obtener** (*like* **tener**); **conseguir** (**i, i**) (**ga**) (12)

occasion: on occasion **de vez en cuando** (9)
ocean **océano** (11)
o'clock: it's . . . o'clock (sharp) **es la... / son las... (en punto)** (P)
October **octubre** *m.* (7)
of **de** (P); of course **claro que sí** (1); **¡por supuesto!** (22)
off: to take off (*clothing*) **quitarse** (7)
offer *v.* **ofrecer** (**zc**) (10)
office **oficina** (1); doctor's office **consultorio** (15); personnel office **dirección** (*f.*) **de personal** (23); post office **correo** (21)
often: how often? **¿con qué frecuencia?** (4)
oil **aceite** *m.* (17)
okay **regular** (P); it's okay **está bien**
old **viejo/a** (3); **antiguo/a** (8)
older **mayor** (8)
on: on time **a tiempo** (11); on top of **encima de** (7); to put on (*clothing*) **ponerse** (7)
once **una vez** (9)
one **un, uno/a** (P); one hundred **cien, ciento** (3, 6); one-way ticket **billete** (*m.*)/**boleto de ida** (11)
only **sólo** (9)
open *v.* **abrir** (*p.p.* **abierto/a**) (4); *adj.* **abierto/a** (4)
operate **funcionar** (12)
or **o** (P)
orange *n.* **naranja** (9); *adj.* **anaranjado/a** (5)
order *v.* **pedir** (**i, i**) (*service, meal*) (6); **mandar** (11); in order to (*do something*) **para** + *inf.* (5)
orderly **ordenado/a** (4)
ordinal **ordinal** (17)
other *adj.* **otro/a** (1, 3); other people **los demás** (22); others *pron.* **los demás** (22)
our *poss.* **nuestro/a(s)** (4)
out (*not at home*) *adv.* **fuera** (9)
outdoor marketplace **mercado al aire libre** (6)
outgoing **extrovertido/a** (8)
outside *adv.* **afuera** (7)
outskirts **afueras** (*pl.*) (19)
oven: microwave oven **horno de microondas** (12)
overcast: it's (very) overcast **está (muy) nublado** (7)
owe **deber** (20)
owner **dueño/a** (10)
ozone layer **capa de ozono** (18)

P

pace: fast pace of life **ritmo acelerado de la vida** (18)
pack: to pack one's bags **hacer** (*irreg.*) **las maletas** (11)
package **paquete** *m.* (21)
pain: to have a pain (in) **tener** (*irreg.*) **dolor** (**de**) (15)
paint *v.* **pintar** (12)
painting **pintura** (12)
pair **par** *m.* (5)
pants **pantalones** *m. pl.* (5)
paper: (piece of) paper **papel** *m.* (1); (term)

paper **trabajo** (12)

pardon **perdón** (P); pardon me **discúlpeme** (14)

parents **padres** *m. pl.* (3)

park *v.* **estacionar(se)** (17)

part **parte** *f.* (8)

partner **pareja** (19)

party **fiesta** (2)

passage **pasaje** *m.* (11)

passbook: savings passbook **libreta de ahorros** (20)

passenger **pasajero/a** (11)

pastime **pasatiempo** (16)

pastry shop **pastelería** (21)

patient *n.* **paciente** *m., f.* (15)

patio **patio** (8)

pay: to pay (for) **pagar (gu)** (2)

peace **paz** *f.* (*pl.* **paces**) (22)

peas **arvejas** *pl.* (9)

peasant **campesino/a** (18)

pedestrian **peatón, peatona** (17)

pen **bolígrafo** (1)

pencil **lápiz** *m.* (*pl.* **lápices**) (1)

people **personas** (1); **gente** *f. s.* (12); other people **los demás** (22)

per **por** (12)

permit *v.* **permitir** (11)

person **persona** (1)

personal **personal** (12)

personnel office **dirección** (*f.*) **de personal** (23)

pet **mascota** (4)

philosophy **filosofía** (2)

photographic equipment **equipo fotográfico** (12)

photographs: to take photographs **sacar (qu) fotos** (12)

physician **médico/a** (15)

physics **física** *s.* (2)

pie **pastel** *m.* (9)

piece: piece of advice **consjeo** (10)

pill **pastilla** (15)

pilot **piloto/a** (11)

pink **rosado/a** (5)

pitcher **jarro** (10)

place *v.* **poner** (*irreg.*) (*p.p.* **puesto/a**); *n.* **lugar** *m.* (1); (*in line, etc.*) **puesto** (11); to take place at (*place*) **ser + en +** *place* (13)

plaid **de cuadros** (5)

plan: to make plans to (*do something*) **hacer** (*irreg.*) **planes para +** *inf.* (16); to plan to (*do something*) **pensar (ie) +** *inf.* (6)

plane **avión** *m.* (11)

plate **plato** (8)

play *v.* (*a musical instrument*) **tocar (qu)** (2); (*a sport*) **jugar (ue) (gu) (al...)** (6); (*a sport*) **practicar (qu)** (15)

please **por favor** (P); pleased to meet you **mucho gusto** (P); **encantado/a** (P); **igualmente** (P)

plug in **enchufar** (18)

plumber **plomero** *m., f.* (23)

political science **ciencias** (*pl.*) **políticas** (2)

pollute **contaminar** (18)

pollution: (air) pollution **contaminación** (*f.*)

(del aire) (18); there's (a lot of / a little) pollution **hay (mucha/poca) contaminación** (7)

pool **piscina** (8)

poor **pobre** (3)

population **población** *f.* (18)

pork chop **chuleta** (*pl.*) **de cerdo** (9)

portable radio **radio portátil** (12)

position (job) **puesto** (23)

possessions **bienes** *m. pl.* (12)

possessive **posesivo/a** (4)

post office **correo** (21)

poster **cartel** *m.* (12)

pot: coffee pot **cafetera** (12)

potato **papa** (9); baked potato **papa al horno** (9); French fried potato **papa frita** (9)

practice *v.* **practicar (qu)** (2)

prefer **preferir (ie, i)** (5)

preposition **preposición** *f.* (7)

prescription **receta** (15)

press *n.* **prensa** (22)

pressure **presión** *f.* (14)

pretty **bonito/a** (3)

price **precio** (6); fixed price **precio fijo** (6)

print medium **prensa** (22)

printer **impresora** (12)

problem **problema** *m.* (1)

profession **profesión** *f.* (23)

professor **profesor(a)** (1)

prohibit **prohibir** (11)

promise *v.* **prometer** (10)

property **bienes** *m. pl.* (12)

protect **proteger (j)** (18)

provided that **con tal (de) que** (21)

psychology **sicología** (2)

public: public services **servicios** (*pl.*) **públicos** (18); public transportation **transporte** (*m.*) **público** (18)

pure **puro/a** (18)

purple **morado/a** (5)

purse **bolsa** (5)

put **poner** (*irreg.*) (*p.p.* **puesto/a**) (7); to put in (*deposit*) **depositar** (20); to put on (*clothing*) **ponerse** (7)

Q

quarter: it's a quarter past . . . **es la... / son las... y cuarto** (P); it's a quarter to . . . **es la... / son las... menos cuarto** (P)

queen **reina** (22)

question: to ask a question **hacer** (*irreg.*) **una pregunta** (7)

quick **rápido/a** (9)

quit (*a job*) **dejar** (23)

quiz **prueba** (8)

R

radio: portable radio **radio portátil** (12)

rain *v.* **llover (ue)** (7); *n.* **lluvia** (7)

raincoat **impermeable** (5)

raise *n.* **aumento** (12)

ranch **rancho** (18)

read **leer (y)** (4)

receive **recibir** (4)

recommend **recomendar (ie)** (10)

recorder **grabadora** (12)

red **rojo/a** (5); red wine **vino tinto** (9)

reductions **rebajas** *pl.* (6)

refrigerator **refrigerador** *m.* (12)

registration **matrícula** (2)

regret **sentir (ie, i)** (12)

relationship **relación** *f.* (19)

relative **pariente** *m.* (4)

remain **quedarse** (7)

remember **recordar (ue)** (13); **acordarse (ue) (de)** (14)

remote control **control** (*m.*) **remoto** (12)

rent *v.* **alquilar** (19); *n.* **alquiler** *m.* (19)

renter **inquilino/a** (9)

repair *v.* **arreglar** (17); repair shop **taller** *m.* (17)

reporter **reportero/a** (22)

reservation **reserva** (21); **reservación** *f.* (21)

resign (from) **renunciar (a)** (23)

resources: natural resources **recursos** (*pl.*) **naturales** (18)

responsibility **deber** *m.* (22); civic responsibility **responsabilidad** (*f.*) **cívica** (22)

rest *v.* **descansar** (11)

restaurant **restaurante** *m.* (10)

résumé **currículum** *m.* (23)

retire **jubilarse** (20)

retirement **jubilación** *f.* (20)

return *v.* **volver (ue)** (*p.p.* **vuelto/a**) (6); (*to a place*) **regresar** (2); (*something*) **devolver (ue)** (*p.p.* **devuelto/a**) (20)

rice **arroz** *m.* (9)

rich **rico/a** (3); **rico/a** (*with food*) (13)

ride a bicycle **pasear en bicicleta** (16)

right *n.* **derecho** (22); right? **¿no?** (5); **¿verdad?** (5); right now **en este momento** (5); **ahora mismo** (11); to be right **tener** (*irreg.*) **razón** (5); to the right of **a la derecha de** (7)

road **camino** (17)

roll *n.* **bollo** (9)

room **cuarto** (1); room and full board **pensión** (*f.*) **completa** (21); room with breakfast and one other meal **media pensión** *f.* (21); room with/without a bathroom **habitación** (*f.*) **con/sin baño** (21); single/double room **habitación** (*f.*) **individual/doble** (21)

roommate **compañero/a de cuarto** (1)

round-trip ticket **billete** (*m.*)/**boleto de ida y vuelta** (21)

routine: daily routine **rutina diaria** (7)

rug **alfombra** (8)

run **correr** (15); to run (into) (collide) **chocar (qu) (con)** (17); to run out of **acabar** (14)

Russian (*language*) **ruso** (2)

S

sad **triste** (4)

sake: for heaven's sake **por Dios** (22)

salad **ensalada** (9)
salary **sueldo** (12)
sales **rebajas** *pl.* (6)
salmon **salmón** *m.* (9)
sandal **sandalia** (5)
sandwich **sándwich** *m.* (9)
Saturday **sábado** (2)
save (*a place*) **guardar** (11); (*conserve*) **conservar** (18); (*money*) **ahorrar** (20)
savings: savings account **cuenta de ahorros** (20); savings passbook **libreta de ahorros** (20)
say **decir** (*irreg.*) (10); to say good-bye (to) **despedirse (i, i) (de)** (13)
schedule **horario** (8)
science: computer science **computación** *f.* (2); natural/political/social science **ciencias** (*pl.*) **naturales/políticas/sociales** (2)
scream *v.* **gritar** (16)
sea **mar** (11)
search *v.* **registrar** (21); in search of **en busca de** (23)
season **estación** *f.* (7)
seat **asiento** (11)
second *adj.* **segundo/a** (17)
secretary **secretario/a** (1)
section: smoking section **sección** (*f.*) **de fumar** (11)
see **ver** (*irreg.*) (10)
sell **vender** (4)
seller **vendedor(a)** (6)
send **mandar** (10)
sentimental **sentimental** (19)
separate *v.* **separarse** (19)
September **se(p)tiembre** (7)
serve **servir (i, i)** (6)
service **servicio** (17); public services **servicios** (*pl.*) **públicos** (18)
seven **siete** (P); seven hundred **setecientos/as** (6)
seventeen **diecisiete** (P)
seventh **séptimo/a** (17)
seventy **setenta** (3)
shame: it's a shame **es lástima** (12); what a shame! **¡qué lástima!** (12)
sharp: it's . . . o'clock sharp **es la... / son las... en punto** (P)
shave **afeitarse** (7)
she **ella**
shellfish **mariscos** *pl.* (9)
ship **barco** (11); cruise ship **crucero** (11)
shirt **camisa** (5)
shoe **zapato** (5); shoe store **zapatería** (6); tennis shoe **zapato de tenis** (5)
shop **tienda** (5); pastry shop **pastelería** (21); (*repair*) shop **taller** (*m.*) (17); tobacco shop **estanco** (21)
shopping **de compras** (6); to go shopping **ir** (*irreg.*) **de compras** (6)
short (*in height*) **bajo/a** (3); (*in length*) **corto/a** (3)
shortage **escasez** *f.* (*pl.* **escaseces**) (18)
shot: to give (someone) a shot **poner(le)** (*irreg.*) **una inyección** (15)
should (*do something*) **deber** + *inf.* (4)
show *n.* **función** *f.* (16)

shower: to take a shower **ducharse** (7)
showing (*of a movie or play*) **función** *f.* (16)
shrimp **camarones** *m. pl.* (9)
sick **enfermo/a** (4); to get sick **enfermarse** (13)
side: to get up on the wrong side of the bed **levantarse con el pie izquierdo** (14)
sign **letrero** (17)
signal: traffic signal **semáforo** (17)
silk **seda** (5)
silly **tonto/a** (3)
sing **cantar** (2)
single (not married) **soltero/a** (3); single room **habitación** (*f.*) **individual** (21)
sink (*bathroom*) **lavabo** (8)
sister **hermana** (4)
sit **sentarse (ie)** (7)
six **seis** (P); six hundred **seiscientos/as** (6)
sixteen **dieciséis** (P)
sixth **sexto/a** (17)
sixty **sesenta** (3)
ski *v.* **esquiar** (11)
skirt **falda** (5)
skyscraper **rascacielos** *m. s.* (18)
sleep **dormir (ue, u)** (6)
sleepy: to be sleepy **tener** (*irreg.*) **sueño** (7)
slender **delgado/a** (3)
slow **lento/a** (14)
small **pequeño/a** (3)
smart **listo/a** (3)
smile *v.* **sonreír (i, i)** (13)
smog: there's (a lot of / a little) smog **hay (mucha/poca) contaminación** (7)
smoke *v.* **fumar** (11)
smoking section **sección** (*f.*) **de fumar** (11)
snow *v.* **nevar (ie)** (7); *n.* **nieve** *f.* (7)
so **así** (20); so-so **así así**; so that **para que** (21)
soccer **fútbol** *m.* (16)
social science **ciencias** (*pl.*) **sociales** (2)
sock **calcetín** *m.* (5)
sofa **sofá** *m.* (8)
soft drink **refresco** (7)
soldier **soldado / mujer** (*f.*) **soldado** (23)
solitude **soledad** *f.* (18)
some **algún, alguno/a** (9)
someone **alguien** (9)
something **algo** (6, 9)
son **hijo** (4)
soon: as soon as *conj.* **en cuanto** (20); **tan pronto como** (20)
sorry: I'm sorry **lo siento** (10); to feel sorry **sentir (ie, i)** (12)
Souls': All Souls' Day **Día** (*m.*) **de los Muertos** (13)
soup **sopa** (9)
soupspoon **cuchara** (10)
south: to the south of **al sur de** (7)
Spanish (*language*) **español** *m.* (2)
speak **hablar** (2)
speed **velocidad** *f.* (17)
spend (*time*) **pasar** (3); to spend time (with) **pasar tiempo (con)** (19)
spoon **cuchara** (10)
sport **deporte** *m.* (2)
spring **primavera** (7)

staircase **escalera** (14)
stamp **sello** (21)
stand: to stand in line **hacer** (*irreg.*) **cola** (11); to stand up **levantarse** (7); tobacco stand **estanco** (21)
star: two- (three-)star hotel **hotel** (*m.*) **de dos (tres) estrellas** (21)
start (*a motor*) **arrancar (qu)** (17)
States: United States **Estados** (*pl.*) **Unidos** (3)
station **estación** *f.* (11); bus station **estación de autobuses** (11); gas station **estación de gasolina** (17); **gasolinera** (17); station wagon **camioneta** (3); subway station **estación** (*f.*) **del metro** (21); train station **estación del tren** (11)
stationery **papel** (*m.*) **para cartas** (21); stationery store **papelería** (21)
stay **quedarse** (7); to stay (*in a place*) (21); to stay in bed **guardar cama** (15)
steak **bistec** *m.* (9)
stereo equipment **equipo estereofónico** (12)
stewardess **azafata** (11)
stick out one's tongue **sacar (qu) la lengua** (15)
still **todavía** (5)
stockings **medias** (5)
stomach **estómago** (15)
stop *v.* **parar** (17); bus stop **parada del autobús** (21); to stop (*doing something*) **dejar de** + *inf.* (15); flight with/without stops **vuelo con/sin escalas** (11)
store **tienda** (5); department store **almacén** *m.* (6); jewelry store **joyería** (6); shoe store **zapatería** (6); stationery store **papelería** (21)
stove **estufa** (12)
straight ahead **todo derecho** (17)
strange: it's strange **es extraño** (12); how strange! **¡qué extraño!** (12)
street **calle** *f.* (17)
strike *v.* **pegar (gu)** (14); *n.* **huelga** (22)
striped **de rayas** (5)
stroll *v.* **dar** (*irreg.*) **un paseo** (16)
student **estudiante** *m., f.* (1)
study *v.* **estudiar** (2)
stuffed-up **congestionado/a** (15)
style: it's in style **está de moda** (5)
subject (*school*) **materia** (2)
suburbs **afueras** *pl.* (19)
subway station **estación** (*f.*) **del metro** (21)
suffer **sufrir** (14)
sugar **azúcar** *m.* (7)
suit **traje** *m.* (5)
summer **verano** (7)
sunbathe **tomar el sol** (11)
Sunday **domingo** (2)
sunny: it's (very) sunny **hace (mucho) sol** (7)
supermarket **supermercado** (6)
surprise **sorpresa** (13)
surprising: it is surprising to me (you, him . . .) **me (te, le...) sorprende** (12)
sweater **suéter** *m.* (5)
sweep **barrer** (12)
sweets **dulces** *m. pl.* (10)

swim **nadar** (11)
swimsuit **traje** (*m.*) **de baño** (5)
syrup: (cough) syrup **jarabe** *m.* (15)

T

table **mesa** (1); end table **mesita** (8)
tablecloth **mantel** *m.* (10)
take **tomar** (2); **llevar** (5); to take a shower **ducharse** (7); to take a trip **hacer** (*irreg.*) **un viaje** (7); to take care of oneself **cuidarse** (15); to take off (*clothing*) **quitarse** (7); (*an airplane*) **despegar** (**gu**) (11); to take out the trash **sacar** (**qu**) **la basura** (12); to take photographs **sacar** (**qu**) **fotos** (12); to take place at (*place*) **ser** (*irreg.*) + **en** + *place* (13); to take (someone's) temperature **tomar(le) la temperatura** (15)
talk **hablar** (2)
tall **alto/a** (3)
tank **tanque** *m.* (17)
tape **cinta** (3); tape deck **grabadora** (12)
tasty **rico/a** (13)
taxes **impuestos** *pl.* (20)
tea **té** *m.* (9)
teach **enseñar** (2)
teaspoon **cucharita** (10)
telephone: by telephone **por teléfono** (2)
television (set) **televisor** *m.* (7)
tell **decir** (*irreg.*) (10)
teller: automatic teller machine **cajero automático** (20); bank teller **cajero/a** (20); teller's window **ventanilla** (20)
ten **diez** (P)
tenant **inquilino/a** (19)
tennis **tenis** *m.* (16); tennis shoe **zapato de tenis** (5)
tenth **décimo/a** (17)
term paper **trabajo** (12)
test **examen** *m.* (3)
textbook **libro de texto** (1)
thank: thank you (very much) **(muchas) gracias** (P); thanks for **gracias por** (9)
Thanksgiving **Día** (*m.*) **de Gracias** (13)
that *conj.* **que** (P); *adj.* **ese/a** (8); *pron.* **eso** (8); in that way **así** (20); provided that **con tal (de) que** (21); so that **para que** (21); that (*over there*) *adj.* **aquel, aquella**; *pron.* **aquello** (8); that's why **por eso** (3); that which **lo que** (11)
theater **teatro** (16); movie theater **cine** *m.* (10)
then **entonces** (6); **luego**; back then **en aquel entonces** (14)
there **allí**; there is/are **hay** (P); there is not / are not **no hay** (P)
these **estos/as** (3)
thin **delgado/a** (3)
thing **cosa** (1)
think **creer** (**y**) (4); **pensar** (**ie**) (6)
third **tercer, tercero/a** (17)
thirsty: to be (very) thirsty **tener** (*irreg.*) **(mucha) sed** (9)
thirteen **trece** (P)

thirty **treinta** (P, 3)
this *adj.* **este/a** (3); *pron.* **esto** (8); at this very moment **en este momento** (5)
those *adj.* **esos/as** (8); those (*over there*) **aquellos/as** (8)
thousand **mil** (6)
three **tres** (P); three hundred **trescientos/as** (6); three-star hotel **hotel** (*m.*) **de tres estrellas** (21)
throat **garganta** (15)
through **por** (17)
Thursday **jueves** *m. inv.* (2)
thus **así** (20)
ticket **billete** *m.* (11); **boleto** (11); **pasaje** *m.* (11); one-way ticket **billete/boleto de ida** (11); round-trip ticket **billete/boleto de ida y vuelta** (11); ticket booth **taquilla** (16); ticket (*for a performance*) **boleto** (16); **entrada** (16)
tie *n.* **corbata** (5)
time **tiempo** (7); ahead of time **con anticipación** (21); at times **a veces** (4); at what time . . . ? **¿a qué hora... ?** (P); from time to time **de vez en cuando** (9); leisure time **ratos** (*pl.*) **libres** (16); on time **a tiempo** (11); to have a bad time **pasarlo mal** (11); to have a good time **divertirse** (**ie, i**) (7); **pasarlo bien** (11); to spend time (with) **pasar tiempo (con)** (19); what time is it? **¿qué hora es?** (P)
tire: (flat) tire **llanta (desinflada)** (17)
tired **cansado/a** (4)
to **a** (P)
toast **pan** (*m.*) **tostado** (9)
toaster **tostadora** (12)
tobacco shop/stand **estanco** (21)
today **hoy** (2)
together **junto/a** (4)
tomato **tomate** *m.* (9)
tomorrow **mañana** (2); day after tomorrow **pasado mañana** (2); see you tomorrow **hasta mañana** (P)
tongue: to stick out one's tongue **sacar** (**qu**) **la lengua** (15)
tonight **esta noche** (5)
too *adv.* **demasiado** (13); too much **demasiado** (13); *adj.* **demasiado/a**
tooth **diente** *m.* (15); to extract a tooth **sacar** (**qu**) **una muela** (15)
top: on top of **encima de** (7)
tourist **turista** *m., f.* (21); tourist class **clase** (*f.*) **turística** (11)
trade (*job*) **oficio** (23)
traffic **circulación** *f.* (17); **tráfico** (17); traffic signal **semáforo** (17)
train **tren** *m.* (11); train station **estación** (*f.*) **del tren** (11)
tranquil **tranquilo/a** (14)
transportation: means of transportation **medios** (*pl.*) **de transporte** (11); public transportation **transporte** (*m.*) **público** (18)
trash: to take out the trash **sacar** (**qu**) **la basura** (12)
travel *v.* **viajar** (11); to travel by boat **navegar** (**gu**) **en barco** (11); travel agency

agencia de viajes (11); travel agent **agente** (*m., f.*) **de viajes** (11)
traveler **viajero/a** (21); traveler's check **cheque** (*m.*) **de viajero** (11, 20)
tray **bandeja** (10)
tree **árbol** *m.* (18)
trip: to take a trip **hacer** (*irreg.*) **un viaje** (7)
trophy **trofeo** (12)
try: to try to (*do something*) **tratar de** + *inf.*
T-shirt **camiseta** (5)
Tuesday **martes** *m. inv.* (2)
tuition **matrícula** (2)
tuna **atún** *m.* (9)
turkey **pavo** (9)
turn *v.* **doblar** (17); to turn off (*a light or appliance*) **apagar** (**gu**) (14); to turn on (*a light or appliance*) **poner** (*irreg.*) (*p.p.* **puesto/a**) (7); **encender** (**ie**) (18)
TV channel **canal** *m.* (22)
twelve **doce** (P)
twenty **veinte** (P)
twice **dos veces**
two **dos** (P); two hundred **doscientos/as** (6); two-star hotel **hotel** (*m.*) **de dos estrellas** (21)

U

ugly **feo/a** (3)
uncle **tío** (4)
under(neath) **debajo de**
understand **comprender** (4); **entender** (**ie**) (6)
unintentional: it was unintentional **fue sin querer** (14)
United States **Estados** (*pl.*) **Unidos** (3)
university **universidad** *f.* (1); university campus **campus** *m.* (19)
unless **a menos que** (21)
unpleasant **antipático/a** (3)
until *conj.* **hasta que** (20)
use **usar** (5); (*expend*) **gastar** (17)
utensils: eating utensils **utensilios** (*pl.*) **de comer** (10)

V

vacation: to be/go on vacation **estar** (*irreg.*)/ **ir** (*irreg.*) **de vacaciones** (11)
vacuum **pasar la aspiradora** (12)
VCR **videocasetera** (12)
vegetables **verduras** *pl.* (9)
verb **verbo** (1)
very **muy** (2); at this very moment **en este momento** (5)
veterinarian **veterinario** *m., f.* (23)
view **vista** (19)
violence **violencia** (18)
volleyball **vólibol** *m.* (16)
vote *v.* **votar** (22)

W

wagon: station wagon **camioneta** (3)
wait: to wait (for) **esperar** (9); to wait in line

hacer (*irreg.*) **cola** (11)
waiter **camarero** (10)
waiting area **sala de espera** (11)
waitperson **camarero/a** (9)
waitress **camarera** (10)
wake up **despertarse (ie)** (7)
walk **caminar** (14)
wall **pared** *f.* (8); to paint the walls **pintar las paredes** (12)
wallet **cartera** (5)
want **desear** (2); **querer** (*irreg.*) (5); where do you (*form. s.*) want to live? **¿dónde quiere vivir?** (19)
war **guerra** (22)
warm: to be warm **tener** (*irreg.*) **calor** (7)
wash **lavar** (12)
washing machine **lavadora** (12)
watch *v.* **mirar** (2); *n.* **reloj** *m.* (5); to watch over **guardar** (11)
water **agua** *f.* (*but* **el agua**) (9); mineral water **agua mineral** (9); water bed **cama de agua** (8)
way: in that way **así** (20)
wear **llevar** (5); **usar** (5)
weather **tiempo** (7); it's (very) good/bad weather **hace (muy) buen/mal tiempo** (7); what's the weather like? **¿qué tiempo hace?** (7)
wedding **boda** (19)
Wednesday **miércoles** *m. inv.* (2)
week **semana** (2)
weekend: (on) the weekend **el fin de semana** (2)
welcome: you're welcome **de nada** (P)
well **bien** (2); to get along well (with) **llevarse bien (con)** (19); (very) well **(muy) bien** (P); well . . . **pues...** (10)
well-being **bienestar** *m.* (15)
west: to the west of **al oeste de** (7)
what **lo que** (11); what? **¿qué?** (P): **¿cómo?** (P); at what time . . . ? **¿a qué hora... ?**

(P); what kind of person are you? **¿cómo es usted?** *form. s.* (P); what's the date? **¿cuál es la fecha?** (7); what's the weather like? **¿qué tiempo hace?** (7); what's your name? **¿cómo te llamas?** *fam. s.* (P); **¿cómo se llama usted?** *form. s.* (P); what time is it? **¿qué hora es?** (P)
when? **¿cuándo?** (2)
where? **¿dónde?** (P); where do you (*form. s.*) live? **¿dónde vive Ud.?** (19); where do you (*form. s.*) want to live? **¿dónde quiere vivir?** (19)
which *conj.* **que** (P); that which **lo que** (11)
which? **¿cuál?** (P)
while **mientras (que)** (15); a while **un rato** (8)
white **blanco/a** (5); white wine **vino blanco** (9)
who? **¿quién?** (1)
why? **¿por qué?** (4); that's why **por eso** (3)
wife **esposa** (4); **mujer** *f.* (4)
win *v.* **ganar** (12)
window **ventana** (1); teller's window **ventanilla** (20)
windshield **parabrisas** *m. s.* (17)
windy: it's (very) windy **hace (mucho) viento** (7)
wine: red wine **vino tinto** (9); white wine **vino blanco** (9); wine glass **copa** (10)
winter **invierno** (7)
with **con** (2); flight with stops **vuelo con escalas** (11); with me **conmigo**; with you **contigo** (*fam. s.*)
without **sin** (4); flight without stops **vuelo sin escalas** (11)
witness **testigo/a** (22)
woman **mujer** *f.* (1)
wool **lana** (5)
word **palabra** (P)
work *v.* **trabajar** (2); **funcionar** (12); *n.* **trabajo** (12); written work **trabajo** (12)

worker **obrero/a** (22); farm worker **campesino/a** (18)
world **mundo** (5)
worried **preocupado/a** (4)
worse **peor** (8)
would: would you be so kind as to . . . ? **¿sería tan amable de... ?** (21); would you mind . . . ? **¿le/te importaría... ?** (21)
write **escribir** (4)
wrong: to be wrong **no tener** (*irreg.*) **razón** (5); **equivocarse (qu)** (14); to get up on the wrong side of the bed **levantarse con el pie izquierdo** (14)

Y

yard **patio** (8)
year **año** (7); New Year's Day **Día** (*m.*) **de Año Nuevo** (13); New Year's Eve **Noche** (*f.*) **Vieja** (13); to be . . . years old **tener** (*irreg.*)... **años** (4)
yellow **amarillo/a** (5)
yes **sí** (P)
yesterday **ayer** (8); day before yesterday **anteayer**
yet **todavía** (5); **aún**
you *sub. pron.* **tú** *fam. s.*; **usted (Ud.)** *form. s.*; *obj. of prep.* **ti** *fam. s.* (7); and you? **¿y tú?** *fam. s.* (P); **¿y usted?** *form. s.* (P)
young **joven** (3)
younger **menor** (8)
your *poss.* **tu(s)** *fam.* (4); **su(s)** *form.* (4); **vuestro/a(s)** *fam. pl. (Sp.)* (4)
you're welcome **de nada** (P)

Z

zero **cero** (P)

INDEX

In this index, Study Hints, pronunciation, and vocabulary topic groups are listed only under those headings. **Antes de leer, De aquí y de allá, Notas comunicativas,** and **Notas culturales** sections appear only as a group, under those headings.

ABOUT THE AUTHORS

▼ ▼

Thalia Dorwick is Publisher of Foreign Languages and ESOL for McGraw-Hill, where she is responsible for the foreign language college list in Spanish, French, Italian, German, Japanese, and Russian, as well as for ESOL materials. She has taught at Allegheny College, California State University (Sacramento), and Case Western Reserve University, where she received her Ph.D. in Spanish in 1973. Dr. Dorwick is the coauthor of several textbooks and the author of several articles on language teaching issues. She was recognized as an Outstanding Foreign Language Teacher by the California Foreign Language Teachers Association in 1978.

Ana María Pérez-Gironés is an Adjunct Assistant Professor of Spanish at Wesleyan University, Middletown, Connecticut, where she teaches and coordinates Spanish language courses. She received a Licenciatura en Filología Anglogermánica from the Universidad de Sevilla in 1985, and her M.A. in General Linguistics from Cornell University in 1988. She is also an ACTFL certified Oral Proficiency Interview Tester.

Marty Knorre was formerly Associate Professor of Romance Languages and Coordinator of basic Spanish courses at the University of Cincinnati, where she taught undergraduate and graduate courses in language, linguistics, and methodology. She received her Ph.D. in foreign language education from The Ohio State University in 1975. Dr. Knorre is coauthor of *Cara a cara* and *Reflejos* and has taught at several NEH Institutes for Language Instructors. She received a Masters of Divinity at Mc-Cormick Theological Seminary in 1991.

William R. Glass is Assistant Professor of Spanish at The Pennsylvania State University, where he teaches both undergraduate and graduate courses in language and applied linguistics. He received his Ph.D. from the University of Illinois at Urbana–Champaign in 1992 in Spanish Applied Linguistics with a concentration in Second Language Acquisition and Teacher Education (SLATE). Professor Glass has presented numerous papers on second language reading and on input processing in second language acquisition. He recently coauthored *Manual que acompaña ¿Sabías que... ?,* another McGraw-Hill textbook series.

Hildebrando Villarreal is Professor of Spanish at California State University, Los Angeles, where he teaches undergraduate and graduate courses in language and linguistics. He received his Ph.D. in Spanish with an emphasis in Applied Linguistics from UCLA in 1976. Professor Villarreal is the author of several reviews and articles on language, language teaching, and Spanish for Native Speakers of Spanish. He is the author of *¡A leer! Un paso más,* an intermediate textbook that focuses on reading skills.

Mandatos y frases comunes en la clase *Commands*

LOS ESTUDIANTES

Practice saying these sentences aloud. Then try to give the Spanish as you look at the English equivalents.

Tengo una pregunta (que hacer).	*I have a question (to ask).*
¿Cómo se dice *page* en español?	*How do you say "page" in Spanish?*
Otra vez, por favor. No entiendo.	*(Say that) Again, please. I don't understand.*
¿Cómo?	*What (did you say)?*
¡(Espere) Un momento, por favor! No sé (la respuesta).	*(Wait) Just a minute, please! I don't know (the answer).*
(Sí,) Cómo no.	*(Yes,) Of course.*

LOS PROFESORES

After you read these Spanish sentences, cover the English equivalents and say what each expression means.

¿Hay preguntas?	*Are there any questions?*
¿Qué opina (cree) usted?	*What do you think?*
Escuche. Repita.	*Listen. Repeat.*
Lea (en voz alta).	*Read (aloud).*
Escriba/Complete (la siguiente oración).	*Write/Complete (the next sentence).*
Conteste en español.	*Answer in Spanish.*
Prepare (el ejercicio) para mañana.	*Prepare (the exercise) for tomorrow.*
Abra el libro en la página _____.	*Open your book to page _____.*
Cierre el cuaderno.	*Close your notebook.*
Saque (un papel).	*Take out (a sheet of paper).*
Levante la mano si...	*Raise your hand if . . .*
Levántese y vaya a la pizarra.	*Get up and go to the chalkboard.*
Pregúntele a otro estudiante _____.	*Ask another student _____.*
Déle _____ a _____.	*Give _____ to _____.*
Busque un compañero.	*Look for a partner.*
Haga la actividad con dos compañeros.	*Do the activity with two classmates.*
Formen grupos de cinco estudiantes.	*Get into groups of five students.*

Selected Verb Forms

Regular Verbs: Simple Tenses and Present Perfect (Indicative)

	PRESENT	PRETERITE	IMPERFECT	PRESENT PERFECT
hablar	hablo	hablé	hablaba	he hablado
comer	como	comí	comía	he comido
vivir	vivo	viví	vivía	he vivido

Common Irregular Verbs: First-Person Singular, Present and Preterite (Indicative)

caer	caigo	caí	**poner**	pongo	puse
dar	doy	di	**saber**	sé	supe
decir	digo	dije	**ser**	soy	fui
estar	estoy	estuve	**tener**	tengo	tuve
hacer	hago	hice	**traer**	traigo	traje
ir	voy	fui	**venir**	vengo	vine
oír	oigo	oí	**ver**	veo	vi
poder	puedo	pude			

Irregular Verbs: First-Person Singular, Imperfect (Indicative)

ir	iba	**ser**	era	**ver**	veía

Regular Verbs: Simple Tenses and Present Perfect (Subjunctive)

	PRESENT	IMPERFECT	PRESENT PERFECT
hablar	hable	hablara	haya hablado
comer	coma	comiera	haya comido
vivir	viva	viviera	haya vivido

Regular and Irregular Verbs: Future and Conditional

hablar	hablaré	hablaría
comer	comeré	comería
vivir	viviré	viviría

caer	cabré	cabría	**poner**	pondré	pondría
decir	diré	diría	**saber**	sabré	sabría
hacer	haré	haría	**tener**	tendré	tendría
poder	podré	podría	**venir**	vendré	vendría